RAPID POPULATION GROWTH

Consequences and Policy Implications

RAPID POPULATION GROWTH

Consequences and Policy Implications

VOLUME II
RESEARCH PAPERS

*Prepared by a Study Committee
of the Office of the Foreign Secretary
National Academy of Sciences
with the support
of the Agency for International Development*

Published for
the National Academy of Sciences by
The Johns Hopkins Press, Baltimore and London

Published 1971 by The Johns Hopkins Press
Manufactured in the United States of America

The Johns Hopkins Press, Baltimore, Maryland 21218
The Johns Hopkins Press Ltd., London

ISBN 0-8018-1263-1 (clothbound edition)
ISBN 0-8018-1264-X (paperbound edition of volume I)
ISBN 0-8018-1427-8 (paperbound edition of volume II)

Originally published, 1971
Second printing, 1972
Paperbound edition, 1971
Second printing, 1972

Preface

Rapid Population Growth is the result of deep concern about the world population problem and about the way those who make policy understand the implications of that problem. In its entirety the work contains a summary and recommendations, Volume I, and a collection of research papers in Volume II by scholars representing several disciplines—economics, political science, sociology, demography, social ethics, education, and public health. We hope that our conclusions will appeal to a wide audience, but we realize that many potential readers, especially busy and preoccupied government officials, are unlikely to have the time to study the more technical research papers upon which the policy recommendations are based. We have therefore decided that publication should take two forms: a clothbound edition containing both sections of the study, and a low-priced paperback edition of Volume I, the summary and recommendations. The paperback edition of Volume I is a self-contained unit and can be read as such; however, for the interested reader, references are made in the footnotes to the more detailed discussions in Volume II.

This special paperback edition of Volume II, published for the use of the Agency for International Development, should be read in conjunction with Volume I. It consists of 17 chapters by individual authors, prepared at the request of a special study committee of the National Academy of Sciences. The members of the committee have carefully reviewed and criticized these papers, but the final responsibility for them rests with the authors.

The aim of this volume is not to cover all the consequences of population growth, but to summarize the present state of knowledge and insight in some of the factors that must be considered in forming population policies. Thus the chapters by Philip Hauser, Dudley Kirk, and Nathan Keyfitz discuss, respectively, the probable future course of population growth in different world regions, the factors that may bring about changes in fertility and mortality rates, and the demographic effects of these changes. Theodore W. Schultz reviews the prospects for future world food supplies; Harley L. Browning presents some results of studies of urbanization in developing countries; T. Paul Schultz discusses the interactions between economic change and population growth; and J. Mayone Stycos describes public and elite attitudes towards birth control policies and programs. Arthur J. Dyck and Paul Demeny consider, respectively, the foundations in ethics and welfare-economics on which population policy should be based. Abdel R. Omran describes the large increase in induced abortion, often with serious consequences for the health of women, which seems to occur in many countries in the early stages of the transition from high to low birth rates. Joseph L. Fisher and Neal Potter show that, on a worldwide basis, natural resources will probably be adequate in quality and quantity for the next 30 years, despite anticipated population growth, but that several poor countries may be severely handicapped by the uneven distribution of resources in the earth.

The remaining papers deal more directly with specific aspects of the consequences of rapid population growth. Harvey Leibenstein discusses some of the factors that have not usually been taken into account in conventional economic models of these consequences. The serious handicaps in meeting health and educational needs imposed on less developed countries by their own high birth rates and high rates of population increase are described by Gavin W. Jones and the co-authors Leslie Corsa, Jr., and Deborah Oakley. The possible consequences for physical and mental health of crowding and rapid changes in population density are examined by John Cassel. Myron Weiner shows that the chief political consequence of rapid population increase, with its accompanying urbanization and large-scale internal migration, is exacerbation of conflicts between ethnic, racial, or religious groups within countries. Joe D. Wray summarizes the large body of evidence that suggests that the welfare and development of children are markedly and adversely affected by large family size or by close spacing of births. These effects on children, and other adverse consequences for families, communities, and villages may be the most serious aspect of high birth rates and unprecedented rates of population increase in the less developed countries.

The Committee

Roger Revelle, Chairman
Ansley J. Coale
Moye Freymann
Oscar Harkavy
Hans Landsberg
Walsh McDermott

Norman Ryder
T. W. Schultz
George Stolnitz
Harold A. Thomas
Samuel Wishik
W. Murray Todd, Staff

Acknowledgments

Among the many people who have contributed to this study we wish to express our gratitude to the following: James W. Brackett, Philander Claxton, Arthur Devany, John Durand, Jason Finkle, Harald Fredericksen, Amos Hawley, Bert F. Hoselitz, Robert Hume, John Keppel, Howard J. Lewis, Juanita Mogardo, R. T. Ravenholt, Richard Reed, James Shannon, Alan Sweezy, Pauline Wyckoff, and George Zaidan.

A special note of thanks must go to Mrs. Carol Picard and Mrs. Sharon Bauer, who ably helped with the organization and production of the study, and Mrs. Jane Lecht, who edited our manuscripts.

Contents

VOLUME II
REASEARCH PAPERS

Introduction

Volume II — Research Papers

The Study Committee acknowledges with gratitude the research and thought devoted to the preparation of these papers. We believe the authors represented have made a valuable contribution to the understanding of a very complex pattern of interacting forces—sometimes labeled the survival of the species. We hope the data presented will contribute to the examination of policy alternatives and will inspire further systematic study of the thorny problems of population growth.

We have profited greatly from discussions and arguments with the authors of these papers, but each paper stands on its own merit and is the work of the author. In some cases there are differences of opinion between individual committee members and authors, and there are inconsistencies between and among authors. We have tried to encourage a high level of scholarship and acceptance of a few common definitions, but we have not imposed either our standards or our definitions on these scholars.

Readers may well ask why this group of authors was selected rather than some other group. Many well-known American experts are conspicuous by their absence, and no scholars from abroad are included. The answer is simply that in order to provide modestly comprehensive coverage of the topics considered most important in the time allotted to the study, some arbitrary decisions had to be made. It was important to bring together the authors and committee members at the summer review and study sessions held in 1968 and 1969 at Woods Hole, Massachusetts. This meant limiting ourselves largely to those authors who were available for these meetings. We were also limited by the availability of authors in general. More simply put, this would have been a thicker volume if previous commitments, sabbatical leaves, the demands of existing research projects, and other academic impedimenta had not stood in the way.

We regret not having contributions from abroad. The scheduling and costs of bringing any significant number of people from around the world to our numerous committee and authors' meetings seemed, however, to make this a substantial problem.

We do not suggest that this is "the definitive volume on the consequences of population growth," nor do we believe all aspects of the problem have been covered with equal depth, clarity, or comprehensiveness. In some ways this is a compendium of research recognized as "needed" when we began the study in 1968. This is a perennial problem for any group attempting to approach a rather specific set of issues in a timely fashion. We do believe that these papers can significantly advance the insight of policymakers and planners and will help them design policies that will reflect what is known about the consequences of rapid population growth. And that was our goal.

The papers are presented in an order that will, we hope, permit the reader to analyze "the population problem" from several distinct, but linked, points of view.

I

World Population:
Retrospect and Prospect

Philip M. Hauser

World population at the beginning of 1969 numbered 3.5 billion. About one and a half generations ago, in 1930, it was 2 billion. About eleven or twelve generations ago, in 1650—the onset of the modern era—it was only half a billion. In little more than one human generation hence, 2000, world population could easily reach 7 billion and possibly exceed this number. In about two human generations from now, 2020, world population could approximate 10 billion; and in about four human generations, 2070, world population could exceed 20 billion. These are the numbers that have led demographers, the students of population, to employ such dramatic language as "population explosion."*

WORLD POPULATION GROWTH

Although the first complete census of mankind has yet to be taken, it is possible to estimate, within reasonable error limits, the population of the world from the end of the Neolithic period (the new Stone Age). At that time, world population is estimated to have been 10 million. At the beginning of the Christian era the population of the world probably numbered between 200 and 300 million. At the beginning of the modern era (1650) world population reached about 500 million. At the beginning of 1969 world population totaled 3.5 billion. A relatively simple analysis of these numbers discloses that an enormous increase in the speed, or rate, of world population growth has occurred, especially during the past 3 centuries.

Man, or very close kin to man, has been on the face of the earth for perhaps 2 to 4 million years. Although it is not known exactly when *Homo sapiens,*

Philip M. Hauser is Professor of Sociology and Director of the Population Research Center, University of Chicago.

*Most of the statistics relating to the population of the world are drawn from publications of the United Nations, especially (1, 2). Previous works of the writer have been drawn upon in the preparation of this paper.

the present version of man, first appeared, he was in evidence something like 40,000 to 50,000 years ago. It has been estimated that for the some 600,000 years of the Paleolithic Age (the old Stone Age) population growth perhaps approximated 0.02 per 1,000 per year (3). During the 3 centuries of the modern era population growth increased from about 3 per 1,000 to 10 per 1,000 per year between World Wars I and II. The rate of world population growth continued to accelerate after World War II, so that in 1965 it approximated 20 per 1,000 per year. In the course of man's inhabitation of this globe, then, his rate of population growth has increased from a rate of about 2 percent per millennium to 2 percent per annum, a thousandfold increase in growth rate.

From time to time there has been interest in the answer to the question, "How many people have lived on the earth?" Estimates in an effort to answer this question vary somewhat, but a good answer is about 69 billion up to 1960 (4). This would mean that of the total number of people ever born up to 1960, some 4 percent were living in 1960.

Population data prior to the modern era are admittedly speculative. But they provide a reasonably sound perspective and permit a very firm conclusion: Whatever his precise numbers may have been, during his habitation of this planet man has experienced a great increase in his rate of growth.

This conclusion is supported by placing in perspective the present rate of world population increase, estimated by the United Nations as approximately 2 percent per year. Although 2 percent per year may seem like a small return on investment, it is a tremendous rate for world population growth. For example, to produce a population of 3.6 billion world population in 1969, one dozen persons increasing at a rate of 2 percent per year would have required only 976 years. Yet *Homo sapiens* alone has been on this earth at least 40,000 to 50,000 years. Similarly, the same one dozen persons reproducing at the rate of 2 percent per year since the year A.D. 1 could by 1965 have had over 400 million descendants for each person actually present in 1965.

Further appreciation of the meaning of a 2 percent rate of increase per year is gained by observing the population that this growth rate would produce in the future. In about 650 years there would be one person for each square foot of land surface on the globe, including mountains, deserts, and the arctic wastes. It would generate a population which would weigh as much as the earth itself in 1,566 years. These periods of time may seem long when measured by the length of an individual lifetime. But they are but small intervals in the time perspective of the evolutionary development of man.

It is possible to summarize quickly the remarkable acceleration which man has experienced in his growth rate. Between 1650 and 1750, at an annual rate of growth of 0.3 percent, world population would have required 231 years to double. Between 1850 and 1900, the growth rate had risen to 0.6 percent per year, and the period required to double world population had declined to 116 years. By the decade 1930 to 1940, world growth, at 1 percent per year, would have doubled the population in 69 years. At the present rate of growth, 2 percent per year, world population would double in 35 years.

EXPLANATION OF ACCELERATED GROWTH

During the 3 centuries of the modern era, from 1650 to 1950, world population multiplied about fivefold, from 0.5 to 2.5 billion. (See Table 1.) But over this time span the population of Europe increased almost sixfold; the population of Europe and European descendants combined, about seven-fold. The population of northern America (north of the Rio Grande) increased about 168-fold and that of Latin America about 23-fold. During the same period the population of Asia increased less than fourfold in contrast to what may have been a much slower increase before that time. (In absolute numbers the increase was greater than that of all other continents combined.) Numbers in Africa only doubled.

It is clear that greatly accelerated growth occurred first among the nations that first experienced modernization, the combination of "revolutions"— the agricultural revolution, the commercial revolution, the industrial revolution, the scientific revolution, and the technological revolution. Explosive population growth, the "vital revolution," did not reach significant proportions among the two thirds of mankind in Asia, Latin America, and Africa until after World War II—less than one human generation ago.

The reason for the population explosion is to be found in the interaction of the components of population growth—births (fertility) and deaths (mortality) for the world as a whole, and fertility and mortality and net migration for any subdivision of the world. To explain the population explosion demographers have a theory of the *demographic transition*. In brief, the explanation lies in the fact that man is the only complex culture-building animal on this globe and in building his culture he has effected great reductions in the death rate well in advance of any corresponding declines in the birth rate. Although research indicates that there have been large regional variations in mortality and fertility changes, the greatly accelerated rate of population growth is the product of natural increase, that is, the excess of births over deaths.

Decrease in Death Rate

The decrease in the death rate may, in general, be attributed to a number of causes (8):

1. Increased productivity ushered in by the agricultural, commercial, and industrial revolutions resulting in higher levels of living—including better nutrition, better living conditions, and better health.

TABLE 1

Estimates of World Population by Regions, 1650-1950

(millions)

Estimates and Dates	World Total	Africa	Northern America[c]	Latin America[d]	Asia (Except U.S.S.R.)[e]	Europe and Asiatic U.S.S.R.[e]	Oceania	Area of European Settlement[f]
Carr-Saunders' estimates:[a]								
1650	545	100	1	12	327	103	2	118
1750	728	95	1	11	475	144	2	158
1800	906	90	6	19	597	192	2	219
1850	1,171	95	26	33	741	274	2	335
1900	1,608	120	81	63	915	423	6	573
United Nations estimates:[b]								
1920	1,834	136	115	92	997	485	9	701
1930	2,008	155	134	110	1,069	530	10	784
1940	2,216	177	144	132	1,173	579	11	866
1950[g]	2,515	222	166	162	1,381	571	13	935

[a]Carr-Saunders, (5).

[b]United Nations, (6, p. 10; 7, Table II). The 1940 figures are unpublished estimates of the United Nations.

[c]United States, Canada, Alaska, St. Pierre and Miquelon.

[d]Central and South America and Caribbean Islands.

[e]Estimates for Asia and Europe in Carr-Saunders' series have been adjusted so as to include the population of the Asiatic U.S.S.R. with that of Europe, rather than Asia. For this purpose, the following approximate estimates of the population of the Asiatic U.S.S.R. were used: 1650, 3 million; 1750, 4 million; 1800, 5 million; 1850, 8 million; 1900, 22 million. Figures for 1950 include all of U.S.S.R. with Europe.

[f]Includes northern America, Latin America, Europe and the Asiatic U.S.S.R., and Oceania.

[g]Revised for more recent United Nations' estimates.

Source: (2, p. 11).

2. The emergence of national governments with the elimination of internecine warfare and the emergence of national markets which permitted a more equitable distribution of the nation's product.

3. Improvements in environmental sanitation and personal hygiene, resulting in uncontaminated food and potable water and a decrease in the probability of infection and contagion.

4. The natural disappearance of some of the agents of disease and death; for example, scarlet fever.

5. The development of modern medicine, climaxed by chemotherapy and the availability of pesticides.

During the modern era, these developments upset the equilibrium between the birth rate and the death rate that characterized most of the millennia of human existence. In the Netherlands in the 1840's, for example, of 1,000 infants born one fourth had died by age 2.5 years and one half by age 37.5 years. In contrast, a century later one fourth had not died until age 62.5 years; and one half, not until 72.5 years (9). As a result of such decreases in death rates, the 100 million Europeans of 1650 had, 3 centuries later, about 940 million descendants.

The areas that are today classed as "developed" or "economically advanced" achieved reductions in mortality throughout the modern period—but mainly since the mid-19th century. In fact, expectation of life at birth has increased more since 1850 than in the preceding 200 years (9). Death rates decreased; birth rates remained at relatively high levels. Therefore, natural increase—the excess of births over deaths—greatly accelerated in the economically advanced regions, primarily Europe, northern America, and Oceania. This was the first population explosion. However, growth rates through natural increase alone rarely exceeded rates of 1.5 percent per annum.

The rapid growth of population in the industrialized nations continued through the 19th century and into the early part of the 20th century, despite the onset of declines in fertility. In France and the United States the birth rate was dropping early in the 19th century, and that of Ireland declined before the mid-1800's. As a general pattern, birth rates in northern and western Europe dropped during the fourth quarter of the 19th century. The pattern of decline spread to southern and eastern Europe only after 1900. Once the fertility decline began in a country, it continued without interruption, and the decline tended to be steeper where it began relatively late. Yet, despite the decreases in birth rate, fairly rapid, even if somewhat dampened, population growth continued in the West because death rates continued to decline. Appreciable decreases in growth rates occurred only among the nations most seriously affected by the Great Depression, during which both marriage and birth rates plummeted. In the aftermath of World War II, however, fertility increased to accelerate rates of total population growth. By the end of the 1950's, the postwar upsurge in birth rates had generally dissipated in most western countries.

Low Death Rates and High Fertility

Since World War II, the "second population explosion" has occurred in Asia, Latin America, and Africa–the "less developed" or "developing" areas of the world. Although some parts of these regions had experienced declines in mortality before World War II, most of this two thirds of mankind were not exposed to the techniques of "death control" until the postwar period. Since the end of World War II, the death rate in the developing nations has been falling much more rapidly than was ever the case in the industrialized nations of the West. In the economically advanced nations, the means by which the death rate was decreased were developed gradually over the modern era; then they became available to the less developed nations all at once. Ships anchored off Bombay, Rio de Janeiro, or Dakar could carry in their holds all of the material means of reducing mortality which western nations acquired only after 3 centuries of experience and effort. Moreover, the United Nations and the specialized agencies, especially the World Health Organization, have sponsored programs for reducing death rates, including economic development programs and the dissemination of chemotherapy and pesticides.

Longevity, then, is increasing much more rapidly in the less developed areas than it did among Europeans and populations of European stock because of the much more powerful means now available for eliminating the causes of death. For example, the death rate of the Moslem population in Algeria in 1946-47 was higher than that of Sweden in 1771-80, more than a century and a half earlier. Eight years later, by 1955, the decrease in the death rate in Algeria was greater than that which Sweden experienced during the century from 1775 to 1875. Between 1940 and 1960, Mexico, Costa Rica, Venezuela, Ceylon, Malaya, and Singapore were among the nations that decreased their death rates by more than 50 percent. Ceylon's death rate was decreased by more than 50 percent in less than a decade.

While death rates fell sharply in the developing areas, birth rates remained at high levels and some may well have increased. Whereas today the economically advanced areas are characterized by low death rates and relatively low birth rates (mainly between 17 and 23 per 1,000 persons per year), most of the developing regions have birth rates above 40. With either high death rates or low birth rates as a check, the industrialized nations in their entire history have rarely exceeded a growth rate of 1 percent per annum without immigration. Annual growth rates in the developing nations are above 2 percent–many above 3 percent. A 3 percent growth rate doubles a population in 23 years. Since the developing nations contain over two thirds of the world's population, the growth rate of the world as a whole is accelerating despite the historical fertility decline in the developed nations. Among the nonwestern nations of appreciable size, only in Japan has the birth rate declined significantly. The developing nations in Asia, Latin America, and Africa, with their 20th century death rates and medieval birth rates, are perpetuating the second world population explosion.

Although the first and second population explosions have affected, or are affecting, every corner of the globe, the majority of the world's peoples live in seven giant nations. In mid-1968, the seven largest nations in the world contained about three fifths of the world's peoples, some 2 billion. These nations were mainland China, with perhaps 730 million inhabitants; India, with about 525 million; the Soviet Union with 240 million; the United States with 200 million; Pakistan with 125 million; Indonesia with over 110 million; and Japan with about 100 million. These nations share a major responsibility for the population outlook of the world.

Population Growth, 1920 to 1960

An analysis of developments between 1920 and 1960 by the United Nations provides a framework for considering the population prospect for the world and for significant regional and national groupings (10, pp. 13, 133). In those 40 years, world population increased from 1.9 to 3 billion, or by 60 percent. There was a great difference, however, in the growth rates of world regions grouped by level of economic development. The less developed regions of the world (Africa, Latin America, east Asia, and south Asia) increased from 1.3 to 2.1 billion, or about 70 percent. In contrast, the more developed areas (northern America, Europe, the Soviet Union, and Oceania) increased by only 40 percent.

Regions of the world are classed as "less developed" or "developed" on an economic basis. An analysis of population characteristics reveals that differences in the level of human reproductivity sharply distinguish the developed from the less developed areas.

About two thirds of the less developed countries have birth rates ranging from 40 to 50 (births per 1,000 persons per year); whereas two thirds of the more developed areas have birth rates of 17 to 23. There is also a difference between the less developed and the developed countries in death rates. It is not as marked as the difference in birth rates, however, because of the great decline in mortality since the end of World War II. Expectation of life at birth in most of the less developed countries ranges from 30 to 60 years, whereas in most of the developed nations it ranges from about 67 to 72 years. With present trends in public health and other lifesaving programs, the differences in mortality will no doubt diminish further.

Despite the differences between developed and less developed nations in fertility and mortality, there is overlap between them in rates of population growth. Some less developed nations are increasing at rates as low as 1 percent; some developed nations are growing at rates as high as 1.7 percent.

The overlap is produced mainly by relatively high birth rates among a few of the more developed areas—rates which are now declining.

Among the more developed areas, Oceania, with a relatively small population, increased most rapidly between 1920 and 1960, rising from 8.5 to 15.7 million, or by about 85 percent. Northern America increased from 116 to 199 million, a gain of about 75 percent. Next in growth rate, despite great losses during World War II, was the Soviet Union with a population of 155 million in 1920 and 214 million in 1960, an increase of about 38 percent. Lowest in growth rate was Europe (excluding the U.S.S.R.) which, with a population of 325 million in 1920 and 425 million in 1960, had an increase of about 30 percent.

Among the less developed areas, Latin America showed the greatest population growth, from 90 million in 1920 to 212 million by 1960. More than doubling, it increased by 135 percent. Africa registered the next greatest growth, having 143 million persons in 1920 and 273 million in 1960, an increase of about 91 percent. South Asia, with 470 million in 1920 and 865 million in 1960, increased by 84 percent. (However, the estimated difference between Africa and south Asia is well within a statistical margin of error.) Slowest in population growth among the less developed areas was east Asia with an estimated 553 million in 1920 and 794 million in 1960, an increase of about 43 percent. It must be noted, however, that the data for east Asia are most uncertain.

The United Nations has also analyzed the growth rates of the world divided into Northern Areas and Southern Areas, with the Tropic of Cancer serving as the dividing line. The Southern Areas (south Asia, Africa, Latin America, and Oceania) as a group grew more rapidly than the Northern Areas. They almost doubled, increasing from 711 million persons in 1920 to 1.4 billion in 1960. The Northern Areas, in contrast, rose from 1.2 billion persons in 1920 to 1.6 billion in 1960, an increase of 33 percent.

World Population Prospects

In 1966, the United Nations issued revised population projections for the world, and for the developed and developing areas, to the end of the century (10, pp. 13-18, 135). The projections indicate that if present fertility and declining mortality rates were to continue, world population would reach 7.5 billion by 2000.

Three other projections are calculated by the United Nations based on varying declines in the birth rate with different timing. These projections are published as "high, low, and medium variant projections." The high variant gives a world population in 2000 of 7 billion, the medium 6.1 billion, and the low 5.4 billion.

Each of the United Nations projections, except the 7.5 billion projection based on the assumption of present fertility levels, assumes decreased birth rates in the developing areas. However, there is no firm evidence up to this time that such reductions in the birth rate have yet occurred among the mass illiterate and impoverished populations of Asia, Latin America, and Africa; therefore, the projection based on continuing present fertility cannot be dismissed as impossible. In this discussion the U.N. high variant projection will be used. It should be stressed, however, that the discussion and the conclusions reached would not differ significantly if the medium projection were used.

On the basis of the high projection the population of the world as a whole would increase to 7 billion by the year 2000; in other words, it would double during the rest of this century. Comparing anticipated growth in the second half of this century with actual growth during the first half highlights the effect of declining mortality, especially in the less developed areas. Between 1900 and 1950, world population increased by less than 1 billion persons. Between 1950 and 2000, according to the high projection, world population will increase by 4.5 billion persons. That is, the absolute increase in the population of the world during the second half of this century may be four and one-half times as great as that during the first half of the century. During the second half of this century, there could be a greater increase in world population than was achieved in all the millennia of human existence up to the present time.

Projections for Developed and Less Developed Areas

Of special economic and political import for the rest of this century is the difference in the rate of population growth between the developed and the developing areas. The United Nations high projections indicate the developing areas would have a total population of about 5.4 billion persons by 2000, whereas the developed areas would reach about 1.6 billion. (See Table 2.)

According to these projections, then, the less developed areas with a population of 2 billion in 1960 would increase by some 3.4 billion persons by the end of the century, or by 170 percent. In contrast, the developed areas would increase by only 598 million persons, or by about 60 percent. The population increase in the developing areas would be over five times as great as that in the more developed areas. Moreover, the developing areas would increase in the last 4 decades of this century by a number of persons about as great as the population of the globe in 1968.

In 1960, about two thirds of the world population lived in the developing areas and only one third in the developed. By 2000, it is possible that the population in the presently less developed areas would have increased to 77 percent of the world's total, and that the population in the developed areas would have shrunk to 23 percent.

According to the high projections, there would be great variations in growth rates among the regions within both areas. (See Table 2.) Within the

TABLE 2

World Population by Major Areas, 1960 to 2000, According to the
High Variant Projection of the United Nations

(millions)

Area	1960	1970	1980	1990	2000
World total	2,998	3,659	4,551	5,690	6,994
More developed areas	976	1,102	1,245	1,402	1,574
Europe	425	458	492	526	563
Soviet Union	214	254	296	346	403
Northern America	199	233	275	323	376
Oceania	16	19	23	29	35
Less developed areas	2,022	2,557	3,306	4,288	5,420
East Asia	794	956	1,171	1,405	1,623
South Asia	865	1,108	1,448	1,910	2,443
Africa	273	348	463	629	864
Latin America	212	283	383	522	686
Northern Areas	1,632	1,901	2,234	2,600	2,966
Southern Areas	1,366	1,758	2,317	3,090	4,028

Source: (10, p. 135).

developed areas Oceania, with its small numbers, would continue to grow most rapidly, reaching 34.8 million in 2000 from 15.7 million in 1960, more than doubling. Northern America and the Soviet Union would increase at about the same rate, close to 90 percent, between 1960 and 2000. Northern America would reach a total of 376 million, the Soviet Union 403 million. Europe would continue to grow more slowly, rising from 425 to 563 million, an increase of 30 percent.

Among the less developed regions, Latin America and Africa would increase the fastest, each of them more than tripling between 1960 and the end of the century. Africa would reach a total of 864 million by 2000; Latin America, 686 million. South Asia would more than double, increasing from 865 million to 2.4 billion. East Asia, including mainland China, would also more than double, increasing from 794 million in 1960 to 1.6 billion by 2000.

The remarkable upsurge in population growth in the developing regions is dramatized by the contrast in the midcentury populations of northern and Latin America with their projected century-end populations. In 1950, northern America with 166 million persons had a population 4 million greater than Latin America. By 2000, it is possible that Latin America with 686 million inhabitants will exceed the population of northern America by over 300 million.

Projections of Northern and Southern Areas

The contrast in growth rates between the Northern Areas and the Southern Areas which was observed between 1920 and 1960 would continue to 2000. The Southern Areas would almost triple between 1960 and 2000, rising from 1.4 to over 4 billion. The Northern Areas would less than double, increasing by 87 percent, from 1.6 to 3 billion. The Southern Areas had a population nearly 300 million below the Northern Areas in 1960; by 2000 they may exceed the Northern Areas by about 1 billion. This shift in relative size could have great political significance by the end of the century.

Projections of Large Nations

Population projections to the year 2000 for the seven largest nations in 1960 are also available or can be derived from the United Nations estimates. Also based on the high variant, they indicate that mainland China by 2000 could have 1.4 billion persons; India, 1.1 billion; the Soviet Union, 403 million; the United States, some 338 million; Indonesia, about 300 million (estimate by writer); Japan, 139 million; and Pakistan, 342 million. Thus, with the exception of Japan each of these nations would have grown enough by 2000 to retain its present ranking. Japan would drop below Pakistan and possibly below Brazil, if Brazil increases at the average rate for Latin America—to 227 million. It is possible that five more nations will pass the 100 million mark by the year 2000: Brazil, Korea, Mexico, Nigeria, and the Philippines.

Of perhaps greatest interest is the projection that the present seven largest countries would constitute a somewhat smaller proportion of the world population in 2000 than they did in 1960, but their aggregate population by the end of the century—over 4 billion—would exceed total world population in 1960.

Caution about Projections

The projections presented here are fictitious models of what may transpire. The actual course of events may be quite different. Moreover, the projections employed are the high variants of the United Nations, which also presented medium and low variants. As said earlier, even the high projections assume birth rate reductions in high fertility areas of a magnitude that is not yet supported by empirical evidence. Therefore, the high projections may be considered quite plausible. If the low projections are regarded as improbable—and there is justification for this viewpoint—the high projections used may be an intermediate between the results of continued present fertility levels and a new low (the United Nations medium) which also assumes relatively great, and as yet not demonstrated, decreases in birth rates in the high fertility areas.

The major point is that the implications of present and prospective population growth remain essentially the same, whichever of the projections is considered. In the long run such rates of increase cannot possibly persist because the limit of population growth is set by the finite dimensions of the planet.

A special caution on the data for China is necessary. These data are especially defective by reason of the absence of good census statistics and reliable vital statistics. The estimated population for China by 2000, according to different United Nations assumptions, could vary from less than 900 million to about 1.4 billion. Other estimates indicate even greater variation is possible. Obviously the data in Table 2 for east Asia and for the world as a whole are vitally affected by the weakness of the data for China.

AGE STRUCTURE AND DEPENDENCY

Overall numbers and growth rates do not explain all the important changes in the demographic transition. As birth and death rates change, so do the age structure and dependency ratios—the proportion of dependents who are under 15 or over 60. The expectation of life for newborn infants and for those who survive to age 20 also changes.

Table 3 presents a model of demographic profiles of four populations— from the *premodern* period of high birth and death rates, through the *transitional* stages in which death rates decrease, to the *modern* phase of low birth and death rates.

In the later transitional period—through which the fast-growing regions of the world are now passing—the death rate declines and the birth rate remains at a relatively high level. Because of better health conditions and increased survival of women of childbearing age, infants, and children, the proportion of young people under 15 rises to about 45 percent of the population. At the same time, of course, the proportion of old people and of working-age people declines.

As the demographic transition proceeds and birth rates begin to decline along with continuing declines in mortality, the demographic profile becomes that of a modern population. Growth rates, age structure, life expectancy, and dependency ratios change radically, as shown in the last two columns of Table 3.

The relevance of these population models is evident when we examine actual populations. In 1960 about two thirds of the less developed countries had birth rates ranging from 40 to 50. Expectation of life at birth among most of these countries ranged from 30 to 60 years. Population growth rates ranged from 1 to 3.5 percent per year. In 1960, 40 percent of the population was under 15 years of age; only 3.3 percent of the population was over 65; and 56.6 percent was 15 to 64 years old. Hence, in 1960 in the less developed regions of the world there were 76 dependents for 100 persons of working

TABLE 3

Demographic Profiles of Premodern, Early and Later
Transitional, and Modern Populations[a]

Population Characteristics	Premodern	Early Transitional	Later Transitional	Modern
Birth rate	45.6	43.7	45.7	20.4
Death rate	40.6	33.7	15.7	10.4
Annual growth rate (percent)	0.5	1.0	3.0	1.0
Age structure:				
Percent under 15	36.7	37.8	45.4	27.2
Percent 15-59	57.6	56.5	50.3	58.2
Percent 60 and over	5.7	5.7	4.3	14.6
Average age	25.5	25.1	21.8	32.8
Dependency ratio				
(per 100 of age 15-59)	74	77	99	72
Youth	64	67	90	47
Old age	10	10	9	25
Percent surviving to age 15	48.8	55.9	78.8	95.6
Expectation of life at birth	25.0	30.0	50.0	70.0
Expectation of life at age 20	31.2	33.9	43.9	53.4
Average number children born to women by age 50	5.7	5.5	6.1	2.9
Average number children surviving to age 20	2.6	2.9	4.7	2.7

[a]Based on stable populations for "West" female.

Source: (11).

age, defined as 15 to 64 years. India, a good example of a population in transition, had in 1968 a birth rate estimated at 41, a death rate of 16, and a growth rate of 2.5 percent per annum. Expectation of life at birth was 45 years. The proportion of persons under 15 years of age was 41 percent.

The more developed areas, in contrast, possessed a modern population profile in 1960. Two thirds of these areas had birth rates ranging from 17 to 23. Most of the developed nations had expectations of life at birth ranging from 67 to 72 years. Most of these nations were growing at rates of 0.5 to 1.7 percent per year.

In the more developed regions of the world in 1960—with reduced fertility as well as reduced mortality—less than 29 percent of the population was under 15; over 8 percent was 65 and over, and 63 percent was in the intermediate group, 15 to 64 years. Therefore, the dependency burden in the economically advanced regions was much lower, only 59, or about three fourths of the dependency ratio in the less developed regions.

The United Kingdom, an example of a modern population, had a birth rate in 1968 of 17.8, a death rate of 11.7, and a growth rate of 0.5 percent per year. Expectation of life at birth in the United Kingdom was 71 years. Population under 15 years was 23 percent of the total.

The Burden of Dependency

The changes in demographic profiles summarized above have significant social and economic implications on families and on society as a whole (both the micro-familial and macro-social levels). In the premodern population the family experiences the wear and tear of many births and many deaths—especially deaths of infants and children. The economic and emotional burdens carried by parents can be measured by the relatively large number of children ever born and their high mortality.

Under the impact of modernization during the late transitional period, the family experiences rapidly decreasing infant and child mortality while fertility actually rises. With a greatly increased number of children in the household, the family has heavier social and economic burdens, although it experiences less of the psychological pain of high infant and child death rates.

In the late transitional period, the burden of youth dependency increases by more than one third, as the youth dependency ratio rises from 67 to 90. (See Table 3.) Length of life increases at birth from 30 to 50 years, and at age 20, from 34 to 44 more years of life. With the increased youth-dependency burden, however, it is unlikely that increases occur in the quality as well as the length of life. On the other hand, the improved survival of children may well mean increased security for parents in old age.

This increased burden of youth dependency is especially severe in urban areas where children tend to be an economic burden rather than an asset as they may have been in an agrarian setting. Moreover, rapid urbanization is usually a characteristic of the late transitional period. In the West the increase in births and in the survival of children—creating a greater burden in an urban setting—probably contributed to the decrease in birth rates which generated the modern population profile. The burden of supporting more dependents may have offset the increased security that surviving children meant to parents in their old age.

The Modern Population Structure

In the modern population structure, family burdens greatly diminish. The wear and tear of reproduction and death is virtually eliminated as the average number of children ever born decreases and as the average number of children surviving to age 20 becomes almost identical to the number of children born. Although the burden of old-age dependency increases significantly, it is more than offset by the decrease in young dependents. Moreover, expectation of life increases, at birth to 70 years and at age 20 to over 53 more years of life; the average age of the population, because of the greatly reduced birth rate, increases to about 33 years. As a result of the great increase in life expectancy at birth and in adulthood and the increasing tendency to restrict births to the earlier years of marriage, parents are freed of the burden of child care for increasingly greater parts of their lives. Couples whose children have left home for higher education or marriage increase both in number and in years of life remaining after children leave home.

The modern population structure permits great improvements in the quality of life because of the decrease in the number of persons on the micro-familial level and the decrease in growth rate at the macro-social level. On the macro-social level the modern population profile provides the nation as a whole with many relative advantages. Although the growth rate of a modern population of 1 percent per annum is approximately the same as that in the early transitional population model, this growth rate is achieved much more efficiently (with a birth rate of 20 and a death rate of 10) than in the early transitional population (with a birth rate of 44 and a death rate of 34). Moreover, the growth rate of 1 percent per annum of a modern population would double the population in 69 years, whereas a population experiencing the late transition and increasing at an annual rate of 3 percent would double in 23 years.

In the long run, the specter of an ecological disaster or the limits on space will necessitate a zero rate of growth. However, in modern populations the slower rate of growth has bought time. As other contributors to this volume show, slow-growth-rate societies can more readily achieve increases in productivity and translate those increases into higher standards of living. The lower birth rate and growth rate of the modern population operate to increase the proportion of total gross national product (GNP) which can be used to increase productivity; to generate an age structure more favorable to increases in product per capita by increasing the size of the labor force in relation to the number of dependents; to augment the ability to invest in human resources (in education and the transmission of skills); to improve the ability of the economy to create nonagricultural jobs; to improve the opportunity for enriching the quality of life (12).

POLICY IMPLICATIONS

The world population outlook has important policy implications in both the short run and the long run.

The Long Run

In the long run, as said earlier, mankind has no alternative to achieving a zero rate of growth. The present rate of world population growth could not possibly have been sustained over any long periods in the past nor can it continue for very long into the future. Given a finite planet, any positive rate of population growth would eventually produce saturation. In the long run, space is the limiting factor to population growth and, in consequence, long-run policy must aim at bringing the world growth rate to zero.

Moreover, because space is the limiting factor, there can be no doubt that the growth rate will eventually be controlled. The only questions are whether the control will be by nature or by man; and, if by man, whether the control will be rational and desirable or irrational and undesirable. Control by nature, of course, would mean control by famine and pestilence, as discussed by Malthus. Relatively irrational and undesirable control by man would include those other "checks" discussed by Malthus—war and misery. More rational and desirable controls by man would include controls of the type mentioned in the discussion of short-run policy which follows.

In the short run, there is no reasonable alternative to bringing the rate of population growth below present levels. Realistically this does not mean setting a zero rate of growth as a short-run target. For even if it could be achieved in the short run, say by the end of this century, the price of achieving it would probably be greater than mankind would be willing to pay. Furthermore, on the basis of experience to date, there is little prospect that a zero rate of population growth can be achieved by man in the near future, and such a goal is especially not likely to be achieved rapidly in the developing areas of Asia, Latin America, and Africa.

The Short Run

In the short run, what is needed is a realistic setting of growth-rate targets, area by area, over fairly short periods of time—probably not less than a decade.

To achieve realistic goals, the more rational and desirable forms of control are to be employed. These include three types of control, often confused, namely: *conception control, birth control,* and *population control.* Conception control refers to all the means—behavioral, mechanical, chemical, physiological, and surgical—by which conception is prevented. Birth control involves not only conception control but, in addition, abortion, the elimination of the product of conception before birth. Population control involves not only birth control, but also the relationship between fertility, mortality, and net migration—the balance between immigration and emigration and internal in-migration and out-migration. Moreover, it also involves the effects of social, economic, and political changes on the components of population growth.

At the present time, most of the world's family planning movements have concentrated on conception control and only recently have there been situations in which family planning movements have endorsed abortion when conception control fails. However, it is probably true that the most wide-spread method today of limiting births in the world is abortion.* Mehlan (13) has estimated that as many as 40 million are performed annually, including both legal and illegal abortions in all nations. Effective conception control would, of course, eliminate the necessity for abortion, and this is one reason why family planning movements have concentrated on conception control.

Two goals that are common to the family planning movement and to national family planning policies are to enable couples to obtain the number of children they want and to decrease their numbers of children on a voluntary basis.

However, the available data indicate that the number of children people desire is above the levels necessary to control explosive growth (14). It should therefore become the policy of governments and agencies to induce parents to desire a number consistent with adopted goals. Such a policy would involve much more attention to educational efforts—from primary school to adult education and to developing motives and incentives for smaller families.

In respect to the second goal, to achieve reduced growth rates by voluntary methods, there is also need for further consideration. In the economically advanced areas whatever control has been achieved has been on a voluntary basis, often against the wishes and efforts of government. Voluntary control seems to have accompanied increased education, higher levels of living, and the breakup of the traditional order through social change. In the developing areas, however, it may be that these socioeconomic changes—and their impact on family-size norms—will not occur fast enough without more direct intervention by governments.†

Within the past few years many nations and international agencies have become much more aware of the need for decreasing the rates of population growth. Furthermore, there has been greatly increased input into both bio-medical and social research to provide better techniques for population control.

At the present time, there is very little hard evidence by which to evaluate the impact of family planning movements on birth rates in the developing regions. In general, it is still true that most of the nations in Asia, Latin America, and Africa are experiencing both high birth rates and high population growth rates. In contrast, it is mainly in the economically advanced areas in Europe (including the U.S.S.R.), northern America, and Oceania that birth rates have been reduced to a point that growth rates approximate 1 percent per annum. In Asia only Japan can completely match the western experience,

---

*See Abdel R. Omran, "Abortion in the Demographic Transition," in this volume.

†In the form of national family planning policy and programs, for example, of the type now underway in India.

but other areas—Taiwan, Korea, Hong Kong, and Singapore—have been achieving substantial reductions in fertility. At the present time, the giant nations of the world are, in general, attempting in some manner to deal with their problems of population growth; and, in increasing numbers, smaller nations representing virtually all religious, cultural, and racial groups are similarly attempting to face up to their population growth problems.

The physical ability to decrease population growth rates has vastly improved over the past few years by the development of modern means of contraception, including the pill and the intra-uterine device. These improved methods, and other new methods still in the laboratories, will undoubtedly serve to accelerate the reduction of birth rates. However, the evidence to date indicates that improved techniques alone cannot be expected to produce the desired results. It has become increasingly clear that incentive and motivation are at least as essential as contraceptive techniques in achieving fertility control. Moreover, experience has indicated that tradition-bound peasant societies in the developing regions are slow to acquire the necessary incentive and motivation. The family planning movement initially concentrated on the diffusion of birth control clinics; now it must increasingly widen its approach by incorporating such clinics into broader programs, such as maternal and child health centers, by undertaking educational programs at all levels, and by other appropriate programs which will motivate families to control conception (15).

Despite the increasing efforts to lower birth rates, substantial reductions in population growth rates cannot reasonably be expected during the rest of this century. The *generation*, rather than the year or decade, has been the unit of time in which changes in reproductive behavior have been achieved (except for Japan). In the West, birth rates began to decline without the benefit of family planning movements or birth control clinics or modern means of contraception. Changes in reproductive behavior were the result of basic social changes which operated to break down traditional values and to provide incentive for restricting family size. The basic question before the developing nations of the world is whether family size can change before other basic cultural and social changes have transformed the values and goals of their peoples. Certainly the stakes involved are so high that every effort to reduce the birth rate—even in regions that are still mainly traditional peasant societies mired in poverty and illiteracy—is greatly desirable. But it must be recognized that up to this point in human history there has yet to emerge the first example of a population characterized by traditionalism, illiteracy, and poverty that has managed to reduce its birth rate.

The forthcoming results of the censuses to be taken in and around 1970 will begin to provide hard data on the impact of family planning programs on growth rates during the past decade. However, to repeat, it is possible that continued reductions in mortality have more than offset reductions in fertility. Growth rates may not have diminished appreciably. If so, this development should not serve as a discouraging factor. It is only by concerted effort to reduce fertility now that reductions in growth rates can be effected in the next generation. It is clear that reductions in mortality can go only so far; sooner or later reductions in fertility, if they occur, will reduce the rate of population growth. To recognize the difficulties involved is not to be pessimistic. On the contrary, there is every reason for optimism as one looks to the future: the increasing awareness of the problem, the increasing inputs into biomedical and social research, and the rapidly developing action programs. However, such optimism must realistically recognize that for the rest of this century, there is every prospect that the world will experience excessive population growth, with its attendant problems.

In general, the economically advanced nations can control excessive population growth within their borders by doing a little more of what they are already doing to lower their growth rates further or even to achieve a zero rate of growth. In the developing nations, however, much yet remains to be done before the control of the population explosion is assured.

References

1. United Nations, *Demographic Yearbook* (annual) since 1948. New York: Statistical Office of the U.N.
2. United Nations, *Determinants and Consequences of Population Trends.* Population Studies No. 17. New York: U.N. Dept. of Social Affairs, 1953.
3. Wellemeyer, Fletcher, and Frank Lorimer "How Many People Have Ever Lived on Earth?" *Population Bul,* Population Reference Bureau, Vol. 18, February 1962. pp. 1-19.
4. Keyfitz, Nathan, "How Many People Have Lived on the Earth?" *Demography*, Vol. 3, No. 2, 1966. pp. 581-582.
5. Carr-Saunders, Alexander M., *World Population: Past Growth and Present Trends.* Oxford: Clarendon Press, 1963. p. 42.
6. United Nations, *Demographic Yearbook 1949-50.* New York: Statistical Office of the U.N., 1950.
7. United Nations, "The Past and Future Growth of World Population." New York: Statistical Office of the U.N., 1951.
8. McKeown, Thomas, and R. G. Brown, "Medical Evidence Related to English Population Changes in the 18th Century," *Population Studies,* Vol. 9, No. 2, November 1955. pp. 119-141.
9. Stolnitz, George J., "A Century of International Mortality Trends," *Population Studies,* Vol. 9, No. 1, July 1955. pp. 24-55.
10. United Nations, *World Population Prospects.* New York: Statistical Office of the U.N., 1966.
11. Coale, Ansley J., and Paul Demeny, *Regional Model Life Tables and Stable Populations.* Princeton, N.J.: Princeton Univ. Press, 1966.

12. Coale, Ansley J., "Population and Economic Development," *The Population Dilemma*, P. M. Hauser, ed. 2nd ed. New York: Prentice Hall, 1969. pp. 59-84.
13. Mehlen, K.-H., "Abort Bekampfung–eine Aufgabe der Familienplanung," *Artz und Familienplanung.* Berlin: Verlag Volk and Gesundheit, 1968. pp. 67-122.
14. Davis, Kingsley, "Population Policy: Will Current Programs Succeed?" *Science*, Vol. 158, November 10, 1967. pp. 730-739.
15. Hauser, P. M., "Non-family Planning Methods of Population Control," *Population Control: Implications, Trends, and Prospects*, Dr. Nafis Sadik, et al., eds. Lahore, West Pakistan: Sweden Pakistan Family Welfare Project, 1969. pp. 58-66.

II

A New Demographic Transition?

Dudley Kirk

The sheer size and menacing character of population growth in the world today have resulted in widespread demands for action. Popular attention is understandably focused on population policies rather than on the basic economic, social, and cultural forces within which all programs must operate. These forces will very largely determine the future course of population growth. This paper seeks to analyze some of these "natural" forces, particularly as they relate to trends in the birth rate in the less developed regions.*

The basic assumption of most students of human populations is that humanity is midstream in a revolutionary change in its processes of reproduction—a transition from wastefully high death and birth rates to a more efficient and humane reproduction with much lower death and birth rates. As Stolnitz says,

> ... All nations in the modern era which have moved from a traditional, agrarian-based economic system to a largely industrial, urbanized base have also moved from a condition of high mortality and fertility to low mortality and fertility. In so doing they have almost all experienced enormous increases in population along with massive shifts in their relative numbers of children, adults and aged. (1)

Among students of population this process is called "the vital revolution" or, more soberly, "the demographic transition."

The first phase of this transition is death control or, strictly speaking, the postponement of deaths. Death rates are being reduced as the result of public health measures, medical advances, rises in levels of living, and improvements in personal cleanliness and health care. The so-called "population explosion" is a manifestation of this success in reducing mortality throughout the world on a scale totally unprecedented in human history. The more developed

---

Dudley Kirk is Professor of Demography, Food Research Institute and Department of Sociology, Stanford University.

*In this chapter these are defined to include Africa, Asia (excluding Japan and the U.S.S.R.), and the Latin American region (excluding Argentina and Uruguay).

countries have achieved levels of mortality almost certainly far below those ever achieved before in human society. In the less developed countries, death rates are falling far more rapidly than they did historically in the more developed countries. Since World War II, reduction in mortality has become worldwide, aside from temporary reverses as the result of war and civil disorder. Further gains are clearly possible, notably in the less developed nations, and indeed great progress is being made. Between 1960 and 1965 the estimated crude death rate (annual deaths per 1,000 population) in the less developed regions as a whole dropped from 20-22 to 16-17, and this achievement was solely responsible for the rise in the rate of population growth in these regions from 20-22 to 24 per 1,000. The estimated annual birth rate for the less developed regions remained about constant: 41-42 in 1960 and 40-41 in 1965 (2).

In the one third of the world that has experienced major economic and social advance the progressive reduction of the death rate has been followed by reduction in the birth rate. In the early stages this was ascribed to many causes, biological, psychological, and nutritional; but it is now generally recognized that the chief factor in reduction of the birth rate has been the voluntary practice of birth control, including induced abortion.

Although there remain great advances to be made in reducing or postponing deaths, the less predictable factor in national population growth has become the level and trends in the birth rate. The developed countries, with relatively low birth rates, also have relatively low rates of population growth. In these countries the excess of births over deaths is commonly 1 percent or less per year,* and in the absence of large-scale international migration, their rates of population growth are at this level.

Continuation of this 1 percent rate of national population growth will, of course, create problems in the developed areas, although probably of a lesser magnitude than those created by the concentration of population in major metropolitan areas. In the less developed world, however, the problem is more urgent, owing to the unique size and rate of population growth involved. Because of the high birth rate, the annual rate of natural increase is over 2 percent in Asia, 2.5 percent in Africa, and 3 percent in Latin America.†

According to the theory of the demographic transition, one would expect the present less developed countries to follow the experience of western countries in reduction of the birth rate. This must occur if there is to be a humane solution of problems of population growth. There is general agreement that birth rates will drop if these countries achieve major socioeconomic

---

*As of 1968 averaging 0.8 percent in Europe, 0.8 percent in the United States, 1 percent in the Soviet Union, 1 percent in Canada, and somewhat higher in Japan, Australia, New Zealand, Argentina, and Uruguay.

†Data not otherwise documented are drawn from United Nations publications, chiefly (3-5).

advance. A number of less developed countries are now making rapid socio-economic advance and almost all are making some progress, though not as rapidly as desired.

As noted above, the birth rate in the less developed regions fell little, if at all, in the first half of the 1960's. Was there a downturn in the latter half of the decade? Does past experience offer guidelines for judging the probable future course of natality in these regions? The information now available is too fragmentary to permit final answers to these questions. But some preliminary answers may be gleaned from an examination of the validity of the following propositions:

1. Reduction of the birth rate is now occuring widely among peoples of very different cultural backgrounds and ways of life in the less developed regions.

2. Historically there is an acceleration of the rate at which countries move through the demographic transition from high to low birth rates.

3. The higher the natality at the time of entering the transition, the more rapid the rate of the decline.

4. A certain threshold and "mix" of socioeconomic development has been a requirement for initiating a strong downward trend in natality; this threshold and mix of socioeconomic variables is different within the major cultural regions (i.e., east and southeast Asia, the Islamic countries, Latin America, and tropical Africa).

Though the subject is outside the scope of this paper, it is assumed that vigorous government population policies may accelerate reduction of the birth rate and possibly initiate such reduction at an earlier stage of socio-economic development than would otherwise occur.

THE DICHOTOMY IN WORLD NATALITY BEFORE 1960

Experience after World War II and in the 1950's was discouraging with reference to the first proposition. By 1960 one-third of the world's population had relatively low birth rates (under 25 per 1,000) and two thirds lived in countries having high birth rates (over 35 per 1,000). Very few countries fell between, and even fewer could be viewed as "in transition."

A high level of social and economic development has universally been accompanied by a reduction of natality. Relatively low birth rates were the rule in the so-called "developed" world in 1960 and are even more so today. With few exceptions annual birth rates by 1968 were below 20 births per 1,000 population in the developed countries of Europe, the Soviet Union, Japan, Australasia, and northern America.* By contrast, birth rates are generally twice as high in the less developed countries.

*The exceptions were Iceland, Ireland, Portugal, and Spain (which reported birth rates of 20 or 21 in 1968); New Zealand, 22.6; Albania (the only Muslim country in

There were significant differences in natality among the less developed countries prior to the 1960's, but these were variations in high fertility due to differences in age at marriage, in cultural practices relating to marriage and reproduction, and in the prevalence of disease, as well as to the use of modern methods of birth control associated with rising levels of socioeconomic development (6).

With the important exception of Japan all countries with low birth rates in 1960 were of European cultural and ethnic background. This is in no way to imply that non-Europeans could not or would not achieve lower fertility; it is simply an empirical fact that, aside from Japan, they had not done so. Historically, low fertility patterns had diffused from their center in northern and western Europe to southern and eastern Europe and across the Soviet Union in a rather orderly pattern. In overseas countries of European background birth rates were higher, but birth rates in these countries did not remotely approach the levels in the less developed countries or what had existed in the same countries prior to the long downward trend. Today, in overseas countries of European settlement the "baby boom" has receded, and birth rates are substantially lower than they were in the decade following World War II. In the less developed regions, countries with mainly European populations had much lower birth rates than their neighbors. Thus Argentina and Uruguay reported birth rates of 22.3 (1967) and 21.4 (1966) in contrast with an estimate of over 40 for the rest of South America.

Until very recently all countries with low birth rates were in the temperate zones. Again, this does not imply that people living in tropical countries could not or would not achieve reductions in natality. It is simply that as of 1960 they had not done so. Tropical countries almost universally had high birth rates.

In summary, countries that had experienced the demographic transition in birth rates were almost universally "developed," chiefly of European cultural background, and located in the temperate zone. Countries of high birth rates were characteristically less developed, non-European, and tropical.

Contrary to popular assumption, neither religious doctrine (i.e., the position of the Catholic Church) nor political ideology (i.e., communist vs. noncommunist) seem to have been a decisive factor in birth rates. Catholic countries ranged from lowest to highest birth rates, depending upon their level of development. Communist doctrine against population limitation has not been a barrier to the spread of the small family pattern; in fact eastern European countries and the Slavic populations of the Soviet Union now have among the lowest birth rates in the world. Communist policies have, if anything, accelerated reduction of fertility by providing abortions in the health services and

---

Europe), 35.6; and, most interesting, Rumania, 26.3, a rise from 14.3 in 1966 because most induced abortions were outlawed in that year.

by constraints on consumption (e.g., housing) that have contributed to post-ponement of marriage and childbearing.* As of 1960 on the natality side the demographic transition had progressed substantially in almost all countries of European background, whether Catholic or non-Catholic, communist or non-communist, and it has advanced even further today.

Now the dichotomy in natality is beginning to break down. With major socioeconomic changes, an increasing number of less developed countries are experiencing reductions in fertility. These changes since the postwar period give promise of a new continuum of countries at various stages moving from high to low birth rates.

THE PENETRATION OF FORMER BARRIERS TO NATALITY REDUCTION

The scope of the changes that are occurring is evidenced by widespread reduction of birth rates in the 1960's and especially by the growing number of less developed countries in natality transition.

The average less developed country today has a birth rate of 40 or so, more often higher than lower. Some forty-seven less developed countries are listed by the United Nations as having "virtually complete" vital statistics, i.e., at least 90 percent coverage of births. Of these, forty-two report a reduction of the birth rate between the average for 1960-64 and the available data for the second half of the decade.[†] Many of the "countries" listed by the United Nations are small areas. The birth rates for countries of 500,000 or more inhabitants are shown in Table 1.

Various stages in natality transition are clearly observable. In some countries reduction of the birth rate began in the 1950's and continued through the 1960's. In others it was initiated in the 1960's. In several (e.g., Guatemala, Mexico, and Panama) it is too early to state whether or not the drop in the birth rate is the first stage in continuous transition or merely the result of changes in age structure or of vagaries in statistical reporting.[‡]

*Communist experience, and especially the important role of providing free abortion, has not been given the attention it deserves in the family planning programs of the less developed countries. See Abdel R. Omran, "Abortion in the Demographic Transition," in this volume.

†The exceptions are Israel (actually a developed country in an underdeveloped region), Jordan, and three very small areas (Nauru, Norfolk Island, and the U.S. Virgin Islands).

‡Among the influences at work are the following examples: the improvement (less often deterioration) in the completeness of birth registration, which would usually raise recent figures relative to earlier ones; the provisional nature of most recent rates (final figures are often, though not always, somewhat higher than the provisional); changes in age structure, i.e., in the proportion of children and of persons in reproductive ages in the total population; errors in estimates of population used as the denominator in computation of birth rates. The often contradictory effects of these influences will be clarified by the results of 1970 and 1971 censuses where these are being taken.

TABLE 1

Birth Rates for All Less Developed Areas of over 500,000 Population
Designated by the United Nations as Having "Virtually Complete"
Vital Statistics, 1950-1969

	Average Birth Rate				Latest Birth Rate	
	1950-54	1955-59	1960-64	1965[a]	Year	Rate[b]
LATIN AMERICAN REGION						
Chile	33.7	35.9	34.8	31.9	1967	30.9
Costa Rica	49.1	49.1	44.8	40.0	1968	37.7
El Salvador	49.0	49.3	48.6	44.4	1969	41.9
Guatemala	51.3	48.7	47.7	44.0	1968	42.5
Guyana	42.9	43.6	42.0	38.2	1968	35.1
Jamaica	34.8	39.2	40.3	37.0	1968	34.3
Mexico	44.9	45.9	46.0	43.7	1969	42.2
Panama	37.5	39.8	40.6	38.6	1969	38.0
Puerto Rico	36.6	33.7	31.2	26.7	1969	24.5
Trinidad and Tobago	37.7	38.3	36.9	29.0	1968	27.4
NEAR EAST						
Israel	32.5	27.9	25.5	25.5	1969	26.1
Jordan	45.0	40.1	45.9	48.0	1966	47.8
Tunisia[c]	30.8	39.9	42.8	42.7	1968	40.4
ASIA						
Ceylon	38.5	36.6	34.9	32.2	1968	31.8
China (Taiwan)	45.9	42.8	37.1	29.7	1969	25.6
Hong Kong	34.2	36.3	32.8	24.2	1969	20.7
Malaysia (West)	44.1	44.4	40.3	36.4	1967	35.3
Ryukyus	35.5	29.2	24.0	21.4	1969	21.5
Singapore	45.5	42.8	35.6	27.0	1969	22.2
OTHER						
Albania	38.9	41.8	40.1	34.9	1968	35.6
Fiji	40.0	40.7	39.2	33.8	1968	30.2
Mauritius	46.2	41.0	38.9	31.8	1969	27.2

[a] Average 1965 through last year indicated in column 6.

[b] The most recent figures are usually provisional and are subject to later adjustment.

[c] Registered births. As corrected for underregistration the average for 1961-64 is 49.1; the average for 1965-68 is 45.4; and the 1968 figure is 43 (7).

Sources: (3-5).

Although all less developed countries with reasonably reliable vital statistics are included in the above discussion, these obviously comprise only a small part of the total population in the less developed regions. They are also unrepresentative in that there is a relationship between development, good statistics, and progress in the demographic transition. However, there is a wider circle of countries, with less reliable statistics, in which various official statistics and sample surveys also indicate a decline in the birth rate.* As among the countries with more reliable statistics, a majority apparently have experienced reduction of the birth rate in the 1960's.

This leaves the giants of the less developed world unaccounted for—mainland China, India, Pakistan, Indonesia, Brazil, and Nigeria. In these countries available information gives no solid basis for saying with assurance that these countries had a reduction of natality in the 1960's; nor, indeed, is there any better evidence that they did not.†

In order to reach European levels of fertility the birth rate must fall to 20 or below. A rough (though somewhat narrow) measure of countries "in transition" are those with birth rates in the range of 25 to 35. In 1960 there were few such countries, and of these even fewer could be regarded as undergoing initial transition.‡ All but Cuba and Israel have since dropped below this category, but a growing list of new countries was approaching, entering, and passing through this range. (See Table 1.)

In quite recent years there have been important breakthroughs in the cultural and climatic barriers to spread of lower birth rates. The most important of these is the diffusion of lower birth rates in east Asia, first established in Japan and now spreading to neighboring countries. Taiwan and Korea§ are experiencing rapid declines in the birth rate, a trend that antedates the successful family planning programs in these countries, though the latter have surely accelerated adoption of birth control. The birth rates of Chinese populations in Hong Kong, Singapore, and Malaysia are also falling rapidly. Most important is, of course, mainland China. What little evidence is available from very

---

*These countries include South Korea, Iran, Turkey, Lebanon (in number of births), the United Arab Republic, Cuba, Colombia, Ecuador, and miscellaneous smaller areas.

†Indirect evidence suggests the possibility of slight fertility reduction in India (as indicated by the enlarged family planning program and, especially, survey results showing rising use of contraception, especially in urban populations); in Pakistan as a result of the wide acceptance of contraception in the family planning program before the change of government in 1968; in China in connection with the campaign to raise age at marriage and to provide birth control services; and, in tropical Latin America as result of the incidence of induced abortion. In all countries there has been an increase of urbanism, education, and other variables that historically have been associated with reduction of birth rates. Counteracting these influences is the possibility that in some areas birth rates may have risen (as they did earlier in Latin America) as the result of improved health conditions.

‡The countries with birth rates between 25 and 35 were Canada and New Zealand, then still experiencing the postwar "baby boom"; three countries related to Europe: Iceland, Israel, and Malta; and three Caribbean countries: Barbados, Cuba, and Puerto Rico.

§In South Korea official vital statistics are defective, but annual enumerations provide tabulations which show declining proportions of young children, as does the census of 1966. These are confirmed by repeated sample surveys conducted for evaluation of the Korean family planning program.

scanty official data suggests that the birth rate may be relatively low for a less developed country, but this is quite uncertain.*

Breakthroughs in other regions are less dramatic but are impressive in the range of cultures and conditions represented. Reductions in natality are occurring among very diverse peoples. They are occurring in Ceylon, the "Ireland of Asia," in which late marriage as well as birth control have brought about lower birth rates among both the Sinhalese and the Ceylon Tamils (originally immigrants from south India). Change is occurring in the island countries of Mauritius, Reunion, and the Seychelles, with their mixed populations of Africans and Asians, and in the West Indies among peoples of African origin (Barbados and Jamaica), of mixed African and Asian origin (Trinidad), and of chiefly European origin (Puerto Rico and Cuba). In the West Indies major reductions in the birth rate are also reported in the French-speaking islands of Guadelupe and Martinique and in the Netherlands Antilles. On the mainland a rapid reduction in natality seems to be occurring in Costa Rica, the most socioeconomically advanced of the countries of Central America, as well as in Chile, one of the most advanced countries of South America.

Finally, a significant development has been the appearance in very recent years of fertility declines among peoples of Islamic tradition. Until very recently Islam was far more effective than Catholicism in its resistance to the spread of fertility control (8). Now rapid reductions in birth rates are occurring in Albania, in the other Islamic populations of southeastern Europe (e.g., in Yugoslavia), in several of the Soviet republics of Islamic heritage, and quite possibly in Turkey and Tunisia (7, 9).

As cultural barriers are being breached, so for the first time rapid reductions in birth rates are occurring in a number of tropical countries, as widely scattered as Malaysia, Ceylon, and the West Indies.

Very recent experience has demonstrated that the fertility transition can cross major cultural frontiers and is indeed doing so in many areas.

The evidence given above should be tempered by two observations:

First, the countries concerned are generally rather small and, interestingly enough, many are islands. Several of them are experiencing unusually rapid social and economic development and, in some, birth rates have been affected by the emigration of young adults. They are also likely to be countries on the frontiers between major cultural regions and hence more vulnerable to external influence than the larger countries. We do not in fact know whether and to what extent change is under way in other and larger countries, but if it is occurring, it seems likely that the transition is at an earlier stage. Despite these cautions, there is increasing evidence that natality reductions are making headway in a wide variety of cultural situations in less developed

---

*The estimate of the birth rate in mainland China used by the United Nations is 34, a figure given for the year 1957 by the State Statistical Bureau in Peking based on surveys and "reports from areas where registration was considered satisfactory."

regions and may indeed have gone much further than can be measured by reliable data.

Second, in some cases the reduction of the birth rate in the near future may be slowed or even temporarily reversed by prospective changes in the age and sex structure of the countries concerned.* In a number of less developed countries there was a relatively low birth rate during the Depression and during the Second World War, followed by some recovery and a higher birth rate after the War. As a result, larger cohorts of young people are now moving into the reproductive ages than was the case during the mid-1960's. In Taiwan, for example, it will require a considerable acceleration in the reduction of age-specific fertility† to continue the present trend toward a lower crude birth rate (10).

Obviously one would like to have better measures of natality than the crude birth. Reproduction rates, which eliminate most of the variance caused by changing proportions of women in the marriageable and reproductive ages, would provide a better measure of trends. Unfortunately these statistics require accurate information on births by age of mother and on age distribution of women in the reproductive ages—information that is often unavailable for recent years. Where it is available, it shows downward trends paralleling those for crude birth rates.‡ The available data for the 1960's support the reasonable conclusion that, given time and socioeconomic advance, one may expect a general diffusion of lower birth rates in the less developed countries. Clearly the process has begun. But much depends on how fast these reductions will occur and at what level of socioeconomic development they may be expected to begin.

On the first point, do declines in natality, like declines in mortality, accelerate over time?

THE ACCELERATING REDUCTION OF NATALITY IN THE DEMOGRAPHIC TRANSITION

The death rate in the less developed areas is dropping very rapidly—"a decline that looks almost vertical compared to the gradual decline in Western

---

*See Nathan Keyfitz, "Changes in Birth and Death Rates and Their Demographic Effects," in this volume.

† Births per 1,000 women at each age, i.e., 15 to 19, 20 to 24, etc.

‡E.g., for Taiwan, Singapore, Chile, Costa Rica, Puerto Rico, Trinidad and Tobago, and Mauritius. Data on completed fertility, i.e., the total number of children born to women passing through their reproductive years, is the final and most accurate measure of fertility, but it does not measure recent change, which is precisely what we are after here. One cannot get around the basic fact that women have births at changing intervals and over a long period of time. A woman at age 45, who has completed her childbearing, usually had her first child 20 to 30 years previously and her number of children reflects the motivations and socioeconomic milieu existing well before the last decade.

Europe . . . " (11). Recent evidence suggests that, in Latin America at least, the acceleration of reduction in mortality has been even greater than earlier supposed (12).

Furthermore, the *levels* of mortality in Latin America and other parts of the developing world were higher than those in western Europe when the latter began its modern demographic transition. The evidence for Latin America and other parts of the world suggests that acceleration in mortality reduction has been to some extent independent of economic development, and is presumably related to the introduction of cheap public health and medical technology.

Paralleling the established facts about mortality decline is the common assumption that natality changes will occur gradually, perhaps more like the European experience. In western Europe, the transition took 50 years or more, often commencing from much lower levels of natality than those now prevailing in most of the less developed world.

The available evidence does not support this assumption. Rather there has been an acceleration in the rate at which countries move through the demographic transition from high to low birth rates. This proposition is demonstrated in Table 2, in which are compared the reductions of the birth rate now occurring in less developed countries and those that occurred in Euro-

TABLE 2

Years Historically and Currently Required for Countries to Reduce Annual Crude Birth Rates from 35 to 20, 1875 to circa 1969[a]

Period in Which Birth Rate Reached 35 or Below	Number of Countries	Number of Years Required to Reach Birth Rate of 20		
		Mean	Median	Range
1875-99	9	48	50	40-55
1900-24	7	38	32	24-58
1925-49	5	31	28	25-37
1950-	6[b]	15	14	10-26

[a]The following countries are included: 1875-99–Austria, Australia, England and Wales, Finland, Italy, Netherlands, New Zealand, Scotland, United States; 1900-24–Argentina, Czechoslovakia, Germany, Hungary, Japan, Portugal, Spain; 1925-49–Bulgaria, Poland, Rumania, the Soviet Union, Yugoslavia; 1950- –Ceylon, Chile, Hong Kong, Puerto Rico, Singapore, Taiwan. The initial and terminal dates were determined by 3-year averages rounded to 35 and 20 respectively and bracketing continuous downward trend in the birth rate. A number of European countries were not included because their birth rates were already below 35 in 1875.

[b]None of these countries have yet reached a birth rate of 20. The average annual percent decline in the birth rate since reaching a crude birth rate of 35 was in each case extrapolated to estimate the total years required to pass from 35 to 20.

Sources: (3, 13-15). See also Table 3.

pean and other countries at an earlier period. Since the countries of the less developed world are often beginning reduction in the birth rate at a much higher level than European countries, a comparison is made for the years required for the crude birth rate to decline from 35 to 20 at different periods. A crude birth rate of 35 was chosen to eliminate fluctuations in natality unrelated to the widespread adoption of family limitation. In no country entering the transition since 1950 has the birth rate dropped to 20. In these cases the decline in the birth rate to 20 was projected by linear extrapolation of annual average percent reduction actually experienced after reaching the 35 level.

In a number of countries (for example, Australia, Canada, New Zealand, and the United States) the birth rate fell to 20 or below in the initial period of decline, but later returned to somewhat higher levels in the postwar "baby boom." Some of these countries now again have birth rates below 20, but the years in transition were considered only for the initial period of consecutive downward trend.

From Table 2 it will be seen that *the average length of time required for a country to pass through this stage of demographic transition has been greatly reduced, from some 50 years for countries entering the transition in 1875-99 to half that time or less for those countries entering the transition, so defined, since 1950.*

The limited number of countries and years of experience included in Table 2 restricts the conclusions that may be drawn from it. Because the new surge of natality reduction is so recent, relatively few countries were eligible, but all were included.* However, the wider experience reflected in Table 1 supports the evidence, which in any event represents a continuation of historical trends.

An obvious question is whether the countries that have entered this phase of the natality transition since 1950 will in fact reach birth rates as low as 20, or fertility as low as that achieved in European countries. All that may be said is that as yet there is no indiction of a "floor" above those levels. Three of the countries in Table 2 already have birth rates in the lower 20's. At present rates of fertility decline the matter will soon be put to empirical test.

Although the "new" countries may move more rapidly through the transition as defined above, they also have farther to go because their initial birth rates are higher. It therefore seems desirable to compare overall experience

---

*All countries meeting the following criteria were included: (a) over one million population; (b) initiation of continuous decline in birth rate prior to 1960; (c) at least 5 years of birth rates at 35 or below. A number of smaller countries and additional larger countries with more recent fertility declines at higher levels also show much more rapid rates of reduction in the birth rate than were historically recorded for European countries. Among these are Albania, Barbados, Costa Rica, Malaya, Mauritius, Reunion, Trinidad and Tobago and several constituent republics of the U.S.S.R.

since the "take-off." Linear regressions fitted to historical data for thirty-two countries with reliable data are shown in Table 3. In this table "t" is a time trend which is set equal to zero at the onset of fertility decline; the "a" coefficient is the statistically estimated level of the crude birth rate at 1875 or later onset of continuous decline; the "b" coefficient is the estimated average annual amount of decline in the birth rate. Thus for Sweden the initial birth rate (in 1875) as estimated from the regression was 32.6 and the average annual decline (represented by the "b" coefficient) was 0.28 per 1,000 population.

The regressions do not take into consideration reduction of fertility that occurred in western and central European countries before the last quarter of the 19th century.

TABLE 3

Regression Coefficients for Decline of the Birth Rate during Modern
Demographic Transitions, 1875-1969 (Linear Regression in Form of
$y = a + bt$)

Country[a]	Period[b]	Coefficient[c] b	Coefficient[d] a
WESTERN EUROPE AND THE UNITED STATES			
France	1876-1938	−0.15	25.5
Ireland	1875-1939	−0.09	25.1
Belgium	1875-1935	−0.28	33.7
Denmark	1885-1934	−0.31	33.6
England and Wales	1876-1934	−0.37	36.7
Finland	1876-1934	−0.32	38.5
Netherlands	1876-1936	−0.26	37.4
Norway	1878-1935	−0.29	34.2
Scotland	1875-1939	−0.29	36.0
Sweden	1875-1934	−0.28	32.6
Switzerland	1876-1938	−0.27	32.3
United States	1875-1934	−0.28	36.0
Average (excluding France and Ireland)		−0.30	35.1
SOUTHERN EUROPE			
Italy	1884-1953	−0.29	38.8
Portugal	1923-1969	−0.22	31.1
Spain	1885-1952	−0.24	37.8
Average		−0.25	35.9
CENTRAL EUROPE			
Austria[a]	1875-1936	−0.35	37.3
Czechoslovakia[a]	1875-1937	−0.41	42.6
Germany	1875-1932	−0.42	42.7
Hungary[a]	1883-1963	−0.39	44.9
Average		−0.39	41.9

TABLE 3 (Continued)

Country[a]	Period[b]	Coefficient[c] b	Coefficient[d] a
EASTERN EUROPE AND JAPAN			
Bulgaria[a]	1906-1966	-0.49	43.2
Japan	1920-1961	-0.44	37.0
Poland[a]	1898-1967	-0.35	42.3
U.S.S.R.[a]	1897-1967	-0.47	54.0
Average		0.44	44.1
"NEW" COUNTRIES[e]			
Albania	1955-1968	-0.69	43.8
Ceylon	1948-1967	-0.42	40.9
Hong Kong	1957-1969	-1.44	39.2
Malaysia (West)	1956-1967	-0.96	46.1
Puerto Rico	1949-1969	-0.8	41.8
Ryukyu Islands	1950-1969	-1.15	37.8
Singapore	1949-1969	-1.21	50.2
Taiwan	1954-1969	-1.22	46.4
Trinidad and Tobago	1954-1968	-0.85	41.9
Average (excluding Hong Kong)		-0.91	43.6

[a]Unless otherwise indicated, national territories are as of the dates given. The exceptions are Austria and Hungary (present territory); Czechoslovakia, western Czechoslovakia only, and for years before 1901 the old Austrian territories of Bohemia, Moravia, and Silesia; Poland, territory approximating the "Central Provinces" of the interwar period; U.S.S.R., before World War I, the fifty provinces of European Russia.

[b]Initial and terminal dates were determined from 3-year averages marking the beginning and ending of continuous declines in the birth rate. Declines occurring prior to 1875 were ignored. For countries seriously affected by war the relevant years were omitted (e.g. 1915-1921 for World War I and 1941-47 for World War II). Dates for the U.S.S.R. are 1897, 1913 and 3-year averages for 1926-28, 1937-39, 1958-1960, and 1966-68.

[c]The statistical estimates of average annual reduction of the birth rate. R^2 values (not shown) exceed 0.9 for all countries except Ireland, Portugal, Japan, Albania, and Trinidad, indicating that the linear regression model is a good fit to the data except in these countries.

[d]Estimated initial birth rate from linear regression.

[e]With the possible exception of the Ryukyu Islands, birth rates in these areas were still declining as of the terminal dates. Puerto Rican data corrected for underregistration.

Sources: Historical data for Europe (13, 14); for 1930-1969, standard U.N. sources, chiefly (3); for Czechoslovakia, Hungary, Poland, and the U.S.S.R., national statistical sources. For the United States (15).

By 1875 fertility reductions were underway in most of western and central Europe and "bottomed out" in the 1930's. In western Europe and the United States the average reduction of the birth rate was only about 0.3 per year. Had earlier experience been included, these countries would have shown even slower reductions in the birth rate. France and Ireland are special cases that started (in 1875-76) with relatively low birth rates and experienced very modest average annual declines. In central Europe the starting levels were higher and the reductions more rapid (i.e., about 0.4 per year). Southern European countries started later and reached their transition lows only after World War II. Portugal and Spain, in particular, do not fit the general pattern. Eastern European countries started later and from much higher birth rates than western Europe and had more rapid reductions in the birth rate. Because of boundary changes resulting from the World Wars, it is difficult to get strictly comparable historical series, but it is clear that these observations also hold for eastern European areas not included in Table 3.*

There is a major and very important gap between European countries and Japan, and those countries entering the transition later. European countries had all entered the transition by the earlier 1920's. The "new" countries did not begin to enter the transition until after World War II. There was an interval of some 25 years when no major country entered the transition.

Since World War II, there has been a new and quite diverse group entering the transition at high birth rates comparable to those of eastern Europe but showing much more rapid fertility declines, averaging a drop of about one point per year, or three times that experienced in western European countries during their natality transition.[†] The table is restricted to countries showing continuous reductions in the birth rate since before 1960. Experience of areas apparently entering the transition since 1960 is too brief to form firm judgments, but there is no reason to believe that progress will be slower in these areas. Among constituent republics of the U.S.S.R., for example, there have been major declines since 1960 at different levels in the transition.[‡]

Though there are inconsistencies, notably as regards Spain and Portugal, Table 3 shows strikingly the acceleration in fertility reduction over time. This acceleration holds in two senses: (a) between countries commencing transition at different periods; and (b) within each country. The latter is evidenced by the fact that the linear regressions refer to absolute amounts of change in the birth rate. This means progressively higher *rates* of natality decline as the transition progresses.[§] In fact, for many countries squared regressions of the form $a+bt^2$ fit the data as well as or better than linear regressions, i.e., in

---

*Albania is classified in Table 3 as a "new" country rather than eastern European because of its quite different socioeconomic characteristics and demographic behavior.

[†] Ceylon appears to be an exception, but probably only because of a statistical artifact. Birth registration is estimated to have improved from 88 percent completeness in 1953 to 99 percent in 1967. Correction of official figures for this factor would substantially raise the average annual reduction in the birth rate.

[‡] Birth rates for 1960 and 1967 in representative areas declined as follows: White Russia, 24.5 to 16.8; Moldavian Republic, 29.2 to 20.7; Georgia, 24.7 to 19.3; Armenia, 40.3 to 25; Kazakhstan, 36.7 to 24; the Turkmen Republic, 42.4 to 35.6.

[§] This point is of importance in judging the impact of family planning programs. The assumption that birth rates would have declined at the same percent as before in the

these countries there was, if anything, an acceleration in absolute reductions in the birth rate and hence an even more rapid *rate* of decline in the birth rate at the later stages than is implied in the data for linear regressions.

The data in Table 3 less firmly support the proposition that the higher the birth rate at the onset of transition, the more rapid the decline. They do, however, clearly suggest that a high birth rate at onset is not in itself a barrier to rapid transition.

The data in Tables 1-3 refer to the crude birth rate and not to measures of fertility standardized for the age structure of the population. Because of the lack of data, detailed comparisons such as those given in Table 3 are not readily available for more refined measures. Gross reproduction rates* for a few representative countries are shown in Figure 1, which illustrates (a) the

GROSS REPRODUCTION RATES FOR SELECTED COUNTRIES

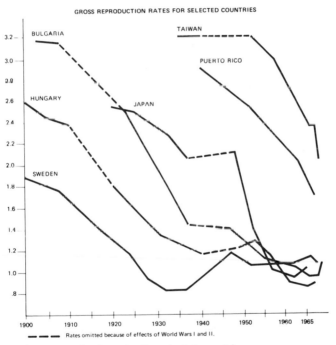

Rates omitted because of effects of World Wars I and II.

Figure 1. Gross reproduction rates for selected countries.

Sources: Unless otherwise noted, data up to 1930, (16); more recent data, (17) and later issues; for Japan, 1920 and 1925, (18); for Puerto Rico 1940-1950, corrected for underregistration, (19); for Bulgaria and Hungary, data are for territory of date.

absence of a family planning program is conservative and may well exaggerate the apparent program effect by understating the decline to be expected.

*Technically defined as the average number of daughters that would be born to hypothetical female cohort if subject to current age-specific fertility rates and zero mortality before the end of the reproductive age.

acceleration of reduction of natality in Europe, proceeding from Sweden (western Europe) to Hungary (central Europe) and to Bulgaria (eastern Europe); (b) the somewhat slower declines in countries where the downward trend began at lower levels of natality (Japan and Puerto Rico), (c) the precipitous decline characteristic of some east Asian countries that have entered the transition since World War II (Taiwan).

If the experience so far is indicative of what may occur in other less developed countries the situation is more hopeful than often described. United Nations projections assume a 5 percent reduction during the first 5 years of sustained fertility decline, followed by about 10 percent for each subsequent 5-year period (20). These projections are conservative as compared with recent experience of countries undergoing transition.

As in the case of mortality, it would appear that a new pattern of fertility change is emerging in quite a few countries of the less developed world. The comparatively slow rate of natality reduction experienced in western Europe is being replaced by a new pattern of precipitous declines.

Recent data suggest that, *once clearly begun*, sustained fertility declines will proceed more rapidly in the less developed regions than they did historically in the West. But *when* such fertility declines will occur, and at *what level of socioeconomic development* are, of course, critical factors. Is there a consistent threshold of socioeconomic development at which sustained reduction in fertility may be expected to occur? Does it differ from one major cultural region to another?

RELATIONSHIP BETWEEN SOCIOECONOMIC DEVELOPMENT AND REDUCTION OF THE BIRTH RATE

The so-called "threshold" hypothesis was examined in some detail for the United Nations study of world natality as of about the year 1960 (6, pp. 148-151). This study was unsuccessful in finding specific threshold values for various socioeconomic indicators, taking all the countries of the less developed world as a single group. However, when the analysis is confined to each of the several major cultural regions, more consistent patterns emerge.

Latin America

In Latin America there is substantial correlation between major indices of development and natality. This is illustrated by data for the Latin American region in Table 4.* The indices include measures of urbanization, of economic structure (percent of economically active males in agriculture), of educa-

*The materials on Latin America are drawn from an unpublished study by K. S. Srikantan and the author of this paper.

TABLE 4

Percent of Variance in Birth Rates Explained by Representative Socioeconomic Variables for Twenty-Five Countries in the Latin American
Region, Circa 1960-1964

Variable (x)	Zero Order[a] Correlations	Percent Variance in Birth Rates Explained by Regression	
		Linear:[b] $(a + \beta x)$	Single Asymptotic:[b] $(a + \beta \mu^Y)$
1. Percent population in places 20,000 or more	-0.75	55	61
2. Percent of economically active males not in agriculture	-0.85***	71	74
3. Percent literate among population 15+	-0.71	47	77
4. Telephones per 1,000 population	-0.94***	87	87
5. Hospital beds per 1,000 population	-0.83***	68	72
6. Newspaper circulation per 1,000 population	-0.80***	62	63
7. Female expectation of life at birth (e_o)	-0.76	55	59

[a]All values statistically significant at 1 percent level, starred items at 0.1 percent
level.
[b]All R^2 values adjusted downward to correct for degrees of freedom.

tion (literacy), of general infrastructure (telephones), of health services (hospital beds), of communication (newspapers), of mortality (expectation of life
for females at birth), and the birth rate. The birth rates are official rates
accepted as reasonably complete by the United Nations or as estimated by
the United Nations agencies from census information for roughly the years
1960-64. These data show a high level of association between the birth rate
and these selected measures of development. Collectively these variables explain some 90 percent of the variance in birth rates in Latin America. Although this is a statistical measure of association, rather than a direct causal
explanation, it confirms the view that levels of the birth rate are closely
linked to development.

It will be noted that these measures relate especially to social and communication variables in which progress is being made in most countries of the
less developed world. The relation of birth rates to strictly economic measures, such as per capita income and average annual growth of GNP, is more

tenuous.* The interrelationship of urbanization and natality is also less stable than other indices shown. When the most urban countries, Argentina and Uruguay, are removed, and the correlation is confined to the remaining twenty-three countries of the region, the correlation coefficient drops from -0.75 to -0.60.† These findings confirm the conclusions, reached by a number of investigators, that in Latin America natality is not so closely linked with industrialization and urbanization as it was historically in Europe. Other aspects of development appear to be more closely related to birth rates in Latin America.

The relationships between socioeconomic indices and natality may take different forms. In Table 4 it will be observed that a curvilinear regression (single asymptotic curve) fits the data somewhat better and explains more of the variance than linear regressions. This is especially true of literacy.

Logically, natality rates should be lagged behind their presumed socioeconomic determinants; but it is not clear what amount of lag is appropriate or that this is a constant among different socioeconomic variables. Further exploration of this subject is required.

On the basis of empirical experience in Latin America, threshold ranges were determined for each of the variables used. This was done by contrasting the indicators for the seven countries of the region that had entered or gone through the transition with those of the eighteen that had not.‡

The threshold range for each socioeconomic indicator is shown in Table 5. This range was much too great for the measure of urbanization (percent of

---

*The seven socioeconomic variables shown in Table 4 were selected from a very much larger number which produced lower but often statistically significant zero order correlations with crude birth rates. The seven variables selected are not only highly correlated with birth rates but also with each other, such intercorrelations ranging in magnitude from 0.64 to 0.94, with an average of 0.78. All the intercorrelations are statistically significant, half of them at the 0.1 percent level.

Correlations between specific economic measures and crude birth rate were: average annual rate of growth of real domestic product, 1960-65 (0.35); per capita gross domestic product, 1963 (-0.42); per capita national income, 1963 (-0.49); gross domestic fixed capital formation as percent of gross domestic product at 1962 market prices (-0.43); percent of income originating in the agricultural (0.47) and manufacturing (-0.21) sectors to the gross domestic product at factor cost, 1962; energy consumption per capita, 1962 (-0.26); percent of economically active males in agriculture (0.85) and in industry (-0.60).

†In a sample of only twenty-five countries and with data of greatly varying quality, single figures should not be taken very seriously. Thus the extraordinarily high correlation of telephones (i.e., a surrogate for modern infrastructure) with natality is reduced from -0.94 to -0.88 when Argentina and Uruguay are excluded.

‡The seven countries are Argentina, Barbados, Chile, Cuba, Puerto Rico, Trinidad and Tobago, and Uruguay. The threshold was determined by the range between the lowest value for the first group of countries and the highest for the second. To take a specific example: the lowest figure reported for female expectation of life at birth (e_0) in the first group was 59 in Chile; the highest in the second group of countries was 67 in Jamaica. The threshold was thus defined as 59 to 67 for this variable and six high-natality countries were in this threshold range. (See Table 5.)

TABLE 5

Threshold Ranges[a] for Socioeconomic Variables
in the Latin American Region, Circa 1962

Variable	Threshold Range[a]	High Natality Countries[b] in Threshold Range
1. Percent population in places over 20,000	16-47	15 countries
2. Percent of economically active males not in agriculture	58-63	Guyana (63), Venezuela (62)
3. Percent literate among males over 15	83-87	Costa Rica (85), Guyana (87)
4. Percent literate among females over 15	74-85	Costa Rica (84), Guyana (75), Jamaica (85)
5. Telephones[c]	2.8-2.9	Panama (2.9), Venezuela (2.9)
6. Hospital beds[c]	3.8-5.3	Costa Rica (4.5), Guyana (5.3), Jamaica (4.0)
7. Daily newspaper circulation[c]	63-109	Costa Rica (75), Guyana (80), Jamaica (71), Mexico (109), Panama (89), Venezuela (70)
8. Female expectation of life at birth (e_o)	59-67	Costa Rica (65), Guyana (63), Jamaica (67), Mexico (60), Panama (63), Venezuela (65)

[a]The range of values for socioeconomic variables at which fertility declines may be expected to occur. See text for explanation of method by which ranges were determined.
[b]Countries with average birth rates above 40 in 1960-64.
[c]Per 1,000 population.

population living in places of over 20,000) to be of any value for prediction. But for the other variables the range was narrow enough to select high fertility countries which as of 1960-64 seemed most eligible for the onset of fertility reduction.

Four countries were in the threshold range for five or more variables (Costa Rica, Guyana, Jamaica and Venezuela), one for four variables (Panama) and one for three variables (Mexico). Of this group Costa Rica and Jamaica have clearly experienced fertility declines since the period of study, both in crude birth rates and in more refined measures of fertility trends. Declines in the birth rate have been reported in Guyana and in Panama (notably in urban areas), but it is too early to state with assurance that these countries have firmly entered the natality transition; a decline in the birth rate has also been recorded for Mexico in very recent years, but, as noted earlier, evaluation of fertility trends in that country and in Venezuela will have to await results of 1970 censuses.

As of 1960-64 the remaining twelve countries of pretransition status were moving toward the threshold ranges, but they were not yet (in 1960-64) at a stage where early fertility reduction would be predicted.

The applicability of the socioeconomic threshold as a predictive device needs more testing, including longitudinal analysis, but the results so far suggest considerable stability in the relation between socioeconomic development and the onset of fertility declines.

A striking feature of the Latin American situation is the high levels of development required for natality transition. Major fertility declines occurred in Europe at much lower levels of literacy, life expectancy, and proportion of the population employed outside agriculture (21). A possible explanation lies in the fact that progress along these lines in Europe was the result of a long and slow historical process, by modern standards. In Latin America many aspects of socioeconomic modernization are occurring much more rapidly than they did in Europe, with less time to change attitudes and practices affecting family size. Urbanization, in statistical terms, is occurring far more rapidly than it did in Europe. By the same token it is reasonable to expect more rapid reduction of fertility, once begun, because of modern technologies of communication and of family limitation, and, indeed, this seems to be happening.

The threshold hypothesis has not yet been examined in detail for other regions but some preliminary conclusions follow.

East and Southeast Asia

In east and southeast Asia* there are also significant relationships between socioeconomic indicators and the birth rate. As is illustrated in Table 6, there appears to be a closer negative relationship between measures of economic achievement and birth rates than in Latin America. This is suggested by the higher correlation coefficients for per capita income and energy consumption in east and southeast Asia.

As might be expected, the threshold of socioeconomic development accompanying fertility decline in this region is substantially lower than the threshold in Latin America. Of the seven areas clearly in natality transition by 1960-64[†] all had experienced the onset of fertility decline with per capita incomes well below $300, roughly the average level for onset of fertility

---

*Including twenty-three areas bounded by Pakistan, Indonesia, and Japan and excluding Asian parts of the Soviet Union. Usable data on most variables are available for only seventeen. All the coefficients presented are statistically significant at the 5 percent level and most at the 1 percent level or better. Nevertheless the countries included are few and scarcely a random sample, so weight should be given to general levels and patterns, not to specific values.

[†]Japan, the Ryukyus, Taiwan, Hong Kong, Malaya, Singapore, and Ceylon.

TABLE 6

Zero Order Correlations of Selected Socioeconomic Characteristics with Birth Rates
in Latin America, East and Southeast Asia, and Islamic Countries, Circa 1962

Socioeconomic Characteristics	25 Countries in Latin American Region	17 Countries in East and Southeast Asia	15 Islamic Countries
Per capita GNP	-0.42^a	-0.67^{bd}	-0.59^a
Per capita energy consumption	-0.26	-0.73^a	-0.38
Percent economically active males not in agriculture	-0.85^b	-0.50^a	-0.27
Percent literate at ages 15 or over	-0.71^b	-0.55^a	-0.82^b
School enrollment as percent of population at ages 5-19	-0.44^a	-0.77^b	-0.80^b
Newspaper circulation[c]	-0.80^b	-0.75^b	-0.82^b
Telephones[c]	-0.94^b	-0.50^a	-0.54^a
Hospital beds[c]	-0.83^b	-0.66^b	-0.33
Female expectation of life at birth (e_o)	-0.76^b	-0.65^b	Not available

[a]Statistically significant at 5 percent level.
[b]Statistically significant at 1 percent level or lower.
[c]Per 1,000 population.
[d]Per capita income.

decline in Latin America, though as pointed out above, income is a poor predictor of natality in Latin America. With the important exception of the Philippines, all countries that reached a per capita income of $200 by 1960-64 were then experiencing, or had experienced (e.g., Japan), a rapid fall in the birth rate. In two countries, Ceylon and South Korea, the onset of natality transition occurred at per capita incomes of about $125.

For cultural reasons and perhaps because the effects of overpopulation are more salient, peoples in this region have undertaken family limitation at a lower level of socioeconomic development than in Latin America. As of 1960-64 three countries fell in the threshold area for several socioeconomic indicators: the Philippines, South Korea, and Thailand. South Korea has since experienced rapid fertility reduction, doubtless accelerated by its unusually successful family planning program. The Philippines and Thailand do not have complete enough vital statistics or survey data to measure year-to-year changes. The great bulk of population in this area, in China, India, Pakistan, and Indonesia, continue to have low indices of socioeconomic development. Although progress has been made and trends are in the right direction, these countries still fall below the threshold for fertility decline indicated by the experience of the more advanced countries of the region. What seems most likely is that some more advanced regions of these countries (such as the

Punjab in India) will shortly reach the thresholds for socioeconomic indicators and will initiate fertility declines in their respective countries. It is to be hoped that national family planning programs in these countries will accelerate the adoption of family limitation before what would occur in the "natural" course of socioeconomic development. Family planning programs are making the population problem more salient, are making knowledge and means of birth control more readily available, and should speed trends initiated by social and economic advance.

The Islamic World

In the Islamic world* measures of education clearly stand out as variables most related to natality levels. It will be noted that in Table 6 the highest correlation coefficients are those for literacy, school enrollment, and newspaper circulation (a crude measure of functional literacy). As noted earlier, fertility declines are apparently occurring in several Islamic countries (i.e., Albania, Lebanon, Malaya, and several Soviet republics of Islamic heritage), all of which clearly lead in education and other indices of socioeconomic development. The evidence is less clear concerning a second rank of countries as determined by measures of achievement in socioeconomic advance and by intermediate levels of natality (i.e., Libya, Syria, Tunisia, Turkey, and the United Arab Republic). As noted earlier, natality seems to be falling in Tunisia and Turkey, but there is insufficient evidence to postulate reduction of fertility or its absence in the remainder. The existing socioeconomic threshold for the reduction of fertility in the Islamic world appears to be higher than that for east Asia but lower than that for Latin America. Again, leading Islamic countries have adopted national family planning policies that may be expected to accelerate the transition in the countries concerned.

Tropical Africa

Analysis of the situation in tropical Africa must rest on the basis of fragmentary material such as scattered censuses, sample surveys, and estimates of fertility made from very limited data. In most parts of Africa, consideration must be given to the possible initial effect of modernization (e.g., improved health conditions) in *raising* rather than reducing fertility, as occurred in Latin America. Although the beginnings of fertility limitation have been observed in a few places such as southern Ghana and Lagos in Nigeria, it is not at all clear what may prove to be the threshold for reduction of fertility in the tropical Africa area.

---

*The fifteen countries with Muslim majorities that have usable data, from Morocco and Senegal in the west to Pakistan and Malaysia in the east. There is some overlap in regions used herein.

The above discussion of socioeconomic "thresholds" for fertility reduction is obviously exploratory and not conclusive. Their predictive value for determining the prospective onset of natality transition is yet to be fully tested. The evidence so far does suggest that there are regularities in the relationships between socioeconomic development and natality within major cultural regions that may prove useful, jointly with other approaches, in forecasting the "take-off" point for sustained fertility declines.*

GENERAL CONCLUSIONS

The examination of recent trends in natality in the less developed regions tends to confirm the first three propositions presented at the outset. The data support the following conclusions about recent changes in natality in less developed regions:

1. A growing number of countries have been entering the demographic transition on the natality side since World War II and after a lapse of some 25 years in which no major country entered this transition.

2. Once a sustained reduction of the birth rate has begun, it proceeds at a much more rapid pace than it did historically in Europe and among Europeans overseas.

3. The "new" countries may reduce birth rates quite rapidly despite initially higher levels than existed historically in western Europe.

4. Where available, the more refined measures of fertility, standardizing for differences in age structure, yield results similar to those for crude birth rates.

5. There is no direct evidence yet that current fertility reductions will terminate at levels significantly higher than those achieved in European countries and Japan.

As earlier noted, the above observations are based primarily on the experience of a relatively few countries with good data. Similar reductions in natality are very likely occurring in a number of other countries lacking reliable annual vital statistics. But there is no evidence yet as to whether reductions in the birth rate have recently occurred, or not occurred, in large countries, such as China, India, Pakistan, and Indonesia. What is happening in these countries will be crucial.

Efforts to identify "thresholds" for the initiation of fertility reduction are at a preliminary stage and their predictive capacity, although promising in

---

*The above analysis has quite consciously used incomplete and sometimes dubious data to evaluate changes that may have appeared in very recent years. It is, of course, not intended to replace much more detailed analysis of better data that will become available in due course. Obviously it complements rather than eliminates the need for study of specific causal relationships between socioeconomic development, changes in motivations regarding desired family size, and the degree of success in the actual practice of family limitation.

some regions, remains to be fully tested. The relation between socioeconomic variables and fertility is clearly different within the different major cultural regions of the less developed world; quite different levels and kinds of development are associated with fertility reductions, for example, in east Asia and in Latin America. This confirms common sense and explains why efforts to relate socioeconomic measures and fertility "across the board" for all less developed countries have led to confusing results.

Finally, is there indeed a new or renewed demographic transition? The evidence suggests that there is. A rapidly growing number of countries of diverse cultural background have entered the natality transition since World War II and after a 25-year lapse in such entries. In these countries the transition is moving much faster then it did in Europe. This is probably related to the fact that progress in general is moving much faster in such matters as urbanization, education, health, communication, and often per capita income. If progress in modernization continues, notably in the larger countries, the demographic transition in the less developed world will probably be completed much more rapidly than it was in Europe.

It would be foolhardy, however, not to end on a word of caution. On any assumptions concerning the reduction of fertility that may occur with socioeconomic progress, it still follows that one may anticipate and must accommodate an enormous increase in the world population and that these increases will be greatest precisely in those countries economically least well-equipped to absorb the increase in numbers.

References

1. Stolnitz, George J., "The Demographic Transition," *Population: The Vital Revolution*, Ronald Freedman, ed. New York: Doubleday, 1964. p. 30.
2. United Nations, *Population Newsletter*, December 1969. p. 3.
3. United Nations, *Demographic Yearbook, 1968*, and earlier issues. New York.
4. United Nations, *Population and Vital Statistics Report*. New York, April 1970.
5. United Nations, *Monthly Bulletin of Statistics*. New York, July 1970.
6. United Nations, *Population Bulletin*, No. 7. New York, 1963.
7. Lapham, Robert J., "Family Planning and Fertility in Tunisia," *Demography*, May 1970. pp. 241-253.
8. Kirk, Dudley, "Factors Affecting Moslem Natality," *Family Planning and Population Programs*, Bernard Berelson, et al., eds. Chicago: Univ. of Chicago Press, 1966. pp. 561-579.
9. Shorter, Frederic C., "Information on Fertility, Mortality and Population Growth in Turkey," *Population Index*, January-March 1968. pp. 3-21.

10. Freedman, Ronald, and T. H. Sun, "Taiwan: Fertility Trends in a Critical Period of Transition," *Studies in Family Planning*, August 1969. pp. 15-19.
11. National Academy of Sciences, *The Growth of World Population*. Washington, D.C., 1963, p. 14.
12. Arriaga, Eduardo E., and Kingsley Davis, "The Pattern of Mortality Change in Latin America," *Demography*, August 1969. pp. 223-242.
13. Kuczynski, Robert R., *The Balance of Births and Deaths*. Vol. I, *Western and Northern Europe*, New York: Macmillan, 1928; Vol. II, *Eastern and Southern Europe*, Washington, D.C.: The Brookings Institution, 1931.
14. Bunle, Henri, *Le Mouvement Naturel de la Population dans le Monde de 1906 à 1936*. Paris: L'Institut National d'Etudes Demographiques, 1954.
15. Coale, Ansley J., and Melvin Zelnik, *New Estimates of Fertility and Population in the United States*. Princeton, N.J.: Princeton Univ. Press, 1963.
16. Kuczynski, Robert R., *Measurement of Population Growth: Methods and Results*. New York: Oxford Univ. Press, 1936.
17. United Nations, *Demographic Yearbook*, 1965 and later issues. New York.
18. Murumatsu, Minoru, ed., *Japan's Experience in Family Planning—Past and Present*. Tokyo: Family Planning Federation of Japan, Inc., 1967.
19. Vasquez, Jose L., "Fertility Decline in Puerto Rico: Extent and Causes," *Demography*, 1968. pp. 855-865.
20. United Nations, *World Population Prospects, 1965-85 as Assessed in 1968*. Population Division Working Paper No. 30. New York: December 1969.
21. Kirk, Dudley, *Europe's Population in the Interwar Years*. The Hague: League of Nations, 1946. Ch. 9, Appendix 2.

III

An Economic Perspective on Population Growth

T. Paul Schultz

A disquieting feature of the postwar period is the increasing rate of population growth in many low income countries. To date, the factors behind this development are not fully understood, nor can its consequences be confidently inferred from existing evidence. Are the acute social strains associated with the contemporary acceleration in population growth a transitory consequence of a once-and-for-all adjustment to the postwar *change* in the rate of population growth, or are they a permanent consequence of a continuing rapid *rate* of population growth? What pressures within the family may work to dampen rapid population growth? How much time is needed for these behavioral mechanisms to take hold, and how effective and humane will they be? Clearly the pace of population growth is, on the surface, alarming, yet uncertainty remains as to what policy priorities should be adopted to cope with this complex problem. Designing and implementing sound social policy requires, principally, a better understanding of the link between individual human behavior and the societal trends we view with concern.

Many impressions of the "population explosion" and its consequences are formed from the perspective of *macro* or *aggregate* analyses. However, perspective both sharpens certain features and conceals others. The object of this paper is to approach rapid population growth from the perspective of *micro-analysis*—that is, from the standpoint of the family, its welfare and behavior. There is, as yet, a dearth of empirical data and analysis that is truly micro in its approach to this issue. Neither is there a firm empirical base for the more familiar macro-analyses of the consequences of population growth (1). The micro-analytic approach of this paper, therefore, relies heavily on a structure of hypotheses, or a logical model, for which the growing body of evidence is still regrettably fragmentary.

A micro-analytic approach to population study seeks to show how additional population pressures arise and impinge on the welfare, goals, opportu-

T. Paul Schultz is Director of Population Research, the Rand Corporation.

nities, and behavior of the family. In particular, an attempt is made here to trace the effects of population growth and economic development on the allocation of family resources. The most difficult problem for such an analysis is to separate cause and effect; the family's changing environment and behavior both cause the acceleration of population growth and simultaneously generate new environmental constraints that presumably exert an influence on family behavior. Formal analysis of these problems within an econometric framework (2, 3, 4) has recently begun, but much more work is needed to make a firm identification of the important interactions between economic and demographic variables in the development process.

The approach of this paper is, first, to develop a simple model of family behavior in which reproductive behavior is central; second, to identify how economic development and the acceleration in population growth affect the family's environment; and third, to infer from this framework what consequences, both transitory and permanent, are likely to follow from mounting population pressures. All the references in this paper pertain to rapidly growing, low income populations unless otherwise stated.

THE VALUE OF CHILDREN: A MODEL

Children certainly are not merely the unintended outcome of sexual activity. On the contrary, children are a source of satisfactions to their parents and the value of these satisfactions depends on an array of psychological, social, and economic needs. I shall assume in this inquiry that reproductive behavior (fertility) is largely a response to the underlying preferences of parents for children, preferences which are constrained by uncertain fecundity and unreliable birth control. Given this working hypothesis, how might these preferences be revealed in micro data? The first task is to search for ways to identify the determinants of demand for children by looking for different aspects of the human environment that are likely to change the demand for children.

The most intractable problem is that of distinguishing between the demand for children and their supply, because parents are both the demanders and suppliers simultaneously (5). If at first one neglects the sources of uncertainty on the supply side of the problem, the desired reproductive behavior of parents is seen to depend on the following underlying values.

With respect to the *demand* there are first, the satisfactions of having a child (psychic utility that appears intangible because of the nonpecuniary context in which these satisfactions are obtained); and second, the tangible returns that accrue to parents because of their child's future contribution to the parents' real income. With respect to the *supply* there are first, the opportunity costs* and psychic cost of the parents' time and effort in bearing and

*Potential loss from not using one's time and energy in alternative activities.

rearing the child. (The nonpecuniary attributes of some of these costs, such as the pain of childbirth, are obvious.) Second, there are the additional resource costs of rearing the child—tangible and, as a rule, pecuniary in nature. These distinctions may appear formal, arbitrary, and unhelpful to some, but they underscore the essential dual function of a child to his parents.* The psychic determinants of both demand and supply are rooted in nonpecuniary values that resist tangible measurement, and are revealed only indirectly by means of micro-analysis, if at all. The second category of determinants is more likely to take a pecuniary form, submit to ordering, and admit to micro-analysis.

Nonpecuniary Returns from Children

We know little about the factors that lead different parents to make different appraisals of the intangible returns from children. On this point, consumer behavior theory is quite empty (6, 7). Economists commonly assume that differences among individuals in appreciating various consumer goods or activities is a function of their particular preferences. In other words, in an economic system people differ in their tastes, and implicitly tastes are taken as primitive or axiomatic to the system. Explicitly, these preferences are treated at a combination of specific tastes, each independently distributed across populations. However, consumer behavior theory provides one relevant implication—that an individual's satisfaction from any particular consumption activity tends to be subject to diminishing returns as that activity is engaged in more extensively. Satisfactions from additional children may diminish with increasing family size or number of surviving offspring.[†]

It is important to probe beneath basic preferences in order to deal with the factors that mould an individual's preferences.[‡] What measurable, variable, and possibly manipulatable elements of an individual, his culture, or his consumption activities determine his preferences for specific activities? Determinants or tastes may be more properly the domain of the sociologist, psychologist, and anthropologist; and a review of their literatures is not intended here. Nevertheless, however conceptualized and quantified, assessing

---

*As discussed in the next-to-last section, the neglect of intangible returns from children pervades the economic literature on population policy and optimum population criteria. On the other hand, some critics from sociology misinterpret the generality of the economic framework properly stated (5), and ignore its compatibility with their viewpoint.

[†]The extreme case can be documented by casual empiricism. For example, Wray (in this volume) reports evidence that the larger the number of children, the greater the jeopardy to the health of the parents and to the physical and mental development of children. If this association is a causal relationship and parents perceive the relationship, then one might argue the nonpecuniary returns to additional children had become strongly negative.

[‡]In the economic literature occasional efforts have been made to express consumption activities in a variety of fundamental dimensions and not to stop with the exhibited demand for goods (7), or to isolate cultural determinants of preference patterns (9).

the influence of culture or genetics on parent appreciation of the intangible returns from children can be pursued only when the tangible pecuniary returns have also been isolated and taken into account properly. None of the behavioral sciences has yet faced this challenge and accomplished the task of sorting out the pecuniary and nonpecuniary determinants of reproductive behavior (8).

Pecuniary Returns from Children

The rest of this paper deals largely with the combined effects of the pecuniary benefits and costs of children on parent demand for offspring. Limiting attention to these two countervailing determinants of parental reproductive behavior is not a reflection of their intrinsically greater importance compared with nonpecuniary factors. To reiterate, this emphasis is chosen because the factors influencing nonpecuniary returns are difficult to observe, conceptualize, and evaluate. Perhaps they are also quite difficult for instruments of public policy to modify. In contrast, the pecuniary returns from children are concrete; they may be interpreted within an established conceptual framework, and they are frequently thought to be directly influenced by the development process and various policies.

The time and resources used in rearing a child may be considered an investment cost applied toward the future productive capacity of a child. Depending on the associated levels of costs and benefits, a child may contribute to his parents a high or low rate of return. However, the apparently simple task of treating a child as though he were a producer good is actually complex. A child presumably consumes more than he can produce for about the first decade of life; at some time thereafter he is increasingly able to produce more than he needs. But what constitutes necessary consumption? After he grows up, how is one to treat a man's support for his wife and children? Should these commitments be viewed as consumption, or as a "surplus" to be credited against his own childhood "deficit"? In comparison with this ambiguous notion of individual consumption within a family, the concept of a man's productive capacity appears more solid, whereas empirical problems of measurement are quite difficult when it comes to assessing the productive capacity of a housewife or child who is not engaged for pay in the full-time labor force.

The family affords the traditional means for greater individual specialization among market, nonmarket, reproductive, and child-rearing activities. Generational cycles in both physical savings and human capital formation in children and adults further constrain and shape consumption opportunities of persons within, or potentially within, a family unit. These life-cycle patterns are affected by individual choice which influences the *measured* level of personal income in a community. One must be cautious, however, not to interpret the sensitivity of measured income in a community to household arrangements, labor force participation, and schooling patterns as entirely a real income phenomenon. More fundamentally, the valuable resource a person commands is his time; its free allocation between market and nonmarket activities, between consumption and investment, between his needs and those of his children should not be interpreted as conclusive evidence of change in welfare or in the real value of personal incomes, though it may change measurable flows of goods and services that are usually construed as income.*

To simplify and avoid problems that arise when the individual standpoint is adopted in such an analysis, I find it useful to regard the family as an integrated decision-making unit with a unified, if not egalitarian, perception of its own welfare. One might assume that parents behave as though they sought to increase the income, or wealth, of parents and children *(intergenerational—family net worth* in physical and human capital) subject to the constraints of necessary and desired paths of consumption for the family over time.

However, desired paths of consumption and the weight attached by parents to the wealth position of present versus future generations may differ systematically among individuals and account for differences in reproductive behavior. For example, poor parents may not be motivated to make a (positive) wealth bequest to their offspring. On the contrary, their aim in having children may be to borrow from them and have them more than "pay" for themselves during the parents' own lifetime. Only recently in the industrialized countries has the state actively taken the side of the child and sharply curtailed the parents' power to exploit the child.[†] At the opposite

---

*The classic statement of consumer decision theory interpreted as the allocation of time is Becker's (10). Efforts to reinterpret the character and structure of modern economic growth from this perspective are as yet limited (11), but theoretical and empirical work in this direction is beginning (2, 12).

[†]To define child exploitation one must distinguish between private welfare (parent and child) and social welfare. First, consider why parents might invest less than some private optimal amount in the development of each of their children—that is, why would they not invest until the private marginal return to additional human investments fell to the equilibrium rate of return in the society? Two reasons are clear: (a) the parents cannot hold enforceable claims on the increment to their offspring's adult productive capacity that are due to the human capital formation the parents might support; (b) the parents may not expect to outlive their children and to be able to collect fully on increments to their child's future productive capacity. Therefore, parents respond by investing less in their children and work them more than would appear to be socially optimal (or optimal from the child's point of view). Were a perfect capital market extended to the rational child, he would presumably be willing to borrow at the equilibrium rate of interest in the society and buy back from his parents his time to invest it in his future productive capacity. Although this institutional arrangement may seem fanciful, child labor and truancy laws, and, more recently, subsidized student loans are all legal mechanisms to redress this institutional shortcoming of the family from the point of view of society's long-run welfare.

extreme, rich parents might view children as instruments for intergenerational (positive) transfers of wealth and the means for perpetuating family influence.

In either case, however, the death of all family heirs might constitute a grave loss to parents. The strong desire to perpetuate the family could cause parents to shift family resources to the support of additional children while they lower their investments in each child as insurance against the family's dying out.*

Clearly, a principal attraction of children as instruments of investment is that a child draws upon resources when they are relatively plentiful and provides a return source of support in old age when the productive capacity of parents is meager and uncertain. Since one general motivation for savings and investment is to level out one's lifetime consumption by giving up consumption in periods of abundance to assure necessary consumption in periods of low earnings, this convenient timing of child costs and returns certainly plays a role in parent demand for children in all cultures.[†] Nevertheless, parents have uncertain claims on their children's future earnings, even in a traditional family-oriented society; therefore, parents may discount children heavily as reliable investments for their own future support. In a stagnant economic setting where there are few opportunities for parents to invest in tangible assets, children may appear attractive as a pecuniary investment for the future. Conversely, where high returns are anticipated from tangible investments, children may be sought only to fulfill nonpecuniary needs of the parents. How parents perceive the limits of the family as an instrument for investment is modified by cultural, institutional, and legal factors, such as inheritance laws, traditional family structure and values, and customs that impinge on marriage transfers and family identity, such as dowries and bride prices (21).

Variable Child Costs: A Crucial Decision. The costs of child rearing are not fixed, particularly in low income, tradition-bound regions. First the parents decide how much to invest in their offspring, and later the child himself may invest further in the development of his productive capacity. In some sense there may be a minimum level of support during a minimum period when a child is completely dependent. But in most developing regions, at a very early age a child becomes potentially capable of contributing to family resources, even though modest increments to his support and nutrition may prove to

---

*See (13) for a more complete discussion of the treatment of uncertainty in the demand for children.

[†]The life-cycle savings hypothesis is discussed and tested against data in a number of recent studies (14-17) and the related survivorship motivation for fertility is explored by various techniques by other investigators (18-20).

yield dramatic advances in his adult mental and physical capacities.* For the rest of his life, the growing productive potential of his time must be allocated between current earnings which may be saved or immediately consumed and earnings foregone which can be invested in his future productive capacity, or human capital (22).[†] To delay a child's entry into the full-time labor force so that he may acquire general education or specific vocational skills, parents must reallocate family resources. They may decide to rear fewer children, reduce family per capita consumption, reduce other forms of household savings and investment, or some combination of these three to increase their investments in their existing children.

Widespread evidence of declining labor force participation rates and increasing school enrollment rates among children in both low and high income countries implies that the costs of rearing and schooling children are rising.[‡] Some of this increase in child costs is directly borne by parents, apparently on a voluntary basis. What has motivated parents to sustain these increasing costs per child at a time when the recent decline in child death rates has led to an increase in the number of children parents must support? (25, 26). Will these concurrent demands on family resources be responsible for new patterns of parent economic and reproductive behavior?

How Parent Demand for Children Changes

In the course of the postwar development process, certain changes in the family environment have hastened the rate of family formation, increased the costs associated with this process, and may have raised the returns from human capital in comparison with those from unskilled labor and physical capital. Several of these changes are examined in this section from the viewpoint of the family, to discern what effects they are likely to have on parent reproductive and economic behavior.

Decline in Death Rates

The immediate cause of the "population explosion" was the abrupt decline in death rates in much of the less developed world shortly after World War II.[§] In general, the reduction in death rates was proportionately greater

---

*See, for example, (23, 24) and Wray, J. D., "Population Pressure on Families: "Family Size and Child Spacing," in this volume.

[†] A formal model of this life cycle process is presented in (12).

[‡] See Gavin W. Jones, "Effect of Population Change on the Attainment of Educational Goals in the Developing Countries," in this volume.

[§] This sharp reduction in death rates is often attributed to the easily transferred techniques of public sanitation and health, including new disease-control measures, such as spraying pesticides. However, there were improvements in consumption levels in the postwar era that led to better nutrition and possibly also facilitated the notable fall in

among infants and young children than among other age groups; therefore, this pervasive change in the regime of mortality had particular impact on parents in the process of forming their families. Many parents now in their 30's and 40's are supporting more children than their parents did at a similar age. This change is not due to noticeably higher fertility or earlier marriage; it is simply a reflection of the fact that more children from the postwar genera- tion have survived. At the social level the increase in child survival and in the speed at which families grow results in a more youthful population; there are fewer adults to work for each child they must feed, clothe, shelter, train, and equip for adult life. This rise in the child dependency rate implies that parents are today less able than were their parents to spread the consumption de- mands of their offspring over their productive lifetimes.

When childbearing is concentrated in a woman's first 10 to 15 years of marriage, and the overlapping period of child dependency is prolonged by increasing child investments, these large concurrent demands on parents' re- sources depress any residual earnings left for physical savings (26). Indeed, in developed countries, such as the United States, household physical savings rates fluctuate widely from periods of substantial dissaving during family formation and child schooling to a period of substantial parental savings after children achieve economic independence (14, 16, 17, 22, 29). With the emer- gence of a similar concentrated childbearing pattern in some low income countries, it is to be expected that differences in household physical savings rates between parents of different ages (stages of family formation) will grow more marked. There are as yet, however, few reliable data on household savings for low income countries by parent age and family size and composi- tion. Thus it is difficult to estimate the effects changing patterns of family formation and age structure have had on savings *

---

death rates. In any case, it is widely believed today that modern medicine and sanitation are not capable of inducing further large-scale reductions in death rates. The precondi- tions are not yet present for controlling the endemic nonmicrobial, diarrhea-pneumonia diseases that still account for a major share of the deaths in low income countries. To cut death rates further, there will have to be a widespread improvement in nutrition particu- larly among young children, and perhaps also a substantial advance in general living levels. See (24, 27, 28).

*Fluctuations in physical savings by age of parents might differ between developed and less developed countries for at least two reasons. First, the availability of consumer debt funding (and our frequent current expense treatment of consumer durables) per- mits young parents to acquire consumption loans that are not likely to be available in a low income country. Therefore, the dissavings rates noted among young parents in the developed countries might not occur. On the other hand, the concentrated childbearing pattern has gradually evolved in countries like the United States, whereas the pattern has emerged more rapidly in the low income countries. If the pattern were anticipated by parents, they might save more before starting to have children, or space their births more uniformly to spread out resource demands. However, in low income countries parents could hardly anticipate the drop in child death rates and the rapid extension of educa- tion. They may be subjected to relatively more severe resource binds and thus be com- pelled to reduce consumption levels or borrow in some fashion against the future when

On the other hand, when household savings are more broadly defined to encompass all additions to family net worth, including investments that parents make in their offspring, it seems that current savings rates in low income countries are not as low as traditionally measured. The concurrent trends of rapid population growth and educational expansion have probably increased total household savings, while depressing only that portion of savings allocated to physical capital formation. Conversely, when and if birth rates do fall in low income countries, the rate of household physical savings could increase as human capital formation rates slow their advance at an aggregate level and more parents have the opportunity to invest in tangible assets once their offspring have gained independence.*

The reduction in death rates also increases returns from having a child; indeed, all forms of human investment would appear to grow more attractive as human life is prolonged and morbidity is reduced. But this increase in pecuniary returns to childbearing need not contribute directly to higher fertility.†

It is reasonable to assume that parents frame their reproductive goals in terms of their preferences for a certain number of surviving children (or sons), not in terms of births. Were this generally valid, parents would want to compensate for the incidence of death among their offspring by seeking the number of births required to give them their desired number of surviving children. At least two mechanisms might function to accomplish such an approximate balance between birth rates and child death rates. To assure its survival and progress, in the Darwinian long run, a society requires institutions that accommodate the prevailing regime of mortality. Social institutions

---

their capacity for physical savings will sharply rebound. Data are clearly needed to explore and to test these predictions. Leff's (15) analysis of aggregate savings behavior across countries is suggestive of what might be found in micro household information, but to my knowledge no satisfactory analysis of micro data has been completed.

*From a societal perspective, Leibenstein has observed how changes in the quality of the labor force take place and concluded that more rapid population growth permits a more rapid replacement of the labor force and consequently a more rapid improvement in the *average "quality" of the labor force.* But because there exist resource constraints both on the public sector's provision of the supply of educational opportunities and on parents' demand for schooling for their children, more rapid population growth is likely to depress the *average "quality" of new entrants to the labor force*, lowering their productive capacity and relative earnings. From the standpoint of new entrants to the labor force, the slower rate of population growth is clearly preferred to a more rapid rate of population growth. Individual and social objectives may conflict in such a case. (See "The Impact of Population Growth on Economic Welfare: Nontraditional Elements," in this volume.)

†The nonpecuniary returns associated with the psychological needs that children fulfill may diminish sharply after a certain number of children have been born. Moreover, the pecuniary returns from children may increasingly favor investing more in each child rather than having greater numbers. This shift in demand from quantity to quality is more likely to occur if parents have only a limited capacity to borrow. Imperfections of this sort in capital markets are a common feature of many low income countries.

and traditional norms appear to play a prominent role in determining the age and extent of marriage, the spacing of births, and the frequency of re-marriage. But research has not shed much light on whether institutional changes occur promptly in response to changes in child death rates.*

Fortunately, a behavioral response at the family level is more likely in the shorter run. Parents are directly confronted by the consequences of the im-proved chances for child survival, and given their limited resources, they are presumably not indifferent to family size. Even though parents retain a rela-tively large family-size goal based on traditional values and constraints, they are likely to seek to regulate their fertility upon reaching their desired family size; institutional change or foresight on the part of parents is not required. Because childhood mortality is concentrated in the first years of life, still-fertile parents can sequentially decide to make an added effort to have an additional child when they lose one. At a community level this short-run replacement mechanism would become important several decades after the onset of the decline in child death rates when a substantial proportion of the fertile women in the population already have the number of surviving chil-dren they wanted and are seeking with some degree of success to avert further births.†

Parents may desire a certain number (and sex distribution) of surviving children, but they undoubtedly realize that they cannot assure the precise outcome they want. Rather, their actions influence only the range and prob-ability of possible outcomes. This recognition of *uncertainty* in the family formation process may induce parents to aim for more or fewer children (births) than they would desire under a predictable (certain) regime of deaths and births. Where parents emphasize having at least a minimum number of children survive and do not regard additional children as a large liability, hedging uncertainty will tend to raise their birth rate. Since the level of child death rates affects the degree of uncertainty attaching to the family forma-tion process, both the direct effect of the postwar decline in death rates and the indirect effect operating through uncertainty will, under such circum-stances, tend to reduce the number of births parents seek. The decline in child death rates could, therefore, be responsible for an overcompensating fall in birth rates, leaving the surviving family smaller than before the demo-graphic transition. In sum, the reduction in child mortality, while raising the

---

*Heer at Harvard is investigating how these changes in mortality are actually per-ceived and translated into behavior in several diverse settings in low income countries.

†Although the death of a child may motivate its mother to seek additional offspring, the effect on her reproductive behavior is difficult to distinguish in the *short run* if she is young, for her age cohort will probably continue having additional children for some time at about the maximal rate regardless of the incidence of child mortality. If on the other hand, the mother is older, say in her late 30's, and a sizeable proportion of her cohort intends to avoid further births, her behavioral response to the child's death will distinguish her sharply from others in her cohort within a relatively short time (3).

returns to child investments, should also foster a reduction in the number of births parents want.

Prospects for Fertility

It may be premature to speculate on the timing and structure of fertility changes that will occur in the less developed world, but available data fall into a consistent pattern. Evidence of fertility levels by age, observed over time, for both high income countries and for the handful of low income countries in which birth rates have recently fallen sharply suggest that declines in fertility do not occur uniformly among women of all ages. Rather, birth rates for women in their 20's remain relatively high, and those for women over the age of 30 fall to relatively low levels after the period of demographic transition. In some countries there is also a concurrent drop in fertility among younger teen-age women, possibly related to delayed marriage, increased demand for adolescent schooling and diminished desired levels of fertility. In the posttransfusion environment parents appear to complete their families more quickly than was the case for earlier generations and to avert additional births rather successfully after the mother reaches the age of 30 or 35. If this pattern of reproductive behavior continues to spread in low income countries, we may anticipate the changes (mentioned earlier) in the allocation of family resources directly linked to the decline of fertility.

Employment of Women

A second aspect of the development process raises the cost of childbearing most notably. A significant part of child costs is the value of a mother's time spent attending to her children. When her most productive activities are easily combined with child rearing in the home, the opportunity cost of her time devoted to them is small and a large family no great inconvenience. However, the household activities traditionally performed by women, such as weaving, processing family food, caring for livestock, and handicraft cottage manufacturing tend to be displaced gradually in the development process by modern food processing and the textile and manufacturing sectors. They are also depreciated by the growing commercial specialization in agriculture. As development proceeds, the woman finds her most remunerative employment opportunities are increasingly outside of the home and even outside of the rural-agricultural sector of the economy (30). These employment opportunities are increasingly difficult to combine with child rearing. In this more specialized economic environment, a large family extracts from parents a growing opportunity cost for the mother's time that may force them to adopt a smaller family-size goal.

This mounting opportunity cost of child rearing reinforces the tendency for a woman to concentrate childbearing in relatively few years to allow her more years of her life to engage in remunerative activities that may help toward increasing family investments in each child's schooling and training.

Shifts in Labor Supply and Demand

A third factor contributing to the change in parent demand for children is the change in the relative scarcity of unskilled labor, skilled labor, and physical capital. From the demand side it appears that modern industrialization calls for an increasing supply of skilled labor that has not been satisfied at past relative wages. Despite the enormous expansion of educational facilities in most low income countries, differences in earnings between individuals with and without primary and secondary educations continue to widen. Although the costs of education certainly have also risen, there are some indications that the pecuniary returns to education have grown with the expansion of the modern sector and the diffusion of new technology. An obvious source of this widening disparity in the earnings of unskilled and skilled labor is the "population explosion" itself, which has caused the supply of labor to increase in the 1960's a third to a half faster than it did in the 1950's.*

With development, the share of national income received by labor has also shown a tendency to rise in comparison with the shares of land or physical capital. In low income countries, labor's share of manufacturing value-added is one half or less, whereas in high income countries the labor share is more like three fourths.† Similar differences probably exist in all economic activity, but the gaps in agricultural data hinder comparisons. In an extreme case of a "labor surplus" economy, Hansen has found that the Egyptian agricultural wage has risen in this century relative to the returns on land, despite the several-fold increase in labor on the nearly fixed physical stock of land. The factor share of land in Egyptian agriculture has secularly fallen, while the share of fertilizers and pesticides has risen, with labor's share virtually unchanged.‡ Comparable evidence is hard to come by for a large number of low income countries, but what information we have suggests that labor's share of income rises with the structure of growth occurring today. Within labor's growing share, evidence indicates a widening dispersion in personal incomes, as the modern sector rewards scarce skills handsomely and the traditional

---

*Kuznets (31), Weiskoff, (32) and Nelson (33) survey data on these developments, though time series are deficient and have many shortcomings. Theoretical and empirical investigations of the complementaries between education and capital formation applied to the United States have been recently investigated in two papers by Griliches (34, 35).

†See (33, Chapters IV, V).

‡See (36, 37). There was some increase in the land brought under cultivation in Egypt during the 1920's and 1930's, and much of the Nile Valley has been shifted to double cropping during this century. The Hansen findings apply only to wage labor, not to family labor. Of course, while the physical stock of land is fixed, land as a unit of production with defined characteristics is not fixed; fertilizer, multiple cropping, etc. can change it.

craft sector, to survive, pays unskilled labor meagerly.* These evidences of change in the personal distribution of income give assurance that rates of return to basic education in the low income countries today are substantial and may be increasing. This situation gives parents an added incentive for furthering the education of their children. As emphasized earlier, parents may view differently these opportunities for investment in their children's future, depending upon their own consumption needs, alternative investment opportunities, and their attitudes toward the family's future.

Uncertainty and Change in Birth Control Technology

Recent developments have also changed the environment in which parents reach their reproductive goals. Three basic sources of uncertainty enter into their supply of children: (a) death may take the lives of more or less of their children than they anticipate; (b) parents may not be able to bear the number (and sex distribution) of children they want; and (c) parents may bear more children than they want. As discussed earlier, improved chances of child survival have markedly narrowed the range of uncertainty a parent must cope with in forming his family. Hedging against catastrophic family losses has become less pressing. To some degree, advances in reproductive biology and improved institutions of adoption may have also reduced the prevalence of sterility or alleviated its impact on family planning. However, the most important change has taken place in the technology of birth control and the administration of health and family planning programs.

The costs of birth control, pecuniary and nonpecuniary, are much more than the money outlays and the inconvenience associated with using a method; they also consist of the task of acquiring and evaluating information about alternative methods. This task may represent an insurmountable obstacle to the natural diffusion of new techniques in a low income, poorly educated country. However, new techniques of birth control provide for highly reliable regulation of fertility at little cost or inconvenience, while family planning programs have improved methods of disseminating these ideas and services to all strata of society. Among the lower social and economic classes of the less developed world, particularly the costs of evaluating, adopting, and using modern birth control are decreasing sharply. Where there is already demand for averting births, this reduction in birth control costs should be reflected in more rapid and humane reductions in fertility.[†]

Many more factors which are linked to the development process in low income countries could be discussed; some might foster and others retard the long-term trends in parents' demand for children.[‡] The changes stressed here

*See (33, Ch. V; 31, 32).

[†] See (33, Ch. VIII; 3).

[‡] Emphasis is here placed on economic factors, though undoubtedly many changes in behavior can also be understood in terms of changes in social values. These variables

all strengthen parents' preferences for having fewer births and for investing more resources in each offspring. The motivation for these changes in parental behavior is found in a microeconomic conceptual framework: the costs of childbearing have risen and the returns to more prolonged education and vocational training have also risen. The next section reviews some empirical evidence in support of this interpretation of the relations between the environment of parents and their reproductive and economic behavior.

EMPIRICAL EVIDENCE OF THE FAMILY PLANNING HYPOTHESIS

To explore a hypothesis regarding the determinants of reproductive behavior, it has been assumed that parents' preferences and the opportunities and constraints of their living environment exert a perceptible influence on their actual reproductive behavior. This hypothesis has been tested by statistical analyses of interregional variation in fertility (birth rates and child/ women ratios) in Puerto Rico, Colombia, Taiwan, and Egypt. Analysis of the environment and reproductive histories of a sample of married women from the Philippines and East Pakistan have also confirmed several aspects of this hypothesis at the family level. These studies are reported fully elsewhere; a summary of the empirical findings must suffice here.*

In each of the six countries, certain relevant features of the parents' environment can be measured, while others cannot. The omission or indirect measurement of some of these variables poses analytical problems. The simultaneous determination of reproductive behavior within the complex of adult decisions pertaining to education, marriage, labor force participation, and migration introduce additional statistical biases that can be dealt with, albeit imperfectly, only in the studies of Egypt, Puerto Rico, and the Philippines. Nevertheless, despite certain specification, measurement, and estimation problems, these empirical investigations find statistically significant multivariate associations between fertility and the features of the parents' environment that are thought likely to modify the number of births parents would want. In particular, two links between the environment and reproductive behavior emerge as quantitatively and statistically significant.

First, birth rates are not independent of death rates. Reduction in child death rates does not necessarily worsen the population problem by accelerating the rate of population growth, except in the short run. In Puerto Rico and Taiwan, the reduction of death rates appears to have fostered the signif-

---

should also be included in conceptual and empirical investigations when they remain independent of the economic environment, or when they adjust only sluggishly to the changes in the observed environment, and when they exert a separate influence on reproductive (and economic) behavior.

*A variety of multivariate linear regression models were employed in these studies, and the general results reported here were insensitive to alternate model specifications examined (2-4, 20, 38).

icant reduction in the birth rate. In the Philippines and East Pakistan, the frequency of earlier child deaths in a family is a good predictor of further births. Although a reduction in child mortality may be associated for 10 or 20 years with an increased rate of population growth, this lag in the decline in birth rates may be seen as a logical consequence of the preferred pattern of family formation discussed before. Parents would appear to bear the number of children they believe they need to bear to reach a desired family size, given the death rates that once prevailed. Adjustment of reproductive behavior becomes noticeable only after the parents have reached their completed family-size goal and seek to avert further births.

As the older group of "family planning" mothers becomes substantial in a less developed country, 10 to 20 years after the reduction in child mortality, there emerges a strong statistical association between the incidence of child death and the birth rate 2 and 3 years later. Indeed in Taiwan, where the data are best designed for examining this relationship, the loss of a child less than age 15 is associated with a rise in birth rates 3 years later more than sufficient to replace the lost child and to increase the number of children likely to survive to age 15.*

The way in which birth rates adjust to the prior level and trend of death rates has been studied in detail in only two countries, Taiwan and Puerto Rico, both of which have experienced relatively low levels of child mortality for a decade or more. It is therefore suggested by some analysts that there is a threshold below which child mortality must fall before parents perceive the change and begin to seek to limit births (18). Perhaps the more modest reductions in child death rates sustained in Egypt and Colombia over the last 2 decades have not been sufficient to initiate a general decline in fertility. No completely satisfactory test of the "threshold hypothesis" has yet been performed, but data now being analyzed for low income, relatively high-mortality regions in East Pakistan provide some evidence at the family level of the anticipated compensatory relationship between child mortality and subsequent fertility.†

*This strong short-run overcompensating relationship appears not to be a manifestation of a biological feedback mechanism (based on lactation, etc.), for it is weakest among the more fertile women between the ages of 20 and 29. Rather the relationship seems to be a behaviorally determined response which is statistically strongest for women over 29, among whom the proportion practicing birth control is greatest. See (3).

†Should some form of the "threshold hypothesis" be confirmed, quite different population policy strategies might prove appropriate to different parts of the world. As a hypothetical example, Egypt and East Pakistan might find it worthwhile to concentrate social investments in health and education until changes in the parents' environment create the demand for restricting fertility and only then employ substantial resources in family planning and birth control services. Perhaps, too, modest investments in prenatal and infant nutritional supplements might be a more cost-effective route to reducing maternal and child mortality below some threshold level than waiting for the general process of development to bring about an improvement in health and living conditions.

The second implication of these studies is that for parents who withdraw their children from the labor force and send them to school fertility is significantly lower. Since work and school for a child are neither mutually exclusive nor necessarily exhaustive of their time, analysis should deal with the allocation of the child's time to both activities. For Puerto Rico and Egypt, both child labor (unpaid family workers) and school attendance, or education, are treated together in the regression analysis, and both have the expected direct and inverse associations with fertility. In Colombia and Taiwan, only child school attendance rates can be measured, and in both countries the enrollment rate is powerfully inversely associated with fertility.*

To interpret this seemingly general association, more information is required on what determines interregional differences in school attendance rates. Is it the limited capacity of the school system, the *supply* of schooling, that is restricting attendance? Or is it the willingness of parents to send their children to receive basic education, the *demand* for schooling, that determines the interregional variation in school attendance rates? The more plausible assumption, as argued earlier, is that although the capacity of school systems, particularly in rural areas, may constrain the acceptance of students in the short run, enrollment rates in the long run reflect the parents' willingness to demand schooling and invest in the education of their offspring.

Adult education may also play a role in facilitating the fall in birth rates, but on this point the findings are mixed. For Colombia and Puerto Rico, adult educational attainment is negatively associated with fertility. But in Taiwan and the Philippines, the association is weak and ambiguous. In Egypt, where a more complex formulation of the model was considered, it appears that women's education contributed to a higher female labor force participation rate, which was in turn associated with somewhat lower fertility.

Neither agricultural employment nor rural residence was in itself a help in accounting for interregional or interpersonal differences in birth rates. Poor health and limited educational opportunities of the agricultural and rural populations fully explain the tendency for these groups to have higher birth rates than those engaged in nonagricultural employment or residing in urban areas. Therefore, interregional and intersectoral migration per se need not influence reproductive behavior.

Much more research is needed to specify adequately a multivariate model of family reproductive and economic behavior in simple terms and to estimate its parameters for a variety of populations from both aggregate and individual family data. Yet, these initial investigations point to important areas of interaction between the parents' environment and their reproductive and eco-

*Caldwell (39, 40) reports a thoughtful and thorough discussion of the interrelationships between education and fertility preferences in regions of Ghana. Jones (in this volume) elaborates a variety of further possible interactions between the educational process and fertility.

nomic behavior that are consistent with the earlier modeling of the determinants of parents' demand for children. The strong associations between variables measuring investments in children (withdrawing them from the work force and putting them in school), child death rates, and fertility suggest that in some countries behavioral self-regulating mechanisms may already be at work within the family to dampen today's rapid rates of population growth.

Though statistical association does not establish causation, one interpretation of the available evidence would run as follows: The development process has somehow precipitated a sharp reduction in death rates, and subsequent changes in the structure and growth of demand for the factors of production have raised the relative returns to human capital. Specialization in both urban and rural markets has exerted pressures on crafts and home industries, depreciating the value of child labor and providing women with stronger incentives to find employment outside of the home. By raising child costs these aspects of development have induced parents to seek smaller families and to concentrate childbearing during a shorter span of years. The parents who succeed in averting unwanted additional births after middle age appear to invest increasing family resources in their children's education.

THE CONSEQUENCES OF POPULATION GROWTH

The current pace of population growth in low income countries is an unprecedented and recent phenomenon, and for this reason, if no other, our understanding of its social and economic significance for human welfare is limited. Previous attempts to deal with this subject are demonstrably inadequate. Yet some inferences for probable social consequences and their time dimensions can be drawn from investigations of the micro repercussions of contemporary population growth.

Two schemes for evaluating the economic consequences of population growth are widely used: a micro-analysis of births as human capital, and a macro-analysis of per capita economic growth in which changes in fertility affect the age distribution of the population. Neither is wholly satisfactory for deriving policy guidelines or for better understanding the basic problem.

The first approach to evaluating the gains of reducing fertility and population growth is associated with the work of Enke.* Applying the human capital analytic framework to a child, Enke shows that a child treated as a producer good generally yields a low rate of return, for the childhood period of dependency absorbs sufficient resources to offset much of the child's expected future earnings as a mature worker. Ohlin has shown that this result is not unique to low income economies. Indeed, under the highly favorable conditions of a high income economy experiencing rapid growth in labor

*For example, see (41, 42).

productivity, the net physical value of a child at birth, discounted by Enke's 10 to 15 percent per year, still yields a substantial negative current value.* Enke concludes that this "social gain" from preventing a birth sets a ceiling on the real resources a society can spend to avert births.

Though Enke's endorsement of various schemes to exhort and to bribe parents into avoiding additional births may be sound in countries with abundant unskilled labor and little human and physical capital, his analytical method for supporting these policy conclusions is inconsistent with the central tenet of welfare economics—that people are the best judges of their own welfare. Enke's analysis neglects altogether the nonpecuniary returns to children (44). Clearly, children represent much more to parents than producer goods.

Viewed *only* as producer goods, children do appear to be a poor social investment. But the rest of the society is not usually asked to bear most of the costs of a child's consumption; parents are willing and able, in most cases, to bear these pecuniary burdens of child dependency in return for intangible parental rewards. For the society to justify policies that seek to change the preferred reproductive patterns of parents, children must also represent a burden that transcends the family unit and poses costs to others than their own kin. On this score, Enke has marshalled no evidence whatsoever that children are a source of external, social diseconomies that warrant social expenditures and interpersonal transfers to reduce birth rates. Enke's computation that a child has a negative net *physical* value at birth is therefore no indication that society and its constituent members would be better off with fewer births.

The second approach to evaluating the gains of slowing population growth has received its most elaborate treatment by Coale and Hoover in their pioneering study of India (15). A reduction in the birth rate reduces the proportion of the population that is not yet of the age when it can participate in the labor force and contribute directly to production. If aggregate income is unaffected by the reduced birth rate (at least for 10 or 15 years), per capita income must rise in comparison with the case of constant birth rates. If savings rates rise in response to this relative increase in per capita income, further long-term advantages accrue to the population experiencing the declining birth rate. This methodology presumes that maximizing per capita income (or consumption) is *the* appropriate social objective and that simple aggregate production functions adequately describe long-term growth pros-

---

*Ohlin (43) states this conclusion which was confirmed by the author. In a later paper by Ohlin, summarized by Easterline (25), it appears that Ohlin has shown that under reasonable assumptions concerning the character of the aggregate production function, children are not a good investment unless the marginal return on capital falls to the rate of growth of the population—an implausible situation in today's world of developing nations. See also Leibenstein's critique of Enke's methodology in (44).

pects for the developing countries. Additional technical assumptions may also be introduced, depending on the study, but they usually lack empirical foundation and are not central to the conclusion this approach yields.

Though it may be untenable to treat population growth as exogenous in the analysis of economic development, the incorporation of population growth into economic growth models remains primitive and controversial because we lack empirical facts on what are the critical interactions, what are the magnitudes of these relationships, and what nontraditional sources of economic growth account for the growth in labor and capital productivity in recent decades.* Without the empirical or theoretical foundation to answer any of these questions, the air of precision attained by such macro-analytic techniques is not particularly helpful today, and may be misleading.†

Moreover, one simply cannot consider per capita income as an adequate indicator of personal welfare for evaluating the effects of demographic trends. As emphasized here, children are much more to parents than a source of future earnings; they also yield intangible and important rewards to parents that elude national income accounts.‡ Nonpecuniary returns can be neglected without harm when one chooses between investments in fertilizer or cement factories, but when the choice is between fewer children and a factory, neglect of nonpecuniary returns biases the selection toward programs and policies that seek to reduce births. Policies that seek to make direct changes in the reproductive preferences of parents should therefore be based on evidence

*Leibenstein (in this volume) questions the usefulness of this approach unless it is accompanied by a more completely specified understanding of the economic growth process, including nontraditional inputs.

†Myrdal disparages the value of this second approach as currently pursued.

This kind of analysis (macro-growth models), in terms of capital investment and output, is typical of the modern approach to the economic problems of South Asian countries. In our opinion it is too mechanistic and schematic. It gives the appearance of knowledge where none exist, and an illusory precision to this pretended knowledge. . . . Increased attention has recently been paid to the economic effects of the change in age distribution resulting from reduced fertility rates, and in consequence more complicated models have been constructed [reference to Coale and Hoover (45)]. . . . But despite their [authors of demographic-economic macro models] disclaimers, they create a false air of precision and a false confidence in their model. A critical examination is therefore justified . . . [and in conclusion] We would not exclude the possibility of constructing models more adequate for this purpose. But such models would have to contain many more parameters and account for many more interrelationships [than Coale and Hoover have]. They would have to be very much more complex in order to be logically consistent and adequate to reality. With the present dearth of empirical data, indulging in this type of preparatory macro-analysis does not seem to be a rewarding endeavor. (1, Vol. III, Appendix 7, pp. 2067-2075.) See also the chapter by Leibenstein in this volume.

‡More narrowly, national income per capita is a poor index for evaluating population policies because consumption requirements are smaller for children than adults. A given level of per capita income clearly means a more satisfactory living standard in an economy where population is growing rapidly and a large fraction of the population are children than in an economy with a low birth rate and a small fraction of children.

of the diseconomies (costs) of population growth that extend beyond the parents and the immediate family and impinge on the welfare of other members of the society. Though these social diseconomies of population growth are undoubtedly substantial for many societies, empirical evidence of their real magnitude has not yet been systematically collected.

If our current stock of knowledge and the capacity of our analytical tools are not up to the task of quantitatively estimating the consequences of population growth on the development process, it is, nonetheless, possible to describe qualitatively the effects of rapid population growth as seen at the aggregate and family levels.

For analytic purposes, the implications of rapid population growth can be divided into two components: those which are associated with rapid population growth in the very long run, and those which arise in the short run when the rate of population growth changes. In general, a more rapid rate of population growth contributes to a somewhat younger composition of the population, and a broader based age pyramid (46). In the long run, the population of labor-force age grows at the same rate as does the total population, creating a need to add more rapidly to the stock of human and physical capital. To sustain any existing capital-labor ratio, a more rapidly growing labor force requires a higher savings rate.*

But the development process is more than a homogeneous process of factor augmentation. Development may be better analyzed as a process that draws an increasing share of the population into distinguishably different and more productive activities. These economic activities require more capital services and other modern inputs per worker than are used elsewhere in the economy; and because they are less routine, they typically require of the labor force more education and skills to cope with their increasingly complex and changing modes of production. The rate at which labor is absorbed into this modern sector of the economy is restrained, and the development process prolonged, by rapid population growth, for many new jobs require that a greater share of output must be saved and invested. In this model of structural change in a dual economy, the savings constraint on development is exacerbated by rapid population growth (33).

In the short run, changes in the rate of population growth can impose further burdens on the family and society, depending on the sources of these changes and their effect on the age structure. The reduction in death rates that initiated the postwar increase in population growth rates affected infants and young children more than other age groups. This rapidly growing younger

---

*For example, if we conservatively assume that the marginal capital-output ratio is equal to the average ratio of, say, three, then a net savings rate from output of 9 percent is required to accommodate a 3 percent annual growth in the labor force without deepening the capital stock or increasing per capita income. This stable state could be achieved with only a 6 percent savings rate if the labor force grew at 2 percent per year.

generation has imposed heavy costs on their parents in the last 2 decades, but is today reaching mature labor-force age, and increasingly the society must contend with a youthful, rapidly growing labor force with its implicit demands for increased savings and investment.

A future change in fertility would also have a clear short-run effect on the age structure. A 10 percent decline in birth rates would within 10 to 20 years reduce the proportion of the population younger than 15 by a comparable fraction. A decline in fertility would, therefore, not only slow population growth, but in the short run it would lead to a sharp reduction in the dependency burden.

Within the family, the acceleration in population growth that began 2 decades ago is today reaching the stage when the burden on family resources of child support and education is likely to be most acute (26). If as a variety of evidence suggests, parents respond to those accumulating economic pressures by seeking to avert additional births when they reach their desired family size, the birth rate among this relatively small group will begin to fall, relieving gradually the burden on family resources. The availability of modern means of birth control may hasten this trend and save parents and society the costs of unwanted births, as appears to be the case in Taiwan.* When and if fertility declines in this manner, it is likely to contribute to a resurgence of household savings and investment in tangible assets.

For similar reasons, the public sector's opportunities to save and invest its resources in tangible productive assets appears first to be eroded by rapid population growth, because public expenditures on social infrastructure (such as schools or hospitals) are closely tied to population growth, urbanization, and the youthfulness of the population. If public and private expenditures on education and health are reconsidered as investments in the future productive capacity of the younger generation, household and public sector savings no longer appear depressed by population growth in the aggregate, though they are probably still strained on a per-child basis.[†] Thus, over a family's formation cycle or over different countries at one moment in time, high fertility, rapid population growth, and high dependency are all associated strongly with low physical savings rates (15-17, 22, 29). But in the case of countries undergoing the postwar acceleration in population growth, the apparently low physical savings rate neglects to show the growing fraction of private and social resources being invested in the human productive agent.

The speed with which birth rates fall may depend critically on public and private efforts to disseminate modern means of birth control. Without such

_____

*Various methods have been used to evaluate the effect of the Taiwan Family Planning Program, and all suggest that substantial reductions in the birth rate may be attributed to the program. For a program evaluation study using multivariate nonlinear regression analysis allied with a behavioral model of fertility as discussed in this paper see (3).

[†]See Leibenstein, "The Impact of Population Growth on Economic Welfare–Nontraditional Elements," in this volume.

efforts, curtailment of fertility may occur in an inefficient and inhumane manner, as shown by the prevalence of abortion performed without medical assistance in many parts of the world today, with consequent maternal morbidity and mortality.*

As with most equilibrium economic models, a change in the rate of growth of one variable has its greatest effect in the short run, whereas after other factors have fully adjusted to the new growth rate, the long-run equilibrium effects on the system are more moderate. In a sense, the family, which was subjected to changing demographic and economic pressures in the postwar period, is adjusting to bring its behavior into equilibrium with the opportunities and constraints of its new environment. In this case the lag in behavioral adjustment has been 2 decades, the time it takes to form a complete family. During this period the transitory pressures are acute and have their most marked effect on household welfare and resource allocation; they generate pressing demands for public sector services as well. But what are the transitory effects of a trend toward long-term family-demographic and -economic equilibrium?

To recapitulate, the postwar decline in death rates creates a transitory burden of children for adult society to rear, train, and equip for modern employment. However, any reduction in fertility that follows will permit a comparable reduction in dependency burden with the associated social opportunities to educate and train the younger generation more adequately and to invest a sufficient amount to employ a larger proportion of it in modern high productivity and high-wage sectors of the economy. From the family's perspective, the population explosion is largely a transitory burden carried by the current generation, a challenge to today's family planning policymakers, and perhaps a promise of future development opportunities if the challenge is met and discharged effectively. Having exchanged one perspective for another, however, one should not overlook the broader outlines of the population problem; though its roots are in the family, the repercussions of the problem do not necessarily stop there.

QUALIFICATIONS AND SUMMARY

For analytic purposes, the postwar increase in population growth rates in low income countries can be divided into two components: that part due to the reduction in child death rates and that part due to the reduction in adult death rates.† The first component is directly responsible for increases in the

*See Abdel R. Omran, "Abortion in the Demographic Transition," in this volume.

†The distinction here is between the reduction in the death rate of children whose parents are still fecund and the reduction in death rates to other persons, mainly adults. About half of the lives saved by the postwar decline in mortality are less than 20 years of age (using standard classes of life tables). The precise fraction of the increase in surviving population which would be children of still-fertile parents would probably be substan-

number of dependent children to feed, support, and educate, while the second, among other things, adds to the demands for jobs and cooperating factors of production required to create new jobs. Though both components can be expressed in common terms, more people, they are not commensurate. Each poses a different underlying problem; each calls for a different method of analysis; and the appropriate policy for one may be different from that for the other. Clearly, socially acceptable policies may not greatly affect adult survival; population policies are largely limited to altering future birth rates—which remain in the domain of the family.

This paper adopts the perspective of the family and has investigated how the family's economic and reproductive behavior may be influenced by population growth. Consequently, attention has centered on the first and probably smaller of the components—the reduction in child mortality—which impinges on parents' well-being directly. This paper has argued that a reasonable model of family decision-making suggests the existence of a feedback mechanism that motivates parents to regulate their fertility in response to major changes in child mortality. Close examination of statistical evidence reveals that this behavioral response is occurring, imperfectly and with lags, in several low income countries. Though parents may find themselves today with more offspring than they had anticipated or wanted, there is within the family unit a homeostatic mechanism that promises to bring the family formation process gradually back toward the privately desired equilibrium size, with the aid of reliable birth control.

But is there a comparable short-run feedback mechanism translating the reduction in adult death rates into pressures on parents to restrict their family size goals? Herein lie the roots of the Malthusian dilemma that may call for policy initiatives that go beyond family planning, that is, beyond the subsidized provision of birth control information, services, and supplies. The social costs and benefits of increasing the number of adults in a community are widely diffused through the society, and although the costs may be hard

---

tially less than half of the total, but this proportion would depend on the initial population structure and mortality regime, as well as the structure of change in mortality levels.

Although for analytical purposes the two initial components of the increase in population growth are of primary importance, derivative sources of population growth would also follow, assuming constant age-specific birth rates and eventually constant age-specific death rates. As adult death rates declined, parents would complete more of their childbearing years in a complete marital union, having, on average, more children. A secondary oscillation in the population growth rate might also ensue from the disproportion in the decline in age-specific death rates. Because the reduction in death rates is generally greater among the young than among adults, the youngest age groups in the population pyramid increase most rapidly. As this postwar wave of surviving babies reaches reproductive age, the changing age composition of the population will foster a rise in crude birth and population growth rates. Eventually, as the composition of the population approaches the stable (ergodic) age distribution dictated by the fixed age-specific birth and death rates, the preponderance of reproductive-aged women in the population will ebb, as will birth and growth rates.

to measure in terms of social welfare or economic development, they may nonetheless be substantial, accumulative, and inequitably distributed. For example, the increased supply of labor directly depresses the returns to unskilled labor, lowering its relative wage and perhaps increasing the rate of unemployment. If this second component of increased population growth is detrimental to social goals but unlikely to lead to a compensating reduction in fertility, how can the public sector equitably transfer the true social costs of reproduction to the parent who is the ultimate decision-maker?

To reiterate, parents may be provided with the means (birth control) to respond appropriately to the decline in child mortality, but they may not be similarly motivated to compensate for the reduction in adult mortality. Such a change in motivation will require a change in parent demand for surviving children. In order to understand what might generate such a change in the demand of parents for children, this paper began by identifying aspects of the parents' environment that were thought to determine the relative attractiveness of having many versus few children. Some of the more fundamental social and economic changes connected with the postwar development process appear to raise, on balance, the relative costs of rearing children. For this reason, one might anticipate that development would slowly foster the adoption of smaller family size goals. Support for the underlying conjecture that fertility is responsive to changing aspects of the parents' environment is drawn from several statistical studies of low income countries.

It is tempting to infer from these exploratory studies that the public sector could effectively hasten the reduction in desired and actual fertility by selective policy measures, such as those aimed at promoting child health, welfare, and education and those assisting women to acquire and employ marketable skills in the paid labor force. But at the moment, understanding of the determinants of family decision-making and its bearing on parent reproductive behavior is too scant to interpret confidently the available evidence. Seen as working hypotheses, however, these inferences might help guide the more extensive micro empirical research and multivariate analysis that is clearly needed in this field. Controversy on the interpretation of the growing supply of micro data on family behavior will probably intensify, not slacken, as different disciplinary perceptions of this broad ecological problem are rigorously formulated and different statistical tools are developed to account for components of observed behavioral, biological, environmental, and cultural change. Though a consensus may not be reached quickly on particulars, there are general grounds for guarded optimism with regard to the micro dynamics of population change.

There are substantial differences in reproductive behavior across regions of low income countries and across individuals in low income communities. The statistical relationships between fertility and the determinants of desired fertility are consistent with the hypothesis that reproductive behavior is responsive to man's environment. This is an optimistic inference in contrast to that drawn by Malthus. But it is not a basis for complacency. The behavioral sciences are being challenged to unravel the exceedingly complex matrix of cultural and economic underpinnings for the environmental changes that correlate consistently with fertility, and discover within them what causes desired and actual patterns of fertility to change. With this augmented stock of knowledge, one may argue from strength for a systematic re-ordering of development priorities and for the adoption of a population policy that will transfer with equity the real social costs of rapid population growth to parents who have been given the choice of modern birth control.

<h2 style="text-align:center">REFERENCES</h2>

1. Myrdal, Gunnar, *Asian Drama*. New York: Pantheon, 1968.
2. Nerlove, M. and T. Paul Schultz, *Love and Life between the Censuses: a Model of Family Decisionmaking in Puerto Rico, 1950-1960*. Santa Monica, Calif.: The RAND Corporation, September 1970, RM-6322.
3. Schultz, T. Paul, "Effectiveness of Family Planning in Taiwan: a Methodology for Program Evaluation." Santa Monica, Calif.: The RAND Corporation, November 1969. P-4069.
4. Schultz, T. Paul, *Fertility Patterns and Their Determinants in the Arab Middle East.* Santa Monica, Calif.: The RAND Corporation, May 1970, RM-5978-FF.
5. Becker, Gary S., "An Economic Analysis of Fertility," *Demographic and Economic Change in Developed Countries*, National Bureau of Economic Research. Princeton, N.J.: Princeton Univ. Press, 1960. pp. 209-240.
6. Johnson, Harry G., "Demand Theory Further Revised or Goods Are Goods," *Economica*, N.S. 25, May 1958. p. 149.
7. Lancaster, Kelvin J., "A New Approach to Consumer Theory," *J P Econ*, Vol. 74, No. 2, April 1966. pp. 132-157.
8. Easterline, Richard A., "Towards a Socioeconomic Theory of Fertility: Survey of Recent Research on Economic Factors in American Fertility," *Fertility and Family Planning, a World View*, S. J. Behrman et al., eds. Ann Arbor, Mich.: Univ. of Michigan Press, 1969. pp. 127-156.
9. Roberts, John M., Richard F. Strand, and Edwin Burmeister, "Preferential Pattern Analysis," *Explorations in Mathematical Anthropology*, Paul Key, ed. Cambridge, Mass.: M.I.T. Press, forthcoming.
10. Becker, Gary S., "A Theory of the Allocation of Time," *Econ J*, Vol. 75, No. 299, September 1965. pp. 493-517.
11. Kuznets, Simon, *Modern Economic Growth; Rate, Structure and Spread.* New Haven, Conn.: Yale Univ. Press, 1966.
12. Ben-Porath, Yoram, "The Production of Human Capital and the Life Cycle of Earnings," *J Pol Econ*, Vol. 75, No. 4, Part 1, August 1967. pp. 352-365.
13. Schultz, T. Paul, "An Economic Model of Family Planning and Fertility," *J Pol Econ*, Vol. 77, No. 2, March/April 1969. pp. 153-180.

14. Ando, Albert, and Franco Modigliani, "The 'Life Cycle' Hypothesis of Savings: Aggregate Implications and Tests," *Amer Econ Rev*, Vol. 53, No. 1, March 1963. pp. 55-84.

15. Leff, Nathaniel H., "Dependency Rates and Savings Rates," *Amer Econ Rev*, Vol. 59, No. 5, December 1969. pp. 886-896.

16. Modigliani, Franco, " The Life Cycle Hypothesis of Saving, The Demand for Wealth and the Supply of Capital," *Social Research*, Vol. 33, No. 2, Summer 1966. pp. 160-217.

17. Tobin, James, "Life Cycle Savings and Balanced Growth," *Ten Economic Studies in the Tradition of Irving Fisher*, W. Fellner, et al. New York. John Wiley & Sons, 1967. pp. 231-256.

18. Heer, David M., and Dean O. Smith, "Mortality Level, Desired Family Size and Population Increase," *Demography*, Vol. 5, No. 1, 1968. pp. 104-121.

19. Immerwahr, George E., "Survivorship of Sons under Conditions of Improving Mortality," *Demography*, Vol. 4, No. 2, 1967. pp. 710-720.

20. Schultz, T. Paul, "Population Growth: Investigation of a Hypothesis," P-4056. Santa Monica, Calif.: The RAND Corporation, April 1969.

21. Goode, William J., *World Revolution and Family Patterns*. Glencoe, Ill.: Free Press, 1963.

22. David, M. H., *Family Composition and Consumption*. Amsterdam: North Holland Pub. Co., 1962.

23. Fichenwald, Heinz F., and Peggy Crooke Fry, "Nutrition and Learning," *Science*, Vol. 163, February 1969. pp. 644-648.

24. McDermott, Walsh, "Modern Medicine and the Demographic Disease Pattern of Overly Traditional Societies: a Technological Misfit." Paper presented at the Institute on International Medical Education of the Assn. of American Medical Colleges. Washington, D.C., 1966.

25. Easterline, Richard A., "Relations between Population Pressure and Economic and Demographic Change." Summary of papers prepared for section 5.4 of the General Conference of the International Union for the Scientific Study of Population. London, September 5, 1969.

26. Lorimer, Frank, "The Economics of Family Formation under Different Conditions," *World Population Conference 1965*. New York: United Nations, 1967. Vol. II, pp. 92-95.

27. Fredericksen, H., "Determinants and Consequences of Mortality and Fertility Trends," *Public Health Reports*. Washington, D.C.: U.S. Public Health Service, 1966. Vol. 81, p. 727.

28. Scrimshaw, Nevin, "Pre-School Child Malnutrition: Primary Deterrent to Human Progress." An International Conference on Prevention of Malnutrition in the Pre-School Child, Washington, D.C., December 7-11, 1964. Washington, D.C.: National Academy of Sciences, Publication 1282, 1966.

29. Eizenga, W., *Demographic Factors and Savings*. Amsterdam: North Holland Pub. Co., 1961.

30. Hymer, S., and S. Resnick, "Responsiveness of Agrarian Economies and the Importance of Z Goods," *Economic Growth Center Discussion*, Paper No. 25. Yale Univ., October 1, 1967.

31. Kuznets, Simon, "Quantitative Aspects of the Economic Growth of Nations: Part VII, Distribution of Income by Size," *Econ Devel & Cult Change*, Vol. 11, No. 2, Part 2, January 1963.

32. Weisskoff, Richard, "Income Distribution and Economic Growth: an International Comparison." Unpublished doctoral thesis, Harvard Univ., May 1969.

33. Nelson, R. R., T. P. Schultz, and R. L. Slighton, *Structural Change in a Developing Economy*, unpublished book manuscript. Santa Monica, Calif.: The RAND Corporation, September 1969. Princeton, N.J.: Princeton Univ. Press, forthcoming 1971.

34. Griliches, Zvi, "Notes on the Role of Education in Production Functions and Growth Accounting," Univ. of Chicago, Report 6839, September 1969.

35. Griliches, Zvi, "A Note on Capital-Skill Complementarity," *Rev Econ & Stat*, Vol. 51, No. 4, November 1969. pp. 465-470.

36. Hansen, Bent, "The Distributive Shares in Egyptian Agriculture, 1897-1961," *Int Econ Rev*, Vol. 9, No. 2, June 1968. pp. 175-194.

37. Hansen, Bent, "Employment and Wages in Rural Egypt," *Amer Econ Rev*, Vol. 59, No. 3, June 1969. pp. 298-313.

38. Harman, Alvin, "Interrelationships between Procreation and Other Family Decisionmaking," P-4267. Santa Monica, Calif. The RAND Corporation, December 1969.

39. Caldwell, John C., "Fertility Attitudes in Three Economically Contrasting Rural Regions of Ghana," *Econ Devel & Cult Change*, Vol. 15, No. 6, January 1967. pp. 217-238.

40. Caldwell, J. C., "The Control of Family Size in Tropical Africa," *Demography*, Vol. 5, No. 2, 1968, Special Issue. pp. 598-619.

41. Enke, Stephen, "The Economics of Government Payments to Limit Population," *Econ Devel & Cult Change*, Vol. 8, No. 4, July 1960. pp. 339-348.

42. Enke, Stephen, "The Economic Aspects of Slowing Population Growth," *Econ J*, Vol. 74, No. 301, March 1966. pp. 44-56.

43. Ohlin, Goran, *Population Control and Economic Development*. Paris: Development Centre, Organization for Economic Co-Operation and Development, 1967.

44. Leibenstein, Harvey, "Pitfalls in Benefit-Cost Analysis of Birth Prevention," *Population Studies*, Vol. 23, No. 2, July 1969. pp. 161-170.

45. Coale, Ansley J., and Edgar M. Hoover, *Population Growth and Economic Development in Low-Income Countries*. Princeton, N.J.: Princeton Univ. Press, 1958.

46. Keyfitz, Nathan, *Introduction to the Mathematics of Population*. Reading, Mass.: Addison-Wesley Pub. Co., 1968.

IV

The Impact of
Population Growth on Economic
Welfare—Nontraditional Elements

Harvey Leibenstein

In an age when there is unusual concern about the population explosion one would think that the concern arises as a result of a solid understanding of the consequences of population growth on the economy. However, much of what is normally understood about the consequences of population growth depends upon the classical approach to the problem. The primary mode of analysis involves inferences about output based on the impact of population growth on the ratios of the traditional inputs of land, labor, and capital. Only in recent years have we had hints that we may be on the wrong track. The viewpoint taken in this paper is that a more useful approach is to consider the problem in terms of a number of nontraditional elements that are likely to be important in determining the rate of economic growth. To be specific, our analysis will emphasize the impact of population growth on those acquired qualities of the population that are important to output and its growth.

THE CLASSICAL MOLD OF THE POPULATION-RESOURCES PROBLEM

The essence of the classical mode of thinking is to emphasize physical resources in relation to population; therefore, land and capital are the basic resources considered. Behind this mode of thinking is the notion of a unique production function. That is to say, there is a one-to-one relation between the inputs for land, labor, and capital and the output that results—for every set of inputs there is a unique and determinate output. Since it is usually argued that land and other natural resources are fixed, then at some point the rela-

Harvey Leibenstein is Member of the Center for Population Studies and Andelot Professor of Economics and Population, Department of Economics, Harvard University.

tion between a growing population and fixed natural resources must lead to diminishing returns per person, other things being equal. Even if we allow for the fact that capital is, in some sense and to some degree, a substitute for natural resources—given the belief that capital becomes a successively less adequate substitute as more capital is substituted for resources—diminishing returns to population growth appear to be valid and reasonable. In principle, output per worker must *eventually* decline as the population grows. The one ameliorating influence is the application of new inventions to the production process.

At first blush, this view seems so reasonable that it is difficult to believe that it could be faulted. Probably most reasoned arguments about the hazards of population growth to economic welfare depend in one way or another on arguments of this type. Such arguments appear to have special relevance for developing countries where the bulk of the output takes place in the agricultural sector and where it often appears that the genuine limiting factor must be cultivable land. In what follows it will *not* be argued that these traditional considerations are of no importance. Far from it. Rather, the thrust of the argument is that such considerations are less important than one would have believed 2 decades ago and that in most instances they are not the factors of prime importance.

The endless stream of arguments about the applicability of neo-Malthusian models rests on two major elements:

1. The consequences of technical change resulting from an endless flow of inventions enable us to avoid indefinitely an approximation to the state of Malthusian equilibrium.

2. The fertility assumptions employed in the neo-Malthusian models no longer hold in view of contemporary contraceptive technology.

Although the second objection is probably a weak one,* the first one seemed to be strong and to have considerable basis in fact. As a consequence, the neo-Malthusian debate frequently turned on whether one happened to be an invention-innovation optimist or an invention-innovation pessimist; i.e., whether one believed that the current rate of material inventions would continue or one believed that this, too, was subject to considerable diminishing returns. The experience of the last half century or so supports the technological optimists. Extrapolating from countries and periods within the last 50 years, during which fairly rapid growth has taken place, it would appear that at least *potential* economic growth is greater than the rate of population growth. The argument of the technological pessimists depends on theory rather than experience, i.e., on the belief that some resources such as land are in fact fixed and that, in fact, the substitutes for such resources are likely to be considerably inferior to the fixed resources so that diminishing returns are likely to result.

---

*Contraceptive technology has no bearing if families *want* to have many children, say between four and six.

The "Residual" and the Acquired Quality of Labor

Research carried out by economists in the last 15 years suggests that, for the most part, growth cannot be explained by increases in the traditional inputs of capital, land, and labor. Although most of this research has been carried out in developed countries, studies by Kuznets refer to periods when the developed countries were relatively underdeveloped.

What has been called the "residual"—that part of economic growth that *cannot* be explained by increases in traditional inputs—comprehends most of the economic growth that takes place. This finding is of great importance. This paper will argue that it is a critical element in any reinterpretation of the neo-Malthusian viewpoint, or of any set of relations between population and resources, or on the impact of population growth on economic development. (Although there has been considerable speculation about the nature of what we may call the "residual" inputs and although we know with some degree of definiteness what some of them must be, we cannot say what all of them happen to be.)

According to Kuznets (1), no more than 10 percent of the growth rate (in a number of European countries, Australia, and Japan) can be accounted for by the traditional inputs.* Kuznets concludes

> ... that the direct contribution of man-hours and capital accumulation would hardly account for more than a tenth of the rate of growth in per capita product—and probably less. The large remainder must be assigned to an increase in efficiency in the productive resources—a rise in output per unit of input, due either to the improved quality of the resources, or to the effects of changing arrangements, or to the impact of technological change, or to all three.

There are a number of studies of the residual. For the most part they concern advanced countries, and the results are frequently less extreme than those found by Kuznets. Nevertheless, it is rare that less than 50 percent is explained by the residual. Traditional inputs explain less than one half, and frequently considerably less than one half, of the growth. †

In addition, some recent studies suggest from a different angle that capital accumulation is relatively unimportant as a contribution to growth. (We

---

*Although the countries used by Kuznets are today developed, the starting period of the analysis (e.g., Norway 1865-74) frequently goes back to a time when they were relatively underdeveloped.

† A number of these studies are summarized in the O.E.C.D. Journal, *Productivity Measurement Review.* See especially (2, 3).

A recent fascinating paper by Krueger (4) shows "that three variables normally associated with the concept of human capital can explain more than half the difference in income levels between the United States and a group of less developed countries for which data are available."

should keep in mind that usually population growth is less than one third of the rate of capital growth.) In a study by the author (5) it has been shown that the incremental capital output ratio varies, in almost all cases, inversely with the growth rate. Patel (6) shows this to be the case for developing countries. A reasonable inference from these studies is that in most cases neither capital nor labor of the existing quality is the major force in growth. Hence, we stress those qualities of the population that result in the improvement of the quality of labor through education and other means of skill acquisition, and those elements that lead to the introduction of innovations and technical change.*

INCENTIVES AND EFFORT RESPONSES

Among the qualities of a population that are likely to be of importance in affecting productivity per worker is the responsiveness of the population to incentives. We may think of it in terms of the degree and directions of effort that the population is willing to put forth in response to the incentives that exist and those that it creates. The rate of population growth is in some sense related to these elements, at least in terms of the impact of differences in family size on nurture and education.

The basic idea to be developed is that human inputs, essentially varieties of labor including management and entrepreneurship, can put forth different degrees of effort in response to different incentives both within firms and in the economy at large. Effort should *not* be interpreted here in a narrow physical sense, although physical effort is one dimension.

Some of many possible dimensions of effort are listed below:
1. various physical activities, each activity being a different dimension;
2. the act of choosing between different activities;
3. the degree of care in carrying out such activities;
4. scanning the "information field" inside and outside the firm;
5. various "search activities," i.e., looking for a new means of performance in terms of techniques of production or characteristics of the product;
6. the degree of perseverance in carrying out activities;
7. the degree of cooperation with co-workers.

Whereas all types of effort are important in production, it is probably true that the forces employed to introduce innovations are the ones that are most significant in promoting economic growth. Such efforts are likely to involve the search for and development of information on new techniques of production and the marshaling of the other inputs required to introduce innovations. This last point is far from trivial. Knowledge of a potential innovation might not be sufficient to induce the entrepreneurial efforts to marshal all of the inputs necessary to put the innovation into effect. Whether the innovation

*A good deal of the evidence is summarized in a paper by Morgan(7).

takes place is likely to depend on three elements of the quality of labor: the actual skills of the labor force which depend upon on-the-job training and formal education; the incentives that exist in the economy; and the degree to which individuals respond to such incentives. Needless to say, incentives also enter the picture in determining the accumulation of physical capital as well as the accumulation of human capital (i.e., education and skills). The point is that part of the acquired qualities of the population that determine development depend upon motivational elements.

If the rate, structure, and pattern of population growth, and its consequences, are in any way related to psychological attitudes concerned with incentives and responsiveness to incentives, then we may obtain a connection between population growth and some of the determinants of economic growth. This relationship may be important despite the fact that there may be aspects of the problem that are exceedingly difficult to measure. We must also include the "negative efforts" to production—the efforts put forth by various people to resist change, to resist the adoption of innovations, whether through legislation, the support of constraints, featherbedding practices, and so on. There is almost no direct evidence on how incentives and degrees of responsiveness to incentives are related to different rates of population growth. As we proceed we shall see that some tenuous clues exist on this matter in the literature on semistarvation, and on the relations between family achievement and family size. There are suggestions that psychological variables, such as apathy in the case of hunger and verbal skill formation in the case of "overcrowded" families, may be of importance. There is also in the literature some exceedingly tenuous evidence on the consequences of maternal deprivation. On this, however, it is exceedingly difficult to know whether it is of any importance from a macro (overall) viewpoint in *any* economy, or whether the incidence is always so small as to be irrelevant for our purposes.

The important aspect of all this is not that the facts themselves—or their possibilities—are especially new. What is of interest in recent research is that it has been shown that the incentive-responsiveness elements are likely to be of great importance (8) in understanding increases in production, although, unfortunately, the relations of these elements to population growth are, at present, not known.

Micro-Demographic Effects*

Associated with the economic state of the system at any time there are a set of demographic characteristics which affect various aspects of the nurture

---

*A brief version of this section was presented at the General Conference, London, September 1969, of the International Union for the Scientific Study of Population.

process and schooling. (See Figure 1.) The nurture and schooling processes have economic consequences which in their turn alter the economic state of the system and may alter some of the demographic causative variables. The system can be viewed, *in part*, as an internally self-generating system. That is, it is a system in which individuals at any time not only transmit their genetic fertility and mortality potentialities in a systematic way to subsequent generations but also transmit certain social, cultural, and physical characteristics. However, it is not a completely self-contained system since part of the economic changes—probably the greater part—are determined outside the demographic system and are, from the point of view of the demographic system, an autonomous set of influences.

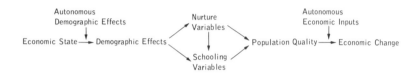

Figure 1. The impact of demographic variables on the economic state of the system.

Now, we delineate what may be viewed as a set of demographic causative effects:

1. *the age-structure-dependency effect*; this effect has been analyzed in detail by Coale and Hoover (9);
2. *the sib-number effect* which considers the consequences of the number of children per family;
3. *the sib-spacing effect*;
4. *the parental-mortality effect* which considers the effects of the possibility of one or both parents being absent during the nurture or schooling period;
5. *the replacement effect.* *

All but one of these listed effects of a greater rather than a lesser rate of population growth are detrimental to the acquired economic quality of the labor force. The main idea is that the quality of the labor force depends (in part) on the growth rate of labor, which in turn depends on the growth rate of the population. The relation between the quality of an input and its

---

*A fairly complete list of demographic effects would also include:
6. *the population-resource ratio effect*
7. *the congestion effect*
Both are likely consequences of population growth. However, these matters will not be treated in this paper.

growth rate is a rather unusual one.* We do not know enough about the facts to examine this element in more than a suggestive way. The discussion that follows suggests that the sib-number effect, the sib-spacing effect, and the parental-mortality effect are all detrimental to the quality of the work force, but we do not know to what degree. The replacement effect, considered at the end of the paper, may operate in the opposite direction from the other effects considered, in some cases.

THE NURTURE-NATURE BORDERLINE: INTELLIGENCE AND FAMILY SIZE

An interesting qualitative aspect of the problem involves the imprecise borderline between nurture and genetic inheritance. A large (although controversial) literature has accumulated which suggests that, on the average, children that come from families with relatively few siblings or with no siblings do disproportionately better at intellectual and related pursuits than those with many siblings (10). Also birth order is in some degree connected with intellectual achievement—on the average the higher the birth order the greater the achievement. It has not been determined whether any of this contains a genetic component.

At present we know little about the relation between population quality, entrepreneurial capacities, innovating capacities, and contact with siblings. There are some data that suggest that an unusual proportion of those who have considerable intellectual achievements to their credit were either only children or from families in which there was a relatively large age gap between siblings (11). It seems plausible that the ability to think abstractly would be developed earlier or would on the whole be greater if children learned the concomitant verbal skills either from adults or from siblings considerably older than themselves (12). Although it is difficult in fact to separate the level of intelligence from acquired skills, there is evidence to suggest that a child's intelligence level can actually be raised by a culturally nurturant upbringing or by training (13), or by the kinds of environmental stimuli available in an urban setting (14, 15); and that there is a connection between family size and intellectual capacity. Intellectual capacity with the attendant ability to manipulate abstractions that typifies educated intelligence is unquestionably important to economic development. It is evident in the contribution of professionalized skills to the economy; i.e., in the work of engineers, lawyers, doctors, architects, and teachers at various levels. It seems likely that acquired intellectual capacities are also related to managerial skills. It would appear then that the smaller the rate of population growth and the smaller the family size, the greater the extent to which these skills could be developed.

*To some degree this idea is found in the concept of "embodied technical change."

Sib-Number and Other Family-Size Effects*

The number of siblings in a family is likely to be important with respect to at least two elements of nurture: nutrition (16, 17) and preschool training. It may also be important in terms of the existence, or absence, of maternal deprivation, but this is not at all clear. With respect to all three of these effects there is some impressive case study evidence although we do not know how widespread these cases are from a statistical viewpoint. Other things being equal, we would normally expect that the number of siblings will determine the nutrition of children and hence the greater the sibling number, the greater the likelihood of malnutrition in low income families (16, pp. 142-143).

For example, J. A. Scott (18) studied a cross-section of children attending ordinary day schools in London. He collected data in 1959 on height and weight of pupils and then linked the results of their "eleven-plus" examinations (verbal reasoning test) with the data. Table 1 shows that as the number of children in the family increases, mean height, weight, and intelligence scores tend to decrease. (Two exceptions—intelligence of a two-child family in 1 G and + height + weight of a four-child family in 1 B.) Conversely—". . . children who belong to small families tend to do better in intelligence tests than children from larger families, and that children from large families are not so tall (or so heavy) at any given age as those from small families."

In Table 2 Scott shows that as average intelligence increases so does the average height. Table 1 shows that intelligence is related to family size and that height is also related to family size. The question is raised as to which of these two variables (height or family size) has the greater influence on intelligence. Table 3 shows that intelligence increases with height and decreases with family size.

Scott therefore says the data suggest that the most intelligent child will be found in the small family.

Similarly, it has been shown that the greater the sibling number the less the effectiveness of informal preschool training on linguistic skills or I.Q. (17, p. 130).†

---

*See also J. D. Wray, "Population Pressure on Families: Family Size and Child Spacing," in this volume, especially the tables.

†There is a large literature on these matters which shows an inverse relationship between intelligence and aspects of family size such as sib number, etc. See (10, 11). Results are questioned by Blackburn (18). See the symposium edited by Scrimshaw and Gordon (19), with report of experiment by Harold Skeels, pp. 353-354. See also Patton and Gardner (20), with report by Thomas, Springfield, Illinois, 1963, in which six cases are cited in which extreme maternal deprivation has been associated with retardation of physical growth and delayed skeletal maturation. However, this last may be the consequence of the accompanying malnutrition rather than maternal deprivation as such.

TABLE 1

Mean Height, Weight, and Standardized Score, by Sex, Year of Examination, and Family Size

Group[a]	Family Size (Number of Children in Family)	Number of Children in Class	Age at Measurement (Years)	Mean Height (cm.)	Mean Weight (kg.)	Mean Standardized Score
Boys 1 B	1	336	11.25	144.2 ± .37	37.01 ± .36	99.9 ± .83
	2	399	11.26	143.4 ± .34	35.23 ± .33	99.1 ± .76
	3	202	11.25	142.4 ± .46	34.15 ± .45	97.5 ± 1.02
	4	79	11.24	142.8 ± .76	34.65 ± .74	96.5 ± 1.71
	5 or more	72	11.27	140.2 ± .78	32.47 ± .78	93.1 ± 1.79
Junior Leaving (11+) Examination in 1959	All	1,088	11.25	143.2 ± .20	35.35 ± .20	98.5 ± .46
Girls 1 G	1	307	11.26	145.3 ± .43	38.67 ± .45	101.8 ± .82
	2	412	11.23	144.8 ± .37	37.08 ± .39	102.4 ± .71
	3	196	11.24	143.9 ± .54	36.15 ± .56	99.5 ± 1.03
	4	106	11.25	142.7 ± .74	34.62 ± .77	97.8 ± 1.40
	5 or more	60	11.23	140.4 ± .98	32.76 ± 1.02	93.9 ± 1.86
	All	1,081	11.24	144.3 ± .23	36.88 ± .24	100.8 ± .44

[a]Children were divided into four main groups:
1 B Boys born between September 1947 and August 31, 1948;
1 G Girls born between September 1947 and August 31, 1948;
11 B Boys born between September 1948 and August 31, 1949;
11 G Girls born between September 1948 and August 31, 1949.

Source: Scott (18).

TABLE 2

Mean Heights[a] of Children from One-Child and Two-Child Families, by Intelligence Score

Verbal Reasoning Standardized Score	Group I				Group II			
	Boys (B)		Girls (G)		Boys (B)		Girls (G)	
	Number of Children	Mean Height	Number of Children	Mean Height	Number of Children	Mean Height	Number of Children	Mean Height
70-86	151	141.8 ± .56	97	142.7 ± .75	92	137.5 ± .68	59	134.6 ± .84
87-95	147	143.1 ± .56	142	144.1 ± .62	126	138.4 ± .58	101	136.7 ± .64
96-104	169	143.9 ± .53	162	145.3 ± .58	157	138.5 ± .52	153	138.1 ± .52
105-113	142	144.7 ± .57	179	145.7 ± .55	135	139.5 ± .56	137	138.7 ± .55
114-140	126	146.0 ± .61	139	147.1 ± .63	158	139.8 ± .52	190	139.3 ± .47
All	735	143.0 ± .25	719	145.2 ± .28	668	138.8 ± .25	640	138.0 ± .25

[a]Standardized for age by simple linear interpolation–Group IB and G 11-25 years and Group II B and G 10-25 years.

Source: Scott (18).

TABLE 3

Average Verbal Reasoning Standardized Scores by Height
and Family Size—Data of Group II G

| Height (cm.) | Number of Children in Family | | | |
| | 1 | 2 | 3 | 4 or More |
	Average Verbal Reasoning Score[a]			
Less than 130.0	96.2 (19)	101.2 (35)	97.5 (16)	94.5 (33)
30.0- 134.9	102.1 (58)	100.4 (88)	101.4 (52)	94.1 (55)
135.0- 139.9	108.4 (70)	107.0 (119)	102.4 (80)	100.7 (44)
140.0- 144.9	108.5 (54)	106.0 (104)	105.9 (37)	99.9 (44)
145 and over	108.5 (43)	107.5 (50)	106.5 (28)	102.8 (16)

[a]Figures in parentheses are numbers of children in each class.

Source: Scott (18).

Maternal Deprivation

Whereas the degree of maternal deprivation may depend to some extent on sib number, it is more likely to depend on sibling spacing and on the maternal morbidity and mortality rates. The effects of extreme maternal deprivation are drastic and impressive in the sense that they affect linguistic skills, I.Q. scores, and success in later life (19-21); the existence or absence of apathy; such physical aspects as height and weight (16, pp. 136-137); as well as the normal immunity from various diseases which is believed to be derived from breast feeding in the early nurture period (19, p. 23).

In 1943 and in subsequent years, Goldfarb (cited in 22) had an opportunity to study communities of children in institutions. Of thirty children aged 34 to 35 months, fifteen who had been brought up in institutions had I.Q.'s lower by 28 points than those of the remaining fifteen who had been in foster homes from the age of 4 months.

Spitz (22) gives the name "anaclitic depression" to the state of dazed stupor found in children deprived of maternal care. The child is apathetic, silent, and sad; he makes no attempt at contact; in many cases he suffers from insomnia; he loses weight and becomes prone to recurrent infections; there is a rapid drop in the developmental quotient. Of the ninety-five children studied by Spitz, this type of depression was observed in almost 50 percent.

Follow-up studies are of particular interest. One of the most important was carried out by Goldfarb who chose two groups of children of similar heredity. Those in the first group had been brought up in institutions until the age of 3 and then placed in the care of foster parents, whereas those in the second group had been handed over to foster parents from the outset. In all cases separation had taken place within the first 9 months of life. The lack of intellectual ability, and particularly the ability to conceptualize, were particularly marked in the group sent to an institution at an early age (22).

On the effects of the length of the intersib interval Anastasi (11) reports on a French study in which

> . . . there were 1,244 two-sibling families . . . both siblings had been tested. These were separated into "long interval" and "short interval" sibships, the latter being defined as those falling at or below the median interval. On the intelligence test, the children with long intersib intervals obtained significantly higher means, these differences persisting within each of the five occupational categories into which the sample was subdivided. With long intersib intervals the scores approximated those of only children —with short intersib intervals, they approximated the scores obtained by 3-child sibships.

Nutrition

It should be stressed that the economic consequences of different levels of nutrition, especially with respect to calories, is probably on a sounder basis than many of the other aspects we have considered. There has been a considerable amount of work on the relationship between the calorie intake and work capacity, and to some degree on the relation between calories and actual output. Unfortunately, the studies involved have not been carried out in less developed countries; therefore, some transference of results is necessary from wartime conditions in advanced countries to the less developed countries. The validity of the transference is to some degree an open question. A good deal of the work is summarized by Keller and Kraut of the Max Planck Institute of Physiology (23). It is of some interest, perhaps, that the relation between calorie change and output change per worker in Germany differed, as we might expect, for different types of work, but the degree of the change for relatively heavy work is quite striking. For example, in a group of coalminers an increase in calories by 33 percent appeared to be associated with a 40 percent increase in output. For steelworkers a 33 percent reduction in calories from an 1,800-calorie level was associated with a slightly larger percentage reduction in output. Although such numbers are at best only suggestive, they nevertheless indicate that at the lower calorie levels, say beginning with 1,800 calories per day and moving downwards, calorie reduction and output reduction may be proportional to each other. One must add, however, that even if it were known that this relationship is true for agriculture in cases where considerable disguised unemployment, or observed unemployment, exists, the reduction in physical capacity per man need not result in an actual reduction in total output. It may simply mean that more of the unemployed become absorbed in the work involved.

Economic Consequences

The economic consequences of all these effects are not entirely clear. Both the sib-number and sib-spacing effects seem to diminish physical size, linguistic skills, relative immunity from disease, and I.Q. (17, p. 130). It should be emphasized that these elements are not entirely separate from one another. Nurture effects will also affect the consequences of formal schooling in the sense that the capacity to absorb formal schooling will depend to a great degree on the nurture aspects.* Thus what appears as part of the economic returns to formal schooling is in fact a return to nurture, since it is the nurture elements that determine the capacity to take advantage of formal schooling. The main element to be noted is that a greater rate of population growth will set in motion demographic causative effects all of which have an adverse impact on economic growth.

The argument presented is that higher rates of population growth (compared to lower rates) are associated with (a) a younger population and hence a higher dependency ratio, (b) usually a higher average sib number, (c) usually closer sib spacing, and *probably* (d) a greater number of pregnancies per woman and *perhaps* higher maternal mortality and morbidity. (This last depends upon the degree to which the higher rate of population growth is a result of lower mortality rather than higher fertility.) The impacts of these four demographic effects on dependency, malnutrition, degree of maternal deprivation, speech and personality formation, I.Q., and on success indicators are all adverse to economic growth and the average *acquired* economic quality of the labor force.

For the most part the data are only suggestive, providing clues to the importance of the elements considered. Unfortunately, there is a lack of statistical information as to how important these elements are from a macroeconomic viewpoint. We do not know what rates of population growth at what level of per capita income will lead to what degree of malnutrition or

*Tanner (16, p. 211) states that Douglas in 1960 reported from a sample of children in Great Britain that "early maturers had gained significantly more successes than late maturers in the examination for entry to secondary schools at age 11. Not only were their test papers better; the reports of the teachers upon their behavior in class also favored them." However, the later maturers catch up when they reach their physical growth spurt.

other detrimental nurture effects or how widespread these effects are on the population.* It may very well be that, despite the dramatic nature of some of the clinical cases, the percent of the population affected in this way may be small. In what follows it will be assumed that the three effects already considered have, in fact, a small impact; for the most part the implications of the replacement effect will be traced.

THE REPLACEMENT EFFECT

The rate at which a population transmits acquired characteristics to subsequent generations will depend in part on the growth rate of the population and its age structure. This is readily seen if we assume that all quality improvements take place among the lower age groups and not the higher ones. For example, nurture and schooling improvements are, for the most part, likely to enter the system during early ages. To the extent that entrants into the work force are of higher quality (i.e., higher education and acquired skills, etc.) than those that leave through retirement or death, the average quality of the labor force improves more rapidly if the rate of population growth is higher (other things equal) rather than lower.

---

*There is some evidence on the effects of starvation that can lead to interesting calculations. For example, Keys (24) determines experimentally the reduction in physical capacities as a consequence of "semistarvation," e.g., a shift from 3,000-plus calories to about 1,600 calories leads in 12 weeks to a decrease in strenuous physical work capacity to 52 percent of the nonstarved group, and, at the end of 24 weeks, to a decrease equal to only 28 percent of the nonstarved group. Of course the initial level based on the diet of well-off American students is unusually high. Perhaps the work capacity is not much lower for a standard below the U.N. Food and Agriculture Organization (FAO) norm but above Colin Clark's (25) calculated norm for west Asia. If so, then we might readily visualize an agricultural family producing grain that would yield 9,600 calories per family per day. Calculating children as two thirds of adults, this would lead a three-child family to have approximately 2,400 calories per adult-equivalent whereas something close to a six-child family would reduce the intake to the semistarvation level of about 1,600 calories. At this level we might apply Keys' results with qualifications. In the Carnegie experiment mentioned by Keys, men's physical capacities were reduced trivially when on a 2,000 calorie low-weight-maintenance diet. See Brown (26) for actual nutritional reference diets, pp. 36, 142-143. See also Clark (25, pp. 123-129). If we raise Clark's figures by some 25 percent for the greater weight and height of Americans to tally with Keys' data, we obtain a norm of about 2,300 calories.

It seems probable that the greatest effects of "semistarvation" are the psychological ones. In Keys' experiments, *apathy* was a major consequence of semistarvation. It was highly correlated with such psychological elements as lack of ambition, decrease in self-discipline, decrease in mental alertness, and a decrease in concentration. On a self-rating scale the increase in apathy and the related psychological characteristics was roughly calibrated at about 1.75 on a range between no apathy (0) and extremely more apathy (5). This was approximately half of the amount of the sense of tiredness reported. Of course, it is very difficult to determine the economic significance of these results, but they are suggestive of the possible relationship between poor diet and the type of resultant characteristics that inhibit economic change.

Among the important factors affecting economic growth are, first, the work skills of the population and, second, the attitudes of the population. The attitudes of the work force are shaped by religious, social, cultural, and political traditions which for the most part are transmitted by the process of nurture, informal education as well as formal training. Among the basic attitudes that affect growth are those that determine degree of adherence to traditional occupations and procedures (9, pp. 108-109). Such attitudinal changes will usually influence the degree of labor mobility, the extent of participation by women in the work force (27), and the age at which people normally enter the work force. In addition, they will affect the willingness of people within a given occupation to accept new techniques, equipment, or new organizational forms. In view of these considerations we visualize an economic quality replacement effect in the sense that those who enter the economically active population have a higher productive capacity than those who leave, and hence they increase the average quality of the labor force.

The extent of quality improvement depends, in part, on the rate of population growth. To see the nature of the possibilities involved, consider some examples based on the following assumptions:

1. Education of a formal or informal nature takes place prior to entry into the labor force.

2. Education expenditures are assumed to be consumption expenditures by the parents of those being educated.

3. There are constant economic returns to education with respect to numbers of people educated.

4. The years of education per person are an independent variable.

5. The mean annual income of those with more education is greater on the average than those with less.*

Figure 2 illustrates what can happen to income per worker under sets of alternative assumptions that emphasize the differences between stationary versus growing populations. In cases I and II we have stationary populations in which 2 percent enter the work force each year and 2 percent leave. Those who enter are assumed to have twice as many years of education and three times the associated income levels as those who leave. In the third case 2 percent exit the work force every year and 5 percent enter every year. Note, for example, that at the end of 25 years the per worker income of the stationary population is $150 (assuming an initial income in year zero of $100) compared to $176 for the case in which the population increases 3

*See Appendix Table A for some sample ratios for a number of developing countries. The assumptions are admittedly extreme since they assume that the entire income differential is a consequence of education. However, the nature of the assumption does not invalidate the main point which is to examine the consequences of the entrants to the work force having different productive capacities than those who leave.

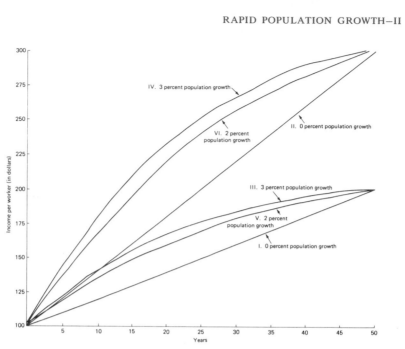

Figure 2. Income per worker at 0, 2, and 3 percent population growth over 50 years.

percent per year. The income per worker is approximately 16 percent higher for the rapidly growing population at the end of 25 years. If we assume a three to one ratio in income of those entering as against those leaving (case IV), the per worker income is 25 percent higher at the end of 25 years. However, at the end of 50 years, when full replacement takes place under all assumptions, the per capita income is the same for all rates of population growth. This, however, omits the likelihood that during this 50-year period further increases take place in the education of those who enter compared to earlier entrants and hence the replacement effect continues to operate until the point is reached where the productivity of those who enter ceases to be higher than the productivity of those who leave.* Also, the illustration omits the effects of higher savings and investment out of the higher income per worker on income growth.

Of course the results depend on the assumption. But we can weaken some of our assumptions without altering the general point made. For example, assume that beyond some point there are diminishing returns to education at

*A model in which there was a gradual shift from 10 percent of the entrants receiving 6 years of education to 100 percent over a period of 10 years gave approximately similar results for the twentieth year. In other words, the 3 percent growth population earned more than 25 percent more income per worker than the stationary population in year 20.

a given level. In that case the replacement effect is somewhat less efficient, but up to a point it still operates in the same direction. The general case is illustrated in Figure 3 in which the X axis represents "general-capital," i.e., physical capital plus human capital. We assume that human capital is the more important component and the major productive element in general-capital. The rays from the origin represent constant ratios of labor and general-capital and they result in a constant income level per worker. If L_0 is the

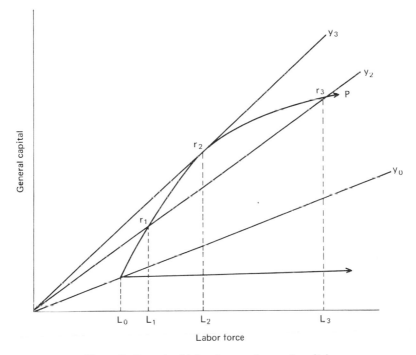

Figure 3. Growth of labor force and general capital.

initial amount of labor and Y_0 is the initial income per worker, then the horizontal arrow shows the consequences of labor force growth under the classical assumptions and constant returns to scale. If education *per person* is an independent variable and a greater number of people implies a higher level of education per worker on the average, then the path of labor force growth is shown by the curved line marked *P*. The tangent of this path with one of the income rays yields the optimum growth of the labor force for the period. It can readily be seen that if actual labor force growth falls short of the optimum labor growth, then the analysis implies the desirability of an increase in the rate of population growth. The figure illustrates the possibility that the lower rate of population growth of r_1 leads to a lower income per worker than the greater rate of population growth r_2.

Expenditures on education in most cases will probably not increase in direct proportion to the number of young people in the population.* Taxing capacity will depend somewhat on real income per person. There are many alternative claims on public revenues. These conflicting claims will vary with the rate and pattern of population growth. In a largely agricultural population, the greater the rate of population growth, the less land per man; the greater the degree of fragmentation of holdings, and usually the smaller the output per man. Also, high growth rates will normally increase the burden of dependency (9, pp. 332-333) and decrease *potential* taxable revenues. Population growth may raise population replacements to a higher production capacity per person, other things equal, *but* it may simultaneously make it more difficult to provide a given amount of education for the same proportion of children entering the population (9, pp. 247-249).

Intuitively we should expect that as population grows, *beyond some rate*, that education per person declines. Under this assumption we have two opposing forces at work. On the one hand, a greater rate of population growth yields a greater replacement effect, but on the other hand, a greater rate of population growth reduces education per person. In principle, the balance of forces can still be in favor of the replacement effect. Thus in Figure 3 the intermediate rate of population growth r_2 yields the highest income per worker.[†]

Educational Inputs

Educational inputs are unlike traditional inputs. Although we know in a general way that education pays off from a productivity viewpoint, we do not know much about the marginal productivity of education. Calculations of the returns to education have been of the *average* returns to marginal years of education. What we do not know very much about are the *marginal* returns to marginal years of education. The author's view is that it is not at all impossible that the marginal returns for some marginal years of education may be zero when a given type of education expands very rapidly.[‡] Education is also complicated by the fact that its inputs are diverse, its quality is rarely constant, and many of its influences on productivity are indirect. This may be one of the reasons why very general types of education, which frequently

*See (28) and Gavin Jones, "Effect of Population Change on the Attainment of Educational Goals in the Developing Countries," in this volume.

[†]r_1, r_2, and r_3 are rates of population growth associated with the alternate amounts of labor force increase L_0L_1, or L_0L_2, or L_0L_3.

[‡]An unpublished study by the author on returns to education in Greece leads him to believe that this may have occurred with respect to secondary education for the period 1960-64.

appear to be unrelated to given vocations, seem frequently to yield relatively high rates of return. We cannot readily assume that we can inject educational inputs and harvest productivity outputs at the other end of the pipeline.*

Similar to education and information, but much more elusive, are the inputs responsible for technological change—especially entrepreneurial capacities. The innovation rate will depend on the perception and the ability to take advantage of economic opportunities, and hence on entrepreneurial capacities. Returning to some assumptions discussed earlier, we might recall that not all inputs necessary for production are marketed and that some are not available to all individuals. Hence, only some people are entrepreneurs. They are likely to be the ones who are able to fill the gaps in necessary inputs or capable of creating substitutes for unavailable inputs, and, in general, are able to perform as "input completers."† Once again entrepreneurship is an elusive input and not easily augmented in the sense in which traditional inputs are augmentable.

The main point of the previous remarks is that, although with the traditional inputs we were able to rely on a production function which is a one-to-one correspondence, in the sense that if we add something tangible to our stock of inputs, we can visualize obtaining at the other end a tangible output. Once we deal with the nontraditional inputs, we can no longer have confidence in such simple input-output relationships.

CONJECTURES AND CONCLUSIONS

In a broad sense human investment—the activities that create the essential changes in the acquired economically valuable qualities of the work force—must be the critical element which determines whether or not population growth in any particular case has adverse economic consequences. Even the process of capital accumulation is not a mechanical one. Obviously entrepreneurial qualities (which are for the most part acquired qualities) are essential elements in the process. Economic growth requires more than the accumulation of capital goods of the type already in use. New types of productive instruments have to be created; new occupations learned, induced, generated, and filled in new contexts and locations; new types of risks have to be assumed; and, to some degree, new social and economic relationships have to be forged. Hence, the characteristics of the population that are transmitted from generation to generation through nurture and education become the vital factors that determine the rate of growth. But the transmission of such characteristics does not result in a replica of the previous generation's occupational skills, and attitudinal characteristics. The transmission process creates the potential for change.

*For a summary of existing knowledge in this area see Bowles (29).
† For a fuller treatment of these matters see the author's (30).

In most instances, economies do not operate at their productive and technical upper bound. Developing countries do not have to invent new techniques. They can borrow techniques and types of capital that already exist. (Of course, in detail, some research and experimentation is frequently necessary to adapt broadly known techniques to specific local conditions.) In view of these considerations, the finding that traditional inputs account for only a small proportion of the growth that takes place is hardly surprising. The old Malthusian argument that additions to the population come into the world with additional hands but without the additional capital or land necessary to produce at the same level as their forebears is not entirely true. The nurture and educational system can create to some degree the additional capital necessary. Whether this "human capital" is adequate or not depends upon the rate of transmission of known and new skills, and the simultaneous introduction of other types of capital into the population. (The word *skill* is used in its broadest possible sense in this context.) The rate of growth of physical capital may be to some extent a function of the growth rate of human capital. The basic argument is neither pro- nor anti-Malthusian. Rather it suggests that the traditional approach misses to a considerable degree the fundamental processes which determine whether or not given rates of population growth are adverse to economic growth.

The point emphasized in this paper is that the research of the last 15 years shows that whereas the output that results from traditional inputs may not be entirely trivial, it is nevertheless not nearly as important as the contribution to output that results from nontraditional inputs. Many of the nontraditional inputs have an elusive quality about them. They cannot be handled from an analytical viewpoint as easily as the traditional ones. The basic conjecture of this paper is that the assumption of a one-to-one correspondence between inputs and outputs is no longer tenable once one gives primary importance to nontraditional inputs. What is new is the rather persuasive evidence that the nontraditional inputs are usually more significant than the traditional ones, and hence the relations between population growth and nontraditional inputs should in most cases become central to the analysis of the "population-resources" problem.

For the most part, this paper is only suggestive. The overall results are inconclusive since we really do not know very much about the economic magnitudes of the demographic factors that are detrimental to economic growth, as against those that are helpful. This lack is especially true of the effects other than the replacement effect. The replacement-effect type of argument is of interest since it suggests that even in developing countries, there may be situations and periods for which relatively high rates of population growth *may* involve some demographic effects that are helpful to economic growth. Whether the beneficial effects are ever the predominant ones is hard to say, but it is a possibility that cannot be entirely ignored. In examining the replacement effect, we do not imply that a 0 percent population growth should attempt to increase its rate of growth to reach the 3 percent level.* Our conclusion is that, other things equal, a population growing at 3 percent will have a temporary advantage over a population growing at 0 percent, in terms of a positive replacement effect, but this advantage cannot be achieved by a gradual increase in the rate of growth of a slower or non-growing population. It simply implies that the more rapidly growing population has a positive aspect which counteracts the negative aspects of rapid growth, and that this aspect is less significant in the slow-growing population.

Whether or not the replacement effect is of interest depends on the acceptability of the assumptions, especially with respect to the assumptions: (a) that the costs of education are consumption costs rather than investment costs, and (b) that the level of education per person provided for later entrants (rather than earlier entrants) is unaffected (or less than proportionately reduced) by positive rates of population growth. We do not have the space here to consider all the possibilities.

Two important qualifications must be made in considering the replacement effect. First, the replacement effect may be negative as well as positive. In other words, if the demographic effects considered in the previous sections are in some sense transmitted from one generation to the next, then a more rapid rate of replacement may lower the acquired economic qualities of such a population. Second, it must, of course, be remembered that even the positive replacement effect must be considered as only one element among many others—most of which probably inhibit economic growth. The positive replacement effect is delineated primarily in the interest of achieving a balanced approach to the question of assessing the consequences of population growth.

*Jones and Gingrich have developed a model in which practically no advantage is gained on the basis of the replacement effect by a population increasing its rate of growth gradually. See (31).

APPENDIX

TABLE A

Schooling and Earnings

Country	Age	Years of Education		Ratio Col. (4)/ Col. (3)	Years of Education 11	Ratio Col. (6)/ Col. (4)
		0-1	5-6			
(1)	(2)	(3)	(4)	(5)	(6)	(7)
Mexico	32	$560	$1154	2.06	$2080	1.45
Colombia	32	$397	$1430	3.60	$2601	1.81
Chile	n.a.	n.a.	$101.4	n.a.	$194.0	1.81
India	32	850 Rupees	1500 Rupees (7 years)	1.76	2565 Rupees	1.71
Venezuela	23-65	3750 Bolivars	7500 Bolivars	2.00	18,000	2.4

n.a. = not available

Sources: Mexico and Colombia (32), Chile and India (33), and Venezuela (34).

REFERENCES

1. Kuznets, Simon, *Modern Economic Growth.* New Haven: Yale Univ. Press, 1966. pp. 80-81.
2. Aukrust, O., "Investment and Economic Growth," *Productivity Measurement Rev*, February 1959. pp. 35-53.
3. Niitamo, O., "Development of Producitivity in Finnish Industry, 1925-1952," *Productivity Measurement Rev*, November 1958. pp. 30-41.
4. Krueger, Anne O., "Factor Endowments and *Per Capita* Income Differences among Countries," *Econ J*, September 1968. pp. 641-659.
5. Leibenstein, Harvey, "Incremental Capital Output Ratios in the Short Run,"*Rev Econ Stat*, February 1966. pp. 20-27.
6. Patel, S. J., "A Note on the Incremental Capital-Output Ratio and Rates of Economic Growth in the Developing Countries," *Kyklos*, 1968, Fasc. I. pp. 147-150.
7. Morgan, Theodore, "Investment Versus Economic Growth," *Econ Devel & Cult Change*, April 1969. pp. 392-414.
8. Leibenstein, Harvey, "Allocative Efficiency vs. X-Efficiency," *Amer Econ Rev*, June 1966. pp. 392-415.
9. Coale, Ansley, and E. M. Hoover, *Population Growth and Economic Development in Low Income Countries, a Case Study of India's Prospects.* Princeton: Princeton Univ. Press, 1958.

10. Altus, William D., "Birth Order and Its Sequelae," *Science*, January 7, 1966. pp. 44-49.

11. Anastasi, Anne, "Intelligence and Family Size," *Psychol Bul*, May 1956. pp. 187-209.

12. McCarthy, Dorothea A., "Language Development in Children," *Manual of Child Psychology*, L. Carmichael, ed. New York: John Wiley & Sons, 1946. pp. 558-559.

13. Haggard, E. A., "Social Status and Intelligence," *Genetic Psychol Monographs*, Vol. 49, 1954. pp. 141-186.

14. Jones, H., "The Environment and Mental Development," *Manual of Child Psychology*. L. Carmichael, ed. New York: John Wiley & Sons, 1946. p. 655.

15. Smith, S., "Language and Non-Verbal Test Performance of Racial Groups in Honolulu before and after a Fourteen-Year Interval," *J Genetic Psychol*, Vol. 26. pp. 51-93.

16. Tanner, J. M., *Growth at Adolescence*. Oxford: Blackwell's 2nd ed., 1962.

17. Tanner, J. M., "Galtonian Eugenics and the Study of Growth," *Eugen Rev*, September 1966. pp. 127-128.

18. Scott, J. A., "Intelligence, Physique, and Family Size." *Brit J Prev Soc Med*, October 1962. pp. 165-173.

19. Blackburn, Julian, "Family Size, Intelligence Score, and Social Class," *Population Studies*, June 1947. pp. 165-176.

20. Scrimshaw, Nevin S., and John E. Gordon, eds., *Malnutrition, Learning and Behavior*. Cambridge: M.I.T. Press, 1968. pp. 353-354.

21. Patton, Robert Gray, and Lytt I. Gardner, *Growth Failure in Maternal Deprivation*. St. Louis: C. C. Thomas, 1963.

22. Lebovici, S., "The Concept of Maternal Deprivation: a Review of Research," *Deprivation of Maternal Care; a Reassessment of Its Effects*. World Health Organization Public Health Papers, Vol. 14. Geneva, 1962. pp. 75-95.

23. Keller, W. B., and H. A. Kraut, "Work and Nutrition," *World Review of Nutrition and Dietetics*, G. H. Bourne, ed. New York: Hafner Pub. Co., 1962. Vol. III.

24. Keys, Ancel, *Biology of Human Starvation*. Minneapolis: Univ. Minnesota Press, 1950.

25. Clark, Colin, *Population Growth and Land Use*. London: Macmillan, 1967. pp. 123-129.

26. Brown, Lester R., *Man, Land and Food*. Washington, D.C.: U.S. Dept. of Agriculture, Economic Research Service, Regional Analysis Division, 1963. pp. 36, 142-143.

27. International Labor Organization, "The World's Working Population, Some Demographic Aspects," p. 173.

28. Harbison, Frederick H., and Charles A. Myers, *Education, Manpower, and Economic Growth, Strategies of Human Resource-Development*. New York: McGraw-Hill, 1964. p. 19.

29. Bowles, Samuel, *Planning Educational Systems for Economic Growth.*
    Cambridge, Mass.: Harvard Univ. Press, 1969. Chs. 1-3.
30. Leibenstein, Harvey, "Entrepreneurship and Development," *Amer Econ
    Rev*, May 1968. pp. 72-83.
31. Jones, Gavin, and Paul Gingrich, "The Effects of Differing Trends in
    Fertility and of Educational Advance on the Growth, Quality and Turn-
    over of the Labor Force," *Demography*, Vol. 5, 1968. pp. 226-248.
32. Carnoy, Martin, "Aspects of Labor Force Mobility in Latin America," *J
    Human Res*, Fall 1967. pp. 528-9.
33. Selowsky, Marcelo, "Education and Economic Growth: Some Interna-
    tional Comparisons," *Economic Development Report No. 83.* CIA,
    Cambridge, Mass.: Harvard Univ. p. 49, Table 14, p. 60, Table 19.
34. Shoup, Carl S., *A Report. Fiscal System of Venezuela.* Baltimore: Johns
    Hopkins Press, 1959. p. 407.

V

The Economics of Population Control *

Paul Demeny

Attempts to analyze the effects of population change on human welfare have been among the earliest preoccupations of economists. The possibility that less than optimal demographic patterns might emerge was also recognized early; so it is not surprising that speculations about the desirability of deliberately influencing population size, or population change, to facilitate the achievement of some economic objective can also be traced back to the earliest recorded economic thought. Similarly, economic objectives have almost always played a prominent role in shaping practical policies, such as there were, aimed at modifying various demographic processes. Thus the present-day attention to economically motivated population control schemes is by no means novel, either in economic theorizing or in the field of practical policy.

THE CONTEMPORARY PROBLEM

Nevertheless, the intensity of the current interest in such schemes, as well as the magnitude of the economic issues underlying that interest, are unquestionably without precedent in human affairs. The primary reason for this is to be found in the historically unparalleled rates of population growth that have been generated by the success in reducing mortality in the less developed countries during the past few decades. The portent of this demographic phenomenon is amplified by the fairly general expectation that a corresponding downward adjustment of fertility will occur spontaneously only after a considerable time lag; as a consequence, achieving a sustained development in the foreseeable future will be a much more difficult task than it was in the now

Paul Demeny is Director of the East-West Population Institute of the East-West Center and Professor of Economics, University of Hawaii.

*This paper was originally presented at the 1969 General Conference of the International Union for the Scientific Study of Population in London, England, and appears in the Proceedings of that Conference; it appears here, with minor editorial changes, by permission of the IUSSP.

industrialized nations during the corresponding phase of their historical development.

Many distinguishing characteristics of the contemporary world add further dimensions to this concern: the comparatively large absolute size of many of the national populations affected by these high rates of population growth; the low initial levels of income per head as well as other correlated economic indices; the prospects of a widening income differential between developed and developing nations and the implications of such a widening gap in a world with modern transportation and communication; and the vastly increased role assumed by national governments in economic management and their pursuit of explicit development goals that are typically cast in terms of income per head, or, in terms of quantitative objectives with respect to employment and/or shifts in the industrial composition of their labor force—indices that are sensitive to differentials in population growth. Under such circumstances policymakers come to regard population not as an exogeneously determined datum but, at least potentially, as another, if special, variable that may be subjected to conscious manipulation by, and in the interest of, society as a whole.

Variables That Influence Population

The immediate levers of such manipulation may be fertility, mortality, and migration. This paper will consider economic issues of population control only with respect to possible measures affecting the first of these three variables. Although such a treatment leaves out some economic considerations that are relevant in formulating a general economic policy, it reflects reasonably closely the actual focus of public attention and debate on population control. There are some obvious reasons why fertility is the only potentially important variable in this context.

Briefly, the possibilities of a reduction of mortality that could appreciably affect the intrinsic rates of population growth have either been already exploited, even in the developing world, or such mortality gains are in the process of being rapidly attained. A reversal, as a matter of deliberate policy, of the public health and related policies that are responsible for these achievements must be considered inconceivable if only because of the high valuation, even in narrow economic terms, that should be attached to survival per se; and, second, because of the strong presumption that multifarious positive connections exist between low mortality on the one hand and economic modernization of a society, interpreted in the widest sense (including the eventual modernization of traditional patterns of fertility as well) on the other hand. Naturally, these arguments leave unsolved many vexing problems with respect to mortality control, such as determining the optimum level of allocation of scarce resources that should be devoted to public health. However, as mentioned earlier, the mortality-reducing measures will be increasingly irrelevant to influencing population growth and size, at least until changes in medical technology permit a major extension of the human life span.

Other policies might influence population growth and size through international migration, but their potential importance as population control measures in the contemporary world are limited, because in most instances the magnitude of the possible international flows is dwarfed by the magnitude of the natural increase. Furthermore, a deliberate encouragement of out-migration is bound to be an undesirable policy from the economic standpoint because of the strongly selective nature of modern migratory movements. (Young adults with valuable skills are most likely to migrate.)

Evaluating Fertility Control Policies

Ideally a satisfactory evaluation of policies aimed at controlling fertility should be based on a comparison of the costs and benefits, both direct and indirect, of such policies. However the vast majority of writings on this subject is cast in somewhat different, narrower terms. Either because the possibility of a purposeful interference with a fertility trend is not contemplated or because of the assumption that the economic cost of such interference is negligible, the usual approach is merely to analyze the economic consequences of hypothetical or observed differences in fertility, bypassing the question of how those differences are to be explained in the first place. Thus, for instance, starting from a given initial situation, in the fashion of the by-now classic study of Coale and Hoover (1), alternative courses of fertility over time may be specified as affecting the same initial population, and the consequences on various economic indicators may be worked out by plugging the alternative population trends into an appropriate model describing the workings of the economy in question.

The pertinence of such a procedure to a full cost-benefit analysis of population control programs is evident. Once the net economic benefits of a reduced fertility are worked out (as a rule tacitly assuming that the reduction itself involved no economic costs), the level of those benefits may be related to the net costs of any proposed scheme that is capable of engineering the fertility reduction specified in the calculation. A rate of return to investment in such a scheme may then be calculated. The scheme will be supported or rejected on economic grounds depending on whether the rate of return so calculated is higher or lower than the return that may be earned in feasible alternative uses of the funds involved. While somewhat awkward, this two-step procedure corresponds to the logical, and to the historical, sequence of the emergence of contemporary proposals for controlling fertility. In the first stage the interest centers around the economic effects of alternative courses of fertility. The results obtained are then examined with respect to their implications on the formulation of public policies that might influence fertility in the desired direction. The discussion in this paper is organized under two main headings corresponding to these two stages. The fact that the exposition here focuses on the economics of fertility *reduction* merely reflects the nature of the contemporary debate. The framework of the cost-benefit analysis itself is, of course, perfectly general and, mutatis mutandis, would be equally well suited for an examination of the economic case for any proposed pronatalist policy.

The Economic Effects of Reducing Fertility

An adequate treatment of this topic would have to embrace virtually all important problems having to do with the economics of development and could be handled satisfactorily only in a general equilibrium framework involving fertility itself as a dependent variable. No such treatment yet exists or is in sight, but the literature on various aspects of the general problem is broad and is rapidly growing. Because of the limitations imposed on this paper, only the briefest reference will be given here to the main themes of this literature. For a comprehensive survey of the state of the art in this field the reader may be referred to the materials of the 1965 World Population Conference,* as well as to some more recent reviews (5, 6) and recent representative studies (7-12). It was assumed that the usefulness of the present discussion will be enhanced if it focuses primarily on the deficiencies and analytical weaknesses, rather than on the achievements, of the existing framework.

As a matter of simple description, in the present-day world the frequency distribution of countries according to the level of their fertility is pronouncedly bimodal. Accordingly, while there is considerable variation within each broad group, countries may be labeled as having either "high" or "low" fertility. The potential reduction of fertility, measured in absolute terms, differs greatly between these two groups. This circumstance, combined with the fact that a separation of countries into the high and low fertility groups pari passu separates the "less developed" economies from the "developed" ones, results in substantial differences in the nature and quantitative importance of the economic effects attributed to fertility change in the two groups.

Countries with High Fertility

With an average crude birth rate in the low 40's, a reduction of fertility of at least 50 percent would be necessary to bring the birth rate in this group

*See in particular (2, 3, 4).

near to the mean value characterizing the low fertility group. As historical experience suggests that such a reduction, if it occurs, may come about fairly rapidly—perhaps within 2 or 3 decades or an even shorter time—the potential impact on the age structure and on the rate of population growth may be quite spectacular. Accordingly and in sharp contrast to the traditional approach that was preoccupied with the relation of population size to "resources," the core of the now prevailing theory on the economics of fertility change focuses primarily on the implications of these two demographic processes: the transformation of the age structure and the change in the rate of population growth.

As fertility drops the young-age dependency falls. With the size of the potential labor force remaining unaffected in the short-run total, output will be as high as it would be in the absence of a fertility decline. But as the given total output is to be distributed among a smaller number of persons, income per head rises relative to what it would be had no fertility decline taken place. The once-and-for-all advantage implicit in the transformation of the age distribution is not lost when eventually a new equilibrium state is reached. This is indicated by the comparison of the high- and low-fertility steady state age distribution.

The decline of fertility will result in a deceleration of population growth and, eventually, in a lower rate of steady state growth than would be the case with maintained high fertility. With a lower rate of growth the efforts required merely to keep the capital stock per head constant will be smaller or, conversely, with a given level of effort the slower-growing population will be able to increase capital per head faster than with a high rate of growth. The effect will be felt to some extent soon after fertility starts to decline but assumes its full importance once the arrival of the cohorts affected by fertility decline starts to slow down the rate of growth in the labor-force ages.

Arguments for and against Lowered Fertility. Further advantages of fertility reduction are discerned by various authors as working through the same mechanisms and amplifying and reinforcing these two major effects.

1. It is often asserted that with higher income per capita not only savings per head will be larger but also that a higher proportion of personal incomes will be saved.

2. The same point is made with respect to government expenditures. Additionally, it is said that the relative decline of the demand for such government services as schooling, maternal health, etc. will permit a shift of the structure of public outlays toward more directly productive investments.

3. Lower fertility may increase female labor force participation rates.

4. The gains in income per capita induced by the fertility decline may have a feedback effect on labor productivity via better nutrition, health, housing, etc.

5. In an economy suffering from technological unemployment or under-employment, the absorption of idle manpower will be accelerated by the higher rate of capital accumulation and, later, also by the lower rate of labor force growth induced by lower fertility.

6. In general, achievement of employment objectives pursued by under-developed economies, such as the relative expansion of the labor force ab-sorbed by the modern (industrial) sector, will be facilitated.

7. The shift in factor proportions implied by a faster rate of growth of the capital stock and a slower rate of growth of the labor force will lessen the pressure for interference in the labor market that results in allocative inef-ficiencies and/or will facilitate the achievement of desired changes toward a more equitable income distribution.

Arguments that dispute the validity of some of these points are usually addressed to the ancillary propositions listed under 1 through 4, or they ques-tion the quantitative importance of the effects described. In particular the empirical validity of the saving-investment relationship is often challenged, mainly with respect to individual saving behavior. In a more positive vein, the possibility of compensating adjustments in labor force participation rates is sometimes stressed and, under the evident influence of the historical experi-ence of the developed economies, it is asserted that high dependency rates stimulate individuals to higher efforts in general and that there is a similar positive effect with respect to government behavior as well. Furthermore, it is argued that a faster growing population provides advantages with respect to the flexibility of the economy in adjusting to structural changes, such as in demand, thereby lessening the penalty for erroneous decisions with respect to investment allocation; and that a younger age and skill composition of the labor force and its faster rate of renewal implied by higher fertility has various beneficial economic effects. Finally, the classic arguments concerning economies of scale and specialization are often invoked and connected with population growth functionally, and some authors stress the presumed rela-tionship between population density and technological progress (7, 13).

Such arguments applied to present-day developing countries appear to take little cognizance of circumstances that invalidate or drastically weaken the importance of the mechanisms involved: (a) the prevailing levels of income per head are so low that little additional stimulus may come from further increasing deprivation; (b) the choice for the foreseeable future is not be-tween demographic growth and a stationary or declining population but be-tween fast growth and somewhat slower growth—so any stimulus conceivably flowing from growth will be amply provided; (c) the point just made is even more evident with respect to internal migration and urbanization; (d) the problem in developing economies is the transfer, adoption, and diffusion of already existing technological knowledge rather than the development of new knowledge said to be stimulated by population pressure; and (e) economies of scale and specialization can be expected to be forthcoming chiefly in the modern sector of the economy, the expansion of which depends on the rate of capital accumulation and on the composition of demand as determined by income per head, rather than on the rate of population growth per se.

Measuring the Effects of Lowered Fertility. On balance the counter-arguments seem to subtract little from the validity of the points that assign a positive economic role to the changes in age composition and population growth consequent upon a decline of fertility. But what is the quantative significance of these effects? A widely quoted estimate (1, p. 280) sets the relative gains in income per capita (adjusted for age distribution) resulting from a 50 percent linear reduction of fertility occurring over a period of 25 years in the Indian setting at about 15 percent after 20 years following the onset of fertility decline and at about 40 percent after 30 years, the difference increasing rapidly afterwards. Thus the short-term gains, while appreciable, would appear to be far from spectacular. Accepting the formal logic of the model on which such calculations are based and accepting as plausible the usually suggested range of the relevant parameter values, it can be effectively argued that the gains attributed to declining fertility could be achieved by a number of alternative means, such as a slightly higher saving-investment rate or slight improvements in labor productivity and/or in the efficiency of using capital (14, 15). Alternatively it may be suggested that the relatively modest results are a consequence of a less than complete exploration of the plausible ranges and combinations of the parameter values that may be relevant (16).

It appears, therefore, that the identification and quantification of the economic effects resulting from a decline of fertility from high levels remains in a less than satisfactory state and that a considerable amount of additional empirical work will be required before the divergences in expert opinion can be expected to be substantially narrowed. More fundamentally, the question is whether the main thrust of future research should continue to be centered on the problems that have dominated the recent debates or whether at least some reorientation of thought and change in emphasis is required. The following four points outline some of these questions.

Reorienting Research toward the Long Run. First, the emphasis that has been given to short-term considerations appears to have been disproportionately strong, in particular to some tangible benefits affecting government expenditures that are attributable to the emergence of low dependency ratios. Perhaps a not always conscious orientation toward policymaking and the implicit assumption that such orientation depends on the analyst's ability to identify quantifiable short-term effects have influenced the research efforts in this field. This emphasis on the short-term becomes explicit in calculations in which the gains from a fertility decline are obtained by aggregating present values of births that did not take place, such present values being determined as the difference between the discounted value of the expected life-time consumption and income streams. The application of a discount rate that is realistic for ordinary investment decisions, that is a rate of the order of magnitude of 10 percent per year or higher, virtually takes away any significance from all effects that will be felt beyond 15 or 20 years. However, it could be argued that population problems are long-run problems par excellence and that it is the special responsibility of economists to clarify the important long-term implications of alternative levels of current fertility, whether or not the incidence of the effects falls within the present time horizon of policymakers. Such clarification is needed quite independently from any economic arguments that would seek to establish the proper rates of time discount that should be applied in formulating public policies.

Second, even if one were prepared to give primacy to short-run considerations, it would seem that the essential economic difference between maintaining fertility at its original high level and drastically reducing it cannot be expressed at all adequately by a catalog of items not consumed because of fewer births and by a quantitative valuation of the items so "saved" and their immediate economic repercussions. Twenty years from now a society that has undergone a revolutionary transformation of the age-old patterns of reproductive behavior will be a society qualitatively different from one in which no such transformation took place. It is difficult to envisage a situation without these qualitative differences also manifesting themselves in multifarious ways in practically all economically significant aspects of human behavior. Massive adoption of new ideas on family size accompanied by action translating these new ideas into reality is inconceivable without a massive breakthrough in spreading and strengthening patterns of rational economic behavior; in inculcating and reinforcing the idea that individual action can improve one's economic status; in effecting favorable changes in economic mobility, initiative, risk-taking, and economic calculus; in promoting modern attitudes on child rearing and education; in raising aspirations and goals of achievement for the individual, his family, and his children; and in changing many other aspects. Much more attention should be given to attempts to verify empirically such intangible relations and, as far as possible, to measure their practical significance.

Third, the same factors that are responsible for an undue emphasis on short-term effects explain why little systematic attention has been given to population size and density as such. To a certain extent the professional literature on this score is in felicitous contrast to much of the popular debate that centers around "overpopulation." A discussion of "resources" and "food" is largely missing in the literature partly because the optimistic notion that sudden changes of fertility could greatly change the parameters of these problems 5 or even 10 years hence is considered a fallacy; and partly because much of the literature, in turn, is more optimistic about the short-term prospects and options available to the developing countries than are the popular conceptions on these matters. Notably, no short-term absolute limitations on "resources" are discerned, and no particular products or expenditure categories are singled out for special attention. The problem of "malnutrition," for instance, is seen as a facet of low income levels in general, as even in the poorest countries the income elasticity of the demand for food is less than unity. The implications of high versus low fertility are envisaged not in terms of choice between "famine and catastrophe" versus "progress" but more correctly, and less dramatically, as a choice between slower and faster rates of economic growth. Nevertheless, paying more attention to longer-run problems would seem to require a reintroduction of many of the familiar classical considerations about size and resources into the debate on the economics of fertility reduction, and these considerations may again gain the upper hand over the concern with population structure and rate of growth as such. Optimistic assumptions as to the longer-run economic prospects for the less developed countries in no way lessen the pertinence of these remarks, as is suggested from the arguments in the next section.

Fourth and finally, according to the received theory there is astonishingly little difference between the various types of high-fertility countries in the magnitude of the potential gains that could be derived from lowering fertility. This attitude is, of course, partly a consequence of the exclusive emphasis placed upon population growth and structure as responsible for the gains: with respect to potential change in these demographic parameters, the less developed countries do exhibit a high degree of uniformity. Nevertheless, it is likely that the presumptions of insensitivity to vastly differing economic characteristics merely reflects the inadequacy of the underlying theoretical apparatus rather than the intrinsic nature of the mechanisms involved. Thus it can be shown that even the simplest disaggregation of the usual single-sector model customarily used to demonstrate the effect of fertility decline would point to important differences in the magnitude, if not in the direction, of these gains, depending on the initial economic conditions of the country affected—particularly the factor endowments which characterize the traditional sector or the nature of international trade relations. Therefore, extensive analysis of the economic effects of fertility change that utilizes more sophisticated and differentiated economic models is urgently needed.

Countries with Low Fertility

Considerations relating to the effects of fertility change occupy a distinctly modest place in debates on the short-term prospects of developed economies. On the one hand, concern with specific resource constraints, formerly a source of antinatalist impulses, has faded with the increasing recognition of the possibilities of substitution for scarce materials and energy sources. On the other hand, institutional changes, such as the adoption of countercyclical fiscal and monetary mechanisms, have removed much of the force of the pronatalist sentiment that was based on stagnationist arguments. Moreover, while the low fertility characterizing the developed countries is consistent with vital rates and age distributions that vary appreciably, the magnitude of the feasible changes (taking each country as a unit) is nevertheless fairly limited when looked at from the standpoint of short-term economic effects. Within the framework of these considerations however, there appears to exist on balance a tentative concensus that population growth at a moderately low rate has some advantages over a zero rate of growth: as a minimum it lessens the need for economic arrangements to compensate for the disadvantages of a stationary age structure.

A Lower Optimal Population. This perspective on growth and on the related age distribution is, however, substantially altered if the implied long-term consequences on population size and density are taken into account. On purely economic grounds the prospects of an increase in size and density seem to appear in a mildly favorable light only in a relatively few advanced countries, and there only if the possibilities of relying on international trade to reap the advantages of specialization and large-scale production are ignored. More significantly, a number of interrelated and overlapping considerations suggest that the very successes of economic growth tend to impose increasing penalties on further demographic expansion.* On the somewhat loose notion of classical population theory, it may be suggested that, on balance, continued economic growth and continued current trends in technological and organizational changes (including trends toward a more integrated world economic system) will tend to lower the population that is optimal for individual countries.

The production of high levels of income per head involves a multiplication of physical artifacts of a staggering variety that create unprecedented demands on space, energy, and raw materials per head. The process of consumption itself has similar effects. Indeed, resource problems in the richest countries have tended to reappear, ironically, in the reverse form of the classical resource problems, i.e., as problems of disposing of a wide range of waste by-products. The pollution of the environment that results, and the costs of coping with such pollution, tend to increase more than proportionately and often discontinuously as the volume of discharge increases. The point is not that population growth is alone or even primarily responsible for the appearance of such problems but merely that the size of a problem for any given income level tends to be at least proportionate to population size. Once a

---

*For relevant discussions and some pertinent obiter dicta see (17-22).

physical saturation level is reached with respect to the per capita consumption of a given item, population growth of course becomes the dominant agent that causes changes in the aggregate volume of the associated waste-making processes. Passenger cars per head, for instance, in some countries are near to such saturation levels.

The income elasticity of demand for living space, travel, space-intensive recreation and, perhaps, solitude and unspoiled nature is demonstrably high and continuation of present trends in income and population is bound to result in increasingly felt scarcities of "nature" and "space," qualities for which only inferior substitutes will be available.

The conventional money measures of income will tend to be considered increasingly irrelevant as a reflection of welfare in a broader sense. The growing complexity of the organizational setup required to ensure the high income levels for a growing population imposes psychic, social, and political costs—notably with respect to privacy, a sense of individual identity, aesthetic satisfactions, freedom from control and excessive regulation, and other related matters.

It is likely that the required growing complexity of the economy and of the social organization in general will tend to render the system increasingly vulnerable to sudden technological and organizational breakdowns and/or will make the costs of insuring against such breakdowns increasingly heavy. It is also likely that uncertainty concerning the long-term implications of the technological adjustments needed to accommodate a growing population at high income levels will continue to be present, and the likelihood that such adjustments will cause unforeseen, irreversible, and undesired consequences, e.g., in man's biological environment, will become increasingly stronger.

It is hardly necessary to underscore that the points outlined above are highly tentative. Little systematic thought has thus far been devoted to exploring the eventual consequences in countries that have effectively escaped from the grips of the Malthusian trap of long-term economic growth while fertility remains at a level that results in positive rates of demographic increase. As a result, the economic prospects for the technologically advanced countries, and the share of population growth in shaping those prospects, remain insufficiently understood.

THE ECONOMIC ARGUMENT FOR FERTILITY CONTROL

The preceding section reviewed the arguments concerning the net economic gain that would be expected to result from a decline of fertility. It follows from these arguments that if a decline does take place *spontaneously*, its occurrence should be welcomed on economic grounds. It is now legitimate to go beyond this proposition and make an economic case for an active policy aimed at *inducing* such a decline? Only too often the answer is taken as self-evident because the potential gains appear to be substantial when compared to the presumed economic costs of various types of policy actions that are usually suggested. However, as illustrated in the preceding section, the discussion of the gain from declining fertility is usually carried out on the macro-economic level and in terms of average indices, such as income per capita. Hence the demonstration that "society" benefits may be less than automatically persuasive as far as individuals or individual families are concerned; collective action aimed at reducing fertility must necessarily operate through individuals or single families rather than through some mythical average man. It is unfortunate that so much of the discussion of the economics of fertility control tends to blur or assume away this elementary point.

If the policies proposed are to be both successful and economically sound, it would be necessary to be quite specific about the distribution of the benefits and the costs that are involved in particular courses of action. This section of the paper is devoted mainly to an outline of the considerations which seem to be pertinent to this issue, and which are neglected in the literature.

To clarify the possible loci of incidence of the benefits and costs in a fertility control program, it may be helpful as a first approximation to picture society as composed of self-perpetuating autonomous units, called families. It will then be useful to distinguish clearly, if only conceptually, between two types of economic justification for a given policy, applicable according to whether the economic consequences—costs and benefits—of any action to reduce fertility taken by an individual family are borne or enjoyed entirely by that family or whether such actions involve certain externalities, i.e., impose burdens or confer benefits on other families as well.

Fertility Control in the Absence of Externalities

If all consequences of fertility decisions remained within the boundaries of the family, the economics of population policy under the usual, if somewhat vague, assumption of a democratic society appear rather simple. Families should be left to judge what they consider best for themselves, and society should accept the decisions of individual families with strict neutrality. The argument that "society" would be better off if only parents had fewer children is as meaningless as to say that society would be better off if only more people worked on Sundays. Clearly the presumed gains that would have accompanied lower fertility would have been by definition derived from the gains concentrated in the very families responsible for that lower fertility. If, in fact, families opted for a higher number of children, ipso facto that option is revealed as preferred. Nevertheless, a policy of pure laissez-faire does not necessarily follow. Our autonomous families do not live in isolation; they organize themselves into a state to serve their interests in carrying out functions that are more efficiently carried out collectively than if they were left to the play of exchange relationships among families through the market. Recognized imperfections in the market and imperfections of the decision-making mechanism within the family itself constitute a prime ground for governmental action.

Providing Information. The case for intervention is strongest with respect to the provision of information. Optimization through private action assumes that families can act intelligently in their own interest, but information available for individual families may be erroneous or lacking for the following reasons:

1. Families may falsely assume that society expects them to follow certain norms of behavior. Thus the psychic cost attached to defying these imagined norms is removed if families are informed that no particular demands on their fertility behavior are imposed from the outside.

2. Families may be unaware of pertinent information concerning types, costs, availabilities, and technical and aesthetic properties, etc. of means for preventing conception or terminating pregnancy, or may have incorrect information on these matters. In either case the resulting decision will necessarily be suboptimal.

3. Choices with respect to parenthood are taken under conditions of uncertainty that can be lessened if parents are provided with pertinent information. Individual foresight in regard to the families' future economic prospects, opportunities, and interests and their appreciation of the dependence of these prospects on their fertility may be more limited than is warranted by the true uncertainty on these matters.

4. Intrinsic imperfections of the "demand" for children also decrease the chances of obtaining results that will be considered optimal ex post: "purchases" of children are "lumpy" and only moderately repetitive, the learning process is slow and largely retrospective. Many of the consequences of having a child are felt only in the long run, and purchases are irreversible.

It is, of course, commonplace that prospective parents seek out and acquire ex ante information on these matters on their own, and it is clear that under ideal circumstances such information would be reasonably well provided by the market or by informal communication. But at least some elements of an optimum informational package would be quasi-collective goods which could not be provided, or would be inadequately provided, by profit-seeking entrepreneurs. Informational messages through the mass media are a good example. Second, and most important, under backward economic conditions, the market mechanism may be simply defective in this field, creating a strong efficiency argument for collective action.

Providing Birth Control Services. It is primarily on the strength of this last argument that governmental intervention that goes beyond providing mere information and extends to providing the means of fertility control can also be justified. As supplies of contraceptives and related services (e.g., physicians) are in no sense collective goods, it would be better, in principle, to provide such items only for appropriate user charges, i.e., at prices that equal the marginal cost of the good or the service provided. Thus, even though government-organized, the quantity of the service consumed would be regulated by ordinary market principles, thereby eliminating the difficulties of setting the appropriate level of expenditures through the political process. On several grounds, however, a different solution may be preferred, notably providing services free or at less than marginal cost. The following arguments are presented:

1. As the provision of birth control services has many common elements with ordinary medical and public health services and as the latter for various reasons is often socialized, a unified treatment for the supply of all such services may be considered natural and/or preferable.

2. The inefficiency resulting from nonprice (or nominal-price) distribution may be considered negligible. Three points are pertinent here. First, all families are engaged in reproduction; hence it can be expected that the benefits will be broadly spread, affecting at some time or another virtually every family. As a consequence, redistributional effects will generally be moderate. Second, the intrinsic nature of the services is such that demand per family is physically constrained; hence, unlike free transportation or even free aspirin, the allocative inefficiency created by a low price, or by no price, will be small. Third, the cost per person may be low and free supply administratively more advantageous.

3. Any distributional effects that *are* involved in a subsidized system may be considered positive because such a system would extend to the poor services that were previously available only to the better-off. The same argument could justify the application of discriminatory pricing, i.e., collecting user charges set by the ability to pay, determined by some appropriate yardstick.

Given the socialized distribution of birth control services, the financing of research and development to improve the efficiency, safety, and acceptability of contraceptive techniques must, by necessity, also be collectively provided. Given the assumption of no externalities, the case for each financing is *not* that it will decrease fertility (although such decrease will be an inevitable by-product, unless compensated for by a reduction of involuntary sterility), just as the case for finding a remedy for headache need not appeal to beneficial effects on labor productivity (although that, too, would be a likely by-product). Rather, insofar as families have any desire to limit their natural fertility, efforts to that effect represent pure costs the reduction of which is desirable per se.

As to the magnitude of such costs and, by the same token, as to the potential increase in "consumers' surplus" that may be derived from the provision of improved techniques, it is enough to refer to the high prices paid, often by the poor, for abortions in countries in which abortions are illegal, and to the historical experience of European populations who achieved fertility control by voluntary means and in the face of social disapproval by methods involving heavy psychic disutilities. If past developments are a guide, the potential pecuniary benefits from research and development in reducing (for a given level of effectiveness, safety, and acceptability) the cost of contraceptives and the amount of personal services required are also large. These arguments seem to establish a solid case for more investment in this field, but in the absence of market tests, naturally the usual difficulties prevail in finding the optimal level.

Birth Control Services without Persuasion. It follows from the logic of the pure no-externalities model that "propaganda" of any form should be absent from it. The information offered should be strictly factual and the means for birth control should be provided cafeteria-style and without fancy packaging. To introduce elements of propaganda or even "persuasion" could be justified only on a frankly paternalistic basis, i.e., on the assumption that the leaders of society, or the elite, somehow know better what is good for the people, or rather that they know it now while the people will know it only later when, like children who grow up and in retrospect are grateful for the firm paternal guidance, they will give a more enthusiastic blessing than they would have earlier. It is difficult to deny that, in a society that expects to undergo rapid economic development which necessarily involves drastic changes in tastes in a fairly predictable direction, there is some element of plausibility in such elitist notions. Yet the argument is evidently a tenuous one; moreover the implied policy is likely to be effective only if the elite has a monopoly on the means of communication. At least, those invoking the argument should be required to be explicit about their assumptions.

In the light of the points just outlined, a double policy conclusion would follow from the no-externalities model. First, societies should leave families free to determine what level of fertility they wish to choose, and second, society should provide the best available information and means to make that freedom meaningful. Broadly speaking, these are the traditional principles followed by the planned parenthood movement and the avowed objectives of practically all governmental family planning programs currently in existence. It is evident, however, that very few countries come even near to fulfilling these ideals. An effective freedom with access to the best of modern technology of birth control is enjoyed by only a minority and is completely beyond the reach of perhaps half a billion families on the earth today.

Fertility Control with Externalities

In any society the assumption that the actions of individual families with respect to fertility do not affect others naturally does not stand up to closer scrutiny. That there are positive externalities (or that there are negative externalities that should be minimized) is explicitly recognized, at least in lip service, by every society's intention to shoulder collectively some of the costs of raising children, notably the cost of schooling. If a policy suggested in the preceding paragraph is actually adopted, its implicit philosophy may be more realistically described as follows: (a) Families should be permitted to act in their best interest as they see it in setting the level of their fertility, and society should extend help to render that freedom effective. (b) Society as a whole should accommodate itself to the sum total of these individual decisions as best as it can. Clearly, such a policy of enlightened laissez-faire is ideal only if the implicit Adam Smithian assumptions about the harmony of private and social interest are actually fulfilled. If externalities are present, utility-maximizing behavior within each family can no longer be trusted to add up to a social optimum and a prima facie case exists for governmental intervention to help achieve such an optimum.

The Case for Governmental Intervention. Consider, as the simplest example, a situation in which externalities manifest themselves merely in the form of an interdependence of individual utilities. Assume that in a society all families traditionally have high fertility, but now each family realizes that it has a choice and may opt for low fertility. Assume furthermore that each family actually prefers to take that option *provided* that all other families do likewise. Under the circumstances the natural expectation about other families' behavior is that it continues to be the traditional one; therefore, the rational choice for each family will be to preserve the old behavior. Government, by maintaining constant communication and assuring each family that if it chooses low fertility, all others will do likewise, can bring about a situation preferred by everyone to the old order and do so without violating in any way the principle of voluntary action by each family.

What happens to voluntariness if the assumptions underlying the game are slightly altered? Suppose again that families do prefer low fertility to high fertility, provided every other family chooses low fertility. But suppose that, once assured that all other families will elect to have low fertility, each family prefers high fertility for itself. A simple-minded example may give some plausibility to such behavioral assumptions. Suppose that children are desired because they provide both (a) parental satisfaction and (b) old age security, and that the traditional norm is six children per family. Suppose that each family would prefer some loss of parental satisfaction (e.g., have only three children) if old age support could be provided by a social security system, and that such a system can actually be set up if low fertility (three children per family) is universally adopted. A social improvement is possible if all families act in concert. However, once each family is assured that the others will have low fertility and that consequently the social security system *will* be set up, private satisfactions now will be maximized by *not* playing the game—to have both social security and full parental satisfaction, i.e., high fertility. Clearly, if each family is permitted to pursue its own interest, the traditional system will be a stable one. Only an enforced agreement among families, in other words government action involving coercion, can bring about a situation that was preferred to the old one by each and every individual family to begin with.*

A more difficult set of problems arises, however, when there are direct conflicts of interest with respect to fertility behavior, i.e., when one person's gain is another person's loss. A first layer of such possible conflicts of interest could be identified within the family itself. If the assumption that the family is a homogenous unit is discarded, there appear at least three potential types of negative externalities attached to high fertility: (a) those imposed on one of the spouses, usually though not always on the mother; (b) those falling on the adult members of the extended family; and (c) those falling on the children already born.

The underlying conflicts will not ordinarily be considered as justifying outside intervention; indeed, theoretically the family offers an ideal frame for dealing with externalities arising within itself because there is constant informal communication, comparison of satisfactions and interests, scope for endless bargaining, flexible compensatory schemes, mutual trust and affection, etc. By the same token the microcosmos of the family admirably illustrates the problems of correcting for externalities. The outcome of the bargaining and bribing process between the husband and wife, for instance, will be considered by an outside observer optimal for the couple only if he accepts the present distribution of power between the partners as desirable—a questionable assumption in the light of the strident feminist coloration of the family planning movement that apparently responded to an only too real need even in the economically advanced countries. Similarly the outcome of the bargain between the couple on the one hand and adult members of the extended family on the other hand (when such familial arrangement is relevant) suggests the possible difficulties in achieving an optimum solution in a political process when substantial interests of the minority—in this instance the couple who may derive prestige and power from their children but bear

---

*For a formulation of this generalized version of the famous "prisoners' dilemma" applied to optimum savings, see (23).

only a fraction of the costs of supporting them—clash with a badly organized majority, the members of which have only moderate objections to the relatively small extra costs imposed upon them by the fertility decisions of the minority. The children, of course, represent a completely disfranchised block, powerless to influence actions that affect their vital interests. The parents may act selfishly or may be simply ignorant of the disadvantages imposed upon their existing children by additional siblings.

Negative Social Effects of High Fertility. Negative externalities consequent upon high fertility pose, of course, much higher-order difficulties within the society as a whole. (One may add that there are analogous difficulties within the society of nations as well, a topic seldom touched upon in the literature.) A nonexhaustive list of these may single out three broad types of effects: undesired consequences of parental decision falling on (a) all other members of the society (as with pollution); (b) affecting some special classes of people (e.g., those whose livelihood is derived from wages only or those paying taxes); and (c) disadvantaging the young generation or, in general, the subsequent generations. As the negative effects are likely to be widely distributed, the possibility of bargaining and arranging for compensatory payments between individual families, and thereby moving toward an optimum, is practically nil. Neither will mere information about the existence of externalities change the behavior from which externalities originate: rational parents will correctly perceive that the effects of their actions on any particular family or on society as a whole are infinitesimally small.

The only workable approach would seem to be governmental intervention seeking to discourage fertility whenever it is found that the social costs of a marginal birth exceed marginal private benefits. Such intervention may take the form of outright coercion; or preferably, an appropriate set of economic incentives or disincentives may be applied to induce socially desirable behavior. It should be recognized, however, that the guidance economists are at present able to give for policymakers on such matters is less than solid. The extremely diffuse nature of the externalities involved; the fact that many of these externalities will manifest themselves through not easily traceable changes in the relative prices of factors and of outputs; the problem of taking into account the numerous positive externalities enjoyed by various segments of the society; the problem of considering the equity of the existing income distribution; the problem of weighing long-term effects against short-term consequences; and the necessity to introduce the intergenerational welfare considerations: all these problems make the applicability of cost-benefit analysis for policy decisions extremely restricted. These difficulties are compounded by the necessity to attach a cost measure to the corrective policy itself: a matter involving complex political, moral, and cultural considerations besides the often considerable purely economic costs.

The urgency of the need for an investigation of the economic aspects of potential alternative policy measures that could be proposed to bring about a more near equality of private and social costs, and most of all the need for a substantial refinement of the analysis and identification of the micro-economic distribution of the net negative externalities resulting from high fertility, could hardly be overemphasized.* Until such advances are forthcoming, the economic foundations of any proposed policy based on the externalities argument will remain unsatisfactory, despite the evident all-pervasive presence of such effects in developing, as well as developed, economies.

CONCLUDING REMARKS

The main conclusion that emerges from this survey is that virtually unqualified economic endorsement can be extended to efforts to ensure the freedom of families to determine their own fertility. Such a policy would require (a) governmental action for removal of positive restrictions on birth control; (b) provision of information that families need to make intelligent choices; (c) provision of the best available means for family planning; (d) development of improved means of contraception. For those who assume that free individual choices add up to a social optimum and for those who hold that society should accommodate its actions to the sum of individual choices in any case, this policy is the best, by definition. For those who hold that these assumptions are unrealistic because free individual choices may result in excessive fertility for society as a whole, the policy is merely a step forward but certainly one in the right direction. Although there will be disagreement whether or not population policy should go "beyond family planning," there should be a broad general agreement on the desirability of the policy per se.

Indeed, differences of opinion on family planning seem to center primarily on the effectiveness of the approach: a technical question involving no differences of principle. In what is probably the severest criticism in print of family planning as a population policy it is argued that, apart from lack of motivation, the policy does not work because the population does not know the means of contraception; because poor people are unable to purchase contraceptives and keep an adequate stock of them; because production facilities that would ensure production of contraceptives in sufficient quantities are lacking in the poor countries; because the import of contraceptives is expensive and is never regular; because there are no adequate channels for the commercial distribution of contraceptives; because contraceptives that are available are inefficient, whereas effective means are expensive and their use is repugnant; and because there is an inadequate network of public health facil-

*On this subject see in particular (25-26).

ities and personnel (27). Such a formulation, of course, implies that an important change with respect to any of the deficiencies listed could have at least some effect in reducing fertility; and that the objections to the policy are based on a set of specific technical and economic assumptions such as on the acceptability of the devices, their efficiency, their prices, etc. But such characteristics are surely amenable to change: prices can be reduced, devices can be made less repugnant, imports can be made more regular, etc. The degree of the change in fertility that can be expected as a result, hence a cost-effectiveness of such measures in terms of a lesser number of births or protection extended per man-year, is an empirical question to which empirical answers can be given.

Fertility Decline and Economic Development

It is often asserted, of course, that fertility decline is a consequence of development and not the other way around. The proposition is well taken, but if offered as a broad historical generalization, it is merely a truism. A detailed examination of the historical experience clearly indicates that even under sharply differing conditions as to contraceptive and communications technology, there existed no simple one-way relationships between the various elements of the development process: indeed a decline in fertility has started at varying levels of development and occurred at varying speeds (28, 29). This circumstance, which has thus far frustrated the attempts to construct a reliable predictive model of fertility behavior, would certainly suggest that the mix of the various components of modernization and the timing of their appearance can be manipulated within fairly wide limits. An early and rapid reduction of fertility, engineered through family planning programs, is thus at least a theoretical possibility not yet contradicted by historical evidence. The potential implications for speeding up economic development are obvious. If such a reduction does occur, it could hardly fail to induce significant feedback effect on other elements of the process of economic change.

This last observation suggests the most general type of positive externality brought forth by fertility reduction and the most plausible economic argument on which a first step beyond family planning, understood in a narrow sense, can be made. In today's less developed countries there exists a wide social consensus that the development processes are to be speeded up by purposive governmental action directed against the general manifestations of backwardness and by the positive promotion and support given to behavior consistent with a modern progressive society, the various facets of which form a mutually reinforcing network. Positive efforts to spread the acceptance of the modern pattern of reproductive behavior is part and parcel of the development process. Indeed, it is perfectly obvious that, once a social choice for modernization has been made, fertility reduction has to come sooner or later. It seems most likely that a fertility decline brought about within a voluntary framework but making use of a carefully engineered set of pressures and inducements would turn out to be less painful than decline under a process of later "natural" demographic adjustment, typically elicited by acute economic distress. Such pressures and inducements should *not* aim at changing the objective economic conditions of families in order to discourage fertility. To the contrary, the pure effects of income change, hopefully, will be consistently positive as development proceeds and as the economic status of the family improves. The policy should focus on changing the subjective image of these conditions in peoples' minds by exposing them to new knowledge and by manipulating their tastes, expectations, ambitions, and time horizons. An elaboration on this theme however is outside the limits of this paper.

The foregoing considerations would powerfully reinforce the argument concerning the economic usefulness of family planning programs, already well established even in the absence of externalities, and suggest that the total program size should be geared to the level of the demand that is being generated, or be determined by organizational and technical rather than budgetary constraints. As to the distribution of funds within the total budget, as long as a sizable demand for the services offered remains to be satisfied, the principle of equating the marginal productivity of the funds in the various subprograms should be applied. This will require continued collection and analysis of program data as to cost-effectiveness, as well as data gauging attitudinal changes and measuring the potential demand for various program outputs.* As a general rule, however, great caution should be exercised not to promote particular types of programs in preference to others on the basis of observed or anticipated short-term results. The returns to programs are necessarily lagged, and the lags are likely to differ significantly from program to program. Informed wisdom under such conditions will be a better guide for action than a narrowly conceived, cost-effectiveness analysis. It is equally important that policy decisions take into account not only the direct demographic effects, but the sociopsychological context of the program and its far-reaching economic ramifications as well.

References

1. Coale, Ansley J., and Edgar M. Hoover, *Population Growth and Economic Development in Low-Income Countries*. Princeton: Princeton Univ. Press, 1958.

*For an analysis of the richest body of data to date see (30). A cost-effectiveness study of selected family planning programs is currently under way under the direction of Professor Warren C. Robinson and will be made public later this year.

2. United Nations, Department of Economic and Social Affairs, *Proceedings of the World Population Conference.* New York, 1966. Vol. I, pp. 305-314.

3. Demeny, Paul, "Demographic Aspects of Saving, Investment, Employment and Productivity," World Population Conference/Working Paper/ 460.

4. United Nations, *Proceedings of the World Population Conference, 1965,* Vols. I-IV. New York, 1966-67.

5. Durand, John D., ed., *World Population. Annals of the American Academy of Political and Social Science,* January 1967. pp. 98-108. (Easterlin article).

6. Ohlin, Goran, *Population Control and Economic Development.* Paris: Organization for Economic Co-Operation and Development, 1967.

7. Clark, Colin, *Population Growth and Land Use.* New York: Macmillan, 1967.

8. Enke, Stephen, "The Economic Aspects of Slowing Population Growth," *Econ J*, March 1966. pp. 44-56.

9. Hoover, Edgar M., and Mark Perlman, "Measuring the Effects of Population Control on Economic Development: A Case Study of Pakistan." *Pakistan Devel Rev,* Winter 1966. pp. 545-566.

10. Meade, J. E., "Population Explosion, the Standard of Living and Social Conflict," *Econ J,* June 1967. pp. 233-255.

11. Stassart, Joseph, *Les avantages et les inconvénients économiques d'une population stationnaire.* Liège, 1965.

12. Tabah, Léon, "Demographie et aide au tiers monde. I. Les modèles," *Population,* May-June 1968. pp. 509-534.

13. Boserup, Ester, *The Conditions of Agricultural Growth.* London: Allen and Unwin, 1965.

14. Kuznets, Simon, "Population and Economic Growth," *Proceedings of the American Philosophical Society,* June 1967. pp. 170-192.

15. Kleiman, E., "A Standardized Dependency Ratio," *Demography,* Vol. 4, No. 2, 1967. pp. 876-893.

16. Myrdal, Gunnar, *Asian Drama.* New York: Random House, 1968. Vol. III, Appendix 7.

17. Baumol, William J., "Macroeconomics of Unbalanced Growth," *Amer Econ Rev,* June 1967. pp. 415-426.

18. Hoyle, F., *A Contradiction in the Argument of Malthus,* University of Hull Publications, 1963.

19. Jarrett, Henry, ed., *Environmental Quality in a Growing Economy.* Baltimore: Johns Hopkins Press, 1966.

20. Keyfitz, Nathan, "Population Density and the Style of Social Life," *Bio-Science,* December 1966. pp. 868-873.

21. Spengler, Joseph J., "The Economist and the Population Question." *Amer Econ Rev,* March 1966. pp. 1-24.

22. Villard, Henry H., "Economic Implications for Consumption of Three Percent Growth," *Amer Econ Rev Pa and Proc,* May 1968. pp. 502-512.

23. Sen, Amartya K., "Isolation, Assurance and the Social Rate of Discount," *Q J Econ*, February 1967. pp. 112-124.
24. Blake, Judith, "Demographic Science and the Redirection of Population Policy." *J Chron Dis*, Vol. 18, 1965. pp. 1181-1200.
25. Davis, Kingsley, "Population Policy: Will Current Programs Succeed?" *Science*, Vol. 158, 1967. pp. 730-739.
26. Berelson, Bernard, "Beyond Family Planning," *Science*, Vol. 163, 1969. pp. 533-543.
27. Podyashchikh, P., "Impact of Demographic Policy on the Growth of the Population," *World Views of Population Problems*, Egon Szabady, ed. Budapest: Akademiai Kiado, 1968. pp. 240-241.
28. Behrman, S. J., L. Corsa, and R. Freedman, eds., *Fertility and Planning: A World View*. Papers by Ansley J. Coale, Dudley Kirk, and Simon Kuznets. Ann Arbor: Univ. of Michigan Press, 1969.
29. Demeny, Paul, "Early Fertility Decline in Austria-Hungary: A Lesson in Demographic Transition," *Daedalus*, Spring 1968. pp. 502-522.
30. Freedman, Ronald, and John Y. Takeshita, *Family Planning in Taiwan: Tradition and Change*. Princeton: Princeton Univ. Press, 1969.

VI

The Effects of Population Growth on Resource Adequacy and Quality

Joseph L. Fisher and Neal Potter

One of the great and abiding questions for any society at any time in history concerns the relation between population and natural resources. In our time of the last few decades of the 20th century a fairly large band of neo-Malthusians remains concerned lest continuing and rapid population increase outrun the supply of food and other raw materials. A larger and very powerful group, especially in the countries that are more highly developed economically, continue to have faith that new discoveries, cheap substitutes, scientific and technological developments, and more rational management will stave off the day of Malthusian catastrophe. A rapidly increasing number of observers are turning their attention away from the quantitative aspects of the population-resource situation to the consideration of the qualitative side. Much more dangerous for the period ahead, they say, is the increasing pollution of water courses, the atmosphere, and the land itself, to the detriment of human and animal health, as well as to an aesthetically pleasing natural environment.

In terms of the sheer availability of adequate supplies of resource commodities—food, fuels, metals, water, and the like—the outlook to the end of this century for the more developed countries is reassuring; whereas for the densely populated, less developed countries (LDC's) the outlook is much more dubious and uncertain. In the qualitative sense, however, the prospect for excessive contamination of the natural environment is at least as discouraging for the more developed countries (MDC's) as for the less developed countries. A case can be made that the more developed a national or regional economy is, the more severe will be the incipient problems of environmental pollution. Developed countries have more industry and a higher proportion of their population living in cities. They consume more fuel and generate more waste residuals that ultimately have to be discharged into the water, the

---

Joseph Fisher is President of Resources for the Future, Inc.; Neal Potter is a member of the RFF professional staff.

atmosphere, or spread on or under the ground. Of course, the more developed countries are better able to plan and otherwise cope with residuals, but they are not always able to muster the investments and social discipline to do so. Less developed countries also have environmental quality problems to a severe degree, but these appear to be somewhat more localized and for the most part have not yet assumed the megasize that one finds in the metropolitan parts of the developed countries.

Of course, the quantitative and qualitative aspects do not occur in separate compartments; they are interrelated in their occurrence, their causes, their consequences, and the ways in which they can be dealt with. For example, upgrading the quality of water in the bays and estuaries of the world, on the shores of which most of the large cities are located, will require upstream storage of larger quantities of fresh water so that the estuarial pollution can be diluted and flushed out into the ocean. The yield of crops from agricultural land is greatly enhanced by the application of fertilizers and the use of pesticides, both of which can have deleterious effects on streams and lakes and even on wildlife and human beings. A solution to the increasing scarcity of certain minerals is to be found by making larger use of lower grade ores, by going to lower quality sources. As one scans the resource field one notices an all-pervading fact: there is a set of trade-offs between the quantity and quality of natural resource commodities. Resource development policies and systems of management must recognize these interconnections. Both the objectives of development and conservation and the means for their achievement will have to include qualitative as well as quantitative aspects if they are to be wise and efficient.

In this paper we shall deal first with the more strictly quantitative side and then turn to the qualitative aspects. Finally, in our comments that bear directly on policies and management we shall be concerned with both the quantitative and the qualitative; neither the statement of the issues nor the presentation of lines of solution can be divorced from either aspect. In considering the quantitative and then the qualitative environmental questions we shall strain a bit to present statistical indicators of trends and conditions. Our indicators will not be as clear-cut and definitive as we would like; however, we do believe that better policy and management will have to be based on more than hearsay and subjective judgment. If our statistical indicators are less than satisfactory, they can at least point the way for future efforts to create a better basis for understanding and then dealing with the problems.

THE QUANTITATIVE TRENDS AND OUTLOOK FOR RESOURCE COMMODITIES

In a recent article we attempted to examine world trends in resources in terms of several indicators of scarcity (1). For each major world region, and for some individual sample countries, we gathered together the best statistics we could find to trace (a) the consumption or output per capita of food, energy commodities, nonfuel minerals, and forest products; (b) the employment-output ratio; (c) the relative price trends; (d) the net import trends. None of these by itself tells as much about the tendency toward or away from scarcity as do all of them taken together. For example, increasing per capita consumption, decreasing employment-output ratio, declining relative price trends of resource commodities to prices generally, and a falling trend of net imports would indicate an easing of scarcity and an increasing plenty of resources.

For the United States, historical data do not point to increasing scarcity in any general sense. Indications as to future technology and supply possibilities, when matched against projected demands to the year 2000, also do not indicate a general tendency toward greater scarcity. There will, indeed, be supply problems for particular resources at particular times and places; but technological and economic progress, building upon an ample and diversified resource and industrial base, gives assurance that supply problems can be met.

For the more developed countries, particularly in western Europe, where the data are reasonably good, the trend is not unlike that for the United States.

For the underdeveloped countries of the world available evidence is far from conclusive, but it does warn against easy generalizations that these countries are either about to run out of raw materials or are going to experience an economic take-off right away because of plentiful supplies of food, energy, and raw materials. The picture is mixed: quite favorable for energy commodities, less so for food. For some less developed but heavily populated countries the race between food and people apparently will be a close one. As with the United States, only more dramatically, much will depend on the rate at which technological advances can be broadly applied and on the ability to keep open the channels of world trade (1).

From this overview we turned to the difficult exercise of projecting resource demands by major world regions. Based on the most recent high population projections of the United Nations (3.295 billion in 1965 projected to 4.551 billion in 1980 and 6.994 billion in 2000), our rough estimates of the materials which would be consumed in the year 2000 were made under each of the following assumptions:

1. The trends in resource consumption during the past decade continue for the next 35 years in the major regions of the world.

2. The average per capita level of consumption for the world as a whole in the year 2000 is at the level attained in the United States in 1965.

3. The average per capita level of consumption in the world in 2000 reaches the level attained by western Europe in 1965.

Food Supply

Tables 1 and 2 summarize our projections for major world regions, first for calorie consumption of food and, second, for consumption of energy in metric tons of coal equivalent. For food, it is interesting to note that the consumption trends of the decade mid-1950's to mid-1960's projected ahead to the year 2000 (Table 1, Column 3) indicate a total only about 10 percent less than what world consumption would be if everyone had the number of calories per day that the average U.S. citizen had in 1965. However, special warning is necessary here. Large and serious deficiencies in animal proteins and vitamins would remain in the world's average diet even if the gap in calories were filled. Figure 1 shows how much lower are the values of the estimated food supplies in the LDC's than those in the developed countries. These differences are due largely to deficiencies in high-value animal products—meat, fish, milk, and eggs—in the diets of less developed countries. Therefore, even the rate of increase of the 10-year base period of the mid-1950's to the mid-1960's (Table 1, Column 3) would not wipe out dietary

TABLE 1

Projections of Calorie Consumption in the Year 2000 Compared
with Prewar and 1965 Actual Consumption

(billions of calories per day)

	Actual		Calorie Consumption in the Year 2000 if[b]		
	Prewar	1965	Trend of 1952-56 to 1963-65 Continues	World Is at U.S. 1965 per Capita Consumption Level	World Is at West Europe 1965 per Capita Level
World	5,200	7,800	19,800	22,100	21,100
Northern America	460	680	1,190	1,190	1,130
Latin America	280	640	2,350	2,170	2,060
Western Europe	750	980	1,440	1,230	1,170
East Europe and U.S.S.R.	800[a]	1,100[a]	2,600[a]	1,800	1,720
Communist Asia	1,100[a]	1,400[a]	2,900[a]	4,400	4,200
Noncommunist Asia	1,400[a]	2,200[a]	7,000[a]	8,500	8,100
Africa	400[a]	710[a]	2,200[a]	2,700	2,600
Oceania	36	60	110	110	100

[a]Very rough estimate by the authors.

[b]United Nations' population projections multiplied by levels of consumption as indicated (see text).

Sources: Prewar and 1965 actual: United Nations' population data multiplied by indicated consumption levels from (2, 3, 4).

TABLE 2

Projections of Energy Consumption in 2000
Compared with 1938 and 1965 Actual
(billions of metric tons of coal equivalent)

	1938 Actual	1965 Actual	Energy Consumption in Year 2000 if		
			Trend in Consumption from 1955 to 1965 Continues	World Consumption Is at U.S. 1965 per Capita Level	World Consumption Is at West Europe 1965 per Capita Level
			(1)	(2)	(3)
World	1.79	5.5	40.5	67.6	23.7
Northern America	.71	2.04	6.45	3.64	1.27
Latin America	.039	.20	2.01	6.63	2.32
Western Europe	.56	1.09	3.84	3.77	1.32
East Europe and U.S.S.R.	.30	1.23	10.98	5.51	1.93
Communist Asia	.027	.32	6.42	13.5	4.74
Noncommunist Asia	.112	.39	9.94	26.1	9.14
Africa	.023	.093	.55	8.36	2.92
Oceania	.018	.061	.33	.34	.12

Sources: Special tabulations of world energy use done at Resources for the Future, Inc. (Washington, D.C.) from United Nations and other data sources.

deficiencies; and there could also be considerable difficulty in maintaining for the next 30 years the rate of increase in food output and consumption achieved in the base period. However, the near tripling of food output by 2000 that is required by a doubling of world population and a one-third increase in per capita output does not appear beyond the range of possibility in terms of sheer calories.

The chief hope for achieving such a target lies, of course, in the application of technology and management in countries at early stages of development. If the less developed countries could attain the yields in basic crops already achieved in North America, Europe, and Japan, the much larger world population at the end of the century could be provided with an adequate supply of calories. If the future levels of yields in the less developed countries equalled those expected in the developed countries, the LDC's would have grains above their requirements for food. This grain surplus could then be a source of more proteins if used for animal feed. Additional increases in output may be secured by cultivating new lands, particularly in Africa and South America, but this is generally less promising than better cultivation as a source of additional food.

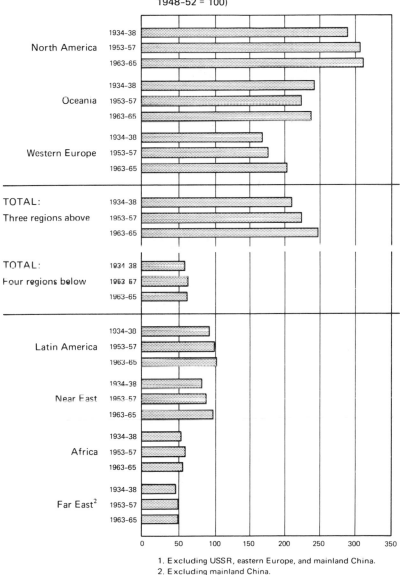

(Price-weighted indices, world[1] average for all food,
1948-52 = 100)

1. Excluding USSR, eastern Europe, and mainland China.
2. Excluding mainland China.

Figure 1. Estimated values of food supplies per capita by world regions, 1930's to 1960's.
Sources: (5, 6).

Many things will be required for a rapid advance in crop yields: more water for irrigation and more skillful application of that water, land drainage in many places, better seeds and methods of cultivation, more fertilizers and pesticides skillfully applied. Also required are a host of social, economic, and institutional changes, most importantly the shift from subsistence agriculture to the market economy. The "Green Revolution" requires heavy application of purchased inputs, such as fertilizer, pesticides, hybrid seeds, and often machinery and fuel. More favorable land tenure arrangements; the incentive of adequate prices for crops; extension and educational programs; adequate credit; better handling, storage, and distribution systems will be needed. Suitable combinations of measures which are designed specifically for both the soil conditions and the social situations in each less developed region are called for.

The problem posed by rapidly increasing populations is to make the necessary cultural and technical changes rapidly enough to stay ahead of the problem and raise standards of living at the same time. Few countries have attained increases in farm output of more than 4 percent per year; none of the developed countries has exceeded 4 percent for more than 5 or 6 years; yet a 3 percent annual increase in population wipes out most of even such a rapid rate of improvement. That the less developed countries can attain even greater rates of advance is shown, however, by Mexico's achievement in the last 14 years–1952-1966: a phenomenal 6 percent annual increase in agricultural output outdistanced a population growth rate of 3.33 percent per year, making possible an increase in farm output per capita of 2.5 percent annually.

The returns from India and a few other countries indicate that new seeds recently developed, in combination with other factors, have greatly raised yields where they are most needed. The story of miracle rice and wheat is beginning to unfold. More extensive utilization of world fisheries is helping to raise the level of protein nutrition in the world, as world catches rise about 6 percent per annum, nearly three times as rapidly as other foods and feeds. Resort to algae culture, and even petroleum and coal, as food sources may become practicable with further scientific and technical improvements. However, for the next few decades at least, the world cannot count on these farther-out possibilities for large contributions to its food supplies.

Institutional and material changes in production methods in the less developed countries could provide sufficient food in nearly all regions of the world. There are, of course, local situations in which the resource base is severely limiting, but few of these are likely to be so restrictive as to prevent a high degree of self-sufficiency. Some of the highest ratios of population to land (total area or agricultural land area) are in Japan and western Europe (see Table 3); yet these regions produce an average of about 80 percent of their food supplies. The cost of the imported 20 percent of the food supplies for these areas is about equal to the cost of their fuel imports, requiring 15 to

TABLE 3

Indicators of Pollution Sources

Country or Region	Area (000 sq. km.) Total (1)	Area (000 sq. km.) Agr.[1] (2)	Population Total 1965 (3)	Population Percent Urban (4)	Percent of Employ. in Nonagr. (5)	Population Density No./Sq. Km. Total Area (6)	Population Density No./Sq. Km. Agr. Area (7)	GNP (1966) Total (billion dollars) (8)	GNP (1966) Per Cap. (dollars) (9)	GNP (1966) Per Hectare of Agr. Area (dollars) (10)	Energy Consump. per Cap. (metric tons) 1965 (11)	DDT and Other Hydrocarbon Imports (mil. kg.) 1968 (12)	Fertilizer Consump./Agr. Area (kg./ha.) 1966-1967 (13)	Paper and Board Consump. per Capita (kg.) (1967) (14)
AFRICA														
Congo Republic	2345	510	15.6	22[a]	31	7	3?	1.73	108	34	.064	...	.04	4
Ethiopia	1222	810	22.6	...	12	18	28	1.48	64	18	.010	1.08	...	.5
Kenya	583	56	9.4	8[b]	12	16	170	1.14	116	200	.141	1.05	6.4	4
Liberia	111	40	1.07	...	20	10	27	.229	210	57	.267	...	...	2
Nigeria	924	220	58.0	16[c]	20	63	260	4.60	77	210	.048	1.46	.3	.7
So. Africa	1221	1020	17.9	47[d]	71	15	18	12.0	578	120	2.76	.46	4.0	35
Sudan	2506	310	13.5	8[e]	22	5	44	1.33[c]	104[c]	43[c]	.085		1.6	.9
MIDDLE EAST														
U.A.R.	1000	28	29.6	38[d]	45	30	1060	4.88	165	1700	.36	3.6[3]	109	6
Iran	1648	180	24.5	39[f]	43	15	140	6.64	263	370	.83	5.31	2.6	4
Iraq	449	110	8.2	44	50	18	75	2.20	262	200	.63	1.42	.6	1.6
Israel	20.7	12	2.56	78[g]	88	124	210	3.92	1490	3300	2.25	.50	33	43
Kuwait	16.0	.01	.48	...	99	30	—	1.70	3460	—	7.3	.05	...	25
Saudi Arabia	2253	20?	6.8	...	22	3	340?	1.12[c]	172[c]	560?	.54	.12	5?	.11
Turkey	781	540	31.1	26[d]	28	40	58	10.4	326	190	.37	1.60	3.5	7

TABLE 3 (Continued)

Country or Region	Area (000 sq. km.)		Population			Population Density: No./Sq. Km.		GNP (1966)			Energy Consump. per Cap. (metric tons, 1965)	DDT and Other Hydrocarbon Imports (mil. kg., 1968)	Fertilizer Consump./ Agr. Area (kg./ha. 1966-1967)	Paper and Board Consump. per Capita (kg.) (1967)
	Total	Agr.[1]	Total 1965	Percent Urban	Percent of Employ. in Nonagr.	Total Area	Agr. Area	Total (billion dollars)	Per Cap. (dollars)	Per Hectare of Agr. Area (dollars)				
	(1)	(2)	(3)	(4)	(5)	(6)	(7)	(8)	(9)	(10)	(11)	(12)	(13)	(14)
ASIA														
China–Taiwan	36	9.0	12.4	...	53	344	1400	3.14	245	3500	.66	.72	269	23
Hong Kong	1.0	.1	3.7	73[g]	93	3700	—	1.17[c]	335[c]	—	.60	.30	...	29
India	3268	1770	487	18[g]	30	149	270	43.8	88	250	.15	21.9[3]	7.0	1.4
Indonesia	1904	180	105	15[g]	34	55	580	10.6	99	590	.13	(.11)	1.1	.6
Japan	370	69	98	68	73	265	1400	98	990	14000	1.93	3.7[3]	307	88
Philippines	300	110	32.3	30[d]	43	108	290	9.0	268	820	.21	11.48	15	7
Thailand	514	110	30.7	18[d]	22	60	280	4.65	147	420	.12	4.05	5.4	3
LATIN AMERICA														
Mexico	1973	1030	44.1	51[d]	48	22	43	21.7	493	210	1.10	1.51	4.3	20
Nicaragua	130	18	1.72	41[c]	41	13	95	.60	349	330	.25	3.92	12	7
Argentina	2777	1380	22.4	63[h]	82	8	16	18.7	818	140	1.47	.8[4]	.4	30
Bolivia	1099	140	3.7	35[i]	35	3	26	.67	178	50	.22	(.06)	.1	2
Brazil	8512	1370	81	45[d]	48	10	60	27.7	333	200	.38	8.02	1.9	10
Chile	757	140	8.6	68[d]	74	11	60	5.14	576	370	1.12	(.54)	11	20
Venezuela	912	220	8.7	67[g]	71	10	40	7.9	879	360	3.2	(.40)	2.3	29

EUROPE, AUSTRALIA

	Col. 1	Col. 2	Col. 3	Col. 4	Col. 5	Col. 6	Col. 7	Col. 8	Col. 9	Col. 10	Col. 11	Col. 12	Col. 13	Col. 14
France	547	340	48.9	63[b]	82	89	140	103	2180	3200	3.3	(2.49)	99	80
Netherlands	36	22	12.3	54[j]	91	342	560	20.7	1660	9400	3.7	(3.40)	262	109
Sweden	450	37	7.7	77	83	17	21C	22.2	2850	6000	2.7	.40[3]	108	171
United Kingdom	244	150?	54.4	77[f]	95	233	36C?	106	1940	7100	5.3	(.66)	110?	117
Ireland	70	47	2.88	46[g]	68	41	60	2.93	1020	620	2.4	...	61	66
Greece	132	86	8.6	43[g]	47	65	100	6.6	764	770	.90	.40	30	22
Spain	505	300	31.6	57[d]	66	63	105	24.6	773	820	1.08	2.9[3]	25	30
Poland	313	200	31.5	49[d]	58	101	160	...	(600)	...	3.6	4.1[3]	72	29
U.S.S.R.	22402	6100	231	48[k]	67	10	38	...	(1000)	...	3.8	(1.63)	10	24
Australia	7687	1000?	11.3	82[g]	90	1.5	10?	25.2	2170	250?	4.7	2.84	11?	104
U.S.	9363	4400	195	70[d]	94	21	45	760	3860	1700	9.7	33.4[5]	29	232
All[2] LDC's	66000	15800	1530	24	32	23	97	218	150	140	.28	...	3.4	4.5
All[2] DC's	33000	8700	675	65	84	20	78	1170	1800C	1300	5.00	...	35.6	127

() or ? = incomplete, doubtful data.

... = unavailable.

— = not computed (relatively meaningless).

[1] Sum of "Arable land and land under permanent crops" and "Permanent meadows and pastures." Omitted are "Forested land," land "Unused but potentially productive," and "Built-on area, wasteland and other." The figures are rounded and in some cases adjusted downward because of the obvious difficulties of drawing a line between "pastures" and "wasteland," particularly where data are footnoted "rough grazing."

[2] Except centrally planned economies (including Yugoslavia among the centrally planned).

[3] Agricultural use in 1966, as reported to U.N. Food and Agriculture Organization.

[4] Agricultural use in 1963, as reported to U.N. Food and Agriculture Organization.

[5] Estimated total consumption in all uses, 1968 (U.S. Department of Agriculture estimate).

a - 1957	e - 1956	i - 1950
b - 1962	f - 1966	j - 1964
c - 1963	g - 1961	k - 1959
d - 1960	h - 1947	

Sources:

Cols. 1 and 2. (7, Table 1 with some adjustments. See reference 1.).

Col. 3. (8).

Col. 4. (9).

Col. 5. (7, Table 5).

Col. 6. Col. 3 ÷ Col. 1.

Col. 7. Col. 3 ÷ Col. 2.

Col. 8 and 9. (10).

Col. 10. Col. 8 ÷ Col. 2.

Col. 11. Resources for the Future computations from U.N. and other data (data in metric tons of hard coal equivalent).

Col. 12. Compiled from export data of principal producing countries which publish detailed tables by commodity and country of import. (Complete data was available for U.S. (1968) and Japan (1967); DDT data only, for France and West Germany (both 1968). Other major insecticide exporters, for which such detailed export data were not available included Netherlands, United Kingdom, Switzerland, and the Soviet Union. Data on chlorinated hydrocarbons reported "used in or sold to agriculture," in 1966 were taken from the U.N. Food and Agriculture Organization's Production Yearbook 1967 (7, Tables 143-148), although in most cases they appeared to be incomplete.

Col. 13. Compiled from (7, Tables 134, 136, and 138) and Col. 2.

Col 14. (11).

20 percent of their foreign exchange annually. This situation appears to pose no serious problem; nor does shipping, for the food tonnage is only about 15 percent of that of imported fuels.

The food imports of the developing countries are much smaller in the aggregate than those of the developed countries, about $6 billion as against $20 billion, but their food imports require about the same 15 percent of their very limited foreign exchange. Unless catastrophic changes occur in the rate of progress shown by the LDC's in the past 15 years, food imports should not be of unmanageable dimensions.*

Energy Resources

The outlook for energy resources is brighter than that for food. By the year 2000 world consumption of energy will quite possibly be about five times what it was in 1965. World consumption of energy in 2000 at the U.S. level in 1965 appears unattainable even though rates of increase in nearly all other parts of the world, and especially in the less developed areas, are expected greatly to exceed that of the United States during the next 30 years. The extrapolation of recent trends in energy consumption in the world does indicate that by the end of the century world consumption could be above the levels obtained in western Europe in 1965, with only Africa falling much below this level. (See Table 2.)

Will reserves be adequate for such an expansion of consumption? World reserves of fossil fuels (coal, oil, and gas) are estimated at 3 to 4 trillion tons of coal equivalent. This is about 500 times current annual consumption, and about 100 times the rate of consumption projected for the year 2000. Additional energy will be available from fissionable materials, for which reserves are estimated to contain several times as much energy as reserves of the fossil fuels, assuming that "breeder" reactors can be perfected. If fusion reactions using hydrogen are developed, they are expected to open up energy resources many times those of fossil fuels or fissionable materials.

Minerals

Reserves of the major metallic minerals, such as iron, aluminum, manganese, and copper must also be assessed. New discoveries, resort to lower-grade ores, and improvements in mining and processing should make it possible to support a growing population and an increasing industrialization during the coming decades. Reserves of metals are not as well known as those of energy materials, but it is clear that available quantities of iron, aluminum, and manganese will supply all projected needs for the next several decades at little increase in cost, and that more remote or lower-grade reserves can cover all

*See also T. W. Schultz, "The Food Supply—Population Growth Quandary," in this volume.

conceivable needs much farther into the future. The prospects are less clear for copper, lead, zinc, and many minor metals because of the conditions of occurrence and lack of adequate data on deposits already discovered. Of all metals and several important nonmetals, however, adequate supplies at present costs will be dependent—in the future as they have been in the past—on new ore discoveries, continued technological advance, and maintaining a world trading and investment system that enables the countries lacking particular mineral resources to draw upon those which have them. Advancing technology and changes in the relative prices of different metals will no doubt bring about substitutions of one metal for another, and of plastics and other more abundant materials for metals. These shifts will help prevent severe shortages. If price rises occur, they can be met by increased recycling of junk materials and other conservation measures that have a large potential for increasing the life of ore reserves.

Although the ultimate depletion of mineral reserves is theoretically inevitable, it is very difficult to say anything scientific about the prospects. For most minor minerals, data on reserves is extremely meager. For the major minerals, total depletion will come only after the world has changed so much in technology and culture that any forecast by the present generation would probably be irrelevant.

Forest Products

Of the major raw materials, our indicators of scarcity register grounds for apprehension and concern only for forest products, especially saw timber. The world will probably want a doubling or more by the year 2000. This may strain the world's capacity to produce, so that prices for timber products will force an even greater resort to substitute materials and unexploited forest zones than we have so far seen. However, the U.N. Food and Agriculture Organization (FAO) data indicate that half the world's output of saw logs and 37 percent of its total wood came from northern America and Europe in 1965, although forest acreage in these two areas was only 22 percent of the world's total. If other forested areas can be brought into more intensive production, the future situation could be greatly eased. Tropical hardwoods and the introduction of faster growing species, including hybrids, in other areas are large potential resources. They would add a bit of optimism to the picture, as would improvements in cutting and management practices in many parts of the world.

Water Supplies

The outlook for water supplies is difficult to assess on a world scale because of lack of statistical information on which to base projections. Furthermore, water statistics by countries or world regions mean very little;

water demand and availability has to be examined on a smaller scale by river basins and even subbasins. Obviously, water is in short supply in the dry and arid parts of the world, some of which are rather heavily populated. Floods constitute the main problem in other places where agricultural land and cities are subjected to devastation from excessive runoff. The problem boils down to one of adjustment of population and economic activities to the hydrologic situation in various places.

A number of possibilities exist for augmenting water supplies. Additional storage reservoirs can be constructed; evaporation and irrigation canal losses can be checked; water-consuming trees and plants can be removed; water can be recycled in industry; salt or brackish water can be substituted for fresh water in cooling and certain other uses; water prices can be raised to curtail consumption; whole river systems can be interconnected; surface and ground water sources can be integrated for more economic use; and so on. In many streams pollution abatement would yield large amounts of higher quality and, therefore, more usable water than is now available. Large gains can be made by legal and institutional changes which would result in some reallocation of water use away from irrigation, which in the United States comprises more than 90 percent of total withdrawals from streams, toward industrial and other much higher value uses. Possibilities for desalinating water exist, but costs are still so high at present that economic use cannot be expected in more than a very few places. It appears that the major water problem in most places for the future will be maintaining and improving its quality, especially in densely populated metropolitan and industrialized regions.

The Problem of Quality

We have seen that the known quantities of natural resources in the world are sufficient to feed the projected populations to the year 2000, if the requisite changes, particularly in agricultural methods, can be brought about. While some of our assumptions may be on the liberal side, others are conservative; for example, we have made no allowance for the increase in land that may become available for food production when machinery is substituted for animals as a source of power. Nor have we mentioned increased yields of food per food-producing animal—a source of large gains in the meat, egg, and milk-producing industries of the United States in the last few decades.

However, the changes we have assumed require the use of large quantities of fertilizers, pesticides, and—in many areas—water to bring output per hectare up to United States and European levels of output. These changes will produce burdens on the natural environment which are potentially quite serious. The "quantity" problem may be solved at the cost of raising difficulties with "quality."

Pesticides have already produced catastrophic impacts on many species of birds. Both the insect-eaters and birds of prey, such as the osprey and the American eagle, appear threatened with extinction by the effects of DDT and other long-lived insecticides. While the effects are heavily concentrated in the countries that use them most, particularly the United States, the nondegradable nature of these pesticides and their gradual worldwide dispersion means that their damaging effects will continue to spread and be greatly accelerated if other countries use them in anything like the quantities used in the United States. Limiting or even stopping the use of this type of insecticide seems imperative in the not-too-distant future; the impact on less developed countries may be serious, particularly as it may affect control of certain insect-borne diseases.

Other drastic impacts on the environment are to be expected from both increasing populations and adoption of new technologies. Primitive agriculture is notorious for its destruction of the soil through overgrazing, single-crop cultivation, and burning of vegetative cover. Larger populations intensify these problems, but new problems often result from the introduction of new technologies and new crops. Fertilizers may produce problems of soil salinity or eutrophy of watercourses and lakes. New plant species may be more vulnerable to disease or drought.

All the major sources of change—larger population, increased urbanization, new technologies, and higher levels of living—tend to create scarcities of the "new" resources of fresh air, pure water, and open space. New in the sense that they have not been allocated in the market place, have not borne a price, and therefore have not been subject to care and economizing, these resources pertain to "quality of the environment." Generally taken for granted, they are only gradually coming into the realm of measurement, analysis, and public policy.

Air Quality

Air quality has diminished rapidly as a result of urbanization, higher living standards, and modern technology. Urbanization, which is increasing much more rapidly than total population, is correlated with higher levels of per capita production (Figure 2) which in turn is closely correlated with higher fuel use (Figure 3). Mineral fuels which provide heat, electricity, and transportation have been the principal detractors from air quality. In some American cities the motor car is charged with producing as much as 80 percent of the total air pollution. In other areas, the principal polluters are ore smelters, blast furnaces, pulp mills, or steam plants for generating electricity. A quick index of overall air pollution is the consumption of mineral fuels, although the degree of impact depends on specific local conditions, including the

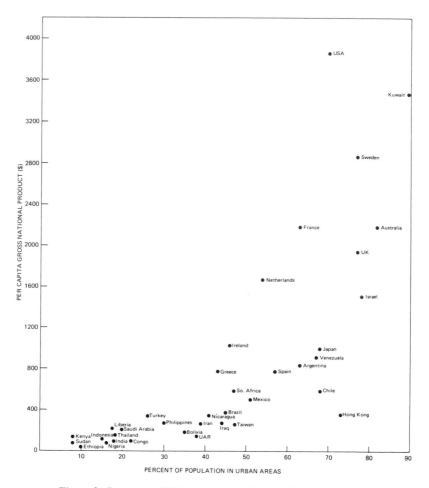

Figure 2. Per capita GNP and percent of population in urban areas.
Source: Table 3.

nature of the fuels used, the equipment used in their consumption, and the
local airshed conditions. Whatever the sources, air pollution is likely to increase with great rapidity.

Pure Water

Pure water has long been recognized as a kind of resource as cities, irrigation agriculture, and some mining areas have faced problems of adequate
supply and potability. Today water is a resource of increasing problems as
populations grow, cities become larger and more densely populated, and
water-polluting industries multiply.

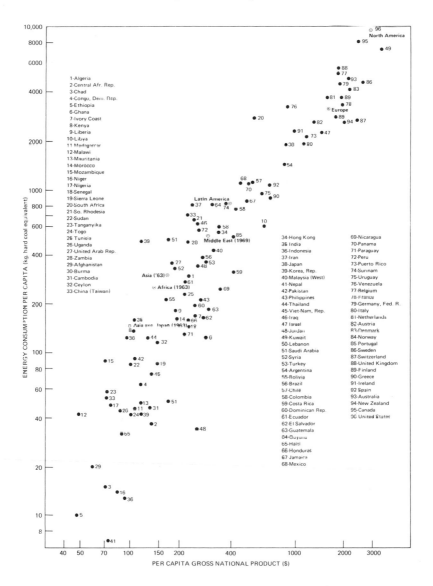

Figure 3. Per capita energy use and GNP, 1965 (excluding communist countries).
Sources: GNP (12), Energy—Resources for the Future tabulations.

As water of high quality and adequate supply and regularity of flow becomes scarcer, increasing public controls will be required, and increasing costs will be encountered in meeting the problems. The polluting industries face higher costs for chemical treatment, settlement ponds, cooling towers, and other devices to limit damage they cause to the environment. Cities face increasing costs for treatment and storage of water supplies and for sewage treatment plants.

Space and Density

Space as a requisite for production, housing, and the amenities of living has been recognized as a resource since early days; land and building rents have allocated it with a strong hand. What is beginning to be recognized now is the importance of common spaces–streets, parks, and the like–and of the spatial relationships among uses; i.e., the planning of employment, residences, transportation routes, etc. so as to minimize costs and congestion and to maximize amenities and conveniences. The growing size of modern cities, the increase of automobile traffic, plus the growth of slums, congestion, and disorder attest to the need for increased attention to planning for orderly city growth in developed and less developed countries alike.

Indicators of Pollution

The two general indicators of pollution sources, or latent environmental degradation, are population density (especially urban population) and gross national product (GNP) per capita (which is generally a result of industrialization). As a country or region moves toward higher levels in these two respects, it becomes increasingly likely to undergo environmental deterioration (air and water pollution, solid waste disposal problems, crowding, etc.) unless countervailing measures are taken to prevent or abate these harmful effects on the environment.

In Table 3 we have gathered some of the indicators of pressures on the natural environment for a wide cross-section of developed and less developed countries, and for all the developed countries, and for the less developed countries taken together (except the communist nations). In the first set of columns are population density, urbanization, and gross national product. Population density and GNP are calculated in relation to agricultural area as well as to total area of each country, in order to show pressures on land that is more intensively used. Mere surface area has limited relevance to either production or pollution problems, especially for such countries as Egypt, Brazil, and Australia.

It can be seen that, contrary to Malthus' thesis, there is little if any correlation between population density and levels of income. Although incomes are low in densely populated countries like India and the Philippines, equally low incomes are found in countries with low population densities, such as the Congo or Brazil; moreover, some of the highest income levels are in the countries with the greatest population densities, such as Japan and the Netherlands. The last two lines of Table 3 show that there is no overall significant relationship between the level of income and availability of land. There are, however, wide differences in urbanization and in output per capita and per hectare between the developed and developing countries. These differences contribute significant burdens on the natural environment. As Figure 2 shows, urbanization and high incomes are positively correlated. Both move up together, causing pollution problems to rise at a far greater speed then urbanization alone.

Population increase, particularly at the rapid rates now experienced by many less developed countries, makes an adequate response to these changes more difficult. Excess population and underemployment on farms rise not only because of improving farm technology but because of a rise in the total population. Urban populations rise under double pressures at rates sometimes as high as 10 percent per year, creating severe problems of planning, as well of capital accumulation to provide a decent living environment.

The last four columns of Table 3 show some indicators of particular types of pollution: fuel consumption as the principal source of air pollution; paper and board consumption as an indicator of solid waste problems; and fertilizer and insecticide use as an indication of land and water pollution arising from agriculture and health measures. Other indicators which might be used include wastes discharged into streams and lakes, scrap metal output, sulfur and other pollutants discharged into the air. Each of these specific indicators of pollution, as well as many others, is more or less closely associated with the two general indicators, population density and production.

In Figure 3 the relationship between GNP per capita and energy consumption is shown. The correlation is rather high, and the regression line is steep, showing that per capita energy consumption rises about fiftyfold for a tenfold increase in per capita GNP. Figure 4 shows a similar relationship between GNP and paper usage. Similar diagrams could be drawn, relating other specific measures of pollution to GNP per capita, population density, or some other aggregate. It seems clear from Figures 3 and 4 that rising income levels tend to add pressure on resources—both in quantitative and qualitative terms—more rapidly than does increase in population. Yet we know that higher incomes also add to the ability to combat pollution and produce substitute materials.

Concluding Remarks on Resource Policy and Management

We have tried thus far to outline major trends and prospects for resource commodities and the natural environment under the impact of continued rapid population growth. We have traced this impact in quantitative and qualitative terms, recognizing from the outset that the two are closely interconnected in the real world. Our major attention has been on world regions and especially economically less developed areas.

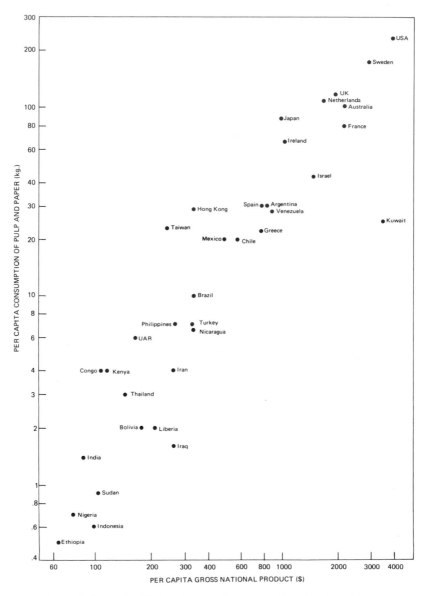

Figure 4. Per capita GNP and per capita consumption of pulp and paper.
Source: Table 3.

Developed Countries

In the perspective of the next 3 decades, our projections of demand for
resource commodities compared to our review of supply possibilities add up

to a mixed outlook. The more developed countries and areas should be able to accommodate the maximum population growth projected for them with due allowance for increasing levels of living, at least as far as *quantities* of resource products are concerned. This accommodation will not happen automatically, however. Scientific and technological advance will have to continue so that new sources of certain resources can be found and utilized and so that cheaper and more plentiful substitute materials can be made available; the channels of world trade will have to be kept sufficiently open so that raw material requirements that cannot be met domestically can be satisfied by imports; careful planning and adequate development investments will continue to be necessary, as will expanded programs of conservation. But there should be enough of the essential raw materials to permit the more developed regions to cope with population increase through the remaining decades of this century, and probably well beyond that.

Eventually any positive rate of population increase will lead to the absurdity of no more standing room on the earth's surface. Long before this comes about, social, psychological, or even biological checks to population increase will no doubt have occurred. It is the task of foresight and planning to set in motion activities which will make more extreme reactions and corrections unnecessary. The recent policy statement of President Nixon regarding population and family planning indicates the growing concern of national leaders with the problems of "overpopulation" even in the United States.

Less Developed Countries

For the less developed countries the outlook in the quantitative sense cannot be as favorable; it will remain in doubt, awaiting the success or failure of measures to check population growth, and programs to increase the supply of food, energy commodities, and other items. We come to the conclusion that the outlook is not as dark as it is frequently painted although the possibility of securing enough food for the underfed 2 billion or more people will remain in doubt for some years to come. Well-conceived plans and strenuous efforts will be necessary, primarily in the poor and less developed countries themselves. Of course, technical and financial assistance from the wealthier nations can help.

Resources

In energy and metal commodities the outlook is more favorable, based on recent production trends and on the outlook for discoveries and development, although even here there will be difficulty at times with regard to particular items. For purposes of human consumption, industry, and agriculture there appears to be enough of sheer global water supply; the issue resolves itself into one of investment, management, and conservation according to the local situation. Changes in policy and patterns of consumption will be necessary in many places if water supplies are to be adequate and cheap.

For some time it has been fashionable to say that although the outlook for resource quantities can be moderately optimistic even in the poor places, the prospects are overwhelming that everywhere the quality of the resource base itself will deteriorate at an alarming and accelerating rate. Comprehensive statistics which would indicate the trends in the condition of the natural environment of land, water, and air are hard to come by.

Environmental Quality

It is a matter of common observation that environmental quality in the great cities of the world, both in the developed and less developed regions, has deteriorated and that air pollution, water pollution, and landscape degradation have increased. At the same time planning and investment in preventive and treatment measures have improved so that human health and life expectancy may be more favorable now than at any time in the past. However, we must not forget that health conditions in any earlier period used for comparison were wretched.

We have tried to present statistically the two basic and overriding trends which, at least in an incipient way, make for pollution and environmental quality problems. We have arrayed a number of countries from the different regions of the world on scatter diagrams which indicate that the more densely populated and the more highly industrialized countries have the incipient conditions for greater environmental pollution. Less industrialized and less densely populated countries can gauge from the diagrams their own likely path toward pollution as they grow in population and industry. Trends in population density and production (or income) per capita are the general indicators of incipient pollution; statistics on fuel consumption, newsprint consumption, and use of DDT and pesticides are among the more specific indicators. All of these are associated with higher levels of economic development.

Whether the developed countries are actually experiencing more—or less—environmental pollution than less developed ones is a complex question. If investment and other efforts to abate or prevent pollution were the same in both, then environmental conditions would no doubt be worse in the more developed places. As things stand now, however, people in the less developed regions seem to be worse off. Their water supplies are usually less pure, both solid waste and sewage problems are severe, housing conditions very bad, and public health levels low. Densely populated urban slums and poverty-stricken rural villages alike are characterized by physical environments of generally poor quality, although specific conditions vary from one situation to another. In the large cities of less developed countries air pollution and congestion will typically be worse than in villages, but public health services, water supply, and job opportunities will be better.

We have spoken of incipient pollution, the conditions in which deterioration of environmental quality is likely to occur. These are potentials that can be circumvented or offset to a considerable extent by preventive and corrective measures, most of which will require planning and investment, public and private discipline, and a willingness to make sacrifices. Clearly it will be helpful for statistical indicators of environmental quality to be improved and extended as a basis for working out better policies and action programs. More complete information might make it possible to demonstrate a clearer relationship between population density and industrialization as indicators of incipient pollution on the one side and the amount of investment in preventive and corrective measures necessary to maintain a particular level of environmental quality on the other side.

In any such relationship between population and industrial density and expenditures on pollution abatement, certain underlying factors will be important. The attitudes of people toward waste creation and handling, as well as the habits and standards they follow, will have considerable effect on the quality of the environment. Some individuals and some nations seem to be almost instinctively tidier and neater than others. Pollution prevention and abatement is done largely through private action as a matter of course; waste paper is not thrown carelessly on the ground; food, building materials, and many other things are more completely utilized; police powers in the interests of public health and welfare are more acceptable; and so on. Some cities, states, and countries are much more inclined to legislate and enforce standards of environmental quality or to provide incentives for private individuals and groups to undertake mitigating activities. The reasons for these differences of attitude and behavior lie deep in the traditions, mores, and perceptions of longer-range social consequences. The structure and emphasis of religious beliefs may even have a bearing on the matter; certainly the sense of aesthetics is relevant. Much of this problem can be summarized by discovering how much awareness a particular group has of the requirements of ecological balance and the consequences of upsetting the balance by permitting an overload of waste residuals to be injected into the system.

Solutions to the problems of natural resource quantities and environmental qualities call for both government and private actions of a high order. In virtually all countries, discovery, development, and conservation of most minerals involve much government support and control; this involvement often provides severe tests of a government's ability to act in the public interest. Effective use of agricultural resources requires great efforts in public education, reform of land tenure systems, road-building, dam-building, and often price adjustments. Dealing with the problems of environmental quality, particularly in the cities, places supreme tests on municipal as well as higher levels of governments—tests which no governments in this country or any other have fully met. The most urgent challenge of economic development is the creation of more adequate political and social institutions for producing resource commodities and maintaining a natural environment of high quality.

REFERENCES

1. Fisher, Joseph L., and Neal Potter, "Natural Resource Adequacy for the United States and the World," *The Population Dilemma*, Philip M. Hauser, ed. Englewood Cliffs, N.J.: Prentice Hall, 1969.
2. U.N. Food and Agriculture Organization, *The State of Food and Agriculture 1968*. Rome, 1968. pp. 176-177.
3. U.S. Department of Agriculture Economic Research Service, Foreign Regional Analysis Division, *The World Food Budget 1970*. Washington, 1964. pp. 100-102.
4. U.N. Food and Agriculture Organization, *Production Yearbook 1958*. Rome, 1959. p. 239.
5. U.N. Food and Agriculture Organization, *The State of Food and Agriculture 1961*. Rome, 1961. p. 30.
6. U.N. Food and Agriculture Organization, *The State of Food and Agriculture 1966*. Rome, 1966. p. 33.
7. U.N. Food and Agriculture Organization, *Production Yearbook 1967*. Rome, 1968.
8. *United Nations Demographic Yearbook 1967*. New York, 1968. Table 4.
9. United Nations Statistical Paper K-3, *Compendium of Social Statistics 1967*. New York, 1967. Table 4.
10. United Nations, *Statistical Yearbook 1968*. New York, 1969. Table 191.
11. *Pulp and Paper*, "1969 World Review Number," June 25, 1969. p. 9.
12. United Nations, *Statistical Yearbook 1967*. New York, 1968. Table 186.

VII

The Food Supply-Population Growth Quandary

Theodore W. Schultz

The steeply rising population curves raise anxious doubts about the supply of food, doubts that loom large over the low income countries. A larger share of the resources of these countries is required to produce food than in the high income countries. This fact has obvious implications for the rest of the economy, including the availability of resources for schools and health facilities. The rapid growth in population implies that even more scarce resources may have to be allocated to the production of food. It also implies that household savings which are spent on children are not available to increase the stock of physical capital. In view of the seriousness of the scarcity of resources in low income countries, the critical unsettled question must be faced: Is the food-producing sector of these low income countries capable of increasing the supply of food enough even to keep up with the demand for food arising from the rapid growth in population?

Using an economic approach, I shall examine mainly the interacting supply and demand developments of food. As per capita income rises, the rate of increase in demand is even higher than the rate of population growth because the income elasticity of the demand for food is relatively high in poor countries. On the supply side, I shall extend the analysis to include the contributions of scientific and technical research to agricultural production. This research will be considered in terms of cost and returns and thus treated as an investment activity. Because the food-producing sector can and should contribute to economic growth, this analysis will not exclude the possibility of going beyond merely staying on a par with hunger (1, Preface).

There are difficulties aplenty whatever the approach. There are the practical short view and the troublesome long view. In the minds of many who are concerned about the population problem, the approach of economics fails to face up to the really long-run implications of population growth. In response to this concern, I shall consider a bit later the limitations of long-range

Theodore W. Schultz is Professor of Economics, University of Chicago.

projections to an economist. The heterogeneity of both the food supply and demand conditions throughout the world are exceedingly difficult to determine and to interpret. For the smaller part of the population—the people who live in countries with high per capita income—the adequacy of the supply of food during the foreseeable future is not in doubt. But for the low income (or "developing" or "less developed") countries, the part of the world where most of the people live, where the rate of population growth is high, and where agriculture has been niggardly, the food-population quandary is all too real (2, 3). No wonder there are fears of famine. Per capita food production in several countries with large populations failed to stay abreast of the increases in population during most of the sixties.* The large stocks of food grains that had accumulated in the high income countries with excess agricultural capacity were drawn down. As recently as 4 years ago the supply prospect seemed grim.

There is a new awareness, however, of the food problem. The recent food grain crisis[†] that became evident in parts of south Asia, mainland China, and even in the Soviet Union during the early 1960's has ruptured the unwarranted complacency that dominated so much of economic planning between 1945 and 1965.

My plan is to examine four issues. First, I shall comment on the state of our knowledge and attempt to distinguish between what is known and what is not known, and I shall also specify the time span under consideration. Second, I shall interpret the economic dynamics that characterizes the world food economy. Third, I shall call attention to some interactions between agricultural productivity and population growth. Last, I shall present the conclusions that emerge along with qualifications to be kept in mind.

KNOWING OR ASSUMING

The food supply controversy could mean that we are not asking the right question. The age-old question, "Will there be enough food?" remains unanswered in the minds of most people. If testimony were required, it has been voiced for centuries in the prayer, "Give us this day our daily bread." Theoretical and empirical analyses have not given us the knowledge to be sure of the answer. The reason why we do not know is due in part to the simplistic nature of the question in coping with an exceedingly complex problem. In part, it is a consequence of the fact that the state of knowledge with regard to food and population consist of fragments, and it is very difficult to integrate them. There is also the additional fact that even the fragments that are known

---

*Food production increased less than population in the developing regions, taken as a whole, between 1959-61 and 1965-67. See (4, Vol. III, Table 4).

†The thrust of my William W. Cook lectures at the University of Michigan, in 1964, is an analysis of the then critical state of the world food problem (5).

do not remain valid for long. They are made obsolete by the advances in the sciences, by new and better materials and skills, and by a wide array of improvements in economic opportunities that affect the production of food. Moreover, the established parts of this knowledge suffer from a high rate of obsolescence. The economist sees disequilibria in the food economy and also in the demographic components determining the growth in population. The responses of farmers and of parents to these disequilibria the world over, some slow and other rapid, contribute to the obsolescence of the knowledge that we possess.

Thus, caution is called for not only in interpreting the abundant agricultural and population statistics, but even more so in projecting the trends that these statistics appear to reveal. Interpretations are no better than the fragments of theory upon which we are dependent in analyzing these data. There is no general food-population theory for the purpose at hand. The processes that determine the rate of obsolescence of these bits and pieces of knowledge are as yet only vaguely understood. From the viewpoint of an economist, I shall mention several reasons why caution is necessary in drawing inferences from the recent past and also in making long-range projections.

We are dependent in large measure upon national aggregates that conceal a vast amount of heterogeneity. The differences among the components that make up the aggregate are often of decisive importance. In the production of food, for example, the heterogeneity of farmland is obvious to anyone who knows agriculture. The large differences in the quality of irrigation structures that are concealed in the total acreage under irrigation is another troublesome aggregate. A similar difficulty characterizes the measurement of each of the major classes of durable capital (6) and of the other inputs, including the skills of the farm labor force (7). It is fair to say that when it comes to explaining the responses of farmers to economic incentives (and linking these responses to agricultural production), these aggregates conceal as much as they reveal (8). Nor is micro-analysis—an examination of farmers—a satisfactory solution of this problem because of the difficulty of integrating the micro fragments, a difficulty which is in no small part a consequence of the gaps between micro and macro theory.

Land as Limitation

That the supply of land is limited is a truism, but as a factor in agricultural production, this limitation is the source of many misleading conclusions. Physically, the area of land within any country is given. The supply of cropland in any country is highly inelastic for any given crop year. If one assumes static economic conditions, the application of additional labor and capital to land is the classical case for diminishing returns; but these assumptions and the production effects derived from them do not explain the gains in productivity of modern agriculture that we observe occurring ever more widely throughout the world. It is a dynamic process, and a major source of the economic dynamics is the advance in scientific and technical knowledge that becomes embodied in new agricultural inputs. As modernization proceeds, the economic importance of land—measured by what it contributes to total agricultural production—declines in relation to the importance of other inputs. High-yielding crops, chemical fertilizers, pesticides, irrigation, and the farming skills to manage them all act as "substitutes" for land. As a consequence, the limitational attribute of land has been modified, making it less severe, markedly so in the technically advanced countries (9, 10). Here too, there is need for caution in interpreting the age-old stranglehold that land has held on the supply of food.*

> ... Yet no less an economist than Colin Clark [11], no longer ago than 1941, in his book, *The Economics of 1960*, came to the conclusion that the world was in for a dramatic rise in the relative price of primary products. Clark did not come to this conclusion by indulging in some easy, intuitive guesses, nor did he rely on a simple projection of past trends. He drew upon his vast stock of data; he proceeded to put them into his "analytical model" with its strong bent for diminishing returns against land, and ground out the following conclusion for 1960. "...the terms of trade for primary produce will improve by as much as 90 percent from the average of 1925-34." To speak of so violent a rise in the relative price of primary products as an "improvement" is a neat twist. ... But what are the facts as of 1960? Clark missed the price target altogether; his shot went off into space in the wrong direction. What went wrong? Did he assume too large a rise in population? On the contrary, the up-surge in population has been much greater than he assumed it would be. Has there been much less industrialization than he anticipated? Again, the answer is in the negative. Clark simply assumed a lot of secular diminishing returns against land and this assumption turned out to be invalid. (9, pp. 25-26; see also 12.)

Long-Range vs. Short-Range Projections

Long-range projections of the supply and demand for food are subject to all manner of doubts. Nevertheless, the propensity of economists to avoid long-range projections is viewed by some biologists and some demographers as one of the serious weaknesses of economics in facing up to the increasing pressure of population on primary (natural) resources. The sins attributed to economics are that it is shortsighted, all too practical, and overcommitted to monetary considerations, thus not sufficiently in touch with real biological

---

*The standard assumption of the highly inelastic nature of the supply of farmland and the implied rise in the supply price of the products from land as industrialization proceeds and populations increase persists.

and natural factors. It is true that the economist is shy in entering upon long-range projections. The reasons for his shyness are both analytical and practical. The rate of discount is a harsh, practical fact in making economic decisions whether they are private or public decisions. It is a strong analytical factor in determining the relevant time horizon. The higher the rate of discount, the shorter the relevant horizon. In a world where the rates of return to investment are high for reasons of new, highly productive economic opportunities to invest, the discount rate tends to be high. Then, too, the uncertainty about future events also shortens the horizon both in practical matters and in analytic terms. Even 5 year plans must be modified, as a rule, each year as new information becomes available. Moreover, economics tells us that one way of coping with the fog of uncertainty that limits our horizon is to remain sufficiently flexible so that one can act efficiently when new and better information becomes available. But such flexibility must be reckoned against its additional costs. In this connection, it is a serious error not to take into account the rate of obsolescence of the knowledge that we have with regard to food and population and the fragmentary nature of that knowledge.

I shall draw rather heavily upon the now-available data and estimates of the United Nations Food and Agricultural Organization (FAO) setting forth a world plan for agricultural development (4). It is a useful study, full of many new insights. The projections are keyed to 1985, a short 15 years from now. I shall be at pains, however, to point out as I proceed that even this short view is subject to important qualifications. New information already at hand makes it necessary even now to modify these projections.

In closing this section, I wish to enter a protest against the many naive long-range projections pertaining to food and population. There are all too many simplistic extensions of past trends. Birth rates are not established by robots. Parents are not fruit flies in breeding up to the food supply. As parents and as farmers, people the world over respond, for example, to changes in death rates and to changes in the opportunities to produce food, and knowledge about these responses is still very tenuous. The simple game of linking the little that is known to the unknown by appealing to convenient assumptions is the source of many misleading projections. In advancing the state of knowledge, conjectures transformed into assumptions are not sufficient.

THE DYNAMICS OF THE FOOD ECONOMY

The basic economic analysis rests on two interacting parts, the demand for and supply of food. For the purpose at hand, much depends on the dynamic properties of both parts. Our knowledge of the factors determining the changes in the demand for food is much better than that pertaining to the supply. The effects of price and income upon the demand for food are in fairly good repair, and also, but to a less extent, the effects of changes in the age composition of a population and in the mix of occupations as a consequence of population growth and industrialization. The demand effects of changes in taste, should they occur, are not known, however.

What the noneconomist often fails to see is that the consumer demand for food, as it is revealed by the behavior of households, is not necessarily a demand for the nutritional requirements of an adequate diet. It should be obvious that man eats foods, not nutrients. Nutritional "food budgets"* have no effect upon the demand for food until the nutritional information is known by consumers and they make it a part of their preferences, or unless the government resorts to income measures and price incentives that shift the demand toward better diets.

In regard to the supply of food, our knowledge of the factors and the processes that explain the increases in supply over time is far from satisfactory. It is weak because the sources of economic growth are, in general, inadequately specified and identified; it follows that all too little is known about the relative costs and returns from these several sources. Economic growth models that depend on national agricultural production aggregates are as yet not capable of explaining the processes that are at work altering the supply of food. The production of food by agriculture, viewed as a dynamic process, accounts for most of it. Yet a large part of this process awaits explanation. The economic dynamics that characterize this set of production activities are primarily a result of the availability of new classes of inputs associated with the modernization of agriculture. However, it is difficult to get at the costs and returns pertaining to each of these inputs. As a first approximation, the following distinction is useful. Farmers cannot obtain the types of agricultural inputs that are necessary to modernize from within agriculture. Hence the key to this modernization is held by persons, private and public, other than farmers. Firms operating for profit, nonprofit private agencies, and public bodies are all *outside of agriculture* in the sense that they do not engage in farming.

It would require a monograph to examine adequately the supply of food, but I am restricted to a brief overview of the farm and food-producing sector. I shall attempt, however, to account for changes in the supply in two situations: first, where agriculture is bound to traditional inputs and is in equilibrium with respect to the economic opportunities that such inputs afford; second, where agriculture is in transition in adopting modern agricultural inputs and is in disequilibrium in exhausting the new economic opportunities

---

*See for example the U.S. Department of Agriculture (USDA) Report, *The World Food Budget 1970* (13). The distinction between what consumers demand and what scientists recommend as an adequate diet is clearly presented in FAO, *Indicative World Plan* (4, Vol. 2, Chapter 13, paragraphs 74-76).

that such modern inputs afford (8). The state of knowledge with regard to the economics of the supply of food can perhaps be summarized best in terms of the following propositions—fluctuations in weather and other natural vicissitudes aside.

1. Farmers in low income countries are not indifferent to changes in economic incentives, i.e., to changes in farm product and factor prices. Empirical analyses of the response of farmers to changes in price leave little room for doubt on this issue; the responses are clear and they are consistent with economic conditions (1, 8, 14-26).

2. Farmers respond to the market demand—including their own demands—provided the market demand is correctly revealed to them in the prices that farmers receive for their products and pay for the inputs they purchase (1, 17, 24, 27-30).

3. The prices that farmers receive for their products can be depressed or enhanced by government policy. How long this can be done is an unsettled question. The governments of several of the larger low income countries were able to depress the prices of farm products during the 1950's and early 1960's, some of them with the assistance of P. L. 480 food grain imports from the United States (1, 29).

4. In some countries farmers are dependent on the factors of production that they are accustomed to and know the value of from long experience, after years of trial and error they have arrived at an economic equilibrium with respect to the production possibilities of these factors. Where these conditions hold, agricultural production is niggardly, in the sense that there are no *gains in productivity* from increases in the application of additional quantities of such factors.* This proposition does not imply that the total production will not increase. What it implies is that the gains in productivity associated with the use of agricultural inputs of better quality, including new forms of superior inputs, will not be realized (1, 5, 8).

5. As modernization of agriculture advances, the supply of food becomes more "elastic." What we observe, however, consists mainly of shifts in the supply schedule. The increasing role of agricultural inputs that are purchased by farmers is a major explanatory factor of the tendency toward a more elastic supply.

6. The favorable shifts in the supply, defined as increases in production at some constant price, or at a somewhat lower price relative to consumer prices, are a consequence of improvements in the underlying agricultural production possibilities.

7. The sources of these improvements are to be found in developments outside of agriculture. They come largely from the following sources:

---

*This proposition is based on an economic conception of *traditional* agriculture as it is formulated in my *Transforming Traditional Agriculture* (8, Chapters 2, 3, 5, 6).

(a) new biological materials from the advances in the biological sciences (31);
(b) reductions in the cost of producing chemical fertilizers (32);
(c) reductions in the cost of transporting these heavy fertilizer materials (better ocean shipping facilities and larger freighters, more economical ways of moving these materials overland—even pipelines to transport nitrogen);
(d) reductions in the cost of applying fertilizer to the field on which the crop is grown (33, 34);
(e) increases in the supply of many new products that are used to protect crops from pests, insects, and crop diseases and to control the growth of weeds (pesticides, insecticides, fungicides, and herbicides) (4, 35);
(f) increases in the availability of diesel motors and of electricity for electric motors to operate tubewells;
(g) more tractors either to supplement or replace draft animals; and
(h) improvements in the skills of farm people, of major economic importance as the process of modernization becomes increasingly complex and as the availability of new types of agricultural inputs increases (7, 36, 37).

An economic perspective of the food supply depends on the interpretation of these propositions as the supply responds and adjusts to changes in the demand. I shall restrict my interpretation mainly to developments that are determining the supply of food of the low income countries. The FAO interpretation is instructive; I shall begin with it. My own interpretation which comes next is more modest. I shall also comment on the effects of agricultural modernization on rice and wheat (the two most important food grains), because they are more telling than any overview.

The FAO Interpretations

The FAO has marshaled an impressive body of technical and economic information on the demand and supply of food (4). It is more comprehensive than either the *Asian Agricultural Survey* (35) or the array of foreign agricultural economic reports of the United States Department of Agriculture (USDA). All these reports, however, supplement each other. It should be borne in mind that the core of the FAO study was prepared under the shadow of near-famine conditions in parts of India during the mid-60's. The remarkable increases in the production of wheat and rice, especially wheat, in India and Pakistan as a consequence of the rapid adoption of high-yielding new varieties that are responsive to fertilizer, along with a large increase in the supply of fertilizer, occurred after the FAO study was almost complete. In several comments throughout the report some account is taken of this development, but is is not an integral part of the model that is employed to guide the empirical analysis. The growth in the demand for food in the developing countries is projected to increase at an annual rate of 3.9 percent.* By comparison the production of food during the 10-year period 1955-57 to 1965-67 increased only 2.7 percent per year and during the first 6 years of the 1960's, it was down to 2.4 percent per year (4).

The urgency which pervades the FAO recommendations for increasing the tempo of agricultural development in the low income countries is strong and clear. The reasons for the urgency are also clear. At that time recent increases in food production had not stayed abreast of the increases in demand. The projected 3.9 percent per year increase in demand, between the FAO base years and 1985, would require an increase in the supply of food exceeding that achieved during the first half of the 1960's by 60 percent (3.9 compared to 2.4). Is such an increase feasible? The FAO answer is in the affirmative. In analyzing the prospect for success, the FAO report presents a very plausible case. The reason for this perspective is stated succinctly in the last volume (4, paragraphs 74 to 79).

I offer three comments on the FAO report. First, it is at its best in analyzing the utilization of land, the biological and chemical inputs, the mechanical components and engineering structures serving agriculture, and the institutional adjustments (land reform, credit institutions, and others). Second, the anticipated increases in the demand for food are probably on the high side with respect to population growth (2.6 percent per year), but somewhat on the low side with respect to income effects on the demand for food. I shall return to the income prospects later.

Third, although this report discusses prices at several points (in addition to Chapter 8 which is devoted to price policies), the treatment of prices is not an integral part of the analysis. The statements on prices are not amiss, but they are essentially ad hoc assertions. The critical role of relative prices of products and of factors of production and changes in these prices in determining the demand and supply is not an explicit variable. The overall economic growth model used in this study is of the fixed-price family of models. For this reason the FAO study does not analyze systematically the function of product and factor prices in the consumption and production of food. The omission of these prices as variables in the model seriously limits the validity and usefulness of the FAO recommendations.

A Modest Interpretation

This interpretation of my seven propositions is not intended to be complete; I simply want to identify several of the more important developments

---

*The "population effect" (increase in population) accounts for 71 percent and the "income effect" (increase in income) for 29 percent of this annual rate of growth in the demand (11, Vol. III, paragraphs 25 to 29).

that in large measure account for the economic dynamics under way in major parts of agriculture in the low income countries. Farmers in these countries are responding to the improved pattern of farm prices. They are beginning to purchase large quantities of new types of agricultural inputs because it is profitable for them to use these inputs. They are investing in durable forms of capital because the expected rate of return is high. I shall not examine the role of large irrigation projects (38, 39) although they are one of the major factors in the high rate of increase in agricultural production in a few countries; for example, Mexico (18). Investments in tubewells (as in Pakistan and India) are highly profitable, accelerating the rate at which they are being installed. The two strong dynamic developments that I shall consider are agricultural research and chemical fertilizers. I shall also present a short overview of developments in the low income regions.

Agricultural Research. The high payoff on agricultural research in the contributions it is making to the production of food grains, and to a lesser extent to that of feed grains, is no longer in doubt. The successful pioneer work on wheat in Mexico by the Rockefeller Foundation in cooperation with the Mexican government is widely known; and similarly, the rice work in the Philippines, which has become a joint research enterprise of the Rockefeller and Ford Foundations. India is also benefiting from research there pertaining to corn, millets, and other crops—first sponsored by the Rockefeller Foundation. These three country-based research enterprises by no means exhaust the list (1, 31, 40-47).

The social rate of return to investment in scientific and technical knowledge that enters into agricultural production activities is high relative to that from most other investment opportunities.* There are as yet no indications of diminishing returns to this class of investment during that part of the future that is relevant for economic decisions. The social rate of return to investment in research pertaining to Asian agriculture is in all probability even higher than it is in the technically advanced countries. It is one advantage in entering late upon the process of modernizing agriculture (1, 29, 40, 45).

In view of the importance of agriculture in India, it is interesting to consider why the agricultural scientists in India delayed so long in taking advantage of the new biological materials. Organized agricultural research was established in India before independence. But until very recently few resources were devoted to the development of high-yielding varieties of rice and wheat.

---

*A number of careful studies have been completed estimating the social rates of return to investment in agricultural research. I have summarized the results of these studies in "The Allocation of Resources to Research" (48). The most comprehensive analysis is that by Evenson (49); it shows a social rate of return for U.S. agriculture of about 50 percent per year. The results of the Ardito-Barletta study (50) on wheat and corn research in Mexico indicate an even higher social rate of return. The pioneer study in this area is (41).

The puzzle is, why this long neglect of the advances in biological information in developing new and better varieties? There were competent agricultural scientists in India who were specializing in rice and wheat. It is my contention that they saw the demand of farmers as a demand for varieties that would perform best, given the depleted soils, the weather uncertainties, the limited control of water, and the poor farm equipment that characterize so much of India. Their assessment was undoubtedly correct. It was also clear to them that the new high-yielding varieties of wheat and rice are strongly dependent upon fertilizer, but they were serving a country with virtually no commercial fertilizer.

To argue ex post that Indian agricultural scientists should have anticipated the recent remarkable increases in the supply of fertilizer available to farmers in India is pointless. It should also be noted that until recently neither the government nor farmers were aware of the modern possibilities of research; therefore, they did not bring their influence to bear in favor of such possibilities. Instead they at least tacitly agreed, particularly with the most talented scientists, that the specialists would engage in the type of scientific and academic pursuits that was their wont. Now that they are aware of new possibilities, government and farmers are using their influence to bring about a change. Now, too, scientists are responding.* They are now actively at work improving the quality of the new wheat and rice varieties as food, determining the proper application of fertilizer that the new high-yielding varieties require, and searching for effective ways to control diseases and pests, for better seeding techniques, and for improvements in land management that the new varieties and the fertilizers call for (43).

Fertilizers. Another development which also has its origin outside of agriculture and which is having a strong positive effect on agricultural production is the large reduction in the price of fertilizer materials. The decline in the price of fertilizer is primarily a consequence of lower cost made possible by gains in productivity that have been achieved by the fertilizer-producing industries.[†] These gains have come, in large part, from advances in industrial technical knowledge. Since the end of the 1930's there have been two series of price declines. The first occurred before 1964-65 and the other since then. The following data show that in the United States fertilizer prices declined by one half relative to farm products prices during the decade from 1939-40 to 1950. (If one were to use the consumer price index, the relative decline would be very much the same.)

---

*I have drawn a part of this paragraph from my previous work (48) and from correspondence with Sterling Wortman of the Rockefeller Foundation.

[†]For an economic analysis of the gains in productivity in producing fertilizer, see Sahota (33, 34).

1939-40	100
1945	62
1950	50
1955	52
1960	49

During this first period, the lower fertilizer prices were transmitted to farmers mainly in western Europe, the United States, Canada, and Japan. The response of farmers in these countries to the cheaper fertilizer accounts for a large part of the increases in crop production. But throughout the low income countries—except for Taiwan (51), Mexico (18), and a few local areas—the cheaper fertilizer did not reach the mainstream of farmers in these countries. During the second period, which began in 1964-65 and is continuing, the cost of producing nitrogen is declining substantially once again as a consequence of an additional major technical advance. Furthermore, the cost of producing potash has also declined as the production of potash has shifted toward Canada.* Now, belatedly, many more farmers in low income countries are obtaining fertilizer at prices relative to the price of food grains so that it makes it profitable for them to use fertilizer, especially where the new fertilizer-responsive varieties of grains are at hand. *But this process of benefiting from cheap fertilizer has only just begun; it will take more than a decade for these low income countries to exhaust the agricultural production opportunities from this source.*

Later, when I turn to the production of wheat and rice, I shall show that the stage is now set throughout major parts of the low income countries to produce food grains at lower real cost than formerly. The availability of cheaper fertilizers, along with the high-yielding varieties of wheat and rice, has become a strong dynamic factor in this process. The following estimates in millions of metric tons (4) provide a perspective of the upward trend in the total quantity of world consumption of fertilizer nutrients.†

1938-39	9.2
1955-56	23.1
1965-66	46.3
1967-68	55.1

The fertilizer tonnage doubled between 1955-56 and 1965-66. The rate of increase has been rising further since then. The less developed countries are

---

*The more recent decline in the price of sulphur is now reducing the cost of producing phosphate fertilizers.

†A very rough measure of the additional crop production that is technically implied is approximately 5 tons of grain for each ton of fertilizer nutrients applied. Thus, the 9 million additional tons of fertilizer used in 1967-68 compared to that of 1965-66, expressed in terms of additional wheat, implies an increase of 45 million metric tons, or 1.66 billion bushels of additional wheat (52).

gaining in relative terms. (See Table 1.) But with the information now available, it is not possible to determine when production and consumption of fertilizer will reach an economic equilibrium.

Modernization. Turning next to a brief overview of farm-food supply developments, the modernization picture is made up of several parts. It is doubtful that agriculture in China is undergoing much modernization, although the evidence is sparse. In the planned economies of eastern Europe and the Soviet Union, the facade of agriculture is being modernized, but

TABLE 1

Increases in the Utilization of Fertilizer
in the World between 1955-56 and 1965-66

	World Total (in Million Metric Tons)		Developing Countries (as Percent of World)		Compound Growth Rates in Fertilizer Utilization in Developing Countries	
					1955-56 to 1965-66	1961-62 to 1965-66
	1955-56	1965-66	1955-56	1965-66		
Nitrogen N	7.1	19.2	17	19	11.6	12.8
Phosphorus Pentoxide P_2O_5	8	14.9	9	12	9.7	10.7
Potassium Oxide K_2O	6.8	12.2	5	10	13	17.8
Total	21.9	46.3	10.6	14.6	11.3	13

Source: (52, Table 2, p. 22).

agriculture continues to perform far below par because of economic inefficiency. The Latin American scene is mixed. Many parts of agriculture continue to stagnate because the economic opportunities to increase production by using modern agricultural inputs are concealed for reasons of economic policy.* The prospects for agriculture in these parts of Latin America remain dim. But the exceptions are noteworthy. Mexico is in the vanguard; agricultural output increased at a rate of 4.6 percent per year from 1940 to 1965 (18). There are some favorable signs in the pampas of Argentina, in regions of Brazil, and in parts of agriculture in some other countries.

Turning to south Asia, it is undoubtedly true that the modernization thrust is fairly strong (29, 35, 44, 53, 54). Important parts of agriculture in India, Pakistan, and Thailand, South Korea, Taiwan, and the Philippines are

*For an extended examination of the Latin American scene, see (1, Part 3, 9.1; 55).

progressing. This forward thrust is mainly a consequence of better farm prices; new varieties of wheat, rice, and other crops that are fertilizer-responsive; and the availability of more and cheaper fertilizer. There is also a boom in tubewells and related water-lifting equipment. It should be noted, however, that the advances in agriculture could be brought to a halt if these countries were to return to the cheap food policies of the recent past or if serious, widespread diseases or pests were to reduce the productivity of the new varieties of crops.

I mentioned earlier that, as the modernization of agriculture proceeds, the contribution of land to agricultural production declines relative to the value of the rest of the agricultural inputs. This process is a consequence of the increases in the use of modern inputs that are purchased by farmers, and this set of inputs increases relative to that of land. This development implies that agriculture becomes increasingly dependent upon other sectors, including imported materials and services. It also implies that agricultural land recedes as the *limitational factor*, contrary to the Ricardo-Malthus approach to food and population (2, 9, 10).

As a rule, the opportunity to modernize agriculture is very unequal within countries. The heterogeneity of agricultural production possibilities, especially in large countries, sets the stage for serious income disparities and for marked differences in the population pressures among farming areas. In other words, the modernization of agriculture alters significantly the *comparative advantage* of the agricultural areas within the country. Except for a few small countries such as Denmark, western countries have also not been spared. Clearly, parts of agriculture in Italy and France have long been depressed. The U.S.S.R., despite her centralized planning and administrated economy, is not spared, and the depressed Appalachia is poignant testimony of the very uneven agricultural development in the United States. Japan, however, appears to have achieved a better record than have most western countries in averting this problem (29).

Mexico and India illustrate the implications of this unequal development. Mexico, which is now well along into the third decade of successful modernization of parts of her agriculture, faces increasingly serious income disparity among major agricultural areas. As the modernization of agriculture in north and middle Mexico has progressed, the stagnant south has become, by comparison, a major depressed area. The internal migration from the depressed south has profound effects on the redistribution of the Mexican population. In India the comparative advantage of agriculture is shifting to the northern parts and to the major "rice bowls" of the southern parts as a consequence of modernization. A large triangle in central India is losing out competitively, and many millions of people who are dependent upon agriculture reside in this large area. They will be left behind. The new fertilizer-responsive varieties of rice, wheat, corn, millet, etc. and the larger, cheaper supply of fertilizer are decisively less productive within this large triangle because of the lack of rainfall and of water for irrigation. *It would be hard to overstate the challenge of discovering policy approaches to cope with this problem that would stand the dual tests of economic efficiency and of welfare and that would be manageable in planning the development of India.*

Modernization is increasing the economic value of educating the farm labor force, especially farmers. The new opportunities and the adjustments in production that modernization entails increase the demand for skills (36, 37, 56). The changes in the demand for farm labor derived from the process of modernization are in general of two parts. First, in the short run, the demand for farm labor increases in the farming areas that are best situated to take advantage of modern agricultural inputs. Second, in the longer run, as more complete modernization takes place, the demand for farm labor declines—at first, relatively, and later on, even absolutely—to the total demand for labor in a growing economy.

An Interpretation Restricted to Wheat and Rice

Wheat and rice are the two principal food grains. They are superior grains in terms of many desired properties. In calories alone, a pound of wheat contains 1,497 and a pound of rough rice, 1,356 calories (57). The production, consumption, and marketing of wheat and rice—and competition between the two—affords still another partial view of the dynamics of the world food supply. Looking toward the next decade, the following inferences emerge (58).

1. Except for P. L. 480 wheat and other concessional supplies, *the substitution* of imported wheat for domestic rice in the heartland of the monsoon areas is not a significant factor, except for Japan and some of the larger coastal cities at the fringe of these areas. Nor are these areas likely to import additional quantities of wheat either to substitute for domestically grown wheat or to supplement it, except in the case of Japan and in areas serving some coastal cities—bad crop years aside.

2. The price of wheat per ton has declined markedly relative to that of rice, with wheat selling at substantially less than half of the price of rice in international markets. This large difference in the prices is decreasing somewhat, but wheat will continue to sell for a good deal less than rice in these markets.

3. The *cereal* production opportunities in Asian agriculture have improved measurably in recent years (29, 54); the reductions in real cost from this development are likely to occur somewhat more rapidly in producing wheat than in producing rice, e.g., in India and Pakistan; therefore, within these countries some domestically produced wheat will be substituted for rice by consumers (43, 54).

4. Except for Argentina, the major countries that produce exportable surpluses of wheat have increased production greatly since World War II by using new and superior agricultural inputs, and they have thereby reduced the real cost of production. Argentina continues to be at a marked disadvantage in this competition because it has not been profitable for Argentine farmers to increase yields. Success in obtaining substantially higher yields depends in large measure upon favorable technical and economic conditions for the utilization of fertilizer, mainly nitrogen.

5. In the major countries that now produce exportable surpluses, such as Canada, Australia, and the United States, additional mechanization is contributing more toward saving labor than toward increasing yields per acre. More important than additional mechanization is the availability and use of fertilizer-responsive grains along with cheap fertilizer and pesticides, as well as the technical possibilities of increasing yields at a profit when fertilizer and pesticides are used.

Until recently, monsoon rice production—the core of the food economy in the monsoon area—has barely managed to stay abreast of the increases in population, except for Japan and Taiwan. World wheat production, however, increased much more than rice. The explanation of the upsurge in wheat production since World War II is fundamentally of two parts: (1) favorable producer wheat prices and (b) improvements in production possibilities from modernization. In western Europe the decline in the price of fertilizer and the high protected price of wheat account for most of it. In Canada and Australia, where mainly dryland wheat is grown, the large gains in production have been due less to modernization via cheap fertilizer than to other improvements and generally profitable wheat prices. (Fertilizer is generally unsuited to dryland wheat.)

In the United States the federal program designed to check the acreage devoted to wheat could not wholly counteract the incentive value of government checks added to the price of wheat. Cheap fertilizer applied where it is not too dry, mechanization, and other new production advances have increased production despite the reductions in wheat acreage. As stated earlier, production in Argentina lagged for want of price incentives and fertilizer. Until very recently in India-Pakistan the producer incentives were also unfavorable; fertilizer was scarce and dear relative to the price of wheat; so there was no inducement to bring in or to develop wheat varieties that would be fertilizer-responsive. Wheat production in the U.S.S.R.—despite the changes in the pattern of producer incentives and the thrust of mechanization—has probably become more rather than less dependent upon weather (59). New and remarkable today are the *recent wheat crops of India-Pakistan—well over 20 million metric tons.*

What are the wheat and rice signals telling us about production and utilization? My interpretation of these signals is as follows:

1. The real cost of producing wheat in countries where wheat production has been modernized has probably declined by more than one half since the mid-1920's.

2. The real cost of producing rice in the countries where rice really counts had not declined until recently, and the recent modernization of some rice production has not as yet had any substantial effect in reducing the price of rice.

3. In countries where rice consumption is important and where the production of wheat and rice overlap to some extent and the production of each is being modernized, wheat has a head start; for example, in India and West Pakistan the recent modernization of wheat production is proceeding more rapidly than that of rice.

4. In general, further reductions in the real cost of producing wheat are likely to match reductions in the real cost of producing rice during the next decade.

5. Wheat may gain somewhat on rice as a food grain in parts of the "rice world," but except for Japan and Taiwan, it will mainly be wheat that is domestically produced.

6. Japan and Taiwan aside, wheat grown in the surplus-producing countries will not make much headway in replacing rice as a food grain in the major monsoon countries, with the exception of some coastal cities.

In the "rice world" the economic dominance of rice over wheat continues to be secure. The all-too-ready explanation is that rice-eaters simply will not eat wheat or wheat products. According to this view, consumer preferences in the "rice world" are strongly set against wheat, and therefore, the declines in the price of wheat relative to rice matter very little. But this widely held view of consumers in the rice-eating part of the world fails to see the lack of consumer incentives to shift to wheat.

If we had a reliable consumer price index for this area and if we had valid estimates of the opportunity costs (the costs of not choosing an alternative) of producing rice under traditional farming conditions in this area, my hypothesis is that they would show that this index and these costs moved virtually horizontally between the mid-1940's and the mid-1960's. It would follow that *there was no economic incentive to substitute wheat for rice* (58; 60, p. 135).

In the domain that belongs to wheat, the price signals are not ambiguous; the underlying supply and demand developments are also clear. In the wheat-producing countries that have modernized wheat growing, the real costs of producing wheat have come tumbling down. All the king's price supports, tariffs, quotas on imports, and programs to manage wheat production cannot put Humpty Dumpty together again. However, it is obvious that in these countries there can be very little substitution of wheat consumption for rice consumption. Moreover, as per capita incomes rise, less wheat is consumed per capita, the inevitable consequence when it becomes an inferior commodity revealed as such by the income elasticity of the demand for wheat as food. The one major outlet for wheat that conceivably could be expanded is to use more of it as a feed grain.

Assuredly, wheat is cheap relative to rice in the "international" trade domain, but this fact in itself tells us little. These prices of wheat do not explain the normal consumption of either wheat or rice in low income countries, because so much that is consumed does not enter the international market. Except for Japan, the recent past movements of wheat into the monsoon rice areas have obviously been in response to food emergencies. In mainland China, it was the aftermath of the "big leap forward." In India, it was the bad monsoons and the availability of P. L. 480 wheat. Tiny Hong Kong and several other similar markets are the exceptions.

In closing this interpretation of the wheat-rice economy, the principal implications are as follows:

1. The supply of these two superior food grains is increasing at a higher rate than that of the demand for them. A declining real price is implied for food grains. The predominant factor shifting the supply is the modernization of wheat and rice production.

2. Agricultural modernization is no longer confined to the temperate zones, nor is it restricted to mechanization. The thrust of modernization is now strong in south Asia. Crops grown under irrigation are showing large gains from the application of fertilizer which is relatively cheap in the world and from the adoption of fertilizer-responsive food grain varieties which are being improved rapidly.

3. The *real costs* of producing food grains are falling. Although particular governments may delay and thwart agricultural modernization by underpricing farm products and other governments may distort the economic efficiency of agriculture by overpricing farm products, they can only postpone, at a high social cost, an adjustment to efficient food grain prices consistent with agricultural modernization as a strong supply factor.

4. World food grain prices are not made in Washington, the Argentine, Japan, or New Delhi—nor by the European Common Market. The market forces at work are much stronger than any of these governments. A particular government can seriously impair the world competitive position of its agriculture, as the Argentine has by thwarting its agricultural modernization.

5. The competition between "cheap" wheat from the high income countries and "dear" rice from the monsoon heartland has been a minor sideshow in the world markets for food grains. However, the modernization of both rice and wheat production within the "rice world" is proceeding impressively today. Although it is not yet certain whether the cost of producing wheat will decline more than that of producing rice, it is more certain that the prices of

food grains are in the process of declining relative to other consumer prices throughout large parts of the monsoon heartland.

ADDITIONAL INTERACTIONS BETWEEN AGRICULTURAL PRODUCTIVITY AND POPULATION GROWTH

The interacting supply and demand developments of food have held the stage up to now. The next scene features the supporting actors. I now turn to the effects of population growth and agricultural productivity upon these factors: the supply of labor—its age composition, schooling, and skill; the demand for farm labor; family savings; the value of children to parents in farm work; internal migration as farming areas become depressed; the income of families generally; and the decisions of parents in having and rearing children. These effects are revealed in additional interactions that occur between agriculture that is gaining in productivity and a population that is experiencing a high rate of growth. I am mindful of the fact that although these effects can be perceived, there is a paucity of information when it comes to determining their quantitative importance. Stating them briefly, and leaving aside the reasons for these interactions, they can perhaps be presented best as a series of tentative propositions.

Farm Labor

For the time being in low income countries the labor force (hired workers, farmers and their families) employed in farming is increasing. In general, the higher the rate of increase in the population as it adds to size of the labor force, the stronger the economic tendency that the employment of additional labor in agriculture will rise during the near future. This proposition implies that in many of these countries the ratio of farm workers to the area of land under cultivation will rise, and in some of them the size of the farms will decline during this period. However, it would be an error to infer from this proposition that the modernization of agriculture cannot proceed under these conditions. Modern agricultural inputs, including farm machinery and tractors, are highly divisible (53). There is little room for doubt on this point in view of the successful agricultural development of Japan (61) and Taiwan (51). The development and adoption of high-yielding varieties of rice, the use of chemical fertilizers (17), and millions of small garden-type tractors are all parts of the successful Japanese experience. It is probably true, however, that the cost of supplying new technical and economic information to farmers by agricultural extension rises for a given farming area (country) as the number of farms increases. The farm income disparities that are in the making within agriculture, and the seriousness of these disparities for the future, are compounded by a high rate of population growth. But this interaction can best be stated in another proposition.

Child Labor

Parents who are motivated to exploit their children and who are self-employed farmers have a wide range of opportunities to do so. The aim of poor parents "in having children may be to borrow from them and have them more than 'pay' for themselves during the parents' own lifetime."* It is obvious that the child has no say whatsoever in the decision of the parents to have the child and virtually no choice but to do the work required by the parents while he is under their control. What is not obvious is the nature of these exploitation opportunities and the extent to which they are exercised. It is clear from the increasing number of social measures in low income countries to protect children that there is a growing awareness that children can be, and to some extent are, exploited. The proposition advanced here asserts that when parents are motivated to exploit their children, the self-employment of farmers affords farm parents the opportunity to do so.

Family Savings

The savings of farm families in low income countries are invested partly in their farm and partly in rearing their children. The effects of agricultural modernization upon savings are far from clear. Where the income from farming rises, the savings of farm families will undoubtedly rise. But what effect the income-increasing modernization will have upon allocation of the total savings between the new high pay-off physical investment opportunities associated with agricultural modernization and the investment of parents in children is an unsettled question. For most families where there is "high fertility, rapid population growth, and high dependency," these demographic attributes may be strongly associated with low physical savings rates.† The process of modernizing agriculture would appear to have two offsetting effects. First, the increase in the rate of return to investment in farming would induce parents to use less of their total savings in having and rearing children in order to increase the proportion of their savings for physical capital formation. Second, modernization increases requirements for farm labor, adding to the value of children for farm work. The increase in total savings would, in other words, permit parents to increase the amounts they invest in both physical and human capital. The question of which of these two effects is the stronger awaits empirical analysis.

*T. Paul Schultz, "An Economic Perspective on Population Growth," in this volume.
†Ibid., citing (62-66).

Disparities in Agriculture

The problem of increasing disparity in income among farming areas is rooted in the heterogeneity of agricultural production possibilities, especially in large countries. Therefore, the opportunities to modernize agriculture are, as a rule, very unequal within a country. Thus, the stage is set for income disparities and for marked differences in population pressures among farming areas even if there were no population growth. The proposition here advanced is that the higher the rate of population growth, the greater the stresses on the economic system, on the political process, and on the people in the depressed areas—because the solution entails a vast amount of internal migration.

Farm Food Prices

Under competitive conditons, the gains in agricultural productivity that are obtained from the adoption and efficient use of modern agricultural inputs are, in general, transferred to the consumers of the farm products as equilibrium is approached. These gains are revealed in lower farm-food prices which are transferred to the benefit of consumers; they become a *consumer surplus.* During any decade the absolute amount of this consumer surplus that is realized from the gains in agricultural productivity necessarily becomes smaller per consumer—when it is distributed among an increasing number of consumers.

Population Responses

Finally, I want to call attention to some of the comprehensive implications concealed in the proposition about parents' choices presented earlier. The expectations of farm people have long been established by the niggardly economic opportunities of traditional agriculture and by general poverty.* These circumstances lead to a complex set of interactions, the core of which is between (a) the substantially better economic opportunities in areas of modernizing agriculture which are accompanied by the availability of cheaper food for the rank and file of the population; and (b) the rate of population growth. The unsettled question is: What are the population responses to the better economic opportunities and cheaper food? In terms of micro theory of the household, farm parents may view their additional income from more modern farming as transitory income. They would then add it to what they otherwise would have saved for investment. Some part of it would be allo-

---

*In (61) the paper by Kaneda, "Long-Term Changes in Food Consumption Patterns in Japan," presents evidence that consumers in Japan were slow in shifting to a more expensive diet as their incomes rose.

cated to having and rearing an additional child, a decision fortified by the improved opportunities for remunerative child labor. The cheaper food implies a higher real income, and the effect of income upon the demand for the satisfactions that parents derive from children would depend on whether children are a "superior good" and, if so, on the income elasticity of the demand for children.

Stated in this way, the interactions under consideration would appear to have disquieting implications. In the past, the settlement of large areas of productive agricultural land in the Americas and Oceania, along with the reduction in the cost of overseas transportation, accounted in large part for the cheaper and vastly increased supply of food, especially during the nineteenth century. The associated high rate of population growth among Europeans and people of European origin should be kept in mind (67). We are at a juncture in economic history during which a vast increase in food grains and of other crops can occur in the long settled, highly populated low income countries. Will there be an analogous growth in the population which is substantially a consequence of more plentiful and cheaper food?* This is indeed one of the major unsettled questions of contemporary history.

CONCLUSIONS WITH QUALIFICATIONS

The food-supply-population quandary is rooted in a complex set of problems, many of which are beyond the reaches of our analytical tools and the knowledge that we now have. I have used food grains in the low income countries as a proxy for the food supply in these countries. It is, however, a simplification, for an all-inclusive concept would include the other food crops, vegetables, fruits, feed to produce animal products, fish, and nonfarm

---

*Wyon has kindly made available to me a preliminary draft of Chapter 11 of the forthcoming book (68). The demographic data for the Khanna Village, rural Punjab, India, show a marked rise since 1966 in the population growth that appears to be a consequence of some in-migration and of a rise in the birth rate. This rise in rate of population growth seems to be strongly associated with the recent rapid agricultural modernization in the village. (See figures 118 and 119 in the book.) Whether this rise in births reflects a permanent increase in the completed size of families that parents plan to have or a temporary consequence of change in the age composition of the population due to youthfulness of in-migrants cannot be ascertained as yet.
I quote the following with permission:

The decade ending with the wheat crop of 1969 witnessed a transformation of agricultural method and an enlarged gross community product. Those segments of society involved in agriculture had strengthened their position, while tradesmen and others were losing place in the village economy. For farm workers, land owners, as well as employed, this was a new way of life, with long hours of work and new skills to learn. Education was recognized as an increasingly valuable asset, for girls as well as for boys. The age of women at marriage advanced well beyond the trend underway in 1959. . . . New investments directed to the land, (fertilizer, high yielding seed, intensified irrigation and mechanically aided cultivation) were yielding more return.

food additives and products. Populations are also heterogeneous aggregates, and whereas people are bound to a country, the technical contributions from the advances in science are not. Commodities are traded, and capital moves from one country to another to a limited extent. Simple projections of food and population trends can be very misleading. The declining ratio of land to man tells us little about the food supply, which is more dependent upon advances in science and economic efficiency than on land.

The scarcity of resources that characterizes the low income countries is pervasive and dominates. Many of the serious resource problems associated with high rates of population growth would remain unsolved even if the food supply in low income countries were to increase at a higher rate than the rate of population growth.

As a step toward clarification, I turn to several conclusions that emerge from the analysis presented in this paper.

On the anxiety with respect to famine there is relief in the following conclusion: The probability is very low that widespread famine will occur during the near future, the next decade or two. Surplus stocks of farm foods are at record levels in the high income countries with excess agricultural capacity. Meanwhile, the production of food grains in the low income countries has risen sharply, notably the production of wheat in Pakistan and India.

The forward thrust of agriculture is strong throughout major parts of south Asia. Wheat and rice production in these long-settled, populous parts of the world is showing gains in productivity resulting from the advances in biological-agricultural research and from the increasing supplies of cheaper fertilizer materials. Barring a return by the governments of these countries to their former cheap food policies, which had depressed the economic incentives of farmers to purchase and utilize modern agricultural inputs, and barring the occurrence of widespread wheat and rice diseases or pests, the supply of domestically produced food grains will continue, during the near future, to increase relative to population growth.

The low income countries in south Asia that were incurring a large and an increasing deficit in food grains, and thus becoming ever more dependent during the 1950's and early 1960's on food grain imports, have already begun to reduce markedly their dependency on imported food grains. The prospects, restricted to the foreseeable short view, are that their dependency on food grains from the countries with excess agricultural capacity will continue to decline. The high income countries with excessive agricultural capacity will undoubtedly be under increasing economic pressure to reduce the quantity of resources allocated to agricultural production.

The real costs of producing farm foods are declining as a consequence of the gains in agricultural productivity. As these lower costs are gradually transformed into lower food costs, they become a consumer surplus. The conclusion that follows is that the economic stage is set for a substantial part of the increases in per capita income that may be realized in many low income countries to originate out of the modernization of agriculture.

Thus far the conclusions have a favorable ring, but they cover only a part of the story. The part that remains raises questions about resource problems that leave little room for hopeful complacency. The problem of depressed areas within agriculture, which is strongly associated with economic growth and agricultural modernization, is likely to become increasingly serious in the larger, agriculturally heterogeneous, low income countries. There are no easy solutions to this problem. Moreover, the problem is compounded by rapid population growth. The massive internal migration of people from these depressed areas to areas that have a comparative advantage in agricultural productivity, or to other locations with job opportunities, places a heavy burden on the political process, on the economic system, and on the people who must bear the cost of migration.

The growth in population under the economic conditions that characterize the low income countries will further increase the supply of the farm labor force. In the farming areas that are favored by agricultural modernization, the demand for farm labor will increase for a considerable period while the marginal product of this labor increases. Farming units may become smaller, but fortunately the divisibility of virtually all modern agricultural inputs is such that the reduction in the size of farms is not giving rise to scale diseconomies, *except* for the public programs that are necessary in disseminating new technical and economic information to farmers, and *except* in rewarding the higher levels of farming skills associated with schooling.

The unsettled question, with perhaps the most serious potential implications, concerns farm people who acquire more real income with which to contribute to the modernization of agriculture and consumers in general who benefit from the lower real cost of food production. *What will they do with the additional savings they acquire as a consequence of these developments?* They may use these additional savings to increase the stock of physical capital or to increase the quality of their children—in terms of health and schooling—or to increase the number of children they have and rear. To the best of my knowledge, we simply do not know the answer to this question.

References

1. Schultz, Theodore, W., *Economic Growth and Agriculture.* New York: McGraw-Hill, 1968.
2. Spengler, Joseph J., "The Economist and the Population Question," *Amer Econ Rev*, March 1966.
3. Bourne, Geoffrey H., ed., "World Hunger: Past, Present, Prospective, That There Should Be Great Famine," *World Rev Nutrition & Dietetics.* New York: Karger, Basel, 1968. Vol. IX, pp. 1-31.

4. United Nations Food and Agriculture Organization, *Indicative World Plan for Agricultural Development*, Rome, August 1969. Vols. I, II, and III.

5. Schultz, Theodore W., *Economic Crises in World Agriculture*. Ann Arbor: Univ. of Michigan Press, 1965.

6. Shukla, Tara, *Capital Formation in Indian Agriculture*. Bombay, India: Vora & Company Publishers, Ltd., 1965.

7. Griliches, Zvi, "Research Expenditure, Education, and the Aggregative Agricultural Production Function," *Amer Econ Rev*, December 1964.

8. Schultz, Theodore W., *Transforming Traditional Agriculture*. New Haven, Conn.: Yale University Press, 1964. Chs. 1, 2.

9. Schultz, Theodore W., "Land in Economic Growth," *Modern Land Policy*, Harold G. Halcrow, ed. Urbana: Univ. of Ill. Press, 1960. Ch. 2.

10. Schultz, Theodore W., "Connections between Natural Resources and Economic Growth," *Natural Resources and Economic Growth*, Joseph J. Spengler, ed. Washington: Resources for the Future, Inc., April 1960.

11. Clark, Colin, *The Economics of 1960*. London: Macmillan, 1943. p. 52.

12. Clark, Colin, *Population Growth and Land Use*. New York: St. Martin's Press, 1967.

13. U.S. Department of Agriculture, *The World Food Budget 1970*. Foreign Agricultural Economic Report No. 19. Washington, D.C., October 1964.

14. Behrman, Jere R., "Supply Response in Underdeveloped Agriculture: A Case Study of Four Major Annual Crops in Thailand, 1937-1963." Unpublished doctoral dissertation, Mass. Inst. of Technology, Cambridge, Mass., September 1966.

15. Hansen, Bent, "Employment and Wages in Rural Egypt," *Amer Econ Rev*, June 1969.

16. Hansen, Bent, "Marginal Productivity, Wage Theory, and Subsistence Wage Theory in Egyptian Agriculture," *J Development Studies*, July 1966.

17. Hayami, Yukiro, and V. W. Ruttan, "Factor Prices and Technical Change in Agricultural Development: The United States and Japan, 1880-1960," Staff Paper P69-19, Univ. of Minn., Institute of Agriculture, St. Paul, Minn., July 1966.

18. Hertford, Reed, "Sources of Change in Mexican Agricultural Production, 1940-65." Unpublished doctoral dissertation, Univ. of Chicago, Chicago, Ill., 1970.

19. Hill, Polly, *The Migrant Cocoa-Farmers of South Ghana: A Study in Rural Capitalism*. London: Cambridge Univ. Press, 1963.

20. Hopper, W. David, "The Economic Organization of a Village in North India." Unpublished doctoral dissertation, Cornell University, Ithaca, N.Y., June 1957.

21. Khusro, A. M., "Indian Society of Agricultural Economics." Presidential address at XXVIIIth Annual Conference, Coimbatore, December 23, 1968. Delhi: Everest Press.

22. Krishna, Raj, "Farm Supply Response in India-Pakistan: A Case Study in the Punjab Region," *Econ J*, September 1963.
23. Krishna, Raj, "Farm Supply Response in the Punjab (India-Pakistan): A Case Study of Cotton." Unpublished doctoral dissertation, Univ. of Chicago, Chicago, Ill. September 1961.
24. Mellor, John W., *The Economics of Agricultural Development*. Ithaca: Cornell Univ. Press, 1966.
25. Rao, C. H. Hanumantha, *Agricultural Production Functions, Costs, and Returns in India*. New York: Asia Publishing House, 1965.
26. Welsch, Delane E., "Response to Economic Incentive by Abakaliki Rice Farmers in Eastern Nigeria," *J Farm Econ*, November 1965.
27. Krishna, Raj, "Agricultural Price Policy and Economic Development," *Agricultural Development and Economic Change*, H. M. Southworth and B. F. Johnston, eds. Ithaca, N.Y.: Cornell Univ. Press, 1967. Ch. 13.
28. Mellor, John W., et al., *Developing Rural India*. Ithaca, N.Y.: Cornell Univ. Press, 1968.
29. Schultz, Theodore W., "Production Opportunities in Asian Agriculture: An Economist's Agenda," *Development and Change in Traditional Agriculture: Focus on South Asia*. East Lansing: Asian Studies Center, Michigan State Univ., November 1968.
30. Southworth, Herman M., and Bruce F. Johnston, eds. *Agricultural Development and Economic Growth*. Ithaca, N.Y.: Cornell Univ. Press, 1967.
31. Moseman, A. H., "National Systems of Science and Technology for Agricultural Development." Presented at the meeting of University Directors of International Agricultural Programs, Univ. of Minn. June 9, 1966.
32. Griliches, Zvi, "The Demand for Fertilizer: An Economic Interpretation of a Technical Change," *J Farm Econ*, Vol. 40, 1958.
33. Sahota, Gian S., "An Analysis of the Causes of the Secular Decline in the Relative Price of Fertilizer." Unpublished doctoral dissertation, Univ. of Chicago, Chicago, Ill., 1965.
34. Sahota, Gian S., *Fertilizer in Economic Development*. New York: Frederick A. Praeger, Inc., 1968.
35. Asian Development Bank, *Asian Agricultural Survey*. Tokyo: Univ. of Tokyo Press, 1968.
36. Chaudhri, D. P., "Education and Agricultural Productivity in India." Unpublished doctoral dissertation, Univ. of Delhi, India, April 1968.
37. Welch, Finis, "Education in Production." *J Pol Econ*, January 1970. pp. 35-59.
38. Hsieh, S. C. and V. W. Ruttan, "Environmental, Technological, and Institutional Factors in the Growth of Rice Production: Philippines, Thailand, and Taiwan." Reprinted from Food Research Institute Studies, Vol. VII, No. 3, Stanford Univ., Stanford, Calif., 1967.
39. Mangahas, Mahar, A. E. Rector, and V. W. Ruttan, "Price and Market Surplus Relationships for Rice and Corn in the Philippines," *J Farm Econ*, August 1966. Part I.

40. Evenson, Robert E., "International Transmission of Technology in the Production of Sugarcane." Unpublished paper, Southern Methodist Univ., Dallas, Tex., September 1969.

41. Griliches, Zvi, "Research Costs and Social Returns: Hybrid Corn and Related Innovations," *J Pol Econ*, October 1958.

42. Hopper, W. David, "The Mainsprings of Agricultural Growth," *Indian J Agric Sci*, June 1965.

43. Hopper, W. David, and Wayne H. Freeman, "From Unsteady Infancy to Vigorous Adolescence: Rice Development," *Economic and Political Weekly, Review of Agriculture*. New Delhi: Rockefeller Foundation, March 1969.

44. "On Progress toward Increasing Yields of Maize and Wheat." Mexico City: International Maize and Wheat Improvement Center (CIMMYT) Report 1968-69.

45. Schultz, Theodore W., "Increasing World Food Supplies: The Economic Requirements," *Prospects of the World Food Supply, A Symposium*. Washington, D.C.: Natl. Academy of Sciences, 1966.

46. Stakman, E. C., Richard Bradfield, and Paul C. Mangelsdorf, *Campaigns Against Hunger*. Cambridge: Belknap Press of Harvard Univ. Press, 1967.

47. Tang, Anthony M., "Research and Education in Japanese Agricultural Development, 1880-1938," *Econ Studies Q*, February and May 1963.

48. Schultz, T. W., *Investment in Human Capital*. New York: Free Press, 1971.

49. Evenson, Robert E., "The Contribution of Agricultural Research and Extension to Agricultural Production." Unpublished doctoral dissertation, Univ. of Chicago, Chicago, 1968.

50. Ardito-Barletta, Nicolas, "Costs and Social Returns of Agricultural Research in Mexico." Unpublished doctoral dissertation, Univ. of Chicago, Chicago, pending 1971.

51. Ho, Yhi-Min, *The Agricultural Development of Taiwan, 1903-1960*. Nashville, Tenn.: Vanderbilt Univ. Press, 1966.

52. Organization for Economic Cooperation and Development, *Supply and Demand Prospects for Fertilizers in Developing Countries*. Paris, 1968.

53. Cummings, Ralph W., Jr., and S. K. Ray, "A Fresh Strategy for Agricultural Development: Relative Contribution of Weather and New Technology to 1968-69 Foodgrain Production and Implications for Future Policy," August 14, 1969. Mimeo.

54. Willett, Joseph W., and Donald Chrisler, "The Impact of New Varieties of Grain." Unpublished paper, U.S. Dept. of Agriculture, December 26, 1968.

55. Reca, Lucio G., "The Price and Production Duality within Argentine Agriculture, 1935-1965." Unpublished doctoral dissertation, Univ. of Chicago, Chicago, Ill., 1967.

56. Chaudhri, D. P., "Farmers Education and Productivity: Some Empirical Results from Indian Agriculture," Human Capital Paper No. 20, Univ. of Chicago, May 1969.

57. Taylor, Harlon D., and Dewell R. Gandy, "Caloric Cost of Rice and Wheat Program," *Am J Agric Econ*, November 1969.
58. Schultz, Theodore W., "Agricultural Modernization Altering World Food and Feed Grain Competition," *The International Conference on Mechanized Dryland Farming*, G. E. Van Riper, ed. Moline, Ill.: John Deere and Company, August 1969.
59. Johnson, D. Gale, "Climatic and Crop Analogies for the Soviet Union: A Study of the Possibilities of Increasing Grain Yields," Ag. Econ. Paper No. 57:16, Univ. of Chicago, Chicago, Ill., December 16, 1957.
60. Wickizer, V. D., and M. K. Bennett, *The Rice Economy of Monsoon Asia.* Stanford, Calif.: Food Research Institute, Stanford Univ. Press, 1941.
61. Ohkawa, Kazushi, Bruce F. Johnston, and Hiromitsu Kaneda, eds., *Agriculture and Economic Growth: Japan's Experience.* Tokyo: Univ. of Tokyo Press, 1969.
62. David, M. H., *Family Composition and Consumption.* Amsterdam: North Holland Publishing Co., 1962.
63. Eizenga, W., *Demographic Factors and Savings.* Amsterdam: North Holland Publishing Co., 1961.
64. Leff, Nathaniel H., "Population Growth and Savings Potential." Preliminary report to the Office of Program Coordination, Agency for International Development, Washington, D.C., 1967. (Forthcoming in *Amer Econ Rev.*)
65. Modigliani, Franco, "The Life Cycle Hypothesis of Saving, The Demand for Wealth and the Supply of Capital," *Social Research*, Summer 1966.
66. Tobin, James, "Life Cycle Savings and Balanced Growth," *Ten Economic Studies in the Tradition of Irving Fisher*, W. Fellner, et al., eds. New York: John Wiley & Sons, 1967.
67. Notestein, Frank W., "Population–The Long View," *Food For the World*, Theodore W. Schultz, ed. Chicago: Univ. of Chicago Press, 1945. pp. 36-57.
68. Gordon, John E., and John B. Wyon, *Population Adaptation in Rural Punjab, India: The Khanna Study.* Cambridge, Mass: Harvard Univ. Press, 1971.

VIII

Migrant Selectivity and the Growth of Large Cities in Developing Societies

Harley L. Browning

Policymakers are not of one mind when it comes to evaluating internal migration, particularly rural-urban migration, in the developing countries. Some see it as a means of speeding up economic development while others believe its consequences are largely undesirable and therefore recommend that it be discouraged. Scholars, too, are divided on this question. Although their positions sometimes emerge out of direct experience, I believe they are predisposed to view cityward migration either favorably or unfavorably by certain fundamental heritages of the various disciplines. To elaborate this point, let us select economics and sociology as contrasting viewpoints, nevertheless acknowledging the considerable diversity of opinion within each discipline.

EVALUATING RURAL-URBAN MIGRATION

Many economists tend to approve internal migration because they take it for granted that in a dynamic economy different regions (and their rural and urban sectors) will grow at different rates and that labor mobility is required to insure the most effective development of the economy. Schultz (1), for example, remarks, "Economic growth requires much internal migration of workers to adjust to changing job opportunities." Increasingly, economists are coming to view migration as an investment in human capital. Schultz believes that "migration of individuals and families to adjust to changing job opportunities" is one of five major ways of improving human capabilities (the

Harley Browning is Associate Professor of Sociology and Director of the Population Research Center, University of Texas.

The author expresses appreciation to Denton Vaughan for his assistance in putting this paper together and to Jorge Balan and Waltraut Feindt for their helpful suggestions.

others being formal education, adult study programs, on-the-job training, and health services).*

In contrast, most sociologists are predisposed by their training to take a different perspective. Inclined as they are to the use of ideal-typical dichotomies (e.g., traditional-modern, folk-urban, *Gemeinshcaft-Gesellschaft*), the city is seen in negative terms because it is characterized by what the village or small community is not. If the small community is said to be characterized by cultural homogeneity, primary interpersonal contacts, and social cohesion, then, by definition, the city must be described in opposite terms. This means, for one thing, that rural-urban migration is conceived of negatively. Social and personal disorganization must inevitably accompany the migrant to the large city because of the very different environment encountered.

Another important reason why some social scientists find social disorganization in the city is that they do not examine a representative sample of the city's population but restrict themselves to certain groups. Consider Lerner's sweeping indictment (3):

> The most conspicuous symptom of the contemporary disorder is what happened to urbanisation in the developing areas. Every student of development is aware of the global spread of urban slums—from *ranchos* of Caracas and *favellas* of Rio, to the *gecekŏndu* of Ankara, to the *bidonvilles* and "tin can cities" that infest the metropolitan centres of every developing country from Cairo to Manila.
>
> The point that must be stressed in referring to this suffering mass of humanity displaced from the rural areas to the filthy peripheries of the great cities, is that few of them experience the "transition" from agricultural to urban-industrial labour called for by the mechanism of development and the model of modernisation. They are neither housed, nor trained, nor employed, nor serviced. They languish on the urban periphery without entering into any productive relationship with its industrial operations. These are the "displaced persons," the DPs, of the developmental process as it now typically occurs in most of the world, a human flotsam and jetsam that has been displaced from traditional agricultural life without being incorporated into modern industrial life.

Lerner's initial problem of "what happened to urbanisation" is converted to an exclusive concern with the "filthy peripheries" of cities. He also argues that migrants from rural areas cannot find employment in the metropolitan center. The bias of the economist, in contrast, is to assume that men migrate in response to economic opportunity and that they do find work. Our purpose here in contrasting these perspectives is not to maintain that one is right and the other is wrong but to show how certain deep-seated features of these

---

*Sjaastad (1962) has developed this argument in (2).

disciplines incline their members to move in one direction rather than another.

The principal problem to be addressed, however, is not one linked to the sociology of knowledge. I want to pose the question, "Who migrates?" because I believe that a satisfactory understanding of the role of migration in developing countries must depend upon some knowledge of the forms and degree of *migrant selectivity*. Migrant selectivity is broadly defined so as to include the factors that distinguish migrants from the general population—not only demographic variables, such as age and sex, and socioeconomic variables, such as education and occupation, but even such elusive psychological characteristics as the propensity to assume risk.

Our task is not ended with the establishment of a set of migration differentials for various developing countries. Migrant selectivity for a given group should not be considered as some invariant property; it may change over time in response to changed conditions. The relationship of migrant selectivity to the urbanization process is a case in point. Increasing urbanization in a country affects the rate and degree of selectivity of rural-urban migration. There are many problems of data and method in a longitudinal approach, but migrant selectivity must be put within a dynamic framework, a context lacking in most studies of this phenomenon.

Restrictions on Scope and Coverage

This investigation is restricted in several ways. Attention is not primarily directed to all forms of internal migration nor even to rural-urban migration but is confined to migration to the large cities of developing countries.

More information is available for this class of cities. Small and medium-size cities up to 100,000 have not received nearly the attention given the larger cities. Even among the latter there is generally an emphasis on the first city or the first two cities. In Latin America, where first-city dominance is especially pronounced, the index of entries by city in a recent bibliography on urbanization in Latin America by Vaughan (4) shows that for nearly every country the first city, or in a few cases the first two cities, account for more entries than all other cities combined.

There are more important reasons for limiting our attention to the large cities. As a group they are growing very rapidly and represent increasingly large shares of both the urban and the total populations of their countries. Put another way, most developing countries are metropolitanizing (growth in places over 100,000) at a faster rate than they are urbanizing, and at a faster pace than was true for most western nations at comparable stages in their urbanization. Table 1 provides support for this statement. Note that in nearly all regions the urban population is growing at least twice as fast as the rural population and the "city" rate is appreciably greater than the "town" rate.

TABLE 1

Per Annum Population Growth Rates,
1950–1960, for Major Developing World Regions

| World Region | Growth Rates | | | | | Ratio | | |
	Total	Rural	Urban	Town[a]	City[b]	Urban/ Rural— Col. (3)/ Col. (2)	City/ Town— Col. (5)/ Col. (4)	Percent City of Total Population[c]
	(1)	(2)	(3)	(4)	(5)	(6)	(7)	(8)
Northern Africa	2.4	1.7	4.3	3.9	4.6	2.5	1.2	21.0
Western Africa	3.4	2.9	6.9	5.8	9.4	2.4	1.6	7.4
Eastern Africa	2.5	2.2	5.5	3.6	10.0	2.5	2.8	4.9
Middle and Southern Africa[d]	1.8	1.3	7.7	5.7	12.0	5.9	2.1	6.0
Middle America	3.1	1.8	4.8	4.4	5.5	2.7	1.2	20.0
Caribbean	2.2	1.7	3.1	2.3	4.2	1.8	1.8	20.7
Tropical South America	3.1	1.6	5.4	3.9	6.9	3.4	1.8	32.1
East Asia	1.8	1.1	6.0	6.1	5.9	5.4	1.0	16.1
Southeast Asia	2.5	2.1	4.6	3.2	5.7	2.2	1.8	12.1
Southwest Asia	2.7	1.9	4.7	3.2	6.5	2.5	2.0	21.8
South Central Asia	1.9	1.8	2.7	1.8	3.5	1.5	1.9	9.8
Oceania	2.7	2.6	4.8	4.8	0	1.8	0	0.0

[a]Less than 100,000.
[b]More than 100,000.
[c]Percent city population is of total population, estimated for 1970.
[d]Excludes Union of South Africa.

Source: Adapted from (6, Table D).

Since the large city category is a terminal one (cities may grow into but not out of it) this means that this category inevitably comes to represent an increasing share of the urban population. To illustrate, in Mexico using population 10,000-and-over as the urban criterion, the 100,000-and-over category rose from 27 percent of the total urban population in 1910 to 64 percent in 1960 (5). We may safely predict an increase in the importance of large city population, both for the urban and for the total population.

As a further restriction on the scope of this paper, comparison of migrant selectivity in the developing countries with that of the developed countries, either at the present time or at comparable periods in their development, has been kept to a minimum not only because of space considerations but also because there is some doubt as to the utility of relying upon the experience of the developed countries as guides for the developing countries.

A final restriction on the discussion is that it generally will be made in terms of voluntary migration—excluding all forced or other involuntary migration as well as the migration of children, at least up until age 15. The migration of married women is more difficult to classify. It can be argued that they migrate only because their husbands do, but in reality they are not always so passive in the making of such decisions. However, there is little doubt that the man's work situation is a key determinant in migration, and much of the following discussion will have men mainly in mind.

The reader is forewarned that world coverage of developing countries will be spotty and unsystematic. Scholars have begun to turn their attention to urbanization and internal migration in developing areas only within the last decade or so. But the trickle has now become something of a flood. Since urbanization and internal migration are multifaceted phenomena, they have attracted the attention of many specialists. At present hundreds of articles and books on these subjects are published each year. Since they appear in many languages and often in fugitive publications, it is impossible to review this output systematically.

In any event, the yield bearing on migrant selectivity from these sources has not, at least until recently, been very great. Although there are a number of studies on the subject, they are generally tangential, not well suited to meet the peculiar methodological requirements of migrant-nonmigrant comparisons. Fortunately, work recently completed or now in progress will soon force a modification of this judgment as more and more researchers, through the use of field surveys, are making migration the focus of their investigations.*

Because I am more familiar with the area, my attention will be concentrated on Latin America. I will also report in some detail the research project I have been engaged in, involving Monterrey, Mexico, as a metropolitan community of destination and Cedral, Mexico, as a rural community of origin for migrants to Monterrey.

The Monterrey and Cedral surveys were explicitly designed to investigate various aspects of the migratory process. The questionnaire instrument included a form in which the complete migratory history (any residences of 6 months or more) was obtained along with marital and work histories. Cedral,

---

*It was the Centro Latinoamerica de Demografía (CELADE) that took the lead in survey studies of internal migration to large cities in Latin America. The pioneer and excellent study was of Santiago, Chile (7, 8). CELADE is sponsoring a number of surveys of other Latin American cities. Mascisco is making a comparative study of all the cities surveyed by CELADE. Hendershot of Vanderbilt is analyzing data collected by the University of the Philippines Population Institute of two rural surveys and one of Manila. Speare at Brown is completing a study of migrants and nonmigrants in Taiwan.

Recent efforts to review systematically and codify the available evidence on migration are also encouraging. Although these efforts are not mainly concerned with migrant selectivity as such, they enable us to locate this topic within a broader framework. Cornelius (9) has done this for migration and socio-politico assimilation in Latin American cities and Nelson (10) has made a somewhat similar review of developing countries not restricted to Latin America. Alers and Appelbaum (11) have done a good job of building a "propositional inventory" for 20th century Peru, drawing upon some "59 major studies."

an agricultural *municipio* of 12,000, is 230 miles south of Monterrey in a region of heavy out-migration to Monterrey and was selected as representative of this type of community.*

Partly to balance somewhat the emphasis given to Latin America and Mexico, and also because it is an impressive study in its own right, the study of rural-urban migration in Ghana as recently reported by Caldwell (12) will be given special attention. His study fits into the orientation of this article because his "urban" designation includes the eight largest cities in Ghana. There are important differences in method between the Mexico and Ghana investigations and substantively there are phenomena found in one country and not the other,[†] but I hope to show that there are also similarities in migratory selectivity of these two countries.

The strategy I have followed is to present propositions (in italics) that bear upon one or another aspect of migrant selectivity. In most cases the available evidence either is so meager or so contradictory that the proposition must be considered as tentative. The advantage of the propositional format is that it is stated in testable terms. Although a comprehensive theory of migrant selectivity is not available at this time, it is possible to begin to accumulate the propositions that would enter into such a theory. I have not, however, attempted to include all conceivable or even relevant propositions.

Origin of Migrants to Large Cities in Developing Countries

The selectivity of migrants to large cities obviously will be much affected by the kinds of communities from which they originate. Migrants may be drawn from the whole range of settlements in a representative fashion, or

*The 1965 Monterrey Mobility Study was a project jointly sponsored by the Centro de Investigaciones Económicas of the Facultad de Economía, Universidad de Nuevo Leon and the Population Research Center of the Department of Sociology at the University of Texas at Austin. The research at both institutions was facilitated in part by grants from the Ford Foundation. The directors of the project are Jorge Balan and Elizabeth Balan (formerly of the Universidad de Nuevo Leon) and Harley L. Browning. The 1967 survey of Cedral was carried out by the Population Research Center by the same directors and again with Ford support.

The Monterrey study has been reported in a number of articles and those pertinent to migration are (13-20).

[†]In Mexico the principal investigation was metropolitan Monterrey, with 1,640 males aged 20 to 60 interviewed, while rural Cedral, with 390 males aged 15 to 64, was subsidiary. In Ghana Caldwell's main concern was with the rural population. He obtained information in 1963 from 1,782 households (13,776 persons) in a reasonably representative sample of villages. He supplemented this with 585 households (3,167) in four cities, with 68 percent of the total obtained in Accra-Tema, Ghana's largest city. In the rural interview information was obtained about persons absent from the village. For further methodological details of the two studies see Caldwell (12, Ch. 1) and Balan, et al. (13, Ch. 1). Substantively, Ghana differs from Mexico in the predominantly male rural-urban migration, in the multilingual character of the society, in the existence of polygamy, and in the pattern of return to village for retirement.

they may be concentrated in one part of the community-size hierarchy. Some writers give the impression that it is the rural areas that provide the great bulk of migrants to the large cities.

Stage Migration

However, there is another conception of the migratory process that would suggest a quite different pattern. I refer to the well-known stage (sometimes known as step) migration model. In its original formulation by Ravenstein (21) in 1885 and set forth as one of his "laws," it maintains that the direction of migration flows will be to successively larger places. Or as Taeuber (22, p. 95) has recently stated, "The stage migration process is one in which the aggregate shift from farms to large cities or suburbs is accomplished not by direct moves but by a series of less drastic moves—from farm to village, from village to town, from town to city, from city to suburb. Many persons participate in these successive displacements, but the typical individual manages only one or two stages in his lifetime."

This formulation carries a significant implication. It suggests that stage migration is an important social mechanism making the urbanization process more tolerable, for it means that migrants are not required to change their environment radically. Few villagers are called upon to go directly to the metropolis. Socialization to large-city life is carried out in progressive stages, with the movement from rural areas to metropolitan centers generally taking two generations or more.

The current evidence bearing on the stage migration model appears to be contradictory. The original study by Ravenstein was based upon the censuses of the United Kingdom. Taeuber finds good support for it in the United States in his study of residential histories for a large representative national survey. Herrick (23), reporting results of the CELADE study of migration to Santiago, Chile, does not directly test the model, but he does note that migrants come disproportionately from other urban places. Except perhaps for Chile, however, these countries are not classed as developing countries, and the evidence from developing countries is very thin. Caldwell (12, pp. 21-22) remarks that for Ghana step migration "has not been of great importance, particularly in recent times, in the Ghanaian rural-urban migration movement," but his findings on this point have not yet been published.

The Monterrey data do not support the stage migration model. Browning and Feindt (19) classified all migrants by last arrival to Monterrey according to their conformity to the model. They found that only 8 percent were in strict conformity; that is, their movement was always to the next largest community-size class. However, by relaxing the requirement to allow for movement to any larger size class (a leapfrog pattern), 42 percent had partial conformity to the model. But this still leaves one half of the migrants who had no conformity whatever to the stage migration model. Nearly one in five violated the model because of return migration, another 11 percent because of migration to the United States, and 20 percent had such a variety of patterns that they were assigned to the "other" category. It is noteworthy that 29 percent of all migrants came to Monterrey from a rural community with no intervening stops.

This is not the place for a full discussion of the appropriateness of the stage migration model, either as it applies to Monterrey or in general. What we are interested in here is its adequacy when applied to large cities; it may have a much better fit when applied to small or medium-size cities. There are, however, several reasons why we should not anticipate a good fit in many developing countries. One assumption of the model rarely made explicit is that the urban-size hierarchy is well developed. In effect, the model assumes a population distribution pattern similar to the Christaller "central place" model in which all parts of a given territory are equally habitable and there is a geometric arrangement of different sizes of communities so that any person randomly selected within the territory (excluding the perimeter areas) would be located the same distance from communities of different size as any other person. In other words, it is assumed that all prospective migrants have the same objective opportunity, as measured by direct-line distance, of access to communities of the next larger size class.

This assumption simply does not hold in many developing countries. The population distribution, due to geographical and historical reasons, is often very uneven and within the urban hierarchy itself there are many "holes." Consequently, many potential migrants would have difficulty in "finding" the properly sized community. Given the top-heavy urban-size hierarchy, reflecting the more rapid rate of growth of large cities as demonstrated by the Davis data (6), it is not surprising to find a good deal of direct rural-to-large-city migration. We may conclude: *The lesser the level of urbanization of a country and the less developed the urban-size hierarchy, the less the conformity to the stage migration model.*

Rural vs. Urban Origins

We are still left with our problem of determining the relative importance of rural versus urban areas in providing migrants to large cities. In the case of Monterrey the community of origin (not place of birth but where respondent spent the greater part of his formative years between ages 5 and 14) of migrants by time of first arrival is as follows:

Rural (less than 5,000)	56%
Small urban (5,000 to 19,999)	21
Medium urban (20,000 to 99,999)	17
Large urban (100,000 and over)	4
Foreign	2
Total	100%

Interestingly enough, when this is broken down by time-of-arrival cohorts, the proportion coming from rural areas does not decline as could be expected because of the steady increase in urbanization in both northeastern Mexico and Mexico as a whole. It is 54 percent rural for those arriving before 1941; 51 percent in the 1941-1950 period; 59 percent in the 1951-1960 period; and 60 percent in the 1961-65 period. As we shall see later on, there are reasons for believing that the earlier migrants to Monterrey were more selective than those arriving later, and this selectivity was manifested in a greater propensity to come from urban areas, even though the country was more rural at the earlier time.

About all that can be safely generalized about the rural-urban balance of migration is: *Large cities in developing areas draw migrants from urban and rural areas, with both being well represented, though not necessarily in close correspondence with national or regional rural-urban ratios.* Weak as this proposition may be, it still guards us against easy assumptions that migrants are nearly all from rural areas or that there is a mechanical relationship between the national or regional rural-urban distribution and the origins of migrants.

Little is known about the factors that affect out-migration from small and medium-size cities because, as already noted, these places have been the object of less investigation than either rural areas or large cities. However, it may be presumed that large cities exercise a strong attraction for many of the inhabitants of small and medium-size cities. In most developing countries it is the large metropolitan centers that benefited most from industrialization, whereas many smaller places have remained economically stagnant. Since the inhabitants of the medium and smaller urban places are generally literate and often, via the mass media, well aware of the superior economic prospects in the large cities, they migrate in the expectation of bettering their socioeconomic situation. Therefore: *Migrants to large cities in developing countries coming from medium or small urban places are positively selective of the populations from which they originate.*

Out-Migration from Rural Areas

Turning to the subject of out-migration from rural areas, we are confronted with one of the most distinctive as well as most important features of developing societies. What makes the situation of these rural areas especially critical at this time is their increasing rate of population growth. While countries, and regions within countries, vary somewhat in this respect, virtually all of them have experienced significant reductions in mortality levels within the last generation. Because fertility has remained high, a pronounced rise in the rate of natural increase has resulted. This in turn has meant an increase, in various degrees and various ways, of population pressure on resources (24).

Not all of the people in rural areas of developing countries are peasant in nature, of course, but peasants unquestionably form an important component of the total rural population in many countries. As a sweeping generalization, it may be said that the social structures of such communities are ill-adapted to cope with the comparatively sudden and sizeable increase in population. Wolf (25) has made an interesting comparison of "closed corporate peasant communities" in two widely separated world areas, Central Java and Mesoamerica. The ability of these communities to absorb additional numbers and their mode of accommodation will depend upon many factors, including availability of raw land, the land tenure arrangement, and the labor requirements of the agricultural system. In a fascinating study, Geertz (26) shows how Javanese villagers have accommodated population increase by agricultural "involution," made possible by the considerable elasticity of labor input that the wet-rice system permits. The social system adjusts to the increased numbers by the practice of "shared poverty." However effective this adjustment may be over the short term, the long-term consequences are indeed grim. In any event, most peasant societies do not have available to them the flexibility of the wet-rice system.

One major form of adaptation to increasing rates of natural increase, and doubtless the most universal one, is out-migration. Sometimes it is likened to a safety valve that works to prevent population pressure on local resources from building up to a danger point. The analogy is a dangerous one, for it implies that out-migration works like an automatic control device. It is anything but that. Anyone who tries to make sense of rural out-migration rates, such as they are for developing countries, soon must acknowledge that they are not to be explained in any mechanistic fashion.

Although rural-urban migration is widespread and well-known, it is still difficult to get reasonably satisfactory statistics on the movement. In any event, migration flows in themselves are insufficient. One better way to evaluate the significance of rural out-migration is in terms of the concept of the "reservoir" of potential rural out-migrants. Barraclough (27) reports some interesting estimates made for seven countries of Latin America. First it was assumed that the out-migration from rural areas that was destined for urban areas represented about one half of the natural increase in the rural areas for the 1950-1960 period. This net rural-urban migration was then stated as the percent of the 1950 rural population of the country. The countries and their percentages are given below:

Chile	29.0%
Argentina	24.9
Brazil	19.0
Ecuador	17.0
Colombia	16.6
Peru	13.6
Guatemala	3.6

One may dispute these figures and the assumptions underlying them, but for our purposes what is important is the illustration of how much variation there is among countries in the extent to which the population of the rural "reservoir" is drawn upon. It is noteworthy that the two most urbanized and advanced countries, Chile and Argentina, have one fourth or more of their total 1950 base rural population removed to urban areas within the decade, whereas Guatemala, the most backward of the seven countries, has by far the lowest—a suspiciously low—figure. As we shall soon see, migration is age-concentrated, so the actual loss in the young adult years is considerably greater than the figures indicate. However, the concept of a migratory "reservoir" is important for any consideration of migrant selectivity. Independent of the characteristics of the migrants, such as education or occupation, it is apparent that the situation in countries such as Chile, in which up to one half of the young adult population leave, does not permit the degree of selectivity that could, though not necessarily would, characterize a country where only 10 percent of the same age group migrated to cities. This important point will be taken up again in another context.

Out-migration from rural areas assumes various forms. Caldwell, in his rural survey, has provided us with some of the best data showing both the amount and form of rural out-migration. In Table 2 the migratory status of

TABLE 2

Migration Classification of Ghana Rural Respondents by Age, 1693

(percent)

Migration Classification[a]	0-9	10-14	15-19	20-24	25-29	30-44	45-64	65+	All Ages
Never migrated	85	83	78	63	55	57	64	73	69
Seasonal migrant	2	3	6	9	8	6	4	2	5
Permanent returnee	3	3	3	6	12	13	17	19	9
Long-term absentee	7	7	12	20	20	21	13	4	14
Other; no entry	3	4	1	2	5	3	2	2	3
Total[b]	100	100	100	100	100	100	100	100	100

[a]Key:
Never migrated—includes those currently "visiting" town, a few of whom may have been previous migrants.
Seasonal migrant—includes those currently in the town and those in the village who intend to migrate again.
Permanent returnee—those who have been either seasonal or long-term migrants but who do not intend to migrate again.
Long-term absentee—includes the long-term absentees resident in the town whether in the town or temporarily visiting the village at the time of the survey.
[b]Number sampled = 6,964.

Source: (12; Appendix 2, p. 240).

the male population is given by age. Since only rural-urban migration is considered and movement to other rural areas is classified as "never migrated," these figures understate the mobility of this group. Nonetheless it is quite impressive that only somewhat more than half of the age group 25 to 44 has never migrated. The female distribution, which is not given here, has a similar profile, but with substantially less migration. (The percentages "never migrated" are 72, 74, and 73 for the age groups 20 to 24, 25 to 29, and 30 to 44, with the total figure being 78 percent compared to 69 percent for males.) However, migrant sex differences are less among the younger ages, and Caldwell suggests that this represents an important change in the migration patterns of Ghana. Seasonal migration, however, remains a predominantly male undertaking regardless of age.

Return Migration. Perhaps most interesting in this table is the "permanent returnee," since it taps a form of migration for which it has always been difficult, especially by means of censuses, to obtain information. In Ghana migration to large cities typically is made with the expectation of returning eventually to the village at retirement age if not sooner (12, pp. 185-200). I do not know how widespread this pattern is in the rest of tropical Africa, but the retirement pattern is not nearly as common in Latin America. Return migration is doubtless quite substantial in all countries, although data deficiencies preclude comparisons. In Cedral, Mexico, where there has been a history of out-migration from a long-depressed area, 34 percent of the men interviewed had left the community as a migrant (defined as those who move away for at least 6 months) and had returned by the time of the survey. Of all men 13 percent were return migrants from Monterrey.

The reasons for return migration to rural areas are many and not easily classifiable. Caldwell's study asked a question about why people return from towns and do not want to go there again. The two main responses were about equal (each about 40 percent): "they preferred village life" or "they did not succeed in the town." Less important (less than 20 percent) was the response, "they had made enough money."

Whatever people report to be the reasons for return migration, a comparative study of the phenomenon would probably find that return migration rates are related to the stability of labor demand in the cities. Mohsin (28, p. 59) states, "The failure of the industrial sector to provide them [migrants] with decent and stable work facilities, and also the seasonal decline of urban employment force these migrants to Indian cities to maintain close ties with their folks at their native places." Gutkind (29) reviewing the evidence for Africa, takes much the same position. In addition to fluctuations in demand for labor, the frequent inadequacies of urban facilities (housing, transportation, etc.) make life difficult. The conclusion to be drawn from this is that if economic opportunity and living conditions in the cities were to be improved, return migration rates would be lower.

Return migration is of special significance in the study of migrant selectivity. It is plausible to assume that much, but by no means all, of return migration serves to "weed out" the less successful migrants. As a proposition: *Return migrants from large cities on the whole will be negatively selective from the total group of migrants, thus increasing the positive selectivity of those who remain in the cities.* The difficulties of testing this proposition are formidable, but it is crucial for migrant-nonmigrant comparisons.

SPECIFIC CHARACTERISTICS OF MIGRANT SELECTIVITY

Let us consider the specific ways in which migrants are selected from the populations from which they originate. A number of comparisons are possible, but the choices will be made in part to indicate the variety of relevant variables. We begin with three conventional demographic variables (age, sex, and marital status), proceed with two socioeconomic ones (education and occupation), and end with a psychological variable (risk-taking propensity).

Age

More than 30 years ago, Thomas (30) in her review of the existing literature on migration differentials—interestingly enough, it was limited almost entirely to developed countries—concluded that there were few empirical regularities in this area that held up through time and space. The one exception that might presume to the status of a law was age-selectivity of migrants. All subsequent work has confirmed this judgment. Whether in developed or developing countries, *migrants to urban places are concentrated in the young adult years.* The distribution may be more or less peaked according to a given country or city but the general configuration remains. For example, the U.N. Mysore Study (31, p. 177) shows that for all in migrant male household heads to Bangalore City, 49.9 percent were within the age range 15 to 29 at the time of their migration to that city. The comparable figure for Mysore City is 44.4 percent. Camisa (32, pp. 408-449) applied the survival ratio technique to the 1950 and 1960 censuses of a number of Latin American countries. Six large cities showed the following percentages of net migration represented by ages up to 30 (in 1960):

Greater Buenos Aires	53%
Metropolitan Caracas	67
Greater Santiago	69
Guayaquil	71
Panama City	73
Mexico City (Distrito Federal)	81

Only in Buenos Aires are "older" migrants important as a percentage of the total.

The age-specific pattern of urbanward migration is so well-known that we sometimes lose sight of its significance. One can even go so far as to maintain that the single feature of migrant selectivity that most benefits the receiving urban community is age, because it is related to so many other characteristics. This judgment applies especially to developing countries where the socioeconomic differences between age cohorts are often very great. Young adults are, on the average, better educated, even when their community of origin is held constant. This, in turn, will affect their occupational attainment. Most men migrate to large cities before the peak of their work careers, which comes quite young in developing countries. Most men must find manual employment, for which physical vitality is an important requisite. Moreover, the adaptability of individuals to different environments and the willingness to change environments is related to youth. Migration is one way for a young man to escape domination by his parents. If he were to remain in a rural area, he would be more likely to orient his work and family life according to parental and kin considerations.

Men in rural areas, at least on the basis of the Cedral data, are keenly aware of the relationship of age to success in the city. This is clearly indicated in the series of three questions reported in Table 3. In the first question asked of all men, there is a clear inverse relationship between age and responses favoring leaving Cedral. However, 42 percent of men 45-and-over still say "go," reflecting the lack of economic opportunity in Cedral, an area with a long tradition of out-migration. When the question is specified for men older and younger than the respondent the effect of age at migration becomes very pronounced. Overwhelmingly, young men are urged to leave, and this has almost no variation by age of respondent. For the older men, the advice is the opposite, though not as pronounced as for younger men. There is somewhat more variation by age of respondent, but not much.

By their comments the men indicated they were well aware of the way in which age influenced successful adaptation to the city. It is fair to conclude that many men in rural areas are there not particularly because they want to be, but because they correctly perceive that job opportunities in large cities for men over 35 or 40 are quite limited. In large cities of developing countries the supply of unskilled labor invariably exceeds the demand, so employers understandably do not hire older men, especially since they are less educated as a group and have few specialized skills.

Sex Ratio

Age specificity of migrants holds up remarkably well through space and time, but the sex ratio (speaking here of the adult population) has no such uniformity. At one time there was a belief to this effect. Ravenstein (21, p. 199) stated as one of his laws, "Females are more migratory than males," but

TABLE 3

The Relationship of Age to Men's Advice Favorable to Migrating
from Cedral, Mexico, to the City, 1967

	Age Category				
	15-24	25-34	35-44	45+	Total

53. "Do you think that to be able to progress the best thing that can be done by a man of your age who lives in a village (*pueblo*) like Cedral is to go to a city as soon as possible?"

	15-24	25-34	35-44	45+	Total
Percent "very much in agreement" or "in agreement"	77	69	52	42	59
Number	(69)	(100)	(77)	(101)	(347)

54. "And in the case of a man older than yourself, what do you think is best?" (Only for respondents less than 55 years old.)

	15-24	25-34	35-44	45+	Total
Percent saying go to the city	37	35	29	23	31
Number	(52)	(81)	(69)	(57)	(259)

55. "And in the case of a man younger than yourself, what do you think is best?" (Only for respondents over 25 years old.)

	15-24	25-34	35-44	45+	Total
Percent saying go to the city		91	92	92	92
Number		(88)	(74)	(109)	(271)

Source: Unpublished data, Cedral survey, Population Research Center, Department of Sociology, University of Texas, Austin.

this assertion was based on his studies of Great Britain and, to a lesser extent, Europe. As evidence came in from other parts of the world, it became apparent that the pattern in west Europe and northern America was not typical, especially with respect to large cities.

Although there are some exceptions, the developing world presents two main patterns: the Latin American one, in which there is a predominance of females among migrants to cities and the Afro-Asian one, in which there is a clear predominance of men. In some large Latin American cities there are among young adults as few as 75 males for every 100 females; in a number of large African and Asian cities there are as many as 150 or more males for every 100 females.

In part the explanation of this difference may be cultural. In Islamic societies and others such as India, unmarried females are not encouraged to leave the household except for marriage. Morris (33) also argues that the joint family restricted the migration of women, for women usually migrated only when whole families moved. In Latin America many unmarried female migrants to large cities are destined for domestic employment service. In effect, they exchange one household environment for another, so the norms of close control of young female behavior are not really contradicted.

But the cultural explanation of the differences between these world areas is not in itself adequate. Although Latin America, Africa, and Asia are all classified as "developing," there are substantial differences in economic organization. Temporary migration to cities is more characteristic of Africa and Asia than it is of Latin America, and, as already mentioned, fluctuating labor demand is part of the explanation. If the labor surplus in large cities of Asia and Africa is greater than in Latin America, females will face greater competition from males for the available positions, and females would be further handicapped by cultural constraints.

In the process of economic development, however, *in the large cities extreme sex imbalances, whether favoring males or females, are inherently unstable and over time they will move toward a more even balance.* Caldwell (12) indicates that a more even balance in the sexes of migrants to cities of Ghana is in process. Bogue and Zachariah (34, p. 45) say with respect to metropolitan areas of India, "Although originally this migration may have some of the aspects of a 'pioneering' movement, comprised predominantly of males, the 1941-51 decade witnessed the removal to the cities of almost as many women as men." In Latin America the same movement is taking place, in part because of the preference of the girls and young women for work other than domestic service.

Marital Status

Marital status is obviously related to the sex balance. The further the sex ratio is from 100, the greater the proportion of migrants who are single. But there is still considerable variation depending upon the willingness of men to leave their families back home. In Asia and Africa this is more common than in Latin America. Nevertheless, Zachariah (35, p. 383) in his study of Bombay states, "In each age-sex group the proportion single was found to be . . . greater than in the general population of the states of origin." Caldwell found that in rural areas of Ghana single males (after he controlled for age) were more likely to be planning to migrate to the cities. Controlling for age, we find that *migrants to large cities are disproportionately single when compared to the populations from which they originate.*

The significance of marital status upon other forms of migrant selectivity can be seen by reference to Kuznets' concept of "detachment" (36, xxxiii). He believes that detachment facilitates economic progress. "Indeed, we cannot exaggerate the importance of this detachment of wide groups of the population, particularly among the young generation, from family origin and surroundings in their movement toward, and placement in, positions within the economic system on criteria that put a premium on maximization of specific capacities that are closely related to measurable economic efficiency." Of course, some sociologists would view detachment quite differently. They believe separation "from family origin and surroundings" results in social deprivation leading to social and personal disorganization. But this is a problem to be addressed later.

Educational Attainment

Migrants to large cities have higher educational attainment than the populations from which they originate. Aside from age, the selective factor of education probably has more generality than any other to be advanced. It is not that migrants have *high* educational attainment; most from rural areas have 6 years of education or less. It means only that they have more than the average of their origin population. For Calcutta (34) and for Bombay (35) it was found that in-migrants had "considerably higher" average educational attainment than the populations of origin, but lower average attainment than the populations in the two communities of destination. Much the same conclusion was reached for Lagos by Ejiogu (37). The Monterrey findings indicate a high degree of educational selectivity. For Cedral, 22 percent of those who had ever migrated had completed 6 years or more of schooling, whereas only 13 percent of the nonmigrants had attained this level.

In the Ghana study the relationship to education is very clear, as indicated by Table 4. The Caldwell study also is of interest in showing the way language competence is related to propensity to migrate. For male rural respondents over 20 years old, the percent who had never migrated by "literacy category" is as follows:

Illiterate	69%
African only	67
English and African	50
English only	38

The educational system stimulates out-migration because it forces young people to leave the community if they are to complete their education. Only rarely do rural communities have facilities going beyond primary school. Since higher educational facilities most often are found in cities, the student has little recourse but to go there. Excepting the few specializations in agriculture, his training is such as to prepare him for urban jobs. In short, everything is stacked against the probability that those who attain an education much beyond the average for the population in their communities of origin will remain there.

TABLE 4

Percentage Distribution of Ghana Rural Respondents over 20 Years of Age
in Each Educational Group by Migration Classification and Sex, 1963

(percent)

Sex and Migration Classification	Highest Level of Education Reached[a]			
	None	Limited Primary Schooling	Extended Primary and Middle Schooling	Secondary Schooling and University
MALE (3,748 respondents)				
Never migrated:				
No plans	65	59	38	17
Planning to do so	4	7	9	8
Ever a seasonal migrant	8	12	9	18
Ever a long-term absentee	19	19	40	49
Visiting; other; no entry	4	3	4	8
Total	100	100	100	100
FEMALE (3,713 respondents)				
Never migrated:				
No plans	77	65	39	26
Planning to do so	3	5	10	13
Ever a seasonal migrant	4	8	8	18
Ever a long-term absentee	12	20	38	43
Visiting; other, no entry	4	2	5	0
Total	100	100	100	100

[a]In this and following tables "migrated" means migrated to urban areas, and current visitors to the town have been put in the residual category because of lack of information about their previous activities.

Source: Caldwell (12, Table 3.3).

Occupational Status

If it can be demonstrated that migrants have higher educational levels than nonmigrants, then it should also follow that *migrants to large cities have, on the average, a higher occupational level than the populations from which they originate.* The stress here should be on "average," for some migrants will have low occupations, just as they will have low educational attainment. Later, this proposition will be demonstrated to hold for migrants to Monterrey. Speare (38) has an interesting comparison of Taiwan male nonmigrants and male migrants before and after their move to Taichung, as given in Table 5. The comparison of nonmigrants and migrants before they moved is clearly favorable to the latter. Speare also shows that 39 percent of the migrants had schooling beyond the primary level, but only 21 percent of the nonmigrants reached this level.

TABLE 5

Occupation Distribution of Migrants and Nonmigrants, Taichung, Taiwan, 1966-1967[a]

(percent)

	Nonmigrants	Migrants before Move	Migrants after Move
Professional, managerial, clerical			
Employees	8.9	19.8	20.2
Self-employed	9.2	4.4	7.6
Sales and service workers			
Employees	3	10	9.8
Self-employed	13.8	12	20.9
Skilled and semiskilled workers			
Employed	6.5	18	17.6
Self-employed	5.1	3.1	4
Transportation workers			
Employees	6	7.8	10.9
Self-employed	0.5	0.9	3.1
Farmers, owners or tenants	40	12.2	2.4
Farm laborers	3.5	5.3	1.3
Not employed	3.5	6.5	2.2
Total	100	100	100
Sample size	370	450	450

[a]Based on results of interview with Taiwanese male migrants to Taichung aged 23 to 42 and Taiwanese males aged 23 to 42 who were living in the area outside Taichung from which the migrants came.

Source: (38).

Propensity to Assume Risk

Propensity to assume risk is a psychological variable, and the proposition may be stated as follows: *Migrants to large cities are, on the average, more disposed to assume risk than the populations from which they originate.** Although this proposition may be plausible, it is the one for which there are least data. It is also difficult to assess its importance independently because the variable is associated with education and occupation. Perhaps it would be easier to reverse the proposition and speak of those loath to assume the risk inherent in moving to a new environment. Many people who should be migration-prone—in terms of the demographic and socioeconomic variables we have discussed—remain at home. They are the people who are less venturesome,

*Although agricultural production is one of the riskiest, I believe that farmers "accept" risk but are not so likely to "assume" it in the active sense of the word.

less ambitious, and less restless. Such characteristics, it should be emphasized, are to be considered independently of general intelligence or willingness to conform to the norms of the village or small-town environments.

Kuznets (36, pp. xxxii), as an economist, places considerable importance on this trait of willingness to assume risk. His argument is as follows:

> Let us assume that, on balance, the in-migrant group, at least in some countries and in many periods, has a greater proportion than the resident population of adventurous and independent individuals capable of adjusting to a variety of circumstances, and also a larger proportion of individuals responsive to economic opportunities and attractions even if qualified by a substantial risk element (necessarily present in the case of most internal migration). If we assume further that the personality characteristics and the greater orientation to economic opportunities involved in such selectivity make for long-term prospects of greater productivity and efficiency, then again it follows that internal migration implies not merely the assured economic growth implicit in supplying the man for the job but further growth resulting from a process of selection that promises an extra gain of productivity over and above the assumption of unselected migration.

Note the qualifications Kuznets introduces. "On balance" means that not all of the individuals who rank high on risk-taking propensity will leave and not all those ranking low will remain. He is careful not to make this feature of migration an invariant property by stating, "at least in some countries and in many periods." And a major unstated assumption is that there *is* a job awaiting the man at the new destination. More than that, it is a job allowing for initiative and permitting increases in productivity. The appropriateness of these assumptions as they would apply to most large cities in developing areas will be challenged by many, but Kuznets, in fairness to his position, really is addressing himself to a prior question, "if we assume that the labor needed for the newly emergent production opportunities in a rapidly growing area can be drawn from the resident population, would the alternative of employing newcomers still be preferable?" (36 pp. xxx). He says yes, in part because of the importance he ascribes to the quality of venturesomeness.

Change in Migrant Selectivity

The point has been made that it is not only important to look for migrant selectivity; it is also necessary to determine if the selectivity itself changes over time. Unfortunately, the evidence is minimal on this question, since adequate information on migrant selectivity is not often available for one point in time, much less as a time series.

Excepting the sex ratio, the various forms of migratory selectivity tend to go together. Thus, the young migrate, and being young, they are more likely to be single, or at least without large families. And in developing countries there are generally pronounced age-cohort differences in educational attainment, so their education will be higher than that of the adult population as a whole. Finally, willingness to assume risk is linked to age, education, and employment, although it is formally distinct. Stated as a proposition: *Forms of migrant selectivity, excepting sex, are interrelated, and when these variables change they will change in the same direction.*

Data from the Monterrey study can be combined with Mexican census results to provide some useful comparisons for education and employment, as shown in Table 6. The categories are noncontiguous groupings of *municipios* (Mexican county equivalents) that are based on socioeconomic criteria. Category I represents highly urban and industrially advanced areas, whereas Category V includes highly rural and backward areas.

A detailed analysis of Table 6 is not possible here (see 17). What is important for our purposes is the demonstration that (a) migrants are selective on both education and employment, with selectivity being extreme for the earlier periods and for the less developed Categories III-V; and (b) excepting for comparisons in Categories I and II that can be explained, selectivity has declined substantially since 1941. In addition to these two variables, it was found that the more recent migrants to Monterrey were more likely to arrive at that place married; and if married, more likely to arrive with children; and if arriving with children, more likely to have two or more children upon arrival.

In all, the Monterrey data provide strong support for the argument that migrant selectivity has declined over the past several decades. The somewhat lengthy explanation of why this happened cannot be reproduced here, especially since it depends in part upon peculiarities of Mexican development. However, the shift from "pioneer" to "mass" migration does have some features of general application and significance. In the course of urbanization, the "reservoir" of rural potential migrants tends inevitably to decline relative to the ever-increasing demands placed upon it by sustained urbanization. Thus, as a larger proportion of the total population of the reservoir is drawn upon, the characteristics of the migrants come to resemble the average of that population. In the Monterrey case the number of migrants by time of arrival rose about sixfold in 30 years. The rural reservoir in the area states providing most of the migrants to Monterrey increased by little more than 50 percent during the same period.

This discussion leads to the following proposition: *The lower the rate of out-migration from rural and small-town areas to large cities, the greater the selectivity.* Stated another way: *The longer a rapid rate of urbanization is maintained, the more probable a decline in selectivity of migrants from rural areas.* Admittedly, the evidence for these propositions is limited, but they touch upon important, if often overlooked, features of migrant selectivity.

TABLE 6

Percentages of Male Migrants to Monterrey Who (a) Have 6 Years or More Schooling and (b) Were Employed in Nonagricultural Activity in Year before First Arrival, by Socioeconomic Category of *Zona* of Community of Origin and Time of First Arrival, with Corresponding Percentages for All Males 15 and Over in Category of *Zonas*

Item and *Zonas* Contributing at Least 2 Percent of Migrants by Category in Terms of Socioeconomic Ranking	Time of First Arrival			Census		Selectivity Indicators	
	Before 1941	1941-50	1951-60	1940	1960	Col. (1) – Col. (4)	Col. (3) – Col. (5)
	(1)	(2)	(3)	(4)	(5)	(6)	(7)
6 years schooling							
All categories[a]	43	35	34				
Category I (highest)	39	51	62	48	51	-9	+11
Category II	31	44	46	14	23	+17	+23
Category III	50	31	25	8	15	+42	+10
Category IV	51	32	27	5	8	+46	+19
Category V (lowest)	34	10	13	3	6	+31	+7
Mexico, total country				12	21		

All categories	71	56	50	89	95	-13	-13
Category I (highest)	76	74	82	36	41	+38	+20
Category II	74	76	61	19	15	+49	+29
Category III	68	36	44	20	18	+41	+29
Category IV	61	46	42	15	13	c	+24
Category V (lowest)	c	68	24	13			+11
Mexico, total country				31	41		

[a]The grouping and ranking of *zonas* by categories is on the basis of three indices of economic development: percent urban, percent in secondary and tertiary activities in the labor force, and worker per capita income.

[b]Percent based on migrants who were employed in year before first arrival. Sample cases number: Before 1941, total-100, I-21, II-23, III-19, IV-31, V-6; 1941-50, 162, 23, 29, 28, 63, 19; 1951-50, 204, 33, 38, 45, 59, 29.

[c]Not calculated; statistic based on fewer than 10 sample cases.

Source: Monterrey 1965 Survey (actual sample) and 1940 and 1960 Mexico census reports.

The Adjustment of Migrants in Large Cities

The discussion so far has been on the forms of migrant selectivity when migrants are compared to the population in the community of origin. Now we can turn to the question of how well migrants fare in the large city. A number of myths on this subject need to be challenged.

First, however, it is necessary to get an idea of the migrant-native composition in large cities. We restrict ourselves, as usual, to a consideration of the adult population. This provides a different picture of migrant-native balance than if we were to deal with the total population.* The migratory composition of the male population aged 21 to 60 of Monterrey is given in Table 7. During the 25 years between 1940 and 1965, the metropolitan area grew at a rate of about 6 percent per annum, enough to double the population every 11 years. This is a rapid rate of growth, but not an extraordinary one. In Mexico eight other places over 50,000 at the 1960 census had 1950-1960 growth rates higher than that of Monterrey. The Davis volume on world urbanization shows that cities 100,000 and above often have growth rates over 5 percent per annum (6, Table E). Consequently, the Monterrey distribution should be characteristic of fast-growing cities throughout the world.

Excluding Migrants by Adoption because their number is insignificant, we have six migratory status groups, defined in terms of exposure to the Monterrey environment. Perhaps the most noteworthy feature of this native-migrant distribution is how few men have temporal "roots" in the city. Second Generation Natives are about one of every seven adult males. If a more stringent criterion were adopted—that both parents be born in Monterrey—only about one of every twenty would qualify. It also should be pointed out that the distinction between Natives by Adoption and First Generation Natives is the accident of whether they were born inside or outside of Monterrey. Of those born in the city, 49 percent have fathers with rural backgrounds compared to 53 percent of First Generation Natives. For well over half of Monterrey men, the rural environment is at most only two generations removed, in a country that has had above-average urbanization during the last 30 years and in a region (northeastern Mexico) that is predominantly urban.

Migration and Kinship Networks

One of the myths about migrants that persists even with mounting evidence to the contrary is that migrants experience social and psychological deprivation because they must exchange the well-integrated interpersonal network of village or small-town environments for the impersonality and lack of

---

*See Arriaga (39) for a discussion of the relative importance of natural increase and net in-migration as contributors to the growth of a number of large Latin American cities.

TABLE 7

Migratory Status of Monterrey Men Age 21 to 60,[a]
Percentage Distribution, 1965

(percent)

Migrant by birth (born outside of Monterrey and community of origin[b] is another place)		54
Short exposure migrants (less than 10 years in Monterrey)	20	
Medium exposure migrants (10-19 years in Monterrey)	20	
Long exposure migrants (20 years of more in Monterrey)	14	
Changes of migratory status		16
Migrants by adoption (born in Monterrey, but community of origin[b] is another place)	1	
Natives by adoption (born outside of Monterrey, but community of origin[b] is Monterrey	15	
Natives by birth (born in Monterrey and community of origin[b] is Monterrey)		30
First generation natives (neither parent born in Monterrey)	17	
Second generation natives (one or both parents born in Monterrey)	13	
Total		100

[a]The sample is a representative one, made so by the initiation of age and income categories underrepresented in the actual sample of 1,640 men.

[b]Community of origin is place where respondent spent most of the time between the ages of 5 and 15.

Source: Monterrey Mobility Study.

kin and friendship ties that characterize the large city. Just why it is assumed that migrants enter an interpersonal void either during the move itself or after their arrival in the large city is hard to explain. The available evidence indicates otherwise. *The great majority of migrants to large cities make the journey to, and the accommodation within, the large city as part of a kinship group.* In Monterrey, only 19 percent of the migrants came alone; 39 percent came with their wives and children, 34 percent with their parents, and 6 percent with both. This pattern probably is not radically different for other developing countries.

Moreover, there are kin and friends known to the migrant already living in the city of destination. In Monterrey, 84 percent had relatives or friends living there. In a study of Jamshedpur, India, Misra (40, p. 78) reports that approximately 75 percent of migrants had relatives or friends there. Caldwell (12, p. 811) in his African study says, "It can be seen that visits to the towns from families without relatives already living there are practically unknown. Only 39 percent of the respondents who had not migrated at the time of the survey came from households where any member was living in the towns at that time, but they provided 98 percent of the current visitors to the towns." These visits generally precede more permanent migration. Caldwell also found in his rural survey that in those households that had members living in town there was a greater likelihood that other members were planning to migrate.

These reports from various parts of the world suggest that it would not be far from the mark to say that *a substantial majority (in most cases at least two thirds) of migrants to large cities in developing areas have relatives or friends already living there.* If migration is not seen as an isolated movement specific in time to one or more individuals but as a process involving people at both ends, then this fact becomes understandable. It therefore is hardly accidental that for Monterrey the 84 percent who had relatives or friends living in Monterrey is very close to the 82 percent who maintain some kind of contact with relatives or friends where they lived longest prior to arrival in Monterrey. Abu-Lughod (41) has emphasized the essential continuity between rural village life and the environment the in-migrant encounters in Cairo.*

Migrant-Native Socioeconomic Differentials

As already noted, a common image of migrants to large cities in developing areas is one of a mass of untutored and unskilled peasants concentrated in slum districts on the outskirts of the cities who are unable to enter "into any productive relationship," to use Lerner's language (3). Since most observers reaching such conclusions have directed their attention only to low income areas of the city, their distortion of the socioeconomic position of all migrants was inevitable.

Investigators who have attempted to take the entire city into account present a different and far more complicated picture. In a study of Recife, Cruz (42, p. 115) found little socioeconomic difference between migrants and nonmigrants, based on a scale combining income and possession of items such

---

*A more detailed picture of the amount of kin and close friend interaction was obtained for Monterrey by asking if, upon arrival, migrants lived with relatives and/or had relatives in the same neighborhood. The relationship of this variable to education and employment is as follows:

Education	Percent in Neighborhood Kinship Network	Number
Primary or less	73	686
Beyond primary	55	190

Last Employment before Monterrey		
Farm	82	292
Nonfarm	62	447

The interesting feature of these data is that higher status individuals are less likely to be imbedded in neighborhood kinship networks. Perhaps the "detachment" Kuznets (36) talks about is manifested in this relationship. But in any event, it should be kept in mind that none of the above groups had less than half of their populations in neighborhood networks. The highest are those from farm backgrounds. They are the group who must make the greatest adjustment in style of living and therefore are presumably most in need of help from relatives and friends.

as a stove, radio, refrigerator. Balan (15) has assembled comparable data on Buenos Aires, Santiago, Mexico City, Monterrey, San Salvador, and Guatemala City. He finds that the socioeconomic gap between natives and migrants in some of these cities is large while in others it is small or nonexistent. Although migrants in nearly all of these cities have lower educational attainments, their occupational distribution, based on a one-digit code, shows they do at least as well as natives in such cities as Santiago, San Salvador, and Guatemala City. In his interpretation of these differences Balan found it useful to consider the position of migrants in terms of the proportion originating in rural areas, their "credentials" (formal requirements such as educational degrees), and the rate of creation of higher status jobs in the community of destination.

The Monterrey data demonstrate that migrant-native differentials are not at all a simple matter. In Table 8 occupation and income data are given for the six Migratory Status Groups, as identified earlier. When the two extreme groups are compared, Short Exposure Migrants and Second Generation Natives, the latter do considerably better even when we control for age. However, there is no steady progression among the six groups, for the Long Exposure Migrants do as well as either the Natives by Adoption or First Generation Natives, and this again holds after controlling for age. The explanation for the superior performance of Long Exposure Migrants is apparently not simply due to their longer exposure in the city, but also to their greater selectivity (17).

The argument advanced here does not deny that in aggregate terms migrants rank below natives on socioeconomic indicators. Doubtless in the great majority of large cities in developing societies they do. But the important point to remember is that overall they do not rank *far* below the natives, or at least as low as would reasonably be expected, considering the important rural component of much of the in-migration to these cities. Whatever the socioeconomic ranking of migrants and natives, the point to be stressed is that *both* groups are lower than is desirable.

There is also the question of migrant-native differences in social mobility or, more precisely, occupational mobility, for that is the way social mobility almost invariably is measured. The argument of Blau and Duncan (43, p. 274), although it derives from their research in the United States, is relevant. They maintain that migration promotes social mobility.

> As a mechanism of selection and redistribution of manpower, migration furthers occupational mobility. Indeed, it is essential for occupational mobility on a wide scale in a highly diversified society because it alone can alter the opportunity structure in which a given man completes.

In terms of the community of destination, in this case large cities, Blau and Duncan maintain that migration facilitates occupational mobility both

TABLE 8

Mean Scores of Occupation and Income by Age for Migratory
Status Groups,[a] Monterrey Men, 1965

Age	Short Exposure Migrants	Medium Exposure Migrants	Long Exposure Migrants	Natives by Adoption	First Generation Natives	Second Generation Natives
			OCCUPATIONAL LEVEL[b]			
21-30	1.26	1.70	–	1.58	1.54	2.14
31-40	1.25	1.43	1.65	2.04	1.82	2.73
41-50	1.32	1.41	2.15	2.07	1.96	2.40
51-60	.91	.81	1.83	1.98	1.85	2.55
Probability, age controlled[c]		.55	.00	.94	.94	.00
Grand mean	1.21	1.33	1.94	1.87	1.76	2.40
Probability, age not controlled[c]		.61	.00	.65	.50	.00
			WEEKLY INCOME[d]			
21-30	2.25	2.89	–	2.55	3.00	3.40
31-40	2.25	2.96	3.23	3.76	3.53	4.58
41-50	2.81	3.03	4.00	3.78	4.05	4.43
51-60	1.83	1.72	3.50	3.88	3.16	4.28
Probability, age controlled[c]		.15	.00	.71	.53	.03
Grand mean	2.32	2.69	3.62	3.34	3.41	4.07
Probability, age not controlled[c]		.06	.00	.21	.74	.00

[a]See Table 7.

[b]A 6-point scale ranging from 0 (unskilled workers) to 6 (managers and professionals).

[c]Null hypothesis that the difference between adjacent Migratory Status Groups is due to chance.

[d]A 9-point scale with unequal intervals, 0 to 8.

Source: Monterrey Mobility Study, actual sample.

directly and indirectly. Directly, because rural migrants to large cities do better occupationally than those who remain in rural areas. Indirectly, because the influx of rural migrants into the lower ranks of the occupational hierarchy creates additional opportunities for upward mobility for the natives. Blau and Duncan found support for this argument in their American data, and it is reasonable to assume that in general the pattern will hold in large cities of developing countries.* A rigorous test of the Blau and Duncan

*Parenthetically, the Blau and Duncan interpretation is in harmony with that of Lipset and Bendix (44) who argue that immigration from Europe to the United States

thesis poses many technical problems (e.g., it presumes data from both communities of origin and destination), but the proposition can be advanced: *Migration to large cities of developing countries increases, on the average, both the occupational mobility of the in-migrants and that of the natives.*

The impact of arrival to the large city upon a man's work status is difficult to determine because information is not often collected for many points in the occupational history. The Monterrey life-history record enables us to make some comparisons. For three age-at-first-arrival-to-Monterrey groups, the percent who were in unskilled employment for three time intervals follows:

	15-19	20-29	30-39
3 years before arrival in Monterrey	93	80	70
First year in Monterrey	83	75	56
Fifth year in Monterrey	68	59	53

Part of the movement out of unskilled employment is a consequence of aging, but, even taking this into account, migrants to Monterrey are not all trapped in unskilled jobs. For Bombay, Zachariah (35, p. 388) states, "Between duration of residence of less than one year, and 15 years or over, the percentages employed in unskilled occupations and in service were nearly halved, while the percentages of craftsmen and those in clerical occupations were nearly doubled."

Social mobility has dimensions not captured in occupational mobility rates. A man's self-perception of how well he is doing is also important. In Monterrey, 92 percent of the migrants reported themselves satisfied with their decision to move to that city. This figure can be discounted; many of the less satisfied left, and some people will report themselves satisfied whatever their current situation. Nevertheless, there can be little doubt that a substantial majority see their migration to Monterrey in favorable terms. A somewhat similar response was obtained in a study of two squatter settlements in Bogotá reported by Cardona Gutierrez (46, p. 63). In response to the question, "Do you consider that you're the same, better, or worse than before migrating?" 87 percent said they were better off and only 3 percent said they were worse off. Caldwell (12, p. 180) found for the urban population in his survey that in response to the question, "Has life in Accra (or Kumasi or Sekondi-Takoradi or Cape Coast) been as good as you thought it

---

fostered upward occupational mobility for the natives. But for nearly all developing countries the reverse holds. Immigrants originating in Europe have done substantially better than the indigenous population (45), and many of them settled in the large cities.

One of the deficiencies of this paper is that it does not take the foreign-born explicitly into account. For a number of large cities their presence has had a considerable impact upon the opportunity structure of both natives and internal migrants.

would when you first came here?" 57 percent said yes. There can be little doubt that "satisfaction" questions are tricky to interpret, much influenced as they are by wording of the question and its placement within the context of other "adjustment" questions. Nonetheless, it is still possible to conclude that most migrants are positive about their move.

In another context, all Monterrey men were asked the question, "Do you consider that your current job is better, the same, or worse than the one your father had at approximately the same age?" Almost two thirds (66 percent) of all migrants reported their jobs as better than their fathers', a higher figure than any of the natives yielded. Only 21 percent of the migrants said their jobs were worse. Another self-appraisal question, "Do you believe your opportunities to live comfortably are greater, the same, or lesser than those of the majority of people in Mexico?" can be used to make the following comparisons:

	Greater	Lesser
Men in Cedral	6%	57%
Men from Cedral but living in Monterrey	15	25
Total sample of Monterrey men	27	15

Clearly the migrants from Cedral to Monterrey are intermediate, with the contrast between Cedral and Monterrey men quite striking.

The large city in developing areas is perceived by those outside as well as inside it as providing greater opportunities than elsewhere. This belief can be held by a man notwithstanding his low occupational status. Men need not evaluate their situation wholly in terms of their own occupation, income, or mobility prospects. For instance, among married men who were 36 or older upon last arrival to Monterrey and who had children, 14 percent reported education as their major reason for migration. At their age, obviously it is their children's education that they have in mind.

Migrants and Differential Personal and Social Disorganization*

The persistent belief that migrants are more prone than natives to all forms of personal and social disorganization has already been mentioned. It undoubtedly derives from a long-standing propensity in the social sciences to impose dichotomies upon reality: folk-urban, mechanic-organic, traditional-modern, etc. This leads, however unintentionally, to a separation of urban and rural into two mutually exclusive social and cultural systems. Scholars thus have reified their theoretical constructs.[†]

*See also John Cassel, "Health Consequences of Population Density and Crowding," in this volume.

[†]As Hauser (49, p. 514) puts it, "The dichotomizations perhaps represent all too hasty efforts to synthesize and integrate what little knowledge has been acquired in

Those who a priori define the city in negative terms fail to look for ways in which the city may favorably affect the in-migrant. For example, Lewis (47) and Butterworth (48), among others, have found that migration to the large city can result in a much greater feeling of personal freedom than was true in rural environments. The gossiping and constant surveillance that serve to maintain social control in small communities are not as pervasive in the city and therefore not as oppressive. Bossism and various forms of terrorism still to be found in villages certainly involve primary or face-to-face relations, but those who are the recipients of real or threatened violence are only too willing to flee to the "impersonality" of the large city. Inkeles (50, p. 224), on the basis of large-scale study involving six countries (Argentina, Chile, India, Israel, Nigeria, and East Pakistan), recently concluded "the theory which identifies contact with modernizing institutions and geographical and social mobility as certainly deleterious to psychic adjustment is not supported by the evidence."

The political dimensions of migrant adaptation can only be touched upon here.* Cornelius (9) takes a position similar to the one presented in this paper. In an up-to-date and thorough review of the literature he is able to demonstrate that the picture presented of urban migration by "developmental theorists and Latin Americanists" bears little relation to that of authors of "empirically-based studies." He first listed six constellations of attitudes and behavior predicted by the "theorists" to be a consequence of cityward migration:

1. felt deprivation, frustration of socioeconomic expectations;
2. personal and/or social disorganization, maladjustment, primary group breakdown;
3. alienation, nonsupportive legitimacy orientations;
4. increased politicization, demand-creation;
5. mass availability, atomization of social relations, reintegration need; and
6. political radicalization, support for, or participation in, disruptive political activity.

Then he reviewed four dozen empirical studies conducted in eleven countries in terms of these six theoretical expectations. None of the six were substantially confirmed; each had some supporting evidence but always involved a small minority. The theory and the evidence simply did not agree.

The re-examination of old beliefs about the city is proceeding on several fronts. In Latin America social anthropologists, such as Mangin (51) and Leeds (52), and urban planners, such as Turner (53), recently have mounted a

---

empirical research. The widespread acceptance of these ideal-type constructs as generalizations, without benefit of adequate research, well illustrates the dangers of catchy neologisms which often get confused with knowledge."

*See also Myron Weiner, "Political Demography: an Inquiry into the Political Consequences of Population Change," in this volume.

frontal attack on the old conception that saw the fringe and squatter settlements (known by various names throughout the region: *barriadas, favelas, callampas, colonias proletarias*, etc.) as festering sores on the urban body politic. In perhaps the most forceful and telling attack on this position, Mangin (51, p. 66) challenged, successfully in my opinion, each of the following "standard myths" attributed to squatter settlements:

1. The squatter settlements are formed by rural people (Indians where possible) coming directly from "their" farms.

2. They are chaotic and unorganized.

3. They are slums with the accompanying crime, juvenile delinquency, prostitution, family breakdown, illegitimacy, etc.

4. They represent an economic drain on the nation; since unemployment is high, they are the lowest class economically, the hungriest and most poorly housed, and their labor might better be used back on the farms.

5. They do not participate in the life of the city; illiteracy is high and the education level low.

6. They are rural peasant villages (or Indian communities) reconstituted in the cities.

7. They are "breeding grounds for" or "festering sores of" radical political activity, particularly communism, because of resentment, ignorance, and a longing to be led.

8. There are two solutions to the problem: (a) prevent migration by law or by making life in the provinces more attractive; or (b) prevent the formation of new squatter settlements by law and "eradicate" (a favorite word among architects and planners) the existing ones, replacing them with housing projects.

Mangin does not maintain that these people have no problems—"I do not mean to minimize the problems of overpopulation, rapid urbanization, poverty, prejudice, and lack of elementary health and social services that play such an important part in squatter settlement life,"—but his "more hopeful and realistic" interpretation is one that views squatter settlements "as a process of social reconstruction through popular initiative."

The Basic Values of Migrants and Natives

The migrant's adjustment to the large-city milieu will be made more difficult if he must undergo a major change of values and norms. One feature of the rural-urban dichotomy is that it leads, however unintentionally, to thinking of rural and urban in terms of exclusive social and cultural systems. If this were literally true, then rural-urban migrants would be forced to abandon whole sets of normative expectations and to take up new ones—an enormous challenge, especially for adults.

But is such a transformation required of most migrants? Satisfactory evidence on this point is not available, but the Monterrey Migratory Status

Groups can be examined with respect to family values and religious orientation, as shown in Table 9. Considering the table as a whole, the striking feature is how little variation there is. The greatest percentage point difference between any of the six groups is 12. The significance of this is enhanced if we recall that the occupational and income differences for the same six groups (Table 8) were quite pronounced, at least between the extreme two groups, Short Exposure Migrants and Second Generation Natives.

TABLE 9

Family Values and Religious Orientation for Migratory
Status Groups,[a] Monterrey Men, Mexico, 1965

Item	Short Exposure Migrants	Medium Exposure Migrants	Long Exposure Migrants	Natives by Adoption	First Generation Natives	Second Generation Natives
	FAMILY VALUES (percent selecting "modern" response)[b]					
1. Divorce	33	33	33	33	34	32
2. Family limitation	44	47	45	53	53	56
3. Wife makes decisions	5	8	9	9	15	14
4. Children may disagree with parents	12	14	9	20	21	19
5. Family obligations	10	10	8	12	7	6
	RELIGIOUS ORIENTATION					
Little or not at all religious	41	47	43	51	46	42
Never attended church	32	39	37	43	42	36

[a]See Table 7.
[b]Those respondents who say they "most agree" with the first alternative of the following five choices:
1. a. If a husband and wife are not happy, they can divorce each other.
    b. Marriage is sacred and should never end in divorce.
2. a. If they want to or need to, parents can limit the number of children.
    b. Parents should never limit the number of children.
3. a. A wife should make her own decisions, even when she disagrees with husband.
    b. A good wife is one who always obeys her husband.
4. a. On some occasions, children should be permitted to disagree with parents.
    b. The most important thing for a child to learn is obedience and respect for the authority of his parents.
5. a. The obligation of a man is only to support his wife and children.
    b. Aside from supporting his wife and children, a man's obligation is also to help his relatives whenever he can, since they too are part of the family.

Source: Monterrey Mobility Study, actual sample.

Other than the narrow range, the other distinctive feature of Table 9 is the slight evidence, if any, of a linear relationship between exposure to the Monterrey environment and the various value or behavioral items. Indeed, for religious belief and practice, Short Exposure Migrants and Second Generation Natives are closer to each other than to any of the other groups.

How are we to interpret this table? There are two possibilities. One is to assume that the Monterrey environment imposes the same standards on everyone, migrant and native alike, so that the migrant must take up new Monterrey values. However, this presumes an extremely effective mode of socialization of incoming migrants, and there is no evidence that this is so. The other alternative, and the more likely one, is simply that there are no great value differences in northern Mexico, rural or metropolitan, at least with respect to such basic institutions as family and religion. Since well over half the Monterrey men have rural origins going back no more than two generations, it can be argued that, if anything, the rural influence is dominant in Monterrey. Among the adult population, natives are definitely in the minority, and the question "Who socializes whom?" must be raised.

In any event, whatever the origins of family and religious values: *Excepting for special groups, such as Indians, migrants to large cities do not differ radically from the natives with respect to their fundamental values.* If this can be confirmed, it suggests that there are not two distinct cultural and normative systems—the rural and the urban—in developing societies that demand unswerving allegiance from their members. All statements suggesting chasmlike differences will be far from the mark. The proposition advanced therefore requires neither that peasants be converted into instant urbanites nor the equally dubious possibility that they become "urban peasants." Life in large cities *does* require of in-migrants from rural areas many changes in style and tempo of life. But these changes need not destroy or greatly affect basic values.

The Ghana study is especially valuable in showing how rural and urban may be amalgamated. The country is in its most intense period of urbanization, but far from there being a violent conflict between tribal life on the one hand and metropolitan existence on the other, these worlds are so closely connected that it is difficult to speak of the one without reference to the other. As Caldwell puts it,

> In the sense that most rural-urban migrants who work their active years out in the town are satisfied about what they have done, there can be no real question about their failure to adjust to the town. It could be said that they failed to embrace town life so exclusively as to be adjusted to the town only; rather is their adjustment one to both town and village. They have a cyclical view of their lives which demands a beginning and an end in the village but which is satisfied and even happy to enjoy an extensive urban experience in the interim. . . .

> The town is essentially a place of activity. There one can work fruit-
> fully during the height of one's powers. There also one can live fully when
> one has the energy to do so. But, as one begins to feel one's age, or as
> sickness brings warning signs of physical troubles, then one begins to think
> of retirement, in a very literal sense of the word, to the village. (12, p.
> 220)

The constant flow of the city dwellers back to the villages for visits and their
eventual retirement there keeps the inhabitants of villages well informed of
urban life. "Rural Ghanaians look upon the large towns as the sources from
which the new patterns of living will come to an extent that would astonish
rural residents in many developed countries." This is not to say that no
differences are perceived between rural and urban life. More than four fifths
of the respondents in both the rural and the urban surveys said that village
life is more "manageable" than town life and nearly two thirds of each group
believed that town life "corrupts." But such judgments do not deny the
attractiveness of town life. More than four fifths of respondents in both rural
and urban areas agreed with the statement, "male migration is a good thing."
While rural-urban contacts in Ghana probably are of an intensity not likely to
be matched in many other developing countries, I would maintain that the
general pattern holds, whereby the migrant is the link between town and
country.

CONCLUSIONS

This review of migrant selectivity has been restricted in various ways. We
have not concerned ourselves with all forms of internal migration, for our
focus has been on migration to the large cities of developing countries. It also
has been restricted to the late adolescent and adult population and has been
concerned mainly with male migration.

Whatever else has been accomplished in this survey, it should be clear that
migrant selectivity is inherently a complex phenomenon. Ideally, one needs
extensive data on migrants and nonmigrants in *both* the communities or
origin and of destination. By this criterion, few if any studies tell us *all* we
would like to know about migrant selectivity. Not only are differences between migrants and nonmigrants difficult to establish unequivocally, but the
fact that migrant selectivity patterns may change is very important. Here we
can echo Bogue (54)

> . . . *migration can be highly selective with respect to a given characteristic
> in one area and be selective to only a mild degree, or not at all, in another
> area.* If the selectivity of migration can vary in both pattern and intensity
> between different places, it is equally plausible that it can vary between
> different periods of time. Hence *it is fruitless to seek permanent inflexible*

differentials in migration that will not vary, to some degree at least, in pattern and intensity with time and place. (Italics in original.)

Possibly age selectivity is the one exception to this statement, but otherwise it is incumbent upon any investigation of migrant selectivity at least to consider the possibility of change in migratory pattern over time.

Studies of migrant selectivity that depend entirely on census information are inadequate. Censuses do provide valuable data, and census bureaus should be encouraged to publish more of the information on migration which they have available, but the census enumeration instrument simply is too restricted in the amount and kind of questions it can cover.

Sample surveys are more flexible and can provide a much wider range of information. The Monterrey Mobility Study convinced me that reliable life histories can be obtained and that the computer makes feasible for the first time the processing and analysis of large numbers of cases. (See 55.) Life histories lend themselves very well to cohort analysis, and this is indispensable for the survey analyst who wishes to escape from static analysis.

Sample surveys on migration are now appearing with increasing frequency, but like the Monterrey study, they are often handicapped in making migrant-native comparisons because of a restriction to one locale. This limitation can be overcome through the use of large national surveys; that by Blau and Duncan (43) is an excellent example. But in order to permit adequate analysis by size of community and by region, a large sample number (N) is required, perhaps as much as 10,000. Such surveys are expensive and difficult to execute in most developing countries, but they provide the best way of determining the importance of various features of migration, including selectivity, on the national level. And if they could be replicated after 10 years or so, one would be able to say with some confidence whether patterns of migrant selectivity are changing.

Finally, the recent surge in output of studies dealing with migration makes it propitious to begin the arduous and tedious task of codifying the findings of these studies, both on a regional and world basis. This task, and my paper is only a gesture in that direction, not only would serve to clarify what we now know about migration, it would tell us where the major gaps in our knowledge are and how they could best be filled.

Notwithstanding the limitations that we have indicated, certain conclusions can be reached on the basis of our survey. Migrants to large cities in developing countries are heterogeneous in their socioeconomic backgrounds. This observation may seem so self-evident as to be trivial, but its acceptance allows us to clear away some of the misconceptions and errors that have occurred frequently in the literature. A number of social scientists have seen the migration process through a glass all-too-darkly. I have tried to explain this trait as originating in the theoretical heritage they have brought to the problem. It has caused many of them to fail to ask whether reality conforms to this preconception.

Migrants to large cities, on an overall basis, are positively selective in relation to the populations from which they originate. (Whether they are also positively selective to small or medium-size cities is an intriguing question, but the evidence is so slight that no conclusion can be reached at this time.) The forms of selectivity (age, education, occupation, risk-taking propensity, etc.) are interrelated and reinforce one another. It was argued earlier in this paper that the allegations (they seldom had more substance than this) of personal and social disorganization in the large cities were exaggerated. If my thesis of positive selectivity is sound, it follows that the migrants, on the average, will be better equipped to cope with conditions in the city.

Although migration to large cities has been found to be positively selective, there are additional questions to be posed as to whether selectivity is changing and, if so, in what direction. Unfortunately, the evidence on these matters is meager. The Monterrey data indicate a clear decline in migrant selectivity over a generation, but we cannot be sure that this holds for other large Mexican cities, let alone cities in other world regions. I think it is safe to assume that if a rapid rate of urbanization is sustained over several decades, selectivity will be lower at the end than the beginning of the period, but this still leaves unanswered questions about the extent and form of this change. In any event, declining selectivity has a host of implications, especially its effects on the city of destination. It suggests that accommodation into the occupational and social structure of the city will become more rather than less of a problem, even though the proportion of the total population represented by migrants steadily declines.

Migrant Selectivity, the Growth of Large Cities, and Economic Development

It should be evident by now that I am more positive than some about the urbanization process in developing countries. In particular the thrust of this paper has been to show the connection between migrant selectivity and the growth of large cities. It is difficult to deny that massive population redistribution is an inherent part of the developmental process, nor that urbanization, as a prominent feature of this redistribution, requires much migration. Large cities draw migrants from other urban centers and from rural areas. As economists often view migration favorably because of its consequences for labor mobility, so can sociologists view it favorably. Blau and Duncan see migration as expanding the life chances available to men. Their conclusion, based upon their investigation of the occupational mobility in the United States, would seem equally appropriate for other societies.

> The community in which a man is raised, just as the race or ethnic group into which he is born, defines an ascriptive base that limits his adult occupational chances. Migration, however, partly removes these ascribed restrictions on achievement by enabling a man to take advantage of opportunities not available in his original community . . . selective migration strengthens the operation of universalistic criteria of achievement and the trend toward increasing selectivity in migration manifests an extension of universalism in our occupational structure (43, p. 275).

Migration also has several desirable implications from the standpoint of the large city. There is positive selectivity, overall, and in particular there is the stream of career migrants from other cities whose importance far exceeds the numbers involved. They are the ambitious ones, anxious to mount and ascend the ladder of success.

Even the migrants from rural areas may contribute more than is generally attributed to them, notwithstanding their limited education and low-level skills. Although the empirical support for it is extremely limited, I am inclined to put a good deal of emphasis upon the risk-taking propensity. Surely the larger cities benefit from the relocation of venturesome and ambitious people.

But at this point critics of cityward migration can be expected to make a vigorous dissent. They will charge that the whole argument is tied to a gigantic *if.* Migrant selectivity can benefit the receiving community only *if* the energies and dedication that migrants bring to the city can be properly put to work. But is there work? Or more precisely, in view of the substantial underemployment to be found in developing countries, is there work worthy of them? Although data are surprisingly limited on this point, there doubtless are many situations, probably the great majority, where the employment absorptive capacities of large cities are not in line with the volume of inmigration. This is indeed a critical point. Perhaps the frequent reference to Monterrey has served to mislead, because this city has had exceptional economic growth (it is the iron and steel center of Mexico and ranks second only to Mexico City in industrial output) over the last 30 years.

But even if the point be granted, this still does not lead us to conclude that rural-urban migration or even that small-to-large-urban migration should be limited in every possible way. In developing countries inadequate work opportunities pervade the entire social structure—rural and urban alike. It is a societal problem, not restricted to one sector. It can be argued that even if employment opportunities in large cities are not as great as they should be, they still are demonstrably superior to those in the rural or small urban communities of origin. And, importantly, educational facilities are much better. Although the migrant himself may not benefit from them, his children can.

Behind the controversies over the relative merits of urbanization and its attendant rural-urban migration is the question of short- versus long-term effects. Many critics of the current pace of urbanization undoubtedly have near-term consequences in mind. In addition to the difficulties of providing employment, the fantastic growth of many large cities in developing countries has strained the meager resources available for providing basic municipal services, much less adequate housing. Is it not reasonable, therefore, to advocate policies that would reduce the volume of rural-urban migration, which, in turn, would slow down the growth of cities, particularly the large ones?

There are several limitations to this approach. First of all, we have very little reason to believe that governments have the necessary administrative tools to manipulate migration rates—even totalitarian governments have not had much success. Moreover, the long-run consequences of retaining people in rural environments are unfortunate. Policies restricting migration may have near-term ameliorative effects, but in time they will become negative. The numerous changes required to bring about the transition to a "developed" status are best made in an urban environment.

I realize the enormous challenge implicit in my "acceptance" of current rates of urbanization in developing countries. I have tried to show, however, that the implications of migrant selectivity, as related to the growth of large cities, makes the prognosis for successful transition to a modern urbanized society more favorable than is sometimes concluded.

REFERENCES

1. Schultz, T. W., "Investment in Human Capital," *Amer Econ R*, 51, 1961. pp. 1-17.
2. Sjaastad, Larry A., "The Costs and Returns of Human Migration," *Investment in Human Beings*, supplement to the *J Pol Econ*, 70, 1962. Part 2.
3. Lerner, Daniel, "Comparative Analysis of Processes of Modernization," *The City in Modern Africa*, Horace Miner, ed. New York: Praeger, 1967. pp. 21-38.
4. Vaughan, Denton R., *Urbanization in Twentieth Century Latin America: A Working Bibliography.* Austin: Institute of Latin American Studies and the Population Research Center, University of Texas, 1969.
5. Browning, Harley L., *Urbanization in Mexico.* Unpublished Ph.D. dissertation, Univ. of Calif. Berkeley, Calif., 1962.
6. Davis, Kingsley, *World Urbanization 1950-1970. Volume I: Basic Data for Cities, Countries and Regions.* Population Monograph Series No. 4, Berkeley: Institute of International Studies. 1969.
7. Centro Latinoamérica de Demografía (CELADE) *Encuesta sobre Inmigración en el Gran Santiago.* E/CN. CELADE/A. 15/C. 64/2. Santiago, Chile, 1964.
8. Elizaga, Juan C., "A Study of Migration to Greater Santiago (Chile)," *Demography.* Vol. 3, No. 2, 1966. pp. 352-377.

9. Cornelius, Wayne, Jr., "The Political Sociology of Cityward Migration in Latin America: Toward Empirical Theory," *Lat Am Ur An.* Beverly Hills, California: Sage Publications, 1970. Vol. I.

10. Nelson, Joan M., "Migrants, Urban Poverty and Instability in New Nations: Critique of a Myth," Harvard Univ., Center for International Affairs. Forthcoming.

11. Alers, J. Oscar, and Richard P. Applebaum, "La Migración en el Perú: Un Inventario de Prosposiciones," *Estudios de Población y Desarrollo* (Peru), Vol. 1, No. 4, 1968. pp. 1-43.

12. Caldwell, John D., *African Rural-Urban Migration.* Canberra: Australian National Univ. Press, 1969.

13. Balan, Jorge, Elizabeth Jelin Balan, and Harley L. Browning, eds., *Movilidad Social, Migración, y Fecundidad en Monterrey Metropolitano.* Monterrey, Mexico: Centro de Investigaciones Económicas, Universidad de Nuevo Leon. 1967.

14. Balan, Jorge, "Are Farmers' Sons Handicapped in the City?" *Rural Sociol,* Vol. 33, No. 2, 1968. pp. 160-174.

15. Balan, Jorge, "Migrant Native Socioeconomic Differences in Latin American Cities: A Structural Analysis," *Lat Am Res R,* Vol. 4, No. 1, 1969. pp. 3-29.

16. Browning, Harley L., and Waltraut Feindt, "Diferencias entre la Población Nativa y la Migrante en Monterrey," *Demogr y Econ* (Mexico), Vol. 2, No. 2, 1968. pp. 183-204.

17. Browning, Harley L., and Waltraut Feindt, "Selectivity of Migrants to a Metropolis in a Developing Country: a Mexican Case Study," *Demography,* Vol. 6, No. 4, 1969. pp. 347-358.

18. Browning, Harley L., and Waltraut Feindt, "The Social and Economic Context of Migration to Monterrey, Mexico," *Latin American Urban Annual,* Vol. 1, Francine F. Rabinovitz and Felicity M. Trueblood, eds. Beverly Hills, California: Sage Publications, 1970.

19. Browning, Harley L., and Waltraut Feindt, "Patterns of Migration to Monterrey, Mexico." Austin: Population Research Center, The University of Texas, no date. Mimeo.

20. Land, Kenneth C., "Duration of Residence and Prospective Migration: Further Evidence," *Demography,* Vol. 6, No. 2, 1969. pp. 133-140.

21. Ravenstein, E. G., "The Laws of Migration," *J Statis Soc,* 48, 1885. Part 2, pp. 167-235.

22. Taeuber, Karl E., Leonard Chiazze, Jr., and William Haenzel, *Migration in the United States: an Analysis of Residence Histories.* Public Health Monograph No. 77. U.S. Dept. of Health, Education, and Welfare. 1968.

23. Herrick, Bruce H., *Urban Migration and Economic Development in Chile.* Cambridge, Mass.: The M.I.T. Press, 1966.

24. Zelinsky, Wilbur, Leszek Kosinski, and R. Mansell Prothero, eds., *Geography and a Crowding World: Essays on Population Pressure upon Resources,* New York: Oxford Univ. Press, 1970.

25. Wolf, Eric R., "Closed Corporate Peasant Communities in Mesoamérica and Central Java," *Southwest J Anthropol*, Spring 1957.
26. Geertz, Clifford, *Agricultural Involution.* Berkeley and Los Angeles: Univ. of Calif. Press, 1963.
27. Barraclough, Solon L., "Agricultural Policy and Strategies of Land Reform," *Stud Comp Int Develop*, Vol. 4, No. 8, 1968-69. pp. 167-197.
28. Mohsin, M., "The Tenor of Indian Urbanism: With Particular Reference to Chittarajan," *Sociol Bull*, Vol. 12, No. 2, 1963. pp. 50-65.
29. Gutkind, P. L. W., "African Responses to Urban Wage Employment," *Int Lab R*, 97, 1968. pp. 135-166.
30. Thomas, Dorothy Swaine, *Research Memorandum on Migration Differentials.* New York: Social Science Research Council, 1938.
31. United Nations, Department of Economic and Social Affairs, *The Mysore Population Study.* Population Studies No. 34. New York: United Nations, 1961.
32. Camisa, Zulma C., "Effects of Migration on the Growth and Population in the Cities of Latin America," *Proceedings of the World Population Conference.* New York: United Nations, E/CONF. 41/5, 4, 1967. pp. 408-411.
33. Morris, David, *The Emergence of an Industrial Labor Force in India: A Study of Bombay Cotton Mills, 1854-1947.* Berkeley: Univ. of Calif. Press, 1965.
34. Bogue, Donald J., and K. C. Zachariah, "Urbanization and Migration in India," *India's Urban Future*, Roy Turner, ed. Berkeley and Los Angeles: Univ. of Calif. Press, 1962. pp. 27-54.
35. Zachariah, K. C., "Bombay Migration Study: A Pilot Analysis of Migration to an Asian Metropolis," *Demography*, Vol. 3, No. 2, 1966. pp. 378-392.
36. Kuznets, Simon, "Introduction: Population Redistribution, Migration, and Economic Growth," *Population Redistribution and Economic Growth, United States 1870-1950.* Hope T. Eldridge and Dorothy Swaine Thomas, eds. Philadelphia: The American Philosophical Society, 1964. pp. xxiii-xxxv.
37. Ejiogu, C. N., "African Rural-Urban Migrants in the Main Migrant Areas of the Lagos Federal Territory," *The Population of Tropical Africa*, J. C. Caldwell and C. Okonjo, eds. New York: Columbia Univ. Press, 1968. pp. 320-330.
38. Speare, Alden, Jr., "Determinants of Rural-Urban Migration in Taiwan," paper presented at the 1969 Annual Meeting of the Population Association of America. Boston, 1969.
39. Arriaga, Eduardo, "Components of City Growth in Selected Latin American Countries," *Milbank Mem Fund Quart*, Vol. 46, No. 2, 1968. pp. 237-252.
40. Misra, B. R., *Socio-Economic Survey of Jamshedpur City.* Patra: Patra Univ. Press, 1959.
41. Abu-Lughod, Janet, "Migrant Adjustment to City Life: The Egyptian Case," *Am J Sociol*, 67, 1961. pp. 22-32.

42. Cruz, Levy, *As Migracoes para o Recife*, Vol. IV. Caracterizacao Social, Recife, Instituto Joaquim Nabuco de Pesquisas Sociais, 1961.
43. Blau, Peter, and Otis Dudley Duncan, *The American Occupational Structure*. New York: John Wiley & Sons, 1967.
44. Lipset, Seymour, and Reinhard Bendix, *Social Mobility in Industrial Society*. Berkeley and Los Angeles: Univ. of Calif. Press, 1959.
45. Bradfield, Stillman, "Some Occupational Aspects of Migration," *Econ Devel & Cult Change*, Vol. 14, No. 1, 1965. pp. 61-70.
46. Cardona Gutiérrez, Ramiro, "Migración, Urbanización y Marginalidad," *Urbanización y Marginalidad*. Bogotá: Asociación Colombiana de Facultades de Medicina, 1968.
47. Lewis, Oscar, "Urbanization Without Breakdown: a Case Study," *Sci Mon*, July 1952. pp. 31-41.
48. Butterworth, Douglas S., "A Study of the Urbanization Process among Mixtec Migrants from Tilantongo in Mexico City," *Am Indig*, Vol. 22, No. 3, 1962. pp. 257-274.
49. Hauser, Philip, "Observations on the Urban-Folk and Urban-Rural Dichotomies as Forms of Western Ethnocentrism," *The Study of Urbanization*, Philip Hauser and Leo Schnore, eds. New York: John Wiley & Sons, 1965.
50. Inkeles, Alex, "Making Men Modern: On the Causes and Consequences of Individual Change in Six Developing Countries," *Am J Sociol*, Vol. 75, No. 2, 1969. pp. 208-225.
51. Mangin, William P., "Latin American Squatter Settlements: A Problem and Solution," *Lat Am Res R*, Vol. 2, No. 3, 1967. pp. 65-98.
52. Leeds, Anthony, and Elizabeth Leeds, "Brazil and the Myth of Urban Rurality: Urban Experience, Work, and Values in 'Squatments' of Rio de Janeiro and Lima," *Conference on Urbanization and Work in Modernizing Societies*. St. Thomas, Virgin Islands, September 2-4, 1967.
53. Turner, John C., *Asentamientos Urbanos no Regulados*, Cuadernos de la Sociedad Venezolana de Planificación No. 36. Caracas: Editorial Latina, 1966.
54. Bogue, Donald, *Principles of Demography*. New York: John Wiley & Sons, 1969.
55. Balan, Jorge, et al., "A Computerized Approach to the Processing and Analysis of Life Histories Obtained in Sample Surveys," *Behav Sci*, Vol. 14, No. 2, 1969. pp. 105-120.

IX

Effect of Population Change on the Attainment of Educational Goals in the Developing Countries

Gavin W. Jones

If there is one article of faith that is almost universally shared in developing countries,* it is that education must be expanded and must be expanded rapidly. Governments emphasize the need to eliminate illiteracy, to provide universal and free primary education, and to produce enough manpower with technical and academic skills to meet the requirements of development plans. Villagers simply have the conviction that, although they did not go to school themselves, their children are going to do so, and the government has a duty to provide schools for them.

The reasoning behind the villager's conviction is clear enough: education is the key to prosperity and to full participation in the rapidly changing social and economic order that he has seen in the towns, even though it may scarcely have reached his village. The motives behind governments' passion for education may be mixed. For example, an architecturally exciting national university is a status symbol for a newly independent country. In any case, however, politicians and government planners cannot fail to take note of the ground swell of popular demand for education. Beyond this, they see clearly enough the need for technicians, for professional people, and for

Gavin Jones is Resident Consultant for the Population Council and Demographer, Manpower Planning Division, National Economic Development Board, Bangkok, Thailand.

*Also called "less developed countries," or "LDC's," and defined roughly as Asia (except Japan), Africa, and Latin America. The countries categorized as "developing" will vary according to the definition used. According to the simple definition of countries with a per capita GNP below $600, the developing countries will comprise all of Africa except Libya, all of Asia except Japan, Israel, Kuwait, and Cyprus, all of Latin America except Argentina and Venezuela; Albania, Malta, Portugal, and Yugoslavia in Europe; and most of Polynesia, Melanesia, and Micronesia. Per capita GNP figures for 1966 are from (1).

literate farmers. They may recognize that even in cold cost-benefit terms, education often pays off better than alternative investments.

Progress and Problems in Expanding Education

The educational progress in developing countries over the last two decades has been truly impressive. As shown in Table 1, enrollments in secondary and higher education in these countries more than doubled during the 1950's and increased by a further two thirds during the first half of the 1960's. The most rapid growth was in Africa, where enrollments, including primary, more than trebled in the 15-year period 1950-1965. In some countries educational developments have been spectacular. Venezuela, for example, cut its illiteracy rate

TABLE 1

Enrollment at Three Educational Levels in Developing
Regions: 1950, 1960, and 1965

				Percent Increase	
	1950	1960	1965	1950-60	1960-65
		(millions)			
AFRICA					
1st level (primary)	8.5	18.9	25.9	122	37
2nd level (secondary)	0.7	2.1	3.6	176	71
3rd level (higher)	0.1	0.2	0.3	168	68
All three levels	9.3	21.2	29.9	128	41
LATIN AMERICA					
1st level (primary)	15.4	27.0	34.7	75	29
2nd level (secondary)	1.7	3.9	6.7	128	72
3rd level (higher)	0.3	0.6	0.9	103	60
All three levels	17.4	31.4	42.3	81	35
ASIA[a]					
1st level (primary)	42.1	74.6	104.1	77	39
2nd level (secondary)	5.4	12.2	19.7	125	61
3rd level (higher)	0.6	1.4	2.6	132	82
All three levels	48.1	88.2	126.4	83	43
TOTAL: LESS DEVELOPED REGIONS					
1st level (primary)	66.0	120.5	164.7	83	36
2nd level (secondary)	7.9	18.2	30.0	131	65
3rd level (higher)	1.0	2.2	3.8	127	75
All three levels	74.8	140.9	198.6	88	41

[a]Excluding China (mainland), North Korea, North Vietnam, and Japan.

Source: (2, Table 2.2).

from 50 percent to 11 percent between 1960 and 1968. Over the same period primary school enrollments doubled, while secondary enrollments and numbers of university students grew about fivefold. Zambia is raising the numbers in secondary schools from fewer than 9,000 in 1964 (excluding Europeans) to a planned 61,300 in 1970 (3).

Demographic Problems

Yet despite these remarkable achievements, the number of adult illiterates throughout the world has increased over the past decade, according to UNESCO (4). One reason is that very large numbers of children drop out of primary school before they have become literate, so that rising percentages in school do not mean very much if they are concentrated in the lower grades. The basic reason, however, is that the steady reduction in the *percentage* of illiterates is not enough to reduce their *absolute* number because the number of children passing through the school-going ages is increasing so rapidly.

Demographic problems facing the educational planners will be discussed later. Here it need only be mentioned that because of massive increases in the size of the youth population, the number of school places must double every 30 years or so just to maintain the same proportion of children in school. The supply of classrooms and teachers must be expanded at the same rate merely to maintain the status quo. Despite this tremendous demographic obstacle, the growth in enrollments has been large enough to narrow the percentage gap between school-going and school-age population:* between 1950 and 1965 the number of countries with more than 50 percent of school-age children in school at the first and second levels grew from 94 to 141, out of a total of 203 countries with relevant data.[†] The steady growth in the proportion of young people in school in Asia during roughly the same period is shown in Table 2.

But the substantial gains over the last decade or two in raising the proportion of children in school, though impressive, do not appear nearly as spectacular as do the increases in the absolute number of enrollments. If the number of children in the developing countries had not increased since 1950, the massive increases in enrollments shown in Table 1 would have been enough to provide school places for 82 percent of primary school age children by 1965, but as it is, only 54 percent were in school.[‡] It is a matter of running up the down escalator; it is possible to reach the top, but the effort involved is much greater than it would be if the escalator were halted.

*The gap in absolute terms has remained about the same and possibly has increased slightly.

[†]Derived from UNESCO (2, Table 2.5). Data are adjusted school enrollment ratios; for definition, see Figure 1, footnote a.

[‡]These are rough estimates derived by applying the figures for primary school enrollment to the age group 6 to 13.

TABLE 2

Trends in School Enrollment Rates, Asian Countries, 1955-1964

(percent)

Enrollment Rate[a]	1955[b]	1960	1964	Total Enrollments: Average Annual Rate of Increase 1955-64
First level	46	53	61	6.7
Second level	9	12	15	9.4
Third level	1.6	2.3	3.0	10.1
Total	27	31	36	6.9

[a]Enrollment rate (ER) is enrollment as a percentage of corresponding age group (6 to 12, 13 to 17, and 18 to 21 for first, second, and third levels respectively).

[b]Since the distribution of the population by single years of age and the distribution of enrollment by grades were not available for that year, the 1955 figures were estimated.

Source: UNESCO (5, Table 11).

Figure 1 gives a very rough indication of the extent to which universal education has been attained in the age groups from which primary and secondary students are drawn. African countries are the furthest from providing education for all children. Asian countries range all the way from very underdeveloped educationally (particularly those countries in the region from the Red Sea to the Himalayas) to advanced; a number of Asian countries now provide universal primary education. Latin America is notably further ahead but still lags behind Europe and northern America.* In terms of the measure used in Figure 1—the percentage ratio of enrollments in primary and secondary schools to the estimated school-age population—Pakistan and Nigeria are the least advanced of the world's twenty largest nations.

*Harbison and Myers in (6, pp. 31-34) rank countries around 1960 according to a "composite index" based on enrollment rates at the secondary and higher levels of education. As shown in the following table, the distribution of countries across the range of their index according to continent is roughly comparable to that in Figure 1, although their table highlights more clearly the differences between Latin America and the developed countries, both because of the earlier data and because they give no place to primary school enrollment rates, in terms of which differences between developed and developing countries are less pronounced.

Harbison and Myers' Composite Index, around 1960

	0-10	10-30	30-50	50-80	80+
	(Number of Countries)				
Africa	14	3	2	–	–
Asia	2	8	3	2	2
Latin America	1	8	5	2	1
Northern America and Europe	–	–	3	8	9

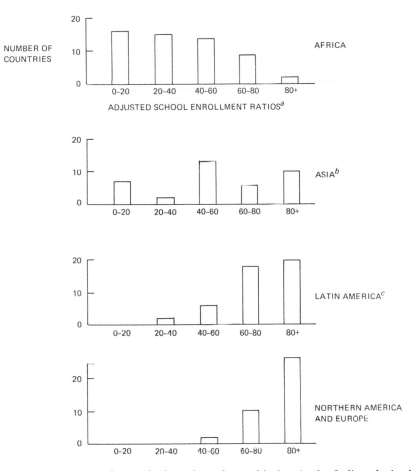

Figure 1. Number of countries in each continent with given levels of adjusted school enrollment ratios, around 1965.

[a]The adjusted school enrollment ratio is a percentage ratio based on the enrollment in primary and secondary schools (including general, vocational, and teacher training schools) related to the estimated population in the age range to which these levels of education apply in the particular country.

[b]Excludes mainland China.

[c]All countries listed by UNESCO under North America, with the exception of the United States, Canada, and Greenland, were included in Latin America.

Source: UNESCO (2, Table 2.5).

The Quality of Education

What has happened to the *quality* of education while these massive quantitative advances have been taking place? Any answer to this question must be tentative because the quality of a school system is difficult to measure and the situation no doubt differs greatly between countries. Nevertheless, it is widely known that a substantial proportion of the effort and money devoted to primary education is wasted. High repeater rates, nonattendance rates, and dropout rates mean that many primary school enrollees do not become even functionally literate. Poor physical facilities, poorly trained teachers, rote learning, and irrelevant courses are only too common. Funds are scarce. In West Pakistan, the total cost of primary education per child per year around 1965 was 90 cents. "Of this sum," says Curle, "an amount less than 5 cents is spent on all such things as paper, equipment, chalk, teaching aids, books. The equivalent figure for a representative American suburban area is $30—at least 600 times as much. In East Pakistan things are even worse" (7).

It is reasonable to assume that popular pressures and perhaps questions of international prestige make some governments answerable regarding the expansion of school places but not regarding the quality of education provided. (After all, parents with little or no school experience themselves have little basis for evaluating the standard of education their children are receiving.) Furthermore, statements on record by ministries of education and by well-placed educational planners lament a deterioration in the quality of education.* From them one can infer that educational quality has been a frequent casualty of the rapid growth of educational systems in less developed countries.

In other countries education has been a casualty of political upheavals. Both China and Indonesia have seen the virtual abandonment of formal education for periods of a year or more during times of political unrest: in Indonesia, in late 1965 and early 1966, and in China during the period of the Cultural Revolution from 1966 to 1968.

Financial Obstacles

The need to raise quality while the drive toward universal education continues is the challenge of the next decade. The obstacles are formidable, the most important being finance. A recent study indicates that educational costs

---

*A number of examples may be cited. The Commission on National Education in Pakistan (1959) stated bluntly that "there can be no doubt that as a consequence of unplanned expansion without adequate funds the system of secondary education has internally collapsed" (8).

A more recent official publication of the Ministry of Education in Pakistan discusses the rapid expansion of education, then adds: "But progress at this pace has its price. . . . to restore standards that may have temporarily fallen in the process is one of the major tasks and challenges we have to face" (9).

The Secretary-General of the Korean Federation of Education Associations, in a recent paper, states: "However, as critics have repeatedly pointed out, it is undeniable that, although Korean education has drastically expanded in quantity during the past two decades, qualitative expansion during the corresponding period fell far short" (10). See also (11).

Educators in Zambia conceded that standards fell drastically in the rush to expand education following independence in 1964. The Education Minister recently stated, "We opened more schools than we could look after" (3).

per student, even when expressed in constant prices, have had a fairly universal tendency to rise over the past 15 years (12, p. 47) primarily because of increasing teacher salary costs. This finding should not be surprising, even though many education ministries have pinned their hopes on the maintenance of constant costs per student at the various levels of education. If wages and salaries are to maintain a given share of total income in the economy* and if teacher salaries are to maintain their position in the salary hierarchy, teacher salaries would have to rise roughly in step with income per worker. Whether in fact they have done so would be a useful subject for detailed international study.

What *is* clear is that in both less and more developed countries, the share of educational expenditures in both the gross national product (GNP) and in government budgets has been steadily rising over the past decade (12, pp. 52-63; 2, Table 2.16; 14). Most industrialized countries "have moved from a point where they were spending between 2 and 4 percent of GNP on education in 1955 (a considerable increase for many over 1950) to the point of spending between 4 and 6 percent by 1965" (12, pp. 52-53). The rise in educational expenditures in the developing countries has been even sharper. In the struggle to expand the coverage of their educational systems, a majority of the countries for which evidence is available have doubled or even trebled their educational expenditures within a period of only 5 or 10 years (12, Appendix 24). The result has been a sharp increase in the share of public educational expenditures in budgets and in GNP (see Table 3).[†] Most countries in Asia were spending between 1 and 2 percent of GNP on education in 1955, and no country was spending more than 3 percent (5, p. 21). The range has since widened, and though most countries are still devoting less than 3 percent of GNP to education, in some the proportion reaches 5 percent. In Latin America, the modal range of expenditure shifted up from 1 to 3 percent in 1960 to 3 to 5 percent 5 years later. The data in Table 4 may somewhat overstate the typical level of expenditure, since data are more often unavailable for the less educationally advanced countries. Nevertheless, the trend between 1960 and 1965 is impressive. Some African countries are now spending the equivalent of 6 percent or more of their GNP on education, if foreign aid is included. Some African and Latin American countries are devoting more than a fifth of the national budget to education, and although the Asian countries as a group cannot match this record, Singapore has been spending even more: 23.5 to 30 percent of the national budget in recent years.

*There is evidence that the share of wages and salaries tends to *rise* (13).

[†]The data in Table 3 and Figure 2 are drawn from the best available source of comparative international data on education (2). They are, however, subject to a variety of weaknesses, not the least of which is that the ratio of private expenditure to public expenditure on education varies between countries. There is unfortunately a dearth of intercountry comparative information on private expenditures on education.

TABLE 3

Distribution of Countries According to Proportion of GNP Spent
on Public Education, 1955 and around 1965, by Continents[a]

(number of countries)

Percent of GNP Spent on Public Education	Asia		Latin America[b]			Africa[b]	
	1955	1965	1955	1960	1965	1960	1965
1 or less	3	–	1	–	–	1	–
1.1 to 2	9	5	5	7	2	5	2
2.1 to 3	3	5	5	6	4	5	4
3.1 to 4	–	2	2	4	7	4	4
4.1 to 5	–	3	–	2	5	4	4
5.1 to 6	–	–	–	–	3	1	3
6.1 to 7	–	–	1	1	–	–	1
7.1 or more	–	–	–	2	1	–	2
Total countries	15	15	14	22	22	20	20

[a]For some countries data for 1955, 1960, or 1965 were not available, and figures for the preceding or subsequent year have been used. For some countries percentages are related to gross domestic product instead of gross national product.
[b]Percentages for Sierra Leone in 1960, Nigeria in 1965, Paraguay in 1960, and Nicaragua in 1965 were calculated by applying the expenditure figures in the UNESCO Statistical Yearbook (2) to gross domestic product figures from the United Nations *Yearbook of National Accounts Statistics* (15). A further adjustment was made to the Nigerian data to allow for expenditure on the third level of education, which was not included in the UNESCO figure.

Sources: (2, Table 2.16; 5, Table 15).

The wealthy countries obviously spend much more on education per head of population than the poor countries. But is it easier for them to devote a greater share of the national income to education? Apparently so; an analysis of the relationship between per capita GNP and the percentage of the national income devoted to public expenditure on education in all countries with available data indicates a strong positive relationship.* However, as shown in Figure 2, there is no relationship at all if we consider only those countries with per capita GNP between $700.† The share of educational expenditures in the national incomes of the poorest countries (those with per capita incomes below $250) range very widely indeed—from 1.5 percent to 8.5 percent. Coupled with the evidence of an upward shift over time in the share of educational expenditures in most countries, these figures indicate that in no sense can low income be considered an immovable barrier to the channel-

*In terms of a simple regression analysis, the relationship can be expressed as follows: $y = .00135x + 3.48692$. $F(1,88) = 32.3$, significant at 0.001 level.
†$F(1,60) = 0.02$, not significant at 0.05 level.

TABLE 4

Projected Enrollments and Financial Requirements up to 1970 for
UNESCO Regional Educational Targets, by Regions

	1965	Percent	1970	Percent	Average Annual Rate of Increase (Percent)
AFRICA					
First level: enrollment	15,279		20,378		5.93
Participation rate (000)		51		71	
Second level: enrollment	1,833.5		3,390		13.08
Participation rate (000)		9		15	
Third level: enrollment	46		80		11.71
Participation rate (000)		0.35		0.55	
Total expenditures (U.S. $ mil)	1,139		1,701		8.35
GNP (U.S. $ mil)	19,694		24,413		4.39
Percentage of GNP		5.78		6.96	
LATIN AMERICA					
First level: enrollment	34,721		43,438		4.58
Participation rate (000)		91		100	
Second level: enrollment	6,230		11,457		12.96
Participation rate (000)		22		34	
Third level: enrollment	665		905		6.35
Participation rate (000)		3.4		4	
Total expenditures (U.S. $ mil)	3,219		4,937		9
GNP (U.S. $ mil)	71,130		90,782		5
Percentage of GNP		4.52		5.43	
ASIA					
First level: enrollment	110,368		148,716		6.15
Participation rate (000)		63		74	
Second level: enrollment	14,545		23,064		9.66
Participation rate (000)		15		19	
Third level: enrollment	2,206		3,320		7.86
Participation rate (000)		3.4		4.1	
Total expenditures (U.S. $ mil)	3,261		4,803		8.05
GNP (U.S. $ mil)	88,319		112,719		5
Percentage of GNP		3.69		4.26	

Source: (12, Appendix 25).

ing of a substantial proportion of income into education. The poor countries
have a wide range of options open to them.

OFFICIAL EDUCATIONAL GOALS

The broad objectives of the future development of education in the LDC's
are well expressed in the final resolution and statement of the Meeting of

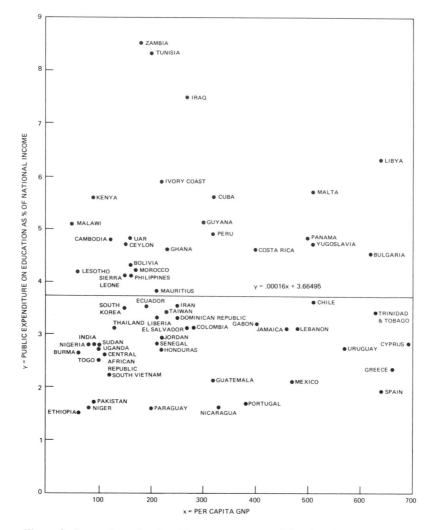

Figure 2. Proportion of national income spent on public education as a function of per capita GNP for 62 selected countries with per capita GNP below $700.
Source: (2).

Ministers of Education at Tokyo (April, 1962), reaffirmed by the subsequent Conference of Ministers of Education and Ministers responsible for Economic Planning of Member States in Asia (Bangkok, November, 1965). As summarized in another UNESCO study (5, pp. 21-22), the major themes that emerged from these statements are:

1. The need for balanced development of education at all levels, with the expansion of secondary and higher levels being determined by the ability of

pupils, availability of financial resources and manpower requirements of the country.

2. The importance of qualitative considerations for development. The need for achieving higher standards at the second and third levels is impera-tive. Even at the primary level the maintenance of proper standards in order to prevent wastage and to provide a satisfactory basis for the higher level is essential.

3. The need for diversification of education by enlarging and strengthen-ing vocational and technical education at the second and third levels in line with the developing capacity of the economy to utilize trained skills.

4. Expansion and improvement of science education at all levels.

5. Promotion of programmes of adult and youth and family education as an integral part of overall educational development.

6. Development of education should reflect the principle of equality of educational opportunity and the promotion of international peace and amity.

After granting these broad goals, educational planners could be excused if they aimed to do no more than maintain the current proportions of children in school, because the school-age population in developing countries is ex-pected to increase by something like 25 percent during the 1970's. However, planners have usually aimed much higher than this. A bird's-eye view of educational goals in the LDC's can be had by examining the ambitious ed-ucational targets adopted a few years ago by UNESCO Conferences of the Ministers of Education in Latin America, Africa, and Asia,* which have been very influential in reinforcing the educational aims of the member countries. The goals for enrollments and enrollment rates, as well as the financial impli-cations, are presented in Table 4.

Table 4 indicates clearly that the educational planners hope to improve very substantially on the 1965 situation by 1970. It is now known that in both Africa and Asia, the growth of education in the 1960-65 period was not quite as rapid as the educational planners had hoped, and the 1965 enroll-ment rates were lower than those shown in Table 4.[†] This makes it less likely that the 1970 goals can be reached, but if they are reached, enrollment rates at the first level of education will reach 71 percent in Africa, 74 percent in Asia, and 100 percent in Latin America. Even greater relative increases are envisaged at the second and third levels. The UNESCO statisticians estimated the cost of meeting these targets. They calculated that in Africa (where enrollment targets at the second and third levels were rather more ambitious than in Asia or Latin America) the countries as a group would have to spend nearly 7 percent of GNP on education by 1970. The Latin American group

*These targets were revisions of targets proposed by UNESCO for the United Nations Development Decade (16, p. 30).

[†]A detailed analysis of the statistical evidence is contained in (17, 18).

would have to spend 5.4 percent of GNP and the Asian group 4.3 percent.* Each case would represent substantial increases over the actual expenditures in recent years,† although as mentioned earlier, the share of the GNP going to education has been moving up in all three regions. However, even these high figures may understate the problem, because it was assumed that various kinds of economy-producing innovations and adjustments would keep unit costs from rising to any extent.‡

The UNESCO conferences also looked beyond 1970 to set longer-term goals for enrollment. For example, the Asian countries adopted the goal of universal primary education, and although target dates were not specified, envisaged that most countries could reach this goal before 1980. Very few countries, however, have developed detailed long-term educational plans although they commonly mention certain long-term targets. For example, Pakistan aims to provide universal primary education of 5 years' duration by 1980 (the target date having been 1975 in earlier documents) and to reduce the wastefully high dropout rate in the early grades. Afghanistan, one of the least advanced countries educationally in the region, aims to reach a 50 percent enrollment rate by 1980. Burma hopes to be able to enforce compulsory education by 1970. In Iran, the 20-year plan (1963-83) aims at providing free and compulsory education for the age group 7 to 13. The national plans typically envisage a vigorous expansion of teacher training, often including in-service training, to meet future needs (5, pp. 22-23).

In setting up these ambitious targets, not all the countries are as courageous as the Indian Education Commission of 1966, which not only proposed large enrollment increases and quality improvements by 1985 but spelled out their financial implications as well. These were formidable enough to be alarming: on the optimistic assumption that India's economy will grow at 6 percent annually throughout this period, educational expenditures will have to expand from 2.9 percent of GNP in 1965 to 6 percent by 1985.

DEMOGRAPHIC OBSTACLES TO THE ATTAINMENT OF EDUCATIONAL GOALS

Official educational goals typically aim to expand the coverage of the school system and to improve its quality so that it may better meet the

*These estimates were predicated on the assumption of an economic growth rate of 5 percent per annum in Latin America and Asia and 4.4 percent in Africa. Available evidence indicates that actual growth in Latin America has averaged 4.8 percent per annum during the 1960-67 period, and growth rates in south Asia and Africa have also been below 5 percent.

†For a statistical analysis, see (19).

‡The exceptions were the assumption of moderate rises for primary education in Africa, and for primary and higher education in Asia.

manpower requirements of economic development, as well as the social, or popular, demand for education. The two most important constraints on attaining these goals are the financial sacrifices the country is willing to make to reach them and, in many cases, the shortage of adequately trained teachers, a shortage that takes time to remedy, particularly when an attempt is made to diversify the system by strengthening areas such as technical education.

Demographic trends in the less developed countries, which are forcing educational planners to aim at a moving target, are an integral part of the problem. In a country with a youth population of 1,000,000 increasing at 3 percent per annum, a rise in the enrollment rate from 50 percent to 75 percent in 10 years means an increase in enrollments, not of 250,000 but of 538,000. This example illustrates only one of the more obvious ways in which demographic trends are of vital importance to educational planning. To explain further the demographic constraints on educational advance, a quick summary of prospective demographic trends is in order.

Population Structure

As Table 5 shows, the less developed areas are sharply divided from the developed ones in terms of fertility, with birth rates more than twice as high as those in the developed regions. Mortality conditions vary more widely among the less developed countries, with crude death rates ranging from 9.5 per 1,000 in "Other East Asia" to 20.9 per 1,000 in Africa. If smaller regions

TABLE 5

Crude Births and Death Rates by Major World Regions 1965-1970
Implied in United Nations Medium Variant Projections

	Crude Birth Rate	Crude Death Rate	Rate of Natural Increase
World Total	32.9	14.4	18.5
More developed countries	18.5	8.5	10.0
Less developed countries	39.4	17.3	22.1
Mainland China	32.3	19.0	13.2
Other east Asia[a]	37.5	9.5	28.0
South Asia	42.1	17.0	25.1
Africa	45.4	20.9	24.4
Latin America	39.0	9.9	29.1
Europe	16.6	9.9	6.7
U.S.S.R.	19.4	7.1	12.3
Northern America	21.3	9.4	11.9
Japan	15.6	7.7	7.9

[a]Excludes Japan.

Source: (21, pp. 34-36).

are compared and more precise measures of mortality employed, the range is wider still. For example, infant mortality rates range from around 25 in Singapore and Hong Kong to more than 200 in some African countries (the African data for 1960-61).*

The significant declines in mortality that have occurred almost universally in the less developed countries are, of course, the primary cause of the accelerated rate of population growth in the postwar years. They have also had some effect on the age structure of the developing areas, an age structure characterized by a much greater share of the population in the school-age and preschool groups than in the advanced countries. (See Table 6.) However, the unbroken history of high fertility has been more influential in shaping the youthful, broad-based pyramid (22, 23).

TABLE 6

Share of the School-Going and Prospective School-Going Age Groups in
the Total Population of Major World Regions, 1970,
United Nations' Medium Projections

	0-4 Age Group	5-14 Age Group	5-24 Age Group
World Total	13.6	22.8	40.8
Mainland east Asia	12.8	22.6	41.3
Other east Asia[a]	16.0	27.1	46.1
South Asia[b]	16.7	25.7	43.9
Africa	17.2	26.0	45.3
Latin America	16.6	25.8	44.2
Northern America	10.1	19.9	37.3
Europe	8.0	16.3	31.9
Japan	7.5	15.2	34.8

[a]Excludes Japan.
[b]Excludes Israel and Cyprus.

Source: (21, pp. 127-32).

The less developed regions also have a somewhat greater share of their population in the school-age and preschool groups today than they did a decade earlier, because the growth of these age groups through the 1960's has exceeded that of the population as a whole. A corollary of this youthful dominance is a much smaller proportion of the population in the working ages, the group which must pay taxes to finance educational programs. This situation is only partly offset by earlier entry into, and later withdrawal from, the work force.

*Of African countries with available data, Dahomey, Upper Volta, and Cameroon had infant mortality rates in excess of 200 per 1,000 live births around 1960-61 (20, pp. 182-83).

These characteristics of the age structure should be considered in relation to the finding that some developing countries can match the share of GNP invested in education in the developed countries. This does *not* mean that they can match the developed countries in terms of the share of GNP spent on education *per head of the school-age population.* One example will suffice. Around 1965, the United Kingdom spent 6 percent of GNP on education, Ghana 5 percent. But the school-age population (5 to 19 years) was about 37 percent of the total in Ghana, 22 percent in the U.K. Therefore Britain was spending about twice as high a percentage of GNP per head of the school-age population as was Ghana.

Future Trends in Mortality and Fertility

Future trends in vital rates are always difficult to predict. Rather severe fluctuations in mortality rates due to civil unrest or famine are by no means a thing of the past, as shown by the terrible toll of the Nigerian civil war. Further steady declines in mortality are, however, in prospect throughout most of the less developed world. In some regions, particularly tropical Africa and middle south Asia, the potential reduction by means of public health programs is still great enough to add a percentage point to the rate of population growth. Such reductions will have relatively little effect on the overall age structure, since they will probably be operative at all ages, but the relative gain in reducing mortality may be greatest at the youngest ages, causing small relative gains at the lower levels of the population pyramid. For educational planning, the important consideration is the trend in infant and early childhood mortality. The expected reduction in mortality at these ages will have precisely the same implications for the educational system as a rise in fertility: an increase in numbers subsequently moving into the school-age groups.

Although fertility may rise slightly during the next few years in some less developed countries, partly because of lowered disease and death rates, the more common trend will almost certainly be downward. More parents will adjust their desired number of births downward in response to changing socioeconomic conditions and the decreased likelihood of infant death. Improved methods of contraception, expansion of family planning programs, and, probably, improvements in commercial marketing channels will make it easier for them to hold the number of children in the family down to the desired number. Thus trends in fertility and in infant mortality will, in most instances, be operating in opposite directions on the number of potential additions to the school population. At current fertility and mortality levels, the *potential* impact of lowered fertility in reducing the increments to the school-age population is substantially greater than that of lowered mortality in raising them, because in most cases death rates are already low while fertility remains high. The extent to which this potential will be realized will depend on the speed and timing of reductions in fertility and mortality.

For the developing countries taken as a whole, the implications of a per-petuation of current high levels of fertility over the next 20 years, combined with prospective declines in mortality, is clear: the school-going age groups would grow very rapidly, and their share of the total population would rise slightly above its current level. With moderate declines in fertility, the United Nations' medium projection indicates that the share of the school-going popu-lation (aged 5 to 14) would remain virtually unchanged up to 1980, since its rate of increase during the 1970's, at 2.2 percent per annum, would be only slightly below that of the total population (21, Annexes 2, 3). In terms of this projection, the school-age population has already reached its maximum rate of growth. The rate is likely to climb higher during the 1970's in rela-tively few areas, notably parts of Africa and southwest Asia.

If widespread and rapid reductions in fertility should occur (and this is not impossible), the growth rate of the school-age population would slacken more quickly although numbers at school age would nevertheless rise very substan-tially during the 1970's and into the 1980's.

If fertility declines at about the rate implied in the United Nations' me-dium projection, the total number of school-age children will still increase rapidly.* The growth rate of the school-age population during the next de-cade will be faster than during the past two decades, and about as rapid as it is at the current time; and two decades from now, the absolute increment to the school-going age groups each year will be about two-thirds greater than it is at present. The financial implications of bringing a higher proportion of this expanding group of "eligibles" into the school system are obvious enough.

The Shortage of Teachers

The age structure that will continue to characterize the developing coun-tries for at least the next decade is an unfavorable one, not only in terms of the high dependency rates, but also in terms of potential teacher supply. In a developing country that has been making rapid progress in expanding school places, the cohorts from which potential teachers must be drawn will be substantially smaller and much more poorly educated. A simple example will illustrate the point. Figure 3 is based on population data from a hypothetical country with high fertility and moderate mortality, whose past educational trends are a composite of those in developing countries for which data are available.† It is striking that the total number of persons in the potential

---

*A number of demographers believe that the United Nations' medium variant is likely to understate the increase in world population between now and the year 2000. For an excellent summary of alternative points of view, see the papers by Macura and Durand in (24).

†The birth rate in this hypothetical country was 44.3 per 1,000, the expectation of life at birth 45 years for males (and the death rate 19.3 per 1,000), and the growth rate

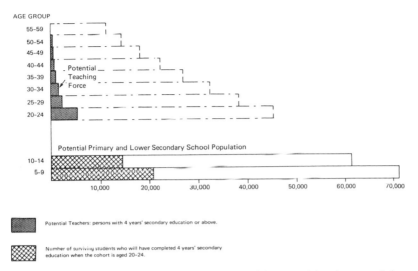

Figure 3. Potential teaching force compared with potential primary and lower secondary school population (ages 5 to 14) in a hypothetical high-fertility country experiencing steady, and recently accelerating, educational development.

teaching ages (20 to 59) who have completed 4 years of secondary education is well below the number who will later do so in the 10 to 14 age group alone. After 10 or 15 years, then, there will be enough extra secondary graduates available to permit a very large expansion of the teaching force. (We are ignoring cost considerations for the moment, as well as the problems entailed in rapidly expanding teacher training facilities.)

But how about the teacher supply problem in the immediate future? Will it, in fact, prove possible to expand enrollment rates at the secondary level as rapidly as postulated? In examining this question, we might note that if all children aged 5 to 14 were to be placed in school immediately, there would be 11.3 such children to every potential teacher (person with 4 years' secondary education). Most of those with 4 years' secondary education, however, will not be available for teaching, representing as they do the source from which a variety of professional, technical, managerial, and clerical positions must be filled. In fact, as shown in Table 7, typically only between one out of three and one out of twelve persons who have reached or surpassed this level of

2.5 percent per annum. The percentages who had completed 4 years' secondary education at ages 20 to 24 and 25 to 29 were derived from the assumed proportions in school when those cohorts were aged 15 to 19, by means of regression equations based on actual country data. The percentages who had completed 4 years' secondary education at ages above 25 to 29 were derived from the ratio of these percentages to the percentage at age 25 to 29 in the ten developing countries for which data were available (25, Appendix, especially Table A-5).

TABLE 7

Ratio of Nonteachers to Teachers among the Labor Force with Secondary Education
or Above, Various Countries

		Some Secondary Education or Above[a]	Completed Secondary Education or Above[b]
India	1961	n.a.	3.4:1
Pakistan	1961	6.0:1	n.a.
Ceylon	1963	6.4:1	3.6:1
Republic of Korea	1960	n.a.	5.4:1
Singapore	1966	11.1:1	9.0:1
Hong Kong	1966	12.4:1	3.9:1
Ghana	1960	11.2:1[c]	n.a.
Barbados	1960	11.7:1	n.a.
Venezuela	1961	6.4:1	8.9:1
Costa Rica	1964	3.0:1	1.8:1
Nicaragua	1964	5.0:1	2.5:1
El Salvador	1964	3.3:1	23.1:1
Honduras	1964	3.7:1	2.1:1
Guatemala	1964	5.2:1	43.0:1

n.a. = not available.

[a]The exact levels of education were: for Pakistan and Ghana, some middle school education; for Ceylon, Standard 8 and above; for Barbados and Venezuela, secondary education or above; for Hong Kong, Senior Middle (Chinese) or Higher Secondary (English) or above; for the Central American countries, some secondary education and above; in Singapore, all persons with some secondary education or more were related to all teachers, the vast majority of whom would have at least some secondary education. (In fact, 57 percent of Singapore's teachers have higher education.)

[b]The exact levels of education were: for India, matriculation or higher secondary and above; for Ceylon, matriculation and above (completed G.C.E. level in Ceylon); for Korea, 10 years of school or above; for Hong Kong, some postsecondary education or above; for Singapore, all persons with completed secondary education or above were related to teachers with at least some higher education; for Venezuela, higher education; and for the Central American countries, some higher education and above.

[c]When the level of education is raised to some secondary (i.e., above middle school education) or above, the ratio falls to 2.8:1.

Source: Population censuses of India, Pakistan, and Venezuela are for 1961; of Barbados and Ghana for 1960; of Ceylon for 1963; and of Hong Kong for 1966; for Singapore, data are from (26). For the Central American countries, data are from (27).

education in the developing countries are teachers and this includes upper secondary and college level teachers.* Thus, if our hypothetical country were to resemble Pakistan in having only one out of six of its secondary school

*The wide spread in this ratio for countries with available data is somewhat surprising. In interpreting the very low proportion of secondary graduates who go into teaching in El Salvador and Guatemala, it must be borne in mind that the number of such graduates is very small.

graduates in teaching, this would mean one such teacher to every 68 children aged 5 to 14. If Singapore's ratio were applicable, there would be only one teacher for every 102 such children.

In such situations, the limited supply of teachers would clearly prevent the immediate enrollment of all children aged 5 to 14. A less than immediate but very rapid rise toward universal education might also prove unattainable, because it might require an unrealistically high wage incentive to attract enough of the small group of potential teachers into teaching. But if expansion of enrollment rates were not pushed too hard—if the date for reaching universal education at ages 5 to 14 were set, say, 15 or 20 years hence—the situation would not appear so grim, because the output of students with 4 years' secondary education would increase much faster during that period than the number of children aged 5 to 14.

The foregoing example is no more than illustrative because the situation varies very widely between countries. India and some countries of Latin America are now producing more secondary school and university graduates than their economies can currently absorb in the types of jobs or at the rates of pay that they expect. Other countries, notably many in tropical Africa, are worse off than our hypothetical country in regard to teacher supply, because their secondary education system was very limited even a decade or two ago.* Many are still forced to rely heavily on expatriate staff at the secondary level, and a few at the primary level. For example, in Papua-New Guinea, expatriate teachers constitute 58 percent of the total teaching service, and although they supply almost the entire secondary teaching force, most of them are teaching in the primary schools (28). In most African countries, expatriate teachers are not required at the primary level, but in secondary schools expatriates constituted 63 percent of teachers in Uganda (1966), 33 percent in Ghana (1967-68), 93 percent in the Ivory Coast (1965) and 90 percent in Zambia (1968) (29, 30, 31, 32).†

Secondary Education

Shortages of educated manpower are clearly serious enough in some countries to make the achievement of universal primary and lower secondary education in the very near future quite inconceivable. But the very rapid achievement of universal education is not an option anyway, because of budgetary and logistic considerations. What *is* normally aimed for is a steady

---

*In 1950, out of a very restricted total school enrollment in Africa, only 8 percent were in secondary schools. The corresponding proportions at the same date were 10 percent in Latin America, 19 percent in Asia, and more than 20 percent in the western countries.

†For data on some other African countries, see (12, p. 195).

and rapid movement *toward* universal education, and shortages of potential teachers per se are unlikely to prevent such rapid movement.* It is, after all, precisely in those countries with serious shortages of secondary graduates (the tropical African countries) that the most rapid increases in enrollments and in the output of secondary graduates are occurring.

Educational authorities can exercise considerable flexibility in setting minimum standards for teacher qualifications. This is adequately demonstrated by a comparison between the poorest countries, where most primary school teachers have had practically no training as teachers and perhaps no more than 6 or 7 years of primary schooling themselves, and the western countries, which normally require at least 2 years of higher education beyond the secondary level for their primary school teachers.† The length of the training course, if any, given to recruits to the teaching force may also be varied. The effect of these shortcuts on the *quality* of education may be a serious concern; indeed, shortages of secondary graduates should perhaps be seen more as a bar to qualitative improvement than to quantitative expansion.

The demographic constraints on teacher supply in developing countries, then, are not absolute constraints; they may in time be effectively eliminated by a balanced expansion of the school system. (As shown later, they can be eliminated more rapidly if the birth rate declines.) In particular, secondary education must be expanded rapidly enough to sustain growth; it must be able to absorb the desired proportion of pupils completing primary school, provide enough primary school teachers and enough entrants to institutions of higher learning to staff the secondary schools themselves subsequently, as well as fill the many other jobs which require a higher education. The need for rapid expansion of secondary education is felt not only in countries in which a shortage of high school graduates has tended to hinder the expansion of primary education and hold down its quality but also in those educationally more advanced countries in which primary education is already universal and where the drive is now toward a broadened and improved system of secondary education. This is particularly true of countries such as the Republic of Korea and Venezuela, in which a burgeoning economy is creating new demands for skilled manpower in many fields.

Teachers and Costs

This need for rapid expansion of secondary education leads us straight to the other aspect of the teacher supply problem—costs. There are a number of interlocking aspects of this problem. One is that an educated person in a less

---

*For an interesting account of the expansion of Kenya's teaching force in the 1950's to keep pace with rapid enrollment increase, see (33).

†For the situation in Asian countries, see (34).

developed country earns relatively much more than an educated person in a developed country. Writing of the situation a few years ago, Lewis stated that "while the average salary of a primary school teacher is less than 1½ times per capita national income in the United States, a primary school teacher gets three times the per capita national income in Jamaica, five times in Ghana and seven times in Nigeria" (35, p. 137).

In secondary education cost per teacher was 30 times per capita income in Nigeria, compared with 12 times in Jamaica and only 2 times in the United States (35, p. 139). Lewis calculated that to give 8 years of primary education to every child would cost about 0.8 percent of national income in the United States, 1.7 percent in Jamaica, 2.8 percent in Ghana, and 4 percent in Nigeria.

The premium for education decreases as the supply of educated persons rises, but in the meantime the cost constraint is formidable. This is particularly so in view of the relatively greater emphasis on expanding secondary and higher education which cost far more per student than does primary education in these countries. For example, in African countries vocational secondary education is fifteen times and university education fifty-nine times as expensive (per student) as primary education, and in Asia vocational secondary education is six times and university education twenty-three times as expensive as primary education.*

The increase in the teacher force could be held down if the size of classes were allowed to increase. In most developing countries, however, this avenue of escape from the inexorable pressures of rising student numbers is already well trodden: pupil/teacher ratios are well above the optimum, and a major aim of educational planning in most countries is to lower them to more efficient levels. It is possible that closed-circuit television and other technological aids will enable countries to break out of the straight jacket of conventional pupil/teacher ratios, but this is a hope for the future rather than a practicable escape route at the moment. Other innovative approaches to the provision of teaching services, such as Iran's quasi-military "education corps," through which young high school graduates spend 14 months teaching in the villages,† should be viewed more as a device to accelerate the expansion of elementary education in the rural areas than as a method of lowering unit costs, although in fact it may achieve this end to a limited extent.

There is also little chance to economize by preventing teacher salaries for any given level of qualification from rising over time. The teaching "industry" is in an invidious position in that it is a labor-intensive industry. A 10 percent salary increase "usually translates into a 7 to 8 percent increase in its total

---

*Calculated as an unweighted country average from UNESCO data (2, Table 2.18). A few of the smallest countries were omitted from the calculations.

†For more details, see (36).

'costs of production.' "* It is also an industry in which it is difficult to measure increases in productivity. In modern industry, by contrast, salaries are a smaller proportion of total cost, and rising productivity permits steady increases in wages and salaries without corresponding increases in the real cost of production. Hence, although there is a strong upward pressure on teacher salaries to keep them more or less competitive with private industry, they tend to lag behind salaries in comparable occupations.

There are, in summary, three major reasons why teacher salary costs are likely to spiral in the developing countries. First, the sharp increase in pupil numbers that is an objective of educational planning in most countries spells more teachers. Second, the emphasis on secondary and higher education means that much of the expansion must be in the form of better educated, much more expensive teachers. Third, there will be an inexorable upward pressure on teacher salaries caused by salary increases for persons of comparable qualifications in other industries with rising productivity. Additionally, if salaries are more strongly linked to qualifications than to length of service, a country that succeeds in upgrading the qualification level of its primary or secondary school teaching force will face substantial increases in costs, even without any increase in the number of teachers.[†] The combination of all these factors spells dramatic increases in costs.

There are many other reasons why costs per student are certain to rise if the school system is to be expanded and improved. One is that the non-teacher salary component of recurrent costs—blackboards, chalk, classroom aids, and so forth—is at present often held to a minimum by restricting these supplies to the point where efficient teaching methods are jeopardized. Another is that elimination of double shifts in school buildings (a common aim, though not necessarily a wise one) would greatly increase the required building program. One further costly item required in the ideal school system in a developing country would be a system of government scholarships to enable gifted children from poor families to continue their education at the secondary and tertiary level. If it is true that ability is distributed roughly equally in all socioeconomic groups, an enormous waste of talent results from the typical situation in the developing countries, in which only children from well-to-do families have much chance of reaching the universities.

---

*An unweighted average for all countries with available data shows that in 1965 teacher salaries constituted 71 percent of total recurrent costs in African countries, 73 percent in Asian countries, and 72 percent in Latin American countries. Even when capital costs are included, teacher salaries constituted more than 60 percent of the total expenditures on education in all three continents (12, p. 35).

[†]Since a rise in the level of qualifications of the teacher force will normally come about through an influx of younger, better qualified recruits, the effect on average teacher salaries will depend on the relative weight given to length of tenure and qualifications in the salary structure. In developing countries level of qualifications is normally given far more weight.

Migration to Cities

Returning to specifically demographic considerations, one that is of direct relevance to educational planners is internal migration. Although there are some instances of large net migrational gains by newly developing agricultural and mining areas, the overwhelming movement throughout the developing countries is from rural to urban areas. The significance of this movement for educational planning is that educational enrollment rates and the standards of educational services in most countries differ widely between rural and urban areas. It is not uncommon for educational enrollment rates to be as high as 80 percent in urban areas and as low as 10 percent in the more isolated rural areas. Educational planning that is predicated on a general steady rise in the average enrollment rate, with predictable trends in costs, may be rather drastically upset by high rates of migration into the cities. Children moving to the cities will need to be accommodated in schools at the 80 percent rate, not the 10 or 20 percent rate applying to the areas from which they came; after all, the greater educational opportunities in the cities may have been a major motive for the move.

Costs in urban areas may also differ widely from those in rural areas, although it is hard to know on a priori grounds which would be the more expensive. Building costs may be substantially lower in rural areas if the villagers supply materials and voluntary labor; on the other hand, teachers may have to be given incentive payments to work there. In urban areas economies of scale may be realized when educational services are centralized in large schools; certainly, the standard of education provided should be superior to that in the small village schools.

ISOLATING THE DEMOGRAPHIC OBSTACLE TO EDUCATIONAL GOALS

Since the demographic obstacle is only one of a number of obstacles to attaining the ambitious educational goals the developing countries have set for themselves, it is necessary to attempt at least a rough measure of the importance of the demographic factor compared with others. There are many possible approaches, but in this section an attempt will be made to isolate the contribution of demographic trends to the rise in student numbers and teacher requirements, and in turn to rising costs, according to a variety of less and more ambitious educational targets.

A very conservative target is merely to attempt to hold constant the proportion of children in school and to leave the pupil/teacher ratio unchanged. In this example, population growth is the only cause of rising student numbers, and of rising teacher requirements as well. It will result in increases of 50 percent or more in 15 years in any country whose youth population is growing by more than 2.5 percent per annum. This will necessitate large increases in expenditure, but probably little change in the proportion of GNP required for education, since GNP will also be increasing.*

The more realistic situation is one in which an attempt is made to raise the proportion of children in school quite rapidly. (See the earlier section on official educational goals.) What is the importance of population growth as a component in burgeoning pupil numbers and teacher requirements in this situation? It is sometimes claimed that when a country begins with only a small proportion of its children in school, the problem of population growth is of only secondary importance. The impact of population growth in raising pupil numbers, it is claimed, is "swamped" by the impact of a sharp rise in enrollment rates.

To study the validity of this claim some hypothetical projections have been computed for a country whose population structure resembled that of many developing countries (particularly those of much of Africa and south and southwest Asia), and in which only 40 percent of children aged 5 to 14 are in school. A series of three population projections were computed, all with the same improvement in mortality (a rise in the expectation of life at birth from 45 years in the first 5-year period to 70 years 40 years later) but with differing assumptions about fertility: continuing high fertility, gradually declining, and rapidly declining fertility. The constant fertility projection assumed that the ratio of female births to women aged 15 to 44 remained constant throughout the projection period;[†] the declining fertility projection assumed that this ratio fell linearly by one half in the first 30 years and remained constant thereafter; and the rapidly declining fertility projection assumed that it fell linearly by half in the first 15 years and remained constant thereafter.[‡]

It was further assumed that the proportion of children in school in the age group 5 to 14 rose geometrically from 40 percent in the base year to 95 percent, but over differing periods of time: 10 years, 20 years, 30 years, and 40 years. Each of these assumptions was applied to each population, and the resultant increases in enrollments were attributed to demographic trends, ER (enrollment rate) trends, or a combination of both by means of standardization techniques.[§] The results are shown in Table 8. In determining teacher requirements, (see Table 9) the pupil/teacher ratio (PTR) was assumed to improve from 40 to 30 in the same length of time as the enrollment ratio took to reach 95 percent.

*A specific example, for Uganda, is contained in (12, pp. 56-57, 204-205).

[†] At 0.103.

[‡] For more details on the population projections, see (25, pp. 228-229).

[§] Specifically, increases attributable to demographic trends were computed by holding ER constant and allowing population size to vary, and those attributable to ER increases were computed by holding population size constant and allowing ER's to vary.

TABLE 8

Disaggregation of Factors Causing Increase in Enrollments in the Period during Which
ER Rises from 40 Percent to 95 Percent, Based on Hypothetical LDC

	Percent Due to			Increase in Pupil Numbers	
	Demography Alone	ER Alone	Both Factors Combined	Absolute	Percent
Very rapid rise in ER: from 40 percent to 95 percent in 10 years					
High fertility	14.3	66.1	19.6	110,000	208
Declining fertility	14.0	66.8	19.2	109,000	206
Rapidly declining fertility	13.0	69.0	18.0	106,000	200
Rapid rise in ER: from 40 percent to 95 percent in 20 years					
High fertility	25.0	40.7	34.3	179,000	338
Declining fertility	20.7	50.8	28.5	143,000	270
Rapidly declining fertility	14.0	66.8	19.2	109,000	206
Slower rise in ER: from 40 percent to 95 percent in 30 years					
High fertility	30.9	26.6	42.5	274,000	517
Declining fertility	22.4	46.9	30.7	155,000	292
Rapidly declining fertility	13.3	55.3	31.4	106,000	200
Slow rise in ER: from 40 percent to 95 percent in 40 years					
High fertility	34.7	17.6	47.7	415,000	783
Declining fertility	23.5	44.2	32.3	164,000	309
Rapidly declining fertility	20.8	50.6	28.6	144,000	272

Source: Author's calculations.

TABLE 9

Disaggregation of Factors Causing Increase in Teacher Requirements in the Period during Which ER Rises from 40 Percent to 95 Percent and PTR Falls from 40 to 30 in Hypothetical LDC

	Percent That Is Separable from Population Growth				Percent That Is Affected by Population Growth		Increase in Number of Teachers	
	Due to ER Rise Alone	Due to PTR Trend Alone	Combined Effect of ER and PTR Trend	Total	Due to Demography Growth Alone	Combined Effect of All Three Factors	Absolute	Percent
Very rapid improvement in ER and PTR: they reach 95 percent and 30 percent, respectively, in 10 years								
High fertility	44.2	10.7	14.8	69.7	9.5	20.8	4,100	311
Declining fertility	44.7	10.8	14.9	70.4	9.3	20.3	4,100	308
Rapidly declining fertility	46.0	11.1	15.3	72.4	8.7	18.9	4,000	299
Rapid improvement in ER and PTR: they reach 95 percent and 30 percent, respectively, in 20 years								
High fertility	28.4	6.9	9.5	44.8	17.4	47.3	6,400	484
Declining fertility	34.9	8.4	11.6	54.9	14.2	42.5	5,200	394
Rapidly declining fertility	44.7	10.8	14.9	70.4	9.5	35.0	4,100	308

Slower improvement in ER and PTR: they reach 95 percent and 30 percent, respectively, in 30 years

High fertility	19.0	4.5	6.3	29.9	22.1	48.0	9,600	724
Declining fertility	32.4	7.3	10.8	51.0	15.5	33.5	5,600	424
Rapidly declining fertility	45.7	11.1	15.3	72.1	8.8	19.1	4,000	301

Slow improvement in ER and PTR: they reach 95 percent and 30 percent, respectively, in 40 years

High fertility	12.8	3._	4.3	20.2	25.2	54.6	14,300	1,078
Declining fertility	30.7	7.4	10.2	48.3	16.3	35.4	5,900	448
Rapidly declining fertility	34.7	8._	11.6	54.7	14.3	31.0	5,230	396

Source: Author's calculations.

Fertility and Pupil Numbers

A number of interesting findings emerge from these tables. One is that if fertility remains at its original, high level, it is only in the rather unrealistic situation in which the enrollment rate reaches the 95 percent target in 10 years that the rise in enrollment rates by itself is able to account for more than half of the increase in enrollments. In the more realistic situation in which 20 or 30 years are required to reach the goal, the rise in enrollments that is attributable to enrollment rate trends alone is much less. In the 30-year example only a quarter of the increase in enrollments can be attributed solely to the rise in enrollment rates, and this is exceeded by the rise caused by demographic trends alone (31 percent of the total increase) and by demographic trends and enrollment rate trends combined (42 percent). It is therefore unrealistic to treat demographic trends in a high-fertility country as only a marginal problem whose contribution to swelling student numbers is swamped by that of rapidly rising enrollment rates. In our specific example, unless the ambitious enrollment rate goals can be achieved in less than about 15 years, less than half of the increase in student numbers can be separated from the effect of population growth.

When one looks at the time ahead only as a succession of short periods, instead of viewing the period in which the ER rises to its maximum as one unit, the contribution of both population trends per se and the ER increase per se to the increase in enrollments appears greater, and the component of the increase attributable to the interaction of the two factors, less. This can be illustrated by Table 10, which analyzes the situation in which it takes 30

TABLE 10

Disaggregation of Factors Underlying Enrollment Increase During Each 5-year Period
When ER Rises from 40 Percent to 95 Percent in 30 Years
in Hypothetical LDC: High Fertility Projection

	Percent Due to		
	Demographic Trends Alone	Rise in ER Alone	Both Factors Combined
1st 5-year period	43.3	50.0	6.7
2nd 5-year period	44.7	48.3	7.0
3rd 5-year period	49.9	42.4	7.7
4th 5-year period	52.0	39.9	8.1
5th 5-year period	50.4	41.7	7.9
6th 5-year period	50.5	41.7	7.8
Entire 30-year period	30.9	26.6	42.5

Source: Author's calculations.

years to reach a 95 percent enrollment rate. As one looks at the 30-year period as a whole, then, the share of the enrollment increase that can be separated from demographic trends decreases. By considering only the short run, it is easy to underestimate the contribution of population growth to the rise in enrollments.

If fertility declines, the growth in enrollments and the demographic contribution to this growth are almost the same as in the high fertility projection if the ER goal is reached in 10 years. (See Table 9.) In the other, more realistic examples the impact of the decline in fertility is reflected in a smaller increase in pupil numbers, and a smaller contribution by population growth to this increase. For example, the ER goal can be reached in 30 years by trebling student numbers in the rapidly declining fertility projection, by quadrupling them when fertility declines moderately, or by raising them sixfold in the high fertility projection. Despite the much slower growth in enrollments required when fertility declines, the contribution of population growth to this increase remains considerable: in the example in which fertility declines moderately, the rise in ER alone can account for less than half the increase in student numbers, provided that the ER goal takes any longer than 20 years to reach.

Fertility and Teacher Requirements

The story is much the same for teacher requirements, although total requirements are boosted by the extra assumption that pupil/teacher ratios are lowered from 40 to 30. This means that in all cases a slightly higher proportion of the rise in teacher requirements than of the increase in enrollments can be isolated from demographic trends. If fertility remains high, less than half the increase in teacher requirements can be isolated from demographic trends if the ER and PTR goals take 20 years or longer to reach, and only a fifth can be isolated from demographic trends if these goals take 40 years to reach. The unlikelihood that the goals could be reached in less than 20 years is illustrated by the vast increase in the number of teachers required: a fourfold increase in 10 years if the goals are to be realized in a decade, and almost a sixfold increase in 20 years if they are to be reached in two decades.

THE CONTRIBUTION OF FERTILITY DECLINE TO EDUCATIONAL GOALS

It has been shown that most developing countries must view population growth as a major component of the increase in enrollments and teaching manpower implied by their educational targets, but the more practical consideration is the saving that could be effected by reducing the rate of population growth. The practical alternative is not "no population growth versus rapid population growth" but rapid population growth versus a gradual slowing of the rate of growth. The rate of growth is already slowing in a number of the developing countries, and even when one allows for the likelihood of continuing declines in mortality, there is a real possibility in many other countries that the growth rate will begin to decline during the next decade as a result of reductions in the birth rate outpacing reductions in the death rate.

Table 11 shows that, in the projections analyzed in the previous section, the savings in enrollments attributable to a rapid decline in fertility are 2.9 percent after 10 years, 30.2 percent after 20 years, and more than 50 percent after 30 years. It is particularly noteworthy that the percentage saving in enrollments caused by declining fertility is precisely the same whether ER's are held constant or are raised more or less rapidly. Viewed in this way, then, a rapid rise in ER's does not "wash out" even slightly the enrollment advantage of reduced fertility. The relative saving in enrollments caused in any given time period by the decline in fertility can be altered only by altering the speed of that decline. The *absolute* saving in enrollments is, of course, larger the more rapidly enrollment rates are raised.

Pakistan Case Study

To test further the potential contribution of a reduction in the rate of population growth to the attainment of educational goals, a series of country case studies is being conducted at the Population Council. In these studies the cost of attaining alternative educational targets is projected for a variety of assumptions about future population trends. Studies have so far been completed for the Republic of Korea, Pakistan, and Ghana (37, 38, 39).* In the following discussion, the findings of the Pakistan study will be briefly summarized.

Two educational targets are contrasted in this study of Pakistan: maintaining the status quo in terms of the coverage and quality of the education system and effecting certain improvements in its coverage and quality. The method was simply to apply to three population projections two different assumptions about enrollment rates at the school-going ages: one that enrollment rates would remain constant at their base-year level, the other that they would increase rapidly, though less rapidly than they would if the ambitious goals set out in Pakistan's Third Five-Year Plan were attained. Two different assumptions about pupil/teacher ratios were applied to the resulting enrollment projections: one that they would remain at their base-year level, the other that the ratio would be lowered, implying an improvement in the

---

*Sudies for Ceylon and Thailand are in process. An important research project on the impact of population change on educational development is currently being undertaken by the International Institute for Educational Planning, and results should be available at the end of 1970.

TABLE 11

Enrollments Saved by Reduced Fertility, According to a Variety of Trends in Enrollment Rates, in Hypothetical LDC

| | Total Enrollments | | | Savings (3) as a Percent of (1) |
| | High Fertility Projection | Rapidly Declining Fertility Projection | Difference | |
	(1)	(2)	(3)	(4)
After 10 years:				
Constant ER	68,734	66,768	1,966	2.9
ER rising to 95 percent after 40 years	85,334	82,892	2,442	2.9
ER rising to 95 percent after 30 years	91,709	89,085	2,624	2.9
ER rising to 95 percent after 20 years	105,920	102,889	3,031	2.9
ER rising to 95 percent after 10 years	163,244	158,573	4,671	2.9
After 20 years:				
Constant ER	97,730	68,251	29,479	30.2
ER rising to 95 percent after 40 years	150,602	105,174	45,428	30.2
ER rising to 95 percent after 30 years	173,959	121,486	52,473	30.2
ER rising to 95 percent after 20 years	232,109	162,096	70,013	30.2
After 30 years:				
Constant ER	137,838	67,081	70,757	51.3
ER rising to 95 percent after 40 years	263,719	128,342	135,377	51.3
ER rising to 95 percent after 30 years	327,365	159,317	168,048	51.3

Source: Author's calculations.

quality of the education system. The projections were computed separately for East and West Pakistan and the results combined for ease of analysis.

Enrollments

As shown in Table 12, the three population projections for Pakistan use the same mortality assumption so that differences in population growth are entirely attributable to trends in fertility. The decline in fertility, it will be noted, is both earlier and sharper in Projection III than in Projection II. Even this rapid decline in fertility, however, takes time to bring down the rate of population growth to moderate levels: the average annual rate of increase in the 1980's is still as high as 2.3 percent. The decline in fertility begins to affect numbers at the primary school ages after about 5 years, and at the

TABLE 12

Assumptions Underlying Educational Projections for Pakistan

---

1. Population Projections

   Mortality: expectation of life at birth rises at a constant rate from its 1960 level[a] to a 1980-85 level of 60.8 years for males and 63.8 years for females in East Pakistan, and 61.3 years for males and 63.8 years for females in West Pakistan.

   Fertility
   Projection I: remains constant at its 1960-65 level throughout the period.
   Projection II: remains constant until 1970 and then declines linearly by 30% to the period 1980-85.
   Projection III: beginning 1965, declines linearly by 50% up to 1980-85.

2. Enrollment Rates: Rising ER Assumption[b]

   Primary level (5-10 years)
   East Pakistan   rises from 37% in 1960 to 90% in 1985 and to 95% in 1990.
   West Pakistan   rises from 30.1% in 1960 to 90% in 1985 and to 95% in 1990.

   Secondary level (11-17 years)
   East Pakistan   rises from 7% in 1960 to 50% in 1990.
   West Pakistan   rises from 14.5% in 1960 to 50% in 1990.

3. Pupil/Teacher Ratios: Improving PTR Assumption[b]

   Primary level
   East Pakistan   falls from 39 in 1960 to 30 in 1990.
   West Pakistan   falls from 33 in 1960 to 30 in 1990.

   Secondary level
   East Pakistan   remains constant at 20.
   West Pakistan   declines from 35 in 1960 to 20 in 1990.

---

[a]49.2 years for males and 46.9 years for females in East Pakistan; 51.1 years for males and 48.7 years for females in West Pakistan.
[b]Except where noted, it is assumed that changes are linear.

Source: (38).

secondary school ages after 12 years. Therefore, as shown in Table 13, enrollments take time to diverge substantially according to trends in fertility, although after 15 years the difference has become quite impressive at the primary level: more than a million fewer pupils according to Projection III than in the other projections, even if the aim is merely to hold enrollment ratios constant. According to this conservative goal of holding enrollment rates constant over the 20 years following 1970, primary enrollments need increase by only 28 percent in Projection III, but by 156 percent in the high fertility projection.

When the aim is the more ambitious one of raising enrollment rates as postulated in Table 12, the interaction of population growth with the rise in proportions in school leads to a tremendous expansion in primary enrollments: these more than double during the 1960's, and fail to double again in the 1970's only in the projection in which fertility declines rapidly. It is noteworthy that even with the rapid decline in fertility postulated in Projection III, it is not until after 1985 that the required increase in enrollment

TABLE 13

Pakistan: Index of Growth in School Enrollments,
Various Assumptions (1960=100)

Assumption	1960	1965	1970	1975	1980	1985	1990
PRIMARY SCHOOL ENROLLMENTS							
Constant enrollment ratios							
High fertility	100	119	134	165	212	273	343
Declining fertility	100	119	134	165	193	221	242
Rapidly declining fertility	100	119	134	146	161	173	172
Rising enrollment ratios							
High fertility	100	159	223	327	490	719	952
Declining fertility	100	159	223	328	446	582	674
Rapidly declining fertility	100	159	223	290	373	457	479
SECONDARY SCHOOL ENROLLMENTS							
Constant enrollment ratios							
High fertility	100	138	173	197	235	297	380
Declining fertility	100	138	173	197	237	280	319
Rapidly declining fertility	100	138	172	199	218	237	256
Rising enrollment ratios							
High fertility	100	235	404	583	845	1,270	1,886
Declining fertility	100	235	404	582	850	1,197	1,582
Rapidly declining fertility	100	235	404	587	784	1,012	1,272

Source: (38, Tables 5 and 9).

drops below a quarter in any 5-year period if the rising enrollment ratio goal is to be reached.

At the secondary level the aim of raising enrollment ratios to 50 percent by 1990 calls for a tremendous increase in enrollments. These would need to increase fourfold during the 1960's from a relatively small base. Toward the end of the 1970's alternative trends in fertility begin to make a difference, but for the decade as a whole enrollments would almost need to double again in Projection III, and more than double in the other two projections. During the 1980's the benefits of the decline in fertility come into their own and enrollment increases would be 62 percent in Projection III, as against 86 percent in Projection II and 123 percent in Projection I.

Teaching Force

The total teaching force required, of course, increases at the same rate as enrollments except where a change is postulated in pupil/teacher ratios. The relatively modest lowering of pupil/teacher ratios that we have postulated makes only a marginal difference to total teacher requirements. The teacher requirements of raising enrollment ratios are much larger. In either case, differences according to fertility are striking and show up earlier in primary than in secondary education. Given rising enrollment rates but no change in pupil/teacher ratios, Projection III would require the teaching force in primary schools to double between 1970 and 1985 (15 years). The high fertility model (Projection I) would require the same doubling in about 9 years, and the more slowly declining fertility model in 10 years.

The actual number of teachers who must be recruited in any given period is much higher than the net increase, because of the need to replace teachers who die, retire, or leave the profession. There are no data on the loss rate to the teaching force in Pakistan, except for a rough estimate by UNESCO that 20 percent of the teaching force must be replaced every 5 years. If this is true, then if enrollment rates are not raised in primary schools, teachers needed for replacement in the high fertility projection outnumber those needed for enrollment increase up to about 1975 and remain at above 40 percent of total teacher requirements up to the end of the projection period. If fertility declines, replacement needs continue to outweigh the needs posed by increasing enrollment throughout the period. If enrollment rates are raised, on the other hand, new teacher requirements for enrollment increase greatly outnumber replacement needs, even in the projection with rapidly declining fertility. In the high fertility projection, they outnumber replacement needs by a ratio of three to one or better.

Cost Alternatives

What are the cost implications of these trends? In an effort to find out, some crude assumptions were made regarding trends in recurrent and capital costs. It was assumed that the average salary per teacher at the different levels of education would increase at the same rate as per capita GNP,* as would the average capital cost per new pupil place. Total GNP was assumed to increase at the same rate in all situations (6 percent per annum), which meant that per capita GNP increased more rapidly in the declining fertility projections. Two assumptions were made about the share of teacher salaries in total recurrent expenditure: one, that this would remain at its 1960 level of 80 percent; the other, that it would fall to 65 percent in 1990, implying an improvement in the quality of education as teachers are better supplied with textbooks, teaching aids, etc.

According to these assumptions, total costs increase spectacularly in all projections, but then so does GNP. The important consideration is whether educational costs rise in relation to GNP. Evidence on this is given in Figure 4, which also shows the percentage of GNP saved in the given years and according to the given targets if fertility declines according to the pattern of Projection III. Clearly, the main factor governing trends in educational costs is trends in enrollment rates. Where these are held constant, the share of GNP required for education rises only slightly especially if fertility declines; where enrollment rates rise as postulated, this share grows manyfold, even if fertility declines rapidly. If pupil/teacher ratios are lowered as well, and the non-teacher salary component of recurrent costs raised, education's share of the GNP climbs to 6 percent and above by 1985, even if fertility declines rapidly. This figure does not include the costs of higher education, including teacher training, which will also be increasing and might well account for a further 1 or 2 percent of GNP by the end of the projection period. At the present time 8 percent of GNP is as much as any country in the world spends on education, and although it would not be impossible for Pakistan to reach this level from the 1.7 percent of GNP actually spent on education in 1965, this would require a very basic reordering of priorities.

A rapid decline in fertility after 1965 will have very little effect on costs for about 10 years, but Figure 4 demonstrates that it will subsequently be of substantial benefit in the struggle to upgrade the education system, and its effect will grow cumulatively as time goes on. By 1990, for example, declining fertility would result in a saving of 1.6 percent of the GNP *each year* in reaching the goal of increased enrollment rates and improved pupil/teacher ratios: a figure almost identical to the entire share of the GNP going to education in 1965.

Moreover, the relative contribution of a decline in fertility to lowering costs is of the same general order of magnitude if attempts are made to raise

*The validity of this assumption will depend largely on the qualification level of new teachers entering the teaching force. Pay scales are linked both to length of service and qualification. When the teaching force is increased sharply, as in the projection with increasing enrollment rates, average length of service of the teaching force will fall. This need not, on balance, lower average salaries if the qualification level of the new recruits is higher than that of the existing teachers.

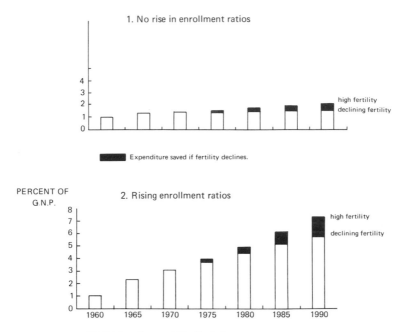

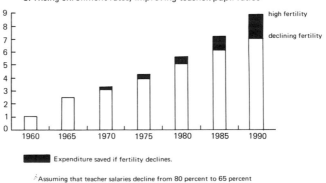

Figure 4. Education costs as a percentage of GNP, 1960-1990.

the quantity and quality of education provided or merely to maintain the status quo.* Nevertheless, in a country such as Pakistan, where enrollment rates are low to begin with, the massive increase in enrollments and teacher

*In 1980 the percent of GNP required in the high fertility case exceeds that in the rapidly declining fertility case by 13.9 percent if enrollment rates are held constant, by 10.4 percent if enrollment rates are raised, and by 9.4 percent if pupil/teacher rates are

requirements needed to effect a rapid increase in enrollment rates is formidable enough even in the absence of population growth. This in no sense weakens the case for population control. It merely underlines the point that a country such as Pakistan would find it impossible to provide universal, high quality education within a decade or two even if fertility were to decline quite rapidly.

Even in the Republic of Korea, where universal primary education has almost been attained, it will not be easy to reach the desired standards of education quickly. The share of the GNP needed for education is likely to rise sharply from an already high figure if the coverage and quality of education are to be improved further, even if there is a modest decline in fertility (37).

RELATIONSHIPS BETWEEN EDUCATIONAL PROGRESS,
DECLINING FERTILITY, AND ECONOMIC DEVELOPMENT

Before the discussion of the policy implications of this analysis, this section will deal with some feedbacks and relationships that have a bearing on policy decisions. The flow diagram (Figure 5) represents an attempt to summarize an extraordinarily complex set of interactions among educational progress, fertility decline, and other elements in the process of economic devel-

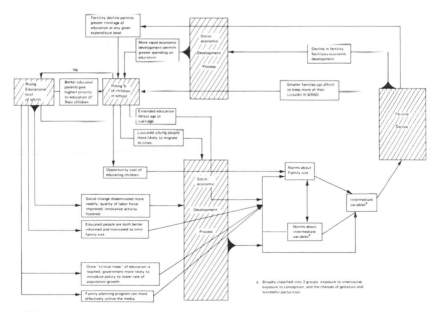

Figure 5. Some interactions among education, economic development, and fertility in a developing country.

lowered in addition. In 1990 the excess in the high fertility case is 38.5 percent, 29.9 percent, and 27.5 percent respectively.

opment. Although some direct causal relationships can be established in both directions between educational expansion and fertility decline, these relationships are seen in true perspective only when viewed as integral components of an ongoing process of socioeconomic development, which is itself both contributing to and benefiting from both the expansion of education and the decline in fertility. The feedback effects depicted are part of the very essence of the development process, part of the reordering of institutions, values, goals, and social relationships that this process requires. They do not, perhaps cannot, occur in isolation.

The diagram is necessarily simplified. To some extent it illustrates an ideal situation rather than the way things always work out in practice. For example, a reasonably well-educated electorate does not necessarily produce good leaders, nor is it necessarily well-informed about the problem of population growth, particularly if this subject is not taught in the schools (as it normally is not). Or again, more rapid economic development permits, but does not ensure, greater spending on education.

What is the evidence for some of the relationships set out in the diagram? Some of it is inferential, some is drawn from survey data, and some from historical association. A few comments on these relationships can begin with the bottom half of the diagram, showing the effects of educational expansion and economic development on fertility. The recognition that education may affect fertility, incidentally, is not new; many of the classical economists speculated about it.*

It is helpful analytically to recognize that changes in socioeconomic variables can act on fertility only through their effects on a number of "intermediate variables" that may be broadly classified in sequence into three groups: exposure to intercourse, exposure to conception, and the chances of gestation and successful parturition.[†] The effect of socioeconomic variables on these intermediate variables, moreover, may be through changes in norms regarding family size and/or one or more of the intermediate variables.

There is no question that the desire to educate their children is very widespread among parents in the developing countries and that even when education is provided free or subsidized by the government, the costs of special fees, uniforms, and perhaps transportation and support away from the home, together with the sacrifice involved in keeping children out of the labor force or at least away from home chores, can contribute powerfully to

---

*"Malthus had hoped that the spread of education would result in greater continence. Senior had hoped that compulsory education would dampen population growth because children would no longer be earning assets to their parents when taken out of the labor market. Mill added an argument for more favorable labor force opportunities for women, so improving the alternatives to marriage and motherhood as to retard population growth still further" (40).

[†]For a more detailed classification, see (41, 42).

the desire to limit family size.* Interestingly enough, Schultz finds in a predictive model for fertility in Taiwan that the association between birth rates and child school attendance rates is more consistent and statistically significant than between birth rates and the proportion of adults with a primary education (45).

Rising school attendance rates result, after a lag, in a rise in the level of education among the adult population, and this contributes to the decline in fertility in a number of ways, none of them completely independent of general socioeconomic development (46). On the personal level, educated couples are more likely to evaluate rationally the pros and cons of an extra birth, and perhaps be less concerned about the various taboos, cultural and religious, on the use of birth control.† They may also understand more clearly the conflicts between "quantity" and "quality" in the raising of children. These effects are likely to be reinforced if population and family life education has been in their school curriculum (47). Through their education they may have developed heightened aspirations and acquired new desires apart from child rearing, some of which directly conflict with child rearing. For example, mobility, which is restricted by a large family, is needed to realize fully the economic and "social status" benefits flowing from education. Whatever the motivation, there is no question that in the developing countries, better educated couples have fewer children and use contraception more than couples with little or no education.‡

*The economic burden is the most frequently cited disadvantage of a large family in surveys conducted in tropical Africa (43, Table 3). As part of this economic burden, the importance of educational costs "climbs steadily from subsistence to cash farming areas and from the latter to the towns, culminating among the urban elite where these costs are the major factor which could lead to the limitation of family size" (43, p. 604). As one specific example, Caldwell reports that in every part of rural Ghana a substantial majority of households reported in a 1963 survey that school attendance not only increases the cost of rearing children while decreasing their labor value, but that the upkeep of school children outweighs their productive value even in the case of 10-to-14-year-old day students. In the towns, the cost of education was sharply felt, particularly among the economically better off classes. Interestingly enough, part of the problem was that educated children tended to expect their parents to spend more on them, and the parents often felt obliged to meet the demand (44, and references cited therein).

†However, among Roman Catholics, extended education in parochial schools may serve to reinforce traditional Catholic values regarding fertility and contraception.

‡Among surveys of knowledge, attitudes, and practice (KAP) of contraception either published or on file in the Population Council, all nineteen studies from eleven countries in Asia and Africa in which practice of contraception was cross-classified by educational attainment of wife, husband, or both showed a positive association between the two variables; in almost all cases the progression in percentages either currently using or ever using contraception was an unbroken one from lowest to highest levels of educational attainment. The inverse relationship between education and fertility is not quite as clearcut, although of twenty-one studies in sixteen developing countries, most showed a steady downward progression in fertility as educational attainment increased, the impact of education on fertility tending to be more pronounced above the primary school level. In a few cases, the progression was broken between two levels of educational attainment;

On the national level, rising levels of education, particularly if linked to effective publicity about the problems of rapid population growth, can lead to growing public support for a government policy to lower the rate of population growth.* Once such a policy is established, its effectiveness is enhanced among a literate population by use of posters, newspapers, and magazine articles to disseminate information about family planning. Children can be made aware in the schools, too, of population problems and the possibility of planning family size.

Apart from its direct links with fertility levels, education contributes to the general process of socioeconomic development,[†] which in turn creates the conditions in which a decline in fertility is likely to come about. For example, a rising proportion of children in school subsequently results in higher literacy levels which facilitate the more rapid dissemination of many kinds of social change (52). It also results in a better educated labor force,[‡] which in turn spells more rapid economic development. The need for educated manpower in those areas of the economy where modern technology reigns supreme—for example, large-scale manufacturing and banking—is clear enough. However, the importance of education in other areas of the economy, and particularly in the process of transforming traditional agriculture, is now well recognized (53, 54).

The process of economic development contributes to a decline in fertility in many and complex ways. For a more detailed discussion see other chapters of this book.[§]

A decline in fertility has a number of effects at the family level which are conducive to economic development. These effects, too, are discussed in

---

in particular, in rural areas in Mysore state, India, according to the Mysore Population Study, and in rural areas of the U.A.R., fertility was found to be lower among those with no education than among those with primary school education. The generally very clear inverse relationship between education and fertility in these studies would appear to contradict the statement in the United Nations' Population Bulletin No. 7 (48, published before most of these research findings became available) that "where negative associations have been found between fertility and educational level or other socio-economic indicators in high-fertility countries, such associations have generally appeared to be weaker and less consistent than they are in low-fertility countries."

*Berelson has shown that size of population and the level of mass education are the two factors most closely associated with either the adoption of a national family planning program, or at least some government involvement in family planning activities (49).

[†]As examples of studies showing the statistical association between education and economic growth, see (50, 51).

[‡]Given the same rise in the proportion of children in school, there is little difference in the length of time taken to replace the bulk of the existing labor force with better educated workers according to whether fertility declines or not; however, it will obviously be easier to raise the proportion in school if fertility declines (25).

[§]See especially Dudley Kirk, "A New Demographic Transition?" in this volume.

detail in other chapters of this book.* One of the effects is to enable parents to keep a higher proportion, and indeed a greater number, of their children in school for any given level of sacrifice. On the national level, as discussed earlier, a decline in fertility permits expansion of education to cover a greater proportion of the eligible population at any given level of expenditure. Since declining fertility facilitates economic development, including higher total output and investment outlays (55, 56, and references cited therein), it should also be possible for the level of educational expenditure to be higher than if fertility remained high.

Government Policy Implications

The feedback effects between fertility decline, educational advance, and other elements in economic development indicate how exceedingly complex a task it is for a development-oriented government to calculate in any precise fashion where it can obtain the best returns from another dollar spent on development. No government, of course, can subsume all other goals beneath that of economic development, and many factors operate to keep the strictly developmental budget within a straitjacket: the priority typically accorded defense expenditures; the strength of the social demand for various services; and, in some cases, the need to maintain a swollen government bureaucracy to provide employment and limit disaffection—to name just three.

However, even if the government is in a position to accord high priority to development goals, it must still rely to a large extent on intelligent guesswork to guide it into a pattern of investment in which the social return from additional expenditures in each area will be equal. Here the specific concern is with the question of government investment in education and in fertility reduction, not because they are any more substitutive for each other than they are individually substitutive for a wide range of other investments, but because they are the two kinds of investment most directly related to the issues discussed in this chapter.

Returns from Expenditures

To date in most developing countries the need to expand education has been considered "self-evident": education has been seen as a basic human right that should not be evaluated merely in cold economic terms; even in these economic terms, the need to break the bottleneck of skilled manpower shortages has seemed justification enough. There were countries where this was not so, notably India and the U.A.R., but these were exceptions.

*See T. Paul Schultz, "An Economic Perspective on Population Growth"; Harvey Leibenstein, "The Impact of Population Growth on Economic Welfare"; and J. D. Wray, "Population Pressure on Families: Family Size and Child Spacing," in this volume.

Similarly, family planning programs contribute so clearly to individual freedom of choice and to the health and welfare of mothers and children that the case for allocating to them the modest funds requires could well be considered self-evident. "Modest" is indeed the correct word to describe the funds allocated to family planning programs so far. In most countries, when such programs are operated by the Ministry of Health, they account for between 1 and 13 percent of the budget of that ministry.* As shown in Table 14, family planning budgets are less than 2 percent of the defense budget in Korea and Pakistan and less than 1 percent in Taiwan and Singapore. Diverting the entire budget of the very successful Taiwan family planning program into education would buy only 1 extra day of education per year; in Ceylon, the figure is a little higher, and in India it reaches 9 days of education. In India, Pakistan, and the Republic of Korea, where the ratio of family planning budgets to educational budgets is highest, diversion of the family planning budget into education would raise the number of children in school by only 3 or 4 percent. Therefore, one could claim that there is not much to lose and possibly much to gain by investing in family planning programs.

As might be expected, some analysts have not been content to view the need for either education or population control as "self-evident" but have applied the familiar cost-benefit technique of evaluating the case for government investments (62). Such studies for education in developed countries normally indicate that investment in education yields better returns than alternative investments; and the limited number of studies for developing countries tend to show an even greater relative advantage for investment in education (63, 64). Very high rates of return on investment in family planning programs have been indicated by studies using the technique of discounting the potential lifetime consumption and production of the unborn child back to the present (65, 66, 67, 68).

In terms of these studies, then, most developing countries may well have underinvested in both education and family planning in recent years, even if the noneconomic benefits are ignored. The rising share of budgets currently and prospectively going into both education and family planning can be seen partly as a recognition of underinvestment in the past.† The rise in India's family planning budget after limited and rather ineffectual spending in earlier years, and in Pakistan's education budget are cases in point.

*One percent in Singapore, 2 percent in Taiwan, 3 percent in Turkey, 12 percent in Pakistan, and 13 percent in India. In Korea it is 17 percent, having been as high as 30 percent in recent years (57). The very low percentages in Singapore, Taiwan, and Turkey may partly reflect a high standard of public health care, and partly (especially in Singapore and Turkey) the fact that family planning expenditures are still increasing as the programs gain momentum. The high percentage in Korea reflects a remarkably small public health budget rather than a large family planning budget.

†In some cases, however, current high levels of expenditure would not have been justifiable until the groundwork has been laid.

TABLE 14

Effect of Diverting Family Planning Budget into Education or
Defense, Various Countries

	Ceylon	India	Korea	Pakistan	Taiwan	Singapore
Days of education that could be bought with family planning budget[a]						
1965	n.a.	n.a.	3	n.a.	1	n.a.
1966	n.a.	5	4	8	n.a.	n.a.
1967	2.5	9	4	7	n.a.	1
1968	n.a.	n.a.	7	n.a.	1	1
Percent by which number of children in school could be raised if the family planning budget were allocated to education						
1965	n.a.	n.a.	1.3	n.a.	0.5	n.a.
1966	n.a.	2.2	1.7	3.6	n.a.	n.a.
1967	1.1	4.1	1.7	3.0	n.a.	0.4
1968	n.a.	n.a.	3.0	n.a.	0.4	0.5
Percent by which defense budget would be increased if the family planning budget were allocated to defence						
1967	n.a.	2.6	1.2	1.8	n.a.	n.a.
1968	n.a.	n.a.	1.6	n.a.	0.2	0.8

n.a. = not available

[a]Total days of education in a year are assumed to be 220.

Sources: Educational expenditure includes both public and private expenditure in India, Korea, Pakistan, and Taiwan; for Ceylon and Singapore, only public expenditure is included. For all countries except Singapore and India, educational budgets have had to be projected beyond 1966 from trends in earlier years. Except for Singapore, figures for defense expenditure were derived from (58).

Data on Family Planning Costs for Korea, Taiwan, and Pakistan have been taken from (59); for India, (60, Nos. 14 and 35); for Singapore, (60, No. 28); and for Ceylon costs are calculated from (61).

However, the current state of rate-of-returns theory with regard to both education and fertility reduction is not such that a government could confidently use it to weigh, even in strictly economic terms, the relative value of an extra million dollars in primary education as against an extra million dollars in rural feeder roads or in an extended network of fieldworkers in family planning programs. A brief discussion of this point is perhaps warranted.

Returns from Education

Rate-of-returns theory, as applied to education, involves a calculation of the discount rate that sets the discounted value of the costs of a certain amount of education equal to the discounted value of the additional future earnings anticipated from it. Lifetime earnings associated with additional education are projected from age-earnings profiles by years of school at a given point in time. Some of the more basic theoretical problems with this approach are the following:*

1. Returns to society are normally computed from returns to individuals who receive them, but there is in fact little evidence on the relationship between the two.

2. It is often very difficult anyway to disentangle the private returns from education in a society in which educational opportunity is closely correlated with wealth and status and in which " 'good breeding' earns more . . . than a good education" (69, p. 45, fn. 1), and this covers many Latin American and Asian countries, though not typically those of tropical Africa.

3. In this as well as in other respects, labor markets in the developing countries are normally very imperfect, and earnings do not, therefore, adequately reflect the relative scarcities of people with different levels of education and skill. This problem can to some extent be overcome by using shadow wages—employing accounting wages for planning purposes which do reflect the relative scarcities of different kinds of labor.

4. In projecting private rates of return from education it is often (probably normally) invalid to assume a close relationship between recent rates of return and future rates of return. The link would appear to be particularly tenuous in a less developed country in which differences in earnings between the better and lesser educated are very wide at the outset because of extreme scarcity of skilled personnel. In such a country differences may either narrow considerably as education becomes more widely disseminated or possibly widen if rapid economic growth boosts the demand for educated personnel, and expansion of education does not keep pace.

5. The developing countries are concerned not with marginal changes, but with massive structural changes, not only in the economy in general but in the education system itself. In such a situation it is extremely difficult to forecast rates of return on investments in education even a few years ahead, since they will be partly a function of the overall pattern of investment that is adopted and the flowback effects that occur. As shown earlier, there are a number of such flowback effects between education and fertility trends.

Returns from Family Planning Programs

The kinds of problems outlines in 4 and 5 apply as well to the analysis of family planning programs, but the application of rate-of-return analysis to these programs faces some additional special problems.

---

*For a more detailed analysis of some of these problems, see (69, Ch. III; 70; 71, pp. 19-30).

1. Family planning programs are so new that the data available barely cover a sufficient length of time to support any kind of rate-of-return analysis. Rates of return based on the early years of a program may bear little relationship to subsequent rates of return. In the early years economies of scale and also of experience have not been fully reaped; and on the other hand, it may have been possible to "skim the cream" by making acceptors out of those women who are strongly motivated to practice family planning.

2. The major "output" from which rates of return can be computed is the number of births averted by the family planning program, but this will always be difficult to measure. There is enough well-founded evidence to be confident that family planning programs have had, in some cases at least, an independent effect on the birth rate.* But measurement of this effect is normally subject to a wide range of uncertainty.[†]

3. A further problem, related to both the foregoing points, is that the potential, as well as actual, impact of a family planning program on the birth rate may change continuously over time. Change in the socioeconomic matrix, in which the family planning program is one element, may after a time render the program obsolete as a method of bringing down the birth rate.

4. There is continuing controversy over the correct rate at which the future consumption and production streams generated by an as yet unborn individual are to be discounted (76). A high rate of discount will "wash out" the production effect almost completely since this does not begin for at least a decade. Other crude aspects of the usual "cost-benefit" analysis of birth prevention, such as the assumption that additional newborn infants will consume at the same rate as the average member of the population they enter, and the tendency to reckon private costs to the public account, have also been questioned (59, 77, 78, 79).

*This evidence is of a variety of kinds. For example, in Taiwan, the rate of fertility decline has accelerated markedly following the introduction of the family planning program in 1963, and both the percent of wives 20 to 44 who had ever practiced contraception and of those who were currently practicing increased by 50 percent in 2 years—1965-67 (60, No. 41, Fig. 7; 72).

A "matching study" which compared the fertility of women accepting intra-uterine devices (IUD's) in the Taiwan program with that of nonacceptors with similar characteristics indicates that the fertility of acceptors fell by 80 percent, whereas that of nonacceptors fell by 48 percent (73).

In Korea the strongest evidence of program impact is the remarkable pace of change in rural areas. The highest acceptance rate for contraception has been among rural women with little or no education, persons who would be the least likely to practice contraception in the absence of the program. The percentage of married women through age 49 currently using contraception in rural areas rose from 6 percent in 1964 (the year the family planning program was initiated) to 18 percent in 1966 (74).

[†]For a concise survey of methods for estimating births averted by family planning programs, see (75).

Given all these drawbacks to the rate-of-returns approach, it is not surprising that governments in developing countries typically ignore this approach to educational planning and instead adopt a "manpower approach," attempting to tailor educational development to projected manpower requirements.* Nor is it surprising that, although the economic benefits of lowering the birth rate have been recognized as a valid reason to invest in family planning programs, strict rate-of-return analysis has often been given a wide berth.[†] But to question our ability to measure accurately the rate of return on either education or family planning and to doubt the appropriateness of relying on the rate-of-returns approach alone are not to deny the place of strict rate-of-returns analysis in a broader cost-benefit approach to the problem of allocating government investment. Such an approach should also take into account welfare criteria, political considerations, and ideally a variety of spinoffs that cannot be measured very precisely, such as the modernizing effect of family planning programs and formal education on people's conception of their ability to influence their own destiny.

The current increase in expenditure on both education and family planning is in itself evidence of the need for a more careful evaluation of the costs and benefits of these expenditures in the future. As noted earlier, one cannot confidently set an upper limit to the possible level of educational expenditures, and a few developing countries have already lifted their spending on education above 7 percent of GNP. A sharp increase in the share of budgets going into education is no doubt difficult to achieve in any country, but the potential for such increases, given a reordering of national priorities, is clear enough. For example, education's toughest competitor for funds in many countries is the military budget, which in Middle Eastern countries averages more than 11 percent of GNP (slightly higher than in the U.S.S.R. and the United States), and in the rest of Asia averages more than 6 percent of GNP (both figures medians).[‡]

Given that education's share of the total budget can, and probably will, be raised in most countries, it becomes urgent that the question be faced: Where is the point at which educational expenditure becomes excessive? Should

---

*This approach is not necessarily any more useful. An incisive critique is contained in (71, pp. 3-18). See also (80).

[†]Recognition of the economic benefits of investing in family planning, of course, is not dependent upon acceptance of the cost-benefit approach outlined above. Given the assumption that family planning programs have an independent effect on the birth rate by aiding people to prevent unwanted births (and thus by definition increasing individual satisfaction), the economic benefits are demonstrated by growth models of the kind cited in (56). Indeed, Simon has derived a figure for the value of a prevented birth from such a model (78).

[‡]In the giant countries of the region—India, Pakistan, and Indonesia—however, a smaller than average share of GNP goes to defense—3.5 percent, 3.9 percent, and 2.5 percent respectively. All figures from (58, Table 4).

India, for example, be attempting to expand the coverage of higher education to the U.S. level? Or to the western European level (which is very much lower)? Or to neither? Similar hard questions will need to be asked about programs to reduce fertility, particularly if governments break out of the usual reliance on family planning programs and begin to use some of the other more costly measures that have been proposed, such as incentive payments to couples for periods of nonpregnancy or nonbirths (81). In either case, the feedback between education and fertility decline is a relevant variable to be taken into account.

One thing is clear from the experience of countries such as India and the Philippines: Once the private returns from education are well recognized among the population at large, the government will find it difficult to control the expansion of education, particularly at the secondary and higher level, even if it wants to. If expansion of public education is too slow, private investment will step in to fill the vacuum, up to the point at which the returns from alternative investments appear more promising. There may be some value in having such a balance established in the market place, although a government with strong egalitarian sentiments would not normally favor leaving too large a share of education in the hands of the private sector, which almost invariably caters mainly to the children of the better-off. This is not only difficult to accept on egalitarian grounds but may also be economically suboptimal insofar as it substitutes education of the less intelligent children of the wealthy for education of the more intelligent children of the poor. However, schemes could be devised to lessen these disadvantages. For example, prospective employers might pay the costs of educating children who would then be committed to work for them for a given length of time;* or public or private agencies could make loans for education to be repaid gradually once the student began to work.†

CONCLUSION

Throughout the Third World, high rates of population growth are proving a barrier to the early attainment of the goals that have been set for quantitative and qualitative expansion of education. Population growth can be viewed either as a factor raising the cost of attaining given educational targets or as a factor stretching out the time period in which such targets can be reached if a ceiling is placed on expenditures. Although the experience of the last decade or two indicates that governments with a commitment to educational progress can expand the coverage of the education system despite population

---

*Disadvantages of this scheme would be its restrictions on mobility and the unlikelihood that it could be operated successfully at the high school level, the level at which most of the students from poor families drop out.

†The possibility of such a scheme for Kenya is discussed in (82).

growth, a rising share of the national product in most countries will have to be invested in education to meet the goals that they have established for themselves. This cost problem demonstrates the need for new approaches— new building methods, new methods of imparting information that will break the requirement for rather inflexible teacher/pupil ratios. It also demonstrates the need for a careful balancing of the costs and benefits of additional spending on education with those of alternative investments. This is easier said than done, for reasons outlined in the previous section, and this is an area for further research.

Additionally, this study indicates that a variety of population projections and their implications need to be studied when long-term educational plans are formulated. Typically only one population projection (the "official" projection) is considered, the rapid growth of numbers at the school-going ages lamented, and schemes for accommodating extra pupils in the school system discussed. The weakness of this approach is evident enough: Who can confidently predict the level of fertility in *any* developing country 15, or even 10, years hence? Employing a number of projections with alternative assumptions for fertility and mortality, though it would add complexity to planning, would make explicit the uncertainty of future trends. Furthermore, it would focus attention on the benefits from a reduction in fertility. Lack of such information, as well as a lack of recognition that population trends can be modified by government action, is probably a major reason why education ministries (and UNESCO) have not typically been strong proponents of efforts to lower birth rates.

References

1. *World Bank Atlas: Population and per Capita Product.* Washington, D.C.: International Bank for Reconstruction and Development, 1968.
2. *UNESCO Statistical Yearbook,* 1967. Paris, 1968.
3. *New York Times,* February 19, 1969.
4. *New York Times,* June 23, 1968.
5. UNESCO, *An Asian Model of Educational Development: Perspectives for 1965-80.* Paris, 1966.
6. Harbison, Frederick H., and Charles A. Myers, *Education, Manpower and Economic Growth.* New York: McGraw-Hill, 1964. pp. 31-34.
7. Curle, Adam, *Planning for Education in Pakistan.* Cambridge, Mass.: Harvard Univ. Press, 1966. p. 107.
8. Pakistan Commission on National Education, *Report of the Commission on National Education, January-August, 1959,* S. M. Sharif. Karachi: Ministry of Education, 1960. pp. 111-112.
9. Government of Pakistan, Ministry of Education, *Achievement in Education, 1958-64.* Karachi: Central Bureau of Education, no date. p. 21.

10. Chong Tae-Si, "Twenty Years of Korean Education through Statistics," *Korea J*, August 1, 1968. p. 4.
11. Hyun Ki Paik, "Basic Problems Facing Korean Education," *Korean Education and Foreign Assistance Programs*. Seoul: Central Education Research Institute, September 1965. p. 8.
12. Coombs, Philip H., *The World Educational Crisis: A Systems Analysis.* New York: Oxford Univ. Press, 1968.
13. Kuznets, Simon, *Modern Economic Growth: Rate Structure and Spread.* New Haven: Yale Univ. Press, 1965. Ch. 4.
14. Edding, F., "Expenditure on Education: Statistics and Comments," *The Economics of Education*, E. A. G. Robinson and J. E. Vaizey. London: Macmillan, 1966. pp. 24-70.
15. *U.N. Yearbook of National Accounts Statistics.* New York: United Nations, annual.
16. *The United Nations Development Decade: Proposals for Action.* Report of the Secretary General. New York: United Nations, 1962. p. 30.
17. UNESCO, "Regional Educational Targets and Achievements 1960-65." Paper presented at the Conference on Education and Scientific and Technical Training in Relation to Development in Africa, Nairobi, July 1968.
18. UNESCO Regional Office for Education in Asia, *Progress of Education in the Asian Region: A Statistical Review.* Bangkok, 1969. pp. 27-32.
19. Blot, Daniel, and Michel Debeauvais, "Les dépenses d'education dans le monde," *Tiers Monde*, June 1965.
20. Coale, Ansley J., "Estimates in Fertility and Mortality in Tropical Africa," *The Population of Tropical Africa*, J. C. Caldwell and C. Okonjo, eds. London: Longmans, Green, 1968. pp. 182-183.
21. United Nations, *World Population Prospects as Assessed in 1963.* Department of Economic and Social Affairs, Population Studies No. 41. New York: United Nations, 1966.
22. Coale, A. J., "The Effects of Changes in Mortality and Fertility on Age Composition," *Milbank Mem Fund Q*, January 1956. pp. 79-114.
23. Coale, A. J., "How the Age Distribution of a Human Population is Determined," *Population Studies: Animal Ecology and Demography.* Cold Spring Harbor Symposia on Quantitative Biology. Cold Spring Harbor, N.Y. Biological Laboratory, 1957. Vol. XXII, pp. 83-89.
24. Farmer, Richard N., John D. Long, and George J. Stolnitz, eds., *World Population—The View Ahead.* Indiana Univ., Internat. Development Research Center Series No. 1, Bloomington, Ind., 1968.
25. Jones, Gavin, and Paul Gingrich, "The Effects of Differing Trends in Fertility and of Educational Advance on the Growth, Quality and Turnover of the Labor Force," *Demography*, Vol. 5, No. 1, 1968. pp. 226-248.
26. Ministry of National Development and Economic Research Centre, University of Singapore, *Singapore Sample Household Survey, 1966.* Re-

port No. 1, Tables Relating to Population and Housing. Singapore: Government Printing Office, 1967. Tables pp. 78 and 99.

27. Consejo Superior Universitario Centroamericano, "Oferta y Demanda Recursos Humanos en Centroamérica." *Estudio de Recursos Humanos en Centroamérica,* No. 6. San José: Univ. of Costa Rica, 1966.

28. "Education in Papua-New Guinea," *Current Affairs Bulletin* (Univ. of Sydney), February 10, 1969.

29. Uganda Government, Ministry of Education, "Education Statistics 1966." Mimeo. p. 7.

30. Ghana Government, Education Statistics, 1967/68. Provisional, Mimeo., n.d.

31. Cerych, L., "L'aide extérieure et la planification de l'éducation en Cote-d'Ivoire." African Research Monographs, No. 12. Paris: UNESCO/IIEP, 1967.

32. Zambia, Development Division, Office of the Vice-President, *Zambian Manpower.* Lusaka: Government Printer, 1969. p. 45.

33. Hansen, W. Lee, "Human Capital Requirements for Educational Expansion: Teacher Shortages and Teacher Supply," *Education and Economic Development,* C. Arnold Anderson and Mary Jean Bowman, eds. Chicago: Aldine Publishing Co., 1965. pp. 63-87.

34. "Review of Educational Progress in the Asian Region," *Bulletin of the UNESCO Regional Office for Education in Asia (Bangkok),* September 1966. pp. 20-23.

35. Lewis, W. Arthur, "Education and Economic Development," *Readings in the Economics of Education.* Paris: UNESCO, 1968. p. 137.

36. Toussi, Mohammed Ali, *Present Educational System in Iran.* Tehran, Iran: General Department of Planning and Studies, Ministry of Education, no date. pp. 33-44.

37. Burke, Meredith, and Gavin Jones, "The Demographic Obstacle to the Attainment of Educational Goals," *Population and Family Planning in the Republic of Korea.* Seoul: Govt., Rep. of Korea, 1970. Vol. I, pp. 485-540.

38. Jones, Gavin W., and Jayati Mitra, "The Demographic Obstacle to the Attainment of Educational Goals in Pakistan." New York: The Population Council, June 1969. Mimeo.

39. Jones, Gavin W., "The Demographic Obstacle to the Attainment of Educational Goals in Tropical Africa." Paper presented to the Conference on Population Growth and Economic Development in Africa, Nairobi, December 14-22, 1969.

40. Blitz, Rudolph C. "Education in the Writings of Malthus, Senior, McCulloch and John Stuart Mill," *Readings in the Economics of Education.* Paris: UNESCO, 1968. pp. 40-49.

41. Freedman, Ronald, "Statement by the Moderator at Meeting A.1: Fertility," *Proceedings of the World Population Conference Belgrade, 30 August-10 September, 1965, Vol. 1: Summary Report.* New York: U.N. Dept. of Economic and Social Affairs. 1966. pp. 37, 48.

42. Davis, Kingsley, and Judith Blake Davis, "Social Structure and Fertility: an Analytic Framework," *Econ Devel Cult Change*, April 1956. pp. 211-235.
43. Caldwell, J. C., "The Control of Family Size in Tropical Africa," *Demography*, 1968.
44. Caldwell, J. C., "The Demographic Implications of the Extension of Education in a Developing Country: Ghana." Paper presented to the Annual Meeting, Population Association of America, Boston, 1968.
45. Schultz, T. Paul, *The Effectiveness of Family Planning in Taiwan: A Proposal for a New Evaluation in Methodology*. Santa Monica, Calif.: The Rand Corp., April 1969. p. 28.
46. Carleton, Robert O., "The Effect of Educational Improvement on Fertility Trends in Latin America," *United Nations World Population Conference*. New York, 1965. Vol. IV., pp. 141-145.
47. Carolina Population Center, University of North Carolina at Chapel Hill, *Approaches to the Human Fertility Problem*. Prepared for the U.N. Advisory Committee on the Application of Science and Technology to Development, October 1968. Ch. VII.
48. United Nations' Population Bulletin No. 7, "Condition and Trends of Fertility in the World." New York, 1964.
49. Berelson, Bernard, "National Family Planning Programs: Where We Stand," *Fertility and Family Planning: A World View*, S. J. Behrman, Leslie Corsa, and Ronald Freedman, eds. Ann Arbor: Univ. of Michigan Press, 1969. pp. 346-348.
50. McLelland, David C., "Does Education Accelerate Economic Growth?" *Econ Devel Cult Change*, April 1966.
51. Bowman, Mary Jean, and C. Arnold Anderson, "Concerning the Role of Education in Development," *Education and Economic Development*, C. A. Anderson and M. J. Bowman, eds. Chicago: Aldine, 1965. pp. 113-134.
52. "Literacy Work and School Education in Economic Development," *Readings in the Economics of Education*. Paris: UNESCO, 1968. pp. 152-157.
53. Schultz, Theodore W., *Transforming Traditional Agriculture*. New Haven, Conn.: Yale Univ. Press, 1964. Ch. 12.
54. Wharton, Clifton R., Jr., "Education and Agricultural Growth: The Role of Education in Early-Stage Agriculture," *Education and Economic Development*, C. A. Anderson and M. J. Bowman, eds. Chicago: Aldine Publishing Co., 1965. pp. 202-228.
55. Demeny, Paul, "The Economics of Population Control." Paper prepared for the 1969 General Conference of the International Union for the Scientific Study of Population, London, September 3-11, 1969. (See also chapter by Demeny in this volume.)
56. Jones, Gavin W., "The Economic Effect of Declining Fertility in Less Developed Countries." Occasional Paper of the Population Council. New York, February 1969.

57. Nortman, Dorothy, "Population and Family Planning Programs: a Fact-book." New York: Population Council, December 1969.
58. *The Military Balance 1968-1969.* London: Institute for Strategic Studies, 1968. Table 4.
59. Robinson, Warren C., "Some Tentative Results of a Cost-Effectiveness Study of Selected National Family Planning Programs." Paper presented at Population Association of America Annual Meeting in Atlantic City, April 1969. Mimeo., c/o National Center for Health Statistics, U.S. Public Health Service.
60. *Studies in Family Planning,* September 1966; April 1968; and August 1968.
61. Perera, Terence, "A Short Review of the National Family Planning Program," July 1968. Mimeo.
62. Prest, A. R., and R. Turvey, "A Survey of Cost-Benefit Analysis," *Surveys of Economic Theory.* Prepared for the American Economic Assn. and the Royal Economic Society. New York: St. Martin's Press, 1966. Vol. III.
63. Selowsky, Marcelo, "Education and Economic Growth: Some International Comparisons," *Economic Development,* Report No. 83. Project for Quantitative Research in Economic Development, Harvard Univ., December 1967, Mimeo.
64. Carnoy, Martin, "Rates of Return to Schooling in Latin America," *J Human Resources,* Fall 1967. pp. 517-537.
65. Zaidan, George C., *Benefits and Costs of Population Control with Special Reference to the United Arab Republic.* Unpublished doctoral dissertation. Cambridge, Mass.: Harvard Univ. 1967.
66. Enke, Stephen, "The Economic Aspects of Slowing Population Growth," *Econ J,* March 1966. pp. 44-56.
67. Enke, Stephen, *Raising per Capita Income through Fewer Births.* Santa Barbara, Calif.: Tempo, General Electric Co., March 1968.
68. Bower, Leonard, "The Returns from Investment in Population Control in Less Developed Countries," *Demography,* 1968.
69. Vaizey, John, *The Economics of Education.* London: Faber & Faber, 1962.
70. Schultz, T. W., "The Rate of Return in Allocating Investment Resources to Education," *J Human Resources,* Vol. 2, No. 3, 1967. pp. 293-309.
71. Blaug, Mark, "A Cost-Benefit Approach to Educational Planning in Developing Countries." Report No. EC-157. Washington, D.C.: Internatl. Bank for Reconstruction and Development, December 20, 1967.
72. Freedman, Ronald, and John Y. Takeshita, *Family Planning in Taiwan: An Experiment in Social Change.* Princeton, N.J.: Princeton Univ. Press, 1969. Ch. XII.
73. Chang, M. C., T. H. Liu, and L. P. Chow, "Study by Matching of the Demographic Impact of an IUD Program," *Milbank Mem Fund Quart,* April 1969. pp. 137-157.

74. Ross, John A., and David P. Smith, "Korea: Trends in Four National KAP Surveys, 1964-1967," *Studies in Family Planning*, June 1969. pp. 6-11, Fig. 4.
75. Mauldin, W. Parker, "Births Averted by Family Planning Programs," *Studies in Family Planning*, August 1968. pp. 1-7.
76. Baumol, William J., "On the Social Rate of Discount," *Amer Econ Rev*, September 1968. pp. 788-802.
77. Fox, Gerald L., "The Net Costs to Society of a Marginal Birth in the Underdeveloped Countries." Northampton, Mass.: Dept. of Economics, Smith College. 1969. (Mimeo.)
78. Simon, J. L., "The Value of Avoided Births to Underdeveloped Countries," *Population Studies*, March 1969, pp. 61-68.
79. Robinson, Warren C., and David H. Horlocher, "Economic Issues in Cost-Benefit Analysis of Family Planning Programs," Dept. of Economics, Pennsylvania State Univ., November 1968. (Mimeo.)
80. Blaug, Mark, "Approaches to Educational Planning," *Econ J*, June 1967. pp. 262-287.
81. Berelson, Bernard, "Beyond Family Planning," *Studies in Family Planning*, February 1969. pp. 1-16.
82. Rogers, Daniel C., "Student Loan Programs and the Returns to Investment in Higher Levels of Education in Kenya." Unpublished paper.

X

Consequences of Population Growth for Health Services in Less Developed Countries–An Initial Appraisal

Leslie Corsa, Jr., and Deborah Oakley

Health—in the traditional sense of the absence of disease and disability or in the ideal of complete physical, mental, and social well-being—has long been one of man's aspirations. Reducing mortality and prolonging life are goals that are rarely in open conflict with other national objectives. However, the effectiveness of health services in comparison with other social and economic forces in achieving these ends has remained uncertain. The proportion of national income devoted to health services has tended to be small, with primary emphasis on alleviating disease and disability, not on preventing them.

Since World War II, the application of new health technology to prevention of disease in many less developed countries (LDC's) has facilitated a more rapid reduction in mortality than previously experienced in any country. Since in most LDC's this development has been combined with negligible net migration and with unchanging high natality rates, the result is new world records for population growth. Many people and their governments are recognizing that present natality levels are producing multiple adverse consequences, not least upon their health and health services. For the first time in history governments are taking purposeful actions to control natality as well as mortality—actions that require utilization of health services (1). Investments in health are beginning to be evaluated for their effect on population growth and per capita income as well as mortality and morbidity (2).

THE APPROACH OF THIS STUDY

How does rapid population growth affect health services in LDC's? Since health services function through use by people to reduce mortality and mor-

Leslie Corsa is Director of the Center for Population Planning, University of Michigan. Mrs. Deborah Oakley is currently a Research Assistant in the Center for Population Planning.

bidity (and now natality), the real test should be the ultimate effect on health (3). Adequate data on mortality, morbidity, and utilization of health services in LDC's do not exist. Instead, the following assumptions are made: with the same amount of service available, a population that is growing, and other conditions held constant, mortality and morbidity will increase; or if the amount of service is increased proportionately to the growth of population, mortality will be held constant. Conclusions must be drawn from limited health service data only. Although this is far from satisfactory, it is the present state of the art.

Any attempt to understand the consequences of population growth for health services should take into account direct *demographic* factors, such as total population, age structure, and geographic distribution, as well as direct *developmental* factors, such as national goals and achievements of specific levels of development, utilization of manpower, world technological developments, and levels of international assistance (Figure 1). What differentiates

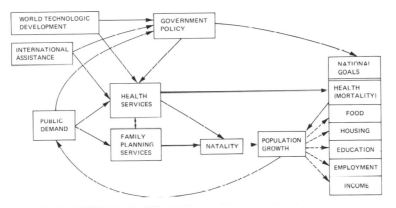

Figure 1. Relationships between population growth and health services.

the consequences of population growth for health services from those for most other topics in this volume is the *more immediate and direct effect* that health services may have on population growth itself through both mortality and natality. In the LDC's today, the effects of population growth upon health services may depend significantly upon what alternative actions are taken by health services to bring natality in closer balance with decreasing mortality.

Objectives of Natality Control

Two essential distinctions between the social objectives of natality control on the one hand and of mortality and morbidity control on the other influence greatly what alternative actions are taken. First, and of greater importance, decrease in mortality is an end in itself; decrease or increase in natality is usually a means to many social ends, one of which is reduction of mortality. Nations and different groups in a given society will seek different social objectives and different specific levels of natality control at any given time. Japan has sought a natality level which would achieve a stable population for its crowded islands at the same time that India seeks a natality level which will increase the rate of social and economic development. Chile seeks a better means of natality control than illegal abortion, and the United States seeks opportunity for the poor to prevent *unwanted* births equal to the opportunity already available to the rest of the population.

Second, the social objectives of natality control usually require a longer time interval for attainment than the social objectives of mortality and morbidity control. The effects of a prevented birth on educational services follows 5 to 20 years after the event, on employment 15 to 60 years later, on health and health services differentially over the life span (Figure 2). Although in time the effects of a prevented infant death are not much different, most health programs affect all age groups; for example, the effect of reduced disability from malaria on employment is relatively rapid.

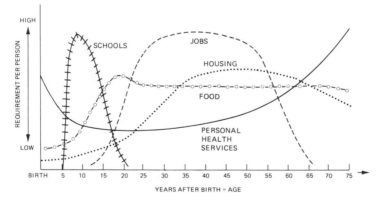

Figure 2. Time relationships between a birth and future service requirements.

The Impact of Health Services

It is beyond the scope of this paper to deal adequately with the relationships between health services and mortality (and morbidity) (3, 4). It is assumed that health services do contribute significantly to lowering mortality (and morbidity), that efforts of health services to control mortality (and morbidity) will continue at present or higher levels, and that mortality (and morbidity) levels of LDC's will continue to decrease toward the levels of more developed countries (MDC's).

It is also beyond the scope of this paper to deal at length with the direct effect of health services on natality, but some discussion is essential since natality control is becoming the prime determinant of population growth. Human reproduction, in a simplified view of a very complicated process, depends upon first, a male and a female capable of reproducing ("natural" fecundity); second, their union (coitus) so that sperm and egg unite; and third, a normal pregnancy of about 10 lunar months. Natality will not occur if one of the partners is not fecund (e.g., sterile from congenital defect, pelvic infection, radiation, surgery, etc.); if union of the partners does not occur (e.g., by delay of marriage or by separation or death of partners); if, although union of the partners occurs, union of sperm and egg are prevented (contraception); or, if pregnancy is terminated by "natural" or induced fetal death.

Health services operate directly to *increase natality* by improving fecundity and reducing maternal and natural fetal mortality and to *decrease natality* by making contraception and induced abortion available. The extent to which health services are likely to improve fecundity in LDC's is not adequately known, but the overall effect on natality in most countries is presumed small since fecundity is already high. In regions with high maternal death rates, health services are likely to contribute to lower maternal mortality and thereby increase the number and proportion of fecund couples. Where health services lower the frequency of fetal death, the degree to which natality will increase is uncertain. Apparently the differences between fetal death rates of LDC's and MDC's is relatively small, but LDC underreporting may be very great. Health services that make induced abortion readily and safely available could have dramatic effects in lowering natality in countries where induced abortion is illegal and relatively infrequent now. However, health services' greatest present and potential effect is in increasing the availability and use of effective contraception.

HEALTH SERVICES–DEFINITION AND CLASSIFICATION

The World Health Organization defines health as complete physical, mental, and social well-being. The closer one approaches this ideal, the more difficult it becomes to define it and to classify what activities are needed to achieve it; so for this paper, health services are defined as organized activities intended to decrease the level of human disease and disability. Major components of health services include manpower, facilities, equipment and supplies (all somewhat translatable, for some purposes, into money). Levels of good health (such as physical or mental fitness, reserves, or endurance) are not included here because the difficulties of measuring either good health or the services required far outweigh immediate relevance.

Classifying health services by type of activity and by type of control is useful in understanding the services and in differentiating the effects of population growth. Four major types of activities are considered here:

1. personal health services—those provided for individuals by doctors, nurses, and health technicians of many kinds to treat illness, prevent disease or disability, or facilitate such normal processes as human reproduction;

2. environmental health activities—those provided on a mass basis by engineers, sanitarians, and others to minimize disease and discomfort by controlling the quality of specific environmental elements such as water, food, air, and housing;

3. public information and education—those provided by individual and mass means to increase public knowledge of health and of conditions affecting it;

4. vital registration and health surveillance—those provided through individual records, sample surveys, and other means to document key events during life, to identify hazardous diseases and conditions, and to measure the level of health and health services in the population.

It is not possible to cover adequately the effects of population growth on all of these major types of activities, nor can one assume that effects will be identical for all of them. The effects of numbers of people alone depend upon the type of service. If it is to individuals, an increase in numbers requires a more or less direct increase in service. If the service is a mass approach to sanitation or information, an increase in numbers may call for little extra service effort; in fact a minimum population size may even be necessary before the service can be started.

Classifying services into those controlled by the *public sector* and those controlled by the *private sector* is important within most countries and essential for comparative analyses of different countries. However, obtaining comparable data for both sectors is diffiuclt within most countries, and much more so between countries. These differences and difficulties are as great among the MDC's as the LDC's.

Personal health services are about equally important for mortality and natality control; they present most of the range of considerations needed to understand the effect of population growth on other health services; and they have data available to consider. Therefore, these services have been selected for attention in this paper.

Levels of Development

A country is defined as *more* or *less developed* at a given time in history on the basis of whether it falls above or below an arbitrary value for one or more of an arbitrary list of interrelated characteristics. Characteristics commonly used (where relevant, on a per capita or family basis) include gross national product (GNP), power consumption, and others shown in Table 1. For this paper, per capita income of less than $600 (U.S.) in 1966 qualified a country as less developed. To provide some comparison with MDC's, data on seven MDC's are included in Table 2.

More relevant than comparisons of various indices among *countries*, however, is the condition of *people* throughout the world. For this purpose, indices must be weighted by the number of people per country. The number of persons per country (in 1965) is the index by which LDC's are ordered in this paper. No country with a population in 1965 of less than 7 million is included because the time required to search for necessary data for the thirty-seven countries listed in Table 1 already exceeded that available. Although sixty-two LDC's were excluded, the thirty-seven include about 90 percent of the population of all LDC's. This ordering re-emphasizes the important frustration in all attempts to describe the condition of people in the LDC's—the unavailability of data about the People's Republic of China, whose population alone is about 30 percent of that of all LDC's combined.

Although levels of natality and mortality are also indices of development, they are of limited value for most countries because births and deaths are not registered with completeness and accuracy. The ability to measure natality and mortality itself requires a high level of development. Modern techniques of population sampling now eliminate the need for complete registration, but the techniques are difficult to apply and have received adequate trial in only a few countries. For example, one's age—knowledge of which is taken for granted in MDC's—can be only approximated in many LDC's, even after great efforts to relate an individual's birth date to memorable national, religious, or natural events (15).

Table 1 includes the present best estimates of overall (crude) live birth and death rates (total live births or deaths per year per 1,000 total population at midyear) and of infant mortality rates (the number of live-born infants in any given year who die before reaching their first birthday per 1,000 born alive in that same year). Infant mortality has long been considered an excellent index for comparing health levels of populations because it reflects a relatively standardized and sensitive condition and is relatively easy to measure (no population estimates are required). Even so, precisely comparable measurements have not yet been achieved even among MDC's (16). Although the degree of completeness and comparability with which live births and infant deaths are recorded in many LDC's seriously limits the reliability of the estimated infant death rate, it remains one of the best single indices of national health available. Figure 3 shows the relationship between per capita gross national products and infant mortality rates in 1965.

Current Levels of Personal Health Services

International comparisons among LDC's are limited and hazardous because national data on health manpower, facilities, and expenditures were collected only very recently and calculated on different bases. In addition, international comparisons must take into account the varying medical and cultural needs of each country. Some countries may have many midwives, while

TABLE 1

Population and Developmental Levels of Largest Less Developed Countries, 1965

Country	Population (millions)	Gross National Product[a] (U.S. $ per Person)	Natality (Live Births per 1,000 Pop.)	(Deaths per 1,000 Pop.)	(Infant Deaths per 1,000 Live Births)	Urbanization (Percent in Cities of over 100,000)	Electric Power (Kwh per Person per Year)	Female Literacy[e] (Percent Illiterate over Age 15)	Radios (per 1,000 Pop.)
	(1)	(2)	(3)	(4)	(5)	(6)	(7)	(8)	(9)
1. China (mainland)	700.0[b]	–	34.0	11.0	–	–	90.0	–	–
2. India	486.8	88	41.7	22.8	139.0	8.8	70.2	86.8	9.2
3. Indonesia	104.9	99	30.6	9.2	87.2	9.9	15.5	70.4	–
4. Pakistan	102.8	125	49.0	18.0	142.0	9.3	38.5	92.6	5.4
5. Brazil	80.7	333	41–43	10–12	170.0	29.8	373.0	–	95.6
6. Nigeria	58.0	77	53–57	–	–	9.0	20.3	–	10.6
7. Mexico	42.7	493	44–45	10–11	60.7	20.4	404.2	39.3	192.9
8. Philippines	32.3	268	24.6	7.3	72.4	12.4	153.3	30.5	–
9. Turkey	31.1	326	43.0	16.0	161.0	19.5	158.6	78.8	78.4
10. Thailand	30.7	147	36.4	7.1	31.2	7.1	45.7	43.9	–
11. United Arab Republic	29.6	189	41.6	14.8	117.3	30.2	184.9	87.6	54.5
12. Republic of Korea	28.4	134	44.7	16.0	–	30.0	107.3	41.8	69.1
13. Burma	24.7	69	50.0	35.0	109.3	5.3	23.5	–	10.5
14. Iran	24.5	263	42.3	6.1	–	22.3	94.1	94.5	–
15. Ethiopia	22.6	64	–	–	–	3.0	10.5	–	–
16. North Vietnam	19.0	–	–	–	–	6.3	29.8	–	–
17. Colombia	18.0	334	41–44	12–14	82.4	32.7	338.8	–	–
18. Republic of Vietnam	16.1	–	27.7	6.4	36.7	11.3	32.4	–	63.6
19. Congo, Democratic Republic	15.6[a]	108	43.0	20.0	104.0	7.2	171.9	97.2	–

20. Afghanistan	*15.1*	60	–	–	–	3.7	13.8	–	13.3
21. Sudan	*13.5*	104	51.7	18.5	93.6	2.7	13.3	98.4	17.1
22. Morocco	*13.3*	185	46.1	18.7	149.0	20.0	96.2	94.0	52.5
23. China (Taiwan)	*12.4*	245	32.7	5.5	22.2	31.3	532.6	62.5	102.1
24. North Korea	*12.1*	–	*38.5*	*10.5*	–	6.2	1,099.2	–	–
25. Algeria	*11.9*	245	48.2	*10.0*	*86.3*	13.9	91.9	–	–
26. Peru	*11.7*	271	44-45	12-14	90.5	21.1	329.5	52.9	185.9
27. Ceylon	*11.2*	151	32.9	8.2	55.8	5.9	37.5	–	39.0
28. Tanzania[a]	*11.2*	70	46.0	24.25	190.0	1.7	19.1	–	–
29. Nepal	*10.1*	99	41.1	20.8	–	1.3	1.4	–	–
30. Kenya	*9.4*	116	50.0	20.0	–	5.8	35.0	–	37.4
31. Portugal	*9.2*	439	22.9	10.3	64.9	12.4	501.8	44.6	127.0
32. Chile	*8.6*	576	34-36	11-12	107.1	35.5	714.2	17.6	–
33. Iraq	*8.2*	262	*15.2*	*4.1*	23.7	34.2	147.4	94.7	88.5
34. Malaysia[d]	*8.0*	316	36.7	7.9	50.0	10.8	264.7	73.5	41.4
35. Ghana	*7.7*	314	47-52	24.0	156.0	13.0	68.2	–	73.6
36. Cuba	*7.6*	–	34-36	8.9	37.7	28.9	484.9	–	180.9
37. Uganda	*7.6*	92	42.0	20.0	160.0	1.9	75.8	–	26.5

– = not available.

[a] For 1966 or nearest available year.

[b] Italicized figures in columns 1, 3, 4, and 5 are less reliable estimates, according to the sources indicated. In some cases expert readers will recognize that some nonitalicized figures are census or survey data from an earlier date which may have been questioned at the time and could certainly be out of date by 1965.

[c] Some data limited to Tanganyika, except columns 7 and 9.

[d] Data for West Malaysia.

[e] For years earlier than 1965.

Sources: Col. 1 (5, Table 4); Col. 2 (6, Table 191) for 1966; Col. 3 (5, Tables 7 and 3); Col. 4 (5, Tables 17 and 3); Col. 5 (5, Tables 12 and 3); Col. 6 (7, Table 5; 8, Table 6; 5, Table 6; Col. 7 (9, Table 147) for total kwh produced; (5) for population denominators; Col. 8 (10, *Supplement*, Table 34; 11, Table 187); Col. 9 (8, Table 209) uses receivers and/or licenses given in this table. (5, Table 4) for population denominators.

TABLE 2

Population and Developmental Levels of Selected More Developed Countries, 1965

Country	Population (Millions)	Gross National Product (U.S. $ per Person)	Natality (Live Births per 1,000 Pop.)	Mortality (Deaths per 1,000 Pop.)	Mortality (Infant Deaths per 1,000 Live Births)	Urbanization (Percent in Cities of over 100,000)	Electric Power (Kwh per Person per Year)	Female Literacy (Percent Illiterate over Age 15)	Radios (Per 1,000 Pop.)
	(1)	(2)	(3)	(4)	(5)	(6)	(7)	(8)	(9)
1. Soviet Union	231	–	18.4	7.3	27.6	23.5	2,198	5.0	320
2. United States	195	3,862	19.4	9.4	24.7	28.4	5,949	2.0	1,233
3. Japan	98	986	18.6	7.2	18.5	40.5	1,961	2.0	209
4. United Kingdom	54	1,944	18.3	11.5	19.5	36.1	3,600	1.5	297
5. France	49	2,181	17.7	11.1	21.9	16.8	2,074	3.6	313
6. Netherlands	12	1,659	19.9	8	14.4	32.9	2,035	1.5	252
7. Sweden	8	2,847	15.9	10.1	13.3	21.7	6,348	1.5	382

Sources: See Table 1; except for col. 6, see (12, 13), for col. 8 (14).

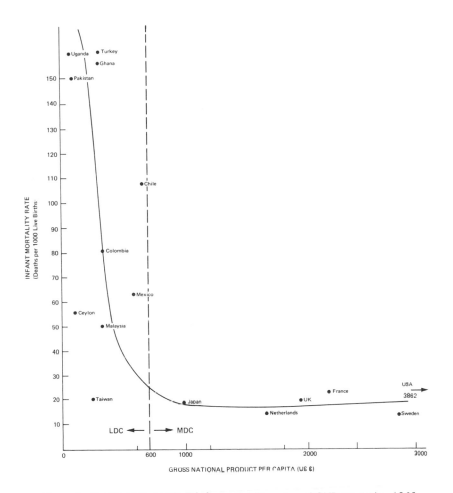

Figure 3. Relationship between infant mortality rate and GNP per capita, 1965.

others will have few; but still the level of health care may be comparable or be affected more by other factors. Health expenditures must be viewed with particular caution, since the private sector is more important in some countries than in others. The World Health Organization (WHO), in particular, is steadily improving the collection and standardization of these data as well as the more difficult indices of mortality and morbidity. Other important sources of health service data are the national development plans and health plans of individual countries. At this stage, however, these plans vary greatly in detail and availability; they may or may not differ significantly from WHO data. Because of these limitations of data, only six indices are used in this paper:

Manpower: (1) doctors (2) nurses (3) midwives
Facilities: (4) hospital beds
Expenditures: (5) total health (6) family planning

Table 3 lists the current level for the first five indices for each LDC listed in Table 1 for which information is available. Table 4 lists similar data for the same MDC's used in Table 2. Table 5 lists family planning expenditures for several national programs.

Health Manpower

Doctors. The range within the LDC's is great—from 2 to 3 per 100,000 population in tropical Africa, Afghanistan, Indonesia, and Nepal to 75 to 89 in the Philippines and Cuba. Most countries of Latin America are over 40, and the average for Asia is under 20. Most MDC's have over 100, the U.S.S.R. over 200. Most doctors in most countries are male, the U.S.S.R. being an important exception.

More important, perhaps, than national averages is that the conditions under which modern doctors perform effectively are those which characterize the MDC's, not the LDC's. Such conditions are present in the major urban areas of LDC's where doctor:population ratios do approximate national ratios for MDC's (17-19). Doctor:population ratios in rural areas of LDC's are low almost everywhere.

Nurses. Again the LDC range is great—from 3 or less in Afghanistan, Nepal, and Ethiopia to 110 in Cuba and 160 in Chile; in comparison with more than 250 in most MDC's. There is a tendency for LDC's with low doctor ratios to have high nurse ratios (e.g., Indonesia, Nigeria, Thailand, Sudan, Tanzania, Kenya, Ghana) and vice versa (e.g., Brazil, Mexico, Turkey, U.A.R., Colombia, Taiwan), but too many exceptions occur for any useful relationship to emerge from these data alone.

Midwives. For trained midwives the range is great for both LDC's (from less than 1 to 40) and MDC's (less than 1 to 74). These figures do not take into account the large number (usually uncounted) of local, untrained midwives or the smaller number of nurse-midwives in many countries. (The latter are included in the nurse category in the tables but can be separated.)

Health Facilities

Hospital Beds. Except for Afghanistan and Nepal with under 20 per 100,000 population; Pakistan, Nigeria, Korea, and Ethiopia with under 50; and Cuba with over 500, most hospital bed:population ratios for LDC's are in the range 80-300, whereas MDC ratios are around 1,000. Hospital beds require a certain amount of health manpower, such as doctors and nurses, to man them, but so little information is available on the kinds and amounts of manpower required for hospitals in LDC's that it seems futile to estimate the health manpower committed to inpatient care. The developmental conditions which are conducive to an urban concentration of doctors apply to modern hospitals as well.

Rural Health Centers. In development plans of most LDC's major emphasis is given to establishing groups of coordinated primary, secondary, and peripheral rural clinics to serve a population of 40,000 to 100,000 people. These clinics are extremely important to the subject of this paper, but they are not included at this time because satisfactory comparable data could not be obtained.

Health Expenditures

The difficulties of obtaining comparable financial data in any field are well known to anyone who has ever attempted to obtain them. Nevertheless, the World Health Organization has moved ahead toward developing governmental health expenditure data which have been utilized in Tables 3 and 4. Despite important unresolved problems affecting the international comparability of these data (23, 24), these kinds of data are being used in national and international planning at present. They are used in this paper to point out the effects of population growth on health services. One hopes their use will also stimulate further improvement of the data themselves.

The range of LDC government health expenditures is much wider than the ranges for manpower and facilities—from 3 U.S. cents per capita per year in Indonesia and 10 in Uganda to 822 in Malaysia and 1,094 in Chile. As a percent of total governmental expenditure, the range narrows considerably— from 0.3 percent in Indonesia to 8.8 percent in Malaysia. Governmental health expenditures in the seven MDC's are much higher—1,363 to 7,777 U.S. cents per capita per year of 4.9 to 13.2 percent of total governmental expenditures.

Among the major problems affecting comparability are:
1. the exclusion of data for the private sector;
2. the degree to which data for state and local expenditures are included;
3. the manner in which development costs, recurring costs, and capital expenditures are included; and
4. differences in what are called health services (e.g., the degree to which medical care costs and various environmental health services are included).

Because of the special significance of family planning services for population growth and the small number of countries with programs more than a few years old, a special effort was made to identify annual expenditures for family planning in countries with active programs. For purposes of this paper,

TABLE 3

Levels of Health Services in Largest Less Developed Countries, 1965[a]

Country	Health Manpower (per 100,000 Pop.)				Health Facilities	Governmental Health Expenditures		
	Doctors	Nurses	Midwives[b]	Change in Doctor Ratio 1955-65 as Percent 1955 Level	Hospital Beds (per 100,000 Pop.)	U.S. ¢ per Capita per Year	Percent GNP	Percent Total Government Expend.[c]
	(1)	(2)	(3)	(4)	(5)	(6)	(7)	(8)
1. China (Mainland)	–	–	–	–	–	–	–	–
2. India	21	10	10	17	59	53	0.6	2.2
3. Indonesia	3.2	19	5.7	129	69	3	0.03[d]	0.3
4. Pakistan	16	7	1.4	140	35	38	0.3	3.3
5. Brazil	42	20	–	6.1	283	150	0.5	4.0
6. Nigeria	2.3	16	7	92	42	30	0.4[d]	7.7
7. Mexico	50	19	–	12	202	264	0.5	6.5
8. Philippines	75	77	41	80	81	139	0.5	5.0
9. Turkey	35	15	2.4	28	178	228	0.7	3.8
10. Thailand	14	24	11	31	82	77	0.5	3.8
11. United Arab Rep.	44	10	7.2	43	168	284	1.6	4.8
12. Rep. of Korea	37	31	20	45	30	16	0.1	0.9
13. Burma	8.4	9	6	3.8	81	62	0.9	4.7
14. Iran	26	12	5.7	21	106	473	1.8	7.5
15. Ethiopia	1.6	3	–	46	41	38	0.6	6.7
16. N. Vietnam	–	–	–	–	–	–	–	–
17. Colombia	40	28	–	17	258	266	0.8	8.7
18. Rep. of Vietnam	3	17	5.2	–	142	–	1.3	2.9
19. Congo, Dem. Rep.	3.7	–	–	–29	–	–	–	–

20. Afghanistan	4.5	3	0.5	150	17	–	–	–
21. Sudan	3.9	27	–	70	99	99	1.0	5.7
22. Morocco	8.2	22	1.2	-22	152	–	–	–
23. China (Taiwan)	41	13	18	-7.1	77	98	0.4	2.8
24. N. Korea	–	–	–	–	–	–	–	–
25. Algeria	12	9	2.0	-44	356	–	–	4.6
26. Peru	46	46	7.8	27	243	233	0.9	5.4
27. Ceylon	24	20	23	24	313	332	2.2	7.9
28. Tanzania^f	5.0	43	3.01^e	0	202	75	1.1	6.4
29. Nepal	2	1	–	–	15	40	0.4^d	4.6
30. Kenya	7.8	53	11	-9.3	129	128	1.1	4.4
31. Portugal	85	70	0.6	13	583	439	1.0	7.0
32. Chile	58	161	8.9	8.1	363	1,094	1.7	7.9
33. Iraq	20	14	1.3	24	189	249	1.0	3.7
34. Malaysia^g	18	49	17	86	363	822	2.6	8.8
35. Ghana	7	35	7.3	–	110	366	1.3	5.3
36. Cuba	89	111	–	-11	553	–	–	–
37. Uganda	5.9	10	4.4	34	109	?0	0.1^d	6.4

– = no data available.

a Data are for 1965 or nearest available year.
b Does not include assistant or auxiliary midwives. Does not overlap with nurses category; nurse-midwives are included in the nursing statistics.
c For countries not listed in (22, Table 3) percentage calculations were made from (9, Table 199).

d Percent gross domestic product.
e Includes midwives and village midwives.
f Figures are for Tanganyika, except for columns 6-8.
g Figures are for West Malaysia only.

Sources: Cols. 1, 2, 5 (20, Tables 2.1, 2.5, 4.1); Col. 3 (20, Vol. III, Table 1; population denominators from 5); Col. 4 (21); Cols. 6, 7 (9, Tables 185, 186, 190, 191, 199; Col. 8 (22, Table 3).

TABLE 4

Health Services in Selected More Developed Countries, 1965[a]

Country	Health Manpower (per 100,000 Pop.)			Health Facilities	Governmental Health Expenditures		
	Doctors	Nurses	Midwives	Hospital Beds (per 100,000 Pop.)	U.S. $ per Capita	Percent GNP	Percent Total Government Expend.
1. Soviet Union	210	340	74	965	–	3.5	–
2. United States	148	464	–	875	51.13	1.4	8.4
3. Japan	109	265	44	892	13.63	1.6	13.2
4. United Kingdom	115	260	37	1,010	65.34	3.6	9.0
5. France	121	255	7	1,021	–	–	–
6. Netherlands	117	125	8	752	12.49	1.0	4.9
7. Sweden	110	313	9	1,373	77.77	3.1	11.3

– = not available.

[a]Data for 1965 or for most recent year closest to 1965.

Sources: Manpower and Facilities: (20, Vol. III).
Expenditures: (9, Tables 185, 191, 199; 22, Table 3; 8, Table 180).

TABLE 5

National Family Planning Program Expenditures in LDC's

Country	Expenditures, U.S. Cents per Capita per Fiscal Year					
	1964	1965	1966	1967	1968	Next Plan Period
India	2.2	2.5	4.1[a]	7.7	8.5	14.6[c]
Pakistan	-	6.6	10.6	14.4	-	23.4[d]
Rep. Korea	4.2	5.1	9.0	9.4	19.8[b]	-
China (Taiwan)	1.2	4.0	3.8	3.5	5.1	-
Malaysia	0	0	0.4	2.9	6.2	-

- = not available

[a]Reflects sudden change in exchange rate from Rs 4.75 to 7.54 per US $; rupee expenditures almost doubled.

[b]Includes large capital investment.

[c]Proposed by Government of India, Draft Fourth Five-Year Plan, 1969-1974, New Delhi, April 1969, p. 312.

[d]Proposed by Government of Pakistan, Planning Commission, Fourth Five-Year Plan 1970-75. p. 242.

Sources: Malaysia 1966-68 from annual reports of National Family Planning Board; others 1964-68 are preliminary data obtained from each country by Warren Robinson, Pennsylvania State University.

family planning expenditures are considered separately whether or not they were included as health expenditures in a particular country.

Family Planning Expenditures

Definition of terms is critical in all international comparative work but particularly so in a new field such as natality control. *Natality control*, as used in this paper, includes all organized activities intended to achieve a specified natality level or a specified growth rate for a population. *Family planning programs*, as used here, are organized activities whose objective is to enable individual couples to act effectively to plan and assure the number and timing of children they want (25). The principal distinction is between societal (governmental) control and individual family control, and the dividing line is very wide and very gray.

Most of the national programs in this field are called *family planning programs*. Where the specified natality goal for a country can be achieved by the sum of individual family planning actions, natality control and family planning programs are for all practical purposes identical. This is the general case today. Most programs operate under policies which specify voluntary family planning as the major means of attaining a natality level. None includes coercion, but all aim at making it easier for families to obtain and use natality control methods than was previously the case. Most specify natality goals that are based upon contraceptive utilization rates that are presumed will occur under voluntary family planning in response to a proposed level of availability of information, service, and supplies at an assumed level of public motivation or of demand potentially present.

In these circumstances (which will almost certainly be altered in some countries by 1985) expenditures for natality control and family planning are considered here as identical.

Family planning expenditures shown in Table 5 are governmental (public sector) expenditures only (although some are used to purchase services in the private sector). The countries were selected because they had national programs at least 3 years old for which expenditure data were available. Since the programs are still in various stages of development in all countries, expenditures per capita are still rising. Levels of at least 10 to 20 U.S. cents per person per year—the same order of magnitude as the cost of malaria-eradication programs (26)—appear necessary in LDC's.

FUTURE LEVELS OF HEALTH SERVICES (1985)

Projecting alternative trends of the factors which affect development of the LDC's—even for 20 years—is becoming as sterile as predicting the most likely combination and outcome is becoming hazardous, but both are necessary for rational planning of man's future.

The effects of population growth on future levels of health services are similar to its effects on other developmental goals which are discussed in this volume—perhaps most like those on education. Levels of health are comparable to levels of knowledge; levels of utilization of health facilities and manpower are comparable to years of schooling; doctor:population ratios to teacher:enrollment ratios; hospital beds to schoolrooms, medical and nursing colleges to teachers colleges; etc. Despite these similarities, substantial differences also exist; for example, needs for schools and needs for health services have different relationships to the age structure of the population (Figure 2) and to the times required to train personnel (doctors vs. teachers).

The effects of population growth on personal health services depend in part upon the probable effects of other factors besides population which help determine what the levels of doctors, hospital beds, and health expenditures will actually be in 1985. First are national decisions regarding the priority position of health relative to other goals, such as food, education, employment, industry, roads, communications, and income; and regarding priorities among health services, such as malaria eradication, clean, piped drinking water, hospital care, and family planning. In those LDC's where mortality is already approaching low levels, less incentive to invest a larger proportion of national development budgets in mortality and morbidity control is anticipated in the next 20 years. Nevertheless, pressures to approach MDC levels of personal health services will persist, and demand for piped water and proper waste disposal will probably increase. Investment in natality control measures above their present low levels can be expected as the effects of high population growth rates are felt.

Second are national decisions made regarding the kinds of health service functions that are best performed by different kinds of health personnel. (Which services during pregnancy can be performed by a midwife and which require a doctor? Who is qualified to insert an intra-uterine device or prescribe oral contraceptives or perform an abortion? What proportion of doctors should be women?) Decisions on these matters by LDC's should differ from those by MDC's, just as the cultures and illness patterns and educational facilities differ.

The criterion of a program's applicability to agricultural village life will remain a dominant consideration for a long time. In a speech (unpublished) at the 1969 World Health Assembly in Boston, WHO Director-General M. G. Candau said,

> . . . the developing nations must not blindly follow old patterns but should design their educational systems to meet their own different health needs. In doing so they must bear in mind the need for re-examining the allocation of responsibility to various members of the health team. Physicians in all countries could be used to better advantage if they were relieved of functions that could be carried out by other members of the team. By this means it should be possible to ameliorate, at least in part, the critical situation of the developing countries where, for at least a generation, there is no possibility of providing enough physicians to carry out all their traditional functions.

Third are world technologic developments. These are the least predictable and most likely to produce profound changes within 20 years. Their overall effect is to accelerate achievement of goals beyond those possible with present technology. However, improper overemphasis on the products of technology can impede progress toward goals; every hospital does not need a heart-lung machine. Because of the great difficulty of prediction, probable improvements in contraceptive technology are not taken into further account here beyond serving as a safety factor for other assumptions.

Fourth are levels of international technical assistance. Since World War II, health assistance has been sizeable through the World Health Organization, the U.S. Agency for International Development, and other governmental and private sources. Except for a few private sources and one small nation—Sweden—technical assistance in family planning was virtually nonexistent before 1965 (27). At recent rates of increase, technical assistance should be substantial over the next 20 years in both health and family planning.

The indirect effects of population growth upon health services are legion; the direct effects follow from (a) numbers of people to be served, (b) their age distribution, and (c) their geographic distribution. For various reasons, such as the frequency of disease at different ages, public perceptions of a doctor's utility, cost to the individual, and local norms regarding the kinds and frequency of health supervision at different ages, the utilization of doctors varies by age of population served (28, 29). There are also differences in utilization and large differences in availability of doctors between rural and urban locations (17, 18, 28, 30). In the absence of good data on utilization rates for LDC's, it is difficult to project or predict the effect of changes in age structure and urban-rural residence on health services in the next 20 years, even if those changes themselves could be accurately predicted. The data that do exist indicate that lower population growth would result in a decrease in doctor utilization as a larger proportion of the population slowly became aged 15 to 45 (a group with lower utilization rates), offset by an increase in doctor availability and utilization as a larger proportion of the population moved into cities. Further discussion of direct population growth effects here will be limited to those resulting from numbers of people.

Changes in the Past Decade

One other important consideration is actual experience with changes in levels of health services in the recent past. Perhaps the best data come from a special WHO report (21) which compares the physician:population ratios of various countries in 1955 and 1965. Data are available for thirty-one of the thirty-seven countries defined as LDC's for this paper and are included in column 4 of Table 3. In the thirty-one countries in 1955, there were 181,891 doctors and 1,017,700,000 people, or 17.9 doctors per 100,000 people. The thirty-one countries showed an average increase from 1955 to 1965 in their doctor:population ratios of 18.5 percent over the 1955 level. Three countries had increases in their ratio of physicians to population by over 100 percent of the 1955 level, four by over 50 percent, and seventeen by less than 50 percent; seven had no change or decreases up to 44 percent. The average increase in doctors per 100,000 population was 3.3. With two exceptions (U.A.R. and Korea), this change by individual country was less then 10 per 100,000 and in nineteen was less then 5. Most of the decreases were in newly independent African countries. For the same time period, the increase in ratio of physicians to population for the United States was 14.4 percent of the 1955 level or 18 doctors per 100,000 population.

The effect of population growth during the decade 1955-65 upon the numbers of new doctors actually required to achieve the increases in doctor: population ratios is shown in Table 6. The requirements for LDC's and the United States are taken as zero in the theoretical case of zero population

TABLE 6

1965 Requirements for Doctors in Thirty-One LDC's and in U.S.A.
as Percent of 1955 Number of Doctors

Change in Doctors per 100,000 Population 1955-65	Population Growth 1955-65	
	Zero	Actual
LDC's		
Zero (remains 17.9)	0	25.6
+3.3 (increases to 21.1)	18.5	49.5
U.S.A.		
Zero (remains 130)	0	17.0
+18 (increases to 148)	14.4	33.5

Source: (21).

growth and zero increase in ratio, since insufficient data are available from the LDC's on replacements needed for death, retirement, and migration, although the actual number in 1965 presumably includes them.

For the LDC's, instead of the 18.5 percent increase in numbers of doctors (33,584) required to move from 17.9 to 21.2 doctors per 100,000 population had no population growth occurred, 49.5 percent was actually required (25.6 percent or 46,611 doctors to maintain the 1955 ratio as population grew and 23.8 percent or 43,360 doctors to increase the ratio for the new population). For the United States, instead of the 14.4 percent increase in numbers of doctors (29,867) required to move from 130 to 148 doctors per 100,000 population had no population growth occurred, 33.5 percent was actually required (17 percent of 35,316 doctors to maintain the 1955 ratio as population grew and 16.5 percent or 34,335 doctors to increase the ratio for the new population).

Population Growth and Health Services in the Next 20 Years

The clearest relationship between population growth and personal health services in the LDC's during the next 20 years is the direct demand more population creates for more health services. This direct effect will be considered here in several ways. One is the requirement to maintain the current level of service under conditions of probable—compared to zero—population growth. This is the familiar measure of how fast one must run to stay in the same place. Another is the requirement to achieve a planned or desired level of service under conditions of probable, compared to zero, population growth. This measures the added burden that population growth adds to developmental costs of health services. Both methods are further complicated by considering two "probable" rates of population growth. One assumes conditions of no change in level or trend of natality from that of the past decade. The other assumes conditions of a decline in natality brought about primarily through organized natality control efforts by the country. Finally, the measure most meaningful to leaders of LDC's is the difference between the actual requirements for the two "probable" rates of population growth. Stated another way, this difference is the savings in investment resulting from effective natality control (Table 7).

TABLE 7

Health Service Requirements under Differing Conditions
of Population Growth and Development

Change in Level of Health Service 20 Years from Now	Population Growth in Next 20 Years			
	Zero	Without Natality Control	With Natality Control	Savings
Zero	A	B	C	B-C
Increased as planned	D	E	F	E-F

Requirements A and D are theoretical, if no population growth occurred. Requirement A has for simplicity been taken as zero in this paper. Requirement D is simply the initial population multiplied by the increase in service: population ratio desired. All requirements are understated to the extent that they do not include replacements necessary for manpower who die or retire or migrate or, in some cases, for facilities and equipment that wear out. In view of the magnitude of requirements and of the difficulties of predicting future retirement and especially migration rates, it has seemed adequate here to assume that neither mortality nor retirement will be significant before 1985 because of the young age distribution of doctors and nurses, and that no real improvement in levels of manpower can occur without developing working conditions that will minimize a "brain drain." Need to replace losses from mortality, retirement, and migration can be great; in the case of Taiwan replacement needs were estimated for the 20 years 1963-1983 to be 76 percent of the total supply of doctors (28, p. 68) in 1963.

Requirements B and E are based upon population projections which assume mortality and natality declining at approximately the 1955-1965 rate (which for most LDC's means no change in natality rate). Requirements C and F are based upon population projections which assume mortality declining at the 1955-1965 rate and natality declining at a more rapid rate than 1955-1965, largely as a result of organized efforts during 1965-1985. Requirements C and F are also based upon assumptions regarding additional requirements for health services when natality control is included.

Neither of these two important assumptions—the additional requirements for health services when family planning is included or the reduction in natality rate resulting from natality control—can be made with precision in the present state of knowledge, but rough guidelines are possible for planning purposes in individual countries.

HEALTH SERVICES REQUIREMENTS FOR FAMILY PLANNING

Semantics can be confusing here. As stated earlier, family planning programs and costs can be considered health service programs and costs. They can also be considered separately and will be so treated here to simplify understanding of alternatives. However, since they utilize some health manpower and facilities, account must be taken of specific health manpower and facilities that must be provided for family planning in addition to that already planned for other health purposes.

If we ignore the possibility that by 1985 technologic advance will make present requirements obsolete, we can reasonably estimate health service requirements for family planning by using available program experience in the world to date.

The requirements for doctors, nurses, and midwives that family planning service will add will depend largely upon decisions made in each country on what specific functions with regard to each method of contraception must be performed by a doctor or nurse or midwife, as well as on the actual availability and utilization rate for various methods. The requirement for doctors for intra-uterine contraception or for oral contraception will be low if most functions are performed by nurses or specially trained assistants and field workers, whereas using present techniques for induced abortion and surgical sterilization may require appreciable amounts of doctor manpower. In summary, much of the manpower required for family planning can be new, specially trained manpower—which will not significantly affect the planned requirements for doctors, nurses, and midwives for other health services.

Pakistan provides one example of an approach to family planning manpower requirements that places minimal strain on the limited medical manpower pool. Convinced that certain functions usually reserved for female doctors (such as pelvic examinations and intra-uterine contraceptive device insertions) could be performed by female high school graduates with one year of specialized training, program leaders established a new cadre of workers—"lady family planning visitors." As a result the program, as projected to 1975

(31, 32), requires only 240 doctors (less than 0.2 doctor per 100,000 population; about 1 percent of all doctors but 5 percent of female doctors). It creates new and socially important work (300 jobs in 1966; 2,460 by 1975) for the small but growing group of female matriculates for whom real job alternatives to childbearing are critical.

The program has also given part-time employment during 1965-1970 to tens of thousands of village midwives (dais) and other village women (and men) to be local contraceptive supply and referral agents. Because most countries traditionally employ females as nurses, health visitors, and midwives, health services are one of the potential sources of greater employment for females in the future. Perhaps more by serendipity than by design, such greater employment of women is also an important indirect natality control measure which could be purposefully expanded. The impossibility of depending upon the pool of female doctors, lady health visitors, and nurse-midwives to provide necessary family planning manpower (e.g., about two doctors per 100,000 population) is well documented in a report from India (33).

No additional requirements for hospital beds result from family planning; rather, in those countries where illegal induced abortion is already so widely practiced that the aftereffects now utilize a sizeable proportion of hospital beds, a case can be made that family planning will result in additional specific savings in bed requirements beyond that related to reduced natality on population growth. On the other hand, if abortion is legalized in more countries, and is both acceptable and accessible, demand for short-term hospital care may increase. Current techniques of aspiration already minimize this demand. It is impossible to predict whether there would be a net increase or a net decrease because of the reduced bed and medical needs to care for complications now ensuing after illegal abortions combined with additional needs created by more legalized, hospital-performed abortions. A large postpartum sterilization program would also increase the need for hospital beds and related services.

The effect of family planning on requirements for other health services, such as maternal and child health, is assumed to be unimportant in most LDC's because demand for other services will greatly exceed the supply under any foreseeable circumstances in the next 20 years. In those few countries with a high ratio of trained midwives to population, reductions in natality rates might result in transient or further underemployment of midwives. In that case the trained midwives would presumably provide family planning services and use of their nursing services would increase as a result of public satisfaction with family planning services from the same source. It seems realistic to treat most family planning requirements during the next two decades as additional to those for other health services, and to assume that the overall effect of adding family planning on requirements for traditional health manpower and facilities will be small in most LDC's.

One other consideration that will not be uniform among LDC's is the extent to which efficiency can be achieved by simply incorporating the administrative and service responsibilities for family planning into existing maternal and child health programs. Ideally, family planning services should be incorporated into maternal and child health services. However, it appears that most maternal and child health programs still have far to go in achieving their prime objectives of basic maternity, infant, and child care. Not only can few economies be achieved, but also a new and controversial service like family planning is unlikely to be introduced effectively if administered as a new objective of maternal and child health. In any case, family planning program costs should be considered as new and additional to other health services in almost all LDC's during the next 20 years. Experience also suggests that, as in the case of malaria eradication, national administration of new family planning programs requires a high and semi-autonomous status in the bureaucracy. In the long run, to the extent that contraceptive technology requires health services, family planning should be incorporated with other family health services. Provisions for such an eventual merger should be part of the planning and implementation of family planning programs from the start.

Reduction in Natality from Family Planning

The effect of family planning services upon natality in the LDC's in the next 20 years will depend mainly upon three factors: the extent to which effective birth control information and services are made readily available to the people; the extent to which natality is modified by means other than birth control (for example, raising the age of marriage); and the extent to which the public wants to use birth control or other means—in other words, how much public attitudes change regarding desired family size and child spacing.

During the next 20 years significant changes in contraceptive practice are more likely than significant changes in age of marriage or the proportion of persons who marry. Contraception involves lesser modifications of agricultural village life, and governments will probably have more effective methods to promote birth control than to change marriage patterns.

In the absence of adequate natality registration in most LDC's, evidence for the effect of family planning programs on natality rests primarily on two propositions:

1. A certain proportion of families of reproductive age use specified methods of family planning provided by the program and not otherwise available or likely to be used.

2. Enough is known of the length of use of different methods of family planning and of the fertility and other characteristics of families using and

not using specified methods that a sound estimate of the number of births prevented can be made.

With regard to both propositions data are becoming available from program service statistics and sample surveys. A rough estimate of the proportion of families of reproductive age (operationally, females 15 to 44 years old) using contraception is available from cumulative data on family planning acceptors and/or users in several national programs (Figure 4). Enough is becoming known also about age, parity, age-specific natality rates, prior use of contraception, and other characteristics of acceptors and on length of use and effectiveness in preventing pregnancy of various family planning methods that, despite variations among LDC's on several of the important variables

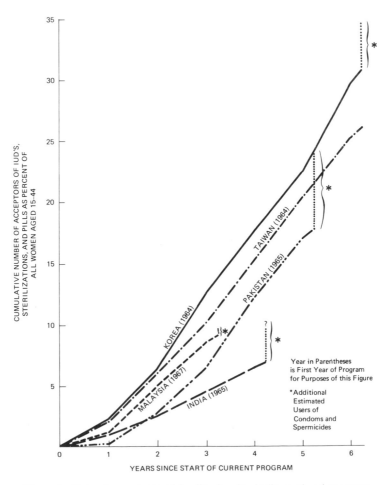

Figure 4. Rate of acceptance of family planning in five national programs.

involved, a useful range of births prevented per acceptor of a given method is emerging.* The least reliable data continue to be on the use of conventional contraceptives, such as condoms and foam. Evaluations of the overall effects of present programs (36, 37) are beginning to indicate what effects sizeable, effective programs can have on natality rates of LDC's in 20 years. The great unknown is what proportion of families will actually use effective contraception if it is made readily available.

By 1985 family planning services should be so available in many countries that the utilization rate of these services (and the resulting natality rates) will be an accurate reflection of public attitudes on family size and spacing (38). As long as contraceptive technology requires health services for delivery and as long as health services for most people are provided by the public sector, family planning services themselves will become and continue to be an important new component of government health services. Before 1985, more governments are likely to have initiated enough new actions such as direct financial, housing, educational, and other incentives and greater educational and employment opportunities for women that it will be possible to measure their effects on desires for family size, on contraceptive use, on age of marriage and on natality.

Present planners in each country attempt to utilize any of the above information that is available to them and relevant to their situations to help determine the kind and size of a family planning program for their country, as well as to estimate the probable effects, particularly on natality and health services. A few examples of such planning are described next.

Some National Examples

Pakistan and Turkey are two countries that have published 20-year goals in terms of specific health-service:population ratios and that already have active family planning programs. Table 8 shows the number of doctors, nurses, and hospital beds that must be added between 1965 and 1985 to achieve those goals in comparison with the numbers required to maintain present ratios, with and without a successful family planning program. Based upon population estimates and health service goals of the Governments of Pakistan and Turkey, these calculations are subject to change with future experience and new data, but they do represent real and reasonably typical situations. Similar data about India from a nongovernmental source are presented in Table 9.

Other countries have established shorter term goals of similar magnitude (43-46). In addition, a series of detailed health manpower studies in Taiwan, Turkey, and Peru (28-30) not only indicate the effects of population growth but also translate the need for doctors, nurses, midwives, etc. into costs,

*See for example (34, 35). Much more unpublished data have been obtained subsequently.

TABLE 8

Requirements for Selected Health Service Goals—1965-1985, Pakistan and Turkey

Population (millions)		1965	1985			
			Zero Population Growth	No Natality Change	Effective Family Planning	Difference
	Pakistan	103.6	103.6	188.0	164.6	23.4
	Turkey	31.4	31.4	58.6	49.7	8.9
Service (per 100,000 Pop.)		Actual Number	Additions Required after 1965 to Achieve Ratio at Left (Percent of 1965 Level in Parentheses)			
		(2)	(3)	(4)	(5)	(6)
		(1)				
Doctors						
Pakistan		16,589	–	13,520 (82)	9,771 (59)	3,749 (23)
Present ratio		16	17,584 (106)	45,451 (274)	37,729 (227)	9,722 (47)
		33ᵃ				

Present ratio	35	11,087	–	9,601 (87)	6,464 (58)	3,137 (28)
Goal	62[a]	–	8,536 (77)	25,245 (228)	19,727 (178)	5,518 (50)
Nurses						
Pakistan						
Present ratio	7	6,848	–	5,581 (82)	4,033 (59)	1,548 (23)
Goal	20[a]	–	12,737 (186)	30,752 (449)	26,072 (381)	4,680 (68)
Hospital beds						
Pakistan						
Present ratio	35	36,171	–	29,499 (82)	21,305 (59)	8,174 (23)
Goal	100[a]	–	67,278 (186)	151,828 (420)	128,429 (355)	23,400 (65)

[a] Actual goals.

Sources: Pakistan population from (39), Turkey (40); Pakistan goals (41), Turkey (42, p. 200); 1965 supply of doctors, nurses, hospital beds from (20, Tables 1 and 3).

TABLE 9

Requirements for Selected Health Service Goals, India, 1966-1981

		1966	1981			
			Zero Population Growth	No Natality Change	Effective Family Planning	Difference
Population (millions)		491	491	731	693	38
Health Service (per 100,000 Pop.)		Actual Number	Additions Required after 1966 to Achieve Ratio at Left (Percent of 1966 Level in Parentheses)			
	(1)	(2)	(3)	(4)	(5)	(6)
Doctors						
Present ratio	21	103,110	–	50,300 (49)	42,420 (41)	7,980 (8)
Goal	50	–	142,390 (138)	262,290 (254)	243,390 (236)	19,000 (18)
Nurses						
Present ratio	12	58,920	–	28,870 (49)	24,150 (41)	4,710 (8)
Goal	50	–	186,580 (317)	306,580 (520)	287,580 (488)	19,000 (32)
Hospital beds						
Present ratio	59	289,690	–	141,600 (49)	118,770 (41)	22,830 (8)
Goal	100	–	201,310 (69)	441,310 (152)	403,310 (139)	38,000 (13)

– = not available.

Sources: (47), hospital beds (48).

timetables, and training programs and point to specific changes urgently needed in medical education and health employment conditions.

Tables can be constructed to show the savings in health services investments like those in Tables 8 and 9 for different rates of development and different rates of natality reduction (population growth). Table 10 is such a table covering the probable range of development goals and natality reduction rates in LDC's in the next 20 years. Requirements for different development goals are shown in column 2. Requirements for population growth without natality control are shown in column 3 for a fixed population growth rate of 3 percent per year. Requirements for lesser population growth rates as a result of natality control are given in columns 4, 5, 6, and 7 and the difference (savings) between them and column 3 are shown in columns 8, 9, 10, and 11. The savings for a country that wants to double its level of health services in 20 years and is able to reduce its average population growth rate for the 20 years from 3 to 2.4 percent per year equal the investment needed to produce and to maintain 41 percent of its initial level (e.g., of manpower and facilities). Expressed as reduction in the requirement or investment needed without natality control the figure would be much less—15.5 percent.

Family Planning and Health Service Costs. Because health service cost projections for 1985 are not available, it is difficult to estimate the reduced investment costs for health services that might result from effective natality control programs. A good guess would appear to come from (a) projecting a nation's development budget to 1985 from recent past experience, (b) assuming that the percent of the development budget for health services in 1985 remains the same as, or increases slightly above, that in 1965, and (c) applying the average percent reduction for that country which would result from calculations like those in Tables 8 and 9. In many LDC's effective natality control could reduce the health services investment needed to achieve goals like those in Tables 8 and 9 by 10 to 50 U.S. cents per capita per year. The direct fiscal benefits for health services of an effective family planning program will certainly be far greater in countries that already spend large amounts on health services or already have high hospital care costs resulting from poorly performed illegal abortions, but such countries are almost by definition well along the scale from less to more developed countries.

If family planning program costs are projected from Table 5 on the assumptions that (a) availability of good services will be increased steadily, (b) the rate of increase of public utilization will slow up, and (c) the cost per user will rise, they can be expected to reach levels of 25 to 50 U.S. cents per capita per year or more.

To summarize, in most LDC's over the next 20 years, the reduction in investment costs in health services resulting from effective family planning is likely to be substantial but does not appear likely to equal the added costs of the family planning program.

TABLE 10

Savings in Health Service Requirements from Reductions in Natality
Rates of LDC's over 20 Years Given Initial Population (Po)
and Initial Health Services (Ho)

Population	No Population Change	No Natality Change[a]	Additions Required to Achieve Ratio in Col. 1 (Percent of Ho) Effective Family Planning[a]				Savings Resulting from Natality Reductions (Percent of Ho)			
Health Services to Population Ratio	Po	1.822 Po	1.751 Po	1.682 Po	1.616 Po	1.553 Po	1.751 Po	1.682 Po	1.616 Po	1.553 Po
(1)	(2)	(3)	(4)	(5)	(6)	(7)	(8) $(3)-(4)$	(9) $(3)-(5)$	(10) $(3)-(6)$	(11) $(3)-(7)$
K_o[b]	0	82	75	68	62	55	7	14	20	27
1.5 K_o	50	173	163	152	142	133	10	21	31	40
2.0 K_o	100	264	250	236	223	211	14	28	41	53
2.5 K_o	150	355	338	321	304	289	17	34	51	66
3.0 K_o	200	446	425	405	385	366	21	41	61	80

[a]Cols. 3, 4, 5, 6, and 7 correspond to annual population growth rates of 3, 2.8, 2.6, 2.4, and 2.2 percent respectively.
[b]$K_o = Ho/Po$.

Source: Author's calculations.

IMPLICATIONS

Leaders of LDC's are concerned with raising the level of all aspects of development of their countries. Since high natality and high population growth rates impede development in most LDC's, most leaders will become increasingly concerned about natality rates in the next 20 years. They will want to know what investments in natality control will result in what reductions in natality rates. They will also want to know what reductions in requirements to meet specific development goals (such as so many hospital beds per capita) will result from reductions in natality rates. They will be interested in the reduced investments that will be needed not only for health and health services but also for education and schools, industrialization and jobs, agriculture and food, housing, national income and its distribution.

Although the savings in investment needed to reach a nation's goals for health services can be estimated with some precision, according to alternative mortality and natality rate projections, it is not yet possible to specify with the precision desired by national planners the reduction in natality and population growth that will result from a given investment in family planning services or the reduction in mortality that will result from a given investment in health services.

Nevertheless, better health remains a goal for the leaders and the public in all countries, and improving health services remains one important means of achieving it. In LDC's, efforts will continue to raise the levels of health services toward the distant goals represented by levels in MDC's. These and other efforts will result in some continuing decrease in the mortality rates of most LDC's, which will continue to increase population growth rates and dependency ratios.

In most LDC's investments in family planning services will result in some reduction in natality rates. Whether they are introduced to enable families, as a basic human right, to have the number of children they want or to enable a society to achieve the size and distribution of its people most consonant with its resources and way of life, investments in family planning are one important means toward achieving a given natality level. They may be a critical factor in initiating natality declines in the present historical circumstances of most LDC's.

The present public expenditure for health services in LDC's ranges from about 2.5 to 7.5 percent of total governmental expenditures. Such investments during the United Nations First Development Decade proved inadequate to meet the moderate goals set by the World Health Organization. Greater investments are needed during the Second Development Decade—the 1970's—but are not in sight in most countries from either internal sources or from all available external sources of technical assistance.

Expenditures for family planning in LDC's are in the range of 5 to 20 U.S. cents per capita per year—approaching those required for malaria eradication.

This level of investment ranges from 5 percent to over 100 percent of present governmental expenditures for health services among the LDC's. Greater investments during the Second Development Decade are in sight as more and more responsible national and international leaders come to recognize the multiple short- and long-term benefits that follow effective family planning and other natality control measures. Among these benefits are direct benefits to health, such as reduced infant and maternal mortality and morbidity and direct benefits to health services, such as reduced investments needed to reach national goals for health personnel and facilities. Although it appears that the cost of family planning programs in the next 20 years will exceed the resulting savings in expenditures required to achieve health service goals, other and much larger direct benefits accrue for major development goals, such as food, housing, education, employment, industrialization, and income.

Although there is no certainty that family planning programs based upon current technology will, of themselves, alter natality rates sufficiently for optimal national development, it is certain that they will contribute to natality reduction and that they will be an essential means through which other natality control measures must operate. The conclusion is inescapable that the World Health Organization and other international and national technical assistance organizations should move rapidly to develop capabilities and resources to assist LDC's over the next 20 years or more with natality control programs of at least the magnitude of the worldwide campaign to eradicate malaria.

REFERENCES

1. Berelson, Bernard, "National Family Planning Programs: Where We Stand" *Fertility and Family Planning*, S. J. Behrman et al., eds. Ann Arbor: Univ. of Michigan Press, 1969. pp. 341-387.
2. Barlow, Robin, *The Economic Effects of Malaria Eradication*. Bureau of Public Health Economics Research Series No. 15. Ann Arbor: Univ. of Michigan, 1968.
3. McKeown, Thomas, "Medicine and World Population," *Public Health and Population Change*, Mindel C. Sheps and Jeanne C. Ridley, eds., Pittsburgh: Univ. of Pittsburgh Press, 1965. pp. 25-40.
4. Newman, Peter, *Malaria Eradication and Population Growth*. Bureau of Public Health Economics Research Series No. 10. Ann Arbor: Univ. of Michigan, 1965.
5. *United Nations Demographic Yearbook, 1967*. New York: United Nations, 1968.
6. *United Nations Statistical Yearbook, 1968*. New York: United Nations, 1969.
7. *United Nations Demographic Yearbook, 1965*. New York: United Nations, 1966.
8. *United Nations Demographic Yearbook, 1966*. New York: United Nations, 1967.

9. *United Nations Statistical Yearbook, 1968.* New York: United Nations, 1969.

10. *United Nations Demographic Yearbook, 1963.* New York: United Nations, 1964.

11. *United Nations Statistical Yearbook, 1964.* New York: United Nations, 1965.

12. United Nations, *Compendium of Social Statistics: 1963.* New York: United Nations, 1963.

13. United Nations Statistical Papers Series K, No. 2. New York: United Nations, 1963. Table 5.

14. Russett, Bruce M., et al., *World Handbook of Political and Social Indicators.* New Haven: Yale Univ. Press, 1964. p. 222.

15. Hashmi, Sultan S., and Iqbal Alam, "The Problem of Obtaining Age Data in Pakistan." Paper presented to International Union for Scientific Study of Population. London, September 1969.

16. Chase, Helen C., *International Comparison of Perinatal and Infant Mortality.* National Center for Health Statistics Series 3, No. 6. Washington, D.C.: U.S. Dept. of Health, Education, and Welfare, March 1967.

17. World Health Organization, *World Health Statistics Annual, 1963.* Geneva, 1967. Vol. III, Table 1.4.

18. World Health Organization, *The Urban and Rural Distribution of Medical Manpower.* WHO Chronicle, Vol. 22, No. 100, 1968.

19. United Nations Children's Fund, Ch. III of volume in preparation on effects of population growth on children. New York, 1969.

20. *World Health Statistics Annual, 1965.* Geneva, 1969. Vol. III.

21. *World Health Statistics Report,* Vol. 22, No. 182. Geneva, 1969.

22. *World Health Statistics Report,* Vol. 21, No. 11. Geneva, 1969.

23. Abel-Smith, Brian, "An International Study of Health Expenditure." World Health Organization Public Health Paper No. 32. Geneva, 1967.

24. World Health Organization, *National Health Planning in Developing Countries.* Technical Report Series No. 350. Geneva, 1967. p. 22.

25. American Public Health Association, *Family Planning. A Guide for State and Local Agencies.* New York, 1968. p. 1.

26. U.S. Department of Health, Education, and Welfare, National Communicable Disease Center, "Malaria Eradication Program, Annual Report, Fiscal Year 1968." Washington, D.C., 1969.

27. Organization for Economic Cooperation and Development, *Population International Assistance and Research.* Paris, 1969.

28. Baker, Timothy D., and Mark Perlman, *Health Manpower in a Developing Economy, Taiwan.* Baltimore: Johns Hopkins Press, 1967.

29. Taylor, Carl E., et al., *Health Manpower Planning in Turkey.* Baltimore: Johns Hopkins Press, 1968.

30. Hall, Thomas L., *Health Manpower in Peru.* Baltimore: Johns Hopkins Press, 1969.

31. Government of Pakistan, Family Planning Council, *Annual Reports* since 1965. Islamabad.

32. Government of Pakistan, Family Planning Division, *Proposals for Family Planning Sector, 1970-75.* Islamabad, 1969.

33. Institute of Applied Manpower Research, "Manpower Requirements of the Family Planning Programme." I.A.M.R. Working Paper No. 1/1968. New Delhi, March 1968.

34. Mauldin, Parket, et al., "Retention of IUD's: An International Comparison." *Studies in Family Planning*, April 1967. p. 1.

35. Jones, Gavin, and Parker Mauldin, "Use of Oral Contraceptives with Special Reference to Developing Countries, *Studies in Family Planning*, December 1967. p. 1.

36. Chang, M. C., T. H. Liu, and L. P. Chow, "Study by Matching of the Demographic Impact of an IUD Program: A Preliminary Report," *Milbank Memorial Fund Quarterly*, April 1969.

37. United Nations Department of Economic and Social Affairs, "Report on an Evaluation of the Family Planning Programme of the Government of Pakistan." U.N. Report No. TAO/PAK/28, April 7, 1969. p. 127.

38. Bumpass, Larry, and Charles F. Westoff, "The Perfect Contraceptive Population: Extent and Implications of Unwanted Fertility," *Science*, 1970 (in press).

39. Government of Pakistan, Central Statistical Office, "Alternative Population Projections of Pakistan." DDS/2/66 May 1966. Islamabad. Assumption I: Table 22 and Assumption III: Table 24.

40. Shorter, Frederick C., "Population Projections for 1965-2000." Unpublished.

41. Government of Pakistan Planning Commission, Outline of the Third Five Year Plan. Karachi, 1965.

42. Republic of Turkey Prime Ministry State Planning Organization, *Second Five Year Plan, 1968-72.* Ankara, 1969.

43. Ceylon, Ministry of Planning and Economic Affairs, *Report on Manpower Resources, 1966-1971.* Colombo, Ceylon. p. 40.

44. Kenya, Ministry of Finance, *Development Plan, 1964-1970.* Nairobi, 1964. p. 107.

45. Federation of Nigeria, Federal Ministry of Economic Development, *National Development Plan 1962-1968.* Lagos, n.d. p. 37.

46. Thailand, National Economic Development Board, *Second National Economic and Social Development Plan, 1967-1971.* Bangkok, p. 182.

47. Tyrrell Burgess, Richard Layar, and Pitawban Pant, *Manpower and Educational Development in India 1961-86.* Edinburgh: Oliver and Boyd, 1968.

48. Government of India, Planning Commission, *Perspectives on Planning—Long-Term Perspectives.* New Delhi. p. 6.

XI

Population Pressure on Families: Family Size and Child Spacing

Joe D. Wray

Today's alarming rates of population growth, appropriately called the population explosion, are produced by the complex interaction of a great many factors. The effects of this growth at global or national levels have only rather recently become a matter of serious concern; the factors which produced the growth have been operating in the West for a long time. It is worth noting, though, that these factors, operating on families, began to produce population pressure at the family level long ago and that there is evidence that people in large numbers recognized the threats to their families imposed by excessive growth.

Let us recall that in the West birth rates began to decline at least a century ago and that this followed not long after death rates began to fall. If this had not occurred, if fertility rates* had remained at their previous high levels, then some western countries might have had a "population explosion" some time ago.

The explosion did not occur. Something happened to prevent it. Decades ago, long before contraceptive technology had approached the convenience or effectiveness demanded today, long before family planning services were readily available, when, in fact, publication of information concerning contraception sometimes brought persecution and imprisonment, fertility rates declined. At a time when national population policies were unheard of and a concern for the long-term effects of population growth was limited to a small band of Malthus' disciples, birth rates fell almost as rapidly as death rates.

What does this mean? It can only mean that thousands upon thousands of families wanted fewer children and managed, somehow, to achieve their goal—so successfully that the aggregate effect produced declines in fertility at

Joe D. Wray is a Field Staff Member for the Rockefeller Foundation, Bangkok, Thailand.

*The number of births per 1,000 women of childbearing age.

national levels. How or why did it happen? Demographers have invoked a variety of explanations. Not long ago Freedman summarized them this way:

> The large declines in fertility in economically developed countries in the nineteenth and twentieth centuries probably are unprecedented. The changes in specific intermediate variables producing the decline varied somewhat from country to country. Most sociologists and demographers would probably agree, however, that the basic causes of the general decline are: (a) a major shift in functions from the family to other specialized institutions, so that there was a decrease in the number children required to achieve socially valued goals, and (b) a sharp reduction in mortality which reduced the number of births necessary to have any desired number of children. (1, p. 53)

While this analysis of causal factors may certainly be correct, it is probable that the great mass of people who made the decisions that produced the phenomenon based their decisions on less abstract rationales. Given the methods of limiting family size available at the time, it seems reasonable to assert that powerful and sustained motivating forces must have been at work to produce the results in large population groups that we recognize in retrospect as unprecedented declines in fertility. It seems equally reasonable to assume that this motivation must have come from the everyday life situation of the people involved—from an immediate awareness of problems felt acutely at the family level, problems clearly recognized as arising from having too many children.

Returning to this century—to this year—and examining the phenomenon so prevalent in many parts of the world of extra-legal abortion, we are driven to a similar conclusion. We know now that the overwhelming majority of such abortions are performed because married women want desperately to limit their family size and have no effective or accessible alternative. Only powerful and immediate motivating forces can account for this decision. They must come from intensely felt pressure at the family level, pressure explicitly associated with family size and the clearly anticipated effects— detrimental effects—associated with having "another mouth to feed."

If this speculation is correct, if it is true that population pressure felt at the family level produced widespread declines in birth rates in industrialized countries and high abortion rates in others, there has been surprisingly little attention paid to it and equally little systematic study of the effects of this pressure at the family level. There have, at least, been recent expressions of the need for such study. Stycos, at a conference on teaching family planning to medical students, referred specifically to the need for more exact knowledge of the health consequences of family size in order to appeal to humanitarian interests in motivating medical students (2). Berelson has also called attention recently to the need to utilize such knowledge in educational campaigns to motivate families (3). If we are to overcome the "tragedy of the commons"* described by Hardin (4), then ways are needed to persuade individuals that their own interests and those of their families, as well as the interests of the community or society at large, require limitation of family size. Similarly, Taylor, in his suggestions for a "five stage population policy" (5), emphasizes the need to go beyond the population that is merely waiting for services and attract those who are not so fully convinced. In both of these cases, *knowledge of the consequences of excessive numbers at the family level would be invaluable.*

Present Knowledge about the Effects of Family Size and Birth Interval

There is a substantial body of evidence concerning the relation between family size, or number of children, and birth interval and a number of factors relevant to health. This evidence was obtained by a diverse array of investigators studying a variety of problems over a period of many years. The studies were carried out in many countries, in all stages of economic development, and among various social classes within a given country. The approaches varied: some were retrospective (based on currently obtained data describing past events), others cross-sectional, still others prospective or longitudinal (identifying children at birth and following them to see what happens).

Each health indicator that has been examined in these studies is produced by complex, and usually obscure, interactions of numerous causal factors. There is undoubtedly a considerable amount of overlap—the same set of interacting causal factors involved in producing various effects. In no case is the total interaction clearly understood, but certainly family size and birth interval operate only as parts of the causal web. In the great majority of these studies, family size and birth interval were among many factors examined as independent variables in relation to a given problem, and not the primary concern of the investigators. Therefore, the interaction between family size, for example, and other relevant variables, such as socioeconomic status is often unexamined. In spite of this, the general pattern of effects suggested by the evidence available is so consistent that it seems reasonable to consider that deficiencies in some studies are, in a sense, compensated for by the adequacy of other studies. We need not, in other words, be compelled to disregard the findings of an investigator who did not control for a given

*To illustrate the fact that a given act may have consequences that seem beneficial to the individual but are harmful to society at large, Hardin uses as an example "the commons," or common pasture. A farmer with two cows adds one more; he gets 50 percent more milk, but his one cow may be enough to push the total population of cows to such a level that the commons may be permanently damaged by overgrazing. The parallel problem with regard to population is obvious.

variable, if the findings of another investigator who could control for that variable show similar results.

The consistent trend of the consequences associated with either increasing family size or decreasing birth interval is striking and uniformly negative. When the full spectrum of these effects is seen, it is, in fact, alarming. No general survey or summary of the evidence concerning these effects could be found in the literature, although one portion of the spectrum, the effects on the survival of fetus and child, was reviewed recently by Day (6).

My intention here is to cover the full spectrum. Where possible, minimum essential information about the methodology of the study is given and relevant examples of the findings obtained are reviewed. The attempt is comprehensive but by no means exhaustive; it is impossible to review all available studies or all the findings of a given study. The chief criterion for inclusion here has been the clarity of the relationships shown by the data. No studies showing significant benefits associated with large families were excluded; none was found, although there were a few studies which showed no effects, either positive or negative.

THE EVIDENCE CONCERNING HEALTH CONSEQUENCES OF FAMILY SIZE

Studies which have examined the effects associated with family size, number of children, number of siblings, or parity of the mother (the number of children born to a mother) are far more numerous than those considering birth or pregnancy interval. Because of the thoroughness and variety of the evidence concerning family size, it will be considered first.

The Effects on Children

Much of the data that are available concern the effects on children and are derived from studies of mortality and morbidity of various types, including malnutrition and anomalies in growth and intelligence.

Family Size and Morbidity. Several factors commonly associated with increased incidence of illness are also associated with increased family size. Among these, economic limitations, crowding, and generally poor sanitary conditions stand out. The stage is set for causal interaction.

The longitudinal study of families of all social classes in Cleveland, Ohio, carried out by Dingle and his associates (7) showed as clearly as any the association between family size and illness. They examined the incidence of various common illnesses by family size. As an example, their findings with respect to infectious gastroenteritis are shown in Table 1. Not only does the total number of episodes per family increase, as might be anticipated on a purely arithmetical basis, but also the number of illnesses per person per year

TABLE 1

Incidence of Infectious Gastroenteritis
by Family Size, Cleveland,
Ohio, 1964

Family Size	Person Days	Family Days	Number of Family Illnesses	Illnesses per Family/Year	Illnesses per Person/Year
3	38,991	12,997	104	2.92	0.97
4	269,604	67,401	869	4.71	1.18
5	399,450	79,890	1,671	7.63	1.53
6	201,396	33,566	1,044	11.35	1.89
7	36,491	5,213	189	13.23	1.89
8	31,104	3,888	180	16.90	2.11

Source: Dingle et al. (7).

increases. Leaving aside a consideration of the precise causal role of family size per se in producing illness, it is obvious that family size increases "pressure" on the larger families simply because of the number of illnesses, more need for maternal care, more expenses for treatment.

One of the most important kinds of morbidity to be found in preschool children throughout the world is that produced by malnutrition (8, 9). In a study of malnutrition in the preschool child population of the rural town of Candelaria, Colombia, my former colleague, Dr. Alfredo Aguirre, and I found that family size is one of the factors involved in the etiology of malnutrition there (10). In a house-to-house survey of the town, the total population of preschool children were weighed and measured and their mothers interviewed. The nutritional status of the children was determined on the basis of internationally recommended standards (11-14). We found 1,094 children under 6 years of age in the survey; 284 of these children were classified as having first degree, 148 second degree, and 14 third degree malnutrition—a total of 41 percent malnourished in varying degrees.

We then examined the data for associations between various social and demographic factors in the families and malnutrition in the children. The effects of family size were explored by grouping all of the children according to the number of living children in their families. The proportion of malnourished children (of all degrees) in each group was then calculated. The results of this analysis are shown in Table 2, where the trend is obvious: children from larger families are more likely to be malnourished than those from smaller families.* In this case, the difference in the prevalence of malnutrition

*Some of the other factors, both social and economic, that were implicated in the cause of malnutrition will be described in the next-to-last section of this chapter. It should be mentioned here that we found in the Candelaria study that as laboring men in

TABLE 2

Malnutrition in Preschool Children Grouped According to the Number
of Living Children in Their Families,
Candelaria, Colombia, 1963

Number of Living Children/Family	Total Number of Children	Malnourished Children	
		Number	Percent
1	75	24	32.0
2	185	63	34.1
3	178	73	41.0
4	204	83	40.7
5	136	57	41.9
6	122	57	46.7
7	62	25	40.3
8 or more	106	49	46.2

Source: Wray and Aguirre (10).

in children from families with four children or less (38 percent malnourished among 642 children) compared with those from families with five or more (44 percent malnourished among 462 children) is statistically significant— highly unlikely to result from sampling fluctuations.*

Quite recently, our students at the Ramathibodi Hospital Faculty of Medicine in Bangkok found a similar relationship in Thai preschool children. In an investigation of the total preschool population of a semirural community near Bang Pa-In, 212 children under the age of 6 years were examined. It was found that 58 percent of those from families with four or more children were malnourished, while 42 percent of those from families with three children or less were so classified (15). This difference was also statistically significant.

Robertson and Kemp carried out one of the few direct studies of family size and child health among children in the group called Coloured in Cape Town, South Africa (16). They sought an association between family size and malnutrition and deaths from causes related to malnutrition. An "unselected control to show the size of families" was obtained from births during 1 week of February, 1962.

Their findings that are particularly relevant here were based on the distribution of families according to the number of living children per family. They

a developing country get older, their income rises but little while family size increases steadily. They seem to attempt to compensate for this by spending a larger proportion of their income for food, but per capita expenditures for food actually fall, and malnutrition in the children increases (10, pp. 95-96).

*That is to say, "p" < .05. The probability of such a difference arising from sampling fluctuations, or from chance, is less than 5 chances in 100.

compared the proportion (percentage) of families of different sizes in their two test groups and in the control and by this method found no evidence of significantly increased risk in children from larger families either of malnutrition or of death from diseases associated with malnutrition.

They concluded that "The size of the family appears to have little effect per se on the health of the younger members, families being 'at risk' because of poverty, accompanied by poor parental capacity" (16, p. 893).

Because, as noted, there are few such studies and the findings of Robertson and Kemp in this study are so different from those of others, a methodological problem involved here deserves careful scrutiny. In treating their data they compared the distribution of differing numbers of children per family in three groups of *families*, each selected quite differently: the first, because there was a malnourished preschool child in the family, the second because a child in the family died of a specified cause, and the third because the mother delivered a newborn infant during a defined period of time. What is needed, however, if we are to understand the effect of family size is a comparison of the prevalence of malnutrition or of death rates in a substantial population of *children* grouped according to family size. Only then can a valid statement be made concerning the presence or absence of increased risk associated with family size.

This point has been spelled out by Chen and Cobb in their paper, "Family Structure in Relation to Health and Disease" (17), in which they state:

> With regard to sampling method, the most important thing is to check that the sampling procedure is the same for cases and controls. It is, for example, wholly inappropriate to compare the distribution of family sizes among patients with the distribution reported in a census. The reason for this is evident on consideration of an hypothetical population consisting of equal numbers of families with one child and ten children. If one picks families and asks how many children there are, one has an equal chance of picking large families or small families and concludes that the average size is 5.5 children. If, on the other hand, one picks individuals and asks them how many siblings they have, the probability of picking a person from a large family is ten times as great as the probability of picking one from a small family. In this situation, one would conclude that average size of family is 9.2 children. . . .
>
> The soundest way to approach this entire problem is, of course, to examine attack rates of disease by size of sibship, but this can only be undertaken when a survey of a total population or sample of the population has been conducted. (17, p. 549)

Family Size and Mortality. Morbidity, or illness, is but a continuum which, in the end, may result in death. There is an abundance of data concerning the association between family size and mortality rates. In one study of a rural population, Gordon and Wyon (18, 19) have described their findings obtained during long-term studies of population dynamics in villages in the Punjab of India. They followed the 1,479 children born in their study villages from 1955 to 1958 and thus could calculate accurate mortality rates in these children. When mortality rates were correlated with maternal parity, which they accepted as a sufficient indicator of family size, they obtained the results summarized in Table 3.

TABLE 3

Mortality of 1,479 Children Born in Eleven Punjab Villages,
by Parity of Mothers, India, 1955-1958

Parity of mother	1	2	3	4	5	6	7-12	Unknown	Totals
Number of births	230	209	210	197	165	136	326	6	1,479
Neonatal mortality (deaths/1,000 infants up to 28 days)	95.7	52.6	81.0	30.5	84.8	51.5	95.1	166.7	73.7
Infant mortality (deaths/1,000 infants up to 1 year)	171.8	116.5	144.9	123.7	171.8	164.2	206.3	166.7	160.6
2nd-year mortality (deaths/1,000 pop.)	75.8	15.6	24.2	92.4	95.7	76.9	95.0	0.0	67.9

Source: Wyon and Gordon (19).

Their figures show clearly that mortality in those infants tended to increase with family size. Among second- or later-born children the trend is most apparent, though in the first month of life, before family or environmental circumstances are as likely to affect the newborn, differences are not great. After 1 month they are striking, and it is important to note that the effect is relatively much greater in the second year of life. Mortality rates for the *first* year among seventh- or later-born children are not quite twice as high as those in second-born children in the first year of life; in the *second* year they are over six times as great.

Similar observations have been made in several countries at the other end of the development scale. Some of the most impressive evidence to be found concerning the association between family size and infant mortality comes from the studies of Morris, Heady, Morrison, and their associates in a study of *all* the births that occurred in England and Wales during 1949 and 1950. They matched the information on the death certificates of all children dying under a year of age with that contained in the birth certificates of the same children. In the case of children born in 1949, they were able to do the same for deaths in the second year. Thus they could examine the association between infant mortality and a number of variables, including the particularly pertinent ones here of maternal age and parity and of social class of the family. Since they were dealing with a huge population—1,322,150 single, legitimate live births—associations that might never have been apparent in smaller groups stand out clearly. The wealth of detailed findings is published in a series of eight papers under the general title, "Social and Biological Factors in Infant Mortality" (20-27).*

Figure 1 shows their data on variations with mother's parity of post-neonatal mortality (deaths between 1 month and 1 year of age) in different social classes (20). Social class differences in mortality rates are clear, as

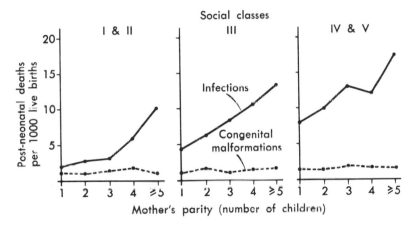

Figure 1. Variations with parity in postneonatal (1 month to 1 year) mortality from infections and congenital malformations in different social classes, England and Wales, 1949-1950, using social class scale of the British General Register Office based on occupation of father, from professionals (I) to unskilled workers (V).

Source: Morris et al. (20).

might have been expected, but equally clear is the increase in mortality with number of children in all social classes. The data depicted also support the contention that deaths due to causes associated with prenatal factors—congenital malformations—do not vary with family size or social class as do those associated with environmental factors, such as infections.

Variations with age and parity of the mother of postneonatal and second-year mortality are shown in Figure 2. The persistence of increasing mortality with increasing family size throughout the first 2 years of life is obvious and

*The data in these papers were subsequently brought together and issued as (28).

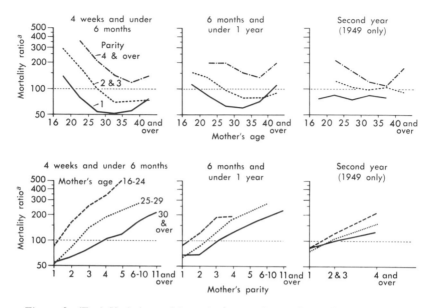

Figure 2. (Top) Variations with mother's age of mortality ratios in infants, comparing mothers of different parities. (Bottom) Variations with mother's parity of mortality ratios in infants comparing mothers of different ages. (England and Wales, 1949-1950.)

[a]Ratio between rates in a given population group and the average rate for the total population.

Sources: Heady and Morris (26), Morrison et al. (27).

appears in all maternal age groups. However, it is clearly more marked in the younger mothers (26).

Finally, they examined variations in mortality rates when each of the three factors—social class, maternal age, and family size—is controlled. When rates are compared, the findings shown in Figure 3 were obtained. Mortality ratios bring out the differences more dramatically, as is evident in Figure 4 (27). Mortality rates increase with family size in all social classes, but the effects are most powerful in the younger mothers, regardless of social class. (A young mother with a large family will, of course, have closely spaced children. Birth interval will be discussed later.) The authors comment:

> The mortality ratio (though not, of course, the actual mortality rate) for fourth and higher children is in fact higher in classes I and II than in the other classes. It is clear, therefore, that the relatively high mortality rates among infants of young mothers with large families are not a phenomenon peculiar to any one social class due to some simple poverty factor. It is also true that the higher death rates in classes IV and V cannot be explained by the concentration of young mothers with large families in these classes. (27, pp. 104-105)

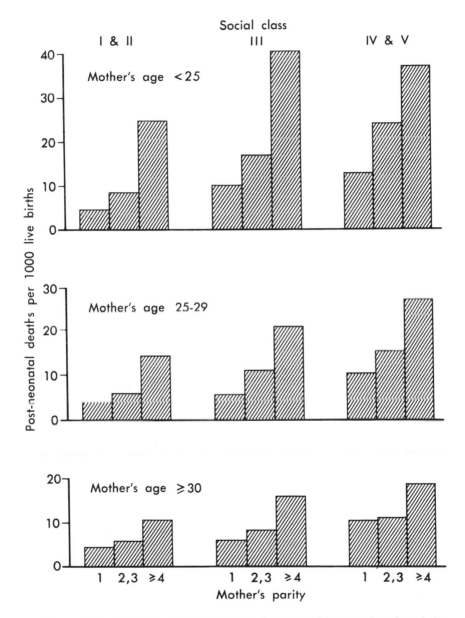

Figure 3. Variations in postneonatal mortality rates with age and parity of the mother and social class of the father, England and Wales, 1949-1950.
Source: Heady et al. (23).

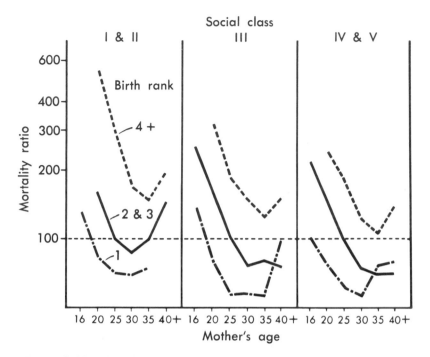

Figure 4. Variations in postneonatal mortality ratios with birth rank of infant (= mother's parity) and mother's age in different social classes, England and Wales, 1949-1950.
Source: Morrison et al. (27).

Evidence from the State of New York that is comparable in many respects to that of Morris and his associates has been provided by Chase (29, 30). She studied "nearly one-half million births" which occurred in New York State, exclusive of New York City, in the years 1950-52. The major study group consisted of single, white fetal deaths and live births. Through examination of death certificates, information was obtained for each child who died within 5 years of birth, and this was related to information from the birth certificate of the same individual. Her data concerning the postneonatal and early childhood deaths are relevant here since environmental factors may be expected to be most important after the neonatal period. The variations in mortality rates by birth rank are shown in Table 4, in which the increase associated with family size is obvious.

Analyses of her data had indicated that increasing mortality rates were associated with prematurity, maternal age, and social class. In her second paper (30) she controlled for prematurity and maternal age by examining the mortality in children whose mothers were 20 to 29 years at the time of their births and whose birth weights were between 2,501 and 3,500 grams. These

TABLE 4

Fetal Mortality and Mortality among Children under 5 Years of Age by
Infant's Birth Rank, New York State, Exclusive of
New York City, 1950-1952

Infant's Birth Rank	Total Births	Fetal		Neonatal		Postneonatal		Early Childhood	
		Deaths	Rate per 1,000	Deaths	Rate per 1,000	Deaths	Rate per 1,000	Deaths	Rate per 1,000
Total	436,045	6,928	15.9	7,002	16.3	2,247	5.3	1,462	3.5
First	135,882	2,252	16.6	2,107	15.8	506	3.8	354	2.7
Second	139,881	1,581	11.3	2,075	15.0	649	4.8	433	3.2
Third	84,393	1,301	15.4	1,345	16.2	481	5.9	295	3.6
Fourth	38,993	717	18.4	682	17.8	256	6.8	177	4.7
Fifth	17,366	396	22.8	354	20.9	137	8.2	79	4.8
Sixth and higher	19,387	636	32.8	437	23.3	218	11.9	123	6.8
Not stated	143	45	(314.7)[a]	2	–	0	–	1	–

– Rates based on less than 100 individuals are not shown.

[a]Based on at least 100, but less than 1,000 individuals; rate high but number of cases low.

Source: Chase (29, Table 6.4, p. 111).

children were considered to represent a "favored" group. She then compared mortality rates within various socioeconomic groups by birth ranks. Her findings are shown in Figure 5. Increasing mortality rates with declining socioeconomic levels are apparent, but equally apparent is the association between increasing mortality and family size *within* the various socioeconomic groups, especially in the postneonatal and early childhood periods.

Similar evidence was found in the longitudinal study of pregnancies on the island of Kauai in Hawaii, reported by Yerushalmy, et al. (31). Their data were obtained during 1953 when all women on the island of Kauai who had experienced at least one pregnancy were interviewed. Their study population included 6,039 women of a total population of around 30,000 on the island. In each interview a complete reproductive history was obtained. This portion of their study was, therefore, retrospective in nature, and the hazards of the method were well known to Yerushalmy and his colleagues. They rigorously scrutinized their findings to test both reliability and adequacy. On comparing their data with that obtained from locally recorded vital statistics, with similar data from elsewhere, and with known facts concerning variations with maternal age and parity, they concluded that it was, indeed, reliable except in regard to the reporting of early fetal deaths (under 20-weeks gestation) on the part of women over 50 years of age.

The particular findings of their study which are of interest here are shown graphically in Figure 6, which shows relative mortality rates in early and late gestation and from birth through 4 years by order of pregnancy. The important point is that at *all* stages, including early and late fetal periods (before and after 20 weeks' gestation) death rates are highest with the higher order pregnancies. Furthermore, when childhood mortality rates were calculated (deaths in age group 1-4 per 1,000 children who survived to age 1), the correlation with birth order was strikingly direct—almost linear. The authors state:

> The pattern of childhood mortality at 1 to 4 years of age exhibits a very orderly and striking variation with order of pregnancies to an even stronger degree than any of the other indices. This indicates that the high rates for the high order of pregnancy may have an environmental origin. (31, p. 87)

Further evidence is offered by Newcombe and Tavendale (32), who compared certain factors relating to 13,556 handicapped children, child deaths, or stillbirths with control data obtained from the birth certificates of 213,353 infants born between 1953 and 1959 in British Columbia. They showed clearly, for example, that congenital malformations of various kinds were associated with maternal age rather than parity—an older woman is more likely to give birth to a child with a congenital malformation regardless of her parity. There were two general exceptions: (a) a statistically significant "in-

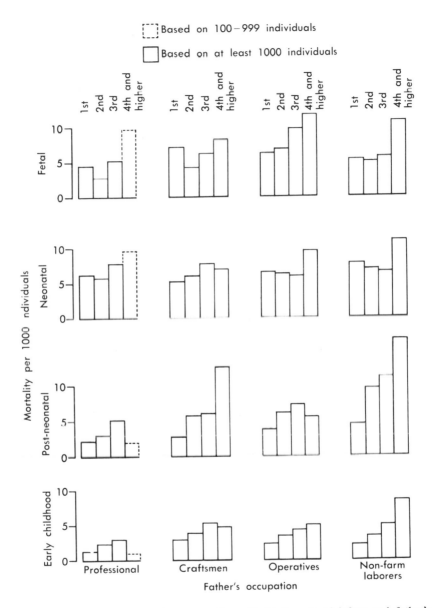

Figure 5. Variations in infant mortality with birth rank of infant and father's occupation, New York exclusive of New York City, 1949-1952.
Source: Chase (30).

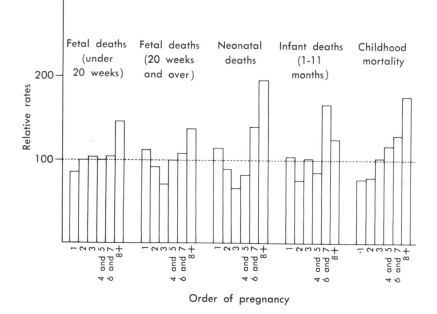

Figure 6. Variations in relative mortality rates with order of pregnancy from gestation to early childhood (relative rates = specific rate expressed as a percentage of the rate for the total–all pregnancies–in each age group), Hawaii, 1953.
Source: Yerushalmy et al. (31).

crease in risk for offspring of advanced birth order for infective and parasitic diseases"–those diseases in which environmental factors must have played an important role; (b) an increased risk associated with higher parity in the younger mothers, as was also observed by Morrison, et al. (27) and shown in Figure 4.

Family Size and Physical Growth. Much of the evidence examined so far relates to the effects of family size on very young children. Evidence of the persistence of these effects is available from several longitudinal studies of physical growth. The data show definite, sustained differences in the growth of children, associated with family size and lasting through adolescence.

In Great Britain the National Survey of Health and Development carefully followed physical growth in a long-term study of 5,386 children born during the first week of March, 1946. The sample was drawn from all parts of Great Britain and included all children born to the wives of nonmanual workers and of farm laborers and 25 percent of those born to the wives of other manual workers and the self-employed. The findings to date (and they are still being followed!) have been described in three books by Douglas and his co-workers (33, 34, 35), and in numerous articles.*

They found that differences in the growth of children associated with family size were not limited to the lower social classes and were established by age 4½ in both sexes (33). Douglas and Simpson have reported the findings at ages 7, 11, and 15 in 1,456 girls and 1,557 boys from their original sample (36). As is apparent in Table 5, differences associated with social class

TABLE 5

Unadjusted Average (Mean) Heights (in Inches) of Boys and Girls, by Social Class and Number of Sibs, Great Britain, 1953-1961

Socioeconomic Class	Boys				Girls			
	Number of Sibs				Number of Sibs			
	0	1	2	3 or More	0	1	2	3 or More
	AT 7 YEARS							
Upper middle	47.17	48.23	47.72	48.65	47.71	48.12	47.79	47.13
Lower middle	47.82	47.62	47.51	47.41	48.03	47.67	47.14	46.57
Upper manual	47.93	47.59	47.15	46.79	48.35	46.95	46.94	46.14
Lower manual	48.15	47.20	47.07	46.29	47.61	46.89	46.48	45.99
	AT 11 YEARS							
Upper middle	55.13	56.40	55.75	56.65	55.86	56.59	56.13	55.78
Lower middle	55.98	55.94	55.36	55.26	57.07	56.28	55.62	55.04
Upper manual	55.70	55.43	55.27	54.54	56.72	55.45	55.78	54.14
Lower manual	57.15	55.34	54.88	54.48	56.03	55.14	54.76	54.14
	AT 15 YEARS							
Upper middle	63.43	64.77	63.59	65.03	62.82	63.43	63.10	62.78
Lower middle	64.73	64.26	63.95	63.44	62.85	63.34	62.63	62.23
Upper manual	64.40	63.52	63.56	62.75	62.84	61.90	62.61	61.78
Lower manual	64.53	63.64	63.48	62.56	62.23	62.33	62.02	61.57

Source: Douglas and Simpson (36).

were found at all ages. An association between height and family size was not apparent in the upper middle class (professional, salaried, or self-employed men with wives from similar backgrounds) but became increasingly apparent with each descent on the social class scale, reaching its maximum in the manual classes. It is noteworthy, however, that only children of both sexes, in all social classes, and at all ages appear to grow equally well.

*See bibliography in (35).

In another British study, Grant (37) followed the growth of 1,310 children living in a London County Council housing estate, most of whom were measured at or near their sixth, tenth, twelfth, and fourteenth birthdays. Her findings parallel those reviewed above, but she also used her data to clarify several points. Taking advantage of the longitudinal nature of her material she showed that the differences in average (mean) measurements (at various ages) associated with family size are, in fact, the product of continuing slower rates of growth in children from larger families. The mean increments over a period of time, for example, between the sixth and tenth birthdays are shown in Table 6, are less in the children from larger families.

TABLE 6

Gain in Height between Sixth and Tenth Birthdays, by Family Size,
London, 1953-1960

Number of Children in Family	Height Gain between Sixth and Tenth Birthdays (cm.)	
	Boys	Girls
1	23.3	23.6
2	23.0	23.4
3	22.9	23.3
4	22.4	22.1
5 or more	22.1	22.6

Source: Grant (37).

She also examined the interaction between family size and birth rank and produced some thought-provoking results. One example is shown in Figure 7 which was constructed from her data. The figure shows only heights in boys, but the same trends are evident in her data for height and weight in both sexes. In order to examine this phenomenon further, she assigned a plus or minus "developmental level" (DL) based on the difference in centimeters between the measured height of a child and the expected average height for his age, using London data for comparison. The DL was assigned on the basis of heights obtained at or near age 8, to avoid growth variations produced by pubertal growth, and it allowed her to compare both boys and girls. She then compared the first and second child in consecutive pairs of children in families of different sizes and obtained the data shown in Table 7. As she noted, "the later-born child of any consecutive pair within a family tended to be taller than the preceding one." In her discussion, she noted:

> . . . that the smaller size of children in larger families is common to all
> of them and that the first-born does not achieve the height and weight of

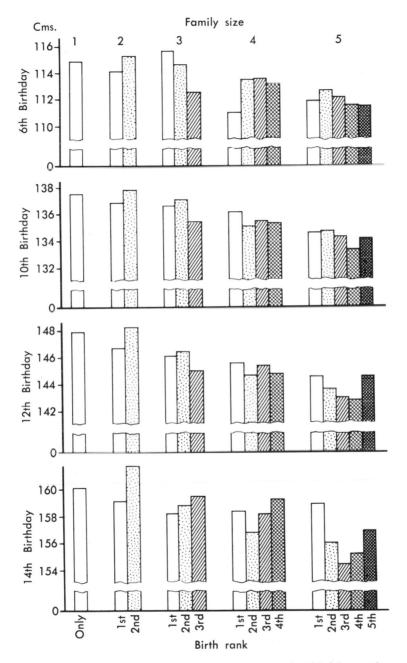

Figure 7. Variations with family size and birth rank in achieved height at various ages in boys followed from age 6 to 14.
Source: Grant (37).

TABLE 7

Developmental Levels, at the Same Age, of Consecutive Children
in Families of Different Size, London, 1953-1960

Number of Children in Family	Birth Ranks	Number of Pairs	Developmental Level[a]	Difference
2	1st and 2nd	103	1st + 1.61	
			2nd + 2.98	+1.37
3	1st and 2nd	106	1st + 0.89	
			2nd + 1.35	+0.46
	2nd and 3rd	79	2nd + 0.06	
			3rd + 2.26	+2.20
4	1st and 2nd	55	1st + 0.20	
			2nd + 0.56	+0.36
	2nd and 3rd	63	2nd − 0.32	
			3rd + 0.46	+0.78
	3rd and 4th	49	3rd + 0.59	
			4th + 0.53	+0.06
5 or more	1st and 2nd	44	1st − 0.32	
			2nd − 0.18	+0.14
	2nd and 3rd	49	2nd + 0.10	
			3rd + 0.51	+0.41
	3rd and 4th	40	3rd − 0.22	
			4th + 0.55	+0.77
	4th and 5th[b]	33	4th + 0.06	
			5th − 0.27	−0.33

[a]Difference in centimeters between the height of a child and average height for age, at or near age 8.
[b]The fifth child in eighteen of these families was not the last but had younger sibs following on.

Source: Grant (37, p. 38).

first-borns who remained only children . . . [the findings] suggest that the advent of each additional child to a family acts as a check on the growth of all preceding sibs. . . . (37, p. 38)

Sexual maturation, another aspect of growth and development, is also associated with family size. Tanner, in discussing the phenomena associated with earlier maturation in man (38), the secular (or long-term) trend, has noted:

The one thing that all authors find significantly related to age at menarche is the number of children in the family. The larger the number the later the menarche and the less the height and weight at all ages, both of the earlier and later born children. . . . (38, p. 27)

He mentions that this has been documented in Czechoslovakia and England and cites malnutrition or increased frequency of diseases, either of which might be associated with increased family size, as possible causal factors.

Douglas and his colleagues also looked into this in the National Survey of Health and Development mentioned earlier. In the first report of their observations (34), only the findings in girls were evaluated because they used menarche as their definitive sign of maturation and lacked an equally satisfactory criterion for boys. Noting the secular trend toward earlier menarche, which has been attributed at least in part to improved nutrition (38, 39, 40), Douglas found no social class differences, in spite of the considerable differences he had observed in growth.

A more detailed study of these families fails to show any positive association between poor living conditions and late puberty; in the middle classes it is the late developers who tend to come from the better homes, from those which were least crowded and best equipped. . . . (34, p. 108)

He did, however, find clear differences associated with family size, as shown in Table 8, in which an obvious relation between family size and menarche is apparent, and only girls may be seen to mature at substantially earlier ages. In a more recent follow-up of these same children, Douglas has

TABLE 8

Age of Puberty among a Sample of Girls in the National Survey of Health and Development by Completed Family Size, Great Britain, 1954-1957

Completed Family Size (Number of Children)	Age at First Period			Total (Percent)	Number of Girls
	Early[a] (Percent)	Average[b] (Percent)	Late[c] (Percent)		
1	53.0	28.3	18.7	100.0	219
2	39.2	36.1	24.7	100.0	502
3	36.0	33.6	30.4	100.0	342
4 or more	33.5	31.9	34.6	100.0	364

[a]Before 12 years 10 months.
[b]12 years 10 months-13 years 9 months.
[c]After 13 years 10 months.

Source: Douglas (34).

reported similar findings in boys, based on a standardized assessment of maturation by physicians who examined the boys at age 15 (35).

Family Size and Intelligence. We have seen that several health indicators reflect the effects of family size. Another important indicator, although perhaps of well-being rather than health per se, is intelligence. Intelligence has been extensively studied in relation to family size, and the existence of a striking negative correlation between the two has been known for many years.

Anastasi reviewed the literature carefully a decade ago (41); Hunt has discussed it thoughtfully more recently (42). Studies of large populations have shown repeatedly that children from large families score significantly lower in intelligence tests. For example, the results of a group intelligence test administered to most of the 11-year-olds in Scotland in 1932 and in 1947 were analyzed by the Scottish Council for Research in Education. In 1932 the sample numbered 87,498, and in 1947 it was 70,805. This represented 87 and 88 percent of the total populations, respectively. In both studies, a negative correlation was found between the test scores and size of sibship (number of children in a family). This negative correlation held true in all social classes, even though the children's scores reflected social class differences. A random sample of 1,215 of the children tested in 1947 were given the Stanford Binet intelligence test; again the negative correlation with sibship was found.* The average I.Q. of only children was 113; that of children with five siblings or more was 91.

A second large-scale study reviewed by Anastasi was carried out in France during 1943-44, when 2 percent of the total elementary school population of France, age 6 to 12, was tested (41). The findings were almost identical: mean test scores decreased with increase in family size. Only children were found to have an average mental age 1 to 2 years higher than children with eight siblings or more, and the differential was apparent in each age group tested. Finally, this study showed the expected social class differences in scores, but the negative correlation between intelligence and family size varied among the classes. It was "clearly apparent" in children of farmers, manual laborers, and clerical workers, "negligible" in children from the managerial class, and "barely discernible" among those from the professional class.

Anastasi also cites numerous other studies of normal children carried out in England, the United States, Greece, and Germany in which it was found that mean intelligence test scores declined with increase in family size. In addition, she notes that Terman, in his study of gifted children, found a negative correlation[†] between I.Q. and number of children in a family (41).

*In this case the correlation coefficient was –.32.
$^†r = -.27.$

As impressive as the correlation data are the test results themselves. Figures from the British National Survey of Health and Development have been published by Douglas (35). The performance of the children studied on the Junior Leaving, or 11-plus, Examination is shown in Table 9, together with their test results at 8 years of age. The expected social class differences in performance are already evident in the younger children, but equally evident at both ages and in all social classes are marked differences associated with family size. It should be noted further that whereas the effects of family size on growth were ameliorated by social class in this same population (see Table 5), such was not the case with intelligence test performance.

Another study has shown the persistence of these differences into adulthood. Vernon (43) analyzed the data from about 10,000 British male National Service Recruits and examined the relation between number of

TABLE 9

Average Intelligence Test Scores[a] by Completed Family Size
and Social Class, Great Britain 1954-1957

Social Class	Age at Test	Completed Family Size							
		1	2	3	4	5	6	7 or More	Unknown
Upper middle	11	59.87	57.31	55.80	56.49	55.65	54.45	54.00	55.00
	8	59.20	56.82	55.44	56.79	54.60	52.14	54.33	63.50
Lower middle	11	54.60	55.27	53.20	52.02	51.81	50.11	47.81	59.00
	8	53.88	54.26	52.64	50.20	50.03	51.43	47.95	58.00
Upper manual working	11	52.74	52.19	49.90	48.61	47.40	45.80	40.54	47.50
	8	52.27	51.64	49.93	48.65	47.31	48.53	42.49	44.00
Lower manual working	11	50.93	48.71	48.16	46.64	45.78	44.86	42.19	44.73
	8	51.54	49.64	48.38	47.44	45.27	45.51	42.44	45.09
All social classes	11	52.96	52.16	50.41	48.57	47.51	46.04	42.49	47.17
	8	52.86	52.09	50.36	48.74	46.87	47.07	43.06	47.00
Social class held constant	11	52.87	51.63	50.27	49.06	48.26	46.97	43.98	49.31
	8	52.83	51.69	50.23	49.07	47.53	48.03	44.61	49.14

[a]These are "T scores which were designed so that the average score for all children in the population is fifty and the standard deviation 10. . . . To convert T scores into I.Q.'s the following formula may be used:

$$I.Q. = 25 + 1.5 \text{ (T score)}." \text{ (34, pp. 34-35)}$$

Source: Douglas (35).

siblings and performance on six mental tests. For purposes of analysis, he considered "four main factors or underlying types of ability: general, verbal-educational, spatial-mechanical, and physical." His findings, which he compared with those of the Scottish Mental Survey, are shown in Table 10.

TABLE 10

Mean Standard Scores of Recruits on Mental Tests of Different Types, by Number of Siblings, Great Britain, 1946

Number of Siblings	Frequency (Percent)	General	Verbal-Educational	Spatial-Mechanical	Physical	Scottish Mental Survey
None	13.3	106.6	107.2	104.6	102.3	105.8
1	22.0	105.8	105.8	104.3	101.6	105.1
2	18.6	101.8	101.7	101.7	100.8	101.6
3	13.8	98.8	98.5	99.5	99.8	98.6
4	10.4	94.9	94.7	96.7	98.7	95.8
5	7.8	93.2	92.9	95.2	97.7	94.2
6	5.2	92.4	92.6	93.5	96.4	92.8
7-8	5.5	88.9	91.6	92.9	96.5	91.8
9-11	2.8	87.9	88.2	90.6	96.2	90.1
12-17	0.4	87.2	86.2	91.6	95.8	86.5

Source: Vernon (43).

Equally clear data are available from the United States. In their extensive study of mental retardation in Minnesota covering the period 1910-1960, Reed and Reed (44) reported on the findings of a subsample of 1,016 families in which I.Q.'s were available for both parents and at least one child—a total of 2,032 parents and 2,039 children. They describe this population with care and, among other points, note that:

> ... the sub-sample seemed to be identical with the expectations for an intelligence curve of a normal population in Minnesota. . . . The striking differences to be presented are certainly not due to testing errors. (44, p. 64)

Their findings for this population are shown in Table 11; the figures require no comment. The figures from their study, as well as those from the Scottish survey and the scores from Vernon's "general" test (43), are shown graphically in Figure 8.

Interesting insight is provided by Scott (45), who in 1959 and 1960 studied over 4,000 London school children aged 10 to 11. Boys and girls were represented about equally, and they were "a cross-section of children attending ordinary day schools in London." Heights and weights, as well as informa-

TABLE 11

Mean I.Q. of Children, by Family Size,
Minnesota, U.S.A., 1910-1960

Family Size	Number of Families	Number of Children Tested	Mean I.Q. of Children
1	141	141	106.37 ± 1.39
2	370	583	109.56 ± 0.53
3	287	606	106.75 ± 0.58
4	122	320	108.95 + 0.73
5	57	191	105.72 ± 1.15
6	21	82	99.16 ± 2.17
7	7	39	93.00 ± 3.34
8	4	25	83.80 ± 4.13
9	5	37	89.89 ± 2.94
10	2	15	62.00 ± 7.55

Source: Reed and Reed, (44).

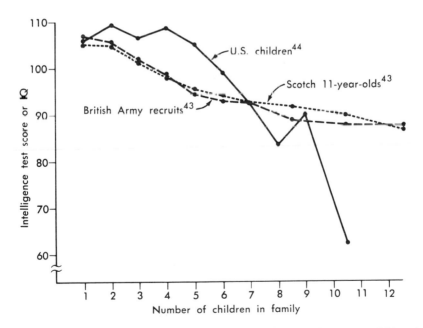

Figure 8. Variations of I.Q. or intelligence test scores with number of children in England, Scotland, and the United States.
Source: Vernon (43), Reed and Reed (44).

tion on family size, were obtained in a survey, and the data were then analyzed with the scores of verbal reasoning tests administered by the schools (the Junior Leaving, or 11-plus, Examination). Scott's findings agreed with those obtained elsewhere: both intelligence test scores and growth decreased as family size increased. In addition, he presents the data shown in Table 12, which shows "a tendency for intelligence both to increase with height and to lessen as family size increases."

Scott concluded that his findings showed:

(a) Height, weight and verbal reasoning scores all tend to decrease as family size increases.
(b) Independently of family size, height and verbal reasoning scores tend to rise and fall in sympathy.
(c) Family size is more closely associated with verbal reasoning than with height. (45, p. 169)

TABLE 12

Average Verbal Reasoning, Standardized Scores
(11+ Examination) by Height and
Family Size, England, 1949

Height (cm.)	Number of Children in Family			
	1	2	3	4 and More
	Average Value Reasoning Scores[a]			
Less than 130.0	96.2 (19)	101.2 (35)	97.5 (16)	94.5 (33)
130.0-134.9	102.1 (58)	100.4 (88)	101.4 (52)	94.1 (55)
135.0-139.9	108.4 (70)	107.0 (119)	102.4 (80)	100.7 (44)
140.0-144.9	108.5 (54)	106.0 (104)	109.5 (37)	99.9 (44)
145 and over	108.5 (43)	107.5 (50)	106.5 (28)	102.8 (16)

[a]Figures in parentheses are the number of children in each class.
Source: Scott (45).

The data in Table 12 also suggest that even if the constellation of causal factors interacting in a large family is such that the children grow well, they are still likely to suffer in their intellectural development. The data seen in Tables 5 and 9 from the British National Survey of Health and Development (35, 36) support this concept, although from a different angle. In the upper-middle families of that study the negative correlation between family size and growth eventually disappeared, but the negative correlation between family size and intelligence remained. These families apparently can and do compensate for increased family size sufficiently to support the growth of their children, regardless of their number. This does not occur with those factors responsible for intelligence. The factors operating to impede intellectual development in children from large families, whatever they may be, are not compensated for even in upper-middle families.

In his 1966 Galton Lecture, Tanner (46) reviewed the evidence gathered to date of the association between height and intelligence, and between those two attributes and family size. He raises an interesting point with regard to findings concerning family size:

> To summarize then: according to present data, children with many sibs in the house are retarded in their height growth from an early age compared with children of the same social class with few sibs. This is especially true of children in poorly-off families. They also score lower in tests of intelligence or attainment. By the time adulthood is reached they have not caught up in intelligence tests, but this may be the result only of the vicious circle in educational opportunity described above. . . . (46, p. 130)

The "vicious circle" mentioned by Tanner is worth describing for those inclined to wonder whether the actual differences in the I.Q.'s found in children of different family sizes are in fact of any real consequence. Tanner noted that a 9-point difference in I.Q. amounts to "two thirds of the standard deviation of the test score, and in the 11+ exam, for instance, corresponds to a difference of about 15 percentile ranks at the level usually used for pass or fail." Later on he notes that children who have that advantage in the 11+ exam "obtain an increasing educational advantage thereafter, simply as a result of passing these tests. Hence they would remain always ahead, an example of the classical self-fulfilling prophecy or positive feedback." The power of the "self-fulfilling prophecy" has been recently documented by Rosenthal and Jacobson (47), who showed convincingly that teacher expectations based on the *reported* test performance (the teachers were shown no actual results) of children have a marked effect on the performance of the children in the classroom situation.

The Effects on Parents

Children are more susceptible to environmental influences and the effects of these influences are more easily measured. Nevertheless, there is some evidence that family size takes its toll of parents, too.

Family Size and Parental Health. Chen and Cobb (27) cited three pertinent studies. One ". . . has shown a direct linear relationship between the frequency of peptic ulcer and number of children for a group of employed men." A study of women showed ". . . a positive association between rheumatoid arthritis and large numbers of children." A study of blood pressures, interestingly enough, has shown no such relationship: ". . . blood pressures are higher among the childless, be they men or women, and . . . in general the greater the number of children the lower the pressure. Furthermore, in a four year interval . . . men and women who added to their families had on the average smaller rises in pressure than those who did not."

Hare and Shaw (48) studied fifty-five British families divided according to the number of children under 16 years of age. They found that both physical and mental ill health in parents increased with family size, and more markedly so in mothers than in fathers. Interestingly, they reported that overall incidence of illness in the children did not increase with family size, but they attributed this to the fact that the mothers of larger families were too busy to take their mildly ill children to their physicians or seek other attention; hence, recorded illnesses in these children were low.

Family Size and Maternal Health. A study of sociocultural factors in the epidemiology of hypertension among the Zulu of South Africa has been reported by Scotch (49). His study, carried out in 1959, included Zulu men and women in two communities, one a rural native reserve and the other an urban "location" near Durban. He found that hypertension was more common in the "location," that women were more affected than men, and that the prevalence increased with age. Among the variables examined was the number of children. In the Zulu women from the "location," the incidence of hypertension increased with the number of children. The difference found in women with five or more children compared with those with four or less was statistically significant.* He did not find this difference among women living in the rural area, and he commented as follows:

> . . . In the city, women with many children had a higher prevalence of hypertension than those with few children, whereas in the rural area there was no relationship between number of children and hypertension. . . . In traditional Zulu society a woman's status is clearly related to her ability to bear children . . . a greater number of children would in no way be stressful. . . . The opposite holds true in the city, where a large number of children must be seen as stressful. . . . As long as a woman has a minimum number her status as a wife is secure. But should she have too many children, life becomes difficult in many ways. . . . (49, p. 1210)

Comparable findings have been reported by Murphy (50), who studied the effects of cultural change on the mental health of Yoruba women in Nigeria. She expected to find evidence of "acculturative stress" among Yoruba women who had been "western educated" in comparison with those who were "unacculturated." Measurement of mental health was "based on systematic questions asked of the women based on psychophysiological sensa-

---

*At the 0.05 level.

tions and psychiatric experiences, and on data regarding each subject's social adjustment given by a knowledgeable informant." The findings did not reveal any significant difference between the mental health of "acculturated" versus "unacculturated" women, but they did show the following correlation between mental health and numbers of children:

> The barren women from both groups have the poorest mental health; the points of optimally good mental health coincide with the women who have 2, 3 or 4 children, and there is again poor mental health in both groups among women with 6 or more children. (50, p. 8)

Finally, from England there are some intriguing data from Pyke's study of the relationship between parity and the incidence of diabetes in women, most of whom were over 45 at the time of onset (51). In a comparison of the number of women in each parity group among the diabetics with that of a control population, the increase in diabetes with increasing parity of the women was dramatic and highly significant statistically, as suggested by Figure 9.

The effects of increasing numbers of pregnancies on mothers must also be mentioned here. A large number of pregnancies is a necessary precondition for a large number of children, although it is obvious that where infant or childhood mortality rates are high, a mother may belong in the "grand multipara" group and yet have only a few living children. Repeated pregnancies followed by prolonged lactation periods will, among other things, produce sustained needs for high quality protein in the diet. In the many parts of the world where these needs are poorly met, the result is what Jelliffe has termed the "maternal depletion syndrome" (14). This process may contribute to low birth weight of their infants, to poor performance in lactation and, ultimately, ". . . this cumulative process plays a part in the premature ageing and early death often seen among women in developing regions."

Direct evidence concerning this condition is scant, although most clinicians who have worked in such countries would certainly agree with Jelliffe. Indirect evidence, however, is available. Wright (52), for example, studied maternal mortality figures for Ceylon during 1962-63 by maternal age group. He found that in age groups 35 to 39, 40 to 44, and 45 to 49 the risk of maternal mortality exceeded the overall average maternal mortality risk by factors of 1.5, 2.0, and 3.3 respectively. Advancing age per se is undoubtedly operating here, but in a country like Ceylon advancing age and advancing parity are closely connected, and Eastman and Hellman (53) have stated that the effects of these two factors on increasing maternal risk are additive—each increases the risk independently.

Perkin (54) has examined similar data from Thailand that tends to confirm the findings from Ceylon. Among other things, he reported that in 1963

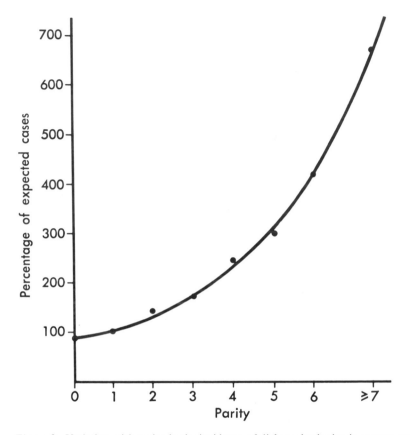

Figure 9. Variation with parity in the incidence of diabetes beginning in women over 45 years of age, England, 1956.
Source: Pyke (59).

women over age 35 contributed 22 percent of the births,* but that 38 percent of all maternal deaths occurred in this age group. Not only does mortality increase but obstetrical complications also increase with maternal age, as is shown by his data in Table 13. Unfortunately, it is impossible here to sort out the effects of age versus those of parity. That high parity is at least present in the older women may be deduced from the fact that the number of live births reported by women in various age groups continues to rise in an almost linear fashion among Thai women over 35 years of age, as shown in Figure 10. Furthermore, we have been able to show from our own data (15, 56) the relatively high proportion of deliveries of a higher order of parity. In

*In the United States in 1965 women over 35 contributed less than 12 percent of all births (55).

TABLE 13

Complicated Deliveries[a] by Age of Mother, Women's Hospital,
Bangkok, Thailand, 1964

Maternal Age	Deliveries	Complicated Deliveries	
		Number	Percent
15-19	1,521	203	13.3
20-24	6,193	693	11.2
25-29	5,956	832	14.0
30-34	2,835	445	15.7
35-39	1,294	257	19.9
40-44	444	104	12.4
45-49	47	10	21.3
	18,291	2,544	13.9

[a]Includes placenta previa, antepartum hemorrhage, postpartum dystocia, abnormal presentation, fetal distress, toxemia.

Source: Perkin (54).

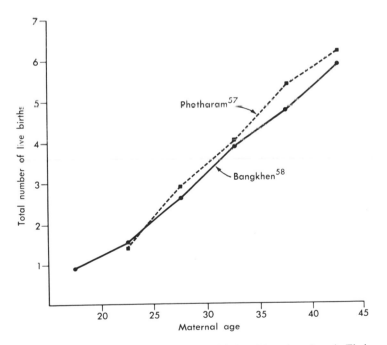

Figure 10. Variations in total number of live births with maternal age in Thai women showing continuing fertility beyond age 35.
Sources: Hawley and Prachuabmok (57), Cowgill et al. (58).

two rural communities not far from Bangkok, 385 women aged 35 to 44 years reported a total of 1,121 previous live births; 447 (39.9 percent) were of birth rank five or higher.

This does not settle the matter, of course; what is needed are studies in which both maternal age and parity are properly controlled. In the meantime, Perkin's contention (54) that older, high parity women constitute a "high risk" group seems reasonable. Knowledge, Attitude, and Practice (K.A.P.) surveys (15, 58) have shown that 85 percent of Thai women over 35 years of age, regardless of parity or number of living children, state that they want *no more* children. If these women could achieve that desire, one might expect to eliminate around a third of the maternal deaths.

The Evidence Concerning Health Consequences of Birth Interval

Although the total number of children occurring in a family is the most important determinant of population pressure within that family, the interval between births is a factor which must not be ignored. Obviously, in the absence of effective family planning, the mother who has children at frequent intervals is likely to have more of them. Equally obvious is the fact that the more young children there are in a household, the greater the demands upon the mother's energy and skills in providing adequate care for them.

Interestingly enough, data relating infant mortality to birth interval have been available for decades. In 1923 Huse published a study carried out in Gary, Indiana, of 1,135 births, excluding first births (59). She found an infant mortality rate of 169.1 (per 1,000 live births) when the interval since the preceding child was less than 15 months, and the rate was 102.8 if the interval was greater than 24 months.

Not long thereafter in 1925 Woodbury published the results of an investigation of some causal factors of infant mortality and included a study of the association between birth interval and infant mortality among 8,196 births* occurring in Baltimore, Maryland (60). He found the following variations:

Birth interval	*1 Year*	*2 Years*	*3 Years*	*4 Years*
Neonatal (up to 28 days) mortality rates	51.2	37.3	36.7	38.1
Infant mortality (up to 1 year) rates	146.7	98.6	86.5	84.9

Eastman, in discussing the effect of birth intervals 20 years later (62), quoted Woodbury's conclusions:

---

*Yerushalmy (61) reports this figure as 7,882, but quotes the same mortality figures as Eastman. I have not personally been able to obtain Woodbury's original monograph.

. . . the infants born after short intervals had a markedly high rate of mortality from all causes. Evidently some factor that is intimately connected with the short interval—perhaps through the influence of frequent births upon the mother's health—affected adversely the chances of life of the infants who followed closely after preceding births. (62, p. 445)

Eastman then went on to say:

Dr. Woodbury's monograph is a reserved and scholarly study, largely objective in character; and it contains no suggestion whatsoever as to what might be done to reduce infant mortality in the short interval groups. But those interested in the furtherance of birth control were quick to see a remedy. Certainly, they reasoned, if conception could be prevented in women during the first year or two after childbirth, the high mortality associated with the short interval could be prevented. And forthwith the Woodbury study became one of the cornerstones of the birth control movement and has remained so ever since. Upon it, indeed, is based the entire rationale, from a medical viewpoint, of so-called "child-spacing," a term which has come to be a sort of euphemism for contraception in general. . . . (62, p. 446)

Dr. Eastman's somewhat disparaging tone was prompted by the fact that his own study, which he was reporting at the time, had failed to reveal a similar association. His study will be discussed later, but students of the history of changes in attitude toward family planning on the part of the medical profession would be rewarded by reviewing the recorded comments in the discussion which followed the presentation of his report in Chicago in 1943.

Since the studies of Huse, Woodbury, and Eastman, there have been a number of further investigations of the effects of birth interval. They are as varied as the studies of family size, although fewer in number, and several of the studies previously referred to examined both variables in analyzing their data. Much of the work has been concentrated upon the fetal, perinatal (around the time of birth), infant, and early childhood mortality; there is surprisingly little data concerning the effects on the mother herself, although one might reasonably expect the "maternal depletion syndrome" mentioned earlier (14) to be aggravated by repeated short intervals as much or more than by excessive numbers of pregnancies.

In the following pages, more recent studies about the effects of birth interval will be discussed.

The Effects on Children

Birth Interval and Mortality. The association between birth interval and mortality from gestation through early childhood was examined in the retrospective study on the island of Kauai by Yerushalmy and his colleagues (31). Their methods were summarized earlier, but one detail is of special interest here. Yerushalmy, in an earlier report (61), had described the effects of prematurity on the association between birth interval and mortality. He gave Eastman (62) credit for pointing out that if a full-term infant is to be born within a year after the termination of a previous pregnancy, conception would have to occur within 3 months of that termination, whereas aborted fetuses or prematurely born infants, conceived 4 months or more after the previous delivery, could still be born within a year of the previous delivery. The high rates of mortality associated with prematurity would therefore artificially inflate the mortality rates of the 1-year-or-less birth interval group.

For this reason, they based their analysis of the Kauai data on pregnancy interval rather than birth interval. In addition, they calculated the relative mortality rates for the various fetal and child age groups in each pregnancy interval in order to bring out the differences more clearly. Their findings are shown in Figure 11, where it is clear that for all child age groups, death rates are highest in the shortest interval groups. For fetal and neonatal deaths, when biological factors are most important, rates are highest in the shortest interval group. They decrease to a minimum with an interval of around 2 years, then increase as the interval increases further, though never equaling the rates in the shortest interval. For postneonatal and early childhood mortality, when environmental factors would be most important, the association is consistent and almost linear: as intervals increase, chances of survival increase.

Yerushalmy had already examined the effect of birth interval on stillbirths (61). He studied all the births and stillbirths that occurred in the United States during the 5-year period 1937-1941. These were classified according to age of mother and parity, and the sample included 7,151,631 births, of which 211,079 were stillbirths. He analyzed the data on the basis of the assumption that, in general, for women in the same age group, the interval between births decreases with increasing parity, and thus provides, as he termed it, an indirect method of studying birth interval. While all of his data need not be reviewed in detail, it is pertinent here to mention two of his observations. First, he noted that when the stillbirth rates were tabulated according to age and parity, the minimum ("best") rates appear in increasingly older age groups as parity increases—as the probable interval between births increased, the stillbirth rates declined. Second, he observed

> It is remarkable that although the level of the stillbirth rate is higher for nonwhite than for total births, and although the effect of the birth-order factor and the effect of the age-of-mother factor by themselves are less pronounced among nonwhite than among total births, the percentage increase or decrease in the stillbirth rate which may be attributed to the factor of interval between births varies in a strikingly similar fashion for nonwhite as for total births.

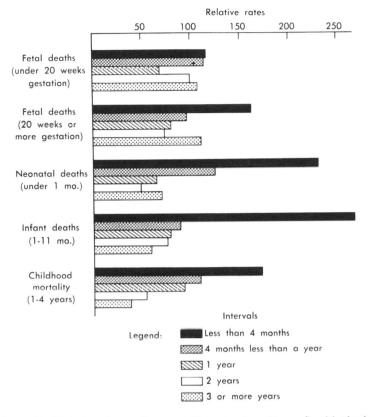

Figure 11. Variations in relative mortality rates (see Figure 6) with the interval between the termination of one pregnancy and the beginning of the next from gestation through early childhood, Hawaii, 1953.
Source: Yerushalmy et al. (31).

Eastman's study (62), mentioned earlier, was also retrospective and was based on 5,158 consecutive births (excluding births to primiparas and also "well-attested criminal abortions") delivered at the Johns Hopkins Hospital between late 1936 and mid-1943. He analyzed his data according to interval since the preceding birth: very brief, less than 12 months; brief, 13 to 24 months; moderate, 25 to 48 months; long, more than 48 months. Abortions, stillbirths, premature delivery, and neonatal deaths were all appreciably higher in the very brief interval group. In all other interval groups these rates were much lower and similar to each other.

Eastman noted that if a previous delivery were followed by a conception that ended in abortion or premature delivery, both deliveries were more likely to take place within a year. His "very brief" was, in other words, artifically exaggerated; so he attributed the differences he had observed to this factor. Because the differences among the other interval groups were minimal, he concluded that birth interval was not a significant factor. Yerushalmy, in discussing this (61), called attention to the time factor affecting prematurity in the brief interval group, as well as possible biases associated with admission policies which might affect a series of patients from only one hospital. He concluded that Eastman's findings did not necessarily contradict those of other investigators.

In the cross-sectional study of all births in England and Wales mentioned earlier, the effect of birth interval was also examined, in this case by another indirect method (27). Having data available concerning duration of marriage, the investigators assumed that the birth interval would be brief in the case of mothers giving birth to a second child after less than 2 years of marriage, or a third after less than 3 years. They therefore considered such births "closely spaced" and compared the mortality rates in that group with the rates in all other births. Their results are shown in Figure 12, where it may be seen that in all maternal age groups and in all social classes the postneonatal mortality rates are higher in the closely spaced group than in the other groups. These rates are also higher in younger mothers, as we saw in the previous data, and a third closely spaced child is at greater risk than a second such child.

They also found, it should be noted, somewhat higher rates among first-borns born after less than a year of marriage in all maternal age groups and all social classes than in first children born later. The differences here were not as great as those between "closely spaced" and "others," but they concluded that " 'duration of marriage', then, apparently reflects something in addition to birth spacing, since first children are also affected by it" (27, p. 105). Clearly children born early in the first year of marriage would either have been born prematurely and exposed to the risks of higher mortality associated with prematurity, or have been conceived premaritally. One can only speculate about the effects of premarital conception, but it seems likely that many mothers in such situations would receive less than optimal prenatal care and be subject to more emotional stress than mothers who conceive their first child after marriage.

Finally, Gordon and Wyon, in their prospective study of children born in Punjabi villages (18, 19) also sought an association between birth interval and mortality rates. They compared the rates in their study children grouped according to the interval between the index child (the individual within a group under study) and the preceding sibling. The data are shown in Table 14. Both neonatal and infant mortality rates were appreciably higher among infants born at short intervals, and the differences observed, even in this relatively small population, were statistically significant.* It is interesting to note that in the environment in which they carried out their study, marked declines in mortality rates occurred only after an interval of 4 years.

*"p" < .01 to .001.

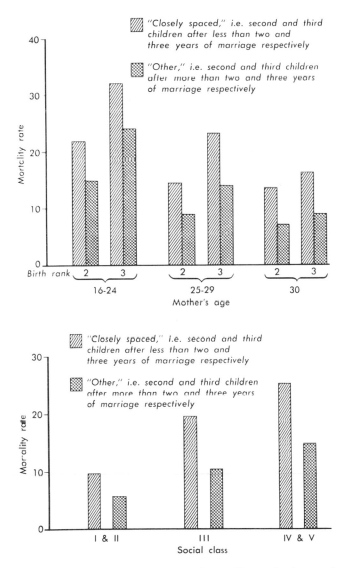

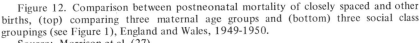

Figure 12. Comparison between postneonatal mortality of closely spaced and other births, (top) comparing three maternal age groups and (bottom) three social class groupings (see Figure 1), England and Wales, 1949-1950.
Source: Morrison et al. (27).

In discussing this finding the authors noted (63) that, "An even greater effect of short interval would be anticipated for the first born of the two siblings" (63, p. 371). On the arrival of a newborn, the preceding child would be deprived of attention from his mother, his nutrition might suffer, or

TABLE 14

Mortality of 1,479 Children Born in Eleven Punjab Villages,
by Interval between Observed and Preceding Child,
India, 1955-1958

Interval between Births in Months	Number of Births	Neonatal Mortality: Deaths per 1,000 Infants Aged Less Than 28 Days[a]	Infant Mortality: Deaths per 1,000 Population Aged Less Than 1 Year[b]	Second Year Mortality: Deaths per 1,000 Population[c]
Primipara	231	95.2	175.4	68.7
0-11	34	88.2	205.9	105.3
12-23	432	97.2	201.9	54.9
24-35	491	57.0	132.2	89.0
36-47	175	57.1	137.9	57.7
48+	112	35.7	108.1	29.0
Unknown	4	0.0	0.0	0.0
Total	1,479	73.7	160.6	67.9

[a] Number = 1479.
[b] Number = 1457.
[c] Number =   854.

Source: Gordon et al. (63).

weaning occur earlier with the consequent weanling diarrhea so often seen in developing countries (64). The younger he is when this occurs, the more serious the consequences are likely to be.

During the period of their study the index children who could be observed for a sufficient length of time after the birth of a subsequent sibling were few in number. The authors report the following, however:

> From the data which exist, the suggestion is that the effect of a short birth interval is more marked for the first child of a pair than it is for the second, as definite as that is. (63, p. 372)

Birth Interval and Morbidity. No studies of the association between acute illness and birth interval have been found. As remarked earlier, however, death is the extreme end of the spectrum of morbid processes, and the clear-cut associations between mortality rates and birth interval in the post-neonatal and 1-to-4-year age groups seen above would surely lead us to expect an increase in illness among closely spaced children.

With regard to more chronic processes—malnutrition, for example—Gordon's remarks above (63) concerning the effects of interval on the preceding child are particularly relevant. It is also pertinent to note that one of the most severe forms of malnutrition seen in developing countries was called *kwashiorkor* by Williams when she first reported it in 1935 (65). In discussing this many years later (66), she reported that in the African tribal language from which she took the term it means "the disease of the deposed baby when the next one is born."

We investigated this situation in our study of malnutrition among pre-school children in rural Colombia. When children were grouped according to the interval between the index, or observed, child and the following sibling and the prevalence of malnutrition calculated for each group, the results shown in Table 15 were obtained. It is clear that only among children who were over 3 years of age at the birth of their following sibling is there an appreciable decline in the prevalence of malnutrition.

TABLE 15

Malnutrition in Preschool Children by Interval until Next Sibling,
Candelaria, Colombia, 1963

Interval between Child and Next Sibling (Months)	Number of Children in Interval Group	Percent of Total Population in Interval Group	Percent of Children in Interval Group Who Are Malnourished
12 or less	50	10.2	40.0
13-18	163	33.3	42.9
19-24	140	28.6	40.0
25-30	71	14.5	50.7
31-36	35	7.2	57.1
37-42	19	3.9	26.3
42	11	2.3	27.3

Source: Wray and Aguirre (10).

The number of preschool children in a family provides an indirect measure of spacing or crowding, since the interval must necessarily be short if there are four or more such children in a family. When the preschool children in Candelaria were grouped in this fashion, the results obtained suggested that this is indeed the case, as may be seen in Table 16. In this case, the difference in the rate among children from families with three or less preschool children, and those from families with four or more is statistically significant.*

Finally, in their study in the district of Bang Pa-In (15), our students in Bangkok investigated the association between interval (again between index child and following sibling) and malnutrition and found a similar, statistically significant effect, as indicated in Table 17.

Birth Interval and Prematurity. Eastman, as mentioned earlier, found high rates of prematurity among children born after a "very brief" interval (62).

*"p" < .05.

TABLE 16

Malnutrition in Preschool Children Grouped by Number of
Preschool Children in Their Families,
Candelaria, Colombia, 1963

Number of Preschool Children/Family	Total Population	Malnourished Children	
		Number	Percent
1	173	59	34.2
2	364	146	40.1
3	366	147	40.2
4	140	66	47.1
5 or more	25	13	52.0

Source: Wray and Aguirre (10).

TABLE 17

Malnutrition in Preschool Children by Interval until Next Sibling,
Bang Pa-In, Thailand, 1969

Interval between Child and Next Sibling (Months)	Total Population	Malnourished Children	
		Number	Percent
Less than 24	43	30	70
More than 24	49	26	53
No child following	119	38	37

Source: *A Health and Demographic Survey of Bang Pa-In* (15).

Douglas, in an investigation of factors associated with prematurity, also examined the effect of birth interval (67). His data were derived from interviews of all mothers who delivered babies during 1 week in March, 1946.* A large number of mothers—90.5 percent, or 13,687—cooperated in the interviews.

Douglas found that social class differences in the risk of prematurity were present but relatively unimportant. Risks appeared to be greatest in "two well-defined groups of working-class women, namely primiparae aged 20 or less, and multiparae with closely spaced pregnancies" (67, p. 159).

After examining his data further, Douglas made the following comment:

... In the present survey 48 percent of working-class mothers spaced their pregnancies either so closely or so far apart that they ran an abnormally high risk of giving birth to a premature baby. If they all could have

*It was from these children that the sample of 5,386 were selected for follow-up in the National Survey of Health and Development in the United Kingdom, referred to earlier (33, 34, 35).

been persuaded to leave intervals of 3 to 6 years between births, the prematurity rate for subsequent pregnancies would have been reduced by 21 percent. (67, p. 158)

It should be added that other factors may have been operating in the longer interval group. These women may have had abnormalities which accounted for infertility and prematurity.

Birth Interval and Growth. In the studies reported from Candelaria (10), growth was used as the indicator of nutritional status and was found to be associated with birth interval. One other study, that of Grant (37), also examined the effect of birth interval. She, too, was concerned about the effect of interval on the *preceding* child. Her conclusions regarding the cross-effects of birth rank and family size may be recalled here: ". . . the advent of each additional child to a family acts as a check on the growth of all preceding sibs. . . ." (37, p. 38).

Her findings for birth interval and growth are presented in Table 18. The differences support the view that birth interval has an effect, but she notes that they are not statistically significant.

TABLE 18

Mean Height at Sixth Birthday Related to Interval between Births, London, 1953-1960

Number of Children in Family		Mean Height (cm.)	
		Boys	Girls
2	Mean for all "first of two"	114.0	113.9
	Mean for 1st when 2nd follows within 2 years	113.0	113.1
3	Mean for all "first of three"	115.6	115.0
	Mean for 1st when 2nd follows within 2 years	116.5	113.0
	Mean for all "second of three"	114.6	112.0
	Mean for 2nd when 3rd follows within 2 years	113.2	109.6

Source: Grant (37).

Birth Interval and Intelligence. We saw abundant evidence of a negative correlation between intelligence test performance (on a wide variety of such tests) and family size. There is no such abundance when it comes to evidence concerning the effects of birth interval. In fact, it appears that only in the British National Survey of Health and Development has the matter been examined. Douglas and his colleagues, who reported the findings in this part of the study in the third book of their series (35), were interested in the effects of spacing on vocabulary as well as upon intelligence ("attainment") tests in general.

In order to investigate vocabulary, they limited their consideration to children of middle-class families in which verbal stimulation, when present, would be at a high level and living conditions would deteriorate relatively little even when births were closely spaced. Upon analyzing the data, they found that

> in each size of middle-class family, the vocabulary scores of the children are relatively high when births are widely spaced and relatively low when they are close together. (35, p. 126)

They also noted that although differences in nonverbal test scores were slight, the vocabulary scores decreased in the test at age 8 as the number of other young children in the families increased. In the same children at age 15 a similar fall was observed in the reading test scores, which are obviously related to vocabulary content.

They also examined the effect of interval on general attainment. Pointing out that in three-child families there are twenty-four possible combinations of sex and rank even before birth spacing is considered, he limited his analysis to the data from two-child families. On comparing test scores for three interval groups—2 years or less, 2 to 4 years, and more than 4 years they found

> . . . remarkably consistent differences in which the highest scores, at each age, are made by those with medium birth intervals. There is no evidence however that those with medium birth intervals increase their lead in the attainment tests between 8 and 15 years, and the effect of birth spacing on performance seems to be fully established by the age of 8, when they were first tested. (35, p. 132)

The Effects on Mothers

Earlier comments on the "maternal depletion syndrome" (14) should apply to mothers whose pregnancies are too close together as readily as to those whose pregnancies are too numerous. Short intervals between pregnancies would provide too little time for recovery, especially among women on diets that are only marginally adequate. Common sense and clinical impressions aside, however, the evidence is extremely scanty.

Eastman, in his Johns Hopkins study (62), has provided the only data available. He examined five factors in relation to birth interval: maternal anemia during pregnancy, toxemia of pregnancy, postpartum hemorrhage, puerperal fever, and maternal mortality. Anemia (hemoglobin less than 10 grams per 100 cc of blood) was more common (34.5 percent) in the "very brief" group (interval less than 12 months), but he considered the group too small to warrant conclusions. The incidence of anemia was lower in the other intervals and the differences among them were not significant, although the lowest rate observed (23.9 percent) was in the "long" (more than 48 months) group.

The "most striking effect" he observed was the association between toxemia of pregnancy and birth interval. As he stated in his conclusion,

> The longer the interval between births, the more likely the mother is to suffer from some form of hypertensive toxemia of pregnancy. The incidence of this complication is lowest when the interval is twelve to twenty-four months, significantly higher when it is twenty-four to forty-eight months, and much higher when it exceeds four years. In the present study this was equally true of white and colored ward patients and private patients. In patients who have had a previous hypertensive toxemia of pregnancy, the likelihood of repetition becomes progressively greater as the interval becomes longer. (62, p. 462)

Eastman was unable in this sample to control for maternal age which is also associated with toxemia of pregnancy. Of course, as interval increases, age of mother increases.

None of the other factors he examined, hemorrhage, infection, or maternal mortality, was found to be associated with birth interval.

The Question of Cause and Effect

Investigations of the causal role of family size or birth interval in regard to the "effects" described earlier are extremely few in number. The problem, as noted from the start, is complicated by the fact that all of these effects are unquestionably the product of many interacting causal factors. Nevertheless, there is some evidence, both direct and indirect, concerning the place of these two factors in the causal web.

Common Sense Effects

Family Size and Food Expenditures. Wherever families are dependent on cash income for the purchase of food, every additional member of the family adds to the strain on the family food budget. Our study in Candelaria (10) showed this clearly, as may be seen in Figure 13, in which per capita food expenditures per week are plotted against the number of living children per family. In situations in which families must buy their food and when food expenditures fall to such an extent in association with increases in family size, then common sense suggests that nutrition would suffer and the increase in malnutrition with family size that we saw in Table 2 should not be surprising.

There is some evidence to show that this phenomenon is not limited to agricultural day laborers in a developing country. In the United States an

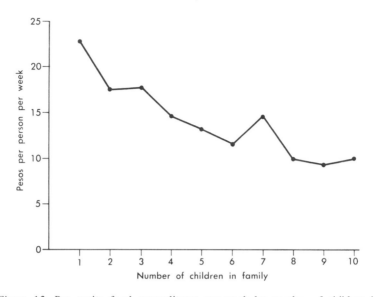

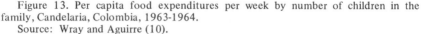

Figure 13. Per capita food expenditures per week by number of children in the family, Candelaria, Colombia, 1963-1964.
    Source: Wray and Aguirre (10).

extensive survey of consumer expenditures and income was carried out by the U.S. Department of Labor and the U.S. Department of Agriculture in 1960-61. Their report (68) includes a detailed review of expenditures by income group as well as by family size.

In Table 19 the figures were obtained simply by expressing the reported expenditures for food as a percentage of the total expenditures in each family size-income class category. The data show two things clearly: as income rises, families spend a smaller proportion of it for food, but as family size increases, a higher percentage is spent for food at all income levels. This parallels the observations in Colombia exactly. In Table 20, however, we see that the end result of spending a higher proportion of income for food is also parallel to the situation in Colombia—the average per person expenditures fall significantly as family size increases. The total family expenditures increase with income, but the average spent per person decreases with family size at every level, including the highest income classes. Furthermore, the decreases are considerable: six-or-more-person families are spending around 40 percent less per person than are the three-person families at every income level up to $15,000 or higher.*

    *The report includes data on expenditures for food prepared at home and food away from home. Only the former were used in these calculations. The rationale for this choice was: (a) It is food prepared at home that largely determines the nutrition of

TABLE 19

Expenditures for Food, as Percent of Total Expenditures for Current
Consumption, by Family Size and Income Class,
United States, 1960-1961

(percent)

Income Class:[a] (U.S. Dollars/ Family/Year)	Family Size			
	3 Persons	4 Persons	5 Persons	6 or More
	Number of Famlies in Sample			
	2,486	2,241	1,449	1,512
$ 1,000- 1,999	28.0	26.5	29.2	34.0
2,000- 2,999	25.0	25.4	27.6	32.1
3,000- 3,999	22.5	22.8	24.1	29.6
4,000- 4,999	20.5	22.2	25.2	27.4
5,000- 5,999	19.7	22.2	22.7	27.1
6,000- 7,499	18.6	20.6	22.4	24.7
7,500- 9,999	17.7	19.0	21.3	22.4
10,000-14,999	14.8	16.2	18.0	20.8
15,000	11.9	13.2	15.4	16.2
Average	18.6	19.7	21.4	24.4

[a]The data for the income class less-than-$1,000 have been omitted; the effect of income taxes at this level, as noted in the Report, made the figures erratic; also the relationship between income and current consumption is often highly erratic.

Source: BLS Report No. 237-93, Part 2, Tables 11D, E, F & G, 1966 (69).

TABLE 20

Calculated Food Expenditures in 1960 Dollars per Person per Week, by
Family Size and Income Class, United States, 1960-1961

($'s/week/person)

Income Class	Family Size			
	3 Persons	4 Persons	5 Persons	6 or More
$ 1,000- 1,999	3.55	2.75	2.23	1.74
2,000- 2,999	4.37	3.86	3.19	2.42
3,000- 3,999	5.24	4.36	3.93	3.09
4,000- 4,999	5.93	4.95	4.48	3.61
5,000- 5,999	6.45	5.73	4.74	4.06
6,000- 7,499	7.25	6.13	5.60	4.44
7,500- 9,999	8.17	6.89	6.21	4.97
10,000-14,999	8.8	7.88	6.67	5.47
15,000	9.78	8.89	8.98	7.04

Source: BLS Report No. 237-93, Suppl. 3-Part A, Tables 28E, F, G & H, 1966 (70).

children; and (b) the expenditures for food away from home represent a significant
proportion of the total food budget only in the higher income groups.

The significance of the figures in Table 20 can be appreciated by relating them to food prices current at the time of the survey. The United States Department of Agriculture periodically issues food plans with costs, devised to provide a nutritionally adequate diet for individuals of both sexes and various ages in a family of four. I have reviewed their plan for October of 1960 (71). Taking the estimated cost of 1 week's food for the "low-cost plan" (and ignoring the "moderate-cost" and "liberal" plans, which are approximately 25 percent and 50 percent more expensive respectively), a crude average of around $5.50 per person per week can be calculated. (The range is from $3.00 per week for children under 1 year of age to $8.60 per week for nursing mothers.) If these estimates are valid, then it is clear that many of the families surveyed in 1960 were not spending enough to provide an adequate diet.

Some benefits from quantity food purchase and preparation are possible in larger families. In an earlier study (72) it was found that 48.7 percent of families of six or more met recommended dietary allowances on expenditures of $4.00 per person per week while only 31.5 percent of the three-person families did so. At expenditures of $4.00 to $5.99 per person per week, 58.1 percent of three-person families and 85.8 percent of six-or-more-person families met the recommendation. "Economy of scale," then, is possible, but it is clear that many larger families, especially in the lower income groups, cannot provide an adequate diet with the amounts they are spending.

Family Size and Medical Expenditures. It is relevant here to examine the effects of family size on medical expenditures as revealed in a Bureau of Labor Statistics (BLS) Report (68-70). Table 21 shows expenditures for medical care, as a percentge of total expenditures, calculated in the same way as in Table 19. The differences in the two tables are interesting. Although actual cash expenditures for medical care increase somewhat, the percentage does not increase with income, as is the case with regard to food expenditures. Unlike food expenditures, medical care expenditures *decrease* as family size increases. In spite of the fact that the need for medical care will increase, as we have seen from the morbidity data associated with family size, expenditures do not. It appears, then, that larger families may be depriving themselves of medical care in order to meet other needs. No data are available to indicate whether the amount of free medical care received by low income families would alter this picture. However, free medical programs would not have any appreciable effect on families with incomes higher than $3,000 or $4,000 per year.

Family Size and Maternal Care. Preschool children are very largely dependent on their mothers. The quality of maternal care provided determines many aspects of child health. With these truisms in mind, it is of interest to review the effects of family size on maternal care, as shown in two British

TABLE 21

Expenditures for Medical Care as Percent of Total Expenditures for Current
Consumption, by Family Size and Income Class,
United States, 1960-1961

(percent)

Income Class	Family Size			
	3 Persons	4 Persons	5 Persons	6 or More
$ 1,000- 1,999	7.4	9.3	6.9	4.9
2,000- 2,999	7.6	6.0	4.5	4.5
3,000- 3,999	7.1	7.9	5.7	5.0
4,000- 4,999	6.8	6.2	5.6	5.5
5,000- 5,999	6.6	6.6	6.4	5.9
6,000- 7,499	6.6	6.4	6.1	5.8
7,500- 9,999	6.3	6.4	6.1	6.1
10,000-14,999	6.3	5.7	6.8	6.3
15,000	6.9	6.2	5.8	4.4
Average	6.6	6.4	6.1	5.8

Source: BLS Report No. 237-93, Part 2, Tables 11D, E, F & G, 1966 (69).

studies that have examined this relationship. In their classic study, *A Thousand Families in Newcastle upon Tyne* (73), Spence and his associates found a statistically significant correlation between "consistently unsatisfactory" maternal care and number of children, although they recognized that other social factors, as well as inadequate housing and overcrowding, were involved.

The matter was examined in more detail in the National Survey of Health and Development, mentioned earlier, and reported in *Children Under Five* (33). Like the authors of the Newcastle study, they experienced difficulty in trying to eliminate subjective judgments from the scoring for quality of maternal care. The differences they observed, however, left them in little doubt that the number of children constitutes a significant factor. They found that the ". . . efficiency of the mother is closely related to the size of her family in each social group, though the relationship is closest in the manual workers' families." Their data for this group are presented in Table 22.

In their subsequent evaluation of the growth of the study children, they made several interesting observations about interrelations between nutrition and maternal care:

The two groups where maternal care appeared to have no effect on growth were at either end of the social scale, i.e., the professional and salaried and the semiskilled and unskilled manual workers. It is possible that when a certain level of material prosperity is reached in the family the nutrition of the child is likely to be adequate whatever the capacity of the mother. Below a certain level, on the other hand, even the best manager

TABLE 22

Proportion of Mothers Rated as Best in All Aspects of Child Care in
Skilled Manual Workers' Families with Varying
Numbers of Dependent Children,
England, 1948-1950

Number of Dependent Children	Proportion of Mothers Rated Best in All Aspects of Care (Percent)	Number of Families
1	44.7	262
2	33.0	441
3	27.3	286
4	16.1	112
5 or more	10.1	80

Source: Douglas and Blomfield (25).

cannot provide an adequate diet for her child with the money available. . . . It is of interest that even in the professional and salaried group maternal care seems to become of importance in relation to the growth of fourth- or later-born children. With blackcoated workers it only *becomes* important after the first child, whereas with skilled manual workers it *ceases* to be important after the third. (33, italics theirs)

The Aggravating Effects of Family Size

In examining the data obtained in the study of preschool children in Candelaria (10), family size was one of several factors found to be associated with malnutrition. Some of the interactions between these factors were examined. The aggravating effect of increasing numbers of children became apparent when cross-correlations were made with some of the other factors associated with malnutrition. Initial analysis of the data, for example, had shown that malnutrition was more prevalent among the children of older mothers. This was rather surprising since we expected that older mothers, having learned from experience, might be more competent. When we controlled for family size, however, the reason became clear. The findings are shown in Table 23, where it may be seen that the prevalence of malnutrition in children of older mothers who have fewer children is well below the communitywide average. The problem in Candelaria is that most older mothers have numerous children and however competent they may be, they were unable to meet the needs of too many children, just as Douglas and Blomfield observed in England.

We also found that children of literate mothers were less likely to be malnourished than those whose mothers were illiterate (38 percent mal-

TABLE 23

The Effect of Numbers of Living Children on Various Factors Correlated
with Malnutrition in Preschool Children,
Candelaria, Colombia, 1963

Factor	Total Population in Category	Malnourished Children	
		Number	Percent
Vulnerable ages (12-35 months)			
5 or less living children	312	154	49.4
6 or more living children	94	53	56.4
Maternal illiteracy			
5 or less living children	235	110	46.8
6 or more living children	71	37	52.1
Maternal age (30 or more years)			
5 or less living children	71	25	35.2
6 or more living children	121	59	48.7[a]

[a]"p" = less than 0.05; X^2 = 3.34.

Source: Wray and Aguirre (10).

nourished among 777 children of literate mothers; 48 percent malnourished among 317 children of illiterate mothers). If we assume that the education of the mothers affects the quality of the care they provide their children, this might have been expected. Here, too, however, numbers made a difference: in the children of illiterate mothers there was a difference in the prevalence of malnutrition between those with fewer and those with more siblings. Even these mothers apparently could cope more effectively if they were not overwhelmed by numbers, as may also be seen in Table 23.

Our basic survey had shown that the children most likely to be malnourished were those between 12 and 36 months of age. Here, too, family size had a negative influence: children in this most susceptible age group from the larger families were distinctly more likely to be malnourished than those from smaller families, as is evident in Table 23.

It seems quite evident that under the circumstances which prevail in Candelaria, parents, poor as they are, are better able to provide for their children if the numbers are not too great. Whether the problem be poverty or ignorance, both of which are almost universally implicated as causal factors in malnutrition, the effects of either are made worse by too many children in the family.

Douglas and Blomfield, in their discussion of the interrelations of family size with other factors affecting growth in the National Study children, made the following comments:

In the early years when the cost of feeding a child is small, growth must depend largely on the patience and conscientiousness of the mother and on the adequacy of her knowledge. And we have seen that the standard of maternal care declines with increasing family size, in the poorer groups especially. At later ages the cost of the food itself becomes important, and the poor growth of the later-born child will be due either to an inadequate family income or unwise spending. The marked relation between the standard of maternal care and growth in those families whose income, though not large, should be sufficient—suggests that spending habits are important. But the lack of such a relationship in the large families of skilled manual workers, and in all families in the poorest groups, suggests that below a certain level of income even the most careful spending will not provide a diet fully adequate for growth. (33)

It seems fair to say that in their families, as in those in Candelaria, family size could be termed an aggravating factor.

Process-of-Elimination Effects

By this rather cumbersome term is meant the effects associated with family size which remain after other factors considered causal are controlled for. The data need not be reviewed in detail here, but several of the studies described earlier presented relevant evidence and three are worth mentioning specifically.

Morris and his associates found that when they controlled for social class and maternal age, infant mortality increased with parity and the increase was relatively greatest in the younger mothers in the *highest* social classes. (See Figure 3.) Whatever benefits one might expect from improved environmental circumstances associated with higher social classes are offset by family size. This is not to say, however, that family size is the only residual variable remaining to account for variations in mortality. Maternal age is also involved, and this prompts a consideration of maternal competence, since it is the younger mothers who have the problem. These two factors, and probably others, are almost certainly interacting.

The data from Douglas and his colleagues also showed clear-cut effects on growth and intelligence associated with family size when social class was held constant. What is clearly evident from their data (see Table 5) is that children from small families in the lowest social classes grow as well as their age peers in the higher social classes. In other words, lower-class mothers can and do overcome, or compensate for, whatever factors are operating to interfere with growth and development, providing the pressure of numbers is not too great. On the other hand, family size has no effect in the higher social classes.

This is not the case, however, with regard to intelligence. Table 9 shows that test scores are higher in the smallest families, but social class differences remain. What is perhaps more important is the fact that the effects of family size are evident within each class, even the highest.

Direct Evidence

There is one study, to my knowledge, in which an hypothesis concerning the nature of the effect of family size was developed and tested. Nisbet tested his hypothesis concerning effects on intelligence among Aberdeen school children (74). His subjects were the children passing from primary to secondary school in 1949 and 1959—around 2,500 each year—who were given a battery of intelligence tests. His idea was that the greater adult contact to be expected in smaller families would stimulate the development of better verbal ability and that this would account for some of the association between family size and intelligence test performance.

He tested this first by examining the association between verbal score (English attainment) and family size, while holding intelligence scores constant. He found, "All these partial correlations are negative and significantly different from zero" (i.e., highly unlikely to occur because of sampling fluctuations). Second, he compared the negative correlation with family size in tests dependent on verbal ability with those of tests more or less independent of such ability. He expected, and found, a greater degree of negative correlation in the verbal test, though the difference was not too great. Finally, he examined the negative correlation at various ages on the assumption that the effect of the environmental influence—the decreased contact with adults in larger families—"will tend to be greater at later ages when the cumulative effect of the environment begins to show itself." The negative correlations were indeed found to increase, both when different groups of children, aged 7, 9, and 11, were compared* and also when the results at ages 7, 9, and 11 of the same children were compared.†

Nisbet concludes

> . . . that part of (though not all) the negative correlation of family size and intelligence test score may be attributed to an environmental influence of the size of family on verbal development and through it on general mental development. (74, p. 286)

Here, then, appears to be some clarification of the role of one element, contact with adults, which may account for variation in intelligence with family size. His data also show that the effect increases with increasing age of the child. Whatever the precise causal interrelations may be, it is clear that the process continues throughout childhood.

*r's = −.256, −.287, and −.333 respectively.
†r's = −.209, −.226, and −.289 respectively.

The Implications of the Evidence

The effects associated with family size on the well-being of individuals—primarily the children—in a family are varied, but serious: increased illness, including malnutrition, serious enough in younger children to increase mortality rates; less satisfactory growth and intellectual development; increased illness in the parents, as well as clear-cut economic and emotional stresses. Family size is not the only cause of these effects, but it is clearly implicated as an important element in the interacting network of causal factors.

The evidence regarding the effects of birth interval is less extensive than that relating to family size but no less disconcerting. At first glance the effects appear to be quite similar—increased mortality, increased morbidity, less satisfactory growth, and less adequate intellectual development. It appears, in fact, that excessive *crowding* of children—too many children too quickly—in a family with a young mother will produce the same effects quickly that excessive *numbers* of children will produce more slowly in larger families.

Do these effects matter? Are the consequences of excessive family size or inadequate spacing of children at the family level sufficiently serious to be of concern to policymakers or economic planners? What is needed for a confident answer to such questions is data that would allow us to move from the qualitative description of effects provided by the evidence available to quantitative estimates of the overall impact of such effects. Such data are not available. In a way this is not surprising. Gunnar Myrdal, an internationally preeminent economist, was compelled, because of a similar lack of data, to justify the provision of health care in developing countries as a "moral imperative" in his monumental *Asian Drama* (75). In the light of the evidence we have seen, one might equally well consider the limitation of family size or the better spacing of children a "moral imperative."

One can, in fact, make some quantitative estimates with the data available—even while acknowledging the need for better information. Given the data from Scotland that the *average* I.Q. of children with five or more siblings is 91, 22 points below that of only children, what are the implications for developing countries? In Candelaria, Colombia, we found that 27 percent of the preschool children had five siblings or more. The implication of the association between family size and intelligence is such that it suggests that a fourth of the population may be subject to serious impairment of its intellectual development. Evidence from the United States has a direct bearing here; the President's Task Force on Manpower Conservation, appointed to investigate why so many youths were unfit for military service, found that 47 percent of all young men rejected on mental grounds came from families with six or more children (76). Similar quantitative data were provided by Pasamanick and Lilienfield (77) in their examination of maternal and fetal factors associated with the development of mental deficiency. They found that the rate of mental deficiency was approximately 40 per 1,000 among firstborn children, rising to 140 per 1,000 for fourth children, and then to 400 per 1,000 in sixth children—a tenfold increase over the rates in first children.

It is also appropriate here to quote a statement published by Dr. Cicely Williams:

> . . . the "survival of the fittest" is a misapplied cliche. It was not recognized that the same conditions that will kill 30 percent of the babies in the first year of life will also produce a large proportion of persons with damaged lives who will be a burden for years and perish at a later date. (78, p. 1280)

Infant mortality rates are no longer so high; infant mortality attributable to family size was probably never that high, though it is interesting to note that in discussing population change in England in the eighteenth century McKeown said:

> . . . Marriage rates were high in the eighteenth century and an increase in the birth rate would have been due chiefly to addition of children to existing families, rather than to an increase in the number of one-child families. Hence any increase in the birth rate would have been offset largely by an *increase in postnatal mortality*. (79, italics mine)

Even though mortality rates have declined since many of the studies relating them to family size were carried out, we know that such rates still prevail in many parts of the world, and there is no reason to doubt that the effects associated with family size are still present. Beyond that, we do know more now about the consequences that might be expected among the children who do not die. For example, the steadily accumulating knowledge concerning the permanent effects of malnutrition on the growth of the brain in young children (9) ought to give pause to anyone concerned about the human resources of a nation. The evidence here is such that any measure that might reasonably be expected to reduce the prevalence of malnutrition is worth supporting to the fullest extent possible.

Would reducing family size, or increasing birth interval, reduce the effects we have seen? Once again, the evidence available is inadequate for an unqualified answer. Such evidence as there is suggests an affirmative answer, derived from the fact that in those studies in which social class as well as family size were examined, the lower-class mothers who had only one or two children seem to have provided as well for their children as the upper-class mothers. This leaves unanswered, of course, the most important question: would the parents of large families have provided better for their children if they had fewer of them? The problem posed here could be stated in the form of two alternative hypotheses:

1. Parents who *do* limit family size are qualitatively different from those who do not. This difference produces (among other things)—
   a. Smaller numbers of children *and*
   b. Healthier, more intelligent children

OR

2. Parents who *do not* limit family size have the same potential as those who do, but—
   a. Because they lack knowledge of, or access to, means of limiting family size, they fail to do so, and,
   b. *Because* of excessive family size, their children are subject to more illness, receive less adequate nutrition, and fail to achieve their full potential for physical and intellectual development.

Until better evidence is available, and such evidence is urgently needed, it will be impossible to assert that either of these is correct. In the meantime, however, there is evidence that mothers *would* like to control their family size. K.A.P. surveys all over the world (80) have shown repeatedly that mothers with three or four children *want no more*. For lack of access to adequate and effective means of limiting family size, many of these *will* have more children, and there is no way to know whether the children they already have would have been better cared for if the ones their mothers did not want had not been born. The evidence, at the very least, suggests that they would have.

For everyone concerned about the welfare of children, everyone who believes that each child born deserves a chance to achieve his own best potential, the message is clear: we must, at the very least, make it possible for parents who do want to control their family size to do so. If effective means are available, there is reason to believe that many will use them—and be better parents as a consequencce.

REFERENCES

1. Freedman, Ronald, *The Sociology of Human Fertility, A Report and Bibliography.* Oxford: Basil Blackwell, 1963.
2. Stycos, J. Mayone, "Demography and Family Planning," *Teaching Family Planning to Medical Students.* New York: Josiah Macy, Jr., Foundation, 1968. pp. 23-40.
3. Berelson, Bernard, "Beyond Family Planning," *Studies in Family Planning*, 38, 1969. pp. 1-16.
4. Hardin, Garrett, "The Tragedy of the Commons," *Science*, 162, 1968. pp. 1243-1248.

5. Taylor, Carl E., "Five Stages in a Practical Population Policy," *Internat Development R*, 10, 1968. pp. 2-7.

6. Day, Richard L., "Factors Influencing Offspring. Number of Children, Interval between Pregnancies, and Age of Parents," *Amer J Dis Child*, 113, 1967. pp. 179-185.

7. Dingle, J. H., G. F. Badger, and W. S. Jordan, *Illness in the Home: Study of 25,000 Illnesses in a Group of Cleveland Families*. Cleveland: Press of Western Reserve Univ., 1964.

8. *Preschool Child Malnutrition: Primary Deterrent to Human Progress.* Pub. 1282, National Academy of Sciences-National Research Council. Washington, 1966.

9. Scrimshaw, N. S., and John E. Gordon, eds., *Malnutrition, Learning, and Behavior.* Cambridge, Massachusetts: The M.I.T. Press, 1968.

10. Wray, Joe D., and Alfredo Aguirre, "Protein-Calorie Malnutrition in Candelaria, Colombia. I. Prevalence; Social and Demographic Factors," *J Trop Pediat*, 15, 1969. pp. 76-98.

11. Gomez, F., et al., "Malnutrition in Infancy and Childhood with Special Reference to Kwashiorkor," *Advances in Pediatrics*, S. Z. Levine, ed. Chicago: Yearbook Publishers, 1955. Vol. VII, pp. 131-169.

12. Bengoa, J. M., D. B. Jelliffe, and C. Perez, "Some Indicators for a Broad Assessment of the Magnitude of Protein-Calorie Malnutrition in Population Groups," *Amer J Clin Nutr*, 7, 1959. pp. 714-720.

13. World Health Organization, *Methods of Planning and Evaluation in Applied Nutrition Programs.* Technical Report No. 340. Geneva: World Health Organization, 1966.

14. Jelliffe, D. B., *The Assessment of the Nutritional Status of the Community.* World Health Organization Monograph Series No. 53. Geneva: World Health Organization, 1966.

15. *A Health and Demographic Survey of Bang Pa-In.* Bangkok: Community Health Care Program, Ramathibodi Hospital Faculty of Medicine, 1969, Mimeo.

16. Robertson, I., and M. Kemp, "Child Health and Family Size," *S Afr Med J*, 34, 1963. pp. 888-893.

17. Chen, Edith, and Sidney Cobb, "Family Structure in Relation to Health and Disease," *J Chronic Dis*, 12, 1960. pp. 544-567.

18. Gordon, John E., "Social Implications of Health and Disease," *Arch Environ Health*, 18, 1969. pp. 216-234.

19. Wyon, J. B., and J. E. Gordon, "A Long-Term Prospective-Type Field Study of Population Dynamics in the Punjab, India," *Research in Family Planning*, Clyde V. Kiser, ed. Princeton: Princeton Univ. Press, 1962. pp. 17-32.

20. Morris, J. N., and J. A. Heady, "Social and Biological Factors in Infant Mortality, I. Objects and Methods," *Lancet*, 1, 1955. pp. 343-349.

21. Heady, J. A., C. Daley, and J. N. Morris, "Social and Biological Factors in Infant Mortality, II. Variations of Mortality with Mother's Age and Parity," *Lancet*, 1, 1955. pp. 395-397.

22. Daley, C., J. A. Heady, and J. N. Morris, "Social and Biological Factors in Infant Mortality, III. The Effects of Mother's Age and Parity on Social-Class Differences in Infant Mortality," *Lancet*, 1, 1955. pp. 445-448.

23. Heady, J. A., et al., "Social and Biological Factors in Infant Mortality IV. The Independent Effects of Social Class, Region, the Mother's Age and Her Parity," *Lancet*, 1, 1955. pp. 499-502.

24. Morris, J. N. and J. A. Heady, "Social and Biological Factors in Infant Mortality, V. Mortality in Relation to the Father's Occupation," *Lancet*, 1, 1955. pp. 554-560.

25. Heady, J. A., and J. N. Morris, "Social and Biological Factors in Infant Mortality, VI. Mothers Who Have Their Babies in Hospitals and Nursing Homes," *Brit J Prev Soc Med*, 10, 1956. pp. 97-106.

26. Heady, J. A., and J. N. Morris, "Variations of Mortality with Mother's Age and Parity," *J Obstet Gynaec Brit Emp*, 66, 1959. pp. 577-593.

27. Morrison, S. L., J. A. Heady, and J. N. Morris, "Mortality in the Post-neonatal Period," *Arch Dis Child*, 34, 1959. pp. 101-114.

28. Heady, J. A., and M. A. Heasman, *General Register Office Studies on Medical and Population Subjects, No. 15, Social and Biological Factors in Infant Mortality*. London: H. M. Stationery Office, 1959.

29. Chase, Helen C. *The Relationship of Certain Biologic and Socio-Economic Factors to Fetal, Infant and Early Childhood Mortality. I. Father's Occupation, Parental Age and Infant's Birth Rank*. Albany, New York: New York State Department of Health, 1961. Mimeo.

30. Chase, Helen C. *The Relationship of Certain Biologic and Socio-Economic Factors to Fetal, Infant and Early Childhood Mortality. II. Father's Occupation, Infant's Birth Weight, and Mother's Age*. Albany, New York: New York State Department of Health, 1962. Mimeo.

31. Yerushalmy, J., et al., "Longitudinal Studies of Pregnancy on the Island of Kauai, Territory of Hawaii, I. Analysis of Previous Reproductive History," *Amer J Obstet Gynec* 71, 1956. pp. 80-96.

32. Newcombe, H. B., and O. G. Tarendale, "Maternal Age and Birth Order Correlations: Problems of Distinguishing Mutational from Environmental Components," *Mutat Res*, 1, 1964. pp. 446-467.

33. Douglas, J. W. B., and J. M. Blomfield, *Children Under Five*. London: Allen and Unwin, Ltd., 1958.

34. Douglas, J. W. B., *The Home and the School*. London: MacGibbon and Kee, Ltd., 1964.

35. Douglas, J. W. B., J. M. Ross, and H. R. Simpson, *All Our Future*. London: Peter Davies, 1968.

36. Douglas, J. W. B., and H. R. Simpson, "Height in Relation to Puberty, Family Size and Social Class, A Longitudinal Study," *Milbank Mem Fund Quart*, 40, July 1964. pp. 20-35.

37. Grant, M. W., "Rate of Growth in Relation to Birth Rank and Family Size, *Brit J Prev Soc Med*, 18, 1964. pp. 35-42.

38. Tanner, J. M., Earlier Maturation in Man," *Sci Amer*, 218, 1968. pp. 21-27.

39. Cone, T. E., "Secular Acceleration of Height and Biological Maturation in Children during the Past Century," *J Pediat*, 59, 1961. pp. 736-740.

40. "Early Maturing and Larger Children" (Editorial), *Brit Med J*, 5250, 1961. pp. 502-503.

41. Anastasi, Anne, "Differentiating Effect of Intelligence and Social Status," *Eugen Quart*, 6, 1959. pp. 84-91.

42. Hunt, J. McV., *Intelligence and Experience*. New York: The Ronald Press Co., 1961.

43. Vernon, P. E., "Recent Investigations of Intelligence and Its Measurements," *Eugen Rev*, 43, 1951. pp. 125-137.

44. Reed, Elizabeth W., and Sheldon C. Reed, *Mental Retardation: A Family Study*. Philadelphia: W. B. Saunders Co., 1965.

45. Scott, J. A., "Intelligence, Physique and Family Size," *Brit J Prev Soc Med*, 16, 1962. pp. 165-173.

46. Tanner, J. M., "Galtonian Eugenics and the Study of Growth" (The Galton Lecture), *Eugen Rev*, 58, 1966. pp. 122-135.

47. Rosenthal, Robert, and Lenore Jacobson, "Teacher Expectations and the Disadvantaged," *Sci Amer*, 218, 1968. pp. 19-23.

48. Hare, E. H., and G. K. Shaw, "A Study in Family Health: I. Health in Relation to Family Size," *Brit J Psyhciat*, III, 1965. pp. 461-466.

49. Scotch, Norman A., "Sociocultural Factors in the Epidemiology of Zulu Hypertension," *Amer J Public Health*, 53, 1963. pp. 1205-1213.

50. Murphy, Jane M., "Cultural Change and Mental Health among Yoruba Women of Nigeria." Mimeo., no date, no place.

51. Pyke, D. A., "Parity and the Incidence of Diabetes," *Lancet*, 1, 1956. pp. 818-820.

52. Wright, N. H., "Maternal Mortality in Ceylon: Trends, Causes, and Potential Reduction by Family Planning." Presented at Association of Obstetrician-Gynecologists of Ceylon, August 21-22, 1968. Unpublished.

53. Eastman, N. J., and L. M. Hellman, *Williams' Obstetrics*, 12th ed. New York: Appleton-Century-Crofts, 1961.

54. Perkin, G. W., "Pregnancy Prevention in High-Risk Women, Strategy for New National Family Planning Programs." Presented at Conference on Family Planning and National Development (IPPF), Bandung, June 1-7, 1969.

55. Ravenholt, R. T., and H. Frederiksen, "Numerator Analysis of Fertility Patterns," *Public Health Rep*, 83, 1968. pp. 449-457.

56. *A Health and Demographic Survey of Villages in Bang Chan, Thailand, 1968*. Ramathibodi Hospital Faculty of Medicine, Bangkok, 1968. Mimeo.

57. Hawley, Amos H., and Prachuabmoh Visid, "Family Growth and Family Planning in Rural District of Thailand," *Family Planning and Population Programs*. Chicago: University of Chicago Press, 1965. pp. 523-544.

58. Cowgill, D. O., et al., *Family Planning in Bangkhen, Thailand*. Bangkok: Center for Population and Social Research, Mahidol University, 1969.

59. Huse, Elizabeth, "Infant Mortality. Results of a Field Study in Gary, Indiana, Based on Births in One Year." Children's Bureau Publication No. 112. Washington: Government Printing Office, 1923. pp. 44-45. Cited by Eastman (62).

60. Woodbury, Robert M., "Causal Factors in Infant Mortality. A Statistical Study Based on Investigations in Eight Cities." Children's Bureau Publication No. 142, Washington: Government Printing Office, 1925. pp. 60-67. Cited by Eastman (62).

61. Yerushalmy, J., "On the Interval Between Successive Births and Its Effect on Survival of Infant. I. An Indirect Method of Study," *Hum Biol*, 17, 1945. pp. 65-106.

62. Eastman, Nicholson J., "The Effect of the Interval Between Births on Maternal and Fetal Outlook" *Amer J Obstet Gynec*, 47, 1944. pp. 445-466.

63. Gordon, J. E., J. B. Wyon, and W. Ascoli, "The Second Year Death Rate in Less Developed Countries," *Amer J Med Sci*, 254. pp. 357-380.

64. Gordon, J. E., I. E. Chitkaru, and J. B. Wyon, "Weanling Diarrhea," *Amer J Med Sci*, 245, 1963. pp. 345-377.

65. Williams, Cicely D., "Kwashiorkor," *Lancet*, 2, 1935. p. 1151.

66. Williams, Cicely D., "The Story of Kwashiorkor," *Courrier*, 8, 1963. pp. 361-367.

67. Douglas, J. W. B., "Some Factors Associated with Prematurity: The Results of a National Survey, *J Obstet Gynaec Brit Emp*, 57, 1950. pp. 143-170.

68. *Survey of Consumer Expenditures.* BLS Report No. 237-93. Washington: U.S. Dept. of Labor, Bureau of Labor Statistics, 1966.

69. Ibid., Supplement 2

70. Ibid., Supplement 3, Part A, May 1966.

71. "Food and Home Notes," October 5, 1960. Washington: U.S. Department of Agriculture, Office of Information, 1960.

72. *Family Food Plans and Food Costs.* Home Economics Research Report No. 20. Washington: U.S. Department of Agriculture, Consumer and Food Economics Research Division, 1962.

73. Spence, Sir James, et al., *A Thousand Families in Newcastle upon Tyne.* London: Oxford University Press, 1954.

74. Nisbet, John, "Family, Environment, and Intelligence," *Education, Economy, and Society*, A. H. Halsey, J. Floud, and C. A. Anderson, eds. New York: Free Press, 1961.

75. Myrdal, Gunnar, *Asian Drama: An Inquiry into the Poverty of Nations.* New York: Pantheon, 1968.

76. *One-Third of a Nation: A Report on Young Men Found Unqualified for Military Service.* The President's Task Force on Manpower Conservation. Washington: Government Printing Office, 1964.

77. Pasamanick, B., and A. M. Lilienfeld, "The Association of Maternal and Fetal Factors with the Development of Mental Deficiency: II. Relationship to Maternal Age, Birth Order, Previous Reproductive Loss and Degree of Deficiency," *Amer J Ment Defic*, 60, 1956. p. 557.

78. Williams, Cicely D., "Kwashiorkor," *JAMA*, 153, 1953. pp. 1280-1285.

79. McKeown, Thomas, "Medicine and World Population," Mindel C. Sheps, and Jeanne C. Ridley, eds. *Demographic History and Population Policy*, Pittsburgh: Univ. of Pittsburgh Press, 1965. pp. 25-40.

80. Mauldin, W. Parker, "Fertility Studies: Knowledge, Attitude and Practice, *Studies in Family Planning*, 7, 1966. pp. 1-10.

XII

Health Consequences of
Population Density and Crowding

John Cassel

The view that crowding and increasing population density are deleterious to health is so widespread and generally accepted as to have become almost a medical axiom. Furthermore, it is currently believed that the harmful effects of crowding not only increase the spread of infectious diseases but also increase the risk of noninfectious disease. Two quotations from a standard text on epidemiology, which with minor variations can be found in all textbooks dealing with the subject, illustrate these opinions.

> It has long been recognized that crowded communities provide a more fertile ground for the spread of infection than more scattered communities. (1)
> The deleterious effects of crowding are not, however, confined to matters concerned with the spread of infection, but are also seen in increased mortality from all causes, both infectious and non-infectious. (1)

The evidence supporting this point of view is derived largely from four sources:

1. The higher death and morbidity rates that traditionally have been reported from the more densely populated urban centers.

2. The dramatic increase in death rates, primarily due to infectious diseases, that have followed industrialization and urbanism.

3. The higher rates of various diseases reported under crowded conditions such as military training camps, nurseries, etc.

4. Animal studies which have shown that as the number of animals housed together increases—with other factors such as diet, temperature, and sanitation kept constant—maternal and infant mortality rates rise, the incidence of atherosclerosis increases, and the resistance to insults such as drugs, micro-organisms, and X rays is reduced.

John Cassel is Professor and Chairman of the Department of Epidemiology, School of Public Health, University of North Carolina.

Examining the Evidence

A careful review of recent data, however, indicates some important inconsistencies in the relationship between crowding and health which throw some doubt on this generally accepted formulation, particularly on the processes through which crowding may influence health. It would appear from these data that the relationship between crowding and health is a far more complex phenomenon than was originally envisaged; while under certain circumstances crowding is clearly associated with poor health states, under other circumstances it may be neutral or even beneficial. The data which cast some doubt on this relationship will be briefly reviewed under the same categories that have provided the evidence used to support the notion that crowding inevitably leads to deleterious health consequences.

Urban-Rural Death and Morbidity Rates

As is shown in Figure 1, death rates for all causes in the United States were indeed higher in urban areas than in rural before 1950. By 1960, however, the ratio had reversed; rural rates were higher than urban, and since 1960 the ratio of rural to urban deaths has been steadily increasing.* Paradoxically,

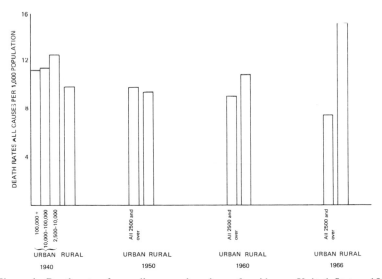

Figure 1. Death rates from all causes by place of residence, United States, 1940, 1950, 1960, 1966.
Sources: (2-7).

---

*The magnitude of these ratios should be accepted as only approximate, especially the data for 1966 which were based on population projections. Further, the differing definitions of "urban" used by the Bureau of the Census (from which the population figures were drawn) and by the National Office of Vital Statistics may introduce a source of bias.

even though cities have been increasing in size since 1940, death rates have fallen more rapidly in these crowded circumstances than in the more sparsely populated rural areas. Part of this phenomenon may be due to the improved medical care and sanitation in the cities and part to the migration of younger people to the cities, which leaves an older, more susceptible population behind in the rural areas. These processes, it could be argued, might overwhelm or obscure the effects of crowding. That they can be only partial explanations for this reversal in the rural-urban health ratios is evident from the data in Tables 1 and 2. The rural excess in incidence from typhoid fever, for example, may well be due to differences in sanitation, and the more effective immunization programs in cities may account for the lower urban rates of diphtheria and pertussis. However, the rural excess in the incidence of scarlet fever can hardly be due to either of these processes, as we do not as yet possess any means to prevent the occurrence of streptococcal infections. Similarly, as far as the migration hypothesis is concerned, this could not explain the excess mortality rates in rural children both black and white, male and female.

TABLE 1

Urban-Rural Differences in Health Status, United States, 1959-1961:
Total Mortality Rates per 100,000 Population

All Causes, Children Age 5-14 Years	Metropolitan Counties	Nonmetropolitan Counties
White Male	48.6	59.7
White Female	32.3	37.6
Nonwhite Male	67.5	82.3
Nonwhite Female	45.5	60.9

Source: (10)

Data from other parts of the world tend to confirm this seeming paradox. DuBos (8), for example, reports that despite the fact that Hong Kong and Holland are among the most crowded areas in the world, they enjoy one of the highest levels of physical and mental health in the world. Even more convincing is the data from Britain, where in 1961 the age-standardized mortality ratios for all causes of death were as follows: * (9)

*Age-standardized mortality ratio as defined by the Registrar General is "the number of deaths occurring in each sex aged 20-64 in a given place of residence expressed as a percentage of the number of deaths that might have been expected to occur if the given place of residence had experienced within each age group the same death rate as that of a standard population. . . . " Thus for each sex group a standardized mortality ratio of 100

	Males	Females
Urban areas population 100,000 or more	101	98
Urban areas population 50,000-99,999	91	90
Urban areas population under 50,000	104	105
Rural areas	91	98

As can be seen from the table, no regular increase in mortality ratios occurs for either sex with increasing population density. In fact, the largest cities have somewhat lower death rates than do the smallest cities, and rural areas have the same, if not lower, rates than cities with populations of 50,000 to 99,999.

TABLE 2

Urban-Rural Differences in Health Status, United States, 1959-1961:
Incidence and Mortality Rates per 1,000,000 Population

Selected Diseases, Children Age 5-14 Years	Incidence		Mortality	
	Metropolitan Counties	Nonmetropolitan Counties	Metropolitan Counties	Nonmetropolitan Counties
Typhoid Fever	3.3	7.0	0.1	0.1
Diphtheria	3.2	7.1	0.2	0.6
Pertussis	111.1	141.1	0.4	1.6
Scarlet Fever and Streptococcal Sore Throat	1,579	2,374	0.5	1.1
Influenza	n.a.	n.a.	13.5	41.9

n.a. = not available.
Source: (11).

The Rise in Death Rates Following Industrialization and Urbanization

Tuberculosis has been used as an example par excellence of a disease that showed a marked increase in rates following industrialization and the accompanying crowding. What is not so well recognized, however, is that in all countries for which data are available, tuberculosis rates rose for 75 to 100 years following industrialization, then started to fall spontaneously, and have continued to fall in the face of ever increasing population density. Improvements in medical care and antituberculosis programs cannot account for this reversal in trends, at least during the initial phase. For example, the diminishing rates in Britain and the United States started in 1850 and 1900 respec-

---

would be the expected death rate for that population with its age distribution if place of residence had no effect.

tively (12), 50 to 100 years before any useful antituberculosis drugs were discovered and several decades before any organized antituberculosis programs were started.

Furthermore, in some relatively recent studies it has been found that, contrary to prevailing theory, tuberculosis does not necessarily occur under crowded conditions. Under some circumstances at least it occurs more frequently in people who are socially isolated. In a careful study conducted in Britain (13), all the families living in a city were X-rayed to determine the prevalence of tuberculosis in relationship to an index of crowding (derived by dividing the number of people in a household by the number of rooms in the house). Although the prevalence varied a great deal with social class, within each social class no relationship between the crowding index and tuberculosis prevalence was found. In fact, lodgers who were living alone in the houses had a tuberculosis rate some three to four times higher than family members even though the lodgers were, by definition, living in uncrowded conditions. Similar results were found in a study in the United States (14). It was found that tuberculosis was occurring most frequently in people living alone in a single room and not in those living under the most crowded conditions.

The Higher Rates of Disease Reported under Crowded Conditions

Although there can be little doubt that outbreaks of disease, particularly acute upper respiratory disease, are more common under the crowded conditions of military training camps, for example, than under less crowded conditions, there is considerable doubt that such outbreaks can be ascribed solely to the physical fact of increased crowding.

In recent years intensive study of outbreaks of upper respiratory infection in recruits in military training camps have indicated that the agent responsible is usually the adenovirus IV. The orthodox explanation for such outbreaks holds that they result from the herding together of large numbers of susceptible young men with a few infected individuals and that crowded conditions facilitate the spread of the agent. Such an explanation, however, fails to account for some of the known facts. For example, the same agent, the adenovirus IV, is widespread in civilian populations, but even under conditions of crowding, as in colleges and schools, has never been implicated in an outbreak of upper respiratory infection. Furthermore, the permanent staff of the military installations, living under the same crowded conditions as the recruits, are not involved in such outbreaks. Finally, immunization experiments against adenovirus IV have been conducted under appropriate double-blind conditions. The immunized companies displayed a reduction in the number of cases ascribed to adenovirus IV, but they experienced just as much upper respiratory illness as had the control companies, now due to a different agent—adenovirus VII.

Studies conducted on Marine recruits in Parris Island, South Carolina (15), on the patterning of such outbreaks, provide further evidence against the orthodox explanation. The basic training program lasts for 8 weeks. The number of upper respiratory infections increases from the first through the third weeks, decreases in the fourth through the sixth weeks, and begins to increase again in the seventh and eighth weeks. As far as can be determined, there are no differences in crowding during these 8 weeks. Furthermore, sick calls from all causes, including gastrointestinal, musculo-skeletal, skin infections, trauma, and so on, display a similar pattern. Not only is this regularity observed for all platoons, but there are systematic differences in the rate of infection between platoons (living under identical conditions), some exhibiting a markedly higher rate for their entire 8 weeks than others.

As will be indicated later in this paper, such data do not necessarily refute the role of crowding in changing susceptibility to disease, but they do provide clues which may necessitate a change in our thinking about how crowding can influence health.

Animal Studies

At first sight the animal data appear convincing. However, they, too, need to be re-examined both in terms of consistency and in terms of the extrapolation that can be made to human populations. Kessler at the Rockefeller Institute, for example, has indicated that mice under extreme conditions of crowding exhibited no increase in pathology once the population had achieved its maximum density and no further population growth was occurring. Under these circumstances asocial behavior was common but physical pathology no more frequent than in the control group living under uncrowded conditions. However, during the phase of rapid population growth that preceded this plateau, disease was much more frequent than in the control group (16).

It is apparent even from these fragmentary illustrative data that population density or crowding does not inevitably lead to poorer health. The rest of this paper will examine some of the reasons that may account for the conflicting data and suggest the need to reformulate some of our conceptual models if the effects of such phenomena are to be better understood.

Part of the reason for the discrepancies in the data presented earlier lies in the well-recognized fact that many studies have used different and often inadequate indicators of crowding. The indicators used have frequently been unable to distinguish between a high population density in some arbitrarily delineated areas of land and increased social interaction. Second, crowding under certain circumstances may be associated with certain factors which themselves can influence health (poverty, poor nutrition, poor housing, etc.) but under other circumstances may be associated with different factors. The relationship of crowding to disease states, therefore, may be a reflection of these other factors rather than the crowding per se.

How Increased Social Interaction
Leads to Disease

Perhaps of greater importance than the inadequacy of the indicators or the presence of "contaminating" factors has been the failure of most investigators to identify explicitly the processes through which increased social interaction can lead to disease. The orthodox model which, implicitly at least, is espoused by the majority of authorities holds that crowding increases the risk of disease mainly through an increased opportunity for the spread of infection. Newer data and re-examination of older data are making this view increasingly untenable. It obviously cannot account for the increase in non-infectious disease which occurs under conditions of crowding; however, even for infectious diseases there is a growing body of opinion which indicates that such a view is at best only a partial explanation for any effects crowding may have. DuBos, the pioneer microbiologist, has perhaps stated this view most clearly:

> The sciences concerned with microbial diseases have developed almost exclusively from the study of acute or semi-acute infectious processes caused by virulent microorganisms acquired through exposure to an exogenous source of infection. In contrast, the microbial diseases most common in our communities today arise from the activities of microorganisms that are ubiquitous in the environment, persist in the body without causing any obvious harm under ordinary circumstances, and exert pathological effects only when the infected person is under conditions of physiological stress. In such a type of microbial disease, the event of infection is of less importance than the hidden manifestations of the smouldering infectious process and than the physiological disturbances that convert latent infection into overt symptoms and pathology. (17)

According to DuBos, then, microbial disease is not necessarily acquired through exposure to a new microorganism. In a large number of cases disease occurs through factors which disturb the balance between the ubiquitous organisms and the host that is harboring them. It may well be that this balance may be disturbed under conditions of crowding, but this disturbance is then not a function of the physical crowding but of other processes. The studies reported above on upper respiratory infections in Marine recruits would tend to support this point of view. They suggest that a large proportion of the recruits are harboring organisms when they enter military training. Something about the military environment, particularly something about the environment of their own platoon or company, leads to the type of physiological stress (to which DuBos refers) that converts latent infection into overt symptoms and pathology. As is discussed later, it would appear that the factors that produce the physiological stress are unlikely to occur in the absence of crowding but are not due necessarily to the physical presence of many infected individuals.

In addition to following an inappropriate set of hypotheses, most research into the health consequences of crowding has failed to take into account the adaptability of living organisms. To a large extent the current views are based upon examinations of health conditions under varying degrees of crowding at one point in time. Fewer studies deal with the reactions of individuals to crowded conditions over the passage of time. The few studies that do indicate that organisms have the power to adapt to a wide range of conditions, including crowding, if the changes to which they are called upon to adapt occur reasonably slowly. These findings suggest that many of the deleterious effects of crowding will occur only, or maximally, in those individuals who are newcomers to the crowded scene. Such a formulation may explain Kessler's findings which, as mentioned earlier, contradict other animal studies that have examined the effects of crowding on first generation animals only.

Toward a Reformulation of the Conceptual Model

A considerable amount of the confusion concerning the health consequences of crowding is due to the lack of utility of the network of hypotheses that have been used to determine research strategy and to interpret research results. Stated in its most simplistic form, the hypothesis implicit in most of existing research holds that crowding is "bad" simply because it increases the opportunity for interpersonal contact and thus facilitates the interchange of external disease agents. That this model does not explain many of the known phenomena and is generally an inadequate guide for the development of research strategy is illustrated in some of the data presented earlier. If, then, the relationships between crowding and human health are to be elucidated in a more satisfactory manner, a more appropriate set of hypotheses needs to be elaborated.

Animal experiments have quite convincingly demonstrated some of the short-term health consequences of increased population density. Of course, these findings cannot necessarily be extrapolated directly to man. They will have to be modified by taking into account the adaptability of biological organisms before one can draw long-term conclusions. However, some of the underlying concepts from such studies may be extremely useful in developing new sets of hypotheses for studies of man. Welch (18), for example, studied the effects of increased population size on mice. He noted that, as the size of the population increases, physiological changes occur in the animal, such as enhancement of the adrenocortical and adrenal medullary secretions. He has postulated that increased population size leads to increased social interaction. Among gregarious animals such increased social interaction enhances emotional involvement and elicits central activation necessary for sensory fixation and recognition even in emotionally neutral encounters. Thus, he postulates that *every such stimulus* contributes to the level of activation of both the brain-stem reticular formation and the major endocrine systems.

Welch's studies seem to indicate that one of the effects of increased population size and density is *to increase the importance of the social environment as a determinant of physiological response to various stimuli*, including the disease-producing agents to which the population is subjected. They suggest that the effect of any disease-producing agent—be it a microorganism, a toxin, or some other physicochemical element—cannot be assessed without knowing the size and nature of the group within which the exposed population interacts and that the larger the interacting group, the more important will these group phenomena be in modifying the responses to disease-producing agents.

Such a formulation receives at least circumstantial support from studies on the level of blood pressure that have been conducted over the last 30 years in every continent in the world (19-43). These studies have indicated that, with few exceptions, populations living in small, cohesive societies tend to have low blood pressures which do not differ in the young and the aged. In a number of these studies, groups who have left such societies and have had contact with western urban culture were found to have higher levels of blood pressure and to exhibit the familiar relationship between age and blood pressure found in studies of western populations.

Disease, Population, and Categories of Individuals

This formulation, useful as it may be as a general proposition, requires further specification and modification if it is to determine future research strategy. Specifically, it seems important to recognize that the influences of increases in population size are going to vary for different categories of individuals. The first such category is determined by hierarchical position within the group. Welch (18) and Mason (44) have shown in animal experiments that the animals occupying subordinate positions within any group tend to respond in a far more extreme fashion to standardized stimuli than do those in dominant positions. Their responses include changes in endocrine secretions as well as manifestations of disease and pathology. To the best of my knowledge, no human studies have been conducted to test whether this particular phenomenon applies in humans, but there seem to be no a priori reasons to suspect that it does not.

For the second category there is both human and animal evidence. It concerns the degree to which the exposed populations have or have not been prepared by previous experience for the demands and expectations of the new situations. In other words, the general formulation needs to be modified by invoking the concept of the adaptability of the biological organisms. Kessler's work indicated that the cohorts of mice born and reared in a situation of extreme population density did not display the same reactions as did their progenitors to whom this was a newer and less familiar set of experiences. Among humans the extraordinary regularity with which various diseases have first waxed and then waned as populations have become exposed and later presumably adapted to urban living and the accompanying industrialization could well be taken as evidence supporting this point of view.

The rise and fall of tuberculosis following industrialization has already been mentioned. As tuberculosis began to decline, it was replaced as a central health problem, in both Britain and the United States, by major malnutrition syndromes. In Britain, rickets was the scourge; in the United States, pellagra. These disorders, in turn, reached a peak and declined for reasons that are only partly understood and were themselves replaced by some of the diseases of early childhood, such as whooping cough, diphtheria, scarlet fever, and diarrhea. These diseases, too, waxed and then waned largely, but not entirely, under the influence of improvements in the sanitary environment and through the introduction of immunization programs, to be replaced between the World Wars by an extraordinary increase in the rate of duodenal ulcer, particularly in young men. This phenomenon, while more marked in Britain, occurred in the United States as well; in both countries, for totally unknown reasons, the rates have declined in a dramatic fashion. Duodenal ulcer has now been replaced by our modern epidemics of coronary heart disease, hypertension, cancer, arthritis, diabetes, mental disorders, and the like. There is some evidence now that some of these disorders have reached a peak and, at least in some segments of the population, are declining. Death rates for hypertensive heart disease, for example, apparently have been declining in the United States since about 1940 to 1950—before the introduction of antihypertensive drugs (45).

Furthermore, there is some evidence in both Britain and the United States that the social class distribution of many of the "modern" diseases is changing. Although 30 years ago coronary heart disease, for example, was more prevalent in Britain among the upper social classes, today there is almost no class difference. This change has occurred coincidentally with the increased length of exposure to urban, 20th century ways of living of the upper classes and (more recently) the migration of many of the lower social classes from rural to urban situations.

Some more direct evidence for this formulation exists. Christenson and Hinkle (46) compared differences in disease prevalence between a group of managers who had completed college and a group with the same job for the same pay in the same company who had not completed college. The managers who had completed college were, with few exceptions, fourth-generation

Americans. They were the sons of managers, proprietors, and white-collar workers, and they belonged to families in middle to high income groups who lived in good neighborhoods. In contrast, the group who had not completed college were hired as skilled craftsmen and later advanced to managerial status. The sons and grandsons of immigrants, this group had fathers who were skilled or unskilled laborers with an average of grammar school education or less. They had grown up in families of low income in modest to substandard neighborhoods. The second group (presumably less well prepared for the demands and expectations of managerial status) shared a significantly greater number of illnesses of all sorts than did the first group.

The findings of a study by Cassel and Tyroler (47) lead to similar conclusions. They studied two groups of rural mountaineers who worked in a factory. One group was composed of individuals who were the first of their family ever to engage in industrial work; the second differed from the first in that they were children of previous workers in the factory—but they worked in the same factory, came from the same mountain coves, were of the same age, and did the same work for the same wages as the first group. The study was undertaken to test the hypothesis that the second group, by virtue of their prior familial experience, would be better prepared for the expectations and demands of industrial living then would the first group and would therefore exhibit fewer signs of ill health. Health status was measured by responses to the Cornell Medical Index and by various indices of sick absenteeism. As predicted, the sons of previous factory workers had lower Cornell Medical Index scores (fewer symptoms) and lower rates of sick absenteeism after the initial few years of service, at each age, than had the "first generation" workers.

Perhaps even more convincing was the study conducted by Haenszel and his associates (48) on death rates from lung cancer in the United States. These investigators discovered that death rates from lung cancer, when controlled for degree of cigarette smoking, were considerably higher in the farm-born who had migrated to cities than they were in lifelong urban dwellers. The study had been designed initially to attempt to quantify the importance of length of exposure to atmospheric pollution of the cities, but despite the lifetime of exposure, urban dwellers had apparently "adapted" better to the effects of such atmospheric pollution than had the migrants.

Group Membership and Health

A further important concept in developing a useful formulation is the strong possibility that, under certain circumstances, group membership can exert a protective influence on the individual. Holmes (14) in his studies on tuberculosis in Seattle, for example, has shown that the disease occurs most frequently in "marginal" people, that is, in those individuals deprived of meaningful social contact. He found higher rates of tuberculosis in the ethnic groups who were distinct minorities in the neighborhoods in which they lived, in people living alone in one room, in those who had had multiple occupational and residential moves, and who were single or divorced than he found in the general population. Similar findings have been found in respect to other respiratory diseases, schizophrenia, accidents, and suicide (49-52). One of the concomitants of increasing population density, particularly when it is associated with increasing urbanization, is the atomization of the groups that provide emotional support and presumably some degree of protection for the individual in rural folk societies. Although, in the course of time, new types of groups develop to fulfill some of the functions originally played by the family and kin group, it is often difficult, particularly for the newcomer to such scenes, to become effectively integrated into such groups.

Finally, the question of a specific relationship between given social factors and particular diseases must be raised. Are the social processes (both positive and negative) inherent in membership in the group and position within the group—particularly under conditions of populations newly experiencing growth and crowding—apt to result in specific disease syndromes or merely in increased general susceptibility to illness? This question is the subject of considerable controversy at the moment, and both points of view have been hotly argued. In a penetrating review on the subject, Thurlow (53) indicates that the argument centers around the question of whether certain stimuli, particularly of a social and psychological nature, operate in a nonspecific fashion to increase general susceptibility to all illnesses or whether such stimuli merely increase the predilection for illness reporting and illness behavior. Another point of view holds that the nonspecific effect of social processes is but a reflection of our ignorance; with further study more specific "agents" will be discovered for which these social processes can be visualized as "vehicles." These agents, it is held, will be related to some specific disease entity. Most of these arguments are based upon the supposition that social and emotional processes are the direct initiators of disease conditions through the activation of inappropriate neuro-endocrine arousal mechanisms. While this may be a useful formulation, the animal work mentioned earlier seems to indicate that a more likely role of social factors is to increase the susceptibility of the organism to disease-producing agents; that is, to act in an indirect fashion in the etiology of any disease syndrome or pattern. In other words, the health consequences of such social processes are likely to be nonspecific. The manifestations of specific disease syndromes will be dependent not upon the specific nature of the social processes but upon the presence or absence of other disease-producing agents of a biological or a physicochemical nature and upon the constitutions, both genetic and experiential, of individuals.

It does not seem unreasonable to suppose that individuals who are deprived of meaningful group membership, exposed to ambiguous and conflicting demands for which they have had no previous experience, frustrated in achieving their goals and aspirations, and who are exposed to the tubercle bacillus, may well be victims of tuberculosis. Similar individuals, not so exposed to the tubercle bacillus, who from childhood have lived on a high-saturated, fatty-acid diet, who tend to be sedentary, who smoke cigarettes heavily may well be victims of myocardial infarction. The point is that if the circumstances under which population density and crowding are deleterious to health are to be elucidated, it would seem important to recognize the limitations of the existing classificatory schemes used to identify disease entities. To a large extent, these schemes have been developed because of their usefulness for therapeutic purposes, but they may not be the best schemes for classifying diseases for the purpose of identifying the factors responsible for the origins of diseases.

Conclusions

On the basis of these findings and the theories that emerge from them, a number of predictions, or "working hypotheses," concerning the health consequences of future population growth and crowding can be advanced.

In most developing countries it can be anticipated that rapid population growth, particularly if associated with a deterioration in housing and nutritional status will, in all likelihood, be accompanied initially by increased death and disease rates. This increased health burden will be greatest on those segments of the population who have had least previous experience with living in crowded conditions. Over a period of some decades, the diseases responsible for high death and morbidity rates will probably decline. Although overall disease rates will decline, "new" diseases will replace the old, requiring a major change in the nature and format of the health services. Whereas the diseases responsible for the initial rise in rates are likely to be diseases caused by acute infections and those associated with undernutrition and malnutrition, the later diseases are more likely to be chronic long-term disorders. Even though the rates for these disorders will be lower than for the acute diseases, the disability resulting from them will pose as great a strain on the national economy as did the high rates of the earlier diseases.

The more rapid the rate of population growth and the more it is accompanied by disruption of important social groups, the more dramatic will these effects be. The rate of population growth and the ensuing crowding will largely determine the ability of the population to adapt successfully to the new situation, and the degree to which new types of social groups can develop to fulfill the function originally played by the family and kinship group will in large part determine how deleterious such changes are.

Although the changing disease patterns are likely to occur in all developing countries undergoing rapid population growth, the *specific* diseases constituting this pattern are likely to vary. The particular diseases which will be most prevalent will depend not so much on the degree and rate of crowding as on the constitution (both genetic and experiential) of the population and the nature of physical and biological agents to which the population is, or has been, exposed.

Finally, if the harmful effects of crowding on health are to be prevented and an orderly and healthful rate of population growth to be planned, the processes through which crowding is related to health need to be understood better than they are today. As indicated earlier, the relatively simplistic notion that crowding exerts its deleterious effects solely through facilitating the interpersonal spread of disease agents is no longer adequate to explain the known phenomena. A more appropriate formulation would seem feasible if we recognize that increased population density increases the importance of the social environment as a determinant of physiological response to various stimuli, including potentially disease-producing agents; that within this social environment the quality of social interactions and position within the group seem to be important factors; and that, given time, adaptation to these social changes can and does occur, but the newcomers to the situation will always be the segment of the population at highest risk.

References

1. Taylor, Ian, and John Knowelden, *Principles of Epidemiology*. Boston: Little, Brown, and Co., 1957. p. 199.
2. *Vital Statistics of the United States, 1939-40 Supplement*. Washington: Dept. of Health, Education, and Welfare.
3. *Vital Statistics of the United States, 1950*. Washington: Bureau of the Census, 1964. Vol. III.
4. *Statistical Abstract of the United States*. Washington: Bureau of the Census, 1964.
5. *Vital Statistics of the United States, 1960*. Washington: Bureau of the Census, 1963. Vol. II.
6. *Vital Statistics of the United States, 1966*. Washington: Bureau of the Census, 1968. Vol. II.
7. Author's calculations of Linear Projections of Population Changes, 1950-1960.
8. DuBos, Rene, "The Human Environment in Technological Societies," The Rockefeller Foundation, 1968. pp. 1-11.
9. The Registrar General's Decennial Supplement England and Wales, 1961, Area Mortality Tables. London: Her Majesty's Stationery Office, 1967.
10. Shapiro, Sam, et al., *Infant, Perinatal, Maternal, and Childhood Mortality in the United States*. Vital and Statistical Monographs APHA. Harvard Univ. Press, 1968.
11. Dauer, Carl C., et al., *Infectious Diseases*. Vital and Statistical Monographs APHA. Cambridge, Mass.: Harvard Univ. Press, 1968.

12. Grigg, E. R. N., "The Arcana of Tuberculosis," *Am Rev Tuberc*, 78, 1958. pp. 151-172, 426-453, 583-603.
13. Brett, G. Z., and B. Benjamin, "Housing and Tuberculosis in a Mass Radiography Survey," *Brit J Prev Soc Med*, Vol. 11, No. 1, January 1957. p. 7.
14. Holmes, Thomas H., "Multidiscipline Studies of Tuberculosis," Phineas J. Sparer, ed., *Personality Stress and Tuberculosis*. New York: International Univ. Press, 1956. pp. 65-152, Ch. 6.
15. Stewart, G. T., and A. W. Voors, "Determinants of Sickness in Marine Recruits," *Amer J Epidem*, Vol. 89, No. 3, May 14, 1968. pp. 254-263.
16. Kessler, Alexander, "Interplay between Social Ecology and Physiology, Genetics, and Population Dynamics." Unpublished doctoral thesis, Rockefeller Univ. 1966.
17. DuBos, Rene, *Man Adapting*. New Haven: Yale Univ. Press, 1965. pp. 164-165.
18. Welch, Bruce L., "Psychophysiological Response to the Mean Level of Environmental Stimulation. A Theory of Environmental Integration," *Symposium on Medical Aspects of Stress in the Military Climate*. Washington: Walter Reed Army Institute of Research, April 22-24, 1964. pp. 39-96.
19. Donninson, C. P., "Blood Pressure in the African Native," *Lancet*, 1, 1929. p. 56.
20. Saunders, G. M., "Blood Pressure in Yucatans," *Am J Med Sci*, 185, 1933, p. 843.
21. Krakower, A., "Blood Pressure of Chinese Living in Eastern Canada," *Amer Heart J*, 9, 1933. p. 376.
22. Kilborn, L. G., "A Note on the Blood Pressure of Primitive Races with Special Reference to the Maio of Kiweichaw," *Chinese J Physiol*, 11, 1937. p. 135.
23. Kean, B. H., "Blood Pressure Studies on West Indians and Panamanians Living on Isthmus of Panama," *Arch Intern Med*, 68, 1941. p. 466.
24. Levine, V. E., "The Blood Pressure of Eskimos," *Fed Proc*, 1, 1942. p. 121.
25. Kean, B. H., "Blood Pressure of the Cuna Indians," *Amer J Trop Med*, 24, 1944 (Supplement). p. 341.
26. Alexander, F., "A Medical Survey of the Aleutian Islands." *New Eng J Med*, 240, 1949. p. 1035.
27. Bibile, S. W., et al., "Variation with Age and Sex of Blood Pressure and Pulse Rate for Ceylonese Subjects," *Ceylon J Med Sci*, 6, 1949. p. 80.
28. Murril, R. I., "A Blood Pressure Study of the Natives of Ponape Island," *Hum Biol*, 21, 1949. p. 47.
29. Murphy, W., "Some Observations on Blood Pressures in the Humid Tropics," *New Zeal Med J*, 54, 1955. p. 64.
30. Whyte, W. M., "Body Fat and Blood Pressure of Natives of New Guinea: Reflections on Essential Hypertension," *Aust Ann Med*, 7, 1958. p. 36.

31. Padmayati, S., and S. Gupta, "Blood Pressure Studies in Rural and Urban Groups in Delhi," *Circulation*, 19, 1959. p. 395.
32. Abrahams, D. G., C. A. Able, and G. Bernart, "Systemic Blood Pressure in a Rural West African Community," *W Afr Med J*, 9, 1960. p. 45.
33. Kaminer, B., and W. P. Lutz, "Blood Pressure in Bushmen of the Kalahari Desert," *Circulation*, 22, 1960. p. 289.
34. Lowell, R. R. H., I. Maddocks, and G. W. Rogerson, "The Casual Arterial Pressure of Fijians and Indians in Fiji," *Aust Ann Med*, 9, 1960. p. 4.
35. Scotch, N. A., "A Preliminary Report on the Relation of Sociocultural Factors to Hypertension among the Zulu," *Ann NY Acad Sci*, 86, 1960. p. 1000.
36. Lowenstein, F. W., "Blood Pressure in Relation to Age and Sex in the Tropics and Subtropics: A Review of the Literature and an Investigation in Two Tribes of Brazil Indians," *Lancet*, 1, 1961. p. 389.
37. Maddocks, I. "Possible Absence of Hypertension in Two Complete Pacific Island Populations," *Lancet*, 2, 1961. p. 396.
38. Fulmer, H. S., and R. W. Roberts, "Coronary Heart Disease among the Navajo Indians," *Ann Intern Med*, 59, 1963. pp. 740-764.
39. Scotch, N. A., "Sociocultural Factors in the Epidemiology of Zulu Hypertension," *Amer J Public Health*, 52, 1963. pp. 1205-1213.
40. Scotch, Norman A., and H. Jack Geiger, "The Epidemiology of Essential Hypertension: II. Psychologic and Sociocultural Factors in Etiology," *J Chron Dis*, 16, 1963. pp. 1183-1213.
41. Cruz-Coke, R., R. Etcheverry, and R. Nagel, "Influence of Migration on Blood Pressure of Easter Islanders." *Lancet*, 1, 1964. pp. 697-699.
42. Mann, G. V., et al., "Cardiovascular Disease in the Masai," *J Atheroscler Res*, 4, 1964. p. 289.
43. Hoobler, S. W., et al., "Influence of Nutrition and 'Acculturation' on the Blood Pressure Levels and Changes with Age in the Highland Guatamalan Indian," *Circulation*, 32, 1965. p. 4.
44. Mason, John W., "Psychoendocrine Approaches in Stress Research," *Medical Aspects of Stress in the Military Climate*. Washington: U.S. Government Printing Office, 1965.
45. Paffenberger, Ralph S., Jr., et al., "Trends in Death Rates from Hypertensive Disease in Memphis, Tennessee, 1920-1960," *J Chronic Dis*, 19, 1966. pp. 847-856.
46. Christenson, William N., and Lawrence R. Hinkle, Jr., "Differences in Illness and Prognostic Signs in Two Groups of Young Men," *JAMA*, 177, 1961. pp. 247-253.
47. Cassel, John, and H. A. Tyroler, "Epidemiological Studies of Culture Change: I. Health Status and Recency of Industrialization." *Arch Environ Health*, 3, 1961. p. 25.
48. Haenszel, William, Donald B. Loveland, and Monroe G. Sirken, "Lung-Cancer Mortality as Related to Residence and Smoking Histories," *J Nat Cancer Inst*, 28, 1962. pp. 947-1001.

49. Dunham, H. Warren, "Social Structures and Mental Disorders: Competing Hypotheses of Explanation," *Milbank Mem Fund Quart*, 39, 1961. pp. 259-310.
50. Mishler, Elliot G., and Norman A. Scotch, "Sociocultural Factors in the Epidemiology of Schizophrenia: A Review." *Psychiatry*, 26, 1963. pp. 315-351.
51. Tillman, W. A., and G. E. Hobbs, "Social Background of Accident Free and Accident Repeaters," *Amer J Psychiat*, 106, 1949. p. 321.
52. Durkheim, Emile, *Suicide*. Glencoe, Ill.: The Free Press, 1957.
53. Thurlow, H. John, "General Susceptibility to Illness: A Selective Review," *Canad Med Ass J*, 97, 1967. pp. 1-8.

XIII

Abortion in the Demographic Transition

Abdel R. Omran

Regulation of the size and distribution of population has been practiced by human communities since time immemorial. The availability of food, the hostility of the environment, and the desire for life's conveniences continue to impinge upon man in his collective setting. In this age-old struggle between large numbers and limited resources, man has been aided by involuntary forces such as epidemics, famines, and wars; however, these scourges alone did not adequately mitigate population pressures. Voluntary methods practiced in an effort to temper the population problem have a long tradition.

Since ancient times, voluntary fertility regulation has included infanticide, abortion, abstinence, and prolonged lactation, as well as attempts at conception control of both a magical and rational nature. From his careful review of the medical history of birth control, Himes (1) cites abortion as the chief means of fertility control in primitive societies. He reports that the earliest known written abortifacient recipe is a Chinese one more than 4,600 years old. Abortion was known in ancient Egypt, Greece, and Rome (1, 2). Several Greek philosophers, including Aristotle (3), sanctioned abortion to limit family size.

Hippocrates, on the other hand, created reluctance among physicians to induce abortion and imbued certain instances of its practice with a sense of criminality (2, p. 459; 4). This reluctance remains with us even today, and the question of "criminality" is still disputed.

Intriguing questions about the impact of abortion on fertility have been raised in recent years. During the past few centuries a successful transition from high death rates and high birth rates to low death rates and low birth rates has occurred in western countries. This *demographic transition* (5) accompanied social, economic, and technological developments. Starting with a gradual decline in mortality, it was followed many decades later by a gradual decline in fertility.

Abdel R. Omran is Associate Professor of Epidemiology, School of Public Health, University of North Carolina.

In other parts of the world, particularly since World War II, the death rate has precipitously declined mainly because of imported medical and other technologies. However, fertility has generally remained at a high level in these developing countries. The inevitable result has been an unprecedentedly high rate of population growth, called the *transitional growth* stage of demographic change (6), in contrast to the *posttransitional*, or *modern*, stage that has been reached by western countries. The problem facing the developing countries is to accomplish the transition from high to low fertility quickly enough to enhance their economic and social development. Whether they can make this transition without the help of induced abortion is a worldwide concern.

Though documentation is not readily available, it is believed that abortion played a significant role in lowering fertility during the demographic transition in many western societies. More conclusive evidence linking abortion and demographic transition exists for Japan, where an accelerated transition from high to low fertility occurred within an unprecedentedly short time span.

This paper will consider some of the major issues concerning induced abortion and demographic change in both developed and developing countries. In particular, the following questions are considered:

1. When developing societies are highly motivated to accomplish or accelerate the transition from high to low fertility, do they usually pass through a phase in which induced abortion becomes a popular method of fertility control?

2. In other words, what should be anticipated when *low fertility determinants* prevail? Will widespread practice of induced abortion occur in response to increased modernization and urbanization?

3. If large-scale induced abortion is somehow forcibly suppressed, what will the effects be? Will the demographic transition be retarded? Will women resort to illegal abortion despite the risks?

4. Can the phase of large-scale induced abortion be avoided, or controlled, in developing countries without slowing down their demographic transition? How effective are contraceptive programs in lowering the incidence of abortion?

5. In countries that have achieved a low fertility level, what success can be attributed to the liberalization of abortion laws? Should high fertility countries liberalize their abortion laws as well?

For the purpose of discussing these issues, countries are arrayed in two main categories: transitional and posttransitional. Then they are further divided according to their abortion laws—restrictive or liberalized, as shown in Table 1.

Although there are difficulties inherent in making international comparisons, the effort here is to put the available statistics together as meaningfully as possible. It is only fair to admit at the onset that in many countries

TABLE 1

Abortion Laws in Transitional and Posttransitional Countries, 1970

Abortion Laws	Stage of Demographic Development	
	Transitional	Posttransitional
Restrictive laws	Asian countries except Japan African countries Latin American countries	Northern American countries[a] Western European countries Southern European countries Oceanic countries
Liberalized laws	Tunisia (since 1966) Mainland China (1960's) Potentially India (1970?) Potentially Chile (1970?)	Northern European countries (since 1930's) Eastern European countries including U.S.S.R. (since 1955) Japan (since 1948)

[a]By mid-1970 a number of states in the United States had liberalized their abortion laws in varying degrees. Included were New York, Maryland, Hawaii, North Carolina, Georgia, California.

abortion statistics are incomplete, unreliable, or both. Whenever possible, data from the less developed countries are used; insofar as appropriate, data from the more developed countries are analyzed as well.

THE PREVALENCE OF INDUCED ABORTION IN TRANSITIONAL SOCIETIES

It is the author's opinion that when developing societies are highly motivated to accelerate their transition from high to low fertility, induced abortion becomes such a popular method of fertility control that it becomes a kind of epidemic. In examining this proposition, both posttransitional and transitional countries are considered. Japan is cited to illustrate possible trends of abortion amidst rapid and profound demographic, social, and economic change. The paucity of abortion data for the period in which other developed countries passed through the transitional stage in the 18th and 19th centuries, however, precludes an examination of demographic correlates of abortion in western societies.

Similarly, we have almost no data on the incidence of abortion in developing countries before the transitional period—before death rates began to decline. Furthermore, current statistics are often inadequate. However, recent studies to show a high prevalence of induced abortion in countries where fertility remains high or is just beginning to decline. In the opinion of investigators and many government officials, the current prevalence is higher than it was in the pretransitional period. Furthermore, possible trends of abortion during the transitional growth stage can be discerned in a few societies, such as Chile and Korea.

Japan's Transition

Although Japan is now considered a developed nation, her recent demographic history illustrates what can occur in a developing country which is propelled through a sequence of accelerated social, economic, and demographic transitions (7). During Japan's transition, fertility and mortality underwent profound changes within the relatively short time in which Japan accomplished this transition.

In Figure 1 the Japanese and Swedish transitions are compared to contrast a recent transition with an earlier one. From 1920 to 1948, the Japanese birth rate remained at a fairly high level, around 35 per 1,000 population. During the same period the death rate declined from 25.4 in 1920 to 14.6 per 1,000 in 1947. The obvious result was a tremendous increase in the Japanese population; it rose from 55,391,000 in 1920 to 78,101,000 in 1947—an overall increase of 41 percent.

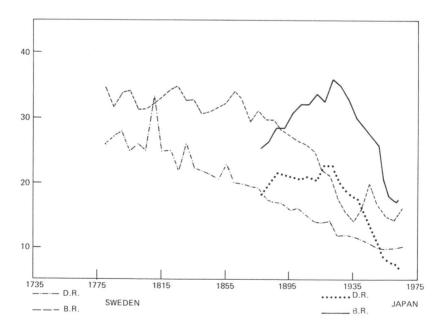

Figure 1. The demographic transition in Sweden and Japan (B.R. = birth rate; D.R. = death rate).
Sources: (9, 10).

A significant change took place in Japan immediately after World War II. Between 1947 and 1957, a phenomenal decline in the birth rate was registered; live births dropped from 35 per 1,000 in 1947 to 17 in 1957—a decline of 50 percent in only 10 years. Such a dramatic decline in fertility is extraordinary in the demographic history of the world. Although contraception has been used in Japan for some time, abortion was the main underlying cause of fertility decline during this period. According to Koya,* the drop in the birth rate was due 80 percent to abortion and 20 percent to contraception.

Even though comprehensive statistics are not available for the prewar period, it does seem evident that abortion was never absent from the natality scene in Japan. Before 1948, it appears that a less spectacular incidence of abortion, together with contraceptive efforts, was responsible for keeping the birth rate in the mid-30's rather than in the mid-40's, as in the present-day developing nations.

Following World War II, abortions reached the high proportion of 716.3 per 1,000 live births in 1957. Table 2 gives the number of legal abortions and

TABLE 2

Trends in Births and Legal Abortions in Japan, 1949-1965

Year	Live Births (in 1,000's)	Legal Abortions (in 1,000's)	Birth Rate per 1,000 Population	Legal Abortions per 1,000 Live Births
1949	2,696.6	246.1	33.2	91.3
1950	2,337.5	489.1	28.2	209.2
1951	2,137.7	638.4	25.4	298.6
1952	2,005.2	798.2	23.5	398.1
1953	1,868.0	1,068.1	21.5	571.8
1954	1,769.6	1,143.1	20.1	646.0
1955	1,730.7	1,170.1	19.4	676.1
1956	1,665.3	1,159.3	18.5	696.2
1957	1,566.7	1,122.3	17.2	716.3
1958	1,649.8	1,128.2	18.0	683.8
1959	1,622.8	1,098.9	17.5	677.2
1960	1,603.0	1,063.2	17.2	663.3
1961	1,586.4	1,035.0	16.9	652.4
1962	1,613.1	985.4	17.0	610.9
1963	1,657.4	955.1	17.3	576.3
1964	1,714.7	878.7	17.7	512.5
1965	1,821.8	843.2	18.6	462.8

Source: (12,13).

*Cited in (8).

their ratio to live births. These officially reported figures, however, are estimated to represent only one third to one half of the actual number of
abortions performed (8).

Figure 2 shows the number of legal abortions per 1,000 live births between
1949 and 1965 for several areas. Although insufficient data preclude ascer-

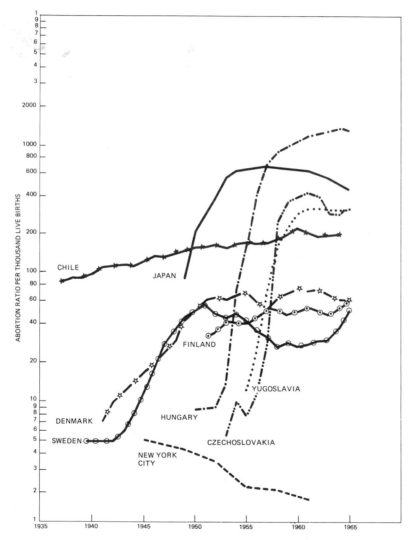

Figure 2. Abortion ratio per 1,000 live births, legal for countries, therapeutic for
New York City.

Sources: Japan, Table 2; Chile, Table 3; New York City, Table 16; European countries, Table 17.

taining the origin of the Japanese curve, we may infer that a moderate, but undetected, wave of abortion occurred before 1949, when the number of legal abortions already exceeded 250,000.

Numerous reasons are advanced for the high prevalence of abortions in postwar Japan. Koya (11) lists the following examples: (a) the amendment of the 1948 Eugenic Protection Law which legalized abortion for medical and social reasons; (b) the moral decay of society after the war; (c) the attitude of physicians toward their patients; (d) the response of the people to the government's efforts to promote family planning and to limit family size. Muramatsu (14) adds that the truly significant fact lies in the strength of motivation among the general public to adjust the number of children to environment.

In Japan abortion is permitted if a pregnancy or delivery threatens the health of the mother because of her physical or financial condition. The assertation that another child will be hard to feed is enough reason for terminating pregnancy. Abortion can be obtained at the cost of about 5 dollars at facilities in both hospitals and specialized abortion centers (8).

It is not possible to assess in exact figures the number of births averted by induced abortion in Japan. However, some detailed studies attempt to determine the extent to which induced abortion was responsible for reducing births during the 1945-53 period. Muramatsu (15) took into account the number of married women of fertile age and their reproductive activities, the level of their fecundity, and their use of contraception and sterilization. Then he used an elaborate procedure to calculate the number of births prevented by induced abortion in 1955. He arrived at three estimates of the expected numbers of births that would have occurred in Japan in 1955 had there been no induced abortion—3.8, 3.4, or 3.1 million live births, both legitimate and illegitimate. The actual number reported for 1955 was 1.73 million. Therefore, 2.1, 1.7, or 1.4 million births were prevented by induced abortions. On the average then, a 50 percent reduction of anticipated births in 1955 is attributed to induced abortion.

It is highly unlikely that the contemporary developing nations will follow the Japanese and effect a dramatic lowering of fertility within such a short period for the following reasons:

1. Japan was more modernized before the war than are most contemporary developing nations.

2. Although Japan had her industrial revolution within the 20th century, her industrial development has been far ahead of other countries in Asia, Africa, and Latin America.

3. Even before the industrial revolution, the fertility level in Japan was not as high as it is in most developing countries today. Japan began her transition with a birth rate of about 35 per 1,000 population. A majority of the developing countries still have a birth rate of 40 to 50 per 1,000.

4. Since the war, a wide use of abortion has been legal in Japan. The developing countries have yet to accept induced abortion as a legitimate method of fertility control, with the exception of Tunisia and possibly mainland China.

Nevertheless, it appears that the Japanese example will inspire countries that wish to enhance their development by slowing down population growth. Some may be willing to accept induced abortion as a practical and legitimate means of fertility control.

Chile

Chile has less adequate abortion data than Japan; however, hospital admission statistics beginning in 1937 indicate an increasing number of abortions in proportion to deliveries.

As shown in Table 3, induced abortion increased tremendously in the period from 1937 to 1964. According to Chilean hospital data for the 24 years ending in 1960, the number of deliveries increased by 1.8 times, whereas the corresponding figure for postabortion hospital admissions increase was 4.4.

The actual occurrence of induced abortion is, of course, much higher, as interview studies as early as 1938 reveal (16-20). These studies are based on selected hospital samples and clearly indicate the widespread prevalence of abortion. (See Table 4, Part A.) More recent studies, based on better sampling procedures, also point to a higher incidence. These studies are summarized in Table 4, Part B (21-24).

Plaza and Briones (25) studied the medical care implications of abortion cases in Santiago and provincial hospitals. The major conclusions summarized in Table 4, Part C, underline the gravity of the abortion problem in a country with limited resources.

In view of the increasing incidence of induced abortion, it may be surprising that the Chilean birth rate has changed only slightly—from 34.6 in 1936 to 32.8 in 1964. Several factors can be mentioned to explain these figures. First, the official birth rate for 1936 may have been subject to underreporting; the actual level probably was higher. Second, the death rate declined 56 percent—from 25.3 in 1936 to 11.2 in 1964; it is likely that improved survivorship together with generally improved health tended to increase fertility by extending the exposure period and by enhancing fecundity. Furthermore, age-distribution changes which have expanded the reproductive-aged segment of the population pyramid are not reflected in the crude birth rate measure which is being compared for the years 1936 and 1964. For these and related reasons, Requena and Monreal's argument that had it not been for abortion the birth rate in Chile for the last 25 years would have been over 40 per 1,000

TABLE 3

Births and Abortion Cases Treated in Chilean Hospitals and Clinics, 1937-1964

Year	Live Births	Abortions	Birth Rate per 1,000 Population	Abortion Ratio per 1,000 Live Births
1935				
1936				
1937	153,354	12,963	32.9[a]	84
1938	154,927	13,982		90
1939	163,589	14,730		90
1940	166,593	16,254	33.4	97
1941	165,004	18,265	32.6	110
1942	170,222	19,242	33.1	113
1943	172,095	20,009	33.1	116
1944	174,864	19,449	33.2	111
1945	178,292	21,581	33.3	121
1946	175,686	23,619	32.4	134
1947	186,784	24,535	33.8	131
1948	189,236	26,448	33.7	139
1949	189,719	28,514	33.2	150
1950	188,323	29,512	32.4	156
1951	191,332	30,571	32.4	159
1952	195,470	32,862	33.6	165
1953	211,808	33,862	34.6	159
1954	209,920	35,748	33.6[b]	170
1955	225,352	39,340	35.0[b]	174
1956	237,268	41,829	36.0	170
1957	262,746	44,945	36.9	171
1958	262,759	49,041	36.0	186
1959	249,799	49,448	35.8	198
1960	256,674	57,368	34.9[b]	223
1961	269,263	55,435	34.0	206
1962	274,440	53,516	34.4[b]	195
1963	277,144	55,873	33.7	202
1964	275,323	56,391	32.8	204

[a]Rate for 1935-39.
[b]Provisional

Sources: (9, 26, 27).

for the whole country and over 50 for the lower socioeconomic groups seems sound (28).

Korea

According to a recent government study (29), the percentage of Korean women experiencing induced abortion rose from 7 to 14 percent between

TABLE 4

Abortion Statistics for Chile: A Summary of Studies

Authors	Sample	Abortions per 100 Pregnancies	Percent of Abortions That Were Provoked	Remarks
A. Hospital material (interviews)				
Matus, 1938 (16)	(a) 484 maternity ward	40.7		Group had 787 abortions of which 234 or 29.7% were followed by admission to hospital
	(b) 816 women	57		
	(c) 140 domestic servants			
Romero & Vildosola, 1952 (17)	3,038 admissions for delivery or abortion or Maternal Clinic attendants	26.5	67	
Manubens, 1952 (18)	1,000 admissions for abortion	48	67	
Mena, 1952 (19)	1,000 in four Obstetrical Departments in Santiago		52	
Walsen, 1954 (20)	3,000 records of abortions admitted (1950-54) in one Maternity Hospital in Santiago			Accounted for 50% of admissions

B. Community studies

Study	Sample		Findings
CELADE Fertility Survey, 1959 (Tabah & Samuel-1961) (21)	Groups in urban (greater) Santiago		1 abortion out of 4 in married women and 1 out of 3 in broken or common law homes
Armijo & Monreal, 1965 (22)	3,776 random sample of child-bearing women 1,890 from Santiago 1,235 from Concepción (North) 651 from Antofagasta (South)	16 22.6 26.2 14.9 26.9	23% of all women had a positive history of abortion. The one-year incidence of abortion was 4.2 per 100 women for the total sample
Requina, 1965a (23) Requina, 1965b (24)	580 random sample of child-bearing, primarily proletarian	23	

C. Medical care studies

Study	Sample		Findings
Plaza & Briones, 1963 (25)	4 general hospitals & 4 emergency departments in Santiago & 5 hospitals in provinces		Abortion accounted for (a) 8.1% of all admissions, (b) 24.3 per 100 deliveries in Santiago & 34.3 in provincial hospitals, (c) 35% of all emergency surgical operations, (d) 17.7% of all blood transfusions, (e) 26.7% of total blood volume in emergency depts. in Santiago

1964 and 1967. The prevalence of abortion was much higher in the urban areas, rising from 15 to 28 percent over the 4-year period. A similar, nearly doubled increase in abortion experience occurred in rural areas where the percentage of women experiencing abortion rose from 4 to 7 percent. During the same period an increase in contraceptive use was noticed, in which the percentage of users rose from 9 to 20 percent of married women.

Individual reports confirm these high rates of abortion and provide more details. In a sample survey among married women in Seoul, Hong (30) found a total of 12,400 pregnancies which resulted in 10,200 live births, 1,500 induced abortions, and 700 spontaneous abortions. The ratio of reported induced abortions was 121 per 1,000 pregnancies and 147 per 1,000 live births. Of those reporting induced abortion, 47 percent had had one and 53 percent, two or more. Of the total reported abortions, 93 percent were induced in private clinics, 4 percent in hospitals, and 3 percent at home. The rates were higher for wives of white-collar workers and for those with large families. The author reported also that rates of abortion throughout the country have risen in recent years. The same author in a later survey (31) found that 5 percent of the women in rural areas, as compared to 25 percent in Seoul, reported having had at least one induced abortion. Of these abortions, 63 percent were performed in cities, 30 percent in towns, and 7 percent in rural areas. Of the women interviewed, 96 percent gave family planning as the reason for induced abortion—90 percent for family limitation and 6 percent for child spacing.

In another study in Seoul, Koh and Song (32) report the ratio of abortions to live births to be 1 to 3. The ratio, it should be noted, is twice that reported by the Ministry for South Korea. While these studies generally indicate a much higher incidence of induced abortion in Korea's urban areas, no significant difference between urban and rural areas was found in a 1966 KAP (knowledge, attitude, practice) survey investigating opinions about legalizing abortion. Of those who expressed an opinion, about 72 percent favored legalized abortion with little difference between urban and rural areas (33).

Other Developing Countries

There is evidence to suggest that the beginnings of a great wave, perhaps even an "epidemic," of induced abortion is already under way in many countries that are experiencing rapid population growth. Despite the apparent limitations of the data from these areas, the gravity of the situation can be demonstrated.

In India, for example, an analysis of pregnancy histories of 5,912 women visiting family planning clinics in New Delhi (34) revealed an average ratio of 9 abortions per 100 pregnancies. Higher rates were observed for women who were more highly educated and whose husbands were employed as officials in the government and earned more than 300 rupees a month.

In Turkey, a study showed that 39.4 percent of the 496 women coming for contraceptive advice in Ankara Maternity Hospital had had induced abortions at some time in their past. More than half had had more than one abortion (35). The report states that some 12,000 maternal deaths occur annually in Turkey because of induced abortion. This seems to be a high estimate, however.

In the United Arab Republic, a sample survey of a rural area in Alexandria governorate found an abortion ratio of 77 per 1,000 live births. Of 3,998 interviewed, 7.1 percent admitted having had an abortion at some time in their lives (36).

In Kenya, Eraj (37) reported that Kenya statistics for 1964 indicate that the number of deaths from abortion was almost half that attributed to malaria. He urges the medical profession to recognize unplanned pregnancy as a social disease which should be dealt with professionally in much the same manner as other social diseases.

In Latin American countries other than Chile, high abortion incidence also exists, as shown in Table 5.

TABLE 5

Induced Abortion Rates in Seven Latin American Cities

	Mexico City	Bogotá	San José	Caracas	Panama	Rio de Janeiro	Buenos Aires
Estimated abortions per 1,000 live births	184	130	191	197	148	167	333
Reported abortions per 1,000 woman-years of exposure	37	26	33	34	24	21	21

Source: (40).

Low Fertility Determinants and Abortion

The widespread occurrence of induced abortion in a developing society is symptomatic of the intense motivation to limit family size which is precipitated by certain *low fertility determinants*. In this discussion three low fertility determinants are singled out for study: the increasing economic liabilities of an additional child; the emancipation of women and their increased use in the labor force; urbanization and modernization. The basic framework used here to investigate possible linkages among abortion, the motivation to limit family size, and specific low fertility determinants was drawn from a conceptual scheme proposed by Spengler for the analysis of the factors affecting the decision to have children. In this scheme, the decision to have an additional child, or voluntary fertility constraint, is a function of three variables: the preference system, the price system, and income (38).

Heer (39) defines these terms broadly. The *preference system* describes the value which a married couple places on additional children relative to all other goals they strive to achieve without the child; the *price system* indicates the net costs of an additional child relative to the costs of attaining all other goals without an additional child; and *income*, the total resources expendable for goal pursuit, includes not only monetary income but the total amount of time and energy that a couple has for pursuit of all their possible goals in life. Heer postulates that the probability of deciding to have an additional child is directly related to the anticipated value of this child and the total resources available for all goals and inversely related to the predicted cost of an additional child. The configuration of these variable relationships determines whether an additional child is considered an asset or liability.

The Increasing Economic Liabilities of an Additional Child

The social and economic changes in developing countries—measured by their impact upon the preference system, the price system, and income—have brought about a general reversal in attitudes toward children as economic assets. In the past the assurance of a surviving son, the economic gain from child labor, and the guarantee that family members would be cared for in their old age have held high priority in the preference system. These norms have encouraged high fertility in transitional societies. Demographic and social changes, such as declining infant mortality, child welfare, compulsory education, and social security schemes, have gradually replaced traditional values with small family norms and low fertility.

Concomitantly, changes in the price system have tended to negate the economic advantages of the large family. The rising costs of housing as a frequent side effect of urbanization, longer periods of child dependency as the result of an expanded educational system, as well as the increasing cost of child care for working mothers, are additional factors which may cause the birth of another child to be an economic liability.

The economic pressure of additional children upon the family has been instrumental in initiating efforts to limit family size. Resorting to abortion continues to be a sure method of terminating an unwanted pregnancy, even though traditional and modern methods of contraception may be used.

Economic motivation to limit family size has been invoked as the reason for abortion in many countries, regardless of the type of abortion law. Nozue (41) reported that 63 percent of all abortions in Japan are performed for socioeconomic reasons. A more intensive study by Koya (42) indicated that

83 percent of the abortions among 1,382 Japanese women were due to fears of difficulty in household financing; the remaining 17 percent were attributed to health reasons.

Studies from eastern Europe and the U.S.S.R. show that women cite low income, inadequate housing, excessive numbers of children, and interference with the mother's work as reasons for induced abortion (43-47).

Studies from France and Sweden revealed that economic indications were responsible for well over half of all abortions (48, 49).

The situation is much the same for Latin America. Rice-Wray (50) reported that among 797 abortions performed among 1,000 interviewed women in Mexico, 46.2 percent were sought as a result of economic pressures compared with 19.9 percent for health reasons. In Chile studies conducted in Santiago, Concepción, and Antofagasta by the Department of Epidemiology at the School of Public Health (22, 51), indicated that for the three cities 48 percent of the recorded abortions were due to economic reasons, 10.7 percent for health reasons, and 10.6 percent because of large family size. In Santiago these figures were 56.5 percent, 7.2 percent, and 8.7 percent respectively. Figure 3 illustrates the relative proportions of induced abortion attributed to various indications in a number of countries.

Emancipation of Women

With increasing frequency, fervor, and logic it is maintained that too many children interfere with the life and leisure of an emancipated woman, particularly if the woman is gainfully employed outside the home. For many coun-

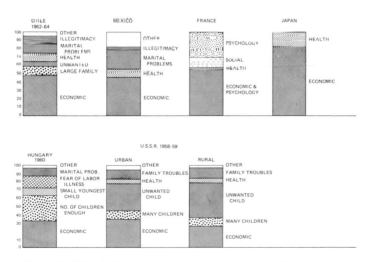

Figure 3. Major indications for induced abortion in various countries.
Sources: (22, 42, 51-53).

tries in which the growing liberation of women has intensified motivation to limit family size, abortion has become a fundamental female right. Baird (54) calls abortion the "fifth freedom."

In eastern Europe this concept is written into justifications for the liberalization of abortion laws. The reasons given in 1955 were twofold. First, it was alleged that there were a large number of abortions being performed illegally, outside hospitals and under unsanitary conditions. Second, the rewriting of abortion laws was in better accord with the Leninist doctrine that no woman should be forced to bear a child she does not desire (55). Consequently, abortion was granted upon request in the Soviet Union, Hungary, Bulgaria, and Romania (56). Many women elsewhere do not find procedures so permissive; nevertheless, many do procure abortions, illegally, or legally on psychiatric or sociomedical grounds.

Two aspects of the emancipation of women are worthy of special mention: educational level and economic activity outside the home. However, these two factors are complex and consequently difficult to isolate in attempting to assess their effects on the dynamics of abortion.

Education of Women. Although more highly educated women tend to use the more effective contraceptives and to practice contraception more effectively, there is still a direct association between the level of a woman's education and her tendency to resort to abortion. Apparently, women with higher education are more highly motivated to limit their fertility by either contraception or abortion.

Studies from Taiwan, as shown in Figure 4, found that the higher the education of women, the higher the probability of their experiencing abortion. In India (34) and Korea (31) investigators reached similar conclusions.

In Lebanon, an interview sample of women who were Lebanese nationals, married only once and for more than 5 years, found that for both Muslims and Christians (Maronite and other Catholic) the educated admitted higher induced abortion rates than the uneducated (58). In the city sample the educated Muslims had higher reported rates than the educated Christians; the reverse was true for the uneducated groups. Both the percentage of pregnancies ending in abortion and the percentage of woman married over 10 years who resorted to abortion were higher among the more educated women regardless of their religion or place of residence.

A study from Cali, Colombia (59), concludes that university graduates have the highest abortion rates. Among primary school graduates, there was a rate of 12.5 abortions per 100 pregnancies; for university graduates, 33.5.

In Japan 2,811 women were questioned regarding their experience with induced abortion. Of the highly educated women 46.5 percent said they had resorted to induced abortion, but only 37 percent of the less educated had done so (60).

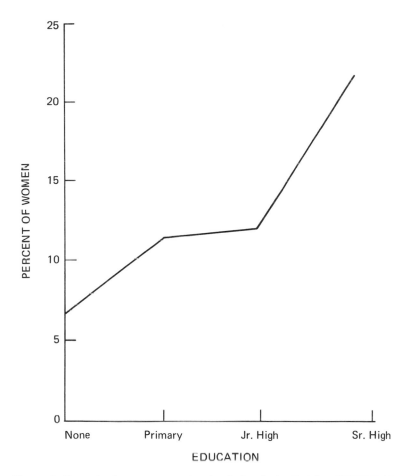

Figure 4. Percent of women experiencing induced abortion by educational level, Taiwan, 1967.
Source: (57).

In the United States, data on therapeutic abortion can be misleading. A strong relationship between educational achievement and abortion is generally reported, but the better educated are generally more able to buy their way into a legal hospital through their private physicians. The definite social discrimination practiced in American hospitals has been revealed in a number of studies.*

In regard to the total abortion picture in the United States, studies by the Institute for Sex Research reported by Gebhard et al. (61) have yielded inconclusive findings as to the association between abortion and educational

*See section of this chapter, "The Need for Liberalizing Abortion Laws."

level. Among the unmarried females in the sample, higher educational level is clearly associated with higher incidence of abortion. Among married women, however, the highest rates of induced abortion were reported for those who did not complete a high school education. Whether one can draw a general conclusion from these findings regarding the total population of married women in the United States is questionable, because the sample was deemed unrepresentative by a statistical committee in 1955 (62).

Women in the Labor Force. Numerous studies from various countries in eastern Europe and the U.S.S.R. have documented the relationship between the participation of women in the labor force and the incidence of induced abortion. For example, a study by Sadvokasova in the U.S.S.R. (54) reported a ratio of abortion of 105.5 per 1,000 working women and only 41.5 per 1,000 for the nonemployed. A study of legal abortions in a Hungarian hospital found 68 percent involved women working outside the home and only 32 percent involved housewives (63). A Czechoslovakian law, under its "special considerations" clause, permits a woman who is the chief or sole supporter of a family to secure an abortion.

These studies indicate that employment of women is a low fertility determinant. However, in regard to the developing countries, the kind of work available to women is important in terms of lowering fertility. In Pakistan, for example, many women work with their husbands for pay in the fields, or even on roads. This factor cannot be expected to lower fertility unless different types of employment for women emerge.

Modernization and Urbanization

Many aspects of modernization and urbanization that motivate couples to limit family size and therefore to increase abortion have been sketched earlier. Modernization, of course, is a many-faceted process in which economics, education, industrialization, women's roles and rights, urbanization, and limited housing are involved. Although measuring modernization and assessing its association with abortion are beyond the scope of this paper, the findings reported throughout this text do suggest that a wave of induced abortion is characteristic of most modernizing countries. Although data for the premodernizing era are missing, it is most likely that the incidence of induced abortion increases as the process of social, economic, and demographic changes gains momentum. In societies in which modernization factors have intensified desires to limit family size, while the availability and acceptance of effective contraceptive methods are limited, there are numerous implications for induced abortion.

The direct effect of urbanization on the prevalence of abortion has been evaluated in several studies by comparing modernizing communities with traditional ones. Requena (23), for example, reported that the frequency of reported induced abortion increased with the length of stay in Santiago. The same author with Monreal provides a rural-urban comparison of the hospitalized postabortion cases per 1,000 women, aged 15 to 45 (23).

	Santiago	Provinces
1961	37.7	24.3
1962	35.6	22.9
1963	30.7	24.2
1964	40.4	18.1
1965	35.8	26.3

As mentioned earlier, the rural-urban differential in South Korea is such that the urban rate was four to five times greater than the rural (31). In the Japanese studies by Koya's group (64) the average number of induced abortions per 100 women was 120 in rural areas, 130 in medium-sized cities, and 140 in large urban areas.

Dissemination of Small Family-Size Norms

A change from large to small family-size norms accompanied the demographic transition in the West during the 19th and 20th centuries. Although the desired family size in the developing nations of Asia, Africa, and Latin America is still larger than that of countries in Europe and North America, a profound shift in attitude has been taking place, and smaller family-size norms and the concept of family planning are gaining acceptance in even the most traditional of societies. (See Table 6.) Apparently this shift has occurred in response to the cultural, economic, and demographic changes that followed World War II.

A striking observation made from abortion surveys is that many women who resort to abortion usually have, or desire, a relatively small number of children. Furthermore, abortion rates tend to show a sharp increase once the desired family size is reached. This trend can be identified in both developed and less developed countries.

In the developed countries of eastern Europe, for example, where actual and desired family size are relatively low, induced abortion appears to be a major determinant of the minimal disparity between actual and desired family size. In Romania, Mehlan (46) reported that in 1963 between 85 and 97 percent of the women applying for abortion had two or fewer children. In Hungary, Miltenyi (66) reported that women with two or fewer living children compose about 70 percent of the abortion clientele—11 percent with no children, 28 percent with one, and 30 percent with two living children. In Czechoslovakia in 1960, 45.3 percent of the sample explained that the ideal family size had been reached; only 12.7 percent gave illness as the reason

TABLE 6

Desired Family Size in Various Countries

Area	Date	Sex of Respondents	Average Number of Children Desired
Austria	1960	F	2.0
West Germany	1960	F	2.2
Czechoslovakia	1959	F	2.3
Hungary	1958-60	F	2.4
Great Britain	1960	F	2.8
	1946	F	2.1
France	1960	F	2.8
	1956	F	2.2
Japan	1961	F	2.8
Switzerland	1960	F	2.9
Puerto Rico	1953	F	3.0
Italy	1960	F	3.1
Norway	1960	F	3.1
Netherlands	1960	F	3.3
U.S.A.	1960	F	3.3
	1955	F	3.4
	1945	F	3.3
	1941	F	3.0
Ceylon	1963	M	3.2
Jamaica	1957	F	3.4-4.2
Turkey	1963	M	3.8
	1963	F	3.2
South Africa	1957-58[a]	F	3.6
Taiwan	1962-63[a]	F	3.9
	1962[a]	M	3.8
	1962[a]	F	3.8
Thailand	1964	F	3.8
Pakistan	ca 1960[a]	M	4.0
	ca 1960[a]	F	3.9
Chile	1959[a]	F	4.1
Canada	1960	F	4.2
India			
Mysore	1952[a]	M	3.7
	1952[a]	F	4.1
	1952[b]	M	4.7
	1952[b]	F	4.6
Central India	1958	M & F	3.8
New Delhi	1957-60[b]	M	4.1
	1957-60[b]	F	4.2
Indonesia	1961-62[b]	M & F	4.3
Korea	1962[b]	M	4.3
	1962[b]	F	4.4
Sungdong Gu	1964[a]	F	3.3
Ghana	1963[a]	M	5.5
	1963[a]	F	5.1
Philippines	1963	F	5.0

[a]Urban sample.
[b]Rural sample.

Source: (65).

(67). In Bulgaria, Starkaleff (68) reported that 90 percent of the aborted women had two or fewer living children.

Several studies of abortion in less developed countries describe a similar pattern, despite the fact that both actual and desired family size is typically higher in these countries.* The Chilean study by Armijo and Monreal (22) found that 77 percent of the provoked abortions in Santiago were concentrated among women who had three or fewer living children. From a study of abortion in three Colombian communities (Candelaria, Popayan, and Manizales, where 86, 90, and 83 percent respectively of the total women interviewed desired a family size of four or less), Mendoza-Hoyos (59) concluded that after the ideal number of children is reached, the abortion rate shows a sharp increase. The data are summarized in Table 7.

TABLE 7

Percentage Distribution of Induced Abortions According to Number of
Pregnancies and Ideal Family Size

(percent)

| | 1-3 Pregnancies | | | | 4 or more Pregnancies | | | | |
| | Ideal Family Size | | | | Ideal Family Size | | | | |
Community	1-4	5-6	7+	Others	1-4	5-6	7+	Others	Total
Candelaria	4.3	0	0	0	73.9	21.8	0	0	100
Popayán	21	0	0	1.8	72	0	3.4	1.8	100
Manizales	5.4	2.2	2.2	0	87	3.2	0	0	100

Source: (59, Table 9, p. 9).

Similar observations were made in South Korea where Hong (31) reported that 90 percent of the rural women in the sample of 2,084 gave family planning as the reason for induced abortion. Child spacing was given as a reason by 6 percent, and 3 percent gave other reasons. In the survey of India previously cited, Agarwala (34) reported abortion rates of 85 per 1,000 pregnancies during the period when contraceptives were not in use and 175 per 1,000 pregnancies during the subsequent period when contraception was being practiced. Abortion rates rose sharply after clinic attendance, which intensified motivation to limit family size. During the period of follow-up, 295 pregnancies occurred among 3,522 women using prescribed contracep-

---

*Surveys of several local areas in Latin America reveal marked disparities between the actual average number of children, which ranged from 4.1 to 5.4 per woman, and the average number of desired children, which ranged from 2.8 to 5.6. The average difference between actual and desired family size for the eight areas investigated was 1.2; however, in two of the areas the difference was well over 2 (59).

tives. Of these pregnancies, 60 were terminated in abortion, yielding an abortion rate of 203 per 1,000 pregnancies.

The Latin American Center of Demography (CELADE) conducted fertility surveys (40) in 1964 to compare the prevalence of abortion, contraception effectiveness, pregnancy rates, and family size among ever-married women in several Latin American cities. The surveys yield further evidence that induced abortion is a popular method for achieving and maintaining a small family size. As indicated by the findings presented in Table 8, the abortion rate per 1,000 pregnant women is highest in cities where the average family size is low *and* where the percentage of contraceptive users is relatively high. Stressing motivation to limit family size as the crucial underlying factor of both contraceptive use and abortion practice, Requena maintained that the highly motivated women practice contraception and, when this fails, induce abortion.

TABLE 8

Fertility, Contraception, and Abortion Characteristics of Ever-Married
Women in Latin American Capitals, 1964

City	Average Number Children per Woman	Level of Contraceptive Effectiveness[a]	Pregnancy Rate per 1,000 Woman-Years	Abortion Rate per 1,000 Pregnant Women	Live Births per 1,000 Woman-Years
Mexico City	3.27	13.75	237	155	201
Bogotá	3.16	21.80	226	117	200
San José	2.98	27.15	207	161	173
Caracas	2.97	27.40	207	163	173
Panama	2.74	–	186	211	162
Rio de Janeiro	2.25	–	147	141	126
Buenos Aires	1.49	41.75	84	246	63

[a]Level of contraceptive effectiveness was computed by adding the percent of women using effective contraceptives in each city and the percent who used ineffective contraceptives multiplied by 0.50.

Source: (40, Table 1, p. 790).

THE CONSEQUENCES OF SUPPRESSING ABORTION

If resort to induced abortion on a large scale is forcibly suppressed and there are no highly effective contraceptive programs to compensate, the transition from high to low fertility will be retarded. Individuals may nevertheless choose to practice provoked abortion outside the law and under unsanitary conditions, with many attendant risks to maternal health and family welfare.

The Demographic Outlook in Developing Countries

National family planning programs in the developing nations of Asia (except for Taiwan, Korea, Hong Kong, and Singapore), Africa, and Latin America have yet to reduce fertility quickly enough to curtail their rapid population growth significantly. The fertility declines in the four exceptions have led Freedman (69) and other optimists to predict similar successes for other regions. Hauser (70), however, does not share Freedman's optimism. He believes that preconditions for the success of family planning programs existed in Taiwan and other successful regions. As a result of modernization, fertility had begun to fall before the family planning programs were begun. He quotes the United Nations population projections—present fertility rates would yield a world population of 7.5 billion by the year 2000; the medium variant projection reduces it to 6.1 billion.*

Most developing countries are in an awkward situation. Their nationwide family planning programs have operated for a number of years, but they have so far been unable to depress fertility. However, these same countries have maintained great reluctance to accept abortion as a curative approach to a problem for which preventive measures alone have not been satisfactory.

If fertility is not significantly reduced in the developing nations, the demographic and economic transitions will be seriously retarded. The demographic gap (the gap between the death rate and birth rate) will be slow to close. It may even increase. The large family norm will continue. The emancipation of women will be delayed as women continue to be burdened with a large number of children. Sustained high fertility will negate gains made in childhood survival by nurturing the disease cycle characteristic of poor home environments (71).†

It is more likely, however, that individuals will not await official sanctions but will resort to abortion to relieve the demographic tension at the family level. A serious problem is created, both for the women who run a higher risk of complications and death and for hospitals and other health services which must cope with a large number of incomplete and often complicated provoked abortions.

To illustrate the gravity of this situation, it may be helpful to discuss the comparative safety of legal abortion in various countries. Unlike illegal abortions, those which have legal sanction are done under medical supervision.

Comparing the Safety of Legal and Illegal Abortion

Current statistics indicate that abortion is becoming increasingly safer from a medical standpoint. There are, however, important differences in the

*See also Philip M. Hauser, "World Population: Retrospect and Prospect," in this volume.

†See also J. D. Wray, "Population Pressure on Families: Family Size and Child Spacing," in this volume.

case fatality rates from country to country. In general, countries with adequate medical services and liberalized abortion laws have lower abortion mortality rates.

The main problem lies in the less developed countries where women, deprived of both medical service and legal sanction, are forced to resort to induced abortion by primitive methods under unsanitary conditions. The women themselves, unskilled neighbors, lay midwives, or medicine men perform the operation.

In the following pages, examples of abortion mortality differentials will be drawn from the experience of various regions.

Northern Europe. The longest available record of maternal mortality due to abortion is from Sweden, as shown in Table 9. This table, which includes only deaths from legal abortion, shows a definite decrease in the case fatality rate over a 25-year period. No comparable long-term information is available on illegal abortion. However, in 1950 a government-appointed committee (73) reported the following statistics based on both legal and illegal abortion in Sweden. Between 1946 and 1951, 28,447 abortions were performed; of these 46 resulted in death, producing a case fatality ratio of 0.16 percent. Combined abortion and sterilization yielded a higher fatality ratio of 0.25 percent, compared with 0.09 percent for abortion alone. The report states that in the latter years of the investigation period (1949-1951) the abortion case fatality ratio decreased to 0.06 percent, which is equal to Sweden's maternal mortality from childbirth during the year 1950. Illegal abortion in the same period resulted in a case fatality ratio of 1.7 percent, based on only 352 cases of illegal abortion, of which 6 died.

Similar abortion mortality statistics have been reported for Finland and Denmark (72, 74).

Despite the significant decline in case fatality ratios in these three north European countries, their current ratios are still higher than those in eastern

TABLE 9

Maternal Deaths from Legal Abortions, Sweden, 1939-1964

Period	Legal Abortions	Maternal Deaths from Abortion	Case Fatality Ratio/100 Abortions
1939-48	13,000	38	0.200
1949-52	23,000	25	0.108
1953-56	18,400	12	0.065
1957-60	12,100	6	0.050
1961-64	14,300	6	0.042

Source: (72).

Europe. This situation is probably due to the fact that a large number of the legal abortions in northern Europe are performed after the third month of gestation—35 percent in Sweden for 1949 and 25 percent in Denmark for 1955-57 (72). The reason for this unfortunate delay is the long procedure of application to a committee which takes its time in reviewing the application and in giving permission for an abortion.

Eastern Europe. Case fatality ratios from legal abortion in eastern Europe are much lower than in northern Europe: first, because the law is more liberal and therefore more apparently healthy, low-risk women are included in the denominator; and second, because most operations are performed in the first 3 months of pregnancy.

In Hungary the mortality due to induced abortion is very low. Klinger (75) states that the number of deaths from permitted abortions is currently 2 or 3 per year. The number of deaths resulting from spontaneous abortion or abortion performed without permission is higher, reaching 20 to 25 annually. Before induced abortion was legalized, the mortality rate was much higher, with 80 to 100 women dying yearly from complications of illegal abortion. Special investigations by Hirschler (76) indicated that the case fatality ratio for the period 1957-58 was 0.0056 percent calculated on the basis of 15 deaths following 269,000 abortions. For the following 4-year period 1960-1963, the ratio dropped to 0.0031 percent, or 21 deaths among 670,000 legal abortions (77).

In Czechoslovakia during the 1957-1960 period (78), 16 deaths occurred among 236,000 legal abortions giving a case fatality ratio of 0.0068 percent. In the following 4-year period 1961-1964, the ratio dropped to 0.0012 percent; there were only 4 deaths among the 140,000 cases studied in 1963 and 1964 (56).

Similar very low abortion death ratios are reported for Yugoslavia (79) and Romania (80).

Japan. The abortion case fatality ratio in Japan in 1950-1963, given in Table 10, is very low. However, the case fatality ratio is not as low as one would expect in a country with such liberal abortion laws. One reason is that many abortionist-doctors underreport nonfatal abortions in an attempt to reduce their income taxes.

Western Europe. The safety of legal abortion in western nations with restrictive laws varies according to the degree of liberality in interpreting the laws, the place where abortion is performed, the stage of gestation, and the health of the woman. The fatality rate is declining in many countries where practitioners are skilled and the use of antibiotics is common practice.

In Switzerland, for example, the abortion laws have been interpreted liberally in recent years. A large number of reasons are accepted for therapeu-

TABLE 10

Maternal Deaths from Legal Abortion, Japan, 1950-1963

Period	Legal Abortions	Maternal Deaths from Abortion	Case Fatality Ratio/100 Abortions
1950-53	2,994,000	253	0.0085
1954-58	5,723,000	334	0.0058
1959-63	5,138,000	210	0.0041

Source: (82).

tic abortion. Abortion mortality for sanctioned operations has decreased in Switzerland, although not to the same extent as in countries with permissive abortion laws. Cloeren and Mall-Haifeli (81) report that while the ratio of abortion to births has increased from 1:20 in 1900 to 1:8 in 1960-1963, the case fatality ratio decreased from 2 percent (1921-1946) to 0.13 percent (1947-1961).*

United States. Abortion statistics in the United States are disappointingly inadequate. The risks of therapeutic abortions are obviously much less than those labelled "criminal" despite the fact that women who seek abortion on medical grounds are more often poorer surgical risks than women who seek abortion outside the law for nonmedical reasons. In the Professional Activities Survey, or PAS (84), or 269 U.S. hospitals in 1963 and 321 hospitals in 1964 and 384 in 1965, the records revealed a total of 2,007 therapeutic abortions. Two deaths were recorded, producing a case fatality rate of approximately 0.1 percent. This rate is 25 times the officially computed rate in Japan and 100 times that in many eastern European countries, despite the efficiency of modern hospitals—no doubt because therapeutic cases are more complicated.

The case fatality rate for criminal abortion is unknown but is estimated to range from 0.5 to 1 percent, based on 5,000 to 10,000 deaths precipitated by an alleged annual 1 million or more illegally performed operations (62). Whatever the actual figure may be, it is a fact that criminal abortion is responsible for a major proportion of maternal deaths in the United States. Its share is increased as other causes of maternal mortality are becoming more controllable. A California study (85), 1955-57, found deaths from abortion to be 21 percent of maternal mortalities. Guttmacher (86) found in the 1961 records of the New York City Health Department that 47 percent of maternal deaths in metropolitan New York were the result of illegal abortions. A 20-year

*For a discussion of the United Kingdom, as of 1966, see (83).

longitudinal study of the New York City Health Department records (87) indicates that abortion was responsible for an increasing proportion of maternal deaths among all ethnic groups. Nonwhites and Puerto Ricans, however, suffered a much higher abortion death ratio, as indicated by the data summarized in Table 11. Niswander (88) speculates that if therapeutic abortion were more readily available, there would be fewer deaths resulting from illegal abortion.

TABLE 11

Mortality Due to Abortion, by Ethnic Group, New York City, 1951-1962

	Abortion Deaths (Total)	Abortion Deaths per 10,000 Live Births	Percent of Maternal Deaths Due to Abortion
All groups			
1951-53	80	1.6	26.1
1954-56	105	2.1	35.1
1957-59	137	2.7	43.6
1960-62	154	3.1	42.1
White			
1951-53	22	0.6	14.4
1954-56	27	0.8	22.9
1957-59	27	0.8	23.3
1960-62	32	1.0	25.2
Nonwhite			
1951-53	43	6.1	35.8
1954-56	61	7.5	47.3
1957-59	68	7.0	50.7
1960-62	87	8.0	49.4
Puerto Rican			
1951-53	15	4.0	44.1
1954-56	17	3.1	32.7
1957-59	42	6.4	65.6
1960-62	35	4.7	55.6

Source: (87, based on Table 1, p. 968).

The Less Developed Countries. In the less developed countries the number of maternal deaths due to abortion is unduly high, primarily because of restrictive abortion laws, insufficient facilities for therapeutic abortions, and even greater insufficiency of trained abortionists who will perform the operation outside the law.

Most of the data on this subject comes from Latin America. The Chilean data in particular indicate that abortion accounts for almost two fifths of maternal deaths in that country. The figures below are for 1963 (22).

Number of live births	294,175
All maternal deaths	803
Maternal mortality per 10,000 live births	27.3
Maternal deaths due to abortion	312
Maternal mortality due to abortion/10,000 live births	10.6
Maternal mortality due to abortion (percent)	38.8

Armijo and Monreal (89) estimate that the case fatality ratio of abortions performed in Chilean hospitals oscillated around 0.5 percent. The burden placed upon Chilean hospitals by postabortion cases has been outlined in Table 4. In 1 year (1960), the care of 57,368 cases required 184,000 bed-days, involving an expenditure well in excess of 1 million dollars. Plaza and Briones calculated the cost of saving the life of a single patient with septic complications to be approximately $3,000 (25).

An interview study of 3,776 women in Santiago, Concepción, and Antofagasta calculated that from 40 percent to 54 percent of all abortions are hospitalized and from 26.7 percent to 40 percent of admittedly induced abortions result in hospitalization (22).

A Brazilian study (90) reported that puerperal infection has been a major cause of maternal mortality since 1931 and that abortion is responsible for a major proportion of puerperal infection. From 1944 to 1962, in one São Paulo department of obstetrics, forty deaths due to puerperal infection occurred. Of these, twenty-four, or 60 percent, were associated with criminal abortion. The study reports that eighteen of forty-two patients with septic shock associated with criminal abortion died, producing a case fatality ratio of 43 percent.

A Colombia study (59) reports a septic abortion case fatality ratio of 4.4 percent in the Child Care Institute of Bogotá (1965-66). This ratio is almost twenty-three times as much as the maternal mortality rate from all causes in the same institution (0.192 percent).

Reports from other developing countries reveal similar findings. As already mentioned, Eraj (91) reported that Kenya statistics for 1964 show that abortion deaths were half again the number of deaths caused by malaria.

A Malaysia report (92) on a study of 1,000 cases of abortion found that 178 were threatened, 102 inevitable, 453 incomplete, 17 complete, 11 missed, and 239 septic. For all types of abortion the ratio to deliveries was 1:6.8 or 14.7 percent. Seven women died, all from septic abortion. This yields a case fatality ratio for septic abortion of 3 percent which is more than four times that for all types of abortion (0.7 percent). Apparently many of these cases were induced in a nonmedical setting.

In 1965 a special medical committee from Australia investigated the incidence of maternal mortality in New South Wales between 1957 and 1960. Abortion accounted for 51 of the 226 maternal deaths, 21.7 percent of the total. Criminal interference was admitted or suspected in 42 of the abortion deaths (93).

A Statistical Model for Differential Abortion Deaths. In 1969, Tietze developed a mathematical model to calculate the relative risks to life associated with contraception (highly effective—the pill—and moderately effective methods), pregnancy, and abortion. The data summarized in Table 12 illustrate the vast difference between the risks of mortality from legal or medical abortion versus criminal abortion. The mortality risks of medical abortion are undoubtedly slight, and, in fact, equal the risks reported for oral contraception (3 per 100,000 users). Tietze concludes that the most rational procedure for the regulation of fertility is the development of a safe, though less than 100-percent-effective, program of contraception *and* the creation of a permissive atmosphere to allow for abortion under hospital operating-room conditions (94).

TABLE 12

Mathematical Model for Maternal Mortality from Pregnancy, Induced Abortion, and
Contraception: Illustrative Annual Rates of Pregnancies and of Deaths
Associated with Contraception, Pregnancy, and Induced
Abortion per 100,000 Women of Reproductive
Age in Fertile Unions

	Pregnancies	Deaths
No contraception, no induced abortion	40,000-60,000	8-12
No contraception, all pregnancies aborted out of hospital	100,000	100
No contraception, aborted in hospital	100,000	3
Highly effective contraception [pill], no induced abortion	100	3
Moderately effective contraception, no induced abortion	11,800-13,000	2.5
Moderately effective contraception, all pregnancies aborted out of hospital	14,300	14.3
Moderately effective contraception, aborted in hospital	14,300	0.4

Source: Tietze (94).

Effective Contraception and Abortion

Unquestionably, successful prevention of pregnancy through contraception is much wiser and safer than terminating a pregnancy through abortion. Nevertheless, amidst the accelerated social and economic changes in developing nations, the complete avoidance of a stage of widespread abortion is unlikely. However, there is evidence that highly effective contraceptive programs, designed to reach a sizable proportion of exposed fertile females, can significantly limit the spread and severity of induced abortion. Such programs will also be effective in limiting the prevalence of resort to induced abortion in developed, low-fertility countries.

Ironically, however, when contraceptive programs are instituted, there may be a temporary increase in induced abortions. Whether programs are directed at selected individuals or the community at large, initial failures are frequent, and those who fail often resort to induced abortion. Because a sizable number of women will continue to resort to abortion, policymakers are faced with the task of limiting or minimizing the hazards of abortion for both humanitarian and public health reasons.

The following discussion focuses on two examples: Japan, a posttransitional society, and Chile, a transitional society. In both countries conscientious efforts to limit induced abortion have been undertaken.

Japan

Japan in the 1950's was confronted with widespread abortion. For every ten women of reproductive age, one or more experienced abortion each year. This problem was widely discussed by experts in demography, economics, sociology, and medicine. The major concern was that large numbers of Japanese women continued to resort to induced abortion despite the availability of improved contraceptive methods.

Intensive educational or "guidance" programs were instituted to promote fertility decline through contraception rather than induced abortion. A report by Koya (11) presents the results of an experimental project in six communities after exposure to 5 years of intensive "guidance" effort. Selected findings of this program are summarized in Table 13. The trends of pregnancies and abortions are depicted in Figure 5. From the original tables and the report, the following observations can be made:

1. The guidance program was intensive and reached a sizable proportion of the couples.

2. There was a pronounced drop in the birth rate, the pregnancy rate, and the induced abortion rate.

3. The trend of decline differed for each rate. There was a progressive drop in the birth rate over the years, indicating a successful combination of contraception and induced abortion. The pregnancy rate began first to in-

TABLE 13

Reproductive History of Japanese Women in Six Communities[a] in Relation
to the "Guidance" Contraceptive Program, 1950's

Reproductive Variable	One Year before Guidance	First Year of Guidance	Second Year	Third Year	Fourth Year	Fifth Year
Couples guided	2,194	2,230	2,219	2,183	1,686	1,645
Live births	435	401	287	227	147	95
Birth rate	27.4	25.6	18.2	14.2	11.1	10.0
Pregnancy rate	37.3	49.0	28.6	21.5	17.3	9.9
Induced abortion/ 100 wives	6.3	9.2	8.6	6.6	4.9	2.1
Induced abortion/100 pregnancies	21.9	30.0	36.5	36.0	33.5	24.8

[a]Condensation of five studies conducted in the 1950's.

Source: (11).

crease and then to decrease progressively as did the induced abortion rate. This pattern suggests that when the contraceptive guidance program was launched, there were a number of initial failures. Some women seem to have accepted pregnancy, and others were determined to terminate pregnancy by induced abortion. However, the abortion rate continued to be higher than in the preguidance year until the fourth year of the guidance program. In Koya's words:

> ... it took five years to achieve any really gratifying results. ... Since it takes experience and skill to practice contraception successfully, failure rates are bound to be high until these are acquired. This is the explanation for the increase in induced abortion at the initial stages of the guidance program.

4. The increase in the abortion-to-pregnancy ratio is due to the number of pregnancies (the denominator) decreasing at a faster rate than did the number of abortions (the numerator). Properly interpreted, this ratio is another expression of the success of the guidance program.

Chile

In Chile concern over increasing induced abortion became manifest around 1962, triggering a series of epidemiological studies to identify and character-

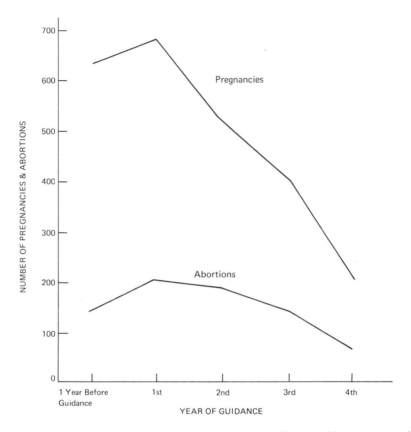

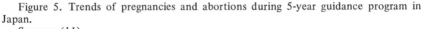

Figure 5. Trends of pregnancies and abortions during 5-year guidance program in Japan.
Source: (11).

ize the problems related to induced abortion. This concern originated among authorities at the University of Chile but soon spread to official governmental agencies. The position of the Chilean government was expressed by the Minister of Health at the inaugural session of the Eighth World Conference of the International Planned Parenthood Federation in Santiago, Chile, in April 1967. Included were the following points (95):

1. Induced abortion is a serious public health problem. Action to control abortion and to offer alternative methods of effective birth control is an imminent necessity.

2. Decisions regarding the limitation and/or spacing of children should be made by free and responsible individual citizens.

3. Educational programs revealing all existing safe and efficient methods of contraception are needed to broaden the range of free choice.

Intensive educational programs were sponsored for both professionals and others who were immediately involved in action programs, as well as the general public. Similarly, a number of research and action-oriented projects in methods of prevention and control of induced abortion were initiated. For the purposes of this paper, a recent report of such a research experiment is selected for consideration (96). The report included the results of a 39-month contraceptive campaign, principally using intra-uterine devices (IUD's), which was aimed at reducing the rates of birth and induced abortion. The study was initiated in the western district of Santiago in 1964 and is still under way. The report covers the period from April 1964, through June 1967.

The program of contraceptive education started in both the hospitals and in the community at large. The contraceptive services included IUD insertions, which were done immediately or soon after an abortion or a delivery, as well as after menses for some women. Other methods were offered, but this report concentrates on the IUD program.

The number of women who accepted the pill totalled 432; those who accepted the IUD totalled 20,416 or approximately 18.5 percent of the total fertile women in the area. The birth rate dropped from over 40 per 1,000 population in 1964 to 28.7 in 1966. Although Viel had calculated this rate to be 73 percent of the preprogram rate in 1963, the curve indicated that the birth rate was already on the decline. Nevertheless, it is evident that this program further hastened fertility decline. So far, the program has had a most significant effect on induced abortion, calculated as a reduction from 31 to 50 percent.

From this and similar programs, the Chilean authors concluded that great effort and substantial expense is necessary to make general a widespread and effective program of contraception. One author has argued that at least 10 to 15 percent of the fertile women need to be protected in order to obtain a reduction in induced abortion and the birth rate (28).

Continued Abortion

The studies from Japan and Chile illustrate that the high rate of induced abortion does not respond immediately to the increasing availability of effective contraceptives. On the contrary, there appears to be a delayed reaction between contraceptive program effectiveness and abortion decline. Several reasons for the continued use of induced abortion during an intensive contraceptive program deserve mention.

During the stages when abortion is widely used, either legally as in Japan or illegally as in Chile, many women become "abortion minded." This attitude is a catalytic result of the modernizing influences which foster upward social mobility. Small family size is perceived as a prerequisite for fulfilling these aspirations. Because of the short supply or failure of contraceptives, induced abortion is perceived as the means to limit family size. Furthermore, many studies from various countries indicate that women who have previously experienced one or more induced abortions have a proclivity to continue this method of birth control.* Even when effective contraceptives become available, this group of vulnerable women may continue to rely on induced abortion as a "tried and true" method of family planning.

Another reason may be that the continued use of induced abortion reveals itself as something of a cohort phenomenon. In the early stage of transition, the socially mobile, upper stratum of society adopts small family-size norms more readily and frequently resorts to induced abortion to limit births. With a rise in educational levels and a stabilization of family-size norms, this group turns increasingly to contraception. Yet while the need to resort to abortion decreases for the upper stratum, the abortion wave is maintained, often at an epidemic level, because each of the lower strata cohorts also pass through a stage of abortion-proneness. The upper-middle, lower-middle, upper-lower, and lower-lower strata replace each other progressively as cohorts vulnerable to induced abortion. This process can continue for long periods of time and can be controlled through vigorous contraceptive programs instituted in such a way that the vulnerable strata are reached.†

Finally, when abortion becomes widely accessible—as in eastern Europe with the sanction of the law or in Latin America without it—there is generally an inclination to relax contraceptive efforts.

The Need for Liberalizing Abortion Laws

This study of abortion in the demographic transition leads to the conclusion that the liberalization of abortion laws is needed to protect maternal and child health in both transitional and posttransitional countries. A legal environment that not only permits "abortion on demand" in a medically approved setting but also provides a supporting structure for abortion would (1) accelerate the transition in high-fertility countries, (2) maintain or increase fertility decline in low-fertility countries, and (3) attenuate the social discrimination typical of practice under restrictive abortion laws. The question today is not whether women *should* resort to induced abortion; it is obvious that many *do*, regardless of the law, the danger, or other factors. The appropriate question asks which policies would best cope with the public health and social aspects of induced abortion.

*See (23; 53; 54, Sadvokasova's study).

†A similar hypothesis, as applied to Latin America, has been proposed by Requena (40).

Increased Cultural Tolerance of Abortion

In many countries cultural tolerance of abortion is increasing despite the historical opposition of several organized religions. At this point it might be well to review the attitudes on abortion of major world religions.

Judaism. According to Guttmacher (97) "unequivocal moral and legal antipathy to abortion originated with the Hebrews." He also indicated that this attitude was inherited unmodified by Christianity.

In a recent article Rabbi Jakobovits (98) presents a relatively more liberal view of the Orthodox Jewish position on abortion. According to Jakobovits, abortion is not equated with murder, and the Talmud permits abortion when the life of the mother is at stake; however, he states that later rabbinical writings clearly forbid abortion on "humanitarian" and eugenic indications.

The practice of induced abortion among Jewish women is more liberal than can be presumed from the official position of Judaism. Hospital studies in the United States have shown a higher abortion rate among Jewish women than among Protestants and Catholics (99). A study in Israel (100) indicated that the national average of abortions per 1,000 live births for 1952-53 was 150 (100, 101).

Roman Catholicism. It is a common belief that the Roman Catholic Church categorically condemns abortion. History, however, will attest that there has been dissension on the issue. Tertullian, the powerful Roman theologian circa A.D. 240, classified deliberate abortion as murder; St. Augustine echoed the same sentiment 300 years later. However, induced abortion before animation of the fetus was not condemned by all of the early Church fathers. The critical point has always been the indeterminancy of when during gestation "the infusion of the soul" occurs (102), after which stage the unbaptized child cannot enter heaven.

Today some of the more liberal clergy, following Thomas Aquinas in this respect, are upholding the theory of delayed animation, but this theory is yet to be accepted by the central hierarchy of the Church (103, 104).

Available data illustrate the difference between the belief system and actual practice. For example, Table 14 provides a comparison of attitudes toward family planning by religious affiliation in the United States and Australia.

Abortion is a method of limiting family size in allegedly Catholic countries. Table 15 presents a study from Mexico.

The outcome of 2,617 pregnancies during 1962-63 in the predominantly Catholic community of Quinta Normal, Chile, were studied (23). The induced abortion rate was 23.4 percent among Catholics, 13.8 percent among "others," and 27.2 percent among those listing no religion. Hutchinson pro-

TABLE 14

Opinions and Attitudes toward Specified
Aspects of Family Planning

(percent)

Place, Year, Question, Number in Sample	Yes or Approve	No or Disapprove	No Opinion
U.S.—Gallup Poll, 1967			
Q. Would it be all right for a woman to have pregnancy interrupted:			
(a) If the pregnancy seriously endangered the woman's health.			
Roman Catholic (1,561)	75	19	6
Protestant (4,411)	89	7	4
Jewish (168)	98	1	1
(b) If the woman had been raped.			
Roman Catholic (1,561)	62	27	11
Protestant (4,398)	74	18	7
Jewish (168)	93	3	4
(c) If the couple could not afford another child.			
Roman Catholic (1,557)	18	77	5
Protestant (4,405)	25	70	5
Jewish (168)	52	41	7
Australia—Public Opinion Poll, 1968			
Abortions should be made legal or allowed in certain circumstances.			
All respondents	64	27	9
Anglicans	69		
Roman Catholics:	49		
Strong church goers	33		
Moderate church goers	50		
Infrequent church goers	67		
Never go	79		

Source: (105).

vides an example from Brazil in which 1,728 married women experiencing
live birth admitted to induced abortion in the following percentages (106):

	Percent
Catholic—nonpracticing	9.8
Catholic—semipracticing	10.9
Catholic—practicing	3.2
Protestant	8.7
Jewish	14.3
Espirita	8.7

	Percent
Other credos	6.7
No religion	19.2

Protestantism. Abortion is not categorically condemned in Prostestantism, but neither is it liberally permitted. According to the 1966 pronouncement by the National Council of Churches of Christ in the United States (107), "Protestant Christians are agreed in condemning abortion or any method which destroys human life except when the health or life of the mother is at stake. The destruction of life already begun cannot be condoned as a method of family limitation." However, certain denominations have taken more permissive stands (108, 109). In perhaps the most permissive statement of all, the 1968 American Baptist Convention urged that legislation be enacted to provide (a) "That the termination of a pregnancy prior to the end of the twelfth week or first trimester be at the request of the individual(s) concerned and be regarded as an elective medical procedure governed by the laws regulating medical practice and licensure"; and (b) "After that period, the termination of a pregnancy shall be performed only by a duly licensed physician at the request of the individual(s) concerned, in a regularly licensed hospital for one of the reasons as suggested by the Model Penal Code of the American Law Institute. . . . Further we encourage our churches to provide sympathetic and realistic counseling on family planning and abortion" (110).

Islam. Islam is liberal in theory whereas in practice Muslim countries are much less tolerant of abortion. The masses of Muslim people are not aware of the liberal position of their religion because it has not been publicized; and because conservative members of the religious hierarchy have imposed unimaginative and restrictive interpretations of the Islamic tradition.

TABLE 15

Induced Abortion by Religion, Mexico[a]

Religion	Women Interviewed	Women Who Provoked Abortion	Percent
Catholic	937	287	30.6
Other or none	63	20	32.7
Total	1,000	307	30.7

[a]The exact date of the survey is not given.

Source: Based on interviews of 1,000 women patients of the clinic of the Asociación Mexicana Pro-Bienestar de la Familia (50).

According to Islamic teaching, the fetus is not instilled with a soul until some time after gestation begins. The Koran describes various successive stages through which the fetus must pass before it becomes a complete human being.* The period for these stages is not categorically fixed, but there is one entry in the Bukhary (111), a leading collection of the Prophet's Tradition, indicating that the soul does not enter the body of the fetus until the eightieth day of gestation, and other sources extend this period to 120 days. In recent writings the longer period has been cited to permit "justifiable" interruption of pregnancy. Beyond this point interruption is considered infanticide since it will destroy a human being complete with body and soul.

A *Fatwa*, or an authoritative religious judgment, was issued by Sheikh Abdul-Majid Salim, the Mufti of Egypt in 1937, that abortion is permissible before the fetal movements occur (112). To avoid indiscriminate abortion practices, the Mufti urged invoking "health" reasons. However, these need not be the only reasons for abortion; other welfare reasons can be equally invoked as long as the procedure is performed early in pregnancy. The *Fatwa* also gave sanction to all types of contraception, although it was emphasized that there be an awareness of human dignity at all times.

Hinduism. Hinduism does not favor abortion as a method of terminating unwanted pregnancy. The Mahabharata stated that letting a women's *Rtu* [fertile period] go waste was the same as embryo-murder (113). Another statement suggests the restrictive attitude of Hinduism toward abortion: "The killer of a priest, or destroyer of an embryo, casts his guilt on the willing eater of his provisions. . . ." (114).

Nevertheless, very few people in India are aware of this view, and abortion is practiced by an increasing proportion of Indian women. In a sample survey of women in Bombay (115), 16.1 percent approved of abortion for economic reasons or as a woman's right. The foremost reason for disapproval in the remaining 83.9 percent was that the operation was harmful to the mother's health.

Countries with Restrictive Abortion Laws

There is considerable variation among nations with regard to both the extensiveness of induced abortion and the liberalization of abortion laws.

*We placed him
As a drop of seed
In a safe lodging
Firmly affixed;
Then fashioned we
The drop into a clot
Then of the clot
We developed
A lump [fetus] ; Then
We developed out of that lump
Bones, and clothed the bones
With flesh;
Then we produced it
As *another creature*
So blessed is God
The Best to Create!

(XXIII-12-13-14)

Whereas the primary effect of liberalized abortion laws in posttransitional, or modernized, countries is to enhance maternal and child health, in transitional countries it appears to be also an integral part of speedier fertility decline.

In nearly all transitional countries, with the recent exception of Tunisia and possibly mainland China, the existing abortion laws are highly restrictive. Restrictive laws have probably curtailed the overall number of induced abortions, but there are large groups of fertile females in all developing countries who are so resolutely determined to limit family size that an illegal abortion is deemed preferable to an additional child. The ever-increasing number of abortions performed beyond the protection of public laws and outside the safety of adequate medical facilities has created a serious health problem—as well as the problems created by a situation in which many women who do not want an expected child fear the repercussions of an illegal abortion.

Although fewer in number and significance, illegal abortions in the more developed countries create the same health problems as those in transitional countries. In several west and south European countries and in most of the United States, therapeutic abortion for medical reasons only is the sole legal basis for terminating a pregnancy.

The United States. In the United States the letter of the law varies considerably from state to state, but the general tone of abortion laws has been overwhelmingly restrictive. As of 1967, abortion was illegal in forty-five states, unless necessary to preserve the life of the woman; and in seven states to prevent the birth of children with high risks of mortality or deformity (116).

In 1959 the American Law Institute proposed a Model Penal Code to modify abortion laws. This code would allow abortion by licensed physicians in cases where (a) there is substantial risk that the mother's physical or mental health may be impaired; (b) the child would be born with serious physical or mental defect; or (c) pregnancy is the result of rape or incest (117). Among both professionals and the general public, attitudes toward acceptance of this code are growing more favorable (118). Based on the recommendations of the American Law Institute, five states—California, Georgia, Maryland, Colorado, and North Carolina—modified their abortion laws in 1967 and 1968. Early in the 1970's a movement began in several state legislatures to make abortion a decision of a woman and her physician, indicating that opinion and policy may be going beyond the Model Penal Code.

One of the inevitable results of restrictive abortion laws is a lack of abortion statistics in the United States. The data reported by hospitals concern only "therapeutic abortions" for which in recent years an approximate ratio of 2 therapeutic abortions per 1,000 live births has been reported (119).

The data available on the total number of abortions in the country is unreliable and is based mainly on "informed guesses" or indirect methods of measurement. Thus, Hall (119) estimated that the ratio of illegal to hospital abortions is 100:1. This figure may be compared to a ratio of 4:1 in Denmark, where laws have been liberalized. A committee of the Arden House Conference on Abortion reported in 1955 (62) that "a plausible estimate of the frequency of induced abortion in the United States could be as low as 200,000 and as high as 1,200,000 per year." Based on the studies of the Institute for Sex Research, Kinsey (62, pp. 50, 54) estimated that among white females 10 percent would have at least one induced abortion before the age of 20 and 22 percent before age 45.

Another result of the restrictive laws is the disgraceful inconsistency of various hospitals in interpreting or implementing the written law. One condition may be accepted as indication for abortion by one hospital and flatly refused as illegal by another hospital in the same city or state. Guttmacher (97) in a provocative critique of the existing laws reported that the abortion committee in a large hospital in Harlem allowed ninety-eight therapeutic abortions. The indications were in accordance with the law in only thirteen cases. In the remaining eighty-five cases, the committee "at least bent the law, if it did not fracture it."

A most serious aspect of the restrictive laws is the discriminatory nature of their application. Gold et al. (87) report that the incidence of therapeutic abortion is five times greater among whites than nonwhites, and twenty-six times greater among whites than Puerto Ricans in New York City. They also noted the higher occurrence of therapeutic abortion among private (mainly white) than "ward" patients (mainly nonwhite). (See Table 16.) In a recent review of therapeutic abortion research, Lyon (120) observed that the "affluent woman is much more likely to be aborted than her indigent sister."

Although not strictly legal, psychiatric indications have been increasingly invoked as reasons for abortions all over the country. These reasons are invoked much more frequently for private patients who can afford the psychiatric consultation and a place in a hospital. In the New York City

TABLE 16

Therapeutic Abortion per 1,000 Live Births
in Several New York Hospitals

Type of Hospital Service	1951-53	1960-62
Proprietary	6.3	3.9
Voluntary:		
Private service	3.6	2.4
General service	1.9	0.7
Municipal	1.2	0.1

Source: (87).

study, illustrated in Figure 6, mental disorders account for two thirds of all abortions in proprietary hospitals, which have the highest abortion ratio, and only one third in the ward services of municipal and voluntary hospitals, which have the lowest abortion ratio. These studies lead Lyon (120) to conclude that abortion for psychiatric reasons is the exclusive "luxury of the rich."*

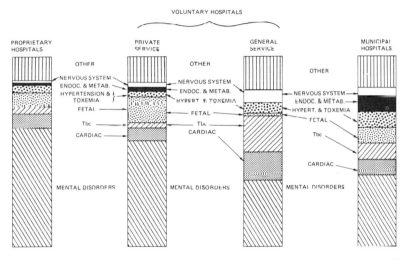

Figure 6. Medical reasons for therapeutic abortions by type of hospital, New York City, 1954-1962.
Source: (87, Table 9).

So long as the actual practice of abortion in American hospitals is inequitable, inconsistent, and largely extra-legal, we can expect a continually large number of abortions to be performed outside the legal hospitals.

Countries with Liberalized Abortion Laws

Among northern European countries, the liberalization of abortion laws began within the last few decades—first, Iceland in 1935; then Sweden in 1938; Denmark in 1939; Finland in 1950; and Norway in 1960. Further liberalization occurred in Sweden in 1946 and again in 1963; and in Denmark in 1956. Although the letter of the law differs from country to country, abortion is generally permitted for five indications: medical, medicosocial, sociomedical, eugenic, and humanitarian. By permission of the National

---

*Hall provides some interesting explanations of this double standard based on the type of patient, available resources, and patient-physician rapport in private and public practice (116).

Board of Health or by two physicians' certificates, Swedish law permits abortion for the following indications (121): (a) illness or weakness, either physical or mental; (b) a medical-social indication; (c) anticipated weakness, if the pregnancy and additional child are likely to lead to serious physical or mental sequelae; (d) impregnation occurring under the gross invasion of the female's freedom of action; and (e) a genetic indication of hereditary risk. (If the mother is the risk, she must be sterilized at the time of abortion.)

Eastern Europe. The liberalization of abortion laws in most east European countries during the 1950's was tantamount to making abortion a legal right of women. In effect, the old laws were removed and public measures to support the practice of abortion were adopted.

Abortion laws in the U.S.S.R. were liberalized as early as 1920, but restrictions which prohibited abortion except for medical indications were introduced in 1936. In 1955, however, a reliberalization took place, and abortion has been a legal method of terminating unwanted pregnancies since that time. Abortion laws were also liberalized in Poland, Hungary, Czechoslovakia, Bulgaria, and Yugoslavia. By 1960, only East Germany and Albania, among all Soviet-bloc countries, had not followed the Russian example (122).

In Hungary abortion is permitted for medical, psychiatric, and fetal indications; for social and family circumstances; and, simply, if any applicant insists on the interruption of pregnancy. In Czechoslovakia abortion is permitted for (a) women of advanced age; (b) mothers of at least three children; (c) loss or disability of husband; (d) disruption of family life; (e) endangering the living standard, especially if the woman is a major supporter of the family; (f) unmarried women; (g) pregnancy resulting from crime or violence. In other socialist countries, indications are formulated in less specific terms. In Poland, for example, abortion is permitted in instances where pregnancy constitutes a serious threat to the social position of the woman; and, in Yugoslavia, for "grave personal or material circumstances" (53).

Japan. In Japan, the legitimation of induced abortion occurred in 1948 when the Eugenics Protection Law was liberally amended. The reader may refer to the earlier discussion for further information concerning the nature and impact of liberalized abortion laws in Japan.

Effect of Liberalization on the Incidence of Abortion

The immediate and most obvious result of abortion law liberalization—or removal—is an increase in the number of legal abortions and, therefore, a decrease in abortion morbidity and mortality. After liberalization, a process of replacement typically sets in whereby women who would have had an illegal abortion now turn to hospitals and clinics. In addition, the appeal of abortion is enhanced by the removal of legal taboos, and abortion cases are more accurately reported. The tremendous increase in both the number and rates of legal abortions in European countries with liberalized abortion laws in indicated in Table 17. In Hungary, for example, the number of abortions has actually exceeded the number of live births in recent years.

The trend of abortion practices in selected areas is depicted in Figure 2. In northern European countries, a striking rise took place in the early 1940's, followed by the curves' leveling off in the 1950's. The curves for east European countries, where liberalized abortion laws became effective in the mid-1950's, depict a similar pattern for the 1950's and 1960's. Japan's curve is similar to that of eastern European countries, even though the earlier phases were not plotted because of inadequate data. The differences in patterns of abortion incidence over time between areas with liberal laws and those with restrictive laws is dramatized in the same figure. Since 1937 increases in the

TABLE 17

Legal Abortions and Abortion Ratio per 1,000 Live Births

Year	Abortions	Abortion Ratio	Abortions	Abortion Ratio	Abortions	Abortion Ratio
	Sweden		Denmark		Finland	
1939	439	5	484	7		
1940	506	5	522	7		
1941	496	5	519	7		
1942	568	5	824	10		
1943	703	6	977	12		
1944	1,088	8	1,286	14		
1945	1,623	12	1,577	17		
1946	2,378	18	1,930	20		
1947	3,534	28	2,240	24		
1948	4,585	36	2,543	30		
1949	5,503	45	3,425	43		
1950	5,889	51	3,909	49		
1951	6,328	57	4,743	62	3,007	32
1952	5,322	48	5,031	65	3,327	35
1953	4,915	45	4,795	61	3,802	42
1954	5,089	48	5,140	67	3,699	41
1955	4,562	43	5,381	70	3,659	41
1956	3,851	36	4,522	59	4,090	46
1957	3,386	32	4,023	53	4,553	52
1958	2,823	27	3,895	52	5,274	65
1959	3,071	29	3,587	48	5,773	69
1960	2,792	27	3,918	51	6,188	75
1961	2,909	28	4,124	54	5,867	72
1962	3,205	30	3,996	51	6,015	74
1963	3,528	31	3,971	48	5,616	68
1964	4,671	38	4,527	54	4,919	61
1965	6,245	51	5,190	60	4,783	61

TABLE 17 (Continued)

Year	Abortions	Abortion Ratio	Abortions	Abortion Ratio	Abortions	Abortion Ratio
	Hungary (in 1,000's)		Yugoslavia (Slovenia) (in 1,000's)		Czechoslovakia (in 1,000's)	
1950	1.7	8.7				
1951	1.7	8.9				
1952	1.7	9.1				
1953	2.8	13.5			1.5	5.5
1954	16.3	72.9			2.8	10.5
1955	35.4	168.3	0.4	12.5	2.1	7.9
1956	82.5	427.9	0.8	25.4	3.1	11.8
1957	123.3	737.4	2.2	73.1	7.3	28.9
1958	145.6	919.2	4.7	166.7	61.4	261.3
1959	152.4	1,007.9	6.4	225.4	79.1	364.5
1960	162.2	1,107.2	8.2	295.0	88.3	406.4
1961	170.0	1,210.8	9.3	320.7	94.3	431.8
1962	163.7	1,258.3	9.5	327.6	89.8	412.9
1963	173.8	1,313.7	9.4	321.9	70.5	298.7
1964	184.4	1,395.9	9.4	321.9	70.7	293.2
1965	180.3	1,355.6	9.9	322.5	79.6	343.7

Source: (123).

abortion ratio have been gradual and moderate in Chile. Yet, in spite of Chile's epidemic level of abortion during the past few decades, serious efforts to legalize abortion have been made only recently. The trend for New York City, while gradual and moderate, reveals a shrinking therapeutic abortion ratio which continues to be drastically lower than that in the other areas.

Effect of Liberalization of Abortion Laws on the Birth Rate

There are various measurements by which the effect of liberalized laws can be determined. Tietze used the birth rate; Fredericksen and Brackett (124) prefer the effect on total fertility; and Muramatsu (15) used a mathematical formula to calculate the number of births which could have resulted had abortion not been practiced. It must be acknowledged that neither of these methods can unequivocally attribute the observed effect to induced abortion alone. In this overall presentation, the birth rate will be used.

Natality trends in various countries are compared in Figure 7. The lower part of the figure compares countries which liberalized their laws in the late 1940's with two countries which did not, the United States and Italy. The upper part of the figure gives a similar comparison between east European countries and the United Kingdom. From these comparisons, it becomes evident that the permissive countries have enjoyed a marked decline in their birth rate in comparison with restrictive countries. It also appears that the

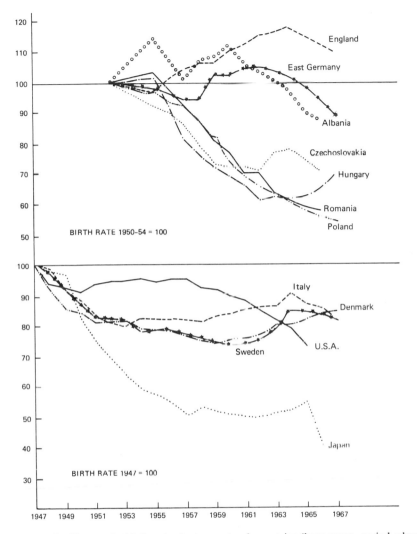

Figure 7. Changes in birth rates in two sets of countries (base years—period when abortion policies were liberalized).
Source: (123).

amount of natality decline is related to the extent of liberalization. Japan has the most impressive decline. Next in magnitude of decline are the east European countries. In contrast, countries with restrictive abortion laws could not bring down their natality trend to the same extent within comparable periods of time. On the contrary, some of the countries showed a slight, though temporary, increase in the trend in the same period.

Of special interest are the two eastern European countries, Albania and East Germany, which did not liberalize their laws and did not experience any appreciable decline in natality. Tietze (123), whose data for Europe have been updated and used for a part of Figure 7, feels that the difference in natality trends between the two groups of countries is sufficiently striking and that, with the demographic and social similarities between these countries, he concludes that "the legalization of abortion has had a depressant effect on the birth rate in most of the countries concerned."

IMPLICATIONS FOR POLICY

This study has emphasized two major themes for policy formation. First, there is no question that prevention of pregnancy through effective contraception is much wiser and safer than termination of pregnancy through abortion. Second, for reasons that vary from one country to another with the dynamics of fertility transition, a margin of induced abortion is to be anticipated and provided for. It follows that the most rational procedure for the regulation of fertility and, hence, population growth, involves both (a) the development of aggressive and effective contraceptive programs, and (b) the creation of a permissive atmosphere wherein abortion is widely available and performed in the safety of adequate medical facilities and with the sanction of law.

Inasmuch as abortion is a crucial ramification of the so-called population problem, responsible policymakers can no longer afford to ignore the demographic, economic, and health consequences of restrictive abortion laws. When the motivation to limit fertility is high and even the most effective contraceptive methods frequently fail, such antiquated laws serve to encourage rather than curb the many abuses of induced abortion. At a minimum, policymakers should move immediately to recognize the personal nature of a decision to abort an unwanted pregnancy, and to respect the discretion of the woman and her physician. In developing countries where the many problems of illicit abortion are coupled with those of high fertility and overburdening population growth, policymakers may be forced to pursue a more rational, more imaginative, and perhaps even drastic course. While the particular issues raised by abortion abuses, unwanted children, and excessive population growth may differ from country to country, in nearly all countries the policy decisions required to treat these issues will entail the following steps:

1. *Policymakers must recognize that induced abortion is a popular and universal practice which poses profound problems for societies and individuals alike.* Beyond doubt, abortion is a worldwide problem. The nature and extent of the problem, as well as its determinants and solutions, differ from one group of countries to another.

The transitional societies face by far the worst dilemma of all; they have a problem every way they turn. On the one hand, if they do not have a sufficient number of abortions, their transition to low fertility will be critically retarded. On the other hand, unless policymakers sanction abortion law reform, criminal abortions—provoked by amateurs under dangerous conditions—will mount and foster an extremely serious public health problem. A deluge of complicated cases will continue to overburden the already inadequate and insufficient medical services that are needed for so many other purposes.

The problem in posttransitional countries that still have restrictive laws is twofold. There is a serious problem of illegal or criminal abortion with all the consequent social, psychological, and racketeering abuses. There is also the problem of inconsistent implementation of ambiguous and outdated laws, very often favoring the wealthy and not the poor who most need relief.

Finally, in posttransitional countries with liberalized laws, abortion prevalence persists despite the fact that contraceptives are widely available.

In all three categories of countries, therefore, policymakers should give immediate recognition to the problem of induced abortion and should plan to phase it out rather than pretend it does not exist.

2. *Whereas the primary goal of every fertility regulation program is the prevention of pregnancy through effective contraception, policymakers should recognize that contraceptive failures do occur.* In such cases, legal abortion is the only rational alternative to the birth of an unwanted child. Policies providing abortion services are needed to ensure that the procedure is performed safely, inexpensively, and without discrimination.

3. *Countries which have already liberalized their abortion laws and those which will do so in the future should be warned against overreliance on abortion to solve fertility problems.* Abortion should be but one option in the pursuit of fertility control.

4. *In all cases, intensive education-guidance programs must be established.* These programs are necessary to aid a smooth transition from abortion-mindedness to the achievement of balanced national and community family planning programs.

5. *Both field and clinical research is needed to provide policymakers with accurate, up-to-date information about the dynamics of abortion.* This is an area that should receive higher priority than ever before. Basic and applied research is needed in many areas, of which the following is only a partial list:

(a) *Research in the epidemiology of abortion.* Intensive and extensive research is needed to characterize the problem of abortion and its determinants in various cultures. Of particular significance is how developing countries can accomplish their demographic transition without precipitating an epidemic wave of abortion.

(b) *Contraceptive research.* There is great need to continue and expand basic research to increase the effectiveness of existing contraceptives, to reduce their side effects, and to develop new methods which are safe, more effective, easily administered, socially and aesthetically acceptable, and, above all, do not require continued motivation. All methods should be subjected to rigorous epidemiologic evaluation before general use.

(c) *Communications research.* While it is advisable to liberalize or repeal abortion laws, continued research is needed in methods of reaching the target population or population at risk of abortion (women with unplanned, unwanted pregnancies) with advice on the benefits of preventive, contraceptive methods.

(d) *Research on abortion techniques.* Since we will have to live with abortion, research is needed to improve existing methods of pregnancy termination and to develop new methods that are easier, safer, less expensive, and that do not require hospitalization. Research on nonsurgical methods of abortion that can be used immediately upon suspicion of an unwanted pregnancy and that do not require the direct assistance of highly skilled medics should be undertaken.

REFERENCES

1. Himes, E. Norman, *Medical History of Contraception.* New York: Gamut Press, 1963 (first published in 1936). p. 4.
2. Guttmacher, Alan F., "Therapeutic Abortions in a Large General Hospital," *Surg Clin N Amer*, April 1957. pp. 459-461.
3. Aristotle, *Politics*, Book VII, Ch. 16 (1335b).
4. *Hippocrates on Intercourse and Pregnancy*, T. U. H. Ellinger, trans. New York: Henry Schuman, 1952.
5. Thompson, Warren, "Population," *Amer J Sociol*, Vol. 34, No. 6, May 1929. pp. 959-975.
6. Notestein, Frank, "Population–The Long View," *Food for the World*, T. W. Schultz, ed. Chicago: Univ. of Chicago Press, 1945.
7. Taeuber, Irene B. *The Population of Japan*, Princeton, N.J.: Princeton Univ. Press, 1958.
8. Pommerenke, W. T., "Abortion in Japan," *Obstet Gynec Survey*, Vol. 10, No. 2, April 1955. pp. 145-175.
9. Keyfitz, Nathan, and Wilhelm Flieger, *World Population: An Analysis of Vital Data.* Chicago: Univ. of Chicago Press, 1968.
10. Taeuber, Irene B., "Japan's Demographic Transition Re-examined," *Population Studies*, Vol. 14, 1960-61, Part I, July 1960. p. 29, Table 1.
11. Koya, Yoshio, "Why Induced Abortions in Japan Remain High," *Research in Family PLanning*, Clyde V. Kiser, ed. Princeton, N.J.: Princeton Univ. Press, 1962. pp. 103-110.
12. Japan Ministry of Health and Welfare, *Report of Statistics on Eugenic Projection.* Tokyo, published annually.
13. United Nations, *Demographic Yearbooks* 1949-1965. New York: U.N. Statistical Office, 1950-1966.
14. Muramatsu, Minoru, "Action Programs of Family Planning in Japan," *Population Dynamics*, Minoru Muramatsu and Paul Harper, eds. Baltimore: Johns Hopkins Press, 1965. pp. 67-76.

15. Muramatsu, Minoru, "Effects of Induced Abortion on the Reduction of Births in Japan," *Milbank Mem Fund Quart*, Vol. 38, 1960. pp. 153-166.
16. Matus Benavente, V., "El problema del Aborto," *Bol Soc Chilena de Obstet y Ginec*, Vol. 3, April 1938. pp. 184-205.
17. Romero, Hernan, and J. Vildosola, "Introduction to the Abortion Problem," *Rev Chilena Hig*, Vol. 14, 1952. p. 197.
18. Manubens, R., "Estudio sobre Aborto Involuntario." Unpublished thesis, Universidad de Chile, Santiago, 1952.
19. Mena, V., "Estudio sobre Aborto Provocado." Unpublished thesis, Universidad de Chile, Santiago, 1952.
20. Walsen, R., "Problema Médico, Social y Médico-legal del Aborto Provocado," *Bol Soc Chilena de Obst y Ginec*, Vol. 19, October 1954. pp. 185-196.
21. Tabah, L., and R. Samuel, "Preliminary Findings of a Survey on Fertility and Attitudes toward Family Formation in Santiago, Chile," *Research in Family Planning*, Clyde V. Kiser, ed. Princeton: Princeton Univ. Press, 1962. pp. 263-304.
22. Armijo, Rolando, and T. Monreal, "The Problem of Induced Abortion in Chile," *Milbank Mem Fund Quart*, Vol. 43, No. 4, October 1965. Part 2, pp. 263-280.
23. Requena, Mariano, "Social and Economic Correlates of Induced Abortion in Santiago, Chile," *Demography*, Vol. 2, 1965. pp. 33-49.
24. Requena, M., "Studies of Family Planning in the Quinta Normal District of Santiago," *Components of Population Change in Latin America, Milbank Mem Fund Quart*, Vol. 43, No. 4, October 1965. pp. 69-94.
25. Plaza, S., and H. Briones, "El Aborto como problema assistencial," *Rev Med Chile*, Vol. 91, April 1963. pp. 294-297.
26. United Nations, *Demographic Yearbooks*, 1953, 1956, 1963, 1964. New York: U.N. Statistical Office, 1954, 1957, 1964, 1965.
27. Armijo, R., and M. Requena, *Epidemiological Aspects of Abortion*. Presented before Joint Session of the Epidemiology and Maternal and Child Health Sections of the Amer. Public Health Assn. at the 94th Annual Meeting in San Francisco, October 31, 1966. Mimeo.
28. Requena, M., and T. Monreal, "Evaluation of Induced Abortion Control and Family Planning Programs in Chile," *Milbank Mem Fund Quart*, Vol. 46, No. 3, July 1968. Part 2, pp. 191-222.
29. Korea Ministry of Health and Social Affairs Evaluation Unit, "Family Planning Evaluation Studies in Korea," Issue No. 5. Seoul, March 1969.
30. Hong, S. B., *Induced Abortion in Seoul, Korea*. Seoul: Dong-A Publishing Co., 1966.
31. Hong, S. B., "Induced Abortion in Rural Korea," *Korean J Gyn Obstet*, Vol. 10, 1967. p. 275.
32. Koh, K. S., and K. Y. Song, "Some Aspects of Fertility and Family Planning in Seoul City, Korea," International Union for the Scientific Study of Population, Contributed Papers, Sydney conference. Sydney, 1967. p. 462.

33. Keeny, M. S., Korea and Taiwan: The Score for 1966," *Studies in Family Planning*, No. 19, May 1967. pp. 1-7.
34. Agarwala, S. N., "Abortion Rate among a Section of Delhi's Population," *Bombay Medical Digest*, Vol. 30, 1962. p. 1.
35. Cillov, Hatûk, "Attitudes on Family Planning in Turkey," International Union for the Scientific Study of Population, Contributed Papers. Sydney, 1967. p. 483.
36. Kamel, W. H., et al., "A Fertility Study in Al-Amria," *The Egyptian Population and Family Planning Review*, Vol. 1, No. 2, December 1968. pp. 83-100.
37. Eraj, Y. A., "The Unplanned Pregnancy," *E Afr Med J*, 43, 1966. p. 298.
38. Spengler, J., "Values and Fertility Analysis," *Demography*, 1966, Vol. 3, No. 1. pp. 109-130.
39. Heer, David M., *Society and Population*. Englewood Cliffs, N.J.: Prentice-Hall, 1968.
40. Requena, Mariano, "The Problem of Induced Abortion in Latin America," *Demography*, Vol. 5, No. 2, 1968. pp. 785-798.
41. Nozue, G., "Abortion in the Far East," *Proceedings of the Eighth International Conference of the International Planned Parenthood Federation, Hereford, England*. New York: International Planned Parenthood Federation, 1967.
42. Koya, Yoshio, "A Study of Induced Abortion in Japan and Its Significance," *Milbank Mem Fund Quart*, Vol. 32, No. 3, July 1954. p. 288.
43. Sadvokasova, E. A., "Some Social and Hygienic Aspects of a Study of Abortion," *Sovet Zdravookhr*, 1963. (Russian.)
44. Miltenyi, Charles, "Social and Psychological Factors Affecting Fertility in a Legalized Abortion System," *Proceedings of the World Population Conference*, 1965. New York: United Nations, 1967.
45. Zikovic, B., "The Problem of Abortion in the Former District of Nove Gradiska," *Lijecn Vjesn*, 1963. (Croatian.)
46. Mehlan, K-H, "Legal Abortion in Romania," *J Sex Res*, 1965.
47. Lakomy, T., "The Problem of Artificial Abortions–Based upon the Material from the Clinic of Obstetrics and Gynecology of the Gdansk Medical School," *Ginek Pol*, 1964. (Polish.)
48. Sutter, T., "Results of a Study of Abortion in the Paris Region," *Population*, 1950. (French.)
49. Jonsson, G., "The Social-Psychological Background of the Woman's Wish for Abortion," *Acta Obstet Gynec Scand*, 1942.
50. Rice-Wray, Edris, "The Provoked Abortion–A Major Public Health Problem," *Amer J Public Health*, Vol. 54, No. 2, February 1964. pp. 313-321.
51. Armijo, R., and M. Requena, "Epidemiological Aspects of Abortion." Paper presented before a Joint Session of the Epidemiology and Maternal and Child Health Sections of the American Public Health Assn., San Francisco, October 1966. Public Health Report, 1968. pp. 41-48.

52. Watson, C., "Birth Control and Abortion in France since 1939," *Population Studies*, Vol. V., 1951-52.
53. Klinger, A., "Abortion Programs," *Family Planning and Population Programs*, Bernard Berelson et al., eds. Chicago: Univ. of Chicago Press, 1966. pp. 465-476.
54. Heer, David M., *Abortion, Contraception, and Population Policy in the Soviet Union*. Boston: Harvard Univ. Center for Population Studies, Contribution No. 3, reprinted from *Demography*, Vol. 2, 1965. pp. 531-539.
55. Baird, D., "A Fifth Freedom?" *Brit Med J*, 1965.
56. Mehlan, K-H, "The Socialist Countries of Europe," *Family Planning and Population Programs*, Bernard Berelson et al., eds. Chicago: Univ. of Chicago Press, 1966. pp. 206-226.
57. Taiwan Population Studies Center, Taiwan Provincial Department of Health, *Taiwan's Family Planning in Charts*. 2nd Ed. Taiwan, 1967. p. 24.
58. Yaukey, David, *Fertility Differences in a Modernizing Country, A Survey of Lebanese Couples*. Princeton: Princeton Univ. Press, 1961.
59. Mendoza-Hoyos, Hernon, "Research Studies on Abortion and Family Planning in Colombia," *Milbank Mem Fund Quart*, Vol. 46, No. 3, July 1968. Table 8, pp. 223-234.
60. "The Population Problems Research Council's Summary of the Sixth National Survey on Family Planning," *The Mainichi Newspapers*. Tokyo, 1962.
61. Gebhard, P. H., et al., *Pregnancy, Birth, and Abortion*. New York: John Wiley & Sons, 1966.
62. The Arden House Conference on Abortion in the U.S., "Report of the Statistical Committee," *Abortion in the United States*, Mary Calderone, ed. New York: Hoebor Harper Book Co., 1958.
63. Ozsvath, I., and S. Rado, "Experience with Interruption of Pregnancy," *Nepegeszsegugy*, 1961. (Hungarian.)
64. Koya, Yoshio, et al., "A Study of Induced Abortion in Japan and Its Significance," *Asian Medical Journal*, 1965.
65. Maulding, W. P., "Fertility Studies: Knowledge, Attitudes and Practice," *Studies in Family Planning*, No. 7, June 1965. pp. 1-10.
66. Miltenyi, Charles, "Induced Abortions in Hungary during the Years 1957-1959," *Demografía*, 3, 1960. p. 424. (Hungarian.)
67. Vojta, M., "New Significance of Abortion and Interruption of Pregnancy for the Development of the Population," *Demograficky Sbornik*, 1961. (Czech.)
68. Starkaleff, I., et al., "The Situation of Abortion in People's Republic of Bulgaria," *Internationale Abortsituation, Abortbekampfung, Antikonzeption*, K-H Mehlan, ed. Leipzig: Georg Thieme, 1961. (German.)
69. Freedman, Ronald, "Family Planning Programs Today: Major Themes of the Conference," *Family Planning and Population Programs*, Bernard

Berelson et al., eds. Chicago and London: Univ. of Chicago Press, 1966. pp. 811-825.

70. Hauser, Philip M., "Family Planning and Population Programs: A Book Review Article." Mimeo. Reprinted in *Demography*, Vol. 4, No. 1, 1967. pp. 397-414.

71. McDermott, W., "Modern Medicine and the Demographic Disease Pattern of Overly Traditional Societies: A Technologic Misfit," *J Med Educ*, Vol. 41, No. 9, Part 2, September 1966. pp. 137-162.

72. Tietze, Christopher, "Induced Abortion as a Method of Fertility Control," *Fertility and Family Planning: A World View.* Sesquicentennial Celebration, November 15-17, 1967. Ann Arbor: Univ. of Michigan, 1967. pp. 1-33. Mimeo.

73. "The Abortion Issue." Report submitted by the 1950 Abortion Committee, Dept. of the Interior, Stockholm. *Statens Offentliga Utredningar*, 1953. p. 298. Swedish.

74. Olki, M., "Die Abortsituation in Finland," quoted by Tietze (72).

75. Klinger, Andras, "Abortion Programs," *Family Planning and Population Programs*, Bernard Berelson, et al., eds. Chicago: Univ. of Chicago Press, 1966.

76. Hirschler, I., "The Situation of Abortion in Hungary," *Internationale Abortsituation, Abortbekampfung, Antikonzeption*, K-H Mehlan, ed. Leipzig: Georg Thieme, 1961. pp. 114-122. German.

77. Szabady, Egan, and Charles Miltenye, "Abortion in Hungary: Demographic and Health Aspects," *Sex and Human Relations: Proceedings of the Fourth Conference of the Region for Europe, Near East and Africa.* London: Internat'l Planned Parenthood Fdtn. (IPPF), 1965. pp. 84-88.

78. Cernoch, A., "Les Autorizations d'interruptions de Grossesse en Tchécoslavaquie: Étude de ses Effets et Consequences," quoted by Tietze (72).

79. Mojic, A., "Abortion as a Method of Family Planning: Experience of the Yugoslav Health Service," *Proceedings of the Third Conference of the Region for Europe, Near East and Africa.* London: IPPF, 1962. pp. 77-79.

80. Coja, N., et al., "Therapeutic Abortion in the Second Clinic of Gynecology and Obstetrics, Cluj," *Obstetrica Ginec, Buc*, 1963. Romanian.

81. Cloeren, S., and M. Mall-Haefeli, "The Abortion Problem," *Praeventivmed*, 1965. Czech.

82. Japan Ministry of Health and Welfare, *Vital Statistics*, published annually. Cited by Tietze (72).

83. Council of the Royal College of Obstetricians and Gynecologists, "Legalized Abortion: A Report," *Brit Med J*, April 1966. pp. 850-854.

84. Tietze, Christopher, "Therapeutic Abortion in the U.S.," *Amer J Obstet Gynec*, Vol. 101, No. 6, July 15, 1968. pp. 784-787.

85. Fox, Leon P., "Abortion Deaths In California," *Amer J Obstet Gynec*, Vol. 98, No. 4, June 15, 1967. pp. 645-653.

86. Guttmacher, Alan F., "Induced Abortion," Editorial, *New York J Med*, 1963. p. 2334.

87. Gold, E. M., et al., "Therapeutic Abortions in New York City: A Twenty-Year Review," *Amer J Public Health*, Vol. 55, No. 7, July 1965. pp. 964-972.
88. Niswander, Kenneth, "Medical Abortion Practices in the U.S.," *Western Reserve Law R*, Vol. 17, No. 2, December 1965. pp. 403-423.
89. Armijo, R., and T. Monreal, "Epidemiology of Provoked Abortion in Santiago, Chile," *Population Dynamics*, M. Muramatsu and P. Harper, eds. Baltimore: Johns Hopkins Press, 1965. pp. 137-160.
90. Neme, B., L. Mathias, and L. Pedro, "Maternal Mortality in Criminal Abortion," *An Brasil Ginec*, 59, 1965. pp. 7-10. Portuguese.
91. Eraj, Y. A., "The Unplanned Pregnancy," *E Afr Med J*, 1966.
92. Hooi, S. C., "Abortion—A Survey of 1000 Cases," *Med J Malaya*, 1963.
93. Australia: Special Medical Committee investigating maternal mortality in New South Wales: Report on Deaths from Abortion, 1957-1960, *Med J Aust*, 1965.
94. Tietze, Christopher, "Mortality with Contraception and Induced Abortion," *Studies in Family Planning*, No. 45, September 1969. pp. 1-7.
95. Valdicieso, D. Ramón, "Normas de las Acciones de Regulación de la Natalidad." Discurso del Ministro de Salud Pública en la Sesión Inaugural de la Octava Conferencia Mundial de la Federación Internacional se Planificación de la Familia, Ministerio de Salud Pública, República de Chile, April 9, 1967.
96. Viel, Benjamin, "Results of a Family Planning Program in the Western Area of the City of Santiago," *Amer J Public Health*, Vol. 59, No. 10, October 1969. pp. 1898-1909.
97. Guttmacher, Alan F., "Therapeutic Abortion in a Large General Hospital," *Surgical Clin N Amer*, April 1957. pp. 459-469.
98. Jakobovits, Immanuel, "Jewish Views on Abortion," *Abortion and the Law*, D. T. Smith, ed. Cleveland: Western Reserve Univ., 1967.
99. Niswander, Kenneth R., Morton Klein, and Clyde L. Randall, "Changing Attitudes toward Therapeutic Abortion," *JAMA*, No. 13, June 27, 1966. pp. 124-127.
100. Halevi, H. S., and A. Brzezinsky, "The Incidence of Abortion among Jewish Women in Israel," *Amer J Public Health*, May 1958.
101. Bachi, Robert, and Judah Matras, "Contraception and Induced Abortions among Jewish Maternity Cases in Israel," *Milbank Mem Fund Quart*, 1963.
102. Eastman, Nicholson J., "Induced Abortion and Contraception, A Consideration of Ethical Philosophy in Obstetrics," *The First Annual Merriam Lecture*. Mimeo.
103. Kelly, G. A., *The Catholic Marriage Manual*. New York: Random House, 1958.
104. Andrews, J. F., Jesuit Denies Abortion in Early Stages is Immoral," *A.S.A. Newsletter*, Vol. 14, No. 4, Winter 1965. p. 6.
105. Jones, Gavin, and Dorothy Nortman, "Roman Catholic Fertility and Family Planning: A Comparative Review of the Research Literature," *Studies in Family Planning*, No. 34, October 1968. Table 5, pp. 20-21.

106. Hutchinson, Bertram, "Induced Abortion in Brazilian Married Women," *America Latina*, Vol. 7, No. 4, October-December 1964. pp. 21-33. Portuguese.
107. "A Pronouncement: A Policy Statement of the National Council of the Churches of Christ in the U.S.A.," *Responsible Parenthood.* Adopted by the General Board, New York, February 23, 1966.
108. 62nd General Convention of the National Episcopal Church, "Resolution on Abortion Law Reform," *Summary of the General Convention Actions*, Secretaries of the House of Bishops and of the House of Deputies, 1968.
109. Wentz, E. K., "Problem of Abortion," *Board of Social Ministry.* New York: Lutheran Church in America, 1967.
110. "American Baptist Resolution on Abortion," Valley Forge, Pa.: American Baptist Convention, May 31, 1968.
111. J. G. (*sic*), "Islam and Birth Control," *Confluent*, 1965. French.
112. Sheikh Abdel-Majid, Salim, the Grand Mufti of Egypt, "Fatwa: Law No. 81, Register 43, 1937," *Journal of the Egyptian Medical Association*, Vol. 20, No. 7, July 1937. pp. 54-56.
113. Thomas, Paul, *Indian Women Through the Ages.* New York: Asia Publishing House, 1964.
114. Haughton, G. C., *Manava-Dherman-Sastra of the Institutes of Menu*, London: Cox and Baylis, 1825. English translation. Vol. II.
115. Jain, S. P., "Fertility Trends in Greater Bombay," International Union for the Scientific Study of Population, Contributed Papers. Sydney conference. Sydney, 1967.
116. Hall, R. E., "Therapeutic Abortion and Sterilization," *Advances in Obstetrics and Gynecology*, 1967. Vol. 1, pp. 248-257.
117. American Law Institute "Model Penal Code: Section 230.3 Abortion," Proposed Official Draft. Philadelphia: American Law Institute, March 4, 1962. Cited in S. Jain and S. Sinding, Monograph No. 2. *North Carolina Abortion Law.* Chapel Hill: Carolina Population Center, 1968.
118. Hall, R. E., "New York Abortion Law Survey," *Amer J Obstet Gynec*, 93, 1965. p. 1182.
119. Hall, R. E., "Abortion in American Hospitals," *Amer J Public Health*, Vol. 57, No. 11, November 1967. pp. 1933-1936.
120. Lyon, Fred A., "Abortion Laws," *Minn Med*, January 1967. pp. 17-22.
121. Aren, P., and C. Amark, "The Prognosis in Cases in which Legal Abortion has been Granted but not Carried Out," *Acta Psychiat Scand*, Vol. 36, 1961. pp. 203-278.
122. Tietze, Christopher, "The Demographic Significance of Legal Abortion in Eastern Europe," *Demography*, 1, 1964. pp. 119-125.
123. Tietze, Christopher, "Abortion in Europe," *Amer J Public Health*, November 1967.
124. Frederiksen, Harald, and James Brackett, "Demographic Effects of Abortion," *Public Health Rep*, Vol. 88, No. 12, December 1968.

XIV

Opinion, Ideology, and Population Problems – Some Sources of Domestic and Foreign Opposition to Birth Control

J. Mayone Stycos

The success of efforts to deal with the problem of world population growth will depend heavily on the extent to which national populations and their leaders are convinced of the seriousness of the problem. This study attempts to assess differences in opinion on population problems among nations and to explicate some of the sources of resistance to family planning among subnational groups in the western hemisphere.

Opinion on any public issue may conveniently be classified as public or private opinion and according to whether it refers to the opinion of elites or the general population. Data for the resulting four types are found in the following characteristic sources:

	Public	*Private*
Elites	(1) Newspapers Books	(3) Unstructured interview
General Population	(2) "Inquiring Photographer" type interview	(4) Poll type interview

It is usually assumed that the "private, anonymous, and confidential" interview provides us with the most "valid" data, or at least the data which best predict behavior. However, the public opinion of politicians or other public figures is certainly more predictive of their behavior than their private opinions which may be almost irrelevant as predictors of their behavior, just as the articulations of an Indian woman in the presence of her in-laws might be a better predictor of her fertility than her more "honest" private thoughts articulated to a stranger with a notebook. Unfortunately, opinion data in the

J. Mayonne Stycos is Director of the International Population Program and Professor of Sociology at Cornell University.

population sphere are heavily concentrated in category 4 (poll type surveys of the general population) and rarest of all in category 2 (public interviews with the general population). Therefore, this paper will deal only with categories 1, 3, and 4 insofar as they relate to opinions on population size and growth on the one hand and to opinions on birth control and family planning on the other.

The Private Opinion of General Populations

Family planning proponents often utilize the results of "KAP" surveys (Knowledge, Attitude, and Practice of Family Planning) to demonstrate public demand for family planning. As measures of national public opinion, especially for purposes of international comparisons, such surveys have a number of limitations:

1. The surveys are usually confined to women in the reproductive age groups and often to women living in relatively stable marital unions. Thus, the opinions of males, older women, and single women are not represented or are underrepresented.

2. Each survey is customarily designed ad hoc so that question wording and sequence of questions are rarely the same from survey to survey.

3. Comparisons between surveys conducted 10 to 15 years apart are often made without regard to time, although there may have been significant shifts of public opinion on population questions over the past decade.

An unusual body of relevant international poll data that is not subject to these limitations has recently been made available. In 1965, the United States Information Agency (USIA) sponsored four questions on population in surveys conducted in twenty-two countries (1, 2). Respondents were not told the sponsorship of the population questions. Local commercial survey organizations and local interviewers were contracted to gather over 17,000 interviews with samples representative of the adult male and female "general population" within each of the places or categories specified in Table 1. (That all the Latin American samples are drawn only from the principal city of the nation and that all the European samples are national must, of course, be borne in mind when one makes cross-national comparisons.)

Perception of National Population Growth

The first question involved the respondents' perception of national population growth:

> Is it your impression that the number of people in [survey country] is increasing, decreasing, or remaining about the same?

In only five countries do more than 10 percent of the respondents fail to answer this question, and three of these nations are European (West Ger-

TABLE 1

Coverage and Sampling in 1965 Surveys on Population

Country	Places	Sample Size	Sample Coverage
WESTERN EUROPE			
Britain	National	1,179	General
France	National	1,228	General
West Germany	National	1,255	General
Italy	National	1,166	General
LATIN AMERICA			
Mexico	Mexico City	493	Urban
Brazil	Rio de Janeiro	501	Urban
Venezuela	Caracas	500	Urban
Argentina	Buenos Aires	507	Urban
Chile	Santiago	511	Urban
FAR EAST			
Japan	National	1034	General
Thailand	Bangkok	500	Urban
Korea	Seoul	500	Urban
Philippines	Manila	500	Urban
Malaysia	Kuala Lumpur	502	Urban
Singapore	National	509	General
NEAR EAST AND SOUTH ASIA			
India	New Delhi	500	Literate, urban
	Bombay	500	Literate, urban
	Calcutta	500	Literate, urban
	Madras	500	Literate, urban
Iran	Tehran	500	Literate, urban
Turkey	Ankara	500	Literate, urban
	Istanbul	500	Literate, urban
Greece	Athens	500	Urban
AFRICA			
Nigeria	Lagos	500	Literate, urban
	Enugu	400	Literate, urban
Kenya	Nairobi	524	Literate, urban
	Mombasa	336	Literate, urban
	Kisumu	218	Literate, urban
	Nakuru	160	Literate, urban
	Machakos/Kitui	295	Literate, urban
Senegal	Dakar	500	Literate, urban

Source: (3).

many, Italy, and Great Britain). In none of the less developed nations do less than three quarters of the respondents believe their population is growing. For all countries, an average (unweighted) of 86 percent believe their nation is growing. It is of interest that in the fastest growing region of the world,

Latin America, the average (mean) is only 80. Indeed, in Caracas, in Rio de Janeiro, and in Mexico City there are over 10 percent who believe their populations are stationary or decreasing in size. On the whole, however, there is virtually a universal awareness of national population growth.

Opinions on Population Growth

The surveys then shifted to three questions of opinion:

> All things considered, do you think having a larger population would be a good thing or a bad thing for this country?
> How about the number of people in the world as a whole? Do you think an increase in the world population would be a good thing or a bad thing?
> All things considered, how would you feel about a birth control program to encourage people in [survey country] to have fewer children—would you approve or disapprove of such a program?

For this set of questions there is a dramatic increase in the "no opinion" category. In seven of the twenty-two countries the number of "no opinions" exceeds 20 percent on the first of the three questions. Four of these are developed countries (Japan, Italy, West Germany, and France), but Rio de Janeiro, Kuala Lumpur, and Singapore also fall in this category. On the second question, referring to world population, the "don't know" and "no opinion" categories range from 1 to 41 percent, with eight countries exceeding 20 percent. Although cultural differences may be of some importance, we conclude that there are serious organizational differences among the pollsters in the ways in which "no answers" are accepted and recorded. To improve comparability, the reported USIA figures have been recomputed, excluding the "no opinions" from the bases used in percentages.* The nations sampled are grouped by continent and the unweighted averages for the three opinion questions are presented in Table 2. Detailed tables including the "no answers" are presented in the appendix to this chapter.

The first noteworthy aspect of Table 2 is the predominance of negative opinion concerning world population growth (Column 2). In only one of the twenty-two sampled areas (Dakar) do less than half of the people with opinions believe such growth is a "bad thing." There is considerable variation, however, both within and between regions. The greatest variation is among the Asian nations, ranging from 95 and 91 percent in India and Turkey to 55 and 61 percent in Bangkok and Manila. Even within Europe the range is great—from a low of 73 percent in Italy to a high of 92 percent in Great Britain. Nevertheless, and this is the second most important aspect of the

---

*Of course statistical "comparability" does nothing about substantive comparability. Excluding the 36 percent "no responses" in Singapore along with the 4 percent in Dakar probably creates or magnifies systematic differences between the two universes which the samples represent.

TABLE 2

Attitudes toward Population Growth and Family
Planning, Twenty-two Countries, 1965

	Percent Believe National Growth a Bad Thing	Percent Believe World Growth a Bad Thing	Percent Approve a National Birth Control Program
Europe			
Unweighted mean	67	86	76
Range	(41-86)	(73-92)	(67-83)
Near East			
Unweighted mean	53	78	74
Range	(22-92)	(61-95)	(62-91)
Far East			
Unweighted mean	53	71	82
Range	(22-81)	(55-91)	(62-99)
Latin America			
Unweighted mean	29	56	74
Range	(19-38)	(52-62)	(61-84)
Africa			
Unweighted mean	33	54	54
Range	(14-47)	(40-61)	(30-71)

Source: (3).

table, there is a sharp division between the figures for Africa and Latin America and those for the rest of the world. Only a narrow majority of the inhabitants sampled in the eight major cities surveyed in these continents believed world population growth to be a bad thing. Within the Latin American region there is very little variation—four of five cities range within 5 percentage points of one another.

The first column of Table 2 reveals a substantial difference in opinion when respondents were asked whether they believe having a larger population would be a good or bad thing for *their* country. Far fewer regard it as bad. France drops by 47 percentage points, Tehran by 44, Athens by 37. Among major geographic regions, the proportional decline is greatest in Africa and Latin America. In these regions a majority of the sampled populations with opinions believe world population increase to be a bad thing, but most people believe it is a good thing for their own country.*

*An unfortunate qualification must be made here. Outside the European region, only respondents who said national growth was a good thing were asked their opinion of world growth; the balance was recorded as having a negative opinion on world growth. Therefore the proportion with a negative opinion on world growth could not be less than that observed for national growth. The assumption seems plausible, though by no means certain; more important is the fact that in Europe, where both questions were asked, the shifts were as substantial as in some of the other regions.

Regarding attitudes toward birth control, a majority of the respondents in every survey (other than in Dakar) favor family planning, as early as 1965. Indeed, in every region there are more people who approve of family planning than who believe that their nation's population increase is a bad thing. This is all the more remarkable when we consider the stringent wording of the question, which refers not merely to the notion of family planning, but to the desirability of *"birth control programs to encourage people to have fewer children."*

According to their responses to this item, countries may be divided into three groups: the Far Eastern countries, three of which have over 85 percent approving and over 50 percent *strongly* approving; Europe, the Near East, and Latin America, where the minimum approval scarcely falls below two thirds; and Africa, where the level of approval is distinctly lower. (The range in Africa however, is very large–from 30 percent in Dakar to 71 percent in Nigeria.) Latin America shows the largest discrepancy between attitudes toward population and toward family planning.

If we disregard the regional classification and rank the countries from 1 to 22 on each of the three items, we discover an interesting pattern–a very close association between rank on attitude toward national population growth and rank on attitude toward world population growth. To measure the degree of association a Spearman Rank-Order Correlation was computed, yielding a value of 0.835. (If there were no relation between the ranks on the two items, the value would be zero; if the ranks were identical, the value would be 1.) Thus, although most countries believe world population growth is a more serious problem than national, their positions vis-à-vis other countries remain about the same. The correlation between attitude toward national growth and attitude toward national birth control programs, however, is much smaller, 0.463, suggesting that national rank on one of these items predicts poorly national rank on the other. If we now divide the countries into two groups on each question, depending on whether they fall in the upper or lower half of the distribution, we emerge with the four types shown in Table 3.

The nations against national growth and in favor of family planning (Group I) are, with the exception of Great Britain, non-Christian, Asian societies all of whom now have active family planning programs. At the opposite pole (Group III), the six nations less in favor of family planning and more in favor of national growth include two Latin American, two African, and two Asian states (Table 3).

The other two categories are especially interesting. One group of countries (II) are rather negative to national population growth but also rather negative to family planning. Italy and Manila, with conservative Catholic populations, might be viewed as nations approving of the ends of population control but not of the contraceptive means. In Group IV–the reverse of the previous group–the Latin American cities are heavily overrepresented. Family

TABLE 3

Attitudes toward National Population Growth and toward a
National Birth Control Program

Attitude toward National Population Growth	Attitude toward Birth Control Program	
	More Positive	Less Positive
Less positive	(I) India Turkey Seoul Japan Singapore Great Britain	(II) Italy West Germany Nigeria Manila Athens
More positive	(III) France Kuala Lumpur Santiago Mexico City Caracas	(IV) Rio de Janeiro Kenya Buenos Aires Bangkok Tehran Dakar

Source: (3).

planning is approved of, but population control (a public policy of discouraging population growth) is not—a position expounded, for example, by
officials of the Chilean government (4).

Before turning to some additional information on reasons for opposition
to family planning, poll data on North American attitudes will help to round
out the picture of world opinion on these topics. Although not a part of the
1965 USIA series, a Gallup poll was conducted in the same year in the United
States. It involved a "modified probability sample" of 3,205 adults (5). A few
of the findings are given in Table 4.

Although the question wording is different, the United States probably
belongs toward that end of the continuum which is concerned about world
population growth, a position it shares with European and eastern nations as
opposed to that of Africa and Latin America. It also appears to share in the
universal tendency to believe that world population problems are more
serious than national ones.

Opposition to Family Planning

Reasons for opposition to family planning are reported only for European
and for two African countries. Within Europe, religious and moral objections
were predominant only in Italy. Of the 26 percent disapproving of birth

TABLE 4

North American Attitudes toward Population
and Birth Control, 1965

Percent who believe that:	
The rate of world population growth is a serious problem.	62
The rate of U.S. population growth is a serious problem.	54
International communism is a more serious problem than world population growth.	71
The U.S. Government should aid states and cities in birth control programs.	63

Source: (5).

control, 8 percent gave religious and 7 percent gave moral objections. In France, the main objection was the need for more people or soldiers (5 of the 18 percent disapproving). In Great Britain and West Germany, the principal objections referred to the potential intrusiveness of government into a private matter; i.e., the objections were less against family planning per se than against the government's possible role in it.

In Dakar, where two thirds of the sample population voiced disapproval of birth control programs (52 percent *strongly* disapproved), the principal reason was that "The country needs men" (37 percent) and an additional 6 percent gave such related reasons as "Overpopulation is no problem" and "There will not be enough children in Senegal."

In Lagos, a survey in 1964 asked:

Would you approve or disapprove of helping people learn how to limit the number of their children if they wish?

Of the 401 respondents, 29 percent disapproved, and the principal reason reflected the Nigerians' belief that more people were needed—both in terms of pure quantity ("Nigeria has plenty of land," "More people are needed to open up underdeveloped lands"—7 percent) and in terms of quality ("Better and more honest leaders, technicians, and men of science" are needed—5 percent). Another 3 percent referred to manpower needs of industry and 3 percent to manpower for war (6).

If we can generalize from these examples, it appears that the small minorities who oppose family planning in Europe did so in 1965 either out of religious conviction (Italy) or, more importantly, out of fear of manipulation by government. In Africa, where much larger proportions of the population opposed family planning, most objections were based on its consequences for *population growth*. This observation is also consistent with the positions of

Italy and of two of the African nations in Table 3, and it reinforces our earlier impression that there are important cultural differences in the way in which the means and ends of family planning are viewed.

With respect to the general public then, we emerge with several conclusions:

1. There is no relation between a nation's growth and a people's concern about that growth. In 1965 the African and Latin American urban populations sampled were largely unconvinced that their nations were growing too large, and most other nations sampled were more concerned about world growth than about the growth of their own nations.

2. In most countries the means (birth control) are less controversial than the ends, insofar as restraint on population growth is considered a major end of birth control. Latin Americans tend to typify the pro-natalist, pro-family-planning position.

3. Countries most committed both to family planning *and* to the notion of excessive national growth were, with the exception of Great Britain, Asiatic nations which have had substantial public family planning programs. Which is cause and which effect is not clear, but it is not unlikely that national public information programs giving attention to both means and ends have had considerable influence in these countries.

THE PRIVATE OPINION OF ELITES

So far we have been dealing with the poll returns as if the opinions of all individuals in a national sample are equal. For purposes of influence on national policy, however, they are not. Unfortunately, most KAP surveys are either confined to lower income classes, or contain so few upper income persons that independent analysis of them is not feasible. In the USIA surveys substantial numbers of upper-class respondents were included, but tabulations were done only for Latin America. Table 5 shows that the classes with the lowest fertility are generally the least favorable to the notion of a family planning program for the nation.

Polls taken in the United States show a contrary tendency. Respondents with more than a high school education are markedly more in favor of the government's participation in family planning programs than those with a grade school education. Among high-school-educated Catholics, however, "there may be a tendency to become *less* liberal as income increases above $7,000" (8).

Latin American Elites

In Latin America, several recent studies have been specifically directed at elite groups. In Bolivia, 97 men and women from law, government, the mili-

TABLE 5

Approval of a National Birth Control Program, by Socioeconomic
Class, Five Latin American Cities, 1965

	Percent Who Approve		
	Upper	Middle	Lower
Buenos Aires	37	49	61
Caracas	48	71	76
Mexico City	60	70	72
Rio de Janeiro[a]	63	62	69
Santiago	70	79	78
	Number in Bases		
Buenos Aires	46	252	209
Caracas	37	160	303
Mexico City	35	161	284
Rio de Janeiro	119	128	254
Santiago	40	170	301

[a]"No Answers" in Rio de Janeiro ranged from 12 percent of the upper class to 20 percent of the lower, and therefore have been removed from the bases before calculating. In other countries, since the total percentage of "No Answers" does not exceed 8 percent for any class category, the "No Answers" have been left in the bases.

Source: (7).

tary, journalism, education, and the clergy were interviewed from a list of 140 "agreed on national leaders." Some representative findings are summarized below:

... 75 percent believe current national population growth to be slow or static.

... 56 percent desire national population growth to be rapid in the next decade.

... 74 percent believe world population growth to be a serious matter.

... 73 percent would favor a national family planning program. (9)

In Medellín, Colombia, a survey of 170 educators, politicians, industrialists, journalists, and female leaders found that although two thirds to all of each of these groups had used birth control, from a third to a half thought physicians should not prescribe contraceptives (10). This response occurred in a nation where, as early as 1966, almost nine out of every ten physicians believed that "it is the physician's duty to prescribe family planning to medical cases that require them, despite the position of the Catholic Church" (11).

A survey of 1,100 male and female adults in Lima, Peru, included a special group of 100 opinion leaders. Selected comparisons between the leaders and the general population are given in Table 6 (12).

TABLE 6

Opinions on Population and Family Planning, Lima, circa 1966

	General Sample	Opinion Leaders
Percent who agree that:		
Rapid population increase slows national progress.	65	51
Steps should be taken to regulate births in Peru.	79	63
To control the number of children is to contribute to the well-being of the family.	91	79
The state should teach people to limit the number of children.	81	75
The state should reward large families.	72	46
Each new child arrives with its own loaf of bread.	42	34
The Catholic woman should not use contraceptives.	54	45
Many children are needed to assure one's old age.	35	12
Number of cases	(1,000)	(100)

Source: (12).

In the first set of questions the leaders are clearly more conservative than the followers, but the reverse is true in the second set. This situation may mean that the former sample, heavily weighted with uneducated respondents, has a greater tendency to agree with any statement (a kind of "yes set") than do the opinion leaders. Or it may mean that uneducated respondents are more genuinely in favor of birth control because they are experiencing the problems of large families; they also want state subsidy of large families because they need the money; and they hold traditional Catholic beliefs without recognizing the contradiction. At least, however, it seems likely that the leaders and followers are not far apart on the basic issues. That half the elite believe the state should reward large families and half believe that population growth does not slow Peruvian progress shows a substantial conservative inclination with respect to population growth and fertility, despite a relatively liberal orientation toward birth control.

In Mexico, a sample of 240 national leaders in political, religious, and professional occupations was found to be quite conservative on the question of population growth (13). When asked the loaded question, "What means should be taken in view of the population growth for the good of Mexico?" only 42 percent were willing to volunteer that the growth should be limited. Not only did over a quarter say "no means," but 28 percent said that population growth should be *stimulated.* Indeed, less than half believe Mexico's population is growing very rapidly, and a clear majority (58 percent) believe that the nation's population growth is increasing its economic potential. Further, four in every five felt the ideal number of children to be five or more, and only four out of ten regard the birth control pills as acceptable; 20 percent felt that control of pregnancy was *never* acceptable. On the few items of which comparisons with a more general survey were possible, leaders were more in favor of families of five or more but more liberal on the acceptability of birth control than were nonleaders. (The high proportion of "don't knows" among the general population on questions concerning specific contraceptives, however, should be considered.)

In sum, the available evidence from Latin American studies of leadership groups indicated that:

1. Large proportions are unconvinced that a population problem exists in their country. Indeed, many believe that rapid population growth is needed.

2. Most leaders favor family planning programs, as opposed to population control programs, but even here substantial minorities are against such programs.

3. There is some evidence that the upper classes are more conservative than the lower, but there are serious methodological problems which cause us to conclude that the question is still open.

While we lack these kinds of studies in other regions, it is of interest that a recent survey of over 600 members of urban elites in Ghana provided corroborative information on the first two points. For example, whereas close to three quarters favored the establishment of family planning clinics and two thirds expressed a willingness to use family planning, only a quarter of the males felt the nation's economic development would be helped if parents had fewer children, and over two thirds of the elite males and females felt the present national rate of population growth to be good, even after being told that it was "increasing much faster than in most parts of the world" (14).

The Public Opinion of Elites

There is no doubt that the upper classes practice family planning much more than the lower and that their fertility is much lower. We have also noted that their private opinions tend to favor family planning, but not policies aimed at limiting population growth. What they say in public, however, is a matter of much greater significance than what they say and do in private. In this context elites may be defined as those who feel strongly enough about population and family planning to speak *publicly* on it, and whose prestige is great enough to merit publication of their views by newspapers or magazines. Since our analysis will concentrate on opposition to birth control programs, it may be helpful first to place both opposition and advocacy in a more general framework.

Table 7 schematizes the nature and source of elitist opinion on family planning and population control, with special reference to groups in the

TABLE 7

Major Elitist Public Arguments in the Western Hemisphere for and against
Family Planning and Population Control, According
to Political Position[a]

	Left	Center	Right
FAMILY PLANNING			
In favor	Individual human right	Anti-abortion Family health & welfare	Responsible parenthood
	New left *Old left*	*Physicians* *Social workers*	*Young clergy*
Opposed	Populationism	0	Hedonism-promiscuity
	Black militants		*Old clergy*
POPULATION CONTROL			
In favor	0	Economic development	Political-economic stability Welfare costs
		Economic planners	*Politicians*
Opposed	Anti-imperialism Revolutionism	Coercion	Nationalism Abundant labor supply Populationism
	Castroites *Peking Communists*	*Liberal intellectuals*	*Military* *Big business*

[a]Italics show examples of groups holding stated positions.

western hemisphere. Aside from the zeros, there is no attempt to indicate relative frequencies in each category. In fact, the scales are probably tipped in the favorable direction toward family planning and possibly narrowly so toward population control, though north-south differences would be especially striking here. Leftist opposition to family planning and centrist opposition to population control are especially small (but vociferous) categories.

Although we have provided an example for each category of a group which tends to maintain such a position, there is no suggestion that all members of the group believe or proclaim it or that there are not other groups who do so. Further, as we have seen from our national poll data, attitude toward family planning does not predict attitude toward limiting population growth; therefore, any group should properly be classified twice in the table. For example, Castroites tend to favor family planning and oppose population control, and many economists favor population control and are not interested in family planning programs.

Groups Opposed to Family Planning or Population Control

Although crude, the scheme provides a springboard for a number of generalizations:

1. The opposition to family planning in this hemisphere is concentrated among the far right and left. Indeed, the Black Muslims on the one hand, and the older hierarchy of the Catholic Church constitute the major organized opposition in the hemisphere, the former for reasons of "populationism" (the equation of numbers and group power); the latter for fear of increasing hedonism and weakening the family as the basic social unit.

2. Opposition to population control, on the other hand, is found at all points of the political spectrum, though for different reasons. As we shall see, the revolutionaries see it as an imperialistic scheme to weaken the likelihood of drastic social and economic change; the rightists see it as an imperialistic scheme to emasculate the Third World.

3. Approval of family planning is based upon its salutary effects on the individual or family. The leftists see it as enhancing individual (especially female) freedom, the centrists as improving family health and welfare, and the rightists as a means of increasing the discipline, responsibility, and stability of the lower classes—the other side of the promiscuity-hedonism coin.

4. Among those favorable to population control, the center sees it as a means of enhancing or accelerating economic development, or as another general public health measure. The right favors it as a way of improving the lot of poor people without excessive disturbance of the distribution of power and as a way of reducing the growing costs of social welfare programs. In regard to the far left, very few in Latin America favor it, and very few in North America have spoken on the subject.

By turning to the published writings of certain of the opponents of family planning or population control in the western hemisphere, some of the categories in Table 7 can be further explicated.* For North America discussion will be limited to the black militants and the new left because so little has been published about these groups and because they are exercising increasing influence on young intellectuals and the elites of tomorrow. The discussion will be organized around three broad values or goals which vary among nations or groups within nations: (a) national power, (b) distributive justice, and (c) individual freedom.

National Power

All nations are concerned with power in international relations, whether power is viewed in terms of military might, gross national product, or pres-

---

*For discussions of Latin American elitist opinion, see the following section on national power and (15-17).

tige. However, among the world's older nations, in developed areas, such as Europe, the less powerful ones have adapted psychologically to their modest power status. National pecking orders of long standing minimize conflict and guarantee an absence of friction over the problem. Of course, acquiescence by small European nations is made much easier by the combination of high per capita incomes and recent efforts at economic and political integration.* Most developing nations, however, are relatively new as nations; they have been exposed to the pecking order for a much briefer time and may not recognize it at all; therefore, as newcomers they are highly concerned with "national mobility." Such countries are invariably poor and thus are denied the psychological comforts of small-country prosperity; nor have they yet developed specializations which would, as in the case of social legislation or sexual freedom in Scandinavia, provide international prestige in a less competitive market. Further, there are special reasons why they might be especially prone to consider population size as a key to national mobility.

First, many of them *are* small in absolute population size, and especially small in the ratio of people to land. Further, this very smallness is often the consequence of actions by colonial powers; slavery, warfare, and the spread of disease are often referred to as decimating native populations of Africa and Latin America. More refined political techniques are often cited, too. The suspicion that the Spanish in Latin America and the British and French in Africa created artificial nations in order to divide and conquer is now matched with the notion that by means of "preventive genocide" and "neo-colonial biological imperialism," the big powers are striving to *keep* these nations small.

In Latin America, a leading voice of nationalism has been the editor of El Salvador's *El Diario de Hoy*, Napoleon Viera Altamirano.† In a 33-month period beginning in mid-1965, no less than fifty-one of his editorials on population have come to our attention. Scarcely a month goes by without at least one editorial, and in several months there have been one or more per week.‡

Slightly shaken (it provoked three consecutive editorials) by Lleras Camargo's flat advocacy of birth control in mid-1965, he reminded Colombia's ex-president that the continent could easily host two or three billion inhabitants and warned him that even serious problems would not warrant

*Even so, a medium-sized nation such as France is not only very concerned over its power position, but especially concerned over the relation of population size to power, largely as a result of manpower losses going back to World War I.

†The following discussion of Altamirano's editorials first appeared in *Demography*, Vol. 5, No. 2, 1968, pp. 850-853; and is included here with minor editorial changes, quoted by permission of the copyright holder.

‡Although most of the editorials quoted here are unsigned, we have, for reasons of style and their editorial position, attributed them to Altamirano. All appeared in *El Diario de Hoy*, a newspaper with a circulation of 56,000 daily and 80,000 on Sunday.

"converting the American mother's womb into a slaughter-house or latrine" (18).

Altamirano's identification of population growth and nationalism is a dominant theme. A heady mix of Juan Bautista Alberdi's demographic slogan with one of Altamirano's favorite biological metaphors produces the following: "To populate continues meaning to civilize, the only difference being that (in this century) the population still needed to civilize America should emerge vigorous and pulsating from the womb of [Latin] American mothers" (19). So vital is population growth that its antonym (birth control) is death's synonym: "When we achieve the demographic density of the great European powers, we shall see if the threat of poverty allows no alternative to suicide" (20).

Little wonder that Altamirano can refer to Lleras' position as one of "extreme pessimism" when his own approaches ethereal optimism:

> The sea is yielding herself to us like a virgin land that once offered herself as a path to unknown territories and fabulous resources. Technology makes the every inch of land a source of riches. Where a tree cannot grow, something else is produced for man. The craggy mountain peak becomes a site to store the water or snow which produces the electricity which in the hands of man will make bread fall from heaven . . . yielding sustenance for all. (21)

Five years ago such optimism was typical of the Latin American intellectual and even, to a lesser extent, of the international agencies. In the past few years, however, Altamirano has had to deal with a growing number of agencies, such as "the FAO, the UNICEF, and even the UNESCO and the OAS, entering the movement under the supreme command of the U.N., spreading the crass error that our population growth is falling behind the increase in food production" (22). His charges against the international organizations soon became more specific, and the new year of 1967 was ushered in with an editorial entitled "Both UNESCO and the FAO in the Racist Plot." It should not be thought, however, that the plot is restricted to the European and North American organizations typically the target of Altamirano's ire. In condemning demography as a new profession created "to manipulate statistics to prove that the whirlpool of population growth requires birth control," he jabs quickly at the Economic Commission of Latin America (ECLA) (23). In other editorials he adds the Inter-American Committee on the Alliance for Progress (CIAP) (24), the Pan American Health Organization, and the Latin American Center of Demography (CELADE), which he terms a "genocidal Center" (25).

Indeed, there are few institutions or classes of people which are exempt from attack. In one editorial he attacks "leader classes, academicians, thinkers and statesmen" (26), and when one hundred Nobel Prize winners called attention to the population problem, the scientists were likened to "monstrous mathematical animals . . . the same scientists who gave us the dreadful arms for nuclear war" (27).

Even the Church cannot remain entirely without suspicion. In a critical editorial devoted to the September 1965 statement of Cardinal Suenens, Altamirano warns darkly that "today there are ideological currents deliberately aimed at destroying the spiritual power of the Church" (28). Soon he is hinting more darkly still at infiltration: "The great fallacious and deceiving argument that demographic growth lags behind economic growth has already been accepted by the Alliance for Progress and some sectors of the Church, as desired by the non-Catholic racists" (29). In disparaging the argument that slowing population growth will improve income distributions, he contemptuously attributes it to "CEPAL, Moscow, Washington, *Rome*, Peking, and Havana" (29, italics added). The changes in the Church are so incomprehensible they can only be attributed to evil forces. He admits he witnessed "with stupefication" how a South American Cardinal during the last ecumenical council "referred with disrespect and blasphemy to the dogma of the Virgin Mary"; and announced forthrightly the source of "the enemies without and the traitors within": it is no less than a community conspiracy. ". . . [T]he Marxist circles, assured that the Church would fall, little by little, into their hand, . . . tried to carry the socialist ideology to the encyclicals, pressuring for all possible agrarian reforms . . . their conspiracy against clerical celibacy. . . . In Colombia Camilo Torres soon appeared . . . then to join the criminal communist gangs" (30).

The reader may have noted a not infrequent reference to a "racist plot," a plot which lies at the heart of Altamirano's crusade, "a vast racist communist and imperialistic conspiracy . . . to socialize, depopulate and de-Catholicize us." The latter phrase is frequently used in the editorials and provides a useful point of departure for explication of his position. Let us consider each of its three terms.

Socialism. The Marxist infiltration of the Church is one small piece of a much grander design. Altamirano sees a "multicontinental, worldwide" effort to "take over." He sees the U.N. "plagued with agents of international leftism" (31) and the FAO "falling into the hands of activists of the socialist left" (32). Naturally, hemispheric institutions have been included. The Alliance for Progress, he feels, has felt the "lethal leftist influence" from its inception, and has been moving farther and farther toward destroying freedom in Latin America (33). The Economic Commission for Latin America is clearly under the influence of socialist economists.

Depopulation. The effort to depopulate Latin America is a part of the socialist conspiracy. The link is on occasion explicitly established.

Not only was it necessary to check demographic growth by birth control, but structural reforms were imposed in order to guarantee a "better distribution of wealth" making possible a true "social justice." In other words the constructive work which the FAO could do was converted into a socialist and Malthusian promotion. (34)

or again:

. . . the leftists not only are trying to check our social development, socializing and regimenting us prematurely, but also holding back our population growth. (35)

At the same time, however, and sometimes in the same editorial, Altamirano can attribute the plot or its financing to "industrial interests of a certain medical kind" (36). Equally unusual for a socialist plot is its success "thanks to the resources made available as much by the U.S. Government as by the contraceptive firms"; (37) or to financing "by racists from the United States and Nordic Europe" (38).

At any rate, there is no doubt that the United States is directly implicated, though it is not singled out for attack as often as in earlier years. Outside of its financial backing, it is usually grouped with other Nordics, Europeans, or "many people" who feel that there are too many "Negroes, Indians, mulattos, and mestizos," and are attempting to prevent "the Central American man from taking firm possession of his land" (39).

Decatholicization and the Fertility Mystique. If the Latin "man" is the ultimate target of this foreign attack, the Latin woman is the medium. Altamirano's view of woman is in the tradition of conservative Catholicism notable in the recent encyclical of Pope Paul. He refers to "the blessed womb of the Central American woman" from which "millions more beings will come to fill the cities" (40). To stop such prolificity would be to stop nature, so that birth control assumes "proportions of genocide in the very maternal cloister of our America" (41). In attacking those who would substitute birth control for abortion, he shows his revulsion for sins of the flesh. "Why should the poor woman have to be taught to sin without conceiving?" (41). The sexual freedom it might bring the woman would be intolerable, as "The mother becomes sterile at will" (42). He sees the "American woman–colored, mestizo, Indian, mulatto, etc." being used in Brazil as "guinea pigs to try out the best methods to check the growth of these peoples" (43) and 40,000 Colombian women "submitting for over two years, to a process of sterilization with chemical contraceptives . . . financed by North American firms and possibly with approval of Alliance functionaries" (44). The fertility mystique and fears of socialism blend nicely in his phrase "regimentation of the womb." His concern over depopulation and his fertility mystique are also blended in the affirmation "a people's will to grow is as authentic as its wish to live, because it is the will to power, a will stemming from the very wellspring of life" (45).

Elsewhere in Latin America, when World Bank President Robert McNamara announced in Argentina that rapid population growth could slow economic development, the reaction was swift and predictable. Inter-American Bank President Felipe Herrera announced that "Latin America is not overpopulated but underpopulated" (46). *El Clarin* termed it an "insulting racism which can indifferently let hundreds of thousands of colored people die in Nigeria and Biafra and which now hopes to avoid future problems by preventing them from being born" (47). President Ongania answered by deeds, quickly supporting new Argentine legislation to stimulate the birth rate by major increases in family allowances. According to the wording of the bill: "This innovation represents only the beginning of a family and demographic policy that would tend to stimulate the increase in the number of births in order to enrich the human potential of our country as an indispensable means to guarantee authentic national justice." In providing additional sums beginning with the third child, the legislation is clearly directed at "the realization of a demographic policy" (48).

The Bolivian National Senate made a long declaration in response to McNamara's statement, maintaining that "Because of its territorial extension and its small population, Bolivia's development depends on the increase in its population, also considering that the chief factor in commerce and industrialization, in addition to the man who produces, is the man who consumes" (49).

Ethnic and Racial Nationalism. Within nations the same phenomenon can be seen with respect to nationalistic minority groups. Blacks often see themselves in a demographic race with whites, and vice versa.

> Right now there are about 3.6 million Europeans living in South Africa and 19.1 million Africans and Asians; about a 5 to 1 ratio. By the year 2000 . . . the gap will have widened to 7 to 1. This projection has struck fear into the "whites." (50)

Cesar Chavez, organizer of the California grape pickers, has stated, "Our only solution is to make the minority much less a minority and make the race progress and multiply" (51); while a small California-based group, EROS (Efforts to Raise Our Size) takes a position very similar to the demographic nationalists of the Third World. As interpreted by Stewart, they maintain that

> The 180,000,000 or more white Americans had sustained an unlimited population growth for over 400 years until they reached the numerical strength they desired. It was their feeling, then, and the feeling is more widespread now, that non-whites who number only 22,000,000 or more need to double this amount in the next 20 years. It is their feeling that the present white majority who had the luxury to grow at their phenomenal

rate should practice birth control to the extent that they maintain a zero or less rate of growth during the next 20 years in order to permit the non-white community to achieve its doubling objective. Through this means they allege we will maintain the ideal growth rate we suggest we need in order to preserve our present quality of life. (52)

In a book by the Black Muslim leader Elijah Muhammad, a section entitled "Do Not Take Birth Control Pills" urges blacks to increase and multiply.

... If you accept Allah and follow me and give birth to 100 children each of you girls and women will be considered more blessed and upright in the eyes of Allah (God) than those who try to kill the birth need.... Why don't they divide the country with you, give you a few of these United States and let you raise all the children you want to. (53)

Reacting to President Nixon's July, 1969, message on population, an officer of the Florida NAACP* stated to the *New York Times:*

I do not think the President's plan is in the best interests of the black people. Our women need to produce more babies, not less. Our problems are mainly economic ones, and until we comprise 30 to 35 per cent of the population we won't be able to really affect the power structure in the country. I don't think this plan will get much support in the black community. The people will consider it an insult. (54)

If one accepts the premises that people are power and that whites are engaged in a "no holds barred" struggle against yellow, brown, or black power, then all manner of ingenious techniques to curb that power can be imagined. Headlines such as

GROUP FINDS LEAD POISONING COMMON WAY TO LEGALLY 'MURDER' BLACK CHILDREN (55)

INFANTICIDE MISSISSIPPI STYLE (56)

THE DELIBERATE POISONING OF GOOD FOOD AND GOOD DRINKS BY THE AVOWED ENEMY (57)

are common in the Black Muslim daily, *Muhammad Speaks.* Two examples of the kind of reasoning behind such accusations are given below:

The spread of narcotic addiction among Black youth is a form of genocide. It's the same tactic of extermination this country has used against Blacks all over the world, only they've taken it out of the Vietnam jungles and put it on the streets of the Black ghetto.... It's made genocide profitable by having the addict pay to poison himself. (58)

*National Association for the Advancement of Colored People.

The Food and Drug Administration ran a series of animal tests on surplus bacon meat that has been radiated and canned for the last three years to avoid spoilage. Results found that among animals that ate the meat there were less and less births. What happened to this surplus food over the last three years? Was it sent as foreign aid to all the darker nations? Is this what they are sending to Biafra right now? (59)

From these plots to exterminate undesirable populations, it is a short step to family planning. Some years ago the Black Muslim leader, Master W. Ford Muhammad, warned his disciples that, "Our enemies, the devils, now seek to prevent us from being a nation through our women, as Pharoah attempted to destroy Israel by killing off the male babies of Israel at birth" (60). More recently Chavez noted that "History is full of cases where they used bullets and weapons of destruction; now they have found a better way . . . they are going to exterminate us before we are ever born" (61).

A recent article penned by Pan-African Press writer Ogun Kakanfo shows how demographic nationalism has both international and intranational implications. Referring to a statement by John D. Rockefeller III that resolution of the population problem by the United Nations could be its greatest contribution to mankind, he comments,

> This contribution . . . involves wiping out 2 billion potential liberation army soldiers in the systematically de-developed nations of Asia, Africa, Central and South America . . . the most hated and bitterly opposed scheme the U.S. Government has plotted since the enslavement of Africans and the near-extinction of North and South American Indians is the world-wide birth control program. (62)

In 1968 in Pittsburgh militant blacks forced the closing of certain Office of Economic Opportunity (OEO) family planning services by threatening to bomb them. In this case Dr. Charles Greenlce, health committee chairman of the Pittsburgh chapter of the NAACP, wrote that "since Congress wouldn't pass a Rat Control Bill it's become popular to kill Black babies by birth control" (63). William Haden, black leader of Pittsburgh's United Movement for Progress, threatened riots and firebombing "if anyone tries to operate a birth control project in the area. I will use any weapon to fight the program and use it against people, black or white, who peddle pills to black women" (64). According to Haden, "The pill can lead to a bigger massacre of black people than the Germans' killing of the Jews" (65). Supported by a grant from the Catholic Dioceses of Pittsburgh, Haden was backed by Msgr. Charles O. Rice, who maintained that the birth control program was "sociological vandalism" and "an invitation to the Negroes to commit race suicide" (66).

The kind of sexual nationalism typified by prewar Germany and Italy, and brought out so clearly in Altamirano's fears of "regimentation of the womb"

(45) are also evidenced among contemporary black militants. Dr. Greenlee's colorful terminology provides us with some examples. In a column regularly entitled "Death in a Douche Bag," Dr. Greenlee frequently referred to contraceptives as "kill pills," to family planning as "Play without Pay," and to the social worker's contraceptive kit as "The Fun Bag." To the macabre blending of sexual joy and death can be added the threat of castration. Whereas Altamirano sees the "Latin American mother's womb becoming a slaughter house" (67), and a conspiracy to "block our growth, cutting the wombs of Latin American mothers, castrating Latin males, before our peoples have grown sufficiently or taken possession of the vast empty lands of the continent" (18), Greenlee refers to

> . . . a group of black men studying how to attack the "Half Women" idea. This group feels that a black woman, taking birth control pills, is the exact same as the black woman who has had her organs removed and for that reason she should be looked upon as an incomplete woman sexually. If this idea catches on, we will have less pill taking and fewer men leaving home in search of a complete sex relation. (68)

Distributive Justice

A characteristic mission of Marxists, new leftists, and, increasingly, young people everywhere is for a more equitable distribution of the world's goods, both among nations and among groups and classes within nations. Even admitting that reduced population growth could accelerate increases in the gross national product, they question whether the benefits would ever by seen by the poor. A larger gross national product, they would argue, means only that the rich get richer or that armies grow larger. The prior, more fundamental task is changing the nature of the social structure in such a way that goods and services will be more equitably distributed. For some, this can only be brought about by revolution, for others by serious and far-reaching economic and social reforms. Proponents of this point of view are determined to suppress anything which deflects attention from their objectives. When they suspect that the deflection is intentional and manipulative, their hostility is understandably even greater.

> The present birth control-population control-family planning program of the present U.S. ruling class must be crushed because it tells people that their economic and political problems—exploitation and racism—are really biological ones—fertility and love of children. The Super Rich, through Ford and Rockefeller money . . . brainwash people into blaming their own strong and creative natural powers of conceiving, bearing and bringing up children for the fact that they are denied educational opportunities, job

opportunities . . . proportionate political power and freedom from war.
(69)

When the South African elites announce their concern over a manpower
shortage of professionals and view the problem as a demographic one, the
blacks analyze the problem quite differently and see a social structural problem:

> The manpower crisis really results from the fact that real Africans are
> denied education, training, jobs, health, housing. . . . (70)

But instead of filling the manpower gap by training black Africans, they say,
the elites are providing birth control programs for the blacks.

In the area of international aid, President Johnson's "dollar for birth control is worth $95" convinced many foreigners that the United States was
either shopping for dubious bargains or looking for ways to reduce its already
inadequate aid to the Third World. Even more sinister were apparent cutbacks
in aid for general programs of health. As Peru's then minister of health put it,
". . . the United States is willing to help in a campaign for the control of
births but not in one to reduce the rate of deaths" (71).

Precisely the same phenomenon can be observed in the United States,
where money and personnel are conspicuously available for family planning,
but where generals of the War on Poverty seem to have declared a truce.
Speaking of young black militants, Douglas E. Stewart writes,

> In the communities where they live there is also a disproportionate
> amount of bad housing, a disproportionate amount of bad health and
> welfare facilities in general, or the non-existence of health and welfare
> facilities, a disproportionate amount of unemployment, and all that ap-
> pears to them to be shiny and bright is our birth control services. "In most
> instances, you people say family planning and use the words planned
> parenthood, which denotes family to us, which means unit to us (one or
> more), and parenthood, which means the production of children, and yet
> we hear very little concern expressed by you people about children already
> born. This lack of expressed concern and action causes us to be suspicious
> of your motives, produces our fear of your programs and raises questions
> in our minds about genocide." (72)

Much of Dr. Greenlee's fire in Pittsburgh was aimed at the unusual attention
being paid to family planning programs when so many other pressing ills were
being neglected. Other black militants have raised similar questions:

> . . . What U.S. hospital has a policy of visiting sick people who skip ap-
> pointments? What welfare group sends volunteers to the homes of people

who miss getting their check or the chance to get welfare food supplies? Do they have "volunteers" to go out and tell people about good jobs . . . ? (73)

Individual Freedom

Among political and sexual conservatives, birth control has never been regarded as a right, and at best is seen as a privilege for the educationally and morally superior classes who can practice it "responsibly." Moralists from Ghandi to Paul VI have recognized the potential for sexual liberation represented by birth control and have condemned it largely for this reason. Both advocated self-restraint as a stone to kill the twin birds of excessive fertility and hedonism. Typified by reactions to the Pope's recent encyclical, the fear of unrestrained sexuality is common among many churchmen and conservatives in Latin America. For example, the Archbishop of Tegucigalpa (Honduras) announced that his government's family planning program tended to "develop prostitution" (74); the Peruvian Bishops congratulated the Pope for his defense of "married life against a reigning hedonism" (75); and a Colombian Monsignor lauded the encyclical as a "violent but necessary brake to sexual corruption in the Western world" (76).

Radicals, on the other hand, have approved of birth control precisely because of its liberating qualities. From the early days of the U.S.S.R., birth control and abortion have been essential components of the movement to liberate women in socialist societies. Another important intellectual movement for sexual liberation was psychoanalysis. An especially vigorous proponent, currently enjoying a comeback with the new left, was Wilhelm Reich, who saw sexual repression as closely linked to both authoritarian and economically underdeveloped societies. "Its function," he wrote in 1942, "is that of laying the foundations for authoritarian, patriarchal culture and economic slavery" (77). A decade later he became convinced that "genital misery" was the key to national underdevelopment.

> No amount of effort to alleviate the great economic misery of the Asiatic masses can ever succeed, unless their emotional and genital misery is alleviated first. It is this misery which renders these millions helpless to do anything or even think about their economic misery [a misery which] cannot even be touched without a clear-cut, thorough and most resolute attack on their genital misery [overpopulation through lack of birth control, cruel moralism, etc.]. . . . (78)

For the new left, female liberation is an essential aspect of the broad revolutionary changes which they seek. As put by Naomi Jaffe of the New York chapter of WITCH,* "The oppression of women is a fundamental part

*Women's International Terrorist Conspiracy from Hell.

of the international division of labor in which nation and people are exploited for the benefit of the U.S. ruling class" (79). One means of escaping such oppression is through power over the childbearing function, or freedom from the penalties of childbearing. In a recent lengthy article in a new left publication, writers Kathy McAfee and Myrna Wood wrote,

> All women are oppressed and exploited sexually. For working class women this oppression is more direct and brutal. They are denied control of their own bodies, when as girls they are refused information about sex and birth control, and when as women they are denied any right to decide whether and when to have children.

The writers recommend the dissemination of birth control information in high schools, liberal abortion reform, and the provision of maternity leaves and child care facilities so that working class women can "free themselves from slavery as sex objects and housewives" (80).

In the June, 1969, Students for a Democratic Society (SDS) Conference in Chicago, controversy over the female liberties issue was heated, not only between the Progressive Labor Party (PLP) wing and the Revolutionary Youth Movement (RYM) but also between factions of the latter. The PLP sees the working class struggle as the dominant issue and insists that black liberation and female liberation must have a *class* character, not a race or sex character. They maintain that male chauvinism is a product of capitalistic exploitation of female workers. This group was expelled from the Conference. The "RYM 2" faction gave more emphasis to female and black liberation movements, both as a way of increasing the consciousness of the working class and as desirable in their own right. In a statement of five principles presented to the Conference, Point II read, in part, as follows:

> . . . The proletariat cannot achieve complete freedom without achieving complete freedom for women. The struggle for women's liberation is a powerful force against U.S. imperialism. We are dedicated to fighting male supremacy, to destroying the physical and spiritual oppression of women by men, and to the achievement of full equality for women in every sphere of life. . . . We support the struggle of women for control over their bodies, and demand the removal of all legal and financial restrictions on abortion, and the provision of free birth control for those women who desire it. (81)

Arguing for the primacy of the women's movement, a WITCH representative echoed the Reichian point of view: "The basic unity of women's oppression is the home, and the family is the basic unit of imperialism" (82). Thus, if women are exploited as workers, she argued, this exploitation is a product of their sexual and family oppression.

The five-point RYM 2 proposal was attacked by the RYM 1 or "Weatherman" faction, however, and defeated. Two of the spokeswomen against it argued that "no change in the status of women could occur until socialism was achieved" (82). Black Panther spokesmen further divided the conference on the female issue by proclaiming in favor of "pussy power," a comment which caused severe negative reactions, unrelieved by a Panther leader's subsequent explanation that "He was only trying to say that you sisters have a strategic position for the revolution—prone" (82).

But if the various factions are divided on the primacy of the strategy of women's liberation movements, it is clear that all white radicals recognize the desirability of female equality and the importance of birth control techniques—contraception and abortion—in achieving this equality. Indeed, such "conservative" approaches can almost be taken for granted. Somewhat more controversial will be such means as are advocated in a "Journal of Female Liberation" entitled *No More Fun and Games* (83):

> As for single women, we advise them to remain single, and to deal with problems of being a woman alone and free, living autonomously in control of her own life. The most demanding and rewarding arrangement is to live completely alone; however, this is sometimes financially impossible. Female communes offer a creative alternative. The commune should be politically rather than socially oriented (liberation, not snagging men, should be the goal) and women should practice self-sufficiency individually and collectively. Possibilities for learning from each other should be exploited, while resisting temptation to fall back on each other for entertainment.
>
> We think one should avoid pregnancy (by abortion if necessary) at this time. If one has talent for dealing with children, she (or he) can work in a nursery school or an orphanage or even set up a child care center. If one has an overpowering need to possess a child of one's own, there are many homeless children and unwanted children soon to be born: there is no need, where the world problem is overpopulation and not underpopulation, to bring still more into the world. However, if one does feel a need to possess and mold a child of one's own, perhaps that is a sign that one has not achieved sufficient maturity and autonomy and is seeking a hopeless fulfillment through neurotic channels.

Black moderates tend to favor family planning for the same reasons as white moderates, but the picture is less clear for black radicals. On the one hand they are not so concerned as white radicals about female liberation. On the other hand, the "virilism" apparent in some factions plus the equation of black power with black numbers tend to bias them against birth control, even as a way of liberating the female. Julius Lester is one of the very few black radicals who sees the positive role of birth control in the achievement of black power:

> Those black militants who stand up and tell women "Produce black babies!" are telling black women to be slaves. . . . To have 11 children and

a welfare check is almost akin to suicide, no matter how much black militants want to romanticize the black mother. . . . There is power in numbers, but that power is greatly diminished if a lot of those numbers have to sit at home and change diapers instead of being on the front lines, where most of them would rather be. (84)

CONCLUSION

Analysis of 1965 world poll data discloses that the general public in most countries surveyed was aware of, and to some extent concerned about, the rapid rate of world population growth. Far fewer were concerned about the growth of their own nations, especially if their nations were in Africa or Latin America, where especially high growth rates prevail. The attitude toward family planning is surprisingly favorable in virtually all countries, though African respondents tended to be less favorable to it than non-African. The lack of correspondence between attitudes toward population growth and attitudes toward birth control suggested that various dimensions of the population problem have to be considered in classifying either nations or individuals. In seeking the sources of opposition to birth control, we identified three basic values—national or group power, distributive justice, and individual freedom—which underlie the opposition of various individuals and groups. Nationalist and radical groups are often unconvinced that birth control will enhance the power of the group or nation, and radicals especially are unconvinced that any potential economic benefits would be distributed to needy populations.

But with the exception of extreme moral conservatives and extremist black groups, wide-ranging leadership groups tend to favor birth control on grounds of individual freedom. The major spokesman on population matters for Cuba, who repeatedly insists that "all revolutionaries believe that at the banquet to which nature has invited us, we will never have too many," still insists a sentence or two later that

> . . . fertility control . . . is an individual matter of the [married] couple, and the socialist society should facilitate the best means for resolving an individual need. (85)

The left wing Central Labor Federation of Chile has declared itself in favor of family planning and "irrevocably" opposed to birth control.

> . . . Considering that the latter hinders the transformation of the socio-economic structures of Latin America. The CUT considers family planning an intimate family phenomenon, within which the family exercises absolute freedom of decision concerning the number of children. Birth control is understood to be an official policy intended to control births to the detriment of the total development process. (86)

A militant spokeswoman for female liberation may write that "when the colony exceeds capitalism's need for menial workers, no longer functions efficiently as a reserve army of labor and develops a revolutionary consciousness which threatens the whole imperialist system, black women's right to bear children is violated through genocidal 'population control' programs"; but in the next sentence she demands to "control our own bodies," and have "completely free and equal access of all women to birth control and abortions" (79). Even contentious Jane Jacobs can accept birth control on certain terms. "It is a great force for the social and economic liberation of women," she writes, "and perhaps a major human right . . . but as a prescription for overcoming economic stagnation and poverty is nonsense. Worse, it is quackery" (87).

If there are lessons here for United States population policy, they first of all point to the need for treating nations differently depending on the way in which they regard family planning and policies to limit population growth. An important question which the United States, and more particularly international agencies, must face is whether to assist nations or subnational groups to increase their fertility levels if such nations or groups define this as in their interest. Just as the Planned Parenthood movement has always stressed its service to infertile couples as well as to those desiring birth control, should population agencies be prepared to assist Argentina and Bolivia to raise their effective fertility levels or better populate their empty lands?

Perhaps, too, it is time to give more thought to the role of population planning in distributive justice. Concern for this area is no longer the exclusive domain of discontented foreign nationals, but of growing groups of American citizens as well. As budgets for national birth control programs increase, citizens have a right to question whether they will do more than increase individual freedom and generate savings for the national economy. They may need to know more clearly how those savings will enrich their own lives.

APPENDIX TABLES

TABLE A

Percentage Distribution of Answers to Question, "Is it your impression that the number of people in (survey country) is increasing, decreasing, or remaining about the same? [If increasing]: Greatly or only somewhat?"

Country/City	Increasing				Decreasing	Remaining Same	No Opinion	Total
	Total	Greatly	Somewhat	Don't Know How Much (Volunteered)				
India	99	88	8	3	–	–	1	100
Nigeria	99	78	18	3	–	1	–	100
Turkey	99	75	16	8	–	–	1	100
Tehran	97	41	54	2	1	1	1	100
Manila	96	82	13	1	–	3	1	100
Bangkok	95	61	23	11	–	–	5	100
Seoul	95	86	7	2	1	1	3	100
Dakar	95	68	25	2	2	2	1	100
France	90	51	29	10	–	5	5	100
Mexico City	88	66	21	1	2	8	2	100
Great Britain	86	55	27	4	3	6	5	100
Kuala Lumpur	86	61	23	2	–	–	14	100
Singapore	84	70	10	4	–	1	15	100
Santiago	82	49	27	6	5	10	3	100
Kenya	82	44	26	12	6	6	6	100
Caracas	80	50	26	4	6	10	4	100
Rio de Janeiro	76	55	19	2	3	8	13	100
Athens	76	33	34	9	14	8	2	100
Japan	76	16	53	7	10	7	7	100
Buenos Aires	72	20	37	15	5	14	9	100
Italy	70	39	17	14	10	5	15	100
West Germany	63	15	40	8	3	23	11	100

Source: (3).

TABLE B

Percentage Distribution of Answers to Question, "How about the number of
people in the world as a whole? Do you think an increase in the
world population would be a good thing or a bad thing?"

Country/City	Bad Thing	Good Thing	Don't Know	Total
India	89	5	6	100
Turkey	86	8	6	100
Great Britain	78	7	15	100
Seoul	74	7	19	100
West Germany	71	8	21	100
France	71	10	19	100
Athens	71	23	6	100
Italy	57	21	22	100
Japan	54	19	27	100
Singapore	44	15	41	100
Tehran	59	31	10	100
Kenya	55	34	11	100
Nigeria	60	39	1	100
Manila	53	34	13	100
Buenos Aires	48	30	22	100
Kuala Lumpur	44	27	29	100
Santiago	48	37	15	100
Bangkok	47	38	15	100
Rio de Janeiro	39	30	31	100
Mexico City	48	43	9	100
Caracas	41	38	21	100
Dakar	35	53	12	100

Source: (3).

TABLE C

Percentage Distribution of Answers to Question, "All things considered,
do you think having a larger population would be a good
thing or a bad thing for this country?"

Country/City	Bad Thing	Good Thing	No Opinion	Total
India	87	8	5	100
Great Britain	73	12	15	100
Seoul	68	16	16	100
Italy	59	21	20	100
Turkey	63	33	4	100
West Germany	51	24	25	100
Japan	51	27	22	100
Singapore	38	26	36	100
Nigeria	47	53	–	100
France	32	46	22	100
Manila	39	54	7	100
Athens	40	56	4	100

TABLE C (Continued)

Country/City	Bad Thing	Good Thing	No Opinion	Total
Rio de Janeiro	29	47	24	100
Kuala Lumpur	29	49	22	100
Kenya	36	59	5	100
Santiago	30	64	6	100
Mexico City	31	65	4	100
Bangkok	20	69	11	100
Buenos Aires	21	71	8	100
Tehran	21	76	3	100
Caracas	18	75	7	100
Dakar	13	83	4	100

Source: (3).

TABLE D

Percentage Distribution of Answers to Question, "All things considered, how would you feel about a birth control program to encourage people in (survey country) to have fewer children—would you approve or disapprove of such a program? Strongly or only somewhat?"

Country/City	Approve		Disapprove		Qualified Answer, Don't Know	Total
	Strongly	Somewhat	Somewhat	Strongly		
Seoul	72	14	3	3	8	100
India	60	24	3	6	7	100
Singapore	55	17	2	3	23	100
Santiago	52	26	6	9	7	100
Kuala Lumpur	46	24	7	6	17	100
France	40	27	7	6	20	100
Caracas	47	25	7	12	9	100
Turkey	59	13	7	12	9	100
Mexico City	41	29	11	11	8	100
Great Britain	37	28	12	6	17	100
Nigeria	53	17	13	16	1	100
Japan	16	42	13	5	24	100
Athens	24	43	12	15	6	100
West Germany	32	29	10	11	18	100
Rio de Janeiro	35	19	7	16	23	100
Tehran	26	36	19	13	6	100
Italy	36	17	6	20	21	100
Manila	30	26	13	21	10	100
Buenos Aires	21	32	14	19	14	100
Bangkok	23	27	15	15	20	100
Kenya	28	25	17	19	11	100
Dakar	17	11	13	52	7	100

Source: (3).

REFERENCES

1. United States Information Agency, "Worldwide Opinions About Some Issues of Population Control," December 1965.
2. United States Information Agency Report R-176-65, "U.S. Standing in Worldwide Public Opinion–1965," December 1965.
3. United States Information Agency, "Worldwide Opinions About Some Issues of Population Control," R-210-65, December 1965.
4. Stycos, J. M., "Problems of Population Policies in Latin America." Proceedings of the 1965 meetings of the International Union for the Scientific Study of Population, forthcoming.
5. The Population Council, "American Attitudes on Population Policy," *Studies in Family Planning*, No. 9, January 1966. pp. 5-8.
6. United States Information Agency, "Some Attitudes in Less Developed Areas Toward Population Control." R-199-64. Washington, D.C., December 1964. Mimeo.
7. United States Information Agency, Attachment #2, Policy Program Directive, No. 10-1-67.
8. The Population Council, "American Attitudes in Population Policy: Recent Trends," *Studies in Family Planning*, No. 30, May 1968. pp. 1-7.
9. Centro Para el Desarrollo Social y Económico. *Encuesta de Opiniones de Líderes sobre Problemas de Población y Familia.* La Páz, no date, c. 1969.
10. Jaramillo, María, "Informe sobre la Evaluación del Programa Experimental de Medellín," *Regulación de ia Fecundidad.* Bogotá: Tercer Mundo, 1968. Vol. II.
11. Mendoza-Hoyos, Hernán, "The Colombian Program for Public Education, Personnel Training and Evaluation," *Demography*, Vol. 5, No. 2, 1968. p. 833.
12. Uriarte, Carlos A., "Encuesta de Actitud sobre el Tamaño de la Familia," *Estudios de Población y Desarrollo.* Líma, 1968. Vol. 2, No. 2.
13. Leñero Otero, Luís, *Investigación de la Familia en México.* México D.F.: Instituto Mexicano de Estudios Sociales, 1968. Ch. 10.
14. Caldwell, John C., *Population Growth and Family Change in Africa.* Canberra: National Univ. Press, 1968.
15. Stycos, J. Mayone, "Opposition to Family Planning in Latin America: Conservative Nationalism," *Demography*, Vol. 5, No. 2, 1968.
16. Stycos, J. Mayone, "American Goals and Family Planning," *World Population and U.S. Government Policy and Programs*, F. T. Brayer, ed. Washington, D. C.: Georgetown Univ. Press, 1968.
17. Stycos, J. Mayone, *Ideology, Faith and Family Planning in Latin America.* New York: McGraw-Hill, 1971.
18. "Tambien Lleras Camargo sobre la Madre y el Niño," *El Diario de Hoy* (San Salvador), August 9, 10, 1965.
19. "La Campaña Mundial a Favor de la Natalidad," *ibid.*, September 23, 1965.

20. "Asamblea Adversa Control de Natalidad," *ibid.*, November 15, 1965.
21. "La Explosión Demográfica y la Conspiración Racista," *ibid.*, January 13, 1966.
22. "La Campaña Racista del Control de la Natalidad," *ibid.*, February 23, 1966.
23. "La Campaña Mundial a Favor de la Natalidad," *ibid.*, September 17, 1965.
24. "También Nos Será Impuesto el Control de Natalidad," *ibid.*, February 11, 1968.
25. "Reunion en Puerto España para Activar el Control de la Natalidad," *ibid.*, November 11, 1967.
26. "El Seminario Anti-Cristiano en Tegucigalpa," *ibid.*, June 13, 1966.
27. "Cien Bárbaros Nobel ante su Santidad," *ibid.*, July 16, 1965.
28. "El Daltonísmo Axiológico del Cardenal Suenens," *ibid.*, October 12, 1965.
29. "Las Falacias Económicas de la Racistas," *ibid.*, September 9, 1967.
30. "Piden Supresion de Leyes contra el Aborto," *ibid.*, September 11, 1967.
31. "Como la UNESCO, también la FAO en el Complot Racista," *ibid.*, June 16, 1967.
32. "La FAO al Servicio de la Conspiración Racista," *ibid.*, April 11, 1967.
33. "La Campaña Racista del Control de la Natalidad," *ibid.*, February 23, 1966.
34. "El Pretexto del Hambre en la Conspiración Racista," *ibid.*, April 14, 1967.
35. ¿"Contra el Hambre o contra el Hombre?" *ibid.*, March 28, 1965.
36. "Reunión en Puerto España," *ibid.*, November 11, 1967.
37. "Gobierno Adversa Control de Natalidad," *ibid.*, December 2, 1967.
38. "Genocidio Malthusiano de Mujeres en Brasil," *ibid.*, July 13, 1967.
39. "Gobierno Adversa Control do Natalidad," *ibld.*, December 2, 1967.
40. "La Santa Misión de Unir Pueblos," *ibid.*, September 15, 1966.
41. "Genocidio Malthusiano de Mujeres en Brasil," *ibid.*, July 13, 1967.
42. "Cien Bárbaros Nobel ente su Santidad," *ibid.*, July 16, 1965.
43. "Genocidio Malthusiano de Mujeres en Brasil," *ibid.*, July 13, 1967.
44. "Esterilizan a 40 Mil Mujeres Colombianas," *ibid.*, February 21, 1967.
45. "El Deber de Poblar y el Derecho de Dejar Nacer," *ibid.*, February 11, 1968.
46. *La Razón* (Buenos Aires), October 28, 1968.
47. *El Clarín* (Buenos Aires), January 2, 1969.
48. *Boletín Oficial* (Buenos Aires), January 2, 1969.
49. *Presencia* (La Páz), October 4, 1968.
50. *Muhammad Speaks* (Chicago), May 30, 1969.
51. *Ibid.*, October 25, 1968.
52. Stewart, D. E., Inter-Office Memorandum, Planned Parenthood World Population, no date, c. 1969.
53. Cited in *Muhammad Speaks* (Chicago), September 6, 1968.
54. Davies, Marvin, cited in the *New York Times*, July 19, 1969.

55. *Muhammad Speaks* (Chicago), September 13, 1969.
56. *Ibid.*, February 7, 1969.
57. *Ibid.*, July 5, 1968.
58. Statements attributed to Ethel Mills, "a street worker in a local community action program to end drug addiction among Black youth," *Muhammad Speaks*, September 20, 1968.
59. Statements attributed to Dr. Charles Greenlee, *Muhammad Speaks*, September 13, 1968.
60. Cited in *Muhammad Speaks*, October 11, 1968.
61. *Muhammad Speaks* October 25, 1968.
62. *Ibid.*, June 20, 1969.
63. *Ibid.* August 16, 1968.
64. *Pittsburgh Press*, July 25, 1968.
65. *Pittsburgh Courier*, August 24, 1968.
66. *Pittsburgh Catholic*, December 22, 1967. Reprinted by *Pittsburgh Courier*, January 6, 1968.
67. *El Diario de Hoy* (San Salvador), June 21, 1963.
68. *Thrust* (Pittsburgh), September 29, 1968.
69. Kakanfo, Ogun, *Muhammad Speaks*, July 11, 1969.
70. *Ibid.*, May 30, 1969.
71. *Caretas* (Líma, Peru), August 28, 1964.
72. Stewart, D. L., "Family Planning, Prejudice and Politics: An Analysis." Paper presented at California Medical Center, September 14, 1968. Mimeo.
73. Kakanfo, Ogun, *Muhammad Speaks*, July 4, 1969.
74. *El Día* (Tegucigalpa), August 19, 1968.
75. *El Espectador* (Bogotá), August 3, 1968.
76. *El Tiempo* (Bogotá), August 8, 1968.
77. Reich, Wilhelm, *Discovery of the Orgone.* New York: Noonday Press, 1966. p. 203.
78. Reich, Wilhelm, *The Murder of Christ.* New York: Noonday Press, 1967. p. 53.
79. Jaffe, Naomi, Letter to the Editor, *Guardian*, July 12, 1969. p. 9.
80. McAffee, K., and Wood, M., "Bread and Roses," *Leviathan*, June 1969. p. 9.
81. *New Left Notes* (Chicago), July 8, 1969.
82. *Guardian* (New York), June 28, 1969.
83. *No More Fun and Games.* Somerville, Mass., February 1969.
84. *Guardian* (New York), August 17, 1968.
85. *Boletín Demográfico* (Havana, Cuba), no date, c. 1969.
86. Population Reference Bureau Press Release, Washington, D.C., August, 1969.
87. Jacobs, Jane, *The Economy of Cities.* New York: Random House, 1969. p. 120.

XV

Political Demography:
An Inquiry into the Political
Consequences of Population Change

Myron Weiner

Political demography is the study of the size, composition, and distribution of population in relation to both government and politics. It is concerned with the political consequences of population change, especially the effects of population change on the demands made upon governments, on the performance of governments, and on the distribution of political power. It also considers the political determinants of population change, especially the political causes of the movement of people, the relationship of various population configurations to the structures and functions of government, and the public policy directed at affecting the size, composition, and distribution of populations. Finally, in the study of political demography it is not enough to know the facts and figures of populations—that is, the fertility, mortality, and migration rates; it is also necessary to consider the knowledge and attitudes that people have toward population issues.

This essay will focus on one aspect of the study of political demography, namely the political consequences of population change: beginning with a brief review of some of the classical statements concerning the relationship between population and politics, then turning to more detail about some of the more recent statements concerning the political consequences of population change. The second part will suggest some ways of thinking about the political effects of population change. The third and concluding section will point to some of the research and policy implications of this analysis.

POLITICAL THEORIES OF POPULATION CHANGE

Many of the issues raised by political demography have long antecedents in political and social theory. The concept of optimum population for political

Myron Weiner is Professor of Political Science and Senior Staff Member, Center for International Studies, Massachusetts Institute of Technology.

order, as well as economic well-being, can be found in the writings of ancient Chinese scholars, Plato, Aristotle, Ibn Khaldun, the physiocrats, the mercantilists, the classical school of economics, and, of course, Malthus. As one writer commenting on theories of political demography noted, "the thesis that excessive growth of population may reduce output per worker, depress the living of the masses, and engender strife is of great antiquity" (1).

Plato, for example, gave attention to the issue of population size as a consideration in the establishment of constitutional government and stable authority. Aristotle, with his concern for the conditions under which forms of government are transformed, considered the relation of population growth to an increase in poverty and hence civil discord. Rousseau, who also considered the relationship between population size and forms of government, concluded that direct popular government was possible only in small countries. And Mill, seeking a rational basis for challenging the argument that democratic forms were not possible in large countries, developed the theory and principles of representation.

Population growth and population movement were of explicit concern to Thomas Jefferson. Jefferson's belief in the special qualities of agrarian life was related to his conviction that there was an association between population density and the form and quality of civic life. Jefferson was also among the few theorists to give attention to the issues of immigration, which he did as part of his concern with the notion of fundamental and inalienable individual rights. Jefferson argued that there existed a "natural right which all men have of relinquishing the country in which birth or other accident may have thrown them, and seeking sustenance and happiness wheresoever they may be able to find them."* Jefferson's view, which runs so contrary to notions of patriotism based upon place of birth, was an important element in American immigration policy throughout its history.

But although a number of social and political theorists gave attention to the effects of population change in the past, it has only been in the last few decades that the issue has become a part of public discourse. Today, rapid population growth has become a popular explanation for many disturbing features of both the developed and developing world. Urban violence, political instability, crime, poverty, communism, and air pollution have all been related to the growth of population.

Concern with Population Decline

It is, therefore, particularly difficult for us to realize that only 30 years ago European scholars and statesmen were concerned with the social, economic, and political consequences of population decline. Myrdal, in his Godkin lectures at Harvard in 1938, focusing on the consequences of a de-

*Quoted in (2).

clining population, expressed the conviction that the problem of decreasing population was one of the central issues and dilemmas of modern democratic states.

> "To my mind no other factor—not even that of peace or war—is so tremendously fatal for the long-term destinies of democracies as the factor of population. Democracy, not only as a political form but with all its content of civic ideals and human life, must either solve this problem or perish" (3).

The dilemma, he noted, was that there was a conflict between the interest of the individual family concerned with maximizing its own well-being and income and, therefore, keeping family size small, and the long-term interest of society in reproducing itself.*

In these lectures, Myrdal specified some of the significant undesirable effects of a declining population. If population did not grow, he said, demand would remain constant and entrepreneurs would then be less willing to take risks. An increasing fear of investment and a decreasing demand for capital goods would lead to a reduction in the total amount of private investment and, therefore, a slowing down of the economic growth rate. A declining population would also mean an older population, and while it might be easier for young people to find jobs, it would also prove to be more difficult for young people to advance in their careers since there would be a larger percentage of older people maintaining their positions through the right of seniority. It would thus take a longer time for young people to achieve responsible positions.

> When on account of the changed age structure individual opportunities to rise socially are blocked, people will get discouraged. They will lose their dynamic interest in working life. Society will lose the mental attitude that goes with progress. Interest in security will be substituted for an earlier interest in social advancement. (3, p. 165)

Moreover, according to Myrdal, the bureaucratic apparatus would increase since in a country with a declining population the economy would also decline and "much less takes care of itself in a declining economy than in one that is growing" (3, p. 166). And since the bureaucracy would be made up of older men, it would be a "static and senile" institution. Finally, he concluded, in a democratic society the aged would use their votes to exercise political pressures on the state to take over the responsibility of providing security for older people at a time when the most fundamental need would be for a policy of redistribution of income so that the costs of children would be

---

*For a contrasting analysis, focusing on the need for a population policy to reduce fertility, see (4, especially chapters 27, 28).

borne by citizens in proportion to their ability to pay taxes, not according to the number of their children.

Myrdal was not alone in worrying about the effects of a declining population on the future of democratic societies. In Britain, the distinguished sociologist T. H. Marshall and a group of well-known scholars, including A. M. Carr-Saunders, H. D. Henderson, R. R. Kuczynski, and Arnold Plant, delivered a series of radio broadcasts dealing with the dangers to Britain of a declining population. Marshall's lecture began with a discussion of a motion introduced into the House of Commons on February 10, 1937, beginning with the words, "This House is of the opinion that the tendency of the population to decline may well constitute a danger to the maintenance of the British Empire and to the economic well-being of the nation" (5; see also 6, 7). H. D. Henderson, the economist, expressed the view in his lecture that the decline in population would mean growing government intervention.

> It was no accident, I am convinced, that the Victorian Age, when numbers were growing very rapidly, should have been the heyday of the philosophy of laissez-faire, of the idea that governments should confine themselves to the task of maintaining law and order and meddle as little as possible with economic matters.
>
> [Today, in contrast] an increasing degree of state intervention and control will be required to deal with the difficult problems of economic adjustment which are consequential on the change in population trends. (8)

In the same series of lectures, Professor R. R. Kuczynski, a well-known demographer, contrasted the decline in the number of white people in the world with the rising number of people belonging to other races. He suggested that the growth of colonialism and the spread of the British Empire could in part be explained by demographic factors. He estimated that in 1770 there were 150 million whites, while by 1938 the white population of the world had increased almost five times to 730 million; and that in 1770 there were only 8 million persons of English descent, while by 1938 there were ten times as many, 80 million (9).*

The same conviction, that power in the international arena required a large population, led the prewar governments of France, Germany, Italy, and Japan to pursue pronatalist policies (11).

Concern with Population Growth

As one reflects upon the current concern for the effects of the worldwide "population explosion," it is striking to see how many of the same effects

---

*A similar argument was expressed a decade later by an Australian demographer who noted that "we who live in the dominions of the British Commonwealth have good reason to be thankful for the fortitude of the Victorian women of Britain who bore their numerous progeny without obvious complaint and who helped thereby to lay the foundations of a mighty Empire" (10).

which were described as costs of population decline are now viewed as costs of population growth. William Vogt, expressing the contemporary view, has written, "the more people we have, the more government we must have" (12). A similar theme is presented by the geochemist Harrison Brown, who noted that "in the future we can expect that the greater the population density of an industrial society becomes, the more elaborate will be its organizational structure and the more regimented will be its people" (13).

Whereas in the 1930's some economists reasoned that a population decline would bring about state intervention in order to cope with a declining economy, many contemporary economists argue that population growth, by impeding an adequate rate of savings and investment in the developing countries, is likely to lead to economic stagnation which can best be overcome through government intervention to restrict consumption, augment savings, and increase the rate of investment.

Though there has been a growing concern with some of the economic, political, and social effects of population growth in the developed world of western Europe and the United States, primary focus of the current neo-Malthusian wave has been on the consequences of population growth for the developing areas. Almost all the political problems of the developing areas— political instability, violence, aggressive behavior, communism, revolution, intense nationalism—have been linked to rapid population growth.

On the relationship between population growth and the development of nationalism, the historian Henry Steele Commager has written that as the rise of European nationalism after the French Revolution coincided with the first great population increases in modern history, so "now it is Asia, Africa, and South America that are experiencing the population explosion, and it is in these continents that we are witnessing the upsurge of chauvinistic and imperialistic nationalism" (14, 15).

On the relationship between population growth and the spread of communism, one writer has focused on the development of communist movements in the south Indian state of Kerala.

> How did a calm and peaceful little part of Asia come to be such a hotbed of communism? There are a number of complicated answers to this question, based on history, politics, and economics. But two underlying reasons stand out. The first is a physical fact: Kerala is so overcrowded that its people simply do not have enough food to keep their living above the concentration camp level. . . . (16)

Many writers have stressed the relationship between poverty, population growth, and political instability. This viewpoint can be found in the writings of Philip Hauser, Irene Taeuber, Kingsley Davis, and many other American demographers. The late Harold Dorn, in a report to the American Assembly on world population growth, stated the viewpoint succinctly: "as population continues to increase more rapidly than ability to satisfy needs and desires,

political unrest, perhaps leading to the violent overthrow of existing governments, becomes almost inevitable" (17, p. 26; see also 18).

Earlier writers saw population growth as a condition for national power;
now many demographers see population growth as a cause of international
conflict. Hauser has presented a modern version of the *lebensraum* argument
in his article "The Demographic Dimensions of World Politics."

> . . . the larger of these nations are not apt to remain hungry and frustrated
> without noting the relatively sparsely settled areas in their vicinity. The
> nations in the Southeast Asian peninsula: Burma, Thailand, and the newly
> formed free countries of Indo-China . . . even parts of thinly settled Africa
> may be subject to the aggressive action of the larger and hungrier nations
> as feelings of population pressure mount. Moreover, Communist China, the
> largest nation in the world by far, faced with . . . already heavy bur-
> dens . . . may not confine her attention only to the smaller nations within
> her reach. (19)

The same argument is presented by Dorn in his report to the American
Assembly (17, p. 16; see also 20, 21, 22, 23), and it is further elaborated by
Thompson in his widely circulating textbook on population (24, p. 503).
Since no one has demonstrated a linkage between population density and
aggressive behavior in international politics, some demographers have turned
to an elusive psychological concept of "felt" population pressure. According
to Thompson, population pressure includes "the relative pressure of population . . . defined as the degree of deprivation 'felt' by a people as it comes to
know of the meagerness of its manner of living as compared with that enjoyed by other peoples. . . ." This notion permits the analyst to explain away
the fact that some aggressive countries have had lower population densities than the countries they attacked. Thompson proceeds to do just that by
arguing that this feeling of population pressure was exploited by the leaders
of Japan, Italy, and Germany in the 1930's and that similar feelings might be
emerging in many developing countries.* In many instances, of course, attitudes and feelings about demographic changes have important effects on
political behavior. This subject is later discussed in detail. However, a relation
between population density and aggressive international behavior, explained
by "felt" pressures, has not been proven nor disproven. If density is high and
the country is aggressive, population is called an explanatory variable; if
density in the aggressive country is lower than in the country under attack,
the analyst can point to "felt" pressure.

*See (24). For earlier statements on "felt" population pressures, see (25, 26). For a
critique of Japanese efforts to claim population pressures as a factor in her military
expansion, see (27). For an application of the concept to postwar Europe, see (28, p.
253) in which Hofstee defines population pressure as the "social tension originating from
an absolute or relative disproportion between population and available resources," a
definition which led him to conclude in 1950 that population pressures in western
Europe in the years ahead could lead to "internal unrest."

Similar reasoning underlies many of the attempts made so far to relate either population growth or population density to political change. First of all, many of the attempts are based upon spurious correlations. Since the less developed countries are in the midst of a "demographic explosion," it is tempting but quite fallacious to assume that there is a relationship between high population growth rates and the political difficulties these countries are encountering. It would be easy to demonstrate that the unstable countries of the developing world have high growth rates. But we should also note that the few countries in the developing areas with comparatively low growth rates such as Angola, Gabon, Mozambique, Haiti, and Argentina, have no special record of stability and that some of the fastest growing countries have often been cited—if not now, then a few years ago—as among the comparatively more stable countries of their region: Malaya, Singapore, Thailand, Mexico, Brazil, and Costa Rica. There is no evidence to suggest that population growth *alone* as an independent variable can explain instability, violence, aggressive behavior, and the rise of radical movements of the left or right.

Socioeconomic Variables

In the second place, many of the analysts fail to distinguish between those political effects which result from changes in the size, composition, or distribution of populations without the influence of socioeconomic factors, and those effects which only result from the conjunction of population changes and socioeconomic changes. For example, if one ethnic group in a society has a higher population growth rate than another, there may be a change in the distribution of power even if there are no accompanying economic changes. On the other hand, the political effects of a growth in the number of young people in the society may be quite different if the increase occurs at a time when the economy is expanding and jobs are readily available for young adults entering the labor force than if the increase occurs in the midst of a depression when there is widespread unemployment. Similarly, a rapid increase in population in a rural society may have one effect if it occurs at a time when industrialization is opening up new opportunities for employment and quite another effect if the expanded population remains in the countryside. In the latter case, a population increase may result in increased fragmentation of landholdings, an economic change often with very significant political consequences. Moreover, if sons have equal inheritance rights, there may be one set of effects, while the effects will be quite different if there is a system of primogeniture. In short, there may be few population changes which have uniform worldwide political effects. The analyst, therefore, must specify the intermediate variables with which demographic changes are associated.

Unfortunately, some of the attempts by demographers and economists to explain the political effects of population change, utilizing intermediate variables, have been based on dubious assumptions. The most common, of course, is to assume that rapid population growth leads to a decline in economic growth which in turn leads to political violence, political instability, insurrectionary movements, or communism. Population growth need not be accompanied by a low rate of economic growth (the reverse was the pattern in many European countries in the 19th century and, more recently, in Hong Kong, Taiwan, South Korea, Malaya, Singapore, and Israel), nor are the most violent areas of the world those with particularly low rates of economic growth. The attempts by Ted Gurr, Harry Eckstein, and other political scientists to find explanations for violence and political instability have led to a much more complex model of interrelated variables than a simple mix of income growth and population growth (29). Moreover, there is strong evidence to support de Tocqueville's familiar argument that periods of economic growth, rather than periods of economic stagnation, are often times of political instability.

Third, in analyzing the political effects of specific demographic changes, it is important to know how these changes are perceived. It is not enough to know, for example, that different religious or racial groups are increasing their number at different rates; we must also know how each of these groups views the change in its relative size. Differential fertility rates among Methodists and Episcopalians may not be perceived as a matter of great importance in the United States, but the differential fertility rates between Catholics and non-Catholics and between whites and nonwhites are seen as matters of great political significance. The beliefs people have as to the effects of real, and sometimes imagined, demographic changes are in themselves of great political importance. For example, the rapid population growth of "coloured" peoples in Britain (partly due to the fact that a large proportion of nonwhite women are currently in the childbearing age) has led some Englishmen to fear that the character of British life would be changed in an undesirable way and, therefore, to believe that restrictive immigration policies should be pursued. Similarly, beliefs concerning the relationship between population size and national power have affected population policies in New Zealand and Australia, although changes in military technology have made such a relationship much less significant than in the past.

Sometimes a change in government policy can affect popular attitudes toward some long-familiar demographic facts. For example, illegitimacy among the poor, as such, was largely ignored by taxpayers until government took on the responsibility of providing aid to dependent children. What was once viewed benignly as simply a way of life among the lower classes has now become an irritant to many middle class Americans.

Demographers, like economists, have been accustomed to working with "hard" data. They often distinguish themselves professionally from other social scientists, such as anthropologists and political scientists, who work with "softer," that is, attitudinal, data. The demographer feels professionally most comfortable with data on fertility rates, mortality rates, and migration rates, and does not customarily work with attitudinal data. Unfortunately, this has not prevented many demographers from making inferences about the attitudes of individuals and groups. Clearly, of high priority in the study of the political, as well as the social, effects of population change is the rigorous collection of data on the ways in which different ages, classes, and ethnic groups perceive population change.

Fourth, we must be more precise concerning the kinds of political effects which might result from population changes. Within a political system, there are at least two types of political effects which seem to be most apparent. One type concerns the political and administrative strains produced by changes in the size, composition, and distribution of the population. For example, marked increases in the number of young people or the number of older people can have great effects on the kinds of services which governments may be asked to provide. An increase in rural density resulting in a fragmentation of landholdings may have an effect on agricultural policy. Or an increase in family size among poor people supported by welfare programs may have effects upon government expenditures. In short, new demands resulting from population changes may affect the size and character of the bureaucracy and the kinds of resources needed by government to meet those demands. A second major type of political effect is on the internal distribution of power. Since in every society—especially, but not exclusively, in democratic societies the distribution of political power is affected by the proportions of age groups, ethnic groups, or social classes, any changes affecting those numbers, whether from differential fertility rates or migration, can affect the balance in a federal system; for example, the changes in ratio between Hindus and Muslims in northeastern India, Catholics and Protestants in Northern Ireland, and blacks and whites in American cities have had dramatic political consequences.

Fifth and finally, not only must we be more precise about the political effects of demographic change; it is also necessary that we be more precise about the demographic variables as well. There are at least five specific types of population changes which appear to have political effects. Four of these changes are largely the consequence of increases in population, and the fifth is primarily a consequence of economic and political factors, though it, too, may be affected by population growth. These five are: (a) changes in the age structure of a population, (b) changes in family size, (c) changes in the size and density of a population, (d) differential population growth rates among different social classes and ethnic groups, and (e) migration.

EMPIRICAL APPROACHES TO THE STUDY OF POLITICAL DEMOGRAPHY

The rest of this essay will deal with each of these five aspects of population change and consider how each may be related to different types of political effects, asking such questions as: (a) How are these population changes perceived and to what extent do they have political effects irrespective of the ways in which they are perceived? (b) In what ways does the cultural, social, and economic environment shape the political effects of population changes, and do the demographic changes have an independent and direct political consequence? (c) How are demands upon the political and administrative framework affected by population changes? (d) And finally, what are the effects of these population changes on the political and social interaction of groups and the distribution of political power within the society?

Political Effects of Changes in Age Structure

Three factors affect the age of a nation's population. The first and most important is simply the number of children women bear. An increase in the number of births will produce a younger population. The second is a drop in the death rate, which favors young people more often than the elderly. A decline in the death rate most often benefits infants and small children. For example, in Sweden 95 percent survive from birth to age 30 today, as compared to 67 percent in 1870 (30). The third factor is the migration rate. Since migrants tend to be young, a large immigration rate generally means a younger population, and a large emigration generally means an older population.

In many countries in the developing areas, fertility rates are higher, mortality rates are lower, and emigration rates less than was the case for many western European countries in the 19th century. Health conditions improved slowly in many European countries, birthrates were often lower, and migration to North and South America was great. In both the 18th and 19th centuries, most European countries had older populations than exist in most developing countries today. And the contrast between the age structure of Asia, Africa, and Latin America and that of the developed world today is quite striking. For example, 47 percent of the Philippine population is below the age of 15, in contrast to only 23 percent of the British population. Half the population of the Congo is under 20, and half of Brazil is under 19.

Wars have also had a substantial effect on the age structure of a population. In World War I, Serbia lost 27 percent of its males between the ages of 15 and 49, Russia lost 16 percent, Turkey 15 percent, Romania 14 percent, and France 13 percent (31). An extended war may also eliminate a generation of infants who would have been born had there been no war. In a society in which women give birth at frequent intervals, the temporary removal of a large number of males will have a permanent effect on population size. But in a society in which family planning is common, war may only lead to a postponement in births with the result that the end of the war is accompanied by a postwar baby boom. Moreover, a generation after the postwar baby boom, when the percentage of women in the childbearing age group increases, the birth rate may again rise.

Populations grow older when the birth rate declines, when there is no longer a decline in infant mortality, or when there is a substantial out-migration. In the United States the in-migration of older people to such warmer climates as Florida or southern California has affected the age structure of those areas.

Different age groups make different demands upon the state. If there is a rise in the number of infants, parents may demand more health services for children and mothers. A rise in the 5-to-15 age group may mean a greater demand for more primary and secondary schools and for the training of more teachers. A rise in the college-age group means that more institutions of higher learning may need to be built, or older ones enlarged, or employment opportunities created for new entrants into the labor force. A large old-age group may demand more medical and social security programs.

Whether the state responds to any of these needs depends upon the following: (a) whether citizens believe the state ought to be responsible for providing new services, (b) whether citizens have the political power to make effective demands upon their government, (c) whether governmental leaders believe the state ought to take on these responsibilities and are responsive to demands made upon them, and (d) whether the government has or can obtain the administrative and financial resources for expanding its services. These four conditions, obvious as they are, are often forgotten by planners who, viewing the changing age distribution of a population, calculate needs for housing, health services, or education without considering that needs may not be felt, that they may be felt but that citizens do not expect them to be met by government, that particular age groups may not have the political power to press their demands upon government successfully, or that government may not have either the will or the resources to respond to these demands or needs. With these factors in mind, let us consider some of the political effects of changes in the number of three different age groups in the population: the school-age group, say from ages 5 to 15; second, the number of young adults; and third, the number of older citizens.

A Rise in the Young Age Group. In most developing countries, the popular desire for education exceeds the supply. Whereas in other areas of national planning, government elites often lament the failures of industrialists and agriculturalists to achieve targets, in the area of educational development quantitative expansion has often been greater than planners had anticipated. Even poor peasant families are becoming aware of the importance of education for changing the status, occupation, and income of their children. The growth in the number of school-age children, with an increased demand by adults for investment in primary and secondary school education, has led most developing countries to invest a substantial proportion of government revenues in education. Even with the doubling of educational investment, the absolute number of illiterates has actually increased in many developing countries with high population growth rates. It is no accident that countries with high birth rates and low national income are those with much illiteracy. Furthermore, the demand for education is so great in many societies that a substantial portion of educational development is outside of the government sector. In the 19th century, religious institutions in Europe provided much of the money for educational development. In India today, the private sector, especially caste associations, has been creating educational institutions. And in parts of southeast Asia, Chinese voluntary associations have also been building their own schools. However, in spite of these efforts in both the public and private sectors, few developing countries have been able to achieve the goal of universal primary education.

The government of a population with an increasing number of school-age children is often under pressure to divert the investment of funds from industry to education in order to achieve universal literacy and universal primary education. Moreover, as long as the number of children in the school-age group continues to grow, educational planners are confronted with a moving target. Substantial increases in governmental expenditure are needed simply to keep the same proportion of children of school age in the schools. In India, for example, the number of children below the age of 15 increased from 138.6 million in 1951 to 180.4 million in 1961, an increase of nearly 42 million or 30 percent.*

If universal education is not achieved and only a portion of the school-age group is actually in school—a pattern in most developing societies—it is invariably the children of the poorest groups who are not in school. The early effects of educational development may thus be to improve the opportunities for the children of the urban middle classes, the children of the peasant proprietors, and perhaps for those of the urban working class, while the children of tenant farmers and landless laborers are left behind. Since occupational levels often coincide with differences in religion or caste or tribe or language, a half-developed system of primary and secondary school education may sharpen both class and ethnic differences.

There is an impressive amount of evidence that many modern revolutionary movements are associated with an increase in the number of young adults. In a stimulating and original article, Moller has argued that in any society, regardless of social and economic conditions, an increase in the number of youths makes for an increase in social turbulence (32). The reason that

---

*See Gavin W. Jones, "Effect of Population Change on the Attainment of Educational Goals in the Developing Countries," in this volume.

people tend to assume a correlation between violence and poverty, he notes, is that poor neighborhoods and poor countries both have high proportions of young people. Moller provides many historical examples to bolster his argument. He notes that during the early part of the 16th century in Germany large cohorts (age groups) of young adults coincided with the rise of the Lutheran Reformation and the Peasants War of 1524-25. In the late 18th century, 40 percent of the French population was between the ages of 20 and 40, and only 24 percent was over 40 years of age. Because of the economic hardships that prevailed between 1785 and 1794, the many underemployed young people formed an explosive population group, contributing to the revolutionary unrest within France and also to the military ventures of the Revolutionary and Napoleonic Wars. Similarly, Italy experienced a rise in the number of young adults at the time that Mazzini was organizing the "Young Italy" movement.*

By the latter part of the 19th century, the proportion of young people was declining in western Europe, but at the same time their number was increasing in eastern Europe, the Balkans, and in Russia, all areas of revolutionary change in the latter part of the 19th and early 20th centuries. The 20-to-45 age group had declined in Germany in the early part of the 20th century with a diminution in births, but the proportion of young adults began to rise sharply in the late 1920's as a result of a natural increase some 20 to 30 years earlier. Thus the Depression hit Germany at the worst possible time—when the age group from 20 to 45 was the largest in modern German history. It was only after Hitler came to power that the proportion of youths began to taper off.

Moller further notes that the violence of American youth in the 1960's has taken place at a time when the postwar babies have entered late adolescence and college age. Moreover, postwar fertility rates rose somewhat more rapidly for Negroes than for the white population, and the increase in the young Negro population has been pronounced in the cities of the North, areas of social turbulence and violence throughout the 1960's.

The proportions of young adults in the populations of the developing areas today are higher than those typically experienced by the European countries or the United States in the 18th or 19th centuries. In France, for example, the age group 15 to 29 was 65 percent of the 30-years-and-over group in 1776, and down to 48 percent in 1900. In Sweden, the highest was 69 percent in the middle of the 19th century, and in Great Britain it reached 77 percent in the 1840's. But in Ceylon today, it is 79 percent, in Brazil 85 percent, in Ghana 85 percent, in Tanzania 93 percent, and in the Philippines

---

*For an important statement on the analysis of the social role of cohorts, see (33). For an analysis of the effects of a youthful population on economic development, using Indonesia as a case study, see (34).

96 percent. These extraordinarily high rates result from the rapidity with which mortality rates have dropped in recent decades, from the higher birth rates in some developing countries than those in 19th century Europe, and from the absence of emigration opportunities for young Asians, Africans, and Latin Americans comparable to the opportunities which Europeans had in the late 18th and 19th centuries (32, p. 251).

Even if fertility rates should sharply drop, the number of young adults in developing societies should rapidly increase in the years ahead since all those who will become young adults in the near future have already been born. In most developing countries, the number of children under 15 far exceeds the number of individuals above the age of 30. There are 180 million children in India under the age of 15 and only 150 million adults over 30, compared with 60 million children in the United States and 93 million adults over 30. Barring a rapid rise in mortality, the number of young adults between 15 and 29 will sharply rise in many developing countries, so that in some countries it will exceed the number of people above the age of 30.

Do these figures necessarily mean that Asia, Africa, and Latin America are destined to have a more turbulent political life than that experienced by Europe and America in the 19th century? Much depends upon the extent to which political attitudes and behavior are linked with age and the extent to which these links transcend cultures. Does the rise in the number of young people, irrespective of the country's economic and social structure, mean a rise in radicalism; and conversely, does an aging population necessarily mean more conservatism? Though insurrectionary movements in Cuba, Vietnam, Angola, and elsewhere in the developing world appear to be essentially movements of young men, as were revolutionary movements in the past, can we not also point to countries with large numbers of young people which have not experienced revolutionary upheavals? If so, one could argue that an increase in the number of young adults may be a necessary, but not sufficient, condition for revolutionary movements. However, one can readily see factors at work in many developing societies which would encourage an increasingly youthful population to be revolutionary.

Insofar as many developing societies continue to be ranked by age and older people, irrespective of their performance, continue to demand both respect and authority, young people are likely to become frustrated at the lack of opportunities made available to them within established institutions. If the young adult population increases more rapidly than job opportunities, then there will be a rapid increase in the number of unemployed or underemployed. Moreover, the movement of many young adults from villages where traditional social controls continue to operate to colleges and universities in the cities means that young adults are concentrated and, therefore, may be more able to organize as a cohesive political force. It does not follow, of course, that young people necessarily share a common political ideology or common political interest, but these factors may mean that a large youthful population is readily capable of being organized by various political groups.

A Rise in Aged Population. Is there any relationship between age and political attitudes or behavior? A few scholars have questioned the widespread belief that youth is linked to liberalism and radicalism and old age to conservatism. Herbert McClosky, for example, has suggested that personality traits are more important than age as a cause of an individual's political views (35). Other studies, however, show that prejudice towards minority groups tends to be greater among older people, and that, in general, social conservatism is greater among the aged than among youth (36, 37). This seems to be the case even when educational levels are constant.

Among the few empirical studies of aged populations is a study by Rainey in the state of Arkansas, which, as a result of substantial emigration of young adults, has an older population than most other states. Rainey reports a growth of political pressures by senior citizens, the presence of growing conservatism on race issues, a decline not only in the number of school children but an even more rapid decline in the number of young teachers, and some evidence that the aged population is opposed to measures to finance new schools, roads, and other projects designed to stem the state's out-migration and attract industry (38).

There may be some validity to the slogan of young radicals, "don't trust anyone over 30," an example of a most un-Marxist position in that it implies that neither income, occupation, nor social class are determinants of radicalism. Is it possible that the decline in revolutionary fervor in the Soviet Union is not an outgrowth of increased affluence, or the growing influence of middle and professional classes, or even the "natural" decline in ideology, but is a result of the fact that the Soviet population has been aging? By the early 1960's the 15-to-29 age group was down to 53 percent of the number over 30. Perhaps the current theory that increased affluence leads to restraint in international relations needs to be re-examined in the light of the possibility that age is a more restraining factor on the part of governments.

An examination of the effects of aging populations should also include consideration of the type of demands made by older citizens as a result of changes in family structure. The aging of populations in developed societies takes place in the context of changes in the family system. The growth of independence on the part of young people and the establishment of the nuclear family system have made older people less able to be dependent on their children and increasingly dependent upon the state for support in their old age. It is ironic that the number of older people in the society is increasing at the very same time that the family system is less able to cope with the needs of older citizens. Now that older people are less likely to live with their children, they are increasingly in need of their own housing, facilities for social recreation, and, above all, state-financed medical facilities. Responsibilities once borne by children are now increasingly being borne by the state through systems of social security.

In considering the structure of a population and its political effects, it is necessary to distinguish between the political role of a particular age group when it constitutes a small portion of the population and its role when its numbers have sharply increased. The young, for example, may be more innovative, more liberal, and more radical than their elders, but they may not be politically active unless they are numerically large. Similarly, a small, conservative, elderly population may be ignored by politicians, but beyond a certain size threshold, it may become a target of competing politicians, as has been the case in California, Florida, and Arkansas. In the 1968 presidential elections in the United States, Senators McCarthy and Kennedy explicitly sought the support of young age groups, just as Mr. Nixon sought the support of middle-aged citizens, and as, 4 years earlier, Mr. Goldwater sought the support of older citizens. In short, in the study of political demography it is not only important to examine the size of different age groups in the population and their attitudes and behavior, but we must also consider the perceptions of politicians as to the importance of certain age groups as constituents.

Political Effects of Changes in Family Size

Though the ideal of the extended multigenerational family is found in most traditional societies, it is during the period of demographic transition that this ideal becomes a reality. In a period of demographic transition, there are fewer infant mortalities, fewer maternal deaths, and an increase in longevity which results in the survival of parents and grandparents. Families have both more children and more adults, frequently extending over several generations.

How large do families become during periods of demographic transition when mortality rates have declined but fertility rates have not? Clark, surveying a large number of studies, reports that of women born from 1870 to 1879 in Brazil, total fertility (excluding childless women) was 7.5 births per woman, among Jamaican women born between 1844 and 1923 it was 5.4, in the United States (1800) it was 5.8, in Japan (1868) somewhere between 6.5 and 7.3. At various times in the 19th century, total fertility for Norwegian women reached 6.5, for British women 6.1, and for German women 5.5.

Among contemporary developing countries, total fertility for completed families was 4.8 in Ceylon (1946), 6.35 in China (1934), 6.4 for Mexico (1960), 7.4 for Brazil (1940), 6.2 for Egypt (1956), 6.5 for Senegal (1965), 6.5 for the Philippines (1950), 5.6 for Indonesia (1955), 6.7 for Singapore

(1959), 5.2 for Vietnam (1945), and 6.4 for nonwidowed, married women in India (1951).*

What are the consequences of a growth in family size? Much depends upon the traditional structures of family life, upon the inheritance system, on the extent of landholding on the part of the family and the availability of new lands, and on the prospects for employment opportunities elsewhere.

Family Size and Housing. One effect, however, is nearly universal and that is the effect of an increase in family size on housing. An increase in family size invariably means that families require more living space. The traditional family dwelling may no longer be able to accommodate grandparents and two or three married children, each of whom have five or six children of their own. Villagers may expand their huts, or extended families may break up as a result of the need for more living space. In cities, wealthier families will move into larger living quarters. Since an increase in family size usually means a diminution in per capita income within the family, poorer families in cities will erect partitions within their homes or live under more crowded conditions. As crowding increases for the urban poor, there is often an outcry, if not from the poor themselves then from socially concerned middle and upper classes, for state intervention to improve housing conditions for poor families. Since poor, large families do not have the income to move to larger quarters, state intervention means the transfer of resources from one sector of society to another.

Family Size and Landholding. A growth in family size in the countryside may affect the size of landholdings. Unless some sons leave the family homestead or new lands are found, existing holdings must be fragmented if each son is to have a piece of land. In some regions, it has become possible for sons with energy to do what their fathers or grandfathers did—convert mountain slopes into usable land, drain a swamp, level a hillside, or clear a forest. In much of Africa, it may still be possible for young men to make "new" land suitable for cultivation. In such areas, a growth in family size will be accompanied by an increase in the amount of arable land. But in other areas the only alternative for young men is migration. In much of Europe in the middle of the 19th century, fragmentation of land had reached a point that it became an important factor in emigration.

Whether the family chooses to respond as a unit to the change in ecology or whether individual members of the family make their own choices has important political and social consequences. Marcus Lee Hanson reports that in Germany in the mid-19th century, men with six children and small landholdings realized that an equal division of the land upon their death would

---

*The dates show the year of the studies or the year of the census used by Clark to assemble his tables (31, pp. 24-26).

doom their children to the status of "potato eaters." To prevent this outcome the family sold the estate and embarked as a unit for America. With the family savings every child could have a farm in America as large as the paternal estate in Germany (39). In the 1840's, the German emigration consisted largely of such parents and their unmarried sons who moved into the rural areas of America.*

In still other families the father and the older sons chose to remain while the younger sons sought their fortunes elsewhere, in factory jobs, in the growing urban centers of Europe, or abroad in America. A system of primogeniture may serve to keep the family estate intact, but in a situation of expanding family size it may serve to divide the family. One can readily picture the tensions within families in Ireland, Germany, Italy, and eastern Europe throughout the 19th century as men quarreled over whether to sell their estates and migrate as a family, whether to divide the estates into uneconomical units, or whether to turn the land over to older sons while the younger ones migrated. If the family is to migrate, should one member go ahead and the others follow later, or should the entire family migrate at once? If one son turns his patrimony over to the others, how should he be compensated? If the entire estate is to be sold, and the family to emigrate abroad, what shall be done with the elderly and the sick? Shall they be taken along or shall they be sent to live with the relatives who remain?

If new agricultural techniques are employed, new crops introduced, or profits from agriculture rise, then there may be little migration. Under these conditions, fragmentation may take place without a drop in income from father to son. Clark has cited a number of historical examples of transformations of agriculture under conditions of rapid population growth—6th century B.C. Greece, 16th century Holland, Britain in the latter part of the 18th century, Japan at the end of the 19th century, and perhaps India today (31, pp. 72-73). In these instances, Clark argues, population growth compelled peasants to change their methods of cultivation and economize in the use of land. There are a variety of ways in which peasants have adapted to changes in the ecological balance within the framework of traditional agriculture—by cultivating what had previously been considered marginal land, by the elimination of pasture lands, by engaging in supplementary occupations, by adopting a few new crops (such as potatoes), or simply by living with a lower income.

Which response to changing family size is made by peasants—the cultivation of new lands, the adoption of new agricultural techniques and crops, the fragmentation of landholdings, or migration—can all be influenced by government policy or the opportunities which exist outside of agriculture.

*Whether any member of the family chooses to move at all under conditions of declining agriculture can have significant political consequences, too. For an examination of the issue—when does a population rebel rather than migrate—see (40).

Sons of upper class families are likely to find a decrease in income and status even less tolerable than the sons of members of the lower classes. In the traditional demographic situation, the family elder may have died in his 40's or early 50's; then authority and income moved to sons who were in their 20's or 30's. With the increase in longevity, younger men often have to wait longer for their patrimony. Moreover, with a larger number of sons to share the family estate, each of whom now survives into his 20's (often with his own family), it becomes self-evident to young men that they will never be able to acquire the status and wealth of their fathers as long as they remain on the land. The movement of the sons of aristocrats away from the land in 18th and 19th century Europe was, in part, brought about by an increase in family size. Some younger members of wealthy Scottish families, for example, took positions in the British Imperial Service, and some sought positions in industry. Young French aristocrats joined the military. And throughout western Europe, the Catholic Church continued to provide opportunities both for the wealthy and for the poor.

Increased family size often promoted occupational diversification within the family. The poor moved into factory occupations; the sons of large land-holders and aristocrats often entered the new expanding bureaucracies—the civil bureaucracy, the military, or the imperial services—where sons in high status occupations could maintain the family heritage and exercise authority over others.

Political Effects of Population Size and Density

Much of the popular discussion of the political effects of population growth has focused on increased density. When we think of population growth, we generally do not think of changes in family size, or changes in the age distribution of the population, or differential fertility rates, or even increased migrations, but simply that there are too many people. "Overcrowding" has been used to explain air pollution, traffic jams, the high cost of housing, the destruction of natural resources, unemployment, and even the psychic and political tensions of modern life, but these are more often the consequences of industrialization and technological change than they are of population growth.

Moreover, density is itself a relative notion with a wide variety of meanings. It customarily refers to the ratio between numbers of people and land area within a country, but this is a most inadequate conception for the purposes of this study which is primarily concerned with the frequency and kind of interpersonal contacts, and a land/man ratio hardly provides us with such a measure. Overall density for a country may be low, but because there is little arable land, population may be highly concentrated. Or density on the land may be increasing, but density per room is declining with an increase in the construction of housing. Or population in the core city may be declining as people move to the less densely populated suburbs while density on the highway is rapidly rising. In short, there are different densities at work, at home, and in transportation, and different densities day and night.

What can be said then about the relationship between population density—or more properly, different kinds of population densities—and various aspects of political and governmental systems? The following discussion will briefly examine six possible relationships: (a) the relationship between population density and political or social stability, (b) the relationship between population size and the interplay of central and subordinate government authority, (c) the relationship between population size and government resources and policy options, (d) the relationship between the dispersal of population and the cost of bureaucratic penetration, (e) the relationship between size and the problems of regional disparity, and (f) the relationship between size and density and the optimal size of government.

Density and Political Instability. As of 1960, the following European countries had population densities of more than 100 per square kilometer:

Netherlands—342	East Germany—150
Belgium—300	Switzerland—130
West Germany—215	Luxembourg—121
United Kingdom—215	Czechoslovakia—107
Italy—164	Hungary—107
	Denmark—106

The following regions in Asia, Africa, and Latin America had populations of more than 100 per square kilometer:

Hong Kong—2,891	Lebanon—158
Singapore—2,813	Ceylon—151
Mauritius—342	Jamaica—142
Taiwan—295	India—136
Puerto Rico—265	Haiti—126
Japan—252	El Salvador—117
South Korea—250	North Vietnam—103
Trinidad—165	Israel—102

Whether one uses as an index of political instability the amount of violence or revolutions or coups d'etats, or the frequency of changes in government, neither of the above lists of densely populated countries correlates well with any list of politically unstable countries. There are both stable and unstable densely populated countries, and most of the unstable countries have a low density. Africa, with an overall population density of 8 per square kilometer, the lowest of any continent in the world, has been one of the most unstable regions during the past two decades. Moreover, even when regional characteristics are weighed as an influence, there is no noticeable relationship between density and political instability. The Philippines, which has been among the more stable countries of southeast Asia, has a density of 93, while Indonesia, one of the least stable countries, has a density of 62. In Africa, Nigeria is high with a density of 38, but the Congo is low with 6, as is Guinea with 12, and Angola with 4. In the Middle East the relatively stable country of Tunisia has a high density of 33 compared to Syria with 25, Egypt with 26, Morocco 26, and Yemen 26. Finally, contrary to popular impressions, population density in mainland China is not high by Asian standards. Its population density is 68, lower than that of India, Pakistan (98), South Korea, North Vietnam, Japan, or Ceylon; and about the same as that of Nepal—67 (41).

In one important respect these simple correlations are, of course, quite misleading, for they do not take into account that some countries, such as mainland China, have large uninhabited areas, so that in some parts of the country density is extraordinarily high. Thus, although the density of Indonesia is lower than some other parts of south and southeast Asia, the island of Java is one of the most densely populated agrarian regions of the world. Similarly, in India, the density of the small state of Kerala, which shares with Java the reputation for being violent and unstable, is three times that of India as a whole. A close examination of the relationship between regional density within a society and levels of violence would be useful. However, one can readily point to many densely populated areas of the world that have been highly stable and to many countries of Latin America and Africa with relatively low population densities on arable land that have been highly unstable. There is, in short, no evidence yet that population density alone is either a necessary or sufficient condition of political stability.

One can, however, discern a relationship between political organization and population density. It is customary for political scientists to consider the growth of political organizations and the articulation of political interests as a consequence of an increased division of labor and, in general, of the growing differentiation of social groups. Marx, for example, saw the differentiation of occupations in relationship to property ownership as the major dimension in the organization of conflicting interests. Modern political scientists following Durkheim and Weber are more likely to see all differentiations of occupations as a determinant of political organization. One can, however, note the striking fact that concentration of populations in a given space is a factor in whether or not political organizations emerge. Dispersed, nomadic, pastoral peoples, for example, appear to be less able to organize to exercise influence on government than are settled agriculturalists; and settled but dispersed tenant farmers seem less able to organize than plantation laborers. Similarly, factory workers are readily organizable, and students in colleges and universities are more easily organized than young people who are not in educational institutions. Institutions which bring large numbers of people together have clearly created one important condition for the creation of political organizations.

But although there may be a threshold of density below which a people do not readily organize politically, can we assume there is another threshold above which people are likely to be violent and aggressive? This hypothesis is stated in a suggestive and much-quoted study by Calhoun. He conducted an experimental inquiry into the effects of high density on the behavior of a domesticated albino strain of the Norway rat. As density was increased, male rats became more engaged in struggles for status, fighting increased, mortality among infants and females increased, homosexuality among male rats grew, and some even became cannibalistic (42, 43).

A difficulty in assessing the social and political consequences of high densities among humans is the need to disentangle the effect of other variables. David Heer (44, p. 32) points out that the central cities with high densities also tend to have older, more crowded housing than suburbs, that they have a higher proportion of lower socioeconomic groups, Negroes, the foreign-born, and persons living alone, and that central cities often have a higher proportion of newer arrivals than their suburbs. These factors, rather than high density, may account for some of the characteristics of high-density urban centers. In short, as in studies of the impact of density on health, it is difficult to sort out other factors which are often associated with crowding, such as low income, poverty, poor housing, and unemployment.* Heer considers some of the conflicting evidence concerning the social effects of density: the increase in mental illness and loneliness versus the evidence and arguments that primary ties are more intense and numerous in the inner city than they are in the suburbs.† Heer concludes by noting that although the social effects of differences in population density are of great significance, they have not been adequately studied, a point that can be made as well with regard to the political effects of population density.

Whether or not the incidence of pathological behavior among humans is higher in densely populated regions than in dispersed areas is an issue on which the empirical evidence is quite unclear, but certainly one of the most universally believed social theories is the notion that those who live in rural areas and small towns are more virtuous, trustworthy, less violent, and more reasonable than those who are born and raised in high-density urban centers. Even among urban dwellers in the United States, there is a popular belief in

*See John Cassel, "Health Consequences of Population Density and Crowding," in this volume.

†See the studies by William Foote Whyte, Michael Young, Peter Wilmott, and Louis Worth cited by Heer (44, p. 33).

the special qualities of public figures who come from the small towns of America, from places like Aberdeen, Kansas, or Libertyville, Illinois. This idea, that a man's location in space is more likely to shape his moral character than his education, his occupation, or even his religious affiliation, though statistically unverified, is a belief widely shared in almost all societies, including, and perhaps especially, those societies which are densely populated.

Density and Central Government. Clearly, the size of a country and its population creates both problems and opportunities. It is, first of all, well to remember that although the density of some European states in the late 18th and early 19th centuries was high, the size of the states by modern standards was quite small. The population of England and Wales in the first census of 1801 was under 9 million, about that of Rhodesia and somewhat less than that of contemporary Ceylon, Nepal, Tanzania, Taiwan, or Peru. In 1800, the Netherlands had 2.1 million people, the same as contemporary Dahomey or Honduras. Italy had 17.2 million people in the early part of the 19th century and was therefore slightly smaller than Ethiopia was in 1962 with 20 million people. France, then the most populated and most powerful country in western Europe, had 28.3 million people, slightly more than contemporary U.A.R. with 27.2 million and slightly less than Turkey, which has 29.2 million. By today's standards, most European states in the beginning of the 19th century were quite tiny: Denmark had 983,000, Finland 830,000, Norway 880,000, Netherlands 2.1 million, Sweden 2.3 million, and Portugal 2.9 million. In population, these states compare with contemporary Chad with 2.7 million, Guinea with 3.2 million, and Niger with 3.1 million.*

Compared to the European states of the early part of the 19th century, many of the developing countries today are extraordinary giants. There are five countries each with populations larger than all of western Europe at the beginning of the 19th century. India has over 500 million people, China around 700 million, and there are two countries with approximately 100 million people each, Pakistan and Indonesia. A fifth country, Brazil, has a population of 80 million and is estimated to pass the 100 million mark sometime in the late 1970's. Few governments in the developed world have ever had to govern populations the size of any of these five giants in the developing world. Even Russia, with its formidable problems of governance,

---

*How much more important the skills and motivations of their populations were in the economic growth of these small European states than population size, density, or the availability of local resources is indicated by the role which European migrants from these countries played in the development of the United States, Canada, Australia, New Zealand, South Africa, and Rhodesia. The development of a small piece of the Middle East by Jewish migrants from Europe provides further support for the argument that skills and motivation are primary, and local resources and population density are relatively less important.

See also Harvey Leibenstein, "The Impact of Population Growth on Economic Welfare—Nontraditional Elements," in this volume.

did not pass the 100 million mark (excluding the Asian regions) until the 1890's. The United States had only 50 million people in the 1880's and did not pass the 100 million mark until around 1917. And Japan at the time of the restoration (1868) had only 33 million people, slightly less than contemporary Thailand, and did not join the United States and the Soviet Union as the third developed country with over 100 million people until the late 1960's.

One consequence of population size, as distinct from either population density or population growth rates, is that it creates special problems in the relationship between central and subordinate units of government. Since it is virtually impossible for a single governmental unit to govern directly a large territory with large numbers of people, some powers are invariably delegated to subordinate governmental units. In large systems, subordinate governmental units have a tendency to seek their own resources, often at the expense of the central government. If central authority is itself weak and divided and its control over resources limited, subordinate authorities may seek greater autonomy. Large underdeveloped states with a weak center are thus particularly vulnerable to conflict between governmental units. When the subordinate governmental units govern distinct cultural regions, as in Pakistan and India (and in Nigeria—the largest African country though it is only half the size of Brazil), then an additional dimension is added to the tensions between central and subordinate authority.

Resources—Small vs. Large States. Governments of large states have greater resources available to them than do the governments of smaller states of comparable per capita income. Though all five of the most populous countries in the developing world rank among the lowest in the world in per capita income, four of these five—India, China, Brazil, and Pakistan—rank among the twenty top nations in national income (21, p. 209). By virtue of their size, these countries have large national budgets. Moreover, each of these countries has a large number of scientists and engineers, which makes it possible to make the technological investments that smaller, less developed states cannot make. Large countries, however poor, can amass sizable budgets from small individual contributions with the result that some advanced technologies— nuclear weapons, missiles, and nuclear power stations—are within the technological and resource capacity of several of these nations if they choose to use their resources in these ways. Small developed countries have similar options, but small underdeveloped countries do not.

Similarly, large countries have the advantages of potentially large internal markets and the technological and financial resources to choose among a large number of possible investments. Smaller countries may seek the benefits of size by establishing common markets or through forms of economic integration. East African states, for example, have sought to cooperate in the establishment of universities and medical schools which would serve the entire region. Larger states are under less compulsion to seek regional cooperation for economic purposes.

Though large states have more resources and, therefore, more options to choose from, there is also likely to be a greater differentiation of political and economic interests seeking to influence the choice of options. The more differentiated the interests, the more difficult it is to maintain the kind of personalized rule that so often characterizes small states. This is not to say that a single individual or a small oligarchy cannot govern; it does suggest, however, that for a small group to govern a large state may require more coercion than is often necessary for an oligarchy governing a small state. The temptation and tendency to establish authoritarian governments is particularly great in large, poor societies—four out of the five largest developing countries in the world are under authoritarian rule. However, the task of managing such states is particularly difficult, as both Ayub Khan and Sukarno have discovered. In recent years even the Chinese have demonstrated how difficult it is for an oligarchy to govern an area as large and populous as China.

Effects of Dispersed Populations. Governments of large territories with small and dispersed populations have a wide range of problems. Not only are government revenues likely to be small, but there are few economies of scale. A country with a dispersed population and low density will require a large number of bureaucrats per citizen to penetrate the countryside. If resources are too small to maintain an adequately large bureaucracy, revenue collection will remain small, local communities will depend more heavily upon traditional structures of authority to settle disputes, and the ability of the central government to play an active role in the development process, even in the process of establishing a school system, is apt to be limited. There are a substantial number of countries in the world, mainly in Africa, which are poor, large in area, and inhabited by small and dispersed populations. The following states, many of which are larger than France (with an area of more than 200,000 square miles) have less than ten people per square kilometer: Central African Republic, Congo, Mauritania, Chad, Mali, Niger, Somali, Angola, Mozambique, Rhodesia, Malagasy, Algeria, Libya, Sudan, Saudi Arabia, Laos, and Mongolia.

Algeria has a fairly large population and one that is not widely dispersed throughout the entire territory. Rhodesia is a relatively well-to-do country, at least as far as its white citizens are concerned, and, therefore, can afford to maintain a bureaucracy which can penetrate large portions of the countryside and establish a measure of governmental control comparable to what is found in more densely populated states. But most of the states on this list have populations so dispersed, communications and transportation so underdeveloped, and governmental resources so small that the prospect for establishing governmental control over the territory, much less using government as an instrument for accelerating development, is very limited. So long as government officers have little local contact, citizens must rely more heavily on informal local networks to settle disputes. The high cost of governing under-populated regions, therefore, tends to preserve systems of local justice. In the absence of substantial external support to finance the expansion of the bureaucratic network and the development of modern communication, the governments of many of these states are not likely to be able to extend their writ much beyond the capital city and a few town and rural areas with concentrated populations. Areas of low density in much of Africa are thus likely to remain ungoverned for a long period of time. And so long as they remain ungoverned, they will remain poor and underdeveloped.

Regional Inequities. There is a strong tendency for the most densely pop-ulated areas with growing populations within a country to attract even more industry and more population. Clark, in an analysis of the relationship be-tween population change and the location of industries, concludes that the effects, particularly in the early stages of economic growth, are to increase income inequalities between regions (31, p. 337). In the classic, monumental study *Population Redistribution and Economic Growth*, Kuznets and his as-sociates show the relationship between regional economic development and population movements in the United States (45). If these hypotheses are correct, that populations tend to concentrate rather than disperse as develop-ment proceeds and that regional inequalities grow as a result, they throw some light on the growth of interregional conflicts which so characterize developing societies and which seem to persist in developed societies as well.

In this connection it should be noted that many city politicians, business-men, and some city planners have pressed for the expansion of cities even while demographers, sociologists, and political scientists have become in-creasingly concerned with the pathologies associated with urban living. Many a Chamber of Commerce, eager to see a rise in the value of urban real estate and concerned with increasing the revenues of the municipal government, has encouraged the establishment of new industries and new real estate developments.

Much of the debate over the advantages and disadvantages of high-density living has to do with the question of whether it is responsible for the poverty, violence, and disease so typically found in crowded areas or whether poor people tend to move into areas which are already dense, since these are areas in which opportunities for employment and higher income are most readily found. There is also a long-standing debate between city lovers and city haters over the benefits and disadvantages of urban living. But even in this debate, the most enthusiastic supporters of cities must admit that once a city has reached a given size, there are few benefits to be gained by increasing density. A city of 7 million cannot improve its park facilities, theaters, selection of concerts and art galleries, or its traffic arteries by increasing its population. Furthermore, given the opportunity to maintain an income, millions of Americans have shown their preferences for low-density areas by moving from the inner city to the suburbs.

The tendency of industries and, therefore, of populations to concentrate raises some fundamental issues of public policy. In the developed areas of the world these tendencies have led to the growth of densely populated urban centers and to the depopulation of rural areas. In the developing areas of the world it also is resulting in increased regional disparities. Both in the developed and in the developing world we must ask whether it is possible to achieve a more even distribution of industry and, therefore, of populations without losing the benefits of modern technology. As population densities increase in the decades ahead, we may very well see governments developing not only family planning policies but population distribution policies as well.*

Population Size and Size of Government. The relation between population size and the optimal size of a government is a question which has occupied the attention of political scientists and social theorists since the time of the Greeks. Until modern times, the concern was very much with the question of what constituted an optimal unit for democratic government, and the answer for centuries was that it should be small enough to permit direct participation. How democracies could function within units larger than city states—in large republics—became an important issue among British and American political theorists in the late 18th and early 19th centuries. Thus there developed the concepts of factions, parties, and representation as ways of linking the citizen to the state in a large republic. More recently, as economic values have grown in importance, there has been a concern with the relationship between the size of government and the cost of government as they are related to the specific functions performed by government. The concept of "economies of scale" has increasingly been applied to considerations of government size. This concept assumes that there are certain "indivisibilities"—that is, there are minimum costs for certain activities irrespective of the numbers of people involved. Thus the costs of a highway of a given size are more or less the same whether the highway is used by a few automobiles or very many. And the costs per unit for electricity or for water are often lower for larger settlements than for small towns. The economies-of-scale argument often leads one to stress the economic advantages of larger units of

*For an excellent statement on the need for a population distribution policy for the United States, see (46).

government.* Those who start with a concern for efficiency and cost are likely, therefore, to emphasize the importance of restructuring existing governments into larger units that may be more capable of solving problems at lower cost. In contrast, those who start with a concern for democratic participation are likely to give attention to how to delegate authority from central, state, and municipal governments to local, neighborhood bodies. The conflict between these two approaches was well stated by Dahl in his presidential address to the American Political Science Association in 1967.

> The larger and more inclusive a unit, the more its government can regulate aspects of the environment that its citizens want to regulate, from air and water pollution and racial injustices to the dissemination of nuclear weapons.
>
> Yet the larger and more inclusive a unit with a representative government, and the more complex its tasks, the more participation must be reduced for most people to the single act of voting in an election.
>
> Conversely, the smaller the unit, the greater the opportunity for citizens to participate in the decisions of their government, yet the less of the environment they can control.
>
> Thus, for most citizens, participation in very large units becomes minimal and in very small units it becomes trivial. At the extremes, citizens may participate in a vast range of complex and crucial decisions by the single act of casting a ballot; or else they have almost unlimited opportunities to participate in decisions over matters of no importance. At the one extreme, then, the people vote but they do not rule; at the other, they rule—but they have nothing to rule over. (47; see also 48)

Without attempting to reconcile these conflicting values, Dahl concludes that the optimal city size is in the broad range from about 50,000 to 200,000, but this number seems to reflect the fact that he lives and works and is obviously happy in New Haven, which falls within this range.

The size of governmental units and the distribution of power from one governmental unit to another is perhaps one of the most significant and correspondingly difficult problems in the political development of both modern and developing societies. In modern societies it is a problem because technological changes have made existing units too small to cope with their problems; and in developing societies it is a problem because populations are often so large, dense, and ethnically divided that highly centralized government is often not acceptable, and provincial and local governments may be

---

*There can be diseconomies of scale, too, since beyond a certain size the costs per unit may begin to rise. Sundquist (46, p. 92) points out that for some large metropolitan areas the costs of water supply, sewage, and solid waste disposal may rise for the simple reason that the water and waste must be carried over longer distances. Moreover, many pollution problems are made worse by high population—air pollution, for example, as a result of the dense concentration of automobiles. The economies-of-scale argument, therefore, cuts both ways.

controlled by traditional interests with little concern for accelerating the processes of modernization.

Political Effects of Differential Population Growth Rates within a Country

Within virtually all societies, some groups increase their numbers more rapidly than others. Mortality rates, especially infant mortality rates and fertility rates, vary markedly from one socioeconomic class to another, from one ethnic group to another, and from one geographic region to another. Insofar as numbers constitute an element in the political power of social groups, we can say that differential population growth rates affect the distribution of political power within a society.

Size and Power. How important is the size of a social group as a determinant of its political power? This is not the place to suggest a theory of power which would indicate the precise importance of numbers, say in relation to the cohesiveness and organizability of a social group, its skill, and financial resources, or its ability to deny goods and services to others. Moreover, the "mix" of such variables depends upon the kind of political system in which the social group operates—whether it is democratic or not, the kind of system of representation it has, or how important elections are in the political system. For our purpose it is sufficient to note first that the size of a particular social group, and particularly of an observable ethnic group, is a factor in its political power, particularly in democratic systems. And second, in many political systems, different ethnic groups, socioeconomic classes, and geographic groups often *perceive* differences in size and growth rates as factors affecting the distribution of power.

A few examples should suffice to demonstrate how changing population growth rates or perceptions of changing growth rates affect the distribution of power within political systems and affect the relationships among social groups.*

Much of the support for family planning programs in Britain in the latter part of the 19th century occurred at a time when there were sharp disparities in fertility rates between upper and middle class Englishmen and the working class. Among each group of 100 women in the upper and middle classes married between 1881 and 1886, there had been born 422 children. In contrast, for each 100 women in the unskilled laboring class there had been born 609 children, and among miners' wives 684 children had been born. In other

---

*The literature on differences in fertility, both within and between nations, is extensive. For a list of some recent significant studies, see Heer (44, pp. 48-53). Heer discusses the controversial literature concerning the inverse relationship between income and fertility, differential fertility rates between Protestants and Catholics, and differential fertility rates between blacks and whites. Though there is a substantial literature on differential fertility rates, less has been written on its social and political consequences.

words, working class women had 50 percent more children than middle and upper class women (24, p. 207). Thompson and Lewis, surveying studies in the United States, England and Wales, France, Germany, and Sweden, concluded that the middle and upper classes generally have fewer children than the working class; that among farmers and workers, the least skilled and those with the lowest income have the largest number of children; and that the less educated have more children than those with more education. The data from England also show that the gap in fertility rates had been growing during the previous 50 years; that is, the upper and middle classes had begun to limit family size earlier than had the working class. We can hypothesize, therefore, that family planning movements grow after the middle and upper classes lower their fertility but before the working classes have begun to do so.

As a second example, the opposition of many non-Catholics in the United States to the Catholic position on birth control stems not only from a concern over the effect of Catholic views on public policy, but also because it is a factor in the higher fertility rates among Catholics. According to Kirk, the Catholic birth rate per 1,000 in 1952 was 36 compared to 25 for non-Catholics. Though Catholics constituted only 20 percent of the childbearing segment of the total population, 30 percent of total births were Catholic. Kirk also reported that in 1953, 70 percent of the Catholic population was under 35 years of age compared to 57.5 percent of the entire U.S. population under 35 (49). The differential fertility rate has led some critics of the Catholic position to argue that "the effect of the official Catholic position against birth control is to increase slowly but steadily the ratio of Catholics to non-Catholics in this country" (50).

It is also of political importance to note that the proportion of Catholics in many American cities has been increasing. This is a reflection of the higher birth rate among Catholics and a higher rate of migration of Protestants to the suburbs. The result is that many American inner cities have high Catholic, as well as high Negro, populations. If the backlash voting in the inner cities, particularly as reflected in the high vote for Governor Wallace in the 1968 elections, is so heavily Catholic, this simply reflects the fact that Catholics constitute a substantial portion of the inner city.

The high fertility rate among Negroes in the United States is also viewed with some concern by many public figures and by some demographers. If the present trend continues, it is estimated that there will be over 50 million nonwhites in the United States by the year 2000, approximately 14 percent of the population, and that by the year 2050 the proportion will reach 20 percent. "The magnitude of the explosive growth of the Negro population," writes Hauser, "will undoubtedly make the problems of intergroup relations even more difficult in the coming years." This explosive growth, he writes, occurs at a time when Negroes are migrating from the South to the North and West. "Without question, the transition would be much easier both for the

Negroes and for the community to which he is migrating if the tempo of growth were dampened" (51). This differential in fertility rates between Negroes and whites (the average number of children born to white women was 2.5 and to Negro women 2.8 in 1960) has been a factor strengthening popular sentiment among whites for providing birth control assistance to poor, especially Negro, women.*

So far we have noted several instances of lower social classes and minority groups having high fertility rates in relation to other social groups. Ireland provides an example of a political problem which was partially relieved by a lower population growth rate within a minority group. From the end of the 18th century through the first third of the 19th century, Ireland had about one third of the population of the United Kingdom. By the 1880's, however, the proportion had dropped to only one seventh. The decline in the Irish population, a decline incidentally not simply in proportion to the English but also in absolute numbers, was due partly to the decline in fertility and partly to the vast outpouring of migrants to the United States. This decline in population made a vast difference in how the United Kingdom was willing to cope with the Irish problem. One need only imagine how the British would have responded to the demand for independence if Ireland had been larger. The British would presumably have been even more fearful of an alliance between the Irish and the French and later between the Germans and the Irish. It should also be noted that from the middle of the 19th century to the middle of the 20th century Ireland's population had decreased by half, but the decline was greater for the Catholic areas of Ireland than for Protestant Ulster.

Changing fertility rates in Northern Ireland have, however, created a new set of problems for the British. The rise of a Catholic civil rights movement in Northern Ireland in the past few years, pressing for the abolition of property restrictions on the right to vote so as to permit greater Catholic representation in legislative bodies comes at a time when the proportion of adult Catholics has markedly increased as a consequence of higher fertility rates among Catholics.

These examples point to a shift from concern with differential fertility rates among socioeconomic classes (an issue in much of western Europe in the 19th century when conflicts were mainly along class lines) to a concern with differential fertility rates among populations having different cultural values. Few writers will speak today as Myrdal did as late as 1938 of "the great and obnoxious fertility differences between the overfertile poor strata and the underfertile middle and upper strata" (3), although many will speak readily of the changing proportions of racial, religious, or tribal groups.

*See J. Mayone Stycos, "Opinion, Ideology, and Population Problems—Some Sources of Domestic and Foreign Opposition to Birth Control," in this volume.

Differential fertility rates among cultural groups are, however, of significance only insofar as the difference is seen as having a significant political effect. In the United States little if any attention is paid to differential fertility rates among Baptists, Methodists, Presbyterians, and Episcopalians, but attention is given to the differentials between Protestant and Catholics and between Negroes and whites. But in most societies a differential in the growth rate of races receives attention since racial differences are generally considered more enduring and less assimilable than are differences in language or religion. In South Africa, for example, considerable attention is given to the higher fertility rates of Bantus, "coloureds," and Asians, compared to that of whites.* And though the Maoris constitute less than 10 percent of the population of New Zealand, there has been some concern in that country because the Maori birth rate is approximately twice that of the white population. "If the white people of New Zealand," wrote one extremist New Zealander, "do not awaken to their responsibilities and if the present trend of Maori population continues, this country will inevitably be populated mainly by a coloured race" (53).

A similar concern with the higher fertility of a racial group can be found in the contemporary debate on race issues in Great Britain. In Britain, the growth in the size of the "coloured" (mainly Indian) population has become a strong argument for barring immigrants and for encouraging nonwhites to emigrate. Indeed, in all three cases, in South Africa, in New Zealand, and in Great Britain, the higher fertility rates of racial minorities have been used as a political argument for restrictive and selective immigration.

Conflicts over the Census. When the representation of ethnic groups in the political system is explicitly based upon numbers, there is often a political struggle over control of the enumerating agency—the census department. Controversies often arise over such issues as which ethnic groups will be employed as enumerators, the reliability of the enumerators in finding and counting specific ethnic groups, whether certain social groups have been under-enumerated, and the criteria employed for indicating race, or religion, or language. In Lebanon, the census itself is such a delicate issue that the Lebanese government has been reluctant to take a census which records religion for fear that a change in the distribution of Muslims and Christians in the country would disturb the existing political balance within the government. In India, religion and language are enumerated but, with certain exceptions, caste is not, since the Indian government does not accept caste as a legitimate social institution.

In fact, India can provide us with a number of examples of how the census can be employed by government or by social groups to change the numbers

---

*According to Strauss (52), the natural population increase for whites in 1960 was 1.6 percent, for Asians 2.8 percent, for "coloureds" 3.3 percent. Reliable data on the Bantus were not available.

of specific social groups so as to affect the distribution of political power within the society. A census, for example, has been a major element in the controversy over language policy in India. The 1951 census showed a substantial increase in the number of Hindi- and Hindustani-speaking people, primarily by grouping under this category languages which had previously not been included. The demographic data, however, shows that the states of Uttar Pradesh and Bihar, the largest Hindi-speaking states in India, have had population growth rates below the national average. In fact, the percentage of India's population living in Uttar Pradesh, the largest Hindi state, has declined from 20.4 percent in 1901 to 16.8 percent in 1961 (54).

The census also played a part in the controversy over the demand to reorganize the Indian states along linguistic lines. For example, in the district of Belgaum, in the northern part of Mysore state bordering on Maharashtra, there has been a dispute between the two major linguistic groups as to whether the entire district should remain in the Kannada-speaking state of Mysore or whether the Marathi-speaking portions should be transferred to neighboring Maharashtra. Because the 1951 census in the town of Belgaum was conducted by the Marathi-speaking staff of the municipal corporation, Kannada politicians argued that Kannada speakers were underenumerated. The quarrel over numbers became so great in the early 1960's that the Mysore state government withheld publication of the 1961 census figures which included linguistic breakdowns in the district.

The 1951 census also showed a decline in the tribal population of India. The census enumerators argued that the British had classified many social groups in the subcontinent as tribal when they ought to have been classified as caste Hindus. But some critics of the government from tribal groups argued that the government was underenumerating tribals in an attempt to circumvent the constitutional provisions giving members of tribes special representation in legislative assemblies and special privileges both in appointments to state governments and in admissions into schools and colleges. The 1961 census, however, showed a rapid increase in the number of people reporting themselves as members of scheduled tribes—a jump of 33 percent from 22.5 million in 1951 to 29.8 million in 1961. This increase is a reflection of a social explosion within India's tribal societies rather than any demographic explosion.

Representation of Groups. Finally, differential fertility rates in different regions of a country can affect the distribution of political power in a representative system. The population growth rate in the large south Indian state of Madras was so low during the 1951-1961 period (11.9 percent against an all-India growth rate of 21.5 percent for the decade, according to the 1961 census) that a number of state politicians have expressed their concern over the long-term position of Madras in the national Parliament, in which representation is determined by population. The difference in growth rate seems largely accounted for by a lower birth rate in Madras—34.9 compared to 41.7 for all of India, according to census estimates. Moreover, if the family planning program of the government of India has any significant effect on fertility rates, the gap between Madras and other states may increase, since a larger proportion of couples have adopted family planning methods in Madras in recent years than in all but three other states. According to a recent study, 18 percent of Madras couples are "protected" against 12.1 percent for the entire country (55).

Both within and between states, the population of ethnic groups has become an important element in the struggle for political power and in influencing public policy decisions. As Indian politicians during the past two decades have become increasingly sophisticated about the relationships between ethnicity, population size, and voting power, they have also become increasingly concerned with changes in the composition and redistribution of populations and with the ways in which such data is recorded in the census.

On these matters, Indian politicians are considerably more advanced than are political leaders in much of Africa, where ethnic groups are often less cohesive politically, where the absence of representative institutions reduces the importance of numbers, and where census-collecting institutions are not yet developed. In the future, we can expect population changes in Africa, especially differential fertility rates and migration rates, to become, as in India, sources of political conflict.

Political Effects of Migration

In traditional societies, redistributions in population groups are generally due to differential fertility and mortality rates. In all modern societies migration is the major element in the *geographic* redistribution of populations. As societies modernize and become more urban, internal migration becomes more important and the geographical redistribution of populations increases. In the United States regional population shifts either into cities or into states have been largely a consequence of migration. In India redistribution of populations between states, at least before 1951, was due primarily to differential natural increases. Zachariah estimates, however, that, since 1951, changes in the proportion of the Indian population living in each of the states are due more to internal migration than to differential natural increases (56, pp. 93-106, especially Table 3; 41).

To what extent is population growth a factor in migration? As population increases, do people move from the densely populated areas of the country to the less crowded regions? On the contrary. In the last two decades in the United States, for example, as urban density has been increasing, half of the 3,000 rural counties have continued to lose population to the crowded cities. Similar trends are seen in many less developed countries where one or two urban areas often dominate the nation—in population growth and in economic activity. Political upheavals and employment opportunities in the cities, teamed with the declining capacity of agriculture to offer profitable employment, have been far more important influences on migration than changes in fertility or mortality rates.

What are the political effects of migration? First of all, by definition, all migration involves a political act. The U.S. census considers that a migrant is any person who has moved from one county to another, but an individual who moves within the county is simply considered a "mover." In India, the census defines a migrant as any person who has moved from one district to another, though Zachariah (56) in his study of internal migration in India uses the state as the unit. Other scholars speak of rural migrants to urban areas, though the migration may be within a single district or within a single county. All these usages, however, have a common requirement that migration involves a move from one political unit to another.

Therefore, there are political implications to the movements of people regardless of why they move. The distinction between migrant and mover emphasizes at least two important repercussions. For one thing, it calls attention to the fact that the political units which are affected by the migration are often able to take steps to encourage or discourage the migrants, or may treat migrants differently from local inhabitants. For example, there may be residential requirements for voting, or, as in the United States, state universities may have low tuition fees only for state residents. Also, welfare benefits often vary from one political unit to another within the same country. A second repercussion is that the migrant, unlike the mover, has changed his political unit. If he votes, his move has changed the electoral composition of two political units—his place of origin and his new location.

Political Migration. There are two major motives for migration. Migration may be a response to differential economic opportunities or it may be a response to coercion or the threat of coercion. The former is generally called *economic migration* and the latter *political migration.* Economic migration is characteristic of modern and modernizing societies and generally reflects increased social mobility. It generally involves the voluntary, individual movement of young adults seeking better employment and higher wages.

Political migration can occur in either premodern or modern societies, involving as it does an increased danger, or threat of danger, to individuals or groups. Since 1947, for example, an estimated 16 to 17 million people crossed between India and Pakistan as political refugees, as a result of the partition of the subcontinent and the violence associated with it. In 1922 and 1923, as a result of an unsuccessful effort by the Greek Army to invade Turkey, some 1,200,000 Greeks from Anatolia fled to Greece. It has also been estimated that something like a million Turks were "repatriated" from

Yugoslavia, Romania, Greece, and Bulgaria between the two World Wars. After World War II, over 600,000 Jews, mainly from Europe, moved into the newly created state of Israel within 14 months of its creation. And most recently, millions of refugees, uprooted from the Vietnamese countryside, have poured into the cities, rapidly making South Vietnam one of the most urbanized regions of southern Asia.

One significant difference between the economic and political migrant is that whereas the economic migrant moves as an individual, the political migrant often moves as a member of a group. The political migrant has chosen to move or, more often, been forced to move because of his identity. It is because other people, for political reasons, have classified him as a Hindu, a Muslim, a Bulgarian, a Turk, a Greek, or a Jew that he is often forced to move, though he himself may not have been concerned with his identity until it was forced upon him by political circumstances. Moreover, since political migrations are generally international migrations, the migrant has assumed a new political identity by changing his nationality.

International political migrations have had widespread political consequences in those parts of the world in which they have occurred. For example, not only was a new Jewish identity created by Jewish migrants who went to Israel, but a new Palestinian Arab identity was created as well. In the future, the struggle in the Middle East may be increasingly between Israeli nationalism and the nationalism of the Palestinian Arabs, who consider themselves, as the Jews did before them, a nationality in search of a state.

Similarly, the partition of India and Pakistan created a cohesive, distinct social and political community among the Sikhs in the partitioned province of the Punjab. The Sikhs who fled from Pakistan into India became a more militant and cohesive political group than they had previously been. The Akali Dal, a political party of Sikhs, won a demand for a separate state in 1966 when the Indian government agreed to partition the Punjab into Sikh-majority and Hindu-majority states.

One of the most typical types of forced political migration is the movement of an ethnic group from the country in which it is a minority to the country in which it constitutes the majority. Such was the pattern of migrations in the Balkans between the World Wars. However, even in these instances the migrant is not always assimilated easily—politically that is—into his new homeland. The Greek refugees who fled in terror to Greece from Anatolia in the early 1920's constituted a distinct political force in their new homeland. It has been suggested that the more than one million refugees who entered Greece decisively changed the complexion of political parties in Greece (57, 58).

Political Behavior of Migrants. One striking difference between the political and economic migrant is the kind of economic milieu into which each moves. Since the economic migrant has chosen to move into an area where the economic opportunities are greater than exist in his place of origin, the economic migrant generally finds more employment opportunities and receives a higher income than the political migrant. In contrast, a migrant who has moved under compulsion cannot often choose to move into an area which is likely to offer more economic opportunities than his home area. The political migrant was often part of a relatively comfortable economic minority in his place of origin. Moreover, while the economic migrant has often moved as an individual, bringing his family only after he has achieved some improvement in his economic position, the political migrant generally moves with his entire family and his large financial responsibilities while he is seeking employment. He is, therefore, often more dependent on society for housing, schools, family medical care, and other facilities. He is more of a burden on the country to which he moves. He is more likely to be restive, violent, and hostile to the existing political order than is the economic migrant who may be pleased with his new opportunities.*

One of the factors which affects the political behavior of the migrant is his motivation for moving, the political or economic circumstances which led him to move. But, the migrant's political attitudes—what group he joins, how he feels about the political system he now lives in, what he demands of government, and how he makes these demands are affected by many other variables. Relevant questions are: Has the migrant moved from one rural area to another? From a rural to an urban area? From one urban center to another? Within the country or across an international boundary? Is the migrant a part of a stream of people who have moved from a common single origin to a single destination, or is he among migrants who come from a wide variety of places? Is the migrant different in language, religion, or race from other migrants in the region in which he now lives? Is he different in these respects from local inhabitants? What kinds of economic opportunities does the migrant find, and are they above or below his expectations? And finally, what kind of political system has the migrant moved into? Is it one which allows him unrestricted rights of participation or one which is politically closed? And insofar as the system is politically open, who organizes the migrant when he arrives—communists or socialists, populists or royalists, local inhabitants or fellow migrants?

---

*For a comparison of the differences in the political behavior of economic and political migrants in Calcutta, see Weiner (59). Much of the theoretical literature on the behavior of migrants to urban areas is based on Park's theory of marginality (60). For an excellent critique of Park, see (61), a study of migrants in Wilmington, Delaware, which shows that genuine uprooting among migrants is not widespread nor is there extensive social disorganization. The authors focus on the mediating role played by kinsmen in easing the adaptation of migrants to the city. For a comprehensive review and critique of much of the literature on the political behavior of urban migrants, see (62).

See also Harley Browning, "Migrant Selectivity and the Growth of Large Cities in Developing Countries," in this volume.

Migration and Political Conflict. Although there is a substantial scholarly literature on the political behavior of the migrant, far less attention has been given to the political behavior of the inhabitants of the region to which the migrant has moved.* The immigration problem is generally seen as one of "absorption" or "assimilation," rarely as one of interaction in which the inhabitant, too, has problems of adjustment and change. Thus when policymakers give attention to the problems created by migrants, they often give more attention to aiding migrants, rather than to cushioning the strains under which the native inhabitants are also placed.

There are a number of reasons why local inhabitants may feel threatened by a large influx of migrants. The migrant may be competing for the same jobs, and if the migrant is willing to work for lower wages, then the threat may be quite real. If the state and private sector are unable to provide new housing, more health facilities, more educational facilities, and other social programs rapidly, then the native inhabitant will sense a deterioration of local services. If migrants organize themselves and seek power in local government, local school boards, and local churches, they threaten the power of local inhabitants. And if the migrant speaks a different language, belongs to a different race, subscribes to different religious beliefs, or has a different sense of cultural identity, these differences may be offensive to a native. Finally, the native inhabitant often feels that the migrant is destroying the long-established "sense of community"—a sense that the people who live in the area share the same outlook and understand one another.

Cultural and political conflict between the migrant and native inhabitant has long been a theme in American political life. The "Know Nothing Party" of the 1850's rallied the anti-immigrant sentiments of the times (40, p. 250; see also 2, 64, 65). The "backlash" movement of the 1960's has had some of the same characteristics as the earlier movement, only this time the native inhabitants are often of Polish, German, Italian, and Irish descent, reacting not against immigrants from abroad but against Negro migrants from the South.

Some of the great cultural clashes in world history have been a consequence of the international movement of different ethnic groups. The conflicts between Germans and Slavs in eastern and southeastern Europe throughout the latter part of the 19th and early 20th centuries can be traced to the earlier migrations of both Germans and Slavs into this region of Europe (66-75). Similarly, the clash between Jews and Arabs is a consequence of earlier Jewish migrations into the Middle East and even earlier political movements which forced Jews to move to one part of the world from another. And in southern Asia the clash between Hindus and Muslims can ultimately be traced back to earlier migrations of the Mughul into south Asia.

*See, for example, (63).

The Multi-Ethnic State. The multi-ethnic state may have attained its characteristics through earlier international migrations into an existing state or through the establishment of national boundaries incorporating many ethnic groups. In such states, internal migration creates new and frequently grave problems. As has been said, the modernization process accelerates the internal movement of peoples. As land becomes a commodity to be bought and sold, peasants may move to improve their economic position. People become willing to move from areas of low income to areas of higher income in the hope that they can personnally benefit from these differences. Modern transportation at relatively low fares makes it possible for people to move easily. New opportunities arise both for working in industry or for starting new businesses. New educational institutions may be far off, and a young man, first moving to seek an education, now remains to find a job. Moreover, the people of one region or ethnic community are likely to migrate to places where people from their own community have preceded them, thus starting a process of chain migration.

As a group of migrants come to feel that they are living in an alien culture, even though it is within their own nation, they begin to take steps to establish, or at least preserve, their cultural distinctiveness. They may create their own schools, start their own newspapers, convert some of their private family or religious festivities into public ceremonies, start their own mutual benefit societies, or even begin to create their own political institutions.

But the same factors which lead the migrant to strengthen his cultural distinctiveness are also at work within the host culture in which he is living. Only a few decades ago, migrants in premodern societies could live as an alien community with little social interaction or conflict with the host culture. Today in a period of universal education, expanding communication, and expanding political participation, it has become increasingly difficult for migrants to remain encapsulated within the host culture. The result is that local inhabitants become antagonistic to the "outsider," even though he belongs to the same nation-state. Migrations in the 19th century to underdeveloped nations in south and southeast Asia, east Africa, and south Africa have led to explosive political problems in the mid-20th century, as nationalism and cultural cohesiveness have grown with increased modernization.

*The Migrant and His Place of Origin.** Migration also has an effect on the area from which the migrant comes. For one thing, migrants often have continued to play an important role in the struggle for independence on the part of their country of origin. Greek expatriates provided money and recruits for the Greek national struggle against the Ottomans in the 1837 war of independence. Similarly, Czech, Slovak, Italian, and Serb migrants to the

*See also Harley L. Browning, "Migrant Selectivity and the Growth of Large Cities in Developing Societies," in this volume.

United States continued to provide moral encouragement, financial support, and sometimes even arms and men in the struggles within their former countries. Moreover, migrants have often been able to influence the foreign policies of their adopted states, certainly an important element in the conduct of American foreign policy in the peace conferences which followed World War I.

Migrants not only influence their place of origin through remittances and through letters. They may return home to visit or to remain. Though the number of international migrants permanently returning home is relatively small, it is greater than one might at first imagine. It is estimated that approximately one sixth of all migrants to the United States in the 19th and early 20th centuries returned home to Europe, and that for some countries in south and southeastern Europe, such as Bulgaria and Serbia, as many as half of all the migrants who originally went to the United States returned home.

Most census reports underestimate and some do not report return migration at all. If the census enumerator asks "were you born outside the county (or state, or country)," he misses all those who have moved and then returned home. As Zachariah points out in his study of internal migration in India, many workers move from their place of birth when they are young and then return at an older age. The net migration figure may, therefore, substantially underestimate the amount of spatial mobility. Moreover,

> ... the number of contacts and relationships established through rural-urban migration is several times more than the net migration between these areal units. The urban migrant maintains constant contact with the village by a sort of pendulum movement between the village and town where he works and frequently settles down in the village when he retires. (56, p. 106)

There is reason to believe that the social and political significance of return migrations in the developing areas is both underestimated and underemphasized.

One of the most important social, economic, or political effects of migration may well be the impact made by a migrant returning from an urban area to his home village. What political role does this returning migrant play? With what ideas does he return? What new political and economic skills does he have? What new resources? And what role, if any, does he play in transforming the economic, political, and social life of his community of origin?

How can returning migrants be classified? Has a migrant returned for a visit or is it a permanent return? Has he returned after a short or a long departure? What was his social status in the community before he left, and what is it after he returns? And what occupation or activity does he assume upon his return?

Migration and Representation. Another political effect of migration, particularly of internal migration, that has received a great deal of attention in the United States is the effect upon the system of representation. Since systems of representation were often created before large-scale internal population movements took place, many modern states have created new forms of "rotten boroughs." A formula established and institutionalized at one time to satisfy the existing distribution of population and power may no longer be satisfactory after an era of rapid population movements. Some state legislatures in the United States are still controlled by rural interests even though the states have become predominantly urban. The recent demand for reapportionment was essentially directed at changing the structure of representation to fit this new distribution of population. And while reapportionment is taking place, gross inequities in the allocation of state and federal funds to rural instead of urban areas still continue.

RESEARCH AND POLICY IMPLICATIONS

It is beyond the scope of this essay to set forth an agenda for research in political demography or to indicate the policies which might be derived from our current limited knowledge of the political effects of population change. Instead this conclusion will try to indicate some of the questions which political scientists could usefully ask and call attention to a few of the policy issues suggested by existing knowledge.

First of all, it should be emphasized that the effects of population growth are bound to be different in highly developed societies, in densely populated countries with low economic growth, in densely populated countries with high economic growth, and in countries with low density. The level of technological development, the existing population density, and the rate and pattern of economic growth will determine the effects of rapid population growth. Population growth, for example, may have no significant effect on the size of landholdings in a technologically developed society, but it may reduce the size of landholdings to uneconomic units in a densely populated society with low levels of technology; or it may result in the more efficient use of land in a region of low density where slash-and-burn agriculture is practiced. Similarly, a society with a high rate of economic growth may take in its stride the new demands for education, housing, and health facilities accompanying rapid population growth, whereas a government with few resources will be able to provide such facilities only by reducing its efforts to increase capital investment. And, as noted earlier, a rapid expansion of the 15-to-25 age group will have one political consequence if it occurs when the economy is expanding and there are employment opportunities for new entrants into the labor force and quite another consequence if it occurs in a stagnant economy in which there are few new jobs. In other words, any assessment of the political effects of population change must take into account the capacity of the social, economic, and political system to respond to the challenge.

Since the adaptive capabilities of systems differ markedly, there may very well be few if any uniform political effects of population growth; certainly the attempts so far to relate population growth to war, violence, political instability, revolution, etc. have not been successful. To suggest, therefore, as some do, that family planning programs in the developing countries are a way of reducing the probabilities of violence, revolution, or war, and to make such claims as a rationale for family planning programs cannot be justified on the basis of existing knowledge.

Nonetheless, there are a few political effects which, if they are not general in character, are at least relevant to certain classes of political systems.

1. All things being equal, a growth in population will result in an increased demand for housing, education, health facilities, and for employment. In a low income country, the increased demand is not only likely to strain the financial resources of the government, but to place a particularly heavy burden on administrative services as well.

2. Since most governments in the less developed countries can only provide educational and health facilities for a portion of the population, it is generally the lowest socioeconomic groups, or the politically powerless, who are left behind in the allocation of government resources. Since income and occupation often coincide with differences in religion, caste, tribe, or language, a half-developed system of primary and secondary school education may sharpen both class and ethnic differences. Thus, rapid population growth, by slowing progress toward universal education, may result in an intensification of both class and ethnic conflict. Therefore, social scientists could pay more attention to the question of who is being left behind in the development process and, in particular, who is not getting an equal share of educational and health facilities.

3. There are very severe problems of governmental management for the half-dozen or so countries of the developing world which are large in both territory and population. The relationship between central authority and subordinate governmental units, and often the political viability of the subordinate governmental units, can be substantially affected by rapid population growth. Since subordinate governmental units are often given primary responsibility for education and health programs, rapidly increasing demands in these areas may weaken subordinate governmental units and cause a strain in their relations with central authority. With respect to these countries, political scientists need to give attention to the size of subordinate governmental units and to the best allocation of functions and resources among governmental units within a political system.

4. Governments of large territories with relatively small and dispersed populations are less likely to be concerned with the negative economic, political, and social effects of population growth than are the governments of more densely populated regions. Indeed, given the high per capita cost of maintaining a bureaucracy in such countries, their capacity to carry out such policies as a family planning program may be small. Moreover, the disadvantages of population growth are likely to be overlooked by governing elites who often see population growth as a way of increasing military manpower, of reducing the per capita costs of government, and, more generally, of increasing national pride.*

5. Although numbers may be decreasing as a source of political power in the developed countries, their importance appears to be growing in those less developed areas where political participation is high. Moreover, numbers may be a more important factor in the politics of ethnicity than in the politics of class conflict: while the size of a socioeconomic class is determined by economic and technological circumstances, the size of ethnic groups is determined by their natural population increase or by migration. Hardly anyone would argue that the working class can increase its political power by having more babies, but there are those among religious, tribal, caste, and racial groups who argue for a pronatal policy or view programs to reduce fertility as politically threatening. For this reason, the politics of population policy, especially in the multi-ethnic, less developed countries, is much more bound up with issues of race, tribe, caste, and religion than with questions of class.

6. There are countries where the number of young men entering the labor force each year will be substantially larger than the number of job opportunities; the disparity may be particularly great if the labor force increases at a time when agricultural mechanization has diminished the need for labor and there has not been a rapid rise in those industries which require a large labor force. In such an economy there may be strong pressures to expand university education to postpone entry into the labor force, pressures to expand employment in the government bureaucracy and the public sector generally, and pressures on businesses to employ the largest number of people which the firm can possibly sustain rather than the minimum necessary to maximize profit; a work ethic which stresses the sharing of employment rather than efficiency in performance is likely to persist; and new opportunities may be provided for political organizers who view the unemployed as a potential political constituency.

7. If, as some social scientists have argued, a high mortality rate leads individuals to be fatalistic about the future, reduces their willingness to try to manipulate their environment, and strengthens religious as opposed to secular

---

*Since it is a vast subject in itself, this paper has not dealt with the impact of political ideologies or religious doctrine on family planning programs. For a review of the literature and a useful bibliography, see (76-78).

sentiments, then a decline in the mortality rate is likely to increase a sense of personal efficacy, strengthen the secular approach, and lead people to become more future-oriented. In short, a change in mortality rates could affect what many political scientists have called the political culture. Students of political socialization would thus be well advised to examine the relationship between declining mortality rates and changes in the political culture.*

8. As Ryder has pointed out, a period of rapid population growth is one in which the relationship of children to adults and of women to men undergoes great changes (80). Modernizing states have affected these relationships through a range of public policies: compulsory education which removes the child from the home, child labor legislation which effectively increases the costs to parents of having children, inheritance legislation which fragments the family property and protects the wife and younger children, age-of-marriage legislation which delays childbearing, and legislation prohibiting discrimination in the employment of women which increases the number of women in the labor force. Although the primary purposes of most of this legislation were to improve the well-being of children and of women or to facilitate economic growth, clearly such legislation also has an impact on family-size norms. If, as some economists and sociologists argue, the costs and benefits of children, the education of women, and the employment opportunities available for women influence the reproductive decisions of couples, then political movements emphasizing equal rights for women and the care and protection of children could have a considerable impact on population growth.†

9. The political effects of high density are at least as unclear as the mental and physical health consequences and are closely related to them. Does high density—at work, at home, or in transportation—increase social conflict and generate aggressive behavior? As human conglomerations increase, can we expect a decline in civic behavior? An increase in anomic behavior? Or alternatively, new forms of social control and new modes of social and political organization?

How do social groups feel when their numbers are increasing and they are confined to a fixed territory while others in the larger society can readily move about? Do black ghetto dwellers feel they are denied the opportunities

---

*Riesman (79) has made a provocative but nonetheless unsuccessful attempt to link demographic change to personality structure. He related his three personality types— "tradition-directed," "inner-directed," and "other-directed" personalities—to three demographic phases: "high growth potential" when birth and death rates are high, "transitional growth" when the death rate declines but the birth rate has not, and "incipient population decline" when total population growth is small because both birth and death rates are low. The theory, never very well formulated in any event, was not applied in any systematic way to cross-cultural or historical data.

†For an account of the impact of demographic change on the rise of legislation affecting youth in England, see (81).

for spatial mobility that other ethnic groups in the ghettoes once had, and, if so, how does this feeling affect their attitudes toward the ghetto as a physical space, toward their own community, and toward the world outside the ghetto?

The interrelationships of poverty, crowding, and political behavior are admittedly among the most difficult relationships to investigate. In the absence of reliable knowledge, however, it is at least useful to be aware of the extent to which unverified hypotheses and myths often guide public policy. Perhaps the most glaring example is the opinion that elites of poor and densely populated countries, such as China, do not value human life to the extent that political elites do in more prosperous, less densely populated regions of the globe, and that their elites are, therefore, likely to behave in irrational and violent ways in international politics. Such an unverified assumption underlies some of the estimates of potential Chinese aggressiveness.

10. The growth of population has often been accompanied by government policies which make use of the distribution of people within a society to bring about other government aims. A population policy, for example, may be directed at extending political control over an area that is not densely populated—as the United States Government intended in the 19th century when it used population growth through migration as a means of promoting its western land policy. Similarly, the Soviet Union is encouraging the settlement of portions of central Asia as part of an overall security policy.

Governments continue to use immigration policies to affect the internal distribution of political power among various ethnic groups. One ethnic group may use its position in government to promote immigration legislation directed at asserting its political dominance over other ethnic groups—as in the policies of South African white racist regimes or the Guyana policy of increasing the black population in proportion to East Indians.*

In this connection it is useful to call attention to the need for political scientists to study the political consequences of internal population movements—not only of rural-urban migration, but also the movement of people from one ethnic group into areas in which other ethnic groups predominate. What new patterns of intergroup relations are created? To what extent do sentiments against "outsiders" emerge? What are the effects on national integration?

If regional economic differentials grow in newly developing areas, will people migrate from one part of the country to another as they did in the United States and Europe, or will ethnic divisions prove to be a barrier to

*According to the *New York Times*, July 6, 1969, the East Indian opposition in Guyana is fearful that the Prime Minister, a Negro, is planning to populate the interior of the country with Negroes imported from the West Indies, partly to develop large underdeveloped portions of the country, but also in order to change the political balance between Indians and Negroes.

large-scale internal migrations? Will, for example, the Ibo of Nigeria be willing to move into regions in which the Hausa and Fulani predominate? Will Bengalis be willing to move to Assam and Tamils to Bombay? Will Montagnards be willing to move to Saigon and Hue? Or will the hostilities which one ethnic group has shown to another discourage individuals from seeking new economic opportunities in their own country wherever those opportunities can be found?

One could continue to add to this list of hypotheses and questions, but to little purpose. The main point is that if there are so many myths and so little research, it is partly because contemporary political scientists have paid so little attention to these issues and left the study of the political aspects of population change to other disciplines.* But there are three reasons why this lack of attention is likely to be corrected in the near future.

The first is that population issues are increasingly a matter of public controversy and public policy, and wherever controversy arises or policies are debated, political scientists are sure to be interested. In both developed and developing societies, there are political controversies over government-sponsored family planning programs, partly based on the belief that various groups have as to the political effects of such policies, and partly based on the beliefs various groups have as to the motivations of those who are carrying out family planning programs. The attacks by some black militants in the United States against what has been called "prenatal genocide" is simply an American version of a controversy that one can find in many multi-ethnic societies. Moreover, as populations grow and densities increase, governments are likely to give more and more attention to population redistribution policies and these controversies, too, are bound to attract the interest of political scientists.

Second, the population dimensions of political changes in the developing countries are so different from the patterns experienced by Europe that scholars must give particular attention to issues in political demography. The decline in mortality, for example, has been much faster than anything experienced by the European states. The result is that the proportion of young people in developing areas is higher than existed in western Europe in the 18th or 19th centuries. There is a particularly acute problem of meeting the demands for educational facilities and, a generation later, of providing employment for a rapidly expanding labor force. Then, too, as noted before, the

---

*The most explicit theoretical statement I can find on the subject matter of political demography is in the writings of Durkheim, who sought to build a branch of population studies in sociology called social morphology in terms similar to those used in this essay. A member of Durkheim's school, Maurice Halbwach, developed the notion further (82). He proposed that a subfield, "political morphology," be established focusing on the location and distribution of people in space as a determinant of the structure and functions of government. To the best of my knowledge, this aspect of Durkheim's work was never pursued by political scientists.

enormous population size of some developing states and the small and dispersed populations of others make the problem of establishing and maintaining central government authority both different and more difficult. Moreover, the opportunities for international migration which permitted more than 60 million dissatisfied and disaffected Europeans to leave the continent are not available to more than a handful of highly skilled technical people in the developing world. The policy option of coping with minority problems by exporting minorities is thus not one available to more than a few developing countries. Internal migration within multi-ethnic states, as also noted earlier, creates problems which hardly existed in more culturally homogeneous societies. Thus, some of the major problems of political development which concern political scientists—the growth of demands and the creation of political institutions to meet these demands, the problems of establishing governmental authority and legitimacy, and the problems of managing ethnic conflict and creating a national civic sense—are all ones which involve population variables.

Finally, if political science continues to develop as it has in the past, it will be increasingly influenced by the enormous progress in demography and by the expansion of historical population studies (83). As perhaps the most syncretistic of the social sciences, political science has readily borrowed from related disciplines, as shown by the existence of political sociology, political anthropology, political psychology, and political economy as branches of political science. In each instance, political scientists have both borrowed and contributed, and some of the most fruitful developments in these fields have come either through the collaboration of scholars in related disciplines or through the efforts of individual scholars to bring the related disciplines together. A similar opportunity now exists for the development of *political demography.*

References

1. United Nations, *The Determinants and Consequences of Population Trends.* New York: U.N., Population Division, Dept. of Economic and Social Affairs, 1953. p. 21.
2. Higham, John, "American Immigration Policy in Historical Perspective," *Law and Contemporary Problems*, Spring 1956. p. 214.
3. Myrdal, Gunnar, *Population: A Problem for Democracy.* 1940; reprint ed. Gloucester, Mass.: Peter Smith, 1962. p. 22.
4. Myrdal, Gunnar, *Asian Drama: An Inquiry into the Poverty of Nations*, 3 vols. New York: Pantheon, Random House, 1968. Especially Chs. 27 and 28.
5. Marshall, T. H., "What the Public Thinks," *The Population Problem: the Experts and the Public*, T. H. Marshall *et al.*, eds. London: George Allen and Unwin, 1938. p. 15.

6. Spengler, Joseph J., *France Faces Depopulation*. Durham, N.C.: Duke Univ. Press, 1938.
7. Reddaway, W. B., *The Economics of a Declining Population*. London: George Allen and Unwin, 1939.
8. Henderson, H. D., "Economic Consequences," *The Population Problem: the Experts and the Public*, T. H. Marshall *et al.*, eds. London: George Allen and Unwin, 1938. pp. 100-101.
9. Kuczynski, R. R., "World Population," *ibid.* p. 107.
10. Borrie, W. D., *Population Trends and Policies: A Study in Australian and World Demography*. Sydney: Australasian Publishing Co., 1948. pp. 3-4.
11. Glass, David D., *Population Policies and Movements in Europe*, 2nd ed. New York: Kelley, 1940.
12. Vogt, William, *People!* New York: William Morrow and Co., 1960. p. 59.
13. Brown, Harrison, *The Challenge of Man's Future*. New York: Viking Press, 1956. p. 256.
14. Commager, Henry Steele, "Overpopulation and the New Nations," *Our Crowded Planet: Essays on the Pressures of Population*, Fairfield Osborn, ed. Garden City, N.Y.: Doubleday, 1962. p. 119.
15. Turner, Frederick C., "The Implications of Demographic Change for Nationalism and Internationalism," *J Pol*, February 1965. pp. 87-108.
16. Robbins, John, *Too Many Asians*. New York: Doubleday, 1959. p. 12.
17. Dorn, Harold F., "World Population Growth," *The Population Dilemma*, Philip M. Hauser, ed. Englewood Cliffs, N.J.: Prentice Hall, 1963. p. 26.
18. Taeuber, Irene B., "Population and Political Instabilities in Underdeveloped Countries," *Population and World Politics*, Philip M. Hauser, ed. Glencoe, Ill.: Free Press, 1958.
19. Hauser, Philip M., "Demographic Dimensions of World Politics," *The Population Crisis*, Larry K. Y. Ng, ed. Bloomington, Ind.: Indiana Univ. Press, 1965. pp. 65-66.
20. Organski, Kathryn and A. F. K. Organski, *Population and World Power*. New York: Alfred A. Knopf, 1961.
21. Davis, Kingsley, "The Demographic Foundation of National Power," *Freedom and Control in Modern Society*, Morroe Berger, ed. New York: Octogon, 1964.
22. Davis, Kingsley, "Population and Power in the Free World," *Population and World Politics*, Philip M. Hauser, ed. Glencoe, Ill.: Free Press, 1958.
23. Barnett, Harold J., "Population and World Politics," *World Pol*, July 1960. pp. 640-650.
24. Thompson, Warren S., and David T. Lewis, *Population Problems*. 5th ed. New York: McGraw Hill, 1965. p. 503.
25. Thompson, Warren S., and P. K. Whelpton, "Levels of Living and Population Pressure," *The Annals of the American Academy of Political and Social Science*, July 1938. pp. 93-100.
26. Huntington, Ellsworth, "Agricultural Productivity and Pressure of Population," *ibid.*, pp. 73-92.

27. Rager, F. A., "Japanese Emigration and Japan's 'Population Pressure,' " *Pac Affairs*, September 1941. pp. 300-321.
28. Hofstee, E. W., "Population Pressure and the Future of Western Civilization in Europe," *Am J Sociol*, May 1950. pp. 523-532.
29. Gurr, Ted R., *Why Men Rebel*. Princeton, N.J.: Princeton Univ. Press, 1969.
30. Coale, Ansley J., "How a Population Ages or Grows Younger," *Population: The Vital Revolution*, Ronald Freedman, ed. New York: Anchor Books, Doubleday, 1964. p. 51.
31. Clark, Colin, *Population Growth and Land Use*. New York: St. Martin's Press, 1967. p. 121.
32. Moller, Herbert, "Youth as a Force in the Modern World," *Com Stud Soc & Hist*, April 1968. pp. 237-260.
33. Ryder, Norman B., "Cohort as a Concept in the Study of Social Change," *Am Sociol R*, December 1965. pp. 843-861.
34. Keyfitz, Nathan, "Age Distribution as a Challenge to Development," *Am J Sociol*, 70, 1965. pp. 659-668.
35. McClosky, Herbert, "Conservatism and Personality," *Am Pol Sci R*, December 1958. pp. 27-45.
36. Lazarsfeld, Paul F., Bernard Berelson, and Hazel Gaudet, *The People's Choice*. New York: Columbia Univ. Press, 1948. p. 25.
37. Durand, John D., "The Trend toward an Older Population," *The Annals of the American Academy of Political and Social Science*, January 1945. pp. 142-151.
38. Rainey, Gene Edward, "Arkansas' Aging Trend: A Portent of Future Politics," *Southwest Soc Sci Q*, June 1964. pp. 37-49.
39. Hansen, Marcus Lee, *The Atlantic Migration, 1607-1860*. New York: Harper Torchbooks, 1961. p. 214.
40. MacDonald, J. C., "Agricultural Organization, Migration and Labour Militancy in Rural Italy," *Econ Hist R*, Vol. 16, No. 1, 1963. pp. 61-75.
41. Thomlinson, Ralph, *Population Dynamics: Causes and Consequences of World Demographic Change*. New York: Random House, 1964. pp. 490-493.
42. Calhoun, John B., "Population Density and Social Pathology," *Sci Am*, February 1962. pp. 13-146.
43. Winsborough, Halliman H., "The Social Consequences of High Population Density," *Law and Contemporary Problems*, 30, Winter 1965. pp. 120-126.
44. Heer, David M., *Society and Population*. Englewood Cliffs, N.J.: Prentice Hall, 1968.
45. Kuznets, Simon, ed., *Population Redistribution and Economic Growth: United States, 1870-1950*. Memoirs nos. 45, 51, 61. Philadelphia: American Philosophical Society, 1957-1964.
46. Sundquist, James L., "Where Shall They Live?" *The Public Interest*, Winter 1970. pp. 88-100.
47. Dahl, Robert A., "The City in the Future of Democracy," *Am Pol Sci R*, December 1967. p. 962.

48. Duncan, Otis Dudley, "Optimum Size of Cities," *Cities and Society: Reader in Urban Sociology*, 2nd ed., Paul K. Hatt and Albert J. Reiss, eds. Glencoe, Ill.: Free Press, 1957.
49. Kirk, Dudley, "Recent Trends of Catholic Fertility in the U.S.A.," *Current Research in Human Fertility: Proceeding of a Round Table at the 1954 Annual Conference*. Milbank Memorial Fund, 1954. pp. 6-7.
50. "The Impact of Uncontrolled Birth on Our Democratic Process," *Humanist*, January-February 1961. p. 5.
51. Hauser, Philip M., "The United States Population Explosion: Consequences and Implications," *Readings on Social Change*, Wilbert Moore and R. Cook, eds. Englewood Cliffs, N.J.: Prentice Hall, 1966. p. 137.
52. Strauss, C. B., "Population Growth and Economic Development," *So Afr J Econ*, June 1963. pp. 138-148.
53. Sinclair, K. I., *Population: New Zealand's Problem*. Dunedin: Gordon and Gotch, Ltd., 1964. p. 91.
54. Bose, Ashish, ed., *Patterns of Population Change in India, 1951-1961*. Bombay: Allied Publishers, 1967. p. xxvi.
55. *Progress of Family Planning*. New Delhi: Government of India Reports, November 1968. m. p.
56. Zachariah, K. C., and J. P. Ambannavar, "Population Redistribution in India: Inter-State and Rural-Urban," *Patterns of Population Change in India, 1951-1961*, Ashish Bose, ed. Bombay: Allied Publisher, 1967. pp. 93-106.
57. Pentzopoulos, Dimitri, *The Balkan Exchange of Minorities and Its Impact upon Greece*. Paris: Mouton, 1962. p. 178.
58. Burks, Richard V., *The Dynamics of Communism in Eastern Europe*. Princeton, N.J.: Princeton Univ. Press, 1961. p. 57.
59. Weiner, Myron, "Urbanization and Political Protest," *Civilisations*, Vol. 17, No. ½, 1967. pp. 1-7.
60. Park, Robert E., "Human Migration and the Marginal Man," *Robert E. Park on Social Control and Collective Behavior: Selected Papers*, Ralph H. Turner, ed. Chicago: Univ. of Chicago Press, Phoenix Books, 1967.
61. Tilly, Charles, and C. Harold Brown, "On Uprooting, Kinship, and the Auspices of Migration," *Int J Comp Sociol*, September 1967. pp. 139-164.
62. Nelson, Joan M., *Migrants, Urban Poverty, and Instability in Developing Nations*. Occasional Papers in International Affairs, No. 22. Cambridge, Mass.: Harvard Univ. Center for International Affairs, September 1969.
63. Handlin, Oscar, *The Uprooted*. Boston: Little, Brown and Co., 1951.
64. Fuchs, Lawrence H., "Some Political Aspects of Immigration," *Law and Contemporary Problems*, Spring 1956. pp. 270-283.
65. Handlin, Oscar, ed., *Immigration as a Factor in American History*. Englewood Cliffs, N.J.: Prentice Hall, 1959.
66. Kirk, Dudley, *Europe's Population in the Inter-War Years*. New York: Columbia Univ. Press, 1946.
67. Kulisher, Eugene Michael, *Europe on the Move: War and Population Changes, 1917-1947*. New York: Columbia Univ. Press, 1948.

68. Ladas, Stephen P., *The Exchange of Minorities: Bulgaria, Greece and Turkey.* New York: Macmillan, 1932.
69. Kostanick, Huey Louis, *Turkish Resettlement of Bulgarian Turks, 1950-1953.* California Univ. Publications in Georgraphy, Vol. 8, No. 2. Berkeley, Calif.: Univ. of California Press, 1957.
70. Frumkin, Gregory, *Population Changes in Europe since 1939: A Study of Population Changes in Europe during and since the Beginning of World War II as Shown by the Balance Sheets of 24 European Countries.* New York: Kelley, 1952.
71. Proudfoot, Malcolm Jarvis, *European Refugees, 1939-1952: A Study in Forced Population Movement.* Northwestern Univ. Studies, Social Science Series, No. 10. Evanston, Ill.: Northwestern Univ. Press, 1956.
72. Kuczynski, Robert R., *Population Movements.* New York: Oxford Univ. Press, 1936.
73. Schechtman, Joseph B., *European Population Transfers, 1939-1945.* New York: Oxford Univ. Press, 1946.
74. Vernant, Jacques, *The Refugees in the Post-War World.* New Haven, Conn.: Yale Univ. Press, 1953.
75. Moller, Herbert, ed., *Population Movements in Modern European History.* New York: Macmillan, 1964.
76. Eldridge, Hope T., "Population: Population Policies," *International Encyclopedia of the Social Sciences.* New York: Macmillan and Free Press, 1968. Vol. XII, pp. 381-388.
77. Spengler, Joseph J., and Otis Dudley Duncan, eds., *Population Theory and Policy: Selected Readings.* Glencoe, Ill.: Free Press, 1956.
78. Sauvy, Alfred, *Fertility and Survival: Population Problems from Malthus to Mao Tse-tung.* New York: Collier, 1963.
79. Riesman, David, *The Lonely Crowd.* New Haven, Conn.: Yale Univ. Press, 1950.
80. Ryder, Norman B., "Cohort as a Concept in the Study of Social Change," *Am Sociol R,* December 1965. pp. 843-861.
81. Musgrove, F., "Population Changes and the Status of the Young in England Since the 18th Century," *Sociol R,* March 1963. pp. 69-93.
82. Halbwach, Maurice, *Population and Society: Introduction to Social Morphology.* Glencoe, Ill.: Free Press, 1960. pp. 55-65 and 186-188.
83. *Historical Population Studies, Daedalus,* Spring 1968.

XVI

Population Policies and Ethical Acceptability

Arthur J. Dyck

Population experts are becoming increasingly alarmed by population growth rates throughout the world, and they are calling for substantial decreases in birth rates. During the past decade, more and more governments have also become concerned with high birth rates and have inaugurated programs aimed at lowering the birth rate. These programs have largely concentrated on voluntary family planning. Bolstered by the development of the loop and the pill, efforts to provide contraceptives and information concerning their use to as many people as possible have markedly escalated.*

Governments and voluntary organizations can offer two very cogent justifications for such family planning programs. First, the distribution of contraceptives assists couples to have only the children they want. Therefore, providing contraceptives and contraceptive information can quite properly be viewed as an extension of human freedom, and government support of family planning programs can be seen as an attempt to help those who are ignorant about contraceptives and those who have difficulty obtaining them. Second, family planning programs enhance the health of individuals, particularly the health of mothers, and through rational spacing of births, the development, health, and welfare of children as well.†

Many advocates of family planning programs see them as a means of curtailing rapid population growth. Some have even argued that ready availability and clear knowledge of modern contraceptives would, in itself, motivate people to reduce the size of their families (4). Thus, some family planning agencies expect that their programs will reduce birth rates and, therefore, help to solve problems associated with rapid population increase.

Arthur J. Dyck is Member of the Center for Population Studies and Mary B. Saltonstall Professor of Population Ethics, Harvard School of Public Health.

*See, for example, works by Berelson and Nortman (1-3).

†See the chapters by Harvey Leibenstein, T. Paul Schultz, and Joe D. Wray in this volume.

Although few would dispute that family planning programs are of actual and potential benefit to individual couples and to the welfare of their children, this approach has been challenged as inadequate and largely irrelevant for the purpose of bringing down birth rates. Four arguments have been advanced against exclusive reliance upon family planning programs as an instrument of population policy.

First, some studies indicate that the introduction and acceptance of contraceptive practices have had little effect upon birth rates (5, 6). Second, the effect of family planning programs depends upon the family-size ideals of the culture or region into which they are introduced. Some demographers have argued that, given the family-size ideals currently prevailing, voluntary family planning can reduce birth rates by no more than 20 percent in the less developed countries, a reduction that would still leave these countries with growth rates high enough to double their populations every generation (7). Such a doubling rate constitutes an increase rapid enough to augment or provoke economic difficulties and to impede governments' efforts to provide health, education, and welfare services.

A third and quite different argument has been advanced against family planning programs as instruments of government population policy. We cannot, so this argument runs, leave the decisions of social issues to individual couples. We cannot expect couples, each pursuing their own interests, to satisfy the interests or needs of society (8, 9).

Still a fourth consideration has arisen. Increasingly, it is said that family planning programs are not the sole way in which governments are involved in influencing the costs and benefits of having children.* For example, child labor laws and compulsory education have the effect of increasing the cost of having children; whereas tax deductions, maternity benefits, baby bonuses, and aid to dependent children subsidize parenthood and reduce its costs.

Given these doubts concerning the efficacy of family planning as a means of implementing population policy and given also the growing realization that governments (deliberately or not) already have programs that go beyond the mere provision of contraceptives, it is not surprising to find a proliferation of population proposals that would augment or supplant reliance upon family planning programs.†

Population policy proposals advocate ways of coping with problems associated with rapid population growth. Defining the problematic character of rapid population growth is an assessment of what is "wrong with the world," or "what is bad for people." Without defining what is harmful about a given demographic situation and specifying the benefits that would follow from changing it by means of a given policy, a recommendation would lack legiti-

---

*An extensive discussion of this appears in the chapter on population policy in Vol. I of this study.

†See Berelson (10) for a review and evaluation of twenty-nine such proposals.

mation. Population policy proposals and population analyses alike make judgments about what is ethically acceptable and unacceptable. In assessing any given population policy recommendation, therefore, it is appropriate to ask not only whether it is likely to work and likely to be adopted, but also whether it is ethically acceptable, that is, whether it is a policy we *ought* to adopt.*

The purpose of this essay is to evaluate the ethical acceptability of population policy proposals and, at the same time, to suggest a framework for making such evaluations.

THE MEANING OF ETHICAL ACCEPTABILITY

In this paper, "ethical acceptability" has two meanings. First, it is used as a normative criterion. One can ask of any given population policy whether it corresponds to what people *ought* to value and whether it resolves conflicts of value in the way that these *ought* to be resolved. These are questions for normative ethics, questions as to what things are right or wrong, good or bad. Among the most universally recognizable normative criteria identified by ethicists are freedom, distributive justice, veracity, and the calculation of benefits and harms, including, at one extreme, harms that threaten survival.[†]

However, normative assessments of the rightness or wrongness of given population policy proposals may differ. Where disagreements exist, it is necessary to specify criteria for adjudicating moral disputes. This brings us to the second meaning of "ethical acceptability." It can refer to what is specified by meta-ethical criteria, i.e., criteria that provide us with reasons, or a set or procedures, for preferring one moral judgment over another.

There is growing agreement among ethicists that the rationality of moral claims is to be judged by the extent to which they satisfy the following criteria: knowledge of facts; vivid imagination of how others are affected by our actions; and impartiality with respect to both our interests and our passions, so that what obtains for one person obtains for another and for our-

---

*In (10), Berelson delineates ethical acceptability as one of six criteria by means of which he evaluates population policy proposals. Berelson does not restrict ethical acceptability to normative meaning but uses it also in a purely descriptive way by asking whether a given proposal is congruent with the values of those who will be affected, whatever those values may be.

[†]See Ross (11) for a more complete list, one which is widely used and referred to among professional ethicists. Ross calls these norms "prima facie duties." Prima facie duties specify recognizable right- and wrong-making characteristics of actions. Specific actions or policies will be right or wrong insofar as they exhibit one or the other of these characteristics. For example, the act of telling a lie to save a friend violates the prima facie duty of truth-telling but satisfies the prima facie duty of not harming others. To decide the rightness or wrongness of particular actions or policies will usually involve a process of weighing conflicting moral claims upon us. The normative criteria I have specified are to be understood as prima facie claims.

selves as well. These criteria are derived from an analysis of moral discourse and describe the kinds of considerations that arise in the processes of formulating or reformulating our own moral judgments, and of attempting to resolve disputes (12-17). They are embodied in our social and institutional practices and appear in classical attempts to describe an ideal moral judge (14).

Using these normative and meta-ethical criteria, this paper will explore the ethical acceptability of some major population policy proposals.

Questions of Distributive Justice

The ethical acceptability of any population policy will certainly hinge on the relation it bears to distributive justice—to the way in which goods and benefits are to be divided. In terms of this paper, achieving a just distribution of goods is governed by two principles: each person participating in a practice or affected by it has an equal right to the most extensive liberty compatible with a like liberty for all; and inequalities are justifiable only where it is reasonable to expect that they will work out for everyone's advantage and provided that the positions and offices to which they attach or from which they may be gained are open to all (18).

Distributive justice is a strongly held value. Gross inequalities with respect to one's share in a society's goods or one's opportunity to change a disadvantageous position (as in slavery) can prompt people to risk death. It is in the interest of society as well as individuals to satisfy the principles of distributive justice.

Population policy proposals that advocate the use of positive or negative incentives are very directly involved in questions of distributive justice. "Positive incentives" means the governmental inducements that take the form of direct payments of money, goods, or services to members of the target population in return for the desired practice of limiting births. "Negative incentives" are tax or welfare penalties exacted from couples that exceed a specified number of children.

Ketchel (19) has described very well some of the forms of injustice that would be generally perpetrated by population policies resorting to positive and negative incentives:

> In underdeveloped countries practically no financial inducements to have children now exist to be reversed, and the imposition of further taxes upon the many poor people would depress their living standards even further and probably only succeed in raising the death rates. In developed countries people in higher economic groups could still afford to have as many children as they wished so the economic pinch associated with having children would be felt mainly by middle-class and lower-middle-class people, to whom the cost of having children, though somewhat eased

by government economic favors, is still relatively high. In order to be effective, economic pressures would probably seriously affect the welfare of the children who were born in spite of the pressures. It seems to me that the same arguments apply to the use of economic pressures to lower the birth rate as are used to argue against the issue of suppressing illegitimacy by cutting off aid to dependent children. If children become a financial burden, there will be fewer of them, but those that are born will be punished by being deprived of precisely those economic advantages they should have, both for humanitarian reasons and for their growth and development into worthwhile citizens. The same objection applies to the use of financial rewards to induce people not to have children because such programs would make the families with children the poorer families. A further objection to the use of economic pressures or rewards is that, since they would be primarily effective against certain economic groups, such methods are discriminatory.

Among the variety of specific proposals to use positive incentives is one that advocates the provision of pensions for poor parents with fewer than N children as social security for their old age (20-22). This particular policy recommendation is perhaps the least unjust of all the proposals involving incentives, especially in less developed countries where pensions are largely unavailable at present and parents depend upon their children for social security.

If social security were provided for those parents who had no more than some specified number of children, this provision would not severely, or directly, affect the lives of children in economic conditions where it is not normally possible to save money. Similarly, it would not discriminate much against parents who exceeded the specified number of children for they would, as has been the custom, look to their children for social security.

It is true that the whole society would bear the cost of this pension plan, but such a cost could be seen as enhancing the general welfare of the society, and, therefore, as a mutually advantageous burden to bear, even though it would discriminate somewhat against the grown children of large families if they were required to support their parents and contribute to the cost of the pension plan as well.

In any estimate of the benefit/harm ratio that would obtain should some policy of positive or negative incentives be initiated, it is important to consider the way in which these benefits and harms are distributed, and to take care particularly not to discriminate against the poor. Generally, the chances that the children of the poor will get a good education, that they will survive to adulthood, and that they will have a good and productive life and thus realize the hopes for the future that the parents have invested in them are not nearly as good as for the children of people at higher incomes. Having only two or three children may, from the vantage point of the poor, look precarious.

In *Children of Crisis*, Coles (23) asks whether many of us understand what a new child means to many of our poverty-stricken mothers, to the men in their lives, and to their other children. To further our understanding, he cites the following very dramatic and articulate account by a black mother:

The worst of it is that they try to get you to plan your kids by the year; except they mean by the ten-year plan, one every ten years. The truth is, they don't want you to have any, if they could help it. To me, having a baby inside me is the only time I'm really alive. I know I can make something, do something, no matter what color my skin is, and what names people call me. When the baby gets born I see him, and he's full of life, or she is; and I think to myself that it doesn't make any difference what happens later, at least now we've got a chance, or the baby does. You can see the little one grow and get larger and start doing things, and you feel there must be some hope, some chance that things will get better; because there it is, right before you, a real, live, growing baby. The children and their father feel it, too, just like I do. They feel the baby is a good sign, or at least he's some sign. If we didn't have that, what would be the difference from death? Even without children my life would still be bad—they're not going to give us what *they* have, the birth control people. They just want us to be a poor version of them only without our children and our faith in God and our tasty fried food, or anything.

They'll tell you we are "neglectful"; we don't take proper care of the children. But that's a lie, because we do, until we can't any longer because the time has come for the street to claim them, to take them away and teach them what a poor nigger's life is like. I don't care what anyone says: I take the best care of my children. I scream the ten commandments at them every day, until one by one they learn them by heart—and believe me they don't forget them. (You can ask my minister if I'm not telling the truth.) It's when they leave for school, and start seeing the streets and everything, that's when there's the change; and by the time they're ten or so, it's all I can do to say anything, because I don't believe my own words, to be honest. I tell them, please to be good; but I know it's no use, not when they can't get a fair break, and there are the sheriffs down South and up here the policemen, ready to kick you for so much as breathing your feelings. So I turn my eyes on the little children, and keep on praying that one of them will grow up at the right second, when the schoolteachers have time to say hello and given him the lessons that he needs, and when they get rid of the building here and let us have a place you can breathe in and not get bitten all the time, and when the men can find work—because *they* can't have children, and so they have to drink or get on drugs to find some happy moments, and some hope about things.

This graphic description of the feelings of one poverty-stricken mother underlines the claims of distributive justice. In any population policy, attention must be given to the problem of poverty—not so much because the poor have relatively high birth rates but rather because the conditions under which it is just and rational to expect anyone to curtail family size do not occur in dire poverty. Infant mortality rates are high enough, educational opportunities scarce enough, job opportunities uncertain enough to undermine the usual rationale for careful family planning. Alleviating conditions of poverty and delivering better health care to the poor must be part of any population policy, if it is to be just and effective.

Clearly, population policies that employ positive and negative incentives will create injustices by discriminating against the poor and by bringing about less advantageous economic conditions, or even poverty where penalties are severe, for the children of parents who are subject to penalties or who fail to gain rewards, unless special adjustments are made for these groups. However, making these adjustments may reduce the effectiveness of incentive programs. In any event, there is no direct evidence that incentives reduce birth rates and, therefore, no assurance that any injustices that might be perpetrated though the use of incentives would be worth the price.

What about the use of compulsion to secure the goals of population policy? Compulsion, on the face of it, is the most predictable and rational way to achieve the exact birth rates considered desirable or necessary for a given nation. Boulding has suggested marketable licenses to have children in whatever number that would ensure a zero growth rate, say 2.2 children per couple: the unit certificate might be the deci-child, and accumulation of ten of these units by purchase, inheritance, or gift, would permit a woman in maturity to have one legal child (24). Another proposal by Ketchel advocates mass use by government of a fertility-control agent that would lower fertility in the society by 5 to 75 percent less than the present birth rate, as needed (19). Such a substance is now unknown but would, he believes, be available for field testing after 5 to 15 years of research. It would be put in the water supply in urban areas and introduced by other methods elsewhere. Variants of compulsory sterilization, both temporary and permanent, and compulsory abortions have been proposed as well (8, 25).

Aside from the obvious technical and administrative difficulties of all of these proposals, especially in less developed countries, the effectiveness of a policy of compulsion is directly dependent upon its ethical acceptability. Any law can be disobeyed, or subverted, and the problem of punishing offending parents is especially acute. Could it be done, for example, without inflicting suffering upon innocent children? Obviously fines and jail sentences would be a hardship for children as well as parents no matter what provision society would make for the children. Compulsory sterilizations and abortions could be used to enforce a specific quota of children per couple, but these methods are ethically unacceptable for reasons that will be discussed later.

Compulsion, like incentives, discriminates against the poor. Restricting the very poor to two or three children would render their lives much less joyous, much less hopeful, and much more precarious. In less developed countries, such restrictions for the poor mean economic losses in the form of reductions both in labor and in security for their old age.

Suppose, however, that the gross poverty in a given population group were virtually eliminated. What other ethical objections to the use of compulsion would remain? The most conspicuous argument against compulsion is that it is incompatible with the freedom to pursue our own happiness and forge our own destiny. How cogent is this argument?

Questions of Freedom

Freedom refers in part to the relative absence of government interference and compulsion concerning those actions that are not harmful to the public interest. It refers also to what we sometimes call equality of opportunity, that is, the opportunity to determine and change one's economic, social, and political status within one's society. Freedom in both the senses I have specified is as strong a value as survival itself. People will risk death to obtain it for themselves and others. They will not trade it off completely for some other actual or potential benefit. Moreover, freedom serves public interests as well as private ones. Some freedom of speech, for example, is an essential component of any society; it is a necessary prerequisite to social intercourse.

However, freedom is not always incompatible with compulsion. One of the ways in which freedom is secured through compulsory regulations is illustrated by the laws governing traffic. Without such laws, it is difficult to imagine how the freedom to drive private automobiles in crowded areas could be maintained. Compulsory education also guarantees and enhances freedom. Compulsion can prevent great harm both to individuals and to society. One example is compulsory vaccination to prevent epidemics, as well as individual suffering. In all of these examples, certain choices are taken away from the individual, and yet his total freedom is increased. Would compulsion in limiting the number of one's children be comparable to any of these examples? To answer this question, one must try to characterize more nearly the kind of decision involved in choosing whether or not to have children and how many to have.

In Plato's *Symposium*, Socrates notes that there are three ways in which people can try to satisfy their deep longing for immortality (26). One way is to have children. Another is to commit a deed or deeds noble and heroic enough to receive the attention of one's community and become a part of its collective memory. A third way is that of scholarly pursuit and authorship. Each attempt to achieve immortality depends for its success upon the receptivity and support of one's community. Children, therefore, provide a deeply gratifying link to the human community and to the future. Decisions about how we will use our reproductive powers are decisions about our own future and about our own contribution to the future of the human community, about how one's life is to count, and how far its influence is to extend.

Sexuality is at once an expression of our individuality, and a gift that each of us receives from others, his parents most immediately, but also from the wider community. Indeed, it is a gift from the human species to the human species. We owe a debt of *gratitude* to these wellsprings of our unique genetic and social individuality for the very possibility of experiencing sexual pleasure, and for the considerable rewards of childbearing and child rearing.

As those who have been chosen to live, we incur an awesome but joyous obligation to see to it that these gifts of life—sexual expression, procreation, and child rearing—have a future. Our obligation to the larger community is particularly vital insofar as each of us has unique genetic endowments and unique talents to offer and to perpetuate. No one else can give to the species what we bring to it. Failure to reproduce is both an individual and a communal act that requires a special justification if it is to be morally responsible. Individual decisions to refrain from having children of one's own are presumably easier to justify in times of rapid population growth.

If these are the values guiding our reproductive decisions, the very dignity and identity of the person as a moral being is at stake in any decision to use compulsion in controlling reproductive behavior. There are those who believe that the dignity and autonomy associated with reproductive decisions is a human right provided for in the United States Constitution. As part of its successful effort to defeat the birth control laws of Connecticut in the Supreme Court, the Planned Parenthood Federation of America argued that these laws, by forcing couples to relinquish either their right to marital sex relations or their right to plan their families, constituted a deprivation of life and liberty without due process of law in violation of the Fourteenth Amendment (27). Earlier Supreme Court decisions were cited affirming the right "to marry, establish a home and bring up children" as among "those privileges essential to the orderly pursuit of happiness by free men" under the Fourteenth Amendment (28-30). In a "Declaration on Population" presented at the United Nations in 1957, thirty nations, including the United States, affirmed their belief "that the opportunity to decide the number and spacing of children is a basic human right" and "that family planning, by assuring greater opportunity to each person, frees man to attain his individual dignity and reach his full potential."*

But it is precisely on this point that the battle has been enjoined. Davis has directly challenged the right of any person to determine for himself how many children he shall have, because, in his view, the assertion of such a right conflicts with society's need to keep the number of children at some specified level (8). In this instance, Davis, like many others, sees a conflict between

*Quoted in (31).

individual rights and interests on the one hand, and societal necessities and interests on the other.

But has Davis correctly characterized those interests we call human rights? I am convinced that it is not correct to think of a human right as something that can come into conflict with our public interests. To identify a human value as a right is to claim that something of value is *so* valuable and *so* precious that society has a stake in it—for example, freedom of speech, which is generally considered to be a human right (30, Article 19).

Rights imply duties.* When we say that freedom of speech is a right, we imply that it is our duty, and the duty of others, to see to it that freedom of expression is generally honored and protected. In claiming that freedom of speech is a right that society should protect, we are not claiming that every utterance ought to be sanctioned regardless of its consequences. Clearly, the right to free speech is not abrogated by considering it a crime to cry "fire" falsely in a crowded theatre (34). The important thing, however, is that the interests in encouraging certain utterances, and in discouraging others, are both public and private. It is of benefit both to individuals and to society to encourage free expression generally, and to discourage certain forms of it under special circumstances.

This is true also of decisions regarding the nature and the number of one's children. In asserting that it is the right of individual couples to make such decisions voluntarily, we are positing both an obligation and an interest of society to see to it that this right is honored. At the same time, it is in the interest both of individuals and of society to curtail the extensive expression of this choice should the consequences of rapid growth rates become too oppressive or threatening. If, therefore, society is to avoid a conflict between two public interests—the interest in maintaining the quality of life against the interest in maintaining the right to decide voluntarily the number of one's children—every effort must be made to provide the information, materials, and conditions that will assist individuals to limit their births voluntarily for their own welfare and for the common good.

For the sake of argument, let us imagine a hypothetical situation in which a particular government has used every conceivable program to bring down its population growth rates, and these programs have failed. As a result, the nation must attain nothing short of zero growth rates very quickly or face consequences that the government and its people feel they must avoid, even at great cost. Under these circumstances, compulsory measures to curb birth rates might be justified as a last resort.

---

*See, for example, books by Carritt (32) and Ewing (33). I would abstractly define a right much in the way Ewing does, to refer to powers or securities that an individual or group can rightly demand of other individuals or groups that they should not normally interfere with them.

However, I wish to argue that *not every compulsory measure can be justified even as a last resort*. The continuation of human life depends upon the exercise of our reproductive powers. To maintain a population at a replacement level requires slightly more than two children per couple at the death rates now prevailing in affluent nations. In principle, every couple in this world could be granted the right and privilege to have at least two children of their own.* The threat of overpopulation is not in itself a sufficient argument for singling out any given type of individual for compulsory sterilizations or compulsory abortions. The suggestion by Davis (8) that abortions be required in cases in which the child would be illegitimate not only dries up the most important source of children for sterile couples but also denies the unwed woman any right to a moral decision regarding either the fate of her fetus or the physical risks to which she will be subjected.

The right to exercise one's procreative powers is not identical with the right to have as many children as one wants through the use of those powers. In a situation of last resort, society might very well decide to ration the number of children per family and try to provide some just means, like a lottery, for deciding who will be permitted to reproduce more than two children. This limits the right to choose how many children one will have but not the right to choose to have one or two children of one's own. Ketchel's proposal threatens this right, since by the use of sterilants that reduce everyone's fertility some people are involuntarily made infertile. Of course, if Ketchel can prevent or offset such mishaps, his proposal could be used as a method of rationing.

The right to have a choice regarding the exercise of one's procreative powers and to be able to retain the capacity to procreate is as fundamental as the right to life.† Choosing to have a child of one's own is a choice as to one's

*In the United States there are sterilization laws in some states that permit the sterilization of certain classes of people. In North Carolina, for example, the mentally ill, the feebleminded, and epileptics may be sterilized (35). Presumably these are voluntary sterilizations in the sense that the consent of guardians is required, but the state can appoint such guardians. The constitutionality of this procedure in the case of the feebleminded was upheld in (36). The North Carolina law and others like it are ethically very questionable. In *Skinner v. Oklahoma*, the Supreme Court did declare a law permitting the sterilization of "habitual criminals" to be unconstitutional (29).

†To say a right is "fundamental" means, in this context, that it is the kind of right that is recognizable as universal, that is, a right belonging to every human being qua human being, as it is in the United Nations, "Universal Declaration of Human Rights," articles 1-3 (30, p. 492). It would be recognized as such by an ideal observer who is fully informed and impartial, and who can vividly imagine how his actions affect others. For a full description of such an ideal moral judge, see Firth (14). Furthermore, a fundamental right has a prima facie claim upon us. (See Ewing (33) for his arguments against absolutistic theories of rights.) A fundamental right, therefore, always has some claim on us, but there may be circumstances in which a particular fundamental right cannot be honored because of a conflict between more than one individual or more than one fundamental right. When one person, for example, attacks another, the person who is

own genetic continuity. One should be free to express one's gratitude to one's parents and to honor their desire for continuity in the human community; one should be free to seek a place in the memory of future generations. If our lives are to be deprived of any choices in establishing these links to the past and the future, we have lost a great deal of what life is all about and, indeed, we have lost the most predictable way known to us of extending our lives on this earth. Very few people achieve immortality on earth in other ways. Compulsory, irreversible sterilization, I would contend, is not an ethically acceptable method of curbing birth rates.

Our draft system is often used as an analogy for justifying the use of compulsion to meet the needs of society. A just war, fought with just means, as a last resort, and in self-defense, would seem to justify conscription. But even in this situation, conscientious objectors are exempted from military service. Population policies should make a similar provision for those who cannot in good conscience submit to sterilization, or have an abortion, or stay for other reasons within a given rationing scheme. Presumably, when population problems are a clear and present danger, most people will wish to limit the number of their children. Precedents in human history are now well known; hunter-gather societies now being studied in the deserts of Africa keep their populations at levels that guarantee them ample food and leisure for what they regard as the good life (37). They have what modern societies will need to develop, namely a very keen appreciation of the limits of their environment and their own technical capacities to benefit from it without harming it.

Although I believe it is wise to sort out in advance what forms of compulsion would be least evil as last resorts, I consider any compulsory control of birth rates unjustifiable now and in the indefinite future for at least three reasons. First, famines and environmental deterioration are not exclusively a function of population growth rates; second, more practical and ethically acceptable alternatives to compulsion exist and have not yet been sufficiently tested; and third, there are distinct benefits associated with small families which can be facilitated and the knowledge of which can be more widely disseminated.

Questions of Benefits and Harms

Nutritional deficiencies and ecological imbalances will not be eradicated simply by reducing or even halting growth rates. To overcome these harms, agricultural development and pollution abatement will be necessary even if

---

attacked may justifiably defend his right to life even when this might necessitate taking the life of the aggressor. In the example cited earlier, the right to free speech is justifiably abrogated in instances when, as in the case of falsely shouting fire in a crowded theatre, it seriously threatens the right to life of a great many people.

zero growth rates were to be immediately achieved throughout the world. The reasons for this are thoroughly discussed elsewhere (38-40).*

Rapid population growth rates do make it more difficult to feed people, to prevent environmental deterioration, and to maintain the quality of life in other ways. Are there population policies that are more beneficial than harmful and which do not involve injustices or serious threats to human freedom? I wish to suggest some.

In a country like the United States, birth rates have been dropping for the past decade. We have time to see how much more can be done by extending voluntary family planning,[†] by providing health services where needed to improve infant and maternal care, by educating people to the bad consequences of continued population growth for the nation as well as the individual family, and by improving educational and job opportunities for everyone, especially blacks, women, and other currently disadvantaged groups.

What about the situation in less developed countries? On the basis of intensive research over a period of 7 years in the Punjab region of India, Gordon and Wyon hypothesize that people in such an area would be motivated to reduce their birth rates if mortality rates for infants and children were sharply decreased, local social units were stimulated to measure their own population dynamics and to draw inferences from them concerning their own welfare and aspirations, and efficient methods of birth control were introduced (6). Initiating these conditions would substantially increase the opportunities to reduce family size without undue fear, to assess more precisely how fertility affects families and their community, and to plan family size more effectively. Whether birth rates would be markedly lowered by bringing about these conditions alone would depend not simply upon the extent to which people in that region stand to benefit from a reduction in fertility but also upon the extent to which they actually perceive such benefits, both social and economic, and believe they are attainable.

Gathering and disseminating information is, therefore, a crucial aspect of this proposal. Without accurate information, a sense of group responsibility cannot exist on a rational basis and will have no perceptible dividend to the individual members. The proposal of Gordon and Wyon assumes that rational and purposeful behavior exists already to some degree and can be modified in the direction of lower fertility by certain modifications in the environment which make small families beneficial and more attainable.

Looking at the total ecological context within which population problems arise in the less developed countries—especially the factors of under-

*See also Joseph L. Fisher and Neal Potter, "The Effects of Population Growth on Resource Adequacy and Quality," in this volume; and "The Consequences of Rapid Population Growth," in Vol. I.

†Liberalized abortion laws are among the methods now being advocated. For a thorough discussion of the wide variety of ethical issues raised by abortion, see (41).

nourishment, poverty, and lack of opportunity—some writers have suggested that nothing less than substantial technological, social, and economic changes would provide the conditions under which birth rates can be sufficiently reduced (40). These changes include industrialization, urbanization, and modern market agriculture. In the demographic history of the West such an environment certainly has been associated with sharp declines in birth rates. Urbanization and industrialization, accompanied as they are by rising levels of literacy, better communications, increased economic opportunities, improved health care, lower infant mortality rates, higher status for women, and higher costs of bearing and rearing children, may be necessary to provide the incentives and the means to control population growth. In these terms, a population policy is an overall social and economic development policy.*

These two policies would not violate any of our ethical criteria. They would enhance human freedom and encourage responsible community behavior. Indeed, on the face of it they do not violate any of the normative or meta-ethical criteria we have introduced in this essay. Both would increase the elements in the decision-making processes of individual couples that contribute to making the morally best decision. They would increase knowledge of the facts, stimulate the imagination of people concerning the effects of reproductive decisions, and encourage impartiality by fostering more universal loyalties that go beyond one's own interests and passions, and those of one's own group.

Gordon and Wyon's proposal has the advantage of introducing a minimum of disruption into a culture. It may, by the same token, be inadequate to induce the requisite behavior without further transformations of the social and economic lot of the people involved. Each of these ethically acceptable population policy proposals relies upon the voluntary decisions of individual couples. Several writers have contended recently that population policies *cannot* rely upon individual couples pursuing their own benefits to satisfy the needs of society.†

Hardin, for example, has argued that in matters of reproduction individual interests are definitely incompatible with collective interests and, therefore, population growth rates will have to be regulated by society (9). How cogent is this argument?

His argument rests on what he calls "the tragedy of the commons." Where a finite amount of grazing land is available to a number of sheepherders, each sheepherder will add sheep to his own flock, ultimately amassing a larger total number of sheep than the land will sustain. Although each individual sheep-herder is aware of this fact, his immediate decisions are determined, nonethe-

---

*See Dudley Kirk, "A New Demographic Transition?" in this volume.

†See, for example, (8, 9, 25, 42).

less, by the profit he contemplates from adding another sheep to his flock. The knowledge that the commons will at some point be overgrazed, if everyone does this, does not suffice to deter him.

All of this seems reasonable enough when one is talking about sheep. But does the analogy extend to decisions of parents regarding the number of their children? Are the benefits of adding a child to our own families even roughly comparable with the benefits that come from enhancing our economic status?

In discussing freedom, I took the view that children are one means of extending our own selfhood into the future, of obtaining some kind of personal continuity. Children are also a way of replenishing the human community in which we hope to live on as a cherished memory. One child surviving into adulthood and having children of his own will suffice to maintain our own continuity. If our self-interest is extensive enough to embrace a concern for the continuation of society and of the species, two or three children will be enough.

However, in some circumstances we may feel disquieted about limiting ourselves to two or three children. When, for example, we live under conditions in which infant mortality is high, we may very well want to have one or two extra children to be sure that two will survive us, or at least will live to have children of their own.

A second set of satisfactions and opportunities is associated with childbearing and child rearing. To the extent that having a child is a quest for the experience of rearing a child, it is not clear that relatively large families are best. For those satisfactions that come from the quality and frequency of one's contacts with one's own children, small families are preferable to large families. In very large families, the older children, not the parents, obtain most of the satisfactions of playing, of training, and of other forms of intimate interaction with the younger ones. Parental contacts with children in a large family are more likely to occur as disruptions for a busy mother than as opportunities for a show of affection and an exchange of ideas.

The benefits of bearing children are somewhat more ambiguous. At present there is no sure knowledge as to the strength of the drive to bear a child and what role this plays in the number people have. The desire to have the experience of giving birth may be satisfied with the birth of one child. Some women, however, may covet the repetition of this kind of experience.* One psychonalyst has expressed his amazement that the desire to bear children is so easily and quickly satiated (43). Such satiation may result from the long period of dependency typical of human offspring, as well as from the physical exertion, pain, and risks of childbirth itself. Whatever joys may be associated with our children, there are also lifelong concerns and anxieties.

*Some women seem to have a strong unconscious urge to bear children even while practicing birth control. Dr. Hilton Salhanick has observed that some women practicing the rhythm method will break or lose their thermometers at the critical juncture in their menstrual cycle.

Spacing the interval between births is good for both children and parents.* It enhances the intellectual development of children and the health and tranquility of mothers. Even in societies where average family size is relatively large, spacing is extensively practiced (6).

A fourth element in reproductive decisions, not present in decisions to add a profit-making sheep to our flock, has been observed by Rainwater.[†] In his intensive studies of working-class parents, he found that among those who had more children than they professed to want there were parents who reported that they had exceeded their own family-size ideals because they did not wish to be seen as selfish by their neighbors. This desire to be seen as an unselfish, kind, and public-spirited person could be used to bring about a wider acceptance of small family-size ideals. In view of the social problems generated by rapid rates of population growth, generous impulses can now best be exhibited by having only the children that society considers desirable or necessary.

Of course, Hardin might contend that the shepherd who adds to his flock is not deterred by the possibility that such additions will be seen as selfish by other shepherds using the same grazing land. In his case, however, *selfishness* and profit are linked; but in childbearing and child rearing, *unselfishness* is linked with benefit.

Where children serve to provide a substitute for a social security system or where they bring economic profit through their labor, the situation begins more nearly to approximate the one depicted by Hardin. Nevertheless, the constraints that we have cited obtain even in the rural villages of less developed countries where children are often economic assets. There are some recent indications that in areas where agricultural productivity is increasing, birth rates are coming down, for example in certain areas of India (46). Given the history of the demographic transition in developed nations, this should hardly come as a surprise. If adding children were like adding sheep to one's flock, however, birth rates should be going up. Surely Hardin's analogy is at best an uncertain one, and, at worst, inappropriate.[‡]

Davis and Blake have also expressed the belief that individual couples will not voluntarily provide for the collective interests of society but will, given the strongly positive public attitude toward parenthood and especially toward motherhood, persist in having relatively large families (8, 42). Like Hardin, they do not take into account any of the four constraining factors we have cited.

---

*See the essays by Harvey Leibenstein, T. Paul Schultz, and Joe D. Wray in this volume.

[†]See (44) and (45), particularly Chapters 5 and 6, in which the concern for unselfish parenthood is documented for the middle class as well as the working class.

[‡]This is not to deny the existence of interests that may in the long run keep family size just high enough to prove troublesome.

One could argue, contrary to Davis and Blake, that we would do well to think of motherhood even more positively and to emphasize the tremendous responsibility entailed by it. If, much more than they now do, societies came to measure the quality of parenthood and motherhood by the achievements and the quality of life of children, the constraints on family size would operate even more effectively. If the concern of parents is for the best possible development of their children, then it is important to space children widely, to expose them as much as possible to the stimuli and warm support of parental interaction, and to be a model of unselfish restraint in keeping down the size of one's family. Responsible parenthood of this kind would include living in accord with whatever national fertility goals may become morally desirable or necessary to maintain the quality of human life and guarantee a future for the human species.

Davis and Blake have stressed the need to improve the status of women by providing better and more extensive opportunities for employment and for contributions to society in ways other than through childbearing and child rearing. Employment for women and opportunities to make a variety of contributions to the human community extend the freedom of women. Better and more extensive education for women also has the effect of contributing to the quality of mothering as well as to other forms of self-realization.

It would seem to be a shortsighted policy to attack the institution of motherhood and parenthood generally. Stressing the quality of mothering and parenthood and, at the same time, providing women with alternative forms of vocation and self-realization would appear to be a morally and demographically superior policy.

To claim, as I have, that individual couples and their children benefit in certain ways from keeping families small is not to claim that these benefits will necessarily suffice to offset other forces that now keep many families large enough to maintain rates of population growth rapid enough to be troublesome to certain countries. I am maintaining, however, that to mitigate these latter forces, it is helpful to study, facilitate, and make known the benefits associated with small families; and to expose some of the fallacies of assuming that individual couples who actively seek the satisfaction of childbearing and child rearing will generally benefit most by having relatively large families or even as many children as they can afford.

Veracity and Meta-Ethical Criteria as Practical Guidelines

There are certain practical guidelines that should be part of the formulation and implementation of population policies. Generally, these guidelines draw in a special way upon the norm of veracity, i.e., truth-telling, and promise-keeping, and the meta-ethical criteria specified earlier.

Knowing the Facts

An ideal program that would evoke the voluntary response of the people affected by it would make an honest case for the reproductive behavior called for in the policy. Parents need to know what benefits will accrue to them from limiting the number of their children. Evaluations of population policy recommendations, therefore, must include specific designations of what counts as a population problem and of what interests individuals and societies have in their children. Research is definitely needed to explore more fully the significance and meaning of children to parents in a wide variety of circumstances.

Often, in discussions of population policy, there are allusions to the use of propaganda. This word threatens to create a credibility gap. If by propaganda we mean trying to persuade people that a certain policy is in their interest, without giving them the facts that will allow them to decide whether it *is* actually in their interest, we violate the canons of veracity. Moreover, we do not satisfy the criterion of giving people as many of the facts as possible, and hence do not respect their potential to make a morally correct decision and to act upon it.

Vividly Imagining How Others Are Affected by Our Actions

In some of the literature, there is a distinct elitist strain, implying that only certain people are in a position to formulate population policy and that the rest of mankind must be propagandized, won over by incentives, or compelled to act in ways considered to be desirable by the experts. In contrast to such elitism, ethically acceptable population policies should be based on sympathetic understanding of the conditions of life and of the aspirations of the people who will be affected. To guarantee this, many voices must be heard.

Black people in the United States are among those who are making apparent the value of wide and diverse participation in the planning process and thereby extending the actualization of democratic ideals and the humanization of social institutions. Ways must always be sought to assure that vivid images of how people live, and of what they feel and desire, will guide and shape the planners and their work.

Universalizing Loyalties: Impartiality

To strive for impartiality or universal loyalties is to strive to discount the influence upon our moral judgments of particular interests and passions. For example, we demand of a judge that he not try his own son and that he disqualify himself in an antitrust suit involving a company in which he is a significant shareholder. Similarly, both our constitutional provisions for separate branches of government and our continuing quest for fair judicial process are attempts to minimize the effect of particular interests or passions by providing representation of diverse interests, while at the same time assuring equitable checks and balances.

Problems of rapid population growth make the need for impartiality, our third meta-ethical criterion, concretely explicit. Though survival values within our species are strong and tenacious, they are usually individualized and tied to relatively small interest groups representing one's social, ethnic, and national identity. For the survival of such groups many would, under certain circumstances, make sacrifices and even die. But population policies, though they must attend to the needs and interests of particular regions and population groups, should endeavor to ascertain and foster the best interests of the entire human species in its total ecological setting, a task that embraces attention to other species and material resources as well. The goals of population policies go beyond the boundaries our societal and national interests set for us.

In defining these goals, population policies would fail utterly to improve the human condition and enlist its deepest loyalties were they to diminish, rather than augment, the extent to which beneficence, freedom, distributive justice, and veracity are realized on the earth. These are not moral luxuries: our survival, and the worth of that survival, depend upon their effective implementation. As the demographer Ansley Coale has so sagely observed, "preoccupation with population growth should not serve to justify measures more dangerous or of higher social cost than population growth itself" (47). It would be the ultimate irony of history if through our population policies we should lose precisely what we seek to save, namely, human rights and welfare.

References

1. Berelson, Bernard, et al., eds., *Family Planning and Population Programs.* Chicago: Univ. of Chicago Press, 1966.
2. Berelson, Bernard, ed., *Family Planning Programs: An International Survey.* New York: Basic Books, 1969.
3. Nortman, Dorothy, "Population and Family Planning Programs: A Fact Book," *Reports on Population/Family Planning.* New York: Population Council, December 1969.
4. Bogue, Donald J., *Principles of Demography.* New York: John Wiley and Sons, 1966. Ch. 20.
5. Cobb, John C., Harry M. Raulet, and Paul Harper, "An I.U.D. Field Trial in Lulliani, West Pakistan." Paper presented at the American Public Health Assn., October 21, 1965.
6. Wyon, John B., and John E. Gordon, "The Khanna Study," *Harvard Medical School Alumni Assn Bulletin*, 41, 1967. pp. 24-28.

7. Leibenstein, Harvey, "Population Growth and the Development of Underdeveloped Countries," *Harvard Medical School Alumni Assn Bulletin*, 41, 1969. pp. 29-33.
8. Davis, Kingsley, "Population Policy: Will Current Programs Succeed?" *Science*, 158, 1969. pp. 730-739.
9. Hardin, Garrett, "The Tragedy of the Commons," *Science*, 162, 1969. pp. 1243-1248.
10. Berelson, Bernard, "Beyond Family Planning," *Studies in Family Planning*, 38, February 1969. pp. 1-16.
11. Ross, W. D., *The Right and the Good*. Clarendon: Oxford, 1930.
12. Baier, Kurt, *The Moral Point of View*. Ithaca, N.Y.: Cornell Univ. Press, 1958.
13. Brandt, Richard B., *Ethical Theory*. Englewood Cliffs, N.J.: Prentice Hall, 1959.
14. Firth, Roderick, "Ethical Absolutism and the Ideal Observer,," *Phil Phenomenol Res*, 12, 1952. pp. 317-345.
15. Frankena, William, *Ethics*. Englewood Cliffs, N.J.: Prentice Hall, 1963.
16. Hare, R. M., *Freedom and Reason*. Clarendon: Oxford, 1963.
17. Mandelbaum, Maurice, *The Phenomenology of Moral Experience*. Glencoe, Ill.: The Free Press, 1955.
18. Rawls, John, "Justice as Fairness," *Phil Rev*, 67, 1958. pp. 164-194.
19. Ketchel, Melvin M., "Fertility Control Agents as a Possible Solution to the World Population Problem," *Perspect Biol Med*, 11, 1968. pp. 687-703.
20. Ohlin, Goran, *Population Control and Economic Development*. Paris: Development Centre of the Organization for Economic Cooperation and Development, 1967.
21. Samuel, T. J., "The Strengthening of the Motivation for Family Limitation in India," *J Fam Welfare*, 13, 1966. pp. 12-14.
22. Spengler, Joseph, "Population Problem: In Search of a Solution," *Science*, 166, December 5, 1969. pp. 1234-1238.
23. Coles, Robert, *Children of Crisis*. Boston: Atlantic-Little Brown, 1964.
24. Boulding, Kenneth, *The Meaning of the Twentieth Century: The Great Transition*. New York: Harper and Row, 1964, 1967 (paper). pp. 135-136.
25. Ehrlich, Paul, and Anne Ehrlich, *Population, Resources, and Environment: Issues in Human Ecology*. San Francisco, Calif.: W. H. Freeman and Co., 1970.
26. *The Dialogues of Plato*, trans. by B. Jowlett. New York: Random House, 1937. Vol. I, pp. 332-334.
27. *Griswold v. Connecticut*, 381 U.S. 479 (1965).
28. *Meyer v. Nebraska*, 262 U.S. 390, 399 (1923).
29. *Skinner v. Oklahoma*, 316 U.S. 535 (1942).
30. United Nations General Assembly, "Universal Declaration of Human Rights," Article 16. Quoted in Richard Brandt, *Value and Obligation*. New York: Harcourt, Brace and World, 1961. p. 494.

31. *Studies in Family Planning*, 26, 1968. p. 3.
32. Carritt, E. F., *Morals and Politics*. Clarendon: Oxford, 1935. Ch. 13.
33. Ewing, A. C., *The Individual, the State, and World Government*. London: Macmillan, 1947.
34. Holmes, Jr., Oliver Wendell, *Shenkwin v. United States* (1919).
35. Woodside, Moya, *Sterilization in North Carolina*. Chapel Hill: Univ. of North Carolina Press, 1950.
36. *Buck v. Bell*, 274 U.S. 200 (1927).
37. Thomas, Harold. Unpublished manuscript.
38. Revelle, Roger, "International Cooperation in Food and Population," *Internat Org*, 22, 1968. pp. 362-391.
39. Goldsmith, Grace, et al., "Population and Nutritional Demands," *The World Food Problem, Report of the Panel on the World Food Supply*. A Report of the President's Science Advisory Comm., the White House, May 1967. Vol. II, pp. 1-135.
40. Revelle, Roger (testimony), *Effects of Population Growth on Natural Resources and the Environment*. Hearings before the Reuss Subcommittee on Conservation and Natural Resources. Washington: U.S. Govt. Printing Office, 1969.
41. Potter, Ralph B., Jr., "The Abortion Debate," *The Religious Situation: 1968*, Donald Cutler, ed. Boston: Beacon Press, 1968. pp. 112-161.
42. Blake, Judith, "Population Policies for Americans: Is the Government Being Misled?" *Science*, 164, 1969. pp. 522-529.
43. Wyatt, Frederick, "Clinical Notes on the Motives of Reproduction," *J Soc Issues*, 23, 1967. pp. 29-56.
44. Rainwater, Lee, *And the Poor Get Children*. Chicago: Quadrangle Books, 1960.
45. Rainwater, Lee, *Family Design*. Chicago: Aldine Publishing Co., 1965.
46. Wyon, John, "Population Pressure in Rural Punjab, India, 1952 to 1969." Paper presented at the Seventh Conference of the Industrial Council for Tropical Health, October 1969, Harvard School of Public Health, Boston, Mass.
47. Coale, Ansley, "Should the United States Start a Campaign for Fewer Births?" *Population Index*, 34:4, October-December 1968. pp. 467-474.

XVII

Changes of Birth and Death Rates and Their Demographic Effects

Nathan Keyfitz

Present rates of birth and death are unstable: they cannot stay as they are. When change occurs, it will have determinable effects, for instance on age distribution. This paper is devoted mainly to examining the effects of changes in rates of birth at specific ages of mothers and death at specific ages on the overall rate of increase of populations and on their age distributions. It is introduced by a brief survey of rates of birth and death in the world according to recent data on which newly computed life tables and other results have been produced.

SUMMARY

An analysis of the great mass of data available on contemporary national births and deaths suggests three population types: (a) high birth and high death rates, mainly in Africa; (b) high birth and low death rates, mainly in Asia and Latin America; and (c) low birth and low death rates, among peoples of European ancestry and in Japan. Continuation of this pattern into the future implies a striking change in relative numbers on the different continents, an even greater divergence than exists today in levels of living, and a deterioration of the environment in both rich and poor continents.

To achieve a stationary population, imposed by the finite area and resources of the planet, either death rates will rise or birth rates will fall. On the optimistic assumption that the needed adjustment will be by birth rates and on the even more optimistic, extreme assumption that birth rates fall imme-

Nathan Keyfitz is Professor of Demography, University of California at Berkeley.

The research behind this chapter has been supported by NSF grant GZ995, by NIH research contract 69-2200, and by teaching grants to the Department of Demography at the University of California at Berkeley from the National Institute of General Medical Sciences (5 TO1 GM01240) and the Ford Foundation.

diately to a level that will ultimately bring a stationary population, we find that substantial growth still occurs. Because of age distributions favorable to fertility, total numbers would continue to rise, by two thirds in the faster growing parts of the world. These regions are in the grip of a kind of demographic inertia: populations that are growing rapidly have, by virtue of that growth, age distributions favorable to reproduction. Even if fertility falls to a stationary level, such regions continue to grow for at least 50 years before tapering off to their stationary values at 60 percent or more above the present numbers. If the adoption of the stationary birth rates is postponed even as little as 15 years, the increase to stationarity would be not 60 percent but nearly 150 percent.

Today's developing countries differ from the developed ones in growing up to five times as fast—say 3.5 percent per year against 0.7 percent per year. More surprising, they differ strikingly from Europe in the 18th century. The typical developing country of today has decidedly lower death rates and much higher birth rates than did European countries when they were on the road to development.

The result is a high dependency burden today; numerous young children add to the difficulties that the capital-poor countries have in accumulation. That this can be contrasted with the rich countries of today is widely known, but the comparison with 18th century Europe is less familiar. The analysis in this paper seeks to find to what degree the advantage of 18th century Europe was due to its lower birth rates and to what extent to its higher death rates; apparently the birth rate differences had more than twice as much influence on childhood dependency as had death rate differences.

The effect of changes in age-specific death rates on ultimate overall increase is found to be small. For example, a one-time decline of death rates at ages past reproduction has no effect at all on the ultimate population increase. Moreover, with modern low mortality the elimination of all remaining deaths up to the end of reproductive life would only slightly increase the growth.

Death rates are subject to policy decisions, for example, on whether funds are to be spent on heart research (for the older population) or accident prevention (for the younger). However, births are more easily affected by policy. Because the dissemination of birth control information and materials strikes the several ages unequally, it is worthwhile to derive formulas for the effects of reduction in the birth rate at different ages of mothers. Because some women die after the age of 20 and before 40, the reduction of the birth rate at the younger age will have more consequence for the rate of natural increase. For a population that is rapidly increasing, however, this is less important than the fact that there may be twice as many women at age 20 than at age 40, because each year's cohort is 3 percent larger than the preceding one. Moreover, studies in Taiwan suggest that the major increase in use of birth control is at the older ages.

The results so far are based on a one-sex model and strictly apply only to the female component of population. A more precise analysis would take account of males explicitly. It turns out, for example, that males are relatively few in the United States today, at the ages at which they become fathers, in comparison with the number of females at the ages at which they become mothers. This observation applies to other countries affected by the postwar baby boom.

The disparity has been called the marriage squeeze. We do not know what sort of adjustment is made by those of marrying age to the fewness or surplus of suitable marriage partners. With sharp drops in birth rates anticipated, consequences such as this call for more research.

ADEQUACY OF DEMOGRAPHIC DATA

Despite all the effort that has been made, present-day statistics are far from complete; for only about 30 percent of the world population do censuses and vital registrations exist that provide a minimal basis for demographic analysis. Fortunately, this coverage includes the three kinds of population as classified by level of mortality and fertility: high birth and high death rates, high birth and low death rates, and low birth and low death rates. The remaining configuration, low birth and high death rates, is not of usual occurrence.

Statistical information is far from equally available for the three groups. Peoples of low birth and low death rates are also those that are most developed economically, and since statistical advance tends to accompany other directions of advance, the existing data overrepresent developed countries. This is particularly true of birth and death registrations, dependent as they are on the education of the public as a whole, as well as of statistical personnel. Machinery for censuses, on the other hand, can be set up more quickly, and a much larger part of the world's population has recently been counted in censuses than has had its births and deaths registered.

The opposite was true of Europe in the 18th century when baptismal and burial records were widespread and often of high quality, but national organizations for census-taking were not yet in being.

Today census-taking is ahead of vital registration not only in extent, but also in completeness. For a census to be more than 20 percent short is rare, but published birth figures sometimes appear to include no more than one half of the births that occurred. Fortunately the relation of births and census age distributions, to be taken up later, enables estimates of birth rates to be obtained from censuses.

The Three Contemporary Patterns of Birth and Death

A brief review of the available data follows. It will be under the three population types mentioned earlier.

High Birth and High Death Rates

Most of the populations in this category are in tropical Africa. An example (off the mainland of Africa, but for which recent data are available) is Madagascar, with 6,163,000 inhabitants in 1966. Its crude birth rate as registered was 45.75 per 1,000 population, and its crude death rate 25.31; therefore, its current rate of increase is about 2 percent per year. A life table for Madagascar for 1966 shows the expectation at age zero to be 37.6 years for males and 38.5 for females. The probability that a boy just born will live to age 50 is 0.386, and a girl 0.401. These numbers may be compared with those of Europe at the beginning of the 19th century. For Europe of that time, as for Africa now, full information was lacking, but some areas did have good statistics. Calculations for Sweden in the 5 years around 1800 show expectations of life of 36 and 38.9 years for males and females respectively, and 0.417 and 0.456 as the probabilities of living to age 50. Madagascar retains the mortality pattern of Europe about 1800, according to published figures; if its deaths are underregistered, then its death rate is even higher than that of early 19th century Europe.

Similar death rates are found in Cameroon, the Central African Republic, and Togo, for all of which less recent official figures are available. Probably these high rates also apply to much of the rest of tropical Africa, for which no figures at all are to be had. Such high death rates appear to be on their way out and are found today among a minority of the world's population.

In respect to birth rates tropical Africa does not resemble Europe of 1800. The crude birth rate of Madagascar in 1966, reported as 45.75 per 1,000, is half as high again as Sweden's in 1800 of 31.21. The difference is important for the rate of increase; Sweden's increase was about 5 per 1,000 inhabitants per year, while that of Madagascar was 20 per 1,000.

No one knows how many of the world's population are in the condition of birth and death typified by Madagascar; perhaps it is half a billion.

High Birth and Low Death Rates

This category includes most of the present developing world. Again up-to-date official information is lacking, though it is not as scarce as for the high death rate countries. Honduras is typical of countries with the most rapid increase, with a birth rate in 1966 of 44.2 per 1,000 population, and a death rate of 8.67. Its expectation of life is 59.2 years for males and 60.7 for females, and the chance of living to age 50 for a boy just born is 0.741, and for a girl 0.764. These mortality figures contrast sharply with those for Madagascar though births for the two countries are at about the same level.

A country with a birth rate of about 44 per 1,000 and a death rate of about 9 will grow at 3.5 percent per year. Such a country would double its population in 20 years. Honduras is not the only country apparently in this condition; Mexico's rates of birth and death are within 1 per 1,000 of Honduras, and so are those of many other countries. The real number of births in these countries may be even higher than registered births. For this group as a whole we may speak conservatively of a birth rate of 40 per 1,000 and a death rate of 10 per 1,000, a growth by natural increase of 3 percent per year. Again we cannot say with precision how much of the world is in this condition, but it is certainly more than half; let us say that it includes around 2 billion people.

One way to see the meaning of a rate of increase is to translate it into doubling time t, obtained as the solution of the equation

$$(1 + r)^t = 2,$$

where r is the fraction of increase per year. The solution for t, obtained by taking natural logarithms, is

$$t = \frac{\ln 2}{r - r^2/2} = \frac{0.693}{r - r^2/2},$$

if terms in r^3 and higher may be disregarded, or very nearly $t - 0.70/r$ for values of r in the range 0 to 0.04. Hence the rule that doubling time is obtained by dividing the percentage annual increase into 70; on this rule Honduras' annual 3.5 percent implies a doubling time of $70/3.5 = 20$ years. On the 2 percent increase of Madagascar the doubling time is 35 years. On the 0.5 percent of Sweden in 1800 the doubling time is 140 years.

Thus over the course of 140 years Honduras would have seven doublings: it would multiply by $2^7 = 128$ times. In the same 140 years Madagascar would double 4 times, a multiplication by 16. And Sweden of 1800 would multiply only by 2. Although the rates of increase 3.5 percent, 2 percent, and 0.5 percent do not seem very different, the numbers 128, 16, and 2 as factors are different indeed. Sweden could continue at the 0.5 percent rate, and indeed it doubled in about 90 years, despite emigration, because of a fall in its death rate. Honduras—with its spatial and other limitations—cannot double seven times in 140 years or any other period, for this increase would cause it to pass the quarter billion mark. Such considerations make us certain that the rate for Honduras cannot continue; either the birth rate will come down or the death rate will go up.

Low Birth and Low Death Rates

For this group of countries we do not need to select examples; they all have good official statistics, and we need merely add to obtain an aggregate figure. In another connection the author has done such a totalling for the countries of Europe, whose population in 1965 was 442 million. Only for Northern Ireland were 1965 figures unavailable. Europe is treated as though it were a single country, and a consolidated life table, intrinsic rates, and other computations are made available. The several countries are implicitly weighted according to their populations. Such consolidated figures are especially convenient for a relatively homogeneous group of countries.

The consolidated European 1965 birth rate was 18.04 per 1,000, the death rate 10.20; hence the rate of natural increase was 7.84. The United States, for which the 1967 figures are 17.97, 9.36, and 8.61 per 1,000 for birth, death, and natural increase respectively, falls in the same demographic classification as Europe. Similar also are the Soviet Union, Canada, Australia, and New Zealand. Japan is an extreme member of the class, with 1966 figures of 13.77, 6.78, and 6.99; its birth and death rates are lower, but its rate of natural increase is very similar to that of other countries in this group.

The death rates appear to be going down in these countries in recent years but probably at a declining rate. The consolidated male life table for Europe, for instance, goes from an expectation of 64.88 years in 1955 to 66.57 in 1960, but only to 67.69 in 1965. The expectation of life for males is rising by 1 year every 5 years now, for females perhaps double this. In the United States, on the other hand, the male expectation of life has been approximately constant over the past few years, while the female expectation has increased by about 1 year per decade.

We can (with much more confidence than for the preceding groups) speak of this part of the world as containing nearly one billion people, a little less than 30 percent of the current world total, and increasing at about 0.7 percent per year.

Table 1 presents a summary of the three demographic types.

PROSPECTS OF CHANGE

This very approximate scheme allows us to think about the consequences for the world's future population if the present rates continue. The first conclusion is that they cannot continue for a century; if they did, the world would contain 38 billion people.

Serious problems will arise if even the European group continues at the present rate of 0.7 percent per year for a century; its population saturates the environment now. Improving technology substitutes less valuable resources for more valuable: nylon (made of coal) for silk, for example, or atomic

TABLE 1

Summary of Three Demographic Types

	High Birth High Death (Mainly in Tropical Africa, Parts of Asia)	High Birth Low Death (Mainly in Asia, Latin America)	Low Birth Low Death (Mainly in Europe, Northern America, Oceania, U.S.S.R., Japan)
	(1)	(2)	(3)
Number about 1970 (billions)	0.5	2.0	1.0
Percent increase/year	2	3	0.7
Time to double (years)	35	23	100
Doublings per century	3	4	1
Number in year 2070 if present rates continue (billions)	4	32	2

Source: Author's calculations.

energy for fuel oil. It increases crop output per unit of land input as well as per unit of labor. But the rising income that goes with improving technology demands more space. It substitutes beef for bread—which is at least a fivefold extension of the land base needed per person; it builds freeways rather than footpaths; it contaminates the air and water. Whether on balance the high-technology-high-income combination has a greater carrying capacity than traditional peasant exploitation of a given area is uncertain, but even if it has, the increase of 0.7 percent per year cannot continue very long.

The same is true, with greater certainty, for the other two groups. We can suppose that the death rate for tropical Africa will go down and that a further decline in the death rate for the less developed world as a whole is in prospect. The few and small countries for which we have registrations over a series of years provide a suggestion of this trend. Mauritius had a crude death rate of 12.86 per 1,000 in 1955, 8.83 by 1966. The Mauritian expectation of life had gone up 6 years for males and 7 years for females during the same period of 11 years. Jamaica rose by 7 and 9 years for males and females respectively from 1951 to 1963; Mexico by 4 years for both males and females from 1960 to 1966. Other countries rose less, but advances in the expectation of life at age 0 of 5 years per decade are typical for the less developed world.

Declines in birth rates appear conspicuously in some of the countries around the rim of Asia: Taiwan fell from a crude rate of 44.20 per 1,000 in 1956 to 31.88 in 1966; Hong Kong from 34.40 in 1961 to 25.84 in 1966; Ceylon from 39.35 in 1953 to 31.56 in 1967; Singapore from 43.22 in 1957 to 25.99 in 1967. These are the parts of Asia with little prejudice against birth control, with energetic and ambitious people, and with the longest and most intense contact with the outside world. Perhaps more encouraging is the fact that one of the developing countries of Latin America, Costa Rica, showed a fall from a crude birth rate of over 50 about 1955 to 41.75 in 1966.

Increases in birth rates over similar recent periods have also occurred. Jamaica's crude birth rate went from 33.87 per 1,000 in 1951 to 39.79 in 1963; Honduras from 42.38 in 1957 to 44.20 in 1966; French Guiana from 31.95 in 1961 to 35.21 in 1964. The last case undoubtedly reflects improved registration of births, and we do not know to what extent the other cases do as well. But a rise in birth rates with the onset of modernization is not a priori unlikely. The relaxation of premodern constraints on reproduction (for example, permitting remarriage of widows in India) usually precedes the adoption of modern means of limiting reproduction, and in the interval between the one and the other the birth rate can rise. The fall in the death rate, insofar as it preserves the individuals through the ages of reproduction, will by itself raise the birth rate. Such linkages among demographic facts are taken up later, particularly in Appendix 1.

Very substantial differences among the countries of the world are shown in Appendix 2, where each country is represented by its latest data. Birth rates range from about 50 per 1,000 population down to about 16, a ratio of three to one, and rates of natural increase from about 35 per 1,000 down to 0 or less. These gross differences in the contemporary cross section have been noted by many writers.

Less often referred to is the comparison between the less developed world today and the countries of Europe when they were starting their modern advance. It might be supposed that Europe of the late 18th century was in a condition demographically resembling that of the tropics today. We shall see that this is not so, and indeed the differences are very great.

The Sweden-Honduras Resemblance and Contrast

In this limited space we cannot discuss all countries, or even all of those for which reliable data can be found. Let us again focus on one less developed country of today and compare it with one less developed country of the early 19th century. The contrast between Honduras of 1966 and Sweden of 1800 tells much about how the world has changed over the interval. The Honduras 1966 population was 2,363,000, and Sweden's 1800 population was 2,352,000—for all practical purposes identical. In respect to national income Sweden was undoubtedly much higher. The labor force of both was engaged largely in agriculture. Both are somewhat mountainous countries, facing an ocean (both Atlantic and Pacific in the case of Honduras).

Sweden's lower birth rate (31.21 against 44.20) was associated with higher ages at marriage and at childbearing: the average age of mothers at the birth of their children was 32.18 years, as against 29.53 years for Honduras in 1966. Late marriage, associated with private property in land, restrained the birth rate in Sweden in a way that is not occurring in Honduras.

With a decidedly lower death rate and higher birth rate Honduras has a very much higher rate of natural increase: projecting the population forward with the respective age-specific birth and death rates we find for Sweden 10 years later 2,478,000, a gain of about 126,000; for Honduras we have 3,398,000, a gain of about 1,000,000. Honduras is having to assimilate somehow a natural increase about eight times as large as that which Sweden had to deal with.

Age differences are also large. In Honduras 51.48 percent of the population in 1966 was under 15 years old; in Sweden in 1800 only 32.60 percent was under 15. The burden of providing schools and other facilities was only a little over 60 percent as great for Sweden as for Honduras, a disadvantage for Honduras even if her economy was able to bear it as well as that of Sweden in 1800.

It is true that Sweden had a greater proportion of people beyond the main working ages: 5.49 percent over 65 in 1800. Honduras has only 1.76 percent over 65 in 1966. But this small disadvantage for Sweden was more than offset by her fewer children. One way of looking at the matter is through the *dependency ratio*, the number of persons under 15 and over 65 per 100 persons between those two ages. We find that Honduras shows a dependency ratio of 113.89 against Sweden's 61.53. (In this respect Honduras is extreme, but several other less developed countries show dependency ratios higher than 100.)

One point of resemblance between Honduras 1966 and Sweden 1800 was their mortality at older ages. Men of 70 had an expectation of life in Sweden of 6.82 years and in Honduras of 8.63 years. At the youngest ages, on the other hand, the contrast was dramatic: infant mortality (deaths under 1 year of age) was 37.24 per 1,000 live births in Honduras, and 248.96 in Sweden.

Could the difference in completeness of registration be responsible for such a gap? According to the United Nations (1, p. 351) the mortality statistics of Honduras are 75 to 85 percent complete. No evidence is available on the completeness of the early Swedish mortality records, and they could have been better. Even if they were perfect, however, only a small part of this gap would be closed. Let us take extreme assumptions: that 25 percent of the Honduras deaths have been omitted, that the omissions are *all* infant deaths, and that all omitted deaths have been included among the births, whereas Swedish deaths were 100 percent complete. Even these extreme assumptions give an infant death rate for Honduras less than half that of Sweden.

Appendix 2 allows the reader to judge in what degree Honduras is typical of developing countries. For 1966 the crude birth rate of Mexico was 43.96 against Honduras' 44.20; death rates were 9.61 and 8.67 respectively.

Especially for death rates, such comparisons are best standardized for age. The Appendix shows what crude rates would be for the several countries if they preserved their age-sex-specific rates but had the age-sex distribution of the United States in 1960. We find for instance that Honduras goes up to 16.44 against Mexico's 13.33, whereas Sweden was 31.11.

Effects of Immediate Drop to Stationary Birth Level

A stationary population is ultimately inevitable. Let us see what would happen if the age-specific birth rates were to drop immediately to the level that would assure a stationary population in the long run. I have made the calculation for the United States, using 1966 data, on the supposition that for each age of mother the birth rate falls in the same proportion, so that though the total childbearing is reduced, the observed pattern of births by age is retained. Death rates that are exactly those of 1966 are assumed to continue indefinitely. The question is what happens as the population is projected forward under these conditions by perfectly standard methods (2).

It would grow for a long time. At first the growth would be at the rate of about 15 million per decade. Even the first decade of the 21st century would show a growth of 10 million, and only after that would the pace slow down. The ultimate stationary population of just under 260 million would be reached about the year 2031. We have the remarkable result that applying the birth rates of a stationary population in 1966 would still allow an increase of over 30 percent from the 1966 total of 196 million.

If one wanted to hold the population down to its present size, on the argument that our present population-related problems are sufficient, we would have to persuade people initially to drop their births to a rate well below that of replacement, indeed to cause them to have no more births than would replace the actual deaths as these occurred. One would take the view that there is only so much land, water, air, minerals, and other facilities, and set the birth target so that each individual who died would be replaced. I do not know that anyone has seriously argued that at the present time this is the appropriate policy, but with high enough density it could come to be so. Precisely in order to avoid such a requirement at some time in the future, it seems necessary to put the brakes on now (3).

The 30 percent by which the United States population would increase if its birth rate immediately fell to replacement level is not a universal constant, but depends on present and past births. For the countries of Europe, with lower birth rates and hence older populations than the United States, the increase would be less, typically about 20 percent. For the less developed world the increase would be much larger. I have made the same calculation for Ceylon, starting with the 1961 population, supposing that 1961 death rates were maintained, and that the birth rates immediately dropped to the level which would secure a stationary population in the long run. The total would increase from just over 10 million in 1961 to well over 15 million by the year 2011. Of course this is less than the threefold or more that it would grow if the 1961 birth rates continued, but it is nonetheless a great deal.

For Latin America, with a history of higher birth rates, the momentum of past growth would be even greater. If Colombia had dropped its births to the stationary level in 1965 when its population was 18 million, it would have risen to a stationary number of 29.8 million, a rise of over 65 percent. Ecuador of 1965 would have gone up by 66.7 percent; Peru of 1963 by 56.9 percent. Insofar as infant deaths have declined in recent years, the percent rise to the stationary population from a jumping-off point in the 1970's would be higher. If the drop in births extends over a period rather than occurring at one moment, then the ultimate stationary population will be correspondingly higher. (See Table 2.)

TABLE 2

Current and Ultimate Stationary Populations on Assumption That
Birth Rates Drop Immediately to Stationary Level

	Current	Ultimate	Percent Increase to Ultimate
Canada 1968	20,264,000	28,562,000	40.9
Chile 1965	8,584,000	12,916,000	50.5
Colombia 1965	17,993,000	29,786,000	65.5
Ecuador 1965	5,109,000	8,518,000	66.7
Ireland 1968	2,910,000	3,684,000	26.6
Italy 1966	53,128,000	62,189,000	17.1
Trinidad and Tobago 1967	1,015,000	1,633,000	60.9
United States 1966	195,857,000	259,490,000	32.5

Source: Author's calculations.

The impact of a one-time fall in the birth rates would be different at different ages. First a decline in the number of young children would appear. The United States projection at stationary rates from 1966 would show a drop in children under 5 of 25 percent, from 20 million to 14.5 million; the number would then go up again to over 19 million by 1986, as women from the high-birth cohorts of the 1950's moved into childbearing. The under-5's would settle down at about 18 million.

The decline of births will have an effect on the number born in the next generation some 25 years later. As the smaller cohorts come into reproductive age, a further fall in the overall birth rate will take place, but it will be less extreme than the initial fall; the under-5's would still be 17.5 million by 1966.

In the late 1980's the cohorts coming into the labor market would decline because of the original drop in births, and labor shortages might develop. Finally, the cohorts of the birth rate decline would reach the oldest ages about the middle of the 21st century when the number over 85 would drop from 4 million to about 3 million, about two thirds of whom would be women.

The social and economic effects of the changed birth rate would be different for the less developed country. For one thing, they would be more intense: the initial reduction in the youngest ages would be greater, though the ultimate population would be much higher above the initial one. Mortality would continue to improve (which it is by no means sure to do in the United States), and this would make the ultimate population greater than that calculated by a constant death rate, so that the 50 to 67 percent increase that we find after the stationary birth regime is adopted seems conservative.

Among the consequences of the sudden drop in fertility would be a smaller number of babies; although the most immediate effect, it would not be the most fundamental. With fewer babies the national income per capita would be higher than if the high birth rates had continued, but this improvement is of a formal character, since the consumption of the babies is not great and their production is zero.

The economic improvement would be more real to the public and to administrators when the smaller cohorts reached school age. With fewer entrants the amount of teaching personnel and facilities devoted to each child could be greater. A larger proportion of the new smaller cohorts could attend school and receive better instruction than would otherwise be possible. In some countries today increasing school budgets are accompanied by smaller fractions of the new cohorts attending school.*

The most important effects of the drop in the birth rate would be seen some 20 years later when entrants into the labor force would decline. Each of the new entrants would have greatly improved possibilities of effective employment, given the sharply limited capital. Members of the smaller cohorts will be able to work with more capital than would have been accessible to them if they were more numerous, and this means more and better jobs. A further possible advantage of their smaller numbers is a larger ratio of managers to workers if management is provided by those older than

*See Gavin W. Jones, "Effect of Population Change on the Attainment of Educational Goals in the Developing Countries," in this volume.

they (even if only 10 years older). Along with capital, managers help to create effective employment.

In fact, no one anticipates an immediate drop in the birth rate. In many countries the rate has not yet started to fall; in some it may still be rising. Suppose that in a country that is now increasing at 3 percent, the drop to stationary birth rates takes place in exactly 15 years from now. This means that the population would first increase by about 50 percent, and after that would taper off to a level about two thirds higher. Combining these two increases shows a ratio of $1.50 \times 1.67 = 2.50$, or an increase by 150 percent to the stationary level. Thus if Mexico were able to arrange a fall in her birth rate to zero increase exactly 15 years from now, she would level off at 125 million (in contrast to a mid-1966 population of 44,145,000).

SMALL CHANGES IN BIRTH AND DEATH RATES AT SPECIFIC AGES

Actually, change will take place more slowly and in small increments. Fertility is not likely to fall uniformly at all ages. Much of the remainder of this paper will discuss the long-term effects of small changes in birth and death rates at specific ages.

Explanation of the Proportion under Age 15 by the Stable Model

That Honduras has a high birth rate and that 51.48 percent of its population is under 15 years of age are intimately related circumstances. Let us see how one follows from the other.

We shall do so by means of what is called the stable model. If a set of age-specific rates of birth and death, the regime of fertility and mortality referred to above, persist over a long enough time in any population, then an age distribution will be reached that is a function of the regime only and in particular is unaffected by the initial age distribution. In the stable distribution the numbers in each group will be increasing at exactly the same rate, say in the ratio λ for each 5-year period. Moreover, the births in this imaginary but mathematically determinate population will also be increasing in the same ratio λ each 5 years, and so will the deaths. For Honduras $\lambda = 1.195$; this corresponds to an annual rate $r = 0.3564$, or 35.64 per 1,000. (Such a rate r is thought of as compounded continuously, a device that considerably simplifies the mathematics and need not detain us here.) The birth rate for the stable condition corresponding to the Honduras regime of 1966 is $1000b = 44.05$ and the death rate $1000d = 8.41$.

The stable condition resembles the actual one closely in some instances, less closely in others. The interrelations in the stable model are in part transferable to real conditions and help to understand them. In other cases the departure from the stable model is itself of interest. For most of the purposes of this article the stable model will be applied to females only, though it may equally well be applied to males and with some complication to the two sexes together.

When the Honduras population of 1966 is considered as a sequence of cohorts, we note that those under 5 were born between mid-1961 and mid-1966; those 5 to 9 at last birthday between mid-1956 and mid-1961. Now, applying the stable model, if the population is increasing uniformly in the ratio λ each 5 years, then the most recent cohort will have increased on the average for about 2½ years since birth, or in the ratio $\lambda^{1/2}$; the cohort 5 to 9 in 1966 has been alive about 7½ years and would have increased in the ratio $\lambda^{3/2}$. People who were born in each earlier time would be related to the size of the population at that time in fixed ratio on the stable assumption. Moreover, some of them would have died in the meantime; with a fixed life table $_5L_0/l_0$ of the average annual births of the preceding 5 years are still alive in 1966; $_5L_5/l_0$ of the average of the 5 years before that, where

$$_5L_x = \int_0^5 l_{x+t}\,dt,$$

if l_x/l_0 is the probability of surviving from birth to age x. Then it follows that in terms of this year's total of births B the number of survivors from the births of the last 5 years is the product $B\lambda^{-1/2}\,_5L_0/l_0$; of the 5 years before that is $B\lambda^{-3/2}\,_5L_5/l_0$. . . . Thus the number under 15 would be the sum of the first three such quantities, the survivors of the three youngest cohorts, and the total number would be the sum of all such cohorts of which any members are now alive.

On this very simple way of looking at population, which assumes implicitly that all age-specific birth and death rates remain fixed, the percent of the population under age 15 would be

$$100 \times \frac{\lambda^{-1/2}\,_5L_0 + \lambda^{-3/2}\,_5L_5 + \lambda^{-5/2}\,_5L_{10}}{\lambda^{-1/2}\,_5L_0 + \lambda^{-3/2}\,_5L_5 + \lambda^{-5/2}\,_5L_{10} + \ldots}.$$

The ratio of increase λ for Honduras at the 1966 age-specific birth and death rates would ultimately be 1.195 as we saw. A life table calculated from the same data provides us with the fact that

$$_5L_0/l_0 = 4.75394;$$

$$_5L_5/l_0 = 4.57996$$

. . . . .

Entering these numbers in the above formula we find that the percentage under 15 on these assumptions is 47.4. We have used data for women only, and the proportion of boys under 15 would be somewhat higher, but we will not go into this. Suffice it to say that on the assumptions constituting a stable model we have accounted for 47.4 percent out of the 51.5 percent actually shown in 1966.

The discrepancy could be due to changes in the birth and death rates, so that the 1966 figure does not represent the condition to which the people then alive had actually been subject, or to erroneous statement in the current ages of the population.

Sweden and Honduras. Let us now turn to Sweden in 1800. Here the percentage of the population under age 15 was 32.6, and the stable calculation made just as before says 29.7 percent. The difference between Sweden and Honduras was thus about 18 percent, and about 13 percent was explained by the stable model. We continue to bear in mind that part of what was not explained could be error and so does not require explanation in these terms.

The contrast between Honduras in 1966 and contemporary Europe is even greater than the comparison with Sweden of 1800. The 51 percent under age 15 of Honduras stands against about 24 percent for our consolidation of Europe in 1965. On the other hand, the United States shows 31 percent under age 15 for 1965, decidedly above Europe. This difference is explained by the fact that the postwar baby boom in the United States was larger than that in Europe.

The discussion to this point has shown substantial differences in the observed proportion of children under age 15 among populations and has shown that the observed proportions are reflected in the stable age distributions calculated from birth and death rates. This relation will enable us to explain observed age differences by stable ones, a happy circumstance, since stable results can be broken down and reassembled in various ways.

Two Methods of Study

To what extent is the difference in the proportion under age 15 between any two countries due to different birth rates and to what extent to different death rates? There are two ways of answering this question:

Holding One Set of Rates Fixed While Allowing the Other to Change. An obvious method is to redo the calculation first using a common set of birth rates and then a common set of death rates. We compare, for example, the effect of birth rates between Honduras 1966 and Sweden 1800 by working out the proportion on the stable model with the same death rates—say with the same Honduras 1966 life table—but using the birth rates appropriate to each. To compare the effect of death rates we use for both the same Honduras 1966 age-specific birth rates, and for each its own life table.

Such an empirical examination of the effects of changes in mortality in the early stages of the demographic transition may be applied to any characteristic: proportion under 15, dependency ratio, median age, mean age. The technique has been introduced elsewhere (4, p. 189) to study the effects of mortality change on mean age. We use it here to analyze the proportion under age 15. Consider the percentages under 15 in the stable age distribution for Sweden of 1800 and Honduras 1966:

(a)	With Honduran mortality and Honduran fertility	47.37
(b)	With Honduran mortality and Swedish fertility	34.45
(c)	With Swedish mortality and Honduran fertility	41.75
(d)	With Swedish mortality and Swedish fertility	29.71

The difference between (a) and (b) gives the effect of fertility difference between the two populations with mortality fixed at the level of Honduras, and amounts to 12.92. The difference between (c) and (d) gives the effects of fertility change, but at the mortality level of Sweden, and amounts to 12.04. The difference between the two differences constitutes interaction, and is a satisfactorily low amount.

Features of the stable populations of Honduras and Sweden are shown as the first and last columns of numbers in Table 3: r, the intrinsic rate of increase, as well as the percent under age 15 and the mean age. The same calculations with the mortality of Honduras 1966 and the fertility of Sweden 1800 are the second column; the difference between the first two numbers in any row tells us the pure effect of fertility under Honduran mortality. This may be averaged with the difference of the last two numbers, which tells us the fertility effect under Swedish mortality.

Proceeding in this way we find the numbers at the bottom of Table 3. Interactions are small enough that no attempt to interpret them is required. On all three of the variables shown fertility makes more difference than does mortality. The fertility effect on the proportion under age 15 and on the mean age was more than twice as important as the mortality effect.

This result would not have been anticipated by common sense, since Honduras has an expectation of life of over 60 years, whereas Sweden's was less than 40; at some ages Sweden's mortality was ten times as high. One might have thought that the high mortality of Sweden would have kept its average age low; death rates, after all, determine the average age at which individuals die. But this is not the same as the average age of the living population, and it is the latter that affects economic and social activity.

Hence the two points to be stressed are: that the lower mortality of Honduras, acting by itself, would lower the mean age by 2.42 years in comparison with Sweden 1800—evidently the survivorship of Honduras was espe-

TABLE 3

Analysis of Effects of Mortality and Fertility in the Differences
between Honduras 1966 and Sweden 1798-1802

Mortality	Honduras 1966	Honduras 1966	Sweden 1798-1802	Sweden 1798-1802
Fertility	Honduras 1966	Sweden 1798-1802	Honduras 1966	Sweden 1798-1802
1,000 r	35.63	17.08	21.67	4.30
Percent under age 15	47.37	34.45	41.75	29.71
Mean age	20.95	27.62	23.38	30.03

	Average Effects of		
	Mortality	Fertility	Interaction
1,000 r	13.37	17.96	1.18
Percent under age 15	5.18	12.48	0.88
Mean age	−2.42	−6.66	−0.02

Source: Author's calculations.

cially superior at young ages; and that the difference in fertility rates acts even more strongly in the same direction, lowering the mean age by 6.66 years.

This first method of decomposition of parameters of age distribution provides numbers but no mathematical analysis.

The Study of Linkages. The second way of answering the question of how changing birth or death rates affect ages is through studying theoretically the linkages in the stable model. This method has the advantage that it provides an understanding of the mechanism of linkage; it enables us to study all kinds of possible changes, not only those that historically occurred in the past. The latter part of this paper will serve to introduce the main ideas in a relatively nontechnical way. Our linkages are a way of tracing the demographic consequences of possible policies.

Policy Options

The birth and death rates with which the present-day demographer deals are subject to deliberate change. A DDT campaign in Nicaragua could save some of the 470 lives that were lost through malaria in 1965 (1, p. 530); a safety campaign in the same country could save some of the 410 lives lost through accidents. But the two causes of death affect quite different ages; of the malaria deaths two thirds were to children under 5, whereas two thirds of accidents were to people 15 to 45 years of age. Malaria deaths affected boy and girl babies equally; accidents resulted in deaths of three males for each female. If a choice is being made between investment in spraying and investment in safety measures, one of the considerations is the population effect: the difference that it makes for future numbers of people and the rate of growth.

The policy options for birth rates are likely to be greater than for death rates. Should birth control information be directed to young couples or to those who have already had some children? What is the effect of reducing the birth rate of women around age 20 as against reducing the rate of those around 40? The demographic considerations with which this paper will be concerned take their place alongside psychological, economic, cultural, and other considerations treated elsewhere in this volume.

Without a Model No Linkages

We have now dealt with sets of death rates specific to each age, and birth rates specific to each age of mother. Such a set of age-specific rates of birth and death, a regime of fertility and mortality, implies an ultimate rate of increase if it continues long enough, and in conjunction with the initial number of individuals of each age and sex, it implies an immediate rate of increase.

To ask about linkages in a simple if slightly abstract way: What is the effect on r (the ultimate rate of increase of a population) of a change in one part of the regime—say the death rate $_5M_x$ of women aged x to $x + 4$ at last birthday?

Suppose we try without a model, and think of the immediate effect on the crude death rate, as obtained from national vital statistics, of a mortality decline. To be specific, what is the effect on the overall death rate of one female death avoided at age 0 to 4 at last birthday as against one death avoided at age 55 to 59? The answer can only be that the effects are identical; with one death fewer at one age the crude death rate goes down exactly as much as with one death fewer at any other age. What is true for one death is true for ten thousand; the crude death rate is in the short run entirely insensitive to the ages at which those deaths occur, whether before, during, or long after the time of reproduction, whether of males or of females.

Yet this answer is as demographically superficial as it is numerically correct. One, or a million, lives saved on a particular occasion is less the subject of demography than are relatively durable changes in death rates. If the life or lives saved may be supposed the result of a durable improvement in medical technique, then we want to know the effect on populations of the continued application of that improvement. With this viewpoint we ask again—what is the effect of a female life saved at age 0 to 4 as against one saved at age 55 to 59?

The female deaths at age 0 to 4 in the United States in 1966 were 43,000, and the deaths at age 55 to 59 were about the same number—that is the reason I chose those ages for the illustration. Now we ask the question in the form, "What is the effect of a fall of 1/43,000 in the death rate at age 0 to 4 as against the same fall in the death rate at age 55 to 59, supposing that the new rates will continue?"

The Stationary Model

Let us first see what will be the effect on the probability $l(a)/l_0$ of living to age a. We first note that the probability of living, $l(a)/l_0$, is equal to the exponential

$$l(a)/l_0 = \exp\left(-\int_0^a \mu(t)dt\right),$$

where $\mu(t)$ is the death rate in the small interval from t to $t + dt$. A rise in the death rate $\mu(t)$ over the age interval x to $x + 1, x < a$, equal to $\Delta\mu_x$, will add this quantity to the integral in the exponential, so that it becomes $\int^a \mu(t)dt + \Delta\mu_x$. Hence $l(a)/l_0$ contains the further factor $e^{-\Delta\mu_x}$ for all $a > x$. Approximately, an increase in the death rate of given amount $\Delta\mu_x$ over the single year of age x diminishes the probabiliyt of living to subsequent ages a in a ratio.

$$e^{-\Delta\mu_x} \doteq 1 - \Delta\mu_x.$$

Thus the decline of 1/43,000 at age 0 to 4 increases the proportion living to all later ages in the ratio $1 + 5/43,000$, and a decline of 1/43,000 at age 55 to 59 increases the proportion living to ages greater than 60 in the same ratio $1 + 5/43,000$.

Where mortality is already low, so that $l(a)/l_0$ is nearly unity to the end of reproduction, further declines in the younger age-specific death rates have little effect on reproduction. With the rates prevailing in the United States, a 100 percent drop in all mortality up to age 50, so that everyone born lives to that age, would increase long-run growth by about 4 percent. The situation was very different in the developing countries of 20 years ago, when the fall in mortality greatly increased the rate of growth and tended to make the population much younger.

The effect of a change $\Delta\mu_x$ on $\overset{o}{e}_0$ may be inferred as a further step. If the probability that a child just born will survive to age x is $l(x)/l_0$, then the expected time it will enjoy in the next dx of age is $l(x)dx/l_0$, and the total expectation of life is the sum of these elements:

$$\mathring{e}_0 = \frac{\int_0^\omega l(x)dx}{l_0}$$

added through all ages up to ω, the upper limit of life. The expectation of remaining life $\mathring{e}_a$ for a person who has already reached age a will contain the same integral from a to ω.

Now if μ_x for one particular age x changes to $\mu_x + \Delta\mu_x$, and $l(a)/l_0$ accordingly changes in the ratio $1 - \Delta\mu_x$, or in the absolute amount $-[l(a)/l_0]\Delta\mu_x$, $a > x$, then the new integral for $\mathring{e}_0$ can be seen to be the old one plus

$$-\int_x^\omega \frac{l(a)}{l_0}\Delta\mu_x da = -\frac{l_x}{l_0}\mathring{e}_x \Delta\mu_x.$$

This is readily translated into 5-year age intervals. The effect on the expectation of life at birth of a rise $\Delta_5 M_x$ in the death rate $_5M_x$ applying to ages x to $x + 4$ at last birthday will be approximated by

$$\Delta\mathring{e}_0 \doteq -5\frac{l_x}{l_0}\left(\mathring{e}_x - 2\tfrac{1}{2}\right)\Delta_5 M_x.$$

In words applied to our problem: A decrease in the death rate at age x will increase the expectation of life more the younger is x, *both* in proportion to the probability of living to that age l_x/l_0 and in proportion to the expectation of subsequent life $\mathring{e}_x$ at that age. For United States females in 1966 the first factor, l_x/l_0, is about 7/8 at age 55 what it is at age 0, and the second factor, $\mathring{e}_x - 2\tfrac{1}{2}$, is about 1/3 at age 55 what it is at age 0. For the two factors combined, an improvement in the age-specific rate at age 0 to 4 increases the expectation of $\mathring{e}_0$ more than three times as much as a similar improvement at age 55 to 59.

But expectation of life is a notion oriented to individuals, and we are interested here in populations, and especially in their increase and decrease. The life table $\mathring{e}_0$ can be translated into population terms as the number of individuals living at any one time, for each birth per year. In this model the births and deaths are the same, and the population total does not change. In such a stationary model the annual death rate d is the reciprocal of the expectation of life:

$$d = 1/\overset{\circ}{e}_0.$$

If the expectation of life goes up by one third as much for a small improvement in the rate at age 55 as it does for the same size of improvement at age 0, then the death rate goes down by about one third as much. Thus on the stationary model it makes three times as much difference for the overall death rate to have an improvement at age 0 as to have the same improvement at age 55. It also makes three times as much difference to the number of persons living at any moment per 1,000 births.

However, in real life deaths and births are not equal, and we can make our model more realistic, at least to the extent of recognizing this inequality. For an increasing population, the above result becomes even stronger. Moreover, by involving birth as well as death we will find that the more important result of an improvement in infant mortality (as against an improvement at ages 55 to 59) is through its impact on the birth rate. We proceed to the study of population replacement through birth and death.

Population Replacement per Generation

The population process seen as the replacement of one generation by another is conveniently summarized by the Net Reproduction Rate, R_0. This is the expected number of girl children to which a girl child now born will in turn give birth, the expectation typically based on the age-specific rates of birth and death in a given year or other period. In the continuous one-sex model,

$$R_0 = \int_a^\beta p(a)m(a)da,$$

where $p(a)$ is the probability of surviving from age 0 to age a, $m(a)da$ the chance of having a girl child between ages a and $a + da$, a and β the lowest and highest ages of possible reproduction. In terms of the observations in 5-year age intervals,

$$R_0 = \sum_a^{\beta-5} \frac{{}_5L_x}{l_0}F_x,$$

where ${}_5L_x$ is the number of women reaching ages x to $x + 4$ at last birthday out of l_0 births, and F_x is the age-specific birth rate to women aged x to $x + 4$ at last birthday. (The need to use two sets of symbols and to produce two formulas arises because theoretical propositions are often expressed and derived in the continuous form, but that form has to be transformed into discrete elements if data are to be applied and numerical results obtained.) The importance of the Net Reproduction Rate, defined as a girl child's expected number of girl children, is that it is equal to the ratio of the population in one generation to the population in the preceding generation implied by a given regime of births and deaths.

The Net Reproduction Rate, being a replacement index, combines fertility with mortality up to the end of the reproductive period. A measure of pure fertility is given by the conditional expectation, known as the Gross Reproduction Rate,

$$GRR = \int_a^\beta m(a)da \doteq 5 \sum_a^{\beta-5} F_x,$$

the number of girl children by which the girl child would be replaced *if* she lived through the reproductive period and was subject to the given age-specific rates of childbearing.

A measure of pure survivorship relevant to childbearing is the ratio of the NRR to the GRR; this was 0.57 in Sweden of 1800 and 0.86 in Honduras of 1966. The probability of a girl child living to reproduce is more than half as high again in Honduras.

Any model of birth, death, and replacement can be applied to males as well, since each boy child has a father just as surely as each girl child has a mother. The female model seems more natural because (a) the data on childbearing by age of mother are more widely available than births by age of father; (b) the range of ages within which women can be mothers is narrower than the range of ages within which men can be fathers; (c) the number of children that can be born to a woman is more limited than the number that can be born to a man. Nonetheless we will later use the one-sex model for males.

Now our subject of linkages requires an investigation of how the Net and Gross Reproduction Rates would respond to changes in birth and death rates. The GRR is simpler: it is unaffected by mortality, and a change in an age-specific fertility rate will make an equal change in the GRR. The United States had a GRR of 1.336 in 1966; the average woman who lives through the child-bearing period has approximately 1.336 girls, and about 1.049 times as many boys, or about 2.736 children altogether, at the rates of 1966. Disregarding differences in fertility of those few women who die before the end of their childbearing period, this is the average completed family implied by 1966 age-specific rates. The rate of childbearing to women of 35 to 39 was 0.0206, among the lowest in the world. American women prefer to bear their children early; they bear enough children before age 35 to provide a Gross Reproduction Rate and even a Net Reproduction Rate of more than unity.

At the age-specific rates of 1966, low though they were, the American population would replace itself even if all childbearing ceased at age 35. As we shall see, other countries are moving toward this pattern of limiting childbearing to the younger ages.

Effect of Change in Death Rates on Replacement

The definition of R_0 shows the effect on replacement of a decrease in the death rate at age 0 to 4. When $_5M_0$ goes down by Δ_5M_0, every subsequent l_{x+t} will go up in the ratio $e^{5\Delta_5M_0}$. Hence the Net Reproduction Rate will go up in the ratio $e^{5\Delta_5M_0}$. The proportional increase in R_0 will be about $5\Delta_5M_0$, the absolute increase $5R_0\Delta_5M_0$. This is very nearly the same as the effect on R_0 of an increase in all of the F_x simultaneously. It matters little for replacement whether mortality of infants and young children declines or fertility increases.

The effect on R_0 of a fall in the death rates $_5M_5$ or $_5M_{10}$ is about the same as in $_5M_0$. But for ages x beyond 15 the fall Δ_5M_x only affects part of the reproductive life of women, a part that diminishes with increase in the age x of the fall.

A change of death rate at age 55 to 59 or higher has no effect on replacement. This clashes with intuition: if the death rate goes down and people live longer, will not the population increase more rapidly? The answer is that the long-run effect of an improvement at age 55 to 59 is to raise the level of the population curve but not its long-run rate of increase. A stylized expression of the difference is to be seen in Figure 1. For purposes of the chart the increase in population has been placed in a step at the moment of its occurrence, though in fact it will be smoother and spread over more time. The

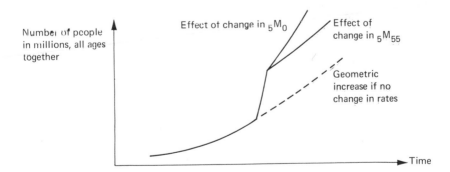

Figure 1. Diagrammatic portrayal of a decrease in $_5M_{55}$ as against the decrease in $_5M_0$. Note that the effect of a change in $_5M_{55}$ is a population curve parallel to that if no change in rates occurs.

chart disregards the gradualness of the adjustment to the new $_5M_x$ and the waves that would take place as the adjustment occurs. Its point is that the effect of both a change in $_5M_0$ and in $_5M_{55}$ will be a rise in the population, but the population curve then resumes in the same direction as before with the ΔM_{55}, while it changes its angle with the ΔM_0.

Even if all deaths between 55 and 100 years of age were to be eliminated the ultimate rate of increase of the population would not be affected. The population curve would turn upwards during the next two or three generations, but would then resume the same geometric sequence that it would follow if the present birth and death rates continued without change. Applying this in practical terms, the conquest of heart disease would not alter the ultimate rate of increase of the population; the advent of antisepsis to eliminate puerperal infection did have a clear permanent effect on the rate of increase.

The effect of a change in an age-specific birth rate on the Net Reproduction Rate is the change multiplied by L_x:

$$\Delta R_0 = L_x \Delta F_x / l_0.$$

Thus a birth change is of more consequence when it occurs to a young age group than to an old, but the difference in this framework is trifling with modern mortality. The survivorship $_5L_x/l_0$ sloped downward from 4.86 at age 15 to 19 to about 4.63 at 45 to 49 for United States women in 1966. Hence a decrease of the birth rate to women 15 to 19 would lower the Net Reproduction Rate only 5 percent more than the same decrease to women 40 to 44. But we will find that for rapidly growing populations the true impact on growth of what the women around their 20's do is fully twice as large as the impact of what the women in their 40's do. In this important respect the Net Reproduction Rate is an inadequate measure.

The Turnover of Generations

A comparison of Canada and the United States for 1967 shows that the Net Reproduction Rate does not tell the whole story of replacement. Canada's NRR was slightly higher than that of the United States, 1.216 against 1.205. The Canadian girl child just born could expect to bear slightly more girl children than the United States girl child at 1967 rates. But the Canadian would marry older and have her children later within marriage; her length of generation—a measure something like the average age of childbearing—was 27.3 years against the United States 26.2 years. This means a more rapid turnover of generations in the United States.

If the length of generation is T years, and the rate of growth compounded momently is r, then the ratio of increase over a year is e^r, and the ratio of increase over T years is e^{rT}. This latter is properly equated to R_0, the Net Reproduction Rate:

$$e^{rT} = R_0,$$

which provides for the United States in 1966 the equation in r

$$e^{26.2r} = 1.205.$$

Taking natural logarithms of both sides gives

$$r = \frac{\ln 1.205}{26.2} = 0.00713$$

against the Canadian $r = 0.00716$. As was said, the rapid turnover of the United States population partly offsets its lower NRR.

We saw that the Net Reproduction Rate is slightly more affected by a small decline of the birth rate at age 15 to 19 than it is by the same decline at 40 to 44; after all, some of the women alive at the younger age die before the older, and for them the number of children they would have had at 40 to 44 does not count. The younger women are also more important because their births imply less time between generations. Furthermore, in a rapidly increasing population there can be twice as many women at age 20 than at age 40, making fertility of younger women of greater importance. All these facts are implicitly incorporated in the intrinsic rate r.

Change in the Intrinsic Rate r Consequent upon Change in an Age-Specific Birth Rate

The intrinsic rate r summarizes a regime of mortality and fertility; it does so by telling us the ultimate rate of increase of any population in which that regime applies. To know how r is affected by a change ΔF_x in the age-specific fertility rate from age x to $x + 4$ at last birthday is one way of extracting the significance for the future of ΔF_x. It is easily shown (4, p. 352) that the corresponding modification of r is in general

$$\Delta r = \frac{e^{-r(y+2\frac{1}{2})}{}_5L_y\Delta F_y}{Kl_0},$$

where K is the mean age of childbearing in the stable population.

From this result it follows that the effect on r of a reduction in the F_y when y is 15 to 19 is very much more than the effect of a reduction when y is

40 to 45. For Taiwan in 1964 r is calculated at 0.02929. Let us tabulate the effects on the intrinsic rate of a fall of ΔF_y in the birth rates at the several ages y to $y + 4$. These are shown in Table 4, along with the age-specific rates. For example, the table says that a drop in the birth rate to women of age 20 to 24 equal to one birth per 1,000 ($\Delta F_{20} = -0.001$) will result in a drop in r of 0.000086, whereas a drop of the birth rate to women aged 40 to 44 of the same 0.001 will result in a drop of 0.000046. Evidently a drop in the age-specific rate is about twice as consequential in the youngest as in the oldest group.

TABLE 4

Effect on Intrinsic Rate r of a Fall in Age-Specific
Birth Rate at the Several Ages, Taiwan 1964

Age y to $y + 4$	Observed Age-Specific Rate F_y	$e^{-r(y + 2\frac{1}{2})}$	$_5L_y$	Effect of a Fall of ΔF_y on $1,000\ r$ $= \dfrac{e^{-r(y + 2\frac{1}{2})}{_5}L_y \Delta F_y}{Klo}$ (K = 28.4 years)
15-19	0.018	0.5989	474,267	$0.100\Delta F_{15}$
20-24	0.123	0.5173	471,375	$0.086\Delta F_{20}$
25-29	0.162	0.4469	467,720	$0.074\Delta F_{25}$
30-34	0.104	0.3861	463,505	$0.063\Delta F_{30}$
35-39	0.058	0.3334	458,333	$0.054\Delta F_{35}$
40-44	0.025	0.2880	451,428	$0.046\Delta F_{40}$

Source: Author's calculations.

We should not underestimate the importance of this comparison because of the zeros after the decimal point. A required diminution in the ultimate increase results from lowering F_{40} by a certain amount, or from lowering F_{20} by *half* of this amount, because half as many women are to be found at the older as at the younger age.

Example of the Assessment of a Fall in Fertility

The relation is important in assessing a fall in fertility, for example that in Taiwan between 1964 and 1966. Table 5 shows the age-specific rates falling in important degree only beyond age 30, and at ages under 25 they rise over the 2-year period. The net effect is downward, the Gross Reproduction Rate going from 2.45 to 2.32. However, the drop in the intrinsic rate r was propor-

TABLE 5

Age-Specific Birth Rates for Girl Children,
Ages 15 to 45, Taiwan, 1964 and 1966

	1964	1966	Change ΔF_y
15-19	0.018	0.019	+0.001
20-24	0.123	0.133	+0.010
25-29	0.162	0.159	-0.003
30-34	0.104	0.092	-0.012
35-39	0.058	0.044	-0.014
40-44	0.025	0.018	-0.007
Total	0.490	0.465	-0.025
Total × 5 = GRR	2.45	2.32	-0.13
Intrinsic rate 1000r	29.29	28.48	-0.81

Source: Author's calculations.

tionately less than this because the generation tended to become shorter over the 2 years, and mortality somewhat improved. In fact, the intrinsic rate r of Taiwan fell from 0.02929 to 0.02848 in the 2-year period, only 52 percent of the proportional drop in the GRR. The change in age-specific rates of Table 5, weighted by the last column of Table 4, provides the net impact on r of fertility change, the remainder being due to improvement in mortality.

The 2-year interval is of little interest by itself; what we really care about is the indication for the future. Suppose that we extend the GRR forward; the drop of 2.45 to 2.32 in 2 years suggests a drop of 0.06 per year, and linear extrapolation suggests that in a further 20 years the population would be just reproducing itself. This agrees with the 1956 to 1964 trend, which showed a slightly greater rate of annual descent of the Gross Reproduction Rate.

But aside from the above proof that, from the viewpoint of controlling r, a fall at the oldest age is worth half or less what a fall at the younger ages is worth, another and much grosser point enters: that the age-specific rate at any age cannot go below zero. This requires no theory for its elaboration. We have implicitly offended against it in projecting the 1964 to 1966 trend of the GRR. On the straight line the birth rate to those over 40 will reach zero within another 5 or so years, and to those over 30 will reach zero in about 10 years. Before that time the overall decline will taper off unless the women below 30 reduce their rates. Quite different long-term projections would be obtained from projecting linearly age by age, taking account of the floor at zero, from those obtained by projecting the total.

These results may seem paradoxical. Is not a birth prevented in a birth control program a reduction of one in the population of the immediate future irrespective of the age of the mother who is persuaded not to have a child? It is, but one judges the success of a continuing birth control program on the degree to which it creates a downtrend in age-specific rates, and the effect of this downtrend on the long-run rate of growth of the population.

The above analysis is concerned with age-specific birth rates, and these are but one mode of analysis. Insofar as there are more women in a population at younger ages, the effort required to lower the age-specific rate F_x would have to be greater for younger than for older women. Moreover, insofar as older women are more willing to protect themselves against further population increase less effort of persuasion is required to bring each one into the program than to bring in a younger woman. On the other hand, insofar as older women are less fertile when unprotected and more likely to resort on their own initiative to traditional methods of birth control, the impact on population increase of each induction of a woman of 40 into modern methods would be relatively less than that of a woman of 20. A rich literature on the probability aspects of contraception is now coming into existence, the main contributors being Mindel C. Sheps and Robert J. Potter, Jr. [See, for example (5, 6).]

Departures from Stability

In using the stable model we have been taking advantage of the extent to which the observed population is approximated by the stable. But the same parameters, and in particular the intrinsic rates of birth and death, enable us to study also the nature of departures from stability.

The characteristics of a population that would result from persistence of its regime of mortality and fertility have been called intrinsic; from r, the intrinsic rate of natural increase, we obtain b, the intrinsic birth rate and d, the intrinsic death rate. All of these may be very different from the observed rates in a population that controls its births to make them accord with the fluctuations of the economy. In 1966 the observed crude death rate of United States females was 8.11 per thousand; if the 1966 age-specific rates of birth and death persisted the crude death rate would steadily increase—to 8.72 in 1971, to 9.06 in 1976, and ultimately to 9.60. The ultimate or intrinsic death rate will be higher than the rate presently observed because the population will be older. This aging arises partly from the improved mortality now in effect gradually leading to an older population and partly from a lower birth rate in the present than in the past.

On the same assumptions, the U.S. female birth rate will move up from 17.61 per 1,000 to 19.30. The reason is that persistence of the 1966 regime would increase the proportion of women of childbearing age in the population. An especially striking difference between crude and intrinsic birth rates appears in the 1959-61 figures, when the projection would lead to an increase from the observed 22.74 to 24.30 in 1970 and to 27.31 ultimately. This increase is due to the action of the age-specific birth and death rates in replenishing the very small generation of women born in the 1930's. The advance 1969 birth figures show a rise in the crude rate without much change from the previous year in age-specific rates, owing to an age distribution more favorable to fertility.

Fortunately for many applications, departures of the observed from the stable age distribution in developing countries are smaller than in the United States.

Various Intrinsic Rates of Natural Increase

The intrinsic rate we have been calculating here answers the question: How fast would the population ultimately increase if its age-specific rates of birth and death continued for a long time? The importance of such an intrinsic rate does not depend on the age-specific rates in fact continuing into the future; it tells us what they mean *now*. Nonetheless the stress on the intrinsic rate as contrasted with the crude rates is justified by the thought that age-specific fertility is more likely to be a continuing characteristic of women than their overall fertility with the (possibly peculiar) age distribution that they happen to have at the present moment.

But other elements than age surely exist—what about marriage? If the proportion of the population married at the moment happens to be higher than the proportion that would be married with the continuance of the current age-specific marriage rates, then it would seem that overall fertility would be higher now than it would be in the long run. The identical argument used to justify the treatment of age in the age-intrinsic rate justifies the corresponding treatment of marriage.

To see the meaning of various possible directions of adjustment for the United States in 1960, consider the following five rates computed by Frank Oechsli (7):

Crude	Crude rate of natural increase	14.7 per 1,000
A	Age-intrinsic rate	20.8
A-N	Age-nuptiality intrinsic rate	18.4
A-P	Age-parity intrinsic rate	23.0
A-N-P	Age-nuptiality-parity intrinsic rate	19.6

The rise when we go from the crude rate in the first line to the age-intrinsic rate in the second means that the observed age distribution was unfavorable to increase—that there was a smaller proportion of women of childbearing age than would be present in the stable condition at 1960 age-specific rates of birth and death. This is a well-known result of the low births of the 1930's.

From the age-intrinsic rate to the age-nuptiality intrinsic rate (from 20.8 to 18.4) we find a decline; that means that the proportion of married women in the observed population of 1960 was greater (in the main ages of child-bearing) than the proportion of married women in the stable condition. If the marriage rates, the age-specific nuptial fertility rates, and the age-specific mortality rates of 1960 are allowed to work themselves out, they would result in a lower overall birth rate than would the age-specific fertility and mortality rates of 1960 disregarding marriage.

Demographers find useful information not only in age and marriage but also in birth order. Registrations customarily record whether a birth is the first, second, third, ... birth to that mother. With complementary information on the number of mothers in the population who have had one, two, three, ... children we can work out rates of childbearing for women who have had one, two, three, ... children. Such rates are called parity-specific. The most useful form of calculation does not abandon the previous classes, but works out rates for the several parities for each age of married woman. These are called age-nuptiality-parity rates, or *A-N-P* for short.

When we go from the age-intrinsic rate to the age-parity intrinsic rate, we find an increase from 20.8 to 23. This can only mean that within each age group the distribution of actual parities is unfavorable to reproduction, and the age-parity intrinsic rate corrects for this. The highest-bearing women are those who have had at most two children, that is, are of parity zero, one and two; apparently the stable condition on 1960 age-parity specific rates would contain relatively more individuals of up to second parity than the observed situation of 1960.

The simultaneous correction for parity and nuptiality brings the rate down. Separation of the married women in the age-parity analysis has so drastic an effect that we find *A-N-P* below the simple age-intrinsic rate *A*. In short, the effect of nuptiality more than offsets the effect of simple parity. Whelpton (8) did the basic work on parity, and Karmel (9) suggested the importance of nuptiality. Oechsli's (7) recent calculations show the importance of both.

The lozenge form of the diagram may help us follow the preceding arguments.

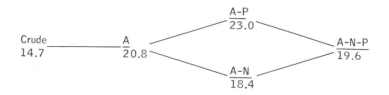

The ideal study would consider all of these elements not for a cross section in time, but following groups of individual women of the same age as they go through reproduction. Such cohorts, as they are called, have different characteristics from cross sections; in particular total fertility and mortality are more constant from one cohort to another than from one period to another. Ryder has made careful studies of the nature of cohort fertility and the distortions it undergoes when translated into period terms (10, and elsewhere).

High Fertility and Low Crude Death Rates

Whereas lower death rates can make a population younger or older, higher birth rates act more simply on age-distribution—they can only make it younger. Because of this fact, the lowest crude death rates in the world today are not shown by the United States and Europe but by Ceylon (7.51 per 1,000 in 1967), Taiwan (5.36 per 1,000 in 1966), and Hong Kong (5.01 per 1,000 in 1966). The United States rate was 9.36 per 1,000 in 1967, and the aggregate of Europe was 10.20 in 1965. Poor countries are tending to have lower crude death rates than rich ones.

A way of showing this by demographic data alone is in terms of standardized rates. The directly standardized death rate on the United States 1960 population tells us what overall death rate would apply in various countries if their age-sex distribution were that of the United States in 1960. By holding constant age and sex we attain an index of mortality, or one might say of unhealthfulness, presumably directly related to poverty. The selected countries charted in Figure 2, including some rich and some poor, show a general inverse relation between crude and standardized rates.

The Two-Sex Model

We now incorporate sex in the model, but drop age. If the number of males at time t is $M(t)$, their birth rate b_m, and their death rate d_m, and the corresponding symbols for females are $F(t)$, b_f and d_f, then we have the equations due to Goodman (11)

$$M'(t) = -d_m M(t) + b_m F(t),$$

$$F'(t) = -d_f F(t) + b_f F(t).$$

Explicit solution is not required for our purposes. Consider only the ultimate sex ratio, analogous to the intrinsic rate of natural increase of our earlier argument. If the sex ratio attains a constant value, then its derivative with respect to time will be zero:

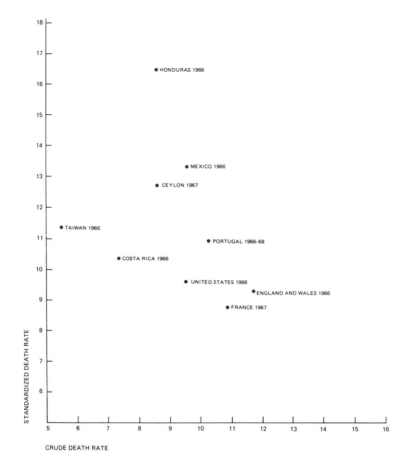

Figure 2. Relation of crude and standardized (on United States, 1960) death rates per 1,000 population.
Source: Author's calculations.

$$\frac{d[M(t)/F(t)]}{dt} = 0,$$

or by the rule for differentiating a quotient

$$\frac{F'(t)}{F(t)} = \frac{M'(t)}{M(t)}.$$

We apply this by dividing the first of the differential equations by $M(t)$ and the second by $F(t)$, and equating the right-hand sides to provide an ordinary equation, containing no derivatives, for $M(t)/F(t)$. Its solution is

$$\frac{M(t)}{F(t)} = \frac{b_m}{b_f + d_m - d_f}$$

as the sex ratio at any time when that ratio is not changing, that is, the ultimate sex ratio (11).

This easily obtained result is instructive. The sex ratio in the population will tend to be lower if the male death rate is higher than the female; it will tend to be higher if the sex ratio at birth b_m/b_f is higher. The latter is not for the moment to be regarded as a policy variable, but it will become one when parents are able to control the probability of a birth being a boy. To find the consequences of such control we would need a model in which the number of births is determined by parents of both sexes. Our present model is called female dominant to signify its restriction; we could easily modify it for male dominance or, what is more realistic, for mixed dominance. To ascertain the consequences of varying sex-ratio at birth on the supply of brides and grooms in the next generation, and hence the ultimate consequences for the birth rate, should be within reach of investigation.

If the crude birth and death rates now prevailing among men and women in the United States were to continue they would lead to a low sex ratio. The crude death rate for males in 1966 was $1000d_m = 10.87$, while the crude rate for females was $1000d_f = 8.11$; birth rates were $1000b_m = 19.05$ and $1000b_f = 17.61$ respectively. We would have for the ultimate sex ratio

$$\frac{M}{F} = \frac{19.05}{17.61 + 10.87 - 8.11} = 0.935.$$

However, the crude rates will not persist if the age-specific rates do, and we want also to see the outcome in the latter case. This is obtained by entering the corresponding intrinsic rates and provides

$$\frac{M}{F} = \frac{20.79}{19.30 + 11.10 - 9.60} = 0.999,$$

a very different result. Apparently with persistence of the age-specific rates the female population becomes older, and this raises its crude death rate and shifts the balance of the sexes towards equality.

Births by Age of Father

The simpler one-sex model recognizing age can be applied to males. Confining it to females omits half the data; in the face of sampling and some other kinds of error we have twice as much information both on mortality and on ages of parents when we use the male data as well as the female. This is if the sexes are moving the same way; if they are not, the male data will tell us something different from what the female data tell; male population may be growing faster than female, and in this case it is even more important to take both sexes into account.

Examples of these two circumstances—true male and female rates of growth being the same, or being different—are provided by England and Wales 1964 and the United States 1966 respectively. England and Wales for 1964 show an intrinsic rate of 11.3 per 1,000 population on the female side, and 11.1 on the male side. One is not tempted to search for the meaning of this difference which may be supposed analogous to sampling variation.

The United States figures for 1966 are a different case: female intrinsic increase was 9.7 per 1,000, and male was 12.8. For females the intrinsic rate is calculated as

$$\frac{\ln R_0}{T} = \frac{\ln 1.289}{26.173} = 0.0097;$$

for males we have

$$\frac{\ln 1.451}{29.026} = 0.0128,$$

where R_0 is the Net Reproduction Rate and T the length of generation.

The U.S. difference of 3 per 1,000 population showed separately in white and nonwhite for 1966. It has built up gradually during the 1960's; early in the decade women had the slightly higher rate, but by 1964 females were 15.7 and males were 17.5. Canada for 1966 shows a difference in the same direction as the United States and about half the amount; its female rate was 10.1 and its male 11.5. Such differences are remarkable, since after all the same babies are born to mothers as to fathers, and the sex ratio of the births is nearly the same in all groups. Why does referring them to fathers make a much higher rate of increase in the population?

A possible answer that first comes to mind is that recent fathers may be younger. If they are younger, then the same children referred to fathers would imply a shorter generation, and hence a faster turnover, and this would make a higher intrinsic rate. To check the point we look up the mean ages of mothers and fathers at childbirth in the stationary population, designated μ. We find for μ in the male and female calculations respectively for the United States:

	Male	Female
1959-61	29.55	26.37
1964	29.62	26.53
1966	29.33	26.35

The relative changes are very small, and could hardly account for the divergence of the male and female intrinsic rates. The new fathers are not sufficiently young in relation to the age of their wives to explain the much higher current male intrinsic rate.

In fact, the explanation is in the male age distribution as a whole rather than in ages of fathers as such. Because the fathers of the mid-1960's are the births of the 1940's and during the 1940's the births were *rising* rapidly, we now suddenly have a much steeper *decline* with age of the number of young men and women than usual: The age distribution has an especially sharp fall from 20 to 30. If women are paired with men on the average 3 years older, then an increase in both men and women of the same ages increases the number of women in the denominator of the age-specific rates more than it increases the number of men. The denominator for women is diluted, so to speak, with women who in the current configuration of ages of husbands and wives cannot have spouses with the usual age difference. This increase of the denominator for women lowers their age-specific rates, and hence the Net Reproduction Rate R_0 and the intrinsic rate r.

The marriage market is constituted by the numbers of males and females of corresponding ages. What are corresponding ages in the United States in 1967 is suggested by the median groom at first marriage being 23.1 years old and the median bride being 20.6 years old, a difference of 2.5 years. The mean age of fathers in the stationary population in 1966 was 29.33, and of mothers in the same year was 26.35, a difference of nearly 3 years.

The numbers at youthful ages in the United States in 1966 were

	Males	Females
10-14	9,861,000	9,542,000
15-19	8,950,000	8,806,000
20-24	6,625,000	6,981,000
25-29	5,632,000	5,840,000
30-34	5,326,000	5,527,000

To compare the women of one age group with the men of the group 5 years older exaggerates the discrepancy but will serve us as an index. We can see from the above data that the biggest disproportion in 1966 is between the women 15 to 19 and the men 20 to 24; as these come to marriage age, which is just about now, the shortage of men will be more serious than 5 years earlier or 5 years later. (Allowance for military personnel stationed outside the United States—omitted from the above official estimates—would somewhat reduce the effect under discussion.)

Japan shows the same phenomenon in its 1966 age distribution:

	Males	*Females*
5-9	3,973,000	3,832,000
10-14	4,499,000	4,346,000
15-19	5,710,000	5,586,000
20-24	4,339,000	4,403,000
25-29	4,198,000	4,261,000

The number of men 20 to 24 is far smaller than the number of women 15 to 19, reflecting a very short-lived baby boom in the 1940's.

This boom in Japan was followed by a dramatic decline in births, and the reverse marriage squeeze appears between men of 15 to 19 and women 10 to 14. As these men and women reach marrying age over the next few years the present excess of women will give place to a shortage. Data for later years should tell us to what extent the decline in fertility of the late 1960's (the crude birth rate fell from 18.6 in 1965 to 13.8 in 1966) is due to the disproportion in the numbers of men and women of corresponding marrying ages. The point will be important for other countries in the wake of successful efforts to control fertility. More research is needed; we have neither adequate data nor adequate theory on the response of marriage and childbearing to disproportionate numbers of the two sexes. This is a major unsolved problem of theoretical demography.

Appendix 1

To trace changes in age-specific birth and death rates to their consequences for overall rates and for age distribution is the main interest of this paper. Its argument depends on a procedure of partial differentiation in the one-sex stable model. The results for birth changes are given in Table A, Appendix 1, which is readable without reference to its derivation.

As an instance of how the table is to be read, if the birth rate m_x increases by the quantity Δm_x, the effect of this on r, the intrinsic rate of natural increase, is an increase of $\Delta r = e^{-rx} p_x \Delta m_x / \kappa$, where p_x is the probability of living to age x for a child just born, and κ is the mean age of childbearing in the stable population. Further down, the fractional effect of the change in the birth rate at age x on the proportion c_a of the population at age a is given as this same value of Δr multiplied by $A - a$, where A is the mean age in the stable population.

Some of the results of the table go back to Lotka (12), some to Coale (13).

Appendix 2

The following collection of materials is part of *Population: The Facts and Methods of Demography*, to be published in 1971 by W. H. Freeman (14). It

TABLE A

Effect of Change in Age-Specific Birth Rates
on Stable Population Parameters

$$\Delta r = \frac{e^{-rx}p_x}{\kappa}\,\Delta m_x$$

$$\Delta b = bA\,\Delta r = bA\,\frac{e^{-rx}p_x}{\kappa}\,\Delta m_x$$

$$\Delta d = (bA - 1)\,\Delta r$$

$$= (bA - 1)\,\frac{e^{-rx}p_x}{\kappa}\,\Delta m_x$$

$$\frac{\Delta c_a}{c_a} = (A - a)\,\frac{e^{-rx}p_x}{\kappa}\,\Delta m_x$$

$$\Delta A = -\,\frac{\sigma^2 e^{-rx}p_x}{\kappa}\,\Delta m_x$$

where

m_x = age-specific birth rate at age x

r = intrinsic rate of natural increase

b = intrinsic birth rate

d = intrinsic death rate

$p_x = l_x/l_0$ = probability of living from birth to age x

$c_a da = be^{-ra}p_a da$ = proportion of population between ages a and $a + da$

$\kappa = {}_a\!\int^{\beta} ae^{-ra}p_a m_a da$ = mean age of childbearing in the stable population

$A = {}_0\!\int^{\omega} ae^{-ra}p_a da / {}_0\!\int^{\omega} e^{-ra}p_a da$ = mean age in stable population

$\sigma^2 = b\,{}_0\!\int^{\omega} (t - A)^2 e^{-rt}p_t dt$ = variance of age distribution in stable population

a = youngest age of childbearing

β = oldest age of childbearing

ω = oldest age to which anyone lives

is based on national publications, correspondence with the statistical agencies of about forty countries, and the very helpful United Nations *Demographic Yearbook*, especially the 1967 edition (1). An extended discussion of these data, and footnotes to their sources, appears in *Population*, which also contains a full description of the methods by which the uniform life tables, intrinsic and standardized rates, and other derived information, were calculated. I am grateful to W. H. Freeman for permission to use this material and the text that discusses it.

TABLE B

Summary of Recent Vital Data

Country	Year	Population at Mid-year 000's	Percent under Age 15	Crude Rates		Rates Standardized on United States 1960		Intrinsic Rates			Expectation of Life at Age 0 $\overset{\circ}{e}_0$	
				Birth	Death	Birth	Death	Birth	Death	Natural Increase	Male	Female
		(1)	(2)	(3)	(4)	(5)	(6)	(7)	(8)	(9)	(10)	(11)
AFRICA												
Algeria	1965	12,134	47.2	43.6	10.0	45.0	9.5	45.2	9.5	35.7	63.0	66.8
Cameroon (West)	1964	1,031	48.6	49.7	25.7	41.5	34.6	45.6	24.1	21.5	34.3	38.1
Central African Republic	1960	1,028	40.0	47.5	25.4	32.4	33.8	37.7	25.1	12.6	34.3	38.3
Guinea	1955	2,582	42.1	54.0	42.5	40.5	42.3	47.1	36.8	10.2	24.3	27.3
Madagascar	1966	6,163	46.5	45.8	25.3	44.5	29.1	46.7	24.2	22.5	37.6	38.5
Mauritius	1966	759	44.2	34.9	8.8	35.4	15.2	38.9	8.4	30.5	59.5	63.7
Reunion	1963	372	45.0	44.4	11.0	43.7	15.7	43.9	8.8	35.1	55.6	62.4
Seychelles Island	1961	42	38.5	41.3	9.9	38.0	11.5	40.2	6.7	33.5	61.9	69.2
South Africa (colored)	1961	1,549	45.1	46.1	15.4	42.0	18.7	46.2	13.4	32.8	49.8	54.6
South Africa (white)	1961	3,129	32.4	24.2	8.6	22.2	10.6	25.0	7.6	17.4	65.3	72.2
Togo	1961	1,544	47.9	54.5	29.0	46.3	29.5	50.3	23.1	27.2	33.6	40.3
Tunisia	1960	4,182	40.8	43.6	12.0	41.3	12.8	40.5	11.6	28.9	55.7	63.2
AMERICA—NORTH AND CENTRAL												
Barbados	1965	244	38.9	28.0	7.8	25.5	9.9	28.0	7.3	20.7	67.0	71.2
Canada	1966-68	19,933	32.1	18.1	7.4	16.8	8.2	17.5	10.1	7.4	68.9	75.5

Costa Rica	1966	1,541	48.2	41.8	7.4	42.4	10.4	43.4	6.8	36.6	65.0	67.7
Dominican Republic	1966	3,498	44.6	36.1	7.6	35.0	10.1	35.9	9.1	26.8	63.6	66.1
El Salvador	1961	2,527	44.8	49.4	11.3	44.0	13.2	46.4	10.7	35.7	56.4	60.6
Greenland	1960	32	44.2	48.8	7.8	44.5	14.9	44.4	6.8	37.6	60.2	64.9
Grenada	1961	92	47.7	44.6	11.1	44.1	12.3	46.7	8.2	38.5	60.5	65.0
Guatemala	1964	4,440	46.0	44.2	15.4	40.9	18.8	43.9	15.4	28.4	49.3	50.9
Honduras	1966	2,363	51.5	44.2	8.7	43.7	16.4	44.1	8.4	35.6	59.2	60.7
Jamaica	1963	1,696	45.1	39.8	8.9	38.5	11.7	42.0	6.7	35.3	62.9	67.2
Martinique	1963	308	42.2	33.2	8.2	33.4	11.2	35.0	6.7	28.3	63.6	68.8
Mexico	1966	44,145	46.3	44.0	9.6	43.1	13.3	43.3	8.7	34.7	59.5	62.8
Nicaragua	1965	1,655	48.3	43.0	7.3	39.6	9.8	41.8	7.3	34.5	64.6	67.9
Panama	1966	1,221	43.4	40.4	7.5	36.6	10.3	40.8	7.1	33.7	65.0	67.2
Puerto Rico	1965	2,626	38.7	30.3	6.7	25.7	8.3	28.9	6.5	22.4	68.0	73.7
St. Kitts, Neville, and Anguilla	1961	59	45.7	42.3	12.1	44.6	13.4	46.0	8.7	37.4	64.0	62.7
Santa Lucia	1960	87	44.3	48.9	14.8	45.2	14.2	47.8	12.6	35.2	54.3	58.0
Trinidad and Tobago	1967	1,010	42.4	28.2	6.7	25.3	20.0	29.0	7.6	21.4	64.1	68.4
United States	1967	197,863	30.3	18.0	9.4	16.7	9.1	17.8	10.4	7.4	67.0	74.2
AMERICA–SOUTH												
Argentina	1964	22,038	29.9	21.9	7.8	20.0	10.0	19.1	10.9	8.2	65.0	71.0
Brazil	1950	51,944	41.9	44.0	20.6	38.0	26.7	40.8	19.8	21.0	41.2	44.1
Chile	1967	9,137	39.8	28.4	9.5	25.5	12.7	28.1	9.7	18.4	59.2	66.2
Colombia	1965	17,993	46.6	38.4	9.9	36.4	13.3	38.8	9.9	29.0	58.2	61.7
Ecuador	1965	5,109	47.0	44.3	11.8	43.4	13.2	44.8	11.5	33.3	57.1	60.2
Fr. Guiana	1964	34	38.6	35.2	11.6	36.8	14.0	40.3	6.3	34.0	58.7	67.4
Br. Guyana	1961	568	46.3	41.9	8.8	40.4	14.1	44.0	7.0	37.0	59.9	64.5
Peru	1963	10,980	44.2	38.4	10.0	38.4	11.9	37.7	10.2	27.6	60.5	62.8
Uruguay	1963	2,648	28.0	21.6	11.3	18.7	12.5	20.1	11.3	8.8	61.4	68.2
Venezuela	1965	8,722	45.4	43.5	7.1	41.8	11.0	44.0	6.4	37.6	63.9	67.7

Table B (Continued)

Country	Year	Population at Mid-year 000's (1)	Percent under Age 15 (2)	Crude Rates		Rates Standardized on United States 1960		Intrinsic Rates			Expectation of Life at Age 0 e_0	
				Birth (3)	Death (4)	Birth (5)	Death (6)	Birth (7)	Death (8)	Natural Increase (9)	Male (10)	Female (11)
ASIA												
Ceylon	1967	11,701	41.9	31.6	7.5	30.0	11.2	32.5	7.9	24.6	65.1	66.8
China (Taiwan)	1966	13,021	43.7	31.9	5.4	31.0	11.4	34.5	6.0	28.5	65.2	69.8
Cyprus	1960	573	36.7	25.3	5.6	22.8	7.5	24.0	7.2	16.8	72.8	75.6
Hong Kong	1966	3,732	40.4	25.8	5.0	28.8	10.7	31.2	5.8	25.4	65.9	72.7
India	1961	439,235	41.1	41.3	19.5	36.5	24.1	41.2	20.0	21.2	46.0	44.0
Indonesia	1961	96,371	42.2	45.0	18.4	35.9	24.9	40.5	17.3	23.2	44.1	47.5
Iran	1956	19,441	44.0	51.0	26.4	47.7	30.3	52.3	26.2	26.1	37.4	37.6
Israel	1967	2,363	31.3	21.4	6.6	20.6	8.5	22.6	7.9	14.7	70.6	74.1
Japan	1966	98,859	25.0	13.8	6.8	10.1	9.3	8.7	19.4	-10.7	68.5	73.7
Korea	1960	24,989	43.1	42.1	12.2	38.7	17.3	40.6	12.2	28.4	54.8	55.7
Kuwait	1966	491	38.0	51.5	5.7	54.6	11.6	53.6	5.9	47.6	64.7	67.0
West Malaysia	1966	8,541	44.2	36.2	7.4	36.1	11.0	38.1	7.2	30.9	63.5	66.8
Pakistan	1961	93,832	44.8	47.2	20.3	43.8	25.6	48.7	21.4	27.3	44.4	42.4
Philippines	1960	27,420	45.7	47.1	10.9	43.8	14.8	44.4	11.0	33.4	55.4	58.7
Ryukyu Islands	1965	930	38.9	23.7	8.0	21.2	11.5	22.7	9.0	13.7	63.9	70.8
Sarawak	1961	745	44.5	37.0	8.0	34.0	12.2	36.9	8.3	28.7	60.6	64.4
Singapore	1967	1,956	42.8	26.0	5.4	26.3	13.4	29.0	6.8	22.2	64.4	70.4
Thailand	1960	26,273	43.2	36.5	8.4	33.8	12.3	33.5	9.8	23.7	58.7	64.4
Turkey	1960	27,506	41.2	45.7	16.6	42.0	21.5	44.6	16.6	28.0	48.3	48.7

EUROPE

	Year												
Albania	1955	1,381	39.1	44.4	15.0	45.8	14.4	44.7	15.4	29.4	54.6	55.4
Austria	1966-68	7,323	23.8	17.4	12.9	17.1	10.0	18.2	10.3	7.8	66.6	73.4
Belgium	1966	9,525	23.9	15.9	12.1	16.1	9.5	16.9	11.0	5.9	67.7	73.8
Bulgaria	1966-68	8,310	23.4	15.6	8.6	13.6	9.0	13.3	14.1	-0.8	68.9	72.9
Czechoslovakia	1967	14,305	24.4	15.1	10.1	13.4	9.7	13.2	13.9	-0.8	67.4	73.8
Denmark	1966	4,801	23.7	18.4	10.3	16.9	8.4	18.0	9.9	8.2	70.4	75.1
Finland	1966	4,639	25.5	16.8	9.4	15.0	11.0	15.7	12.0	3.7	66.0	73.2
France	1967	49,548	25.3	16.9	10.9	17.0	8.8	18.0	9.8	8.2	68.0	75.5
Germany (East)	1966	17,064	23.8	15.7	13.2	15.3	9.6	16.0	11.7	4.3	68.4	73.3
Germany (West)	1967	59,873	23.0	17.0	11.5	16.0	9.5	16.6	11.2	5.4	67.7	73.8
Greece	1966-68	8,716	25.2	18.3	8.2	15.3	8.0	15.2	12.0	3.2	70.6	74.5
Hungary	1967	10,215	22.3	14.6	10.7	13.0	10.1	12.4	15.3	-2.9	66.9	72.0
Iceland	1965	192	34.5	24.6	6.7	24.3	7.2	27.6	5.7	22.0	71.4	76.6
Ireland	1967	2,899	31.3	21.2	10.8	25.1	9.2	26.1	6.8	19.3	69.1	73.5
Italy	1964	52,130	24.2	19.5	9.4	17.0	9.1	17.4	11.0	6.4	67.7	73.2
Luxembourg	1966	334	22.5	15.5	12.1	15.1	10.3	16.1	11.9	4.2	66.3	72.6
Malta	1966	317	32.1	16.8	9.0	15.0	10.9	15.2	13.1	2.0	68.0	71.2
Netherlands	1967	12,598	27.8	19.0	7.9	18.0	7.5	18.9	9.0	9.9	7_.2	76.6
Norway	1967	3,784	24.7	17.6	9.6	18.1	7.4	19.2	8.7	10.4	71.4	76.8
Poland	1965	31,182	31.4	17.5	7.4	16.2	9.9	16.8	11.6	5.3	66.4	72.3
Portugal	1966-68	9,415	28.9	21.4	10.3	18.8	10.9	19.5	11.1	8.4	64.0	69.7
Romania	1965	19,027	26.3	14.6	8.6	12.4	10.3	12.0	16.2	-4.3	66.6	70.6
Spain	1967	32,431	28.0	20.7	8.4	18.8	8.6	19.4	9.3	10.1	69.2	74.6
Sweden	1966	7,808	20.9	15.8	10.0	15.3	7.5	15.4	11.2	4.3	71.9	76.5
Switzerland	1967	5,990	23.3	17.9	9.2	15.3	8.2	15.5	11.3	4.1	69.7	75.9
United Kingdom												
England and Wales	1966-68	48,301	23.2	17.3	11.6	17.0	9.1	18.1	9.9	8.2	63.7	74.9
Northern Ireland	1966	1,425	28.9	23.4	11.5	24.2	10.6	25.0	7.6	17.5	67.0	72.2
Scotland	1966	5,190	25.9	18.6	12.3	18.6	10.6	20.3	9.4	11.0	65.6	72.5
Yugoslavia	1966	19,735	29.3	20.3	8.1	17.0	10.0	17.8	11.9	5.9	65.0	70.2
OCEANIA												
Australia	1967	11,810	29.3	19.4	8.7	18.4	9.2	20.0	9.0	10.9	67.8	74.5
Fiji Islands	1966	477	43.8	34.9	5.2	31.0	8.6	33.5	5.8	27.7	68.1	73.6
New Zealand	1966-68	2,729	32.6	22.4	8.7	21.7	9.2	24.6	7.1	17.6	68.2	74.3

REFERENCES

1. United Nations, *Demographic Yearbook 1967*. New York: United Nations Publication Service, 1968.
2. Whelpton, P. K., "An Empirical Method of Calculating Future Population," *Journal of the American Statistical Association*, 31, 1936. pp. 457-473.
3. Frejka, T., "Reflections on the Demographic Condition Needed to Establish a U.S. Stationary Population Growth," *Population Studies*, 22, 1968. pp. 379-397.
4. Keyfitz, Nathan, *Introduction to the Mathematics of Population*. Reading, Mass.: Addison-Wesley, 1968.
5. Potter, R. G., "Births Averted by Contraception: An Approach through Renewal Theory," *Theoretical Population Biology*, Vol. I. No. 3, Nov. 1970. pp. 251-272.
6. Sheps, M. C., J. A. Menken, and A. P. Radick, "Probability Models for Family Building: An Analytical Review," *Demography*, 6, 1969. pp. 161-183.
7. Oechsli, F., "The Parity and Nuptiality Problem in Demography." Unpublished manuscript, 1969.
8. Whelpton, P. K., *Cohort Fertility: Native White Women in the United States*. Princeton, N. J.: Princeton Univ. Press, 1954.
9. Karmel, P. H., "A Note on P. K. Whelpton's Calculation of Parity Adjusted Reproduction Rates," *Journal of the American Statistical Association*, 45, 1950. pp. 119-124.
10. Ryder, N. B., "The Process of Demographic Translation," *Demography*, 1, 1964. pp. 74-82.
11. Goodman, L. A., "Population Growth of the Sexes," *Biometrics*, 9, 1953. pp. 212-225.
12. Lotka, A. J., *Théorie analytique des associations biologiques*. Part II: Analyse démographique avec application particulière à l'espèce humaine. Actualités Scientifiques et Industrielles, No. 780. Paris: Hermann & Cie, 1939.
13. Coale, A. J., "The Effects of Changes in Mortality and Fertility on Age Composition," *Milbank Memorial Fund Quarterly*, 34, 1956. pp. 79-114.
14. Keyfitz, N., and W. Flieger, *Population: The Facts and Methods of Demography*. San Francisco: W. H. Freeman and Co. Forthcoming, 1971.

Index, Volume II

Abortion, induced: and birth rate, 126*n*, 522-24; compulsory, 624, 628; consequences of suppressing, 500-508; and contraceptive programs, 213, 480, 499-501, 508-12, 525; death from, 169, 501-8; in demographic transition, 124, 126, 479-91; health services for, 371, 385, 390; laws concerning, 481, 513-24; liberalization of, 522-24; and low fertility determinants, 404, 491-500, 511-12; policy formation on, 524-26; prevalence of, 118-19; 129*n*, 169, 370, 481-91; religious attitudes on, 513-16

Africa, 226, 229, 676; attitudes on population in, 539-41, 544, 587; demographic patterns in, 105, 106, 110, 112, 144, 329, 642; education in, 316-18, 321-23, 325, 328, 330, 333, migration in, 284, 288. *See also* Ghana

Age structure: and birth and death rates, 651-75; causes of, 576-77, 580; in demographic transition, 114-17; economic effects of, 180-81, 188, 203, 205, 250, 647; and education, 317, 327, 329, 330-31, 337-38, 346, 384; and fertility, 127*n*, 167-68, 569-70, 640; and health services, 369, 384, 386; political effects of, 576-82, 607-8, 612; of stationary population, 208, 649-51. *See also* Dependency ratio

Aggressive behavior, 572, 588

Agriculture: economic incentives for, 247, 251, 260, 267; employment in, 138, 139, 141, 143, 163; and government policies, 251, 258, 260, 262, 267, 575; increasing yields in, 223, 226, 228, 234, 248-49; and information to farmers,

228, 263, 268; land for, 229-31; and nonagricultural inputs, 250, 251-53; modernization of, 228, 248-68, 354, 631; and regional inequality, 258, 263-65, 268; scientific-technical research for, 245, 247-48, 254-55, 267; skills needed for, 247, 248, 252, 259; traditional, 250, 251, 261, 265. *See also* Food

Agricultural revolution, 105, 228

Air, 235-36, 242

Albania: abortion in, 520, 523; birth rates in, 125, 128, 130, 133*n*

Algeria, 108

Argentina, 126, 257, 260, 282-83

Arkansas, 581

Asia: agriculture in, 246, 257, 262, 267; attitudes on population growth in, 535-39, 541; demographic data on, 106, 112, 678; demographic patterns in, 105, 110, 128, 129, 329, 587; education in, 316, 312, 322*n*, 323, 324-25, 330; migration in, 288; pollution sources in, 230; socioeconomic development of, and fertility, 142-44

Australia, 125-27, 133, 231, 260, 644

Automobile, 235

Baby boom, 577, 641, 674

Barbados, 133*n*, 140

Birth control: definition of, 118, 383; in fertility decline, 124, 130, 168-69, 171, 646; government provision of, 212-14, 217; mortality from, 507; by older ages, 641; uncertainty in, 160-61. *See also* Contraceptives; Family planning programs

681